The
ATLAS
of
WORLD
GEOGRAPHY

The
ATLAS
of
WORLD
GEOGRAPHY

Consultant Editor
Professor Emrys Jones

Introduction by
Magnus Magnusson

Cartographic Editor
Harold Fullard M.Sc.

Sundial

Contents

Introduction

The world we live in is the most marvellous place imaginable. At one time, no one had any idea how the Earth had come about, or how large it was, or what shape it was, or how it fitted into the visible universe of Sun and Moon and planets and stars. They were all great marvels, the ultimate mystery for man's mind to grapple with.

We know that people have always been fascinated by this subject because, as soon as man developed the ability to express his thoughts in writing, some 5,000 years ago, just about the first thing he did was to try to answer some of the riddles of the Universe. Who created it? And why? And how?

Questions of that kind were answered in terms of mythology: the Universe was created by gods, for the enjoyment of mankind. These gods had different functions — a god of the storms, a god of the sea, a god of the plants, and so on. In this way, early man recognized that there were innumerable natural forces which he could observe, but not control; and he tried to come to terms with these natural

phenomena by attributing them to personified gods with whom he could negotiate, or to whom he could pray.

Today we are still asking the same sort of questions: what *is* the Universe? How was it formed? When did it happen? How and when did our planet Earth come into being? What is it made of? What makes the weather happen? What made the mountains? And what is man's place on this great planet, which is such a tiny speck in the infinite vastness of the Universe?

Many of these questions can now be answered with some assurance — and the answers are to be found in this book. There are still marvels and mysteries that are beyond our understanding, of course (and I hope there always will be!); there are almost unimaginable stretches of time and space that are far beyond the reach of even our most powerful telescopes. But we know a great deal now about the world today — about our world, and our place in it.

Finding out about the world has been one of the great achievements of the human mind. The wonder of the world is by no means lessened by knowing more and more about it; on the contrary, it is greatly increased.

Knowledge about our world is not only useful; it is tremendous fun. When you travel from one part of the country to another, or from one part of the world to another, the journey becomes infinitely more exciting if you know why the landscapes are so different, why the people are so different, why customs and languages and styles of living are so different.

Knowing about the world — which means knowing about yourself and all the other people in it, whether they are black, white or yellow — is the beginning of all knowledge. Enjoy it!

Magnus Magnusson

Maps

Acknowledgments

The publishers would like to thank the following individuals and organizations for their kind permission to reproduce the photographs in this book:

Heather Angel 42 below right, 43 below; Aquila Photographics (W S Paton) 6 below right, (P D V Weaving) 40 above right; Ardea Photograhics (Ian Beames) 40 centre right, (M D England) 42 below left, (K W Fink) 40 above left, (Su Gooders) 35 below right, (P Green) 36, (Eric Lindgren) 40 below left, (R F Porter) 44, (Swedberg) 45 above, (R &V Taylor) 43 above left; Barnaby's Picture Library (H Kanus) 55 below; BBC 4-5; Almanna Bokenfeld, Iceland 23; Camera Press Ltd. 24; John Cleare, Mountain Camera 33; Bruce Coleman Ltd. 39, (J Burton) 11 above; Sonia Halliday 49 left; Robert Harding Associates 2-3, 30 above right, 66, (J M Stewart) 51 Above; Angelo Hornak 49 right, 92; Alan Hutchison Library endpapers, 25 above, 68, 71, (S E Porlock) 57, 58; London Features International 86; Photri 87 above; National Coal Board 70; Photo Aquatics (Hermann Gruhl) 43 above right; Pic on Tour/Charlie 40-41 below, 55 above; Picturepoint Ltd. 7, 47 left, 77, 81, 82, 84-85, 85 above, below left and below right, 87 below left and below right, 89 above, 91 below, 94; R K Pilsbury 17, (2) (3) (5) (6) (7) (8) (9) (10); Popperfoto 21, 54, 75, 89 above centre and below centre, 93, (W M Simmons) 91 above; David Prout 12 below; Rex Features Ltd. 14; Spectrum Colour Library 8 below, 16-17, 26, 30-31 below, 31, 35 below left, 41 above, 51 below, 56 right; John Topham Picture Library (Dumas) 42 above, (L Garbison) 35 above, (Mousseau) 45 below left, (M Wilkins) 12 above, (Windridge) 17, (1) (4); A G Waltham 29; Keith Wicks 13 above, 73; ZEFA (R Everts) 27, 82-83, (R Halin) 17 centre below, 32, 62, 63, (H Helbing) 6 above left, 59, (H Hoffmann-Buchardi) 47 right, (Dr Hans Kramarz) 64, (E Landschak) 45 below right, (Photo Leidmann) 1, (Th Luttge) 56 left, (G Marche) 95, (Dr F Sauer) 37, (D H Teuffen) 30 left, (F Walther) 6 above right, 46.

Illustrations by: Diagram Ltd., Eric Jewell Associates, Illustra Design Ltd., Osborne/Marks

Half title page **Tilling with a primitive plough and a donkey near Marrakech in Morocco.**

Title pages **Clouds over Seram, Moluccas.**

Page 6 above left **A modern combine harvester is manoeuvred beside a loading wagon during the harvesting of green crops in Germany.**

Page 6 above right **Peasant farmers ploughing with oxen in the Benares region of Northern India.**

Page 6 below right **A lioness keeps a watchful eye on her cubs at play.**

Page 7 **The women of an Uru Indian family prepare a meal at home in their village at Lake Titicaca in Peru.**

First published 1977 by
Sundial Books Limited
59 Grosvenor Street
London W1
Third impression, 1978

© 1977 Hennerwood Publications Limited

Map section and index, illustrations pages
18-19, 22, 34-35, 48-49, 78 below
© 1977 George Philip & Son Ltd.

ISBN 0 904230 34 1

Printed in Hong Kong by Mandarin Publishers Ltd.

The Physical World

The Earth in Space

To most of us, the Earth seems to be a very big place. Our hands would have to be enlarged more than 100 million times to be able to grasp the Earth. Yet, in their journeys to the Moon, American astronauts saw the Earth appear to shrink until it seemed small enough to hold in their hands. With their own eyes, these men have been able to see just how tiny our world really is in comparison with the great depths of space.

But we, too, can get an idea of our place in the Universe just by looking up into the sky. Only two bodies in the heavens appear to be of any size — the Moon and the Sun. The Moon is a small world, its diameter being only a quarter of the Earth's diameter, whereas the Sun is huge — 109 times greater in diameter than the Earth. But the Sun and Moon look the same size from the Earth because, although the Sun is about 400 times bigger in diameter than the Moon, it is about 400 times farther from the Earth than the Moon is.

Nine main planets move in oval paths around the Sun. The Earth is one of these planets. All the planets are lit by the Sun and do not produce their own light. Some are smaller and some larger but, whatever their size, they are all so far away from the Earth that they appear merely as dots of light in the night sky. Like our world, most of them have one or more moons moving around them, but these are so small that they can be seen from Earth only with the aid of a telescope. The Sun's group of planets, together with their moons and other bodies, such as comets and asteroids (minor planets), is called the Solar System. The orbit of its outermost member, Pluto, averages nearly 6,000 million kilometres (3,750 million miles) from the Sun; your hand would have to be more than 100 million million times its actual size to hold the Solar System!

Almost all the asteroids orbit the Sun in a broad belt between the orbits of Mars and Jupiter. Thousands of asteroids have been discovered and all are extremely small compared with the main planets of the Solar System. Comets are bodies that come from the depths of space. As they approach the Sun, they become visible and usually display a glowing tail of charged particles. After passing close to the Sun, comets travel back to the outer edges of the Solar System. Some comets reappear at regular intervals.

Although the Solar System may seem enormous, in fact it is only a tiny corner of the Universe. A glance into the night sky reveals thousands of stars, many of them like our Sun, which is a common kind of star. The Sun is in fact a member of a vast group of stars called the Galaxy. With the naked eye, we can see only a small proportion of these — the ones that are relatively close or very bright. All together, the Galaxy contains 100,000 million stars, all so distant that they appear, even through the most powerful telescopes, as dots of light. Distances are so great in astronomy that they have to be measured in light-years. One light-year is the distance that light travels in a year, and it is equal to nearly 10 million million kilometres (6.2 million million miles). On this scale, the Galaxy is 100,000 light-years across, and the Universe does not stop there. Scattered throughout space are millions of other galaxies. No one knows how big the Universe really is because it extends beyond the reach of our telescopes. But these instruments have detected bodies that could be as much as 15,600 million light-years away. For comparison, the farthest distance that man has travelled into space — to the Moon — takes light a mere 1¼ seconds to cross.

The Motion of the Earth

Every day, the Sun crosses the sky, rising at dawn in the east and setting at dusk in the west. Night comes as the Sun moves beyond

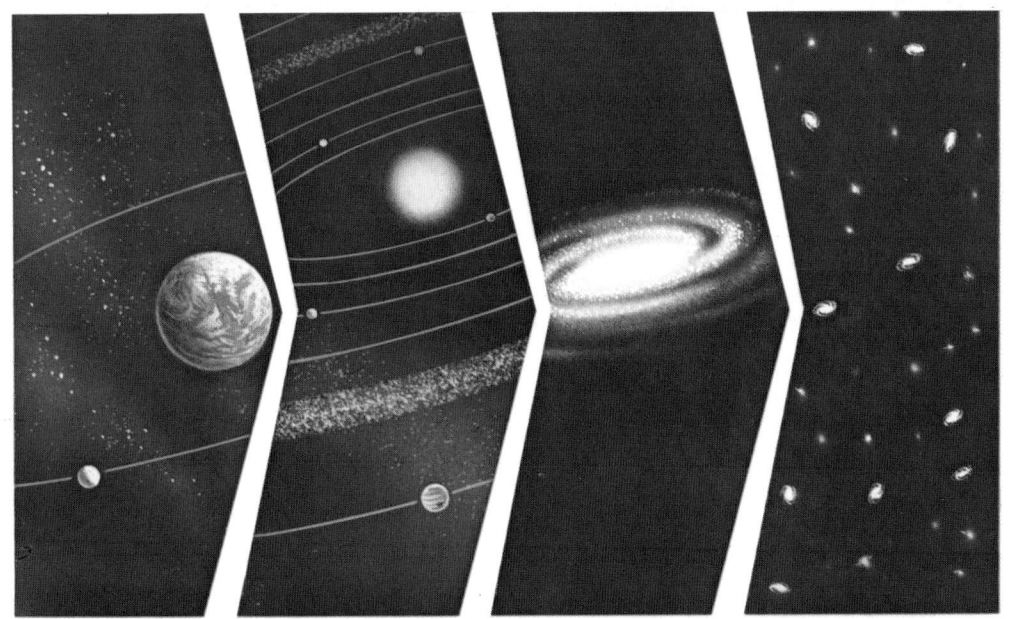

Above: **The planets, to scale, with
their moons (top), and the Solar
System with distances to scale
(bottom). The nine planets, with
their average distances from the
Sun, are:**

1. **Mercury:** 57,900,000 km
2. **Venus:** 108,210,000 km
3. **Earth:** 149,600,000 km
4. **Mars:** 227,930,000 km
5. **Jupiter:** 778,340,000 km
6. **Saturn:** 1,427,000,000 km
7. **Uranus:** 2,869,600,000 km
8. **Neptune:** 4,496,700,000 km
9. **Pluto:** 5,900,000,000 km

**The asteroids, or minor planets,
make up the belt between Mars
and Jupiter.**

Left: **The Earth, as seen from space
by American Apollo astronauts.**

Right: **The Earth is in the Solar
System, which is a small part of the
Galaxy, one of millions of galaxies
in the Universe.**

the horizon to the other side of the world and our side is shaded from its light. We say, for convenience, that the Sun crosses or moves in the sky, but it is, in fact, the Earth that is moving, and not the Sun. The Earth rotates once every 24 hours, spinning in a west-to-east direction but, to anyone on the Earth's surface, the Sun *appears* to move from east to west. With one rotation of the Earth, a day and night passes. However, the length of day and night vary throughout the year. In summer, the days are long and nights short, while winter is a time of short days and long nights. These changes happen because the Earth's axis is tilted. The Earth's axis is an imaginary line about which the Earth rotates; it runs through the middle of the Earth from the North Pole to the South Pole. If this line were exactly at right angles to the plane of the Earth's orbit around the Sun, then all days and nights would be exactly the same length — 12 hours each — and there would be no seasons. But the axis is tilted at an angle of 23½°. As the Earth moves around the Sun in its orbit, first one pole tilts towards the Sun and then the other pole does. The Earth's movement around the Sun thus causes seasonal changes in world climate.

When it is summer in the Northern Hemisphere, the North Pole is tilted towards the Sun, making the Sun appear to be high in the sky at midday. Days are long and it is warm, because the Sun's rays come straight down through the atmosphere and can heat the ground for a long time. At the same time, it is winter in the Southern Hemisphere. The South Pole is pointing away from the Sun, making the Sun appear to be low in the sky in the Southern Hemisphere. The days are short and nights long, and it is cold because the Sun's rays enter the atmosphere at a narrow angle and have little time to heat the ground. Six months later, the poles are pointing the other way and it is winter in the Northern

Hemisphere and summer in the Southern Hemisphere. In between, spring and autumn occurs in each hemisphere. Then neither pole is tilted very much towards or away from the Sun. As a result, days and nights are about the same length during both the spring and autumn months.

The day on which the Sun appears to get to its highest point in the sky is the longest day of the year and is called the *summer solstice.* In the Northern Hemisphere, it is about June 21. The shortest day is called the *winter solstice* and is about December 22 in the Northern Hemisphere. In the Southern Hemisphere, these dates are reversed. On days called *equinoxes,* day and night last exactly the same time all over the world. The vernal (spring) equinox occurs on about March 21 and the autumnal equinox on about September 22. However, these days tend to mark the beginnings of the seasons rather than their midpoints. This is because it takes time for the ground to warm up after winter or cool down after summer.

The Motion of the Moon

The Moon moves around the Earth in an orbit, just as the Earth moves around the Sun, and takes nearly 27⅓ days to go once around the Earth. However, the Moon rotates very slowly, spinning only once in the time it takes to go around the Earth. This means that the Moon always keeps the same face towards the Earth and, from Earth, we can never see the other side.

But the Moon does appear to change. Sometimes, it looks like a crescent, then a semi-circle and a full circle. These changes are called *phases.* They happen because we do not always see all of the side of the Moon that is lit up by the Sun. At new moon, the dark

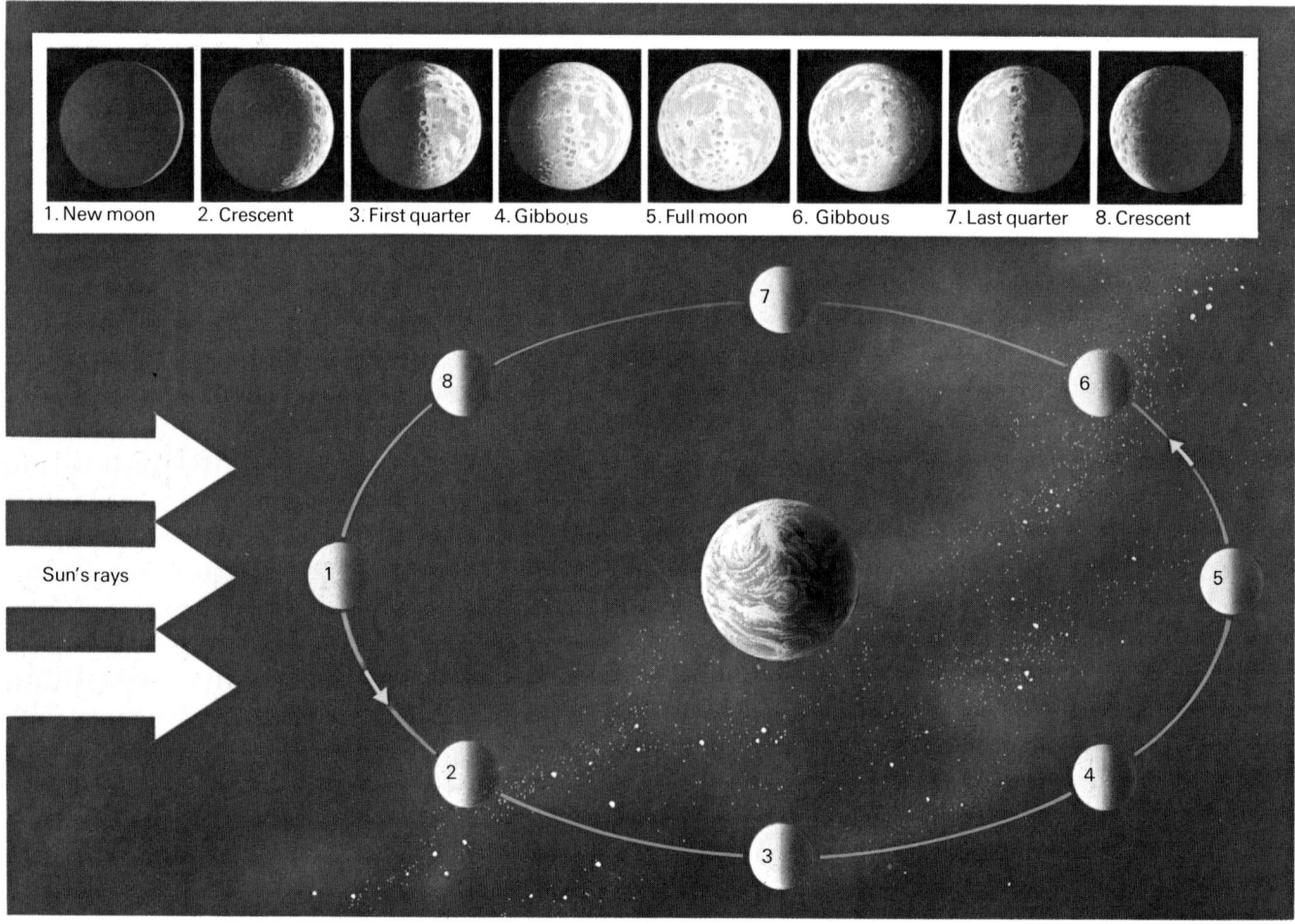

1. New moon   2. Crescent   3. First quarter   4. Gibbous   5. Full moon   6. Gibbous   7. Last quarter   8. Crescent

Sun's rays

side is towards us and we see nothing. Then, as the Moon moves around the Earth, a little of the lit-up side comes into view and we see a crescent. As more of the lit-up side comes round, the crescent grows into a semi-circle and then we have half moon. This grows into a full circle — full moon — when we can see all the lit-up side. Then the full moon shrinks to a half moon and then to a crescent again before we have another new moon. The time it takes for the Moon to go through one complete cycle of phases is just over 29½ days. This is also the length of one complete day and night at any point on the Moon.

The Moon's motion also causes *eclipses* to occur from time to time. When the Moon comes directly between the Earth and the Sun, its shadow sweeps across the Earth's surface. Anyone within the shadow will see the Sun's disc blocked out by the Moon, producing a total eclipse of the Sun, or total *solar eclipse*. Around the Moon's shadow or *umbra*, is a region of partial shadow called the *penumbra*. In places where only the penumbra falls, only part of the Sun's disc is hidden by the Moon. This kind of eclipse is called a partial eclipse. A total eclipse lasts only a few minutes, but a partial eclipse may last for an hour or so. A *lunar eclipse,* or eclipse of the Moon, happens when the Earth comes directly between the Moon and the Sun and the Earth's shadow falls across the Moon, hiding it from view for a short while. Because the orbit of the Moon is tilted, eclipses do not happen every month but usually only once or twice a year.

The Moon also causes tides to occur on the Earth. The gravitational attraction of the Moon slightly raises the level of the ocean beneath the Moon. At the same time, the motion of the Earth causes another rise in level to occur on the opposite side of the world. As the Earth rotates beneath these rises, they appear to move around the world, producing a high tide twice a day. In between, the level falls, giving low tides. The rises in level are also influenced by the Sun. When the Sun is in line with the Moon and the Earth — at new moon and full moon — the rise and fall of the tides is large, giving *spring tides*. Between new moon and full moon, when the Sun, Earth and Moon form a right angle, the rise and fall is small, giving *neap tides*.

Above: **An eclipse of the Moon occurs when the Earth's shadow passes over the Moon.**

Right: **A total eclipse of the Moon occurs when the Moon is completely within the Earth's shadow. Before and after, when it is partly in the Earth's shadow, a partial eclipse occurs.**

Below right: **An eclipse of the Sun occurs when the Moon's shadow falls on the Earth's surface. A total eclipse, in which the Sun is completely obscured by the Moon, occurs only in a small region. But, on either side of this region, the Moon partly shades the surface and a partial eclipse can be seen.**

Left: **The Moon goes through a cycle of phases as it revolves around the Earth. At new moon (1), the dark side is towards the Earth, and the Moon is almost invisible. Then, as the Moon moves in its orbit, the illuminated side comes into view. First we see a crescent moon (2) and this widens into a half moon (3). Then comes a gibbous moon (4) before a full moon is reached (5), when the Moon is halfway through its orbit and the illuminated side faces the Earth. Then the shape shrinks to become gibbous (6), half moon (7) and crescent (8), before we are back to new moon. The whole cycle takes just over 29½ days.**

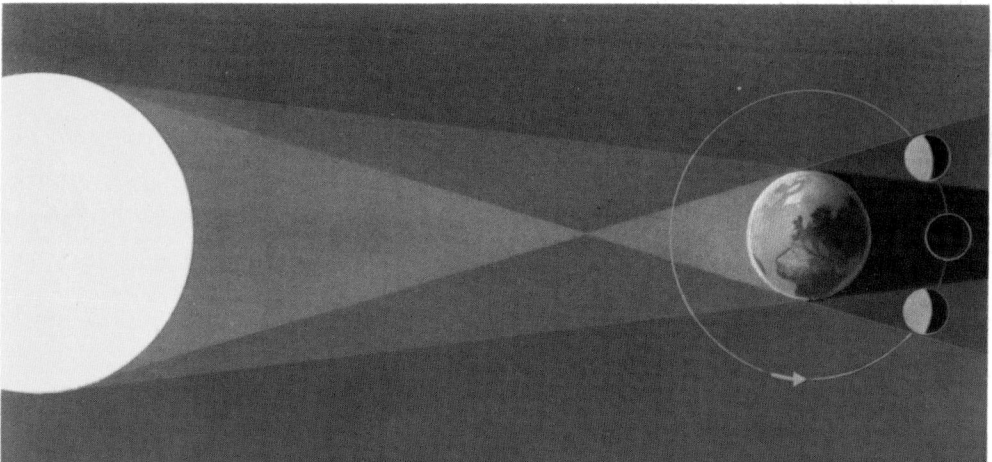

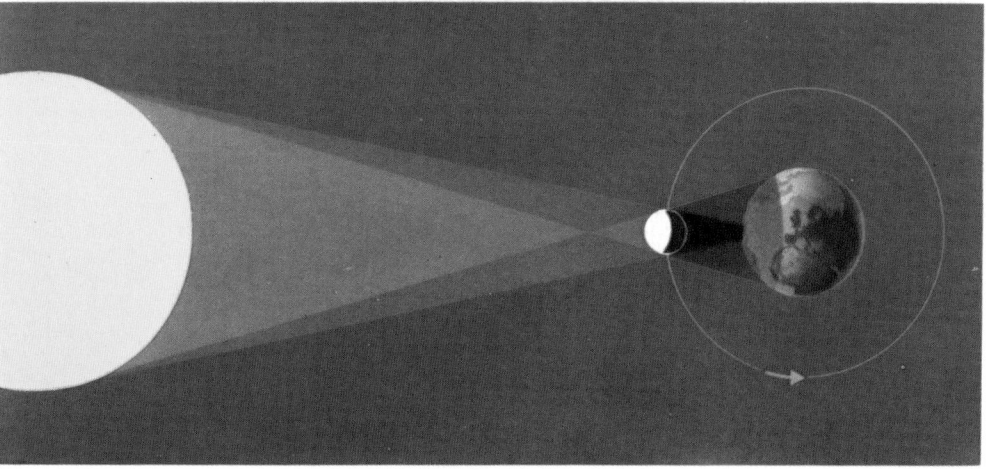

Latitude, Longitude and Time

Latitude and Longitude

Imaginary lines of latitude and longitude divide up the Earth's surface. These lines enable us to locate any place with precision. Latitude shows that a place is on a line running east-west a certain distance north (N) or south (S) of the Equator. The Equator is at 0° latitude, the North Pole at 90°N and the South Pole at 90°S. All other places come somewhere in between. Longitude shows that the place is also on a particular line running north-south. The line of 0° longitude runs from the North Pole to the South Pole through Greenwich Observatory in Britain. All other lines of longitude are related to this line, being up to 180° west (W) or 180° east (E) of it. To find the position of any place on the Earth's surface, it is necessary to give its latitude and longitude. This defines a pair of lines, and the place is at their intersection.

Latitude can be found by observing the positions of certain stars or the Sun in relation to the horizon. Longitude is found by measuring the time at which the Sun or certain stars reach a particular height in the sky.

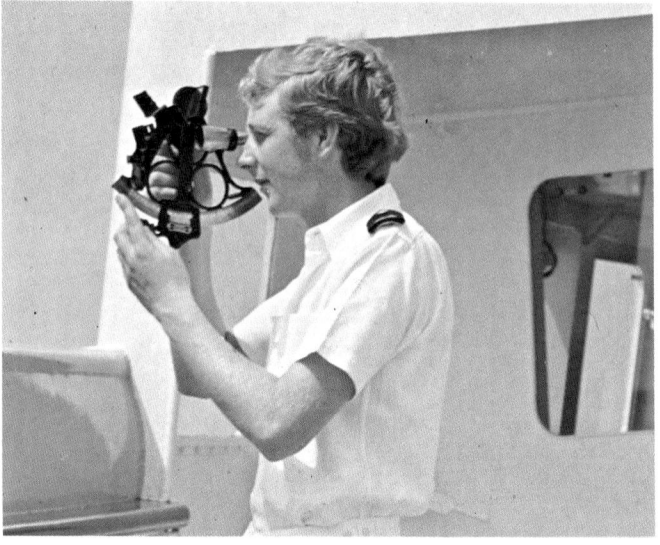

Time

Although we have many kinds of clocks and watches to tell the time, basically time is measured by the motion of the Earth. A day is the time it takes for the Earth to rotate once on its axis in relation to the Sun. This length of time is then divided into 24 hours, each consisting of 60 minutes, each of 60 seconds. This division into hours, minutes and seconds has no special meaning; it is simply convenient for our everyday lives. We also use months in measuring time, but this is a very approximate method as our months vary in length from 28 to 31 days. A year — the time it takes the Earth to go once around the Sun — is a good unit for measuring long periods of time, not only because it is long, but also because it can be measured very precisely. To the nearest second, a year is 365 days 5 hours 48 minutes and 46 seconds.

These odd hours, minutes and seconds have given people a lot of trouble in producing a calendar in which a particular date always occurs at the same time of the year. This is necessary to keep the months and days in step with the seasons. The ancient Egyptians thought that the year was exactly 365 days long, but every new year arrived one quarter of a day too early with such a calendar. After a time, the seasons began to get obviously later in the year. Julius Caesar realized what was wrong and, in 46 BC, produced a calendar in which most years still had 365 days, but every fourth year — a leap year — had 366 days. This made the average year longer by 6 hours, but this was now 11 minutes too much. By the 1500s, the calendar was several days out and, in 1582, Pope Gregory XIII changed the calendar again. He decreed that every century year (for example 1700, 1800) would not be a leap year unless it could be divided by 400 (for example 1600, 2000). This calendar reduced the error in the length of the year to an average of 26 seconds and it is the calendar that we now use.

However, for all this scientific accuracy, our calendar still has months of different lengths named by the ancient Romans, and the same date falls on a different day of the week from year to year. People have worked out a calendar in which every date always falls on the same day of the week. With this calendar, it would not be necessary to print new diaries and calendars every year, as each year would be exactly the same as the one before.

Another problem that occurs with telling the time is one's location on the Earth's surface. Because everyone expects it to be light at noon and dark at midnight (except in polar regions, where it may be light or dark for months at a time), the world is divided into several different time zones.

Left: **A naval officer uses a sextant to find his position. The sextant measures the angle between the horizon and the Sun or a star. With this information and the exact time, he can work out his position.**

Right: **One kind of sundial, man's first reliable clock. The angle of the shadows changes as the Sun moves from east to west, and thus shows the time of day. The length of the shadows at any particular time varies according to the season.**

Below left: **The line of 0° longitude, which is called the prime meridian, passes through Greenwich Observatory in London. All positions of longitude are measured in degrees east or west of this line.**

Below: **The world is divided into several time zones. As people travel from one zone to another, they change their watches to match the local time.**

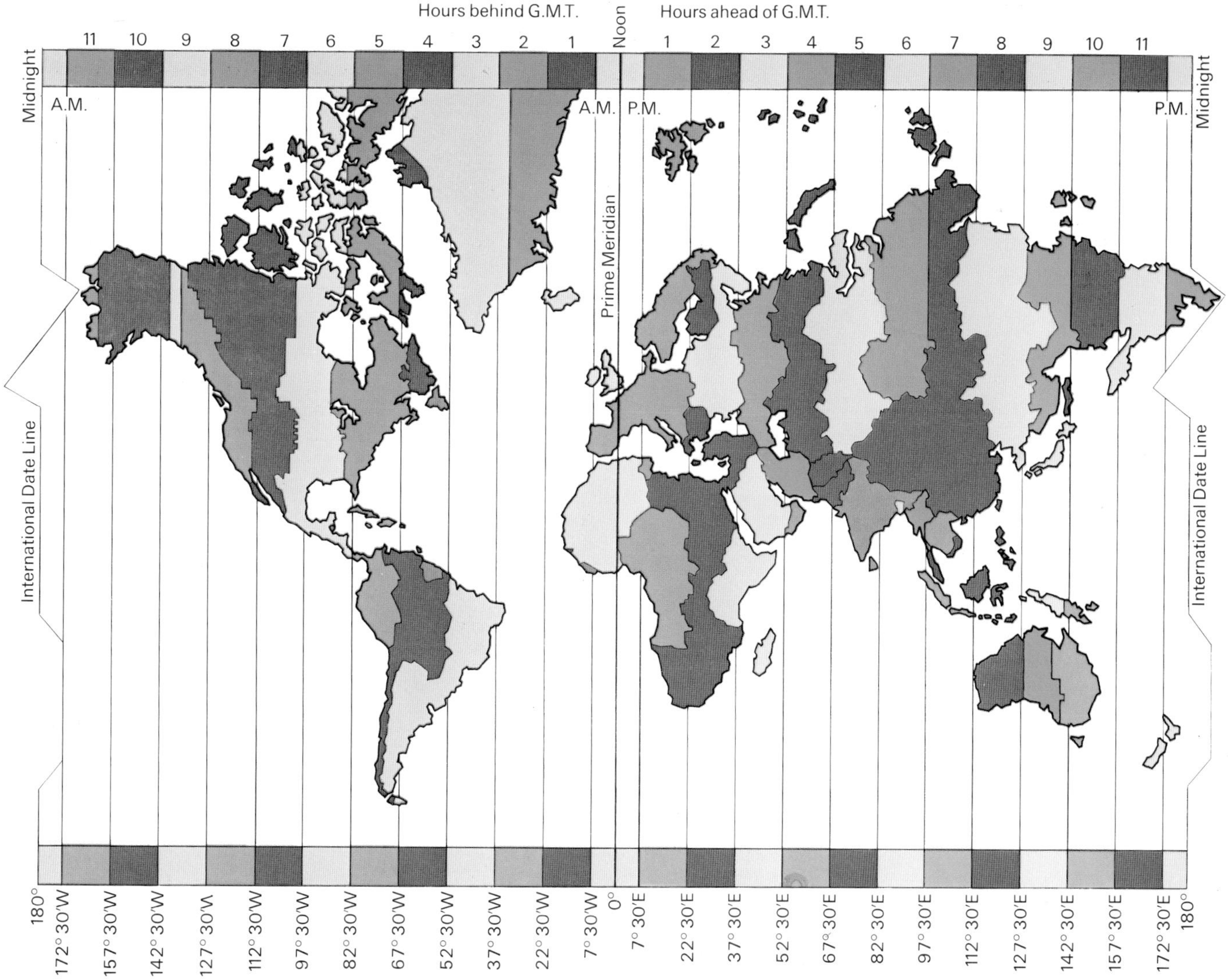

Hours behind G.M.T.   Noon   Hours ahead of G.M.T.

11 10 9 8 7 6 5 4 3 2 1   1 2 3 4 5 6 7 8 9 10 11

Midnight   A.M.   A.M. P.M.   P.M.   Midnight

Prime Meridian

International Date Line   International Date Line

180° 172°30'W 157°30'W 142°30'W 127°30'W 112°30'W 97°30'W 82°30'W 67°30'W 52°30'W 37°30'W 22°30'W 7°30'W 0° 7°30'E 22°30'E 37°30'E 52°30'E 67°30'E 82°30'E 97°30'E 112°30'E 127°30'E 142°30'E 157°30'E 172°30'E 180°

The Atmosphere

About 5,000 million million tonnes of gas make up the Earth's atmosphere. A column of air, weighing about one tonne, is pressing down on our shoulders. But we do not feel this pressure, because it is balanced by the same air pressure within our bodies.

The atmosphere is essential for life on Earth. It contains oxygen for animals and carbon dioxide for plants. The ozone layer in the stratosphere protects life on Earth by absorbing most of the Sun's harmful ultraviolet radiation. And the general circulation of the atmosphere redistributes heat around the globe, thus acting like a giant thermostat.

Dry air is composed of nitrogen (78.09% by volume), oxygen (20.95%) and argon (0.93%), together with minute proportions of other gases, including carbon dioxide, neon, helium, methane, krypton, nitrous oxide, hydrogen, ozone and xenon. The amount of carbon dioxide varies considerably from place to place, being greatest over cities and lowest over countryside. Air also contains tiny specks of dust and other substances, such as salt crystals (derived from ocean spray). There are also varying amounts of water vapour evaporated from the Earth's surface, especially from the oceans.

About five-sixths of the total mass of the atmosphere, including nearly all the water vapour, is confined to the lowest zone — the troposphere. Most of the weather we experience originates in this zone. The temperature in the troposphere decreases upwards to the tropopause — the upper limit of the troposphere. There, the temperature becomes stable at about $-55°C$ ($-67°F$). The height of the tropopause varies between about 8 kilometres (5 miles) over the poles to about 11 kilometres (7 miles) over the middle latitudes and 18 kilometres (11 miles) over the Equator.

Above the tropopause is the lower stratosphere, where conditions are relatively calm and so jet aircraft often fly there. However, strong winds called jet streams blow through the upper troposphere and the lower stratosphere. Reaching speeds of 160 kilometres per hour (100 m.p.h.), these winds can be an obstacle or an aid to high-flying aircraft. Above the tropopause, temperatures remain stable at first but, eventually, they start to rise, reaching about $2°C$ ($36°F$) just above the ozone layer.

Beyond the stratosphere, from about 50 to 500 kilometres (30 to 300 miles) above sea level is the ionosphere. Here, temperatures decrease at first, reaching about $-70°C$ ($-94°F$) at a height of 80 kilometres (50 miles) above sea level. Then temperatures start to rise steadily in the ionosphere, reaching more than $2,000°C$ ($3,600°F$) at 400 kilometres (250 miles). The ionosphere is so called because the thinly-distributed gas molecules are ionized (electrically charged) by solar radiation. These charged particles are important in radio communications because they reflect some radio waves. Radio communications are sometimes interrupted by occasional magnetic storms, when the ionosphere is disturbed by streams of charged particles from the Sun. These particles are deflected through the ionosphere by the Earth's magnetic field. Over the magnetic poles, they collide with molecules in the ionosphere and cause spectacular glowing displays of light called *aurorae*. Beyond the ionosphere lies the exosphere, where the thin air gradually merges into space.

Left: **A weather-satellite photograph of a typhoon, or tropical cyclone, over the Pacific Ocean. These large rotating air systems, which are called hurricanes in the Atlantic Ocean, bring fierce winds and may cause serious flooding and great devastation as they move over coastal areas. Information from weather satellites has enabled meteorologists to study the formation of typhoons, chart their movements and issue advance warnings to shipping and threatened coastal areas.**

Right: **A section through the atmosphere, including the troposphere, stratosphere, ionosphere and exosphere. Alongside the diagram are the temperatures and air pressures at different levels.**

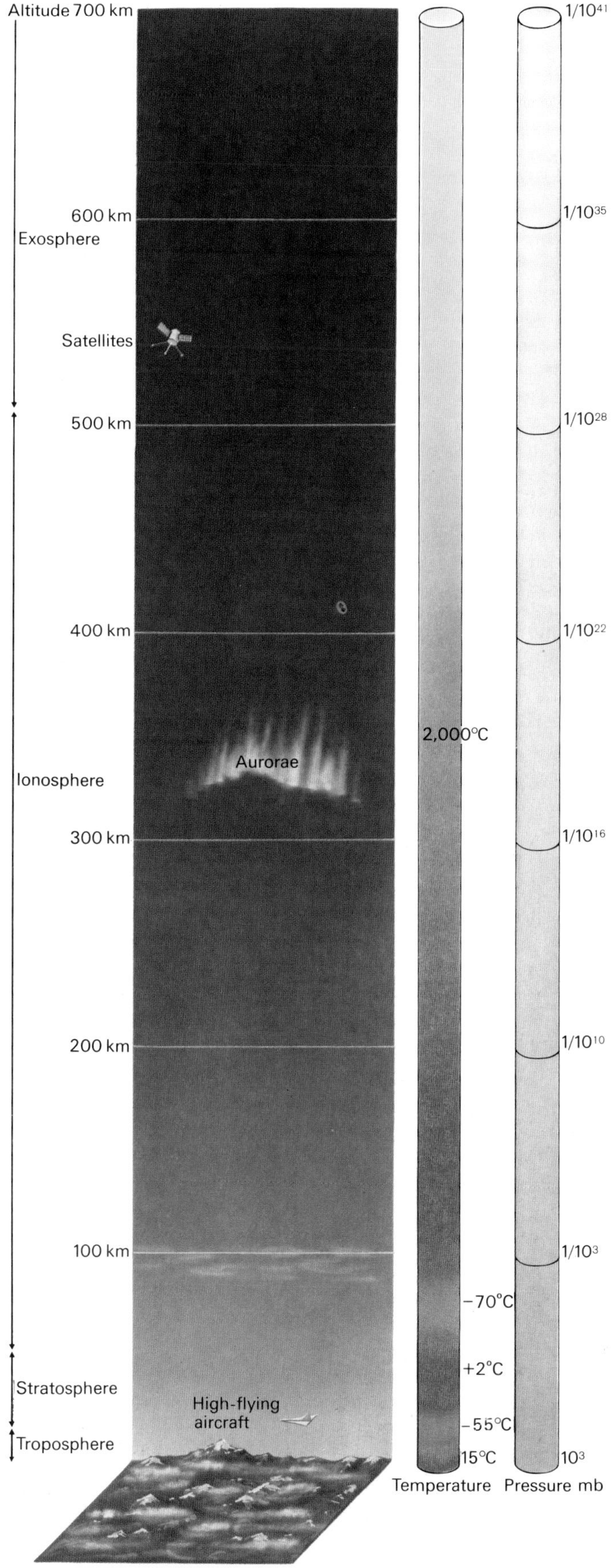

Altitude 700 km

600 km
Exosphere

Satellites

500 km

400 km

Ionosphere

Aurorae

300 km

200 km

100 km

Stratosphere

Troposphere

High-flying
aircraft

2,000°C

−70°C

+2°C

−55°C

15°C   10³

Temperature Pressure mb

1/10⁴¹

1/10³⁵

1/10²⁸

1/10²²

1/10¹⁶

1/10¹⁰

1/10³

Winds

The air in the atmosphere is constantly circulating. It is like a vast machine powered by the Sun. But heat is unevenly distributed, the effect of the Sun being greatest at the Equator, where it passes directly overhead. As a result, there are great variations in air pressure, causing air currents (winds) to flow from high pressure areas towards low pressure areas.

At the Equator, air near the ground is heated, making it expand and rise. As a result, equatorial regions are characterized by a low-pressure air system, called the *doldrums*. On both sides of the Equator, air flows towards the doldrums in the trade-wind belts. The warm air rising above the equatorial zone cools as it ascends and spreads out north and south. Finally it sinks back to Earth around latitudes 30° North and 30° South, creating two high-pressure belts called the *horse latitudes*. At the surface, some of the descending air flows into the trade winds, and some flows polewards in the westerlies. The westerlies meet cold, dense air flowing from the poles along the polar front. The intermingling of warm, light, sub-tropical air with cold, dense polar air creates rotating low-pressure systems, called *depressions*. These bring changeable, stormy weather to middle latitudes.

This simple pattern of atmospheric circulation is complicated by several factors. First, because the Earth spins on its axis, winds do not flow north-south, but are deflected to the right in the northern hemisphere and to the left in the southern hemisphere. Winds are also deflected by mountain ranges. Another important factor is the seasonal development of large and fairly stable air masses. For example, the interiors of large mid-latitude continents heat up in summer. Large low-pressure air masses form, into which winds are drawn. But, in winter, these continental interiors are cold, and so high-pressure air masses form, from which icy winds blow outwards.

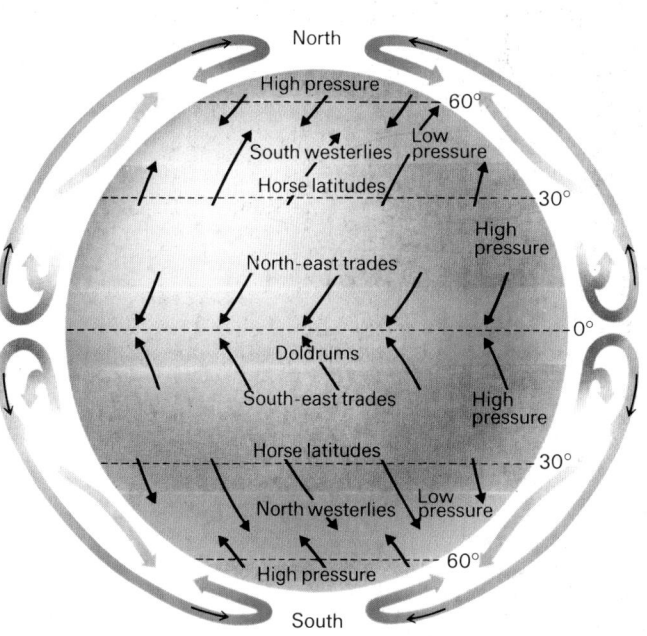

Above: **The main wind belts on the Earth's surface, and the main air-circulation currents in the atmosphere. Air circulates because uneven heating of the Earth gives rise to air-pressure variations in the** atmosphere. **The air moves as winds, from high-pressure to low-pressure regions. The general pattern of prevailing winds shown here does not take account of local and seasonal variations.**

15

Weather

Weather is the day-to-day condition of the air. The chief elements of weather are the temperature and pressure of the air, wind speeds and directions, and the amount of moisture in the air — particularly if the moisture is being precipitated as rain, snow, hail, sleet, dew or frost.

All air contains moisture in the form of water vapour, which is water in gaseous form. Warm air can hold more water vapour than cold air. When warm air is cooled, usually by moving upwards in the troposphere, its capacity to hold water vapour decreases. Finally, *dew point* is reached — that is, the air is completely saturated, having a relative humidity of 100 per cent. Further cooling beyond dew point leads to water vapour condensing around nucleii, such as specks of dust or salt, to form water droplets or, in cold air, minute ice crystals. Large quantities of condensed water vapour form clouds.

There are two main kinds of clouds: cumuliform ('heap' clouds) and stratiform ('layer' clouds). Clouds are classified according to their height. Low clouds, within 2.5 kilometres (1.6 miles) of the surface, include: grey stratus; cumulus, a white heap cloud; cumulonimbus, a heap thundercloud; nimbostratus, a layer cloud often blurred by rain or snow; and stratocumulus, a greyish-white layer cloud. Medium-height clouds, from 2.5 to 6 kilometres (1.6 to 3.7 miles) are the greyish-white, rounded altocumulus, and the altostratus, which is a greyish layer cloud. Above 6 kilometres (3.7 miles) are the high clouds, including the feathery cirrus, cirrocumulus and cirrostratus.

Clouds form part of the water cycle, by which water is continually conveyed from the salty oceans to the land, where it is released from the air as precipitation. This provides the land with the fresh water needed by animal and plant life. Finally, the water completes the cycle by returning to the oceans.

Rainfall is of three main kinds. *Convectional rain* occurs, especially in the tropics, when hot air rises and water vapour condenses into towering, often anvil-topped cumulonimbus clouds. Inside the turbulent clouds, the water droplets collide, fuse together and fall as raindrops. *Cyclonic rain* occurs in depressions when warm air rises above wedges of cold air along cold and warm fronts and occlusions. In the middle latitudes, clouds contain super-cooled water droplets, which are still liquid although their temperature may be as low as $-40°C$ ($-40°F$), and ice crystals. The ice crystals collide with supercooled droplets and grow in size. They then start to fall, melting near the surface to become raindrops or, if the air is cold, they join together to form snowflakes. *Orographic rain* is caused when air rises over a mountain range.

Precipitation is a feature of storms. The commonest storms are thunderstorms, about 45,000 of which break out every day somewhere in the world. Thunderstorms occur when strongly rising air currents cause cumulonimbus clouds to form. As temperatures within the clouds fall, the outer shells of super-cooled water droplets freeze and acquire a positive electrical charge. But, when the core subsequently freezes, it has a negative charge. The core expands as it freezes and shatters the outer shell, tiny splinters of which waft upwards, giving the top of the cloud a positive charge. The heavier cores remain lower down, building up a large negative charge. The air between the cloud and ground normally acts as an electrical insulator. But, when the charge on the cloud becomes great enough, the insulation breaks down and lightning — a gigantic spark — occurs. Along the lightning's path, heat causes a violent expansion of the air, and the resultant compression wave is heard as thunder.

Other storms include large, rotating hurricanes, also called tropical cyclones. Hurricanes strike the coasts of Central America and the southeastern United States about 11 times per year. They cause much damage, especially because strong winds hurl high waves onto the shore, causing flooding. Tornadoes are smaller, measuring about 500 metres (1,600 feet) across. Wind speeds in these rotating, funnel-like columns of air may reach 650 kilometres per hour (400 m.p.h.). In tornadoes, buildings may explode because the air pressure outside the buildings is far lower than the air pressure inside them.

Weather satellites orbiting the Earth help forecasters to track hurricanes and give warnings of their advance, besides supplying much other information. At surface weather stations, on land and at sea, meteorologists take regular measurements of air conditions, including temperature, pressure, humidity, precipitation, and wind speeds and directions. Information about conditions in the upper air is provided by radiosondes — hydrogen-filled balloons carrying instruments.

Information from weather stations is sent to forecast centres, where it is often analysed by computers. Synoptic charts are prepared, summarizing weather conditions over a large area. By comparing the latest synoptic chart with preceding charts, developments are noted. Meteorologists deduce how weather conditions will probably change and express them on a forecast chart, from which forecasts are made for the general public.

Grey stratus clouds

Cumulus clouds

Cumulonimbus clouds

Nimbostratus clouds

Stratocumulus clouds

Altocumulus clouds

Altostratus clouds

Cirrus clouds

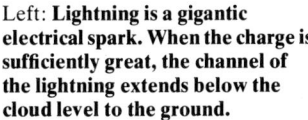

Cirrocumulus clouds

Cirrostratus clouds

Above: **Weather stations use white shelters, called Stevenson screens, to enclose thermometers and, sometimes, other instruments used to measure air conditions. The air can circulate freely through the louvres, so that the instruments, protected from the Sun and the wind, make true readings.**

Left: **Lightning is a gigantic electrical spark. When the charge is sufficiently great, the channel of the lightning extends below the cloud level to the ground.**

Right: **The diagram shows how water continuously circulates from sea to land and back again in the water, or hydrologic cycle. Through this cycle, land areas obtain a regular supply of fresh water, which is essential to the Earth's plant and animal life.**

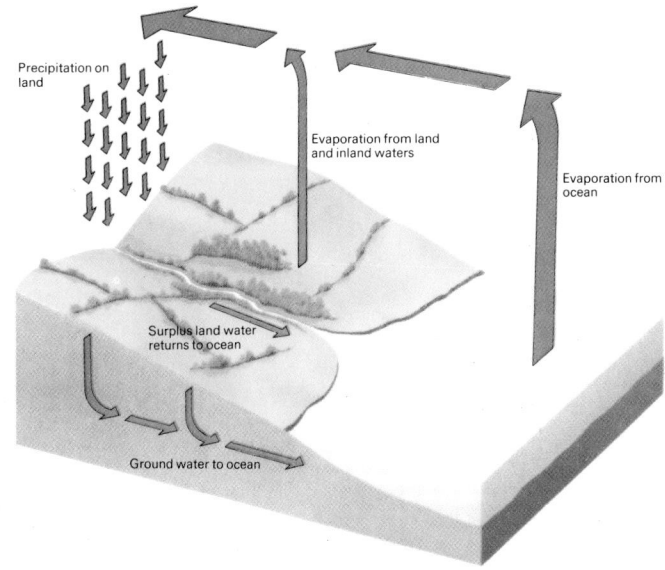

Precipitation on land

Evaporation from land and inland waters

Evaporation from ocean

Surplus land water returns to ocean

Ground water to ocean

Climate

Climate is the typical or average weather of a place based on records covering a period of years. The word climate comes from the Greek word *klima,* which means slope. The Greeks believed that the Earth 'sloped' from the Mediterranean southwards to the hot equatorial zone and northwards to the cold polar region. Hence, a Greek scholar Parmenides suggested in about 500 BC that there were five climatic zones. The central equatorial zone was hot all the year round. The middle latitudes in both hemispheres had summer and winter seasons. And the polar regions were cold all the year round.

But other factors, such as the terrain and the proximity to the sea, complicate this simple pattern. For example, mountains and plateaux have cooler climates than surrounding plains, because temperatures fall, on average, by about 6°C (11°F) for every kilometre (0.6 mile) of altitude. For example, in Kenya, which straddles the Equator, the coastal port of Mombasa has average temperatures of 27°C (81°F) all the year round. But, on the high southwestern plateau in the interior, average temperatures are

10°C to 20°C (50°F to 68°F), and so the plateau has proved more attractive to European settlers than the coast.

The terrain influences the rainfall too. For example, when winds from the oceans are forced to rise over coastal mountain ranges, they lose most of their moisture during their ascent. Beyond the crest of the mountains, the winds are dry and there is often a 'rain shadow' area.

The oceans have a considerable effect on climate. The Sun's rays heat the surfaces of land areas more intensely and faster than they heat the sea. But land areas cool extremely quickly, whereas bodies of water retain heat about two-and-a-half times as readily as land. Generally, in maritime areas, winds from the oceans warm the land in winter and cool it in summer. This moderating influence is particularly pronounced, for example, along the west coasts of land masses in the middle latitudes of the northern hemisphere, where the prevailing winds are southwesterlies. But, beyond the moderating influence of the oceans, the continental interiors have extreme climates. In southwestern Ireland, the

Left: **Climate around the world.**

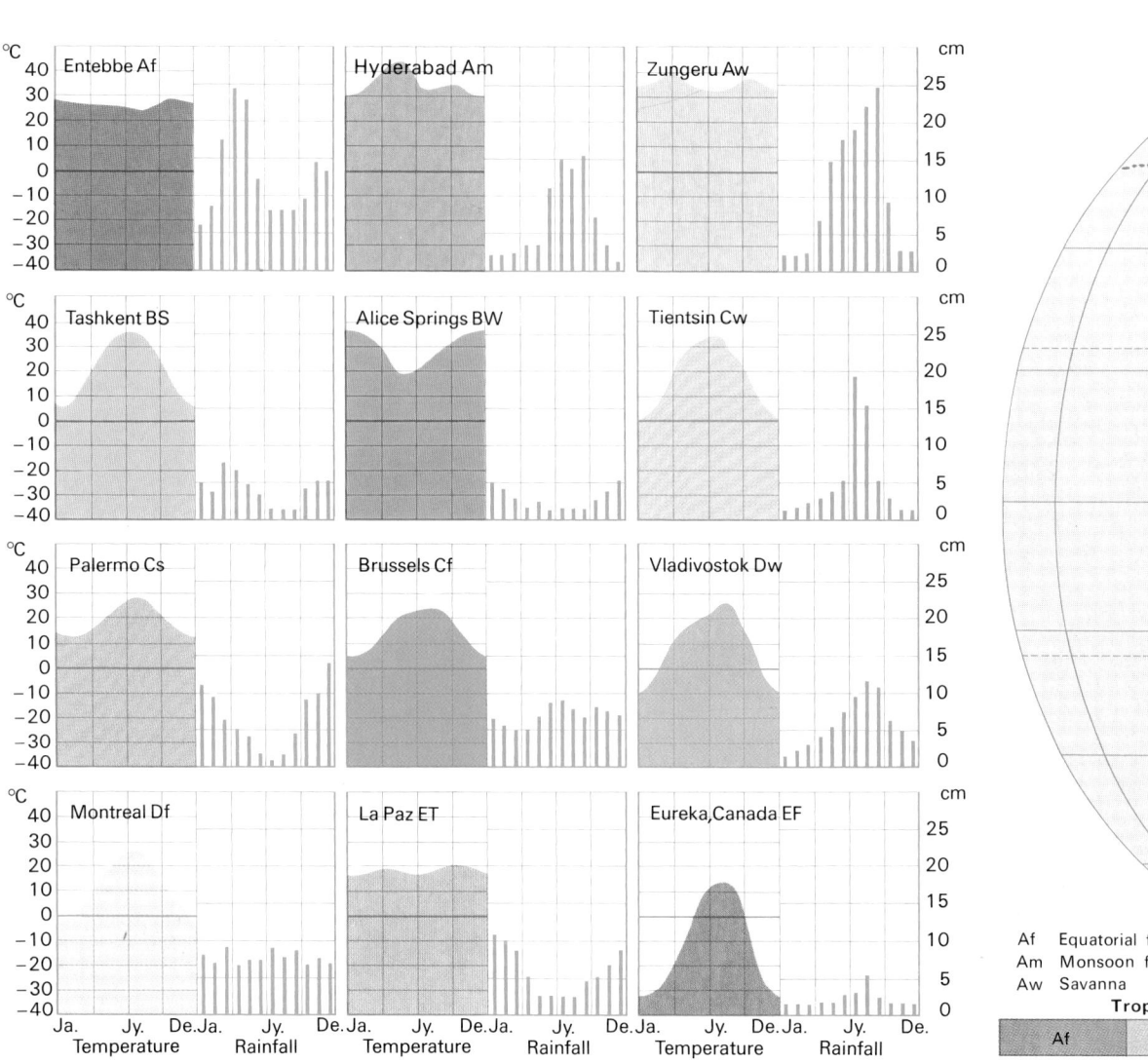

Af   Equatorial forest
Am   Monsoon forest
Aw   Savanna
Tropical climates

| Af | Am | Aw |

average temperature in the coldest month is 5°C (41°F) and the average in the warmest month is 16°C (61°F) — an average annual temperature range of only 11°C (20°F). But, in the same latitude, south of Moscow, the average temperature in the coldest month is −11°C (12°F) and, in the warmest month, it is 21°C (70°F) — an average annual temperature range of 32°C (58°F).

Ocean currents affect climate too. The icy Labrador current flows southwards down the eastern coast of Canada, and St. John's in Newfoundland, for example, has cold winters, with an average temperature in the coldest month of −5°C (23°F). St. John's lies in the same latitude as Brittany, which has mild winters. The coastlands of northwestern Europe are warmed in winter by onshore winds that pass over an extension of the warm Gulf Stream — an ocean current that originates in the Caribbean.

There are various ways of classifying climates, but most classifications used today are based on the work of Russian meteorologist Vladimir Köppen in the early 1900s. Köppen classified climates according to temperature and rainfall. He distinguished five main climatic types, coding them **A, B, C, D** and **E**. Type **A** is the tropical, rainy climate, with average temperatures of over 18°C (64°F) in every month of the year. Type **B** is a dry climate, with an average of less than 250 millimetres (10 inches) of rain per year and a high evaporation rate. Type **C** is the middle-latitude, warm temperate climate, with average temperatures in the coldest month from −3°C to 18°C (27°F to 64°F). Type **D** is a cold and snowy climate, with an average temperature of less than −3°C (27°F) in the coldest month, but the average temperature in the warmest month is more than 10°C (50°F). And type **E** is the polar climate, with an average temperature of less than 10°C (50°F) in the warmest month. Cold, mountain regions, once included in type **E**, are now usually classified **H**.

To distinguish between rainfall patterns, a second group of symbols has been added: **S** (dry steppelands), **W** (deserts), **f** (places with ample, well-distributed rainfall), **m** (monsoon, or seasonal rainfall), **s** (a dry summer) and **w** (a dry winter). To distinguish between polar climates, the code **T** represents tundra and **F** signifies ice-sheet climates. Hence, type **Af** is equatorial forest, which is hot and wet all the year round, whereas **Aw** is tropical savanna, with summer rains and a winter drought.

Other symbols are: **a** (hot summers), **b** (warm summers), **c** (cool summers), **d** (very cold winters), **h** (dry and hot) and **k** (dry and cold). Hence, the code **Cfb** means a middle-latitude, warm temperate climate, with ample, well-distributed rainfall and warm summers — the characteristic climate of northwestern Europe.

Below: **World climate zones.**

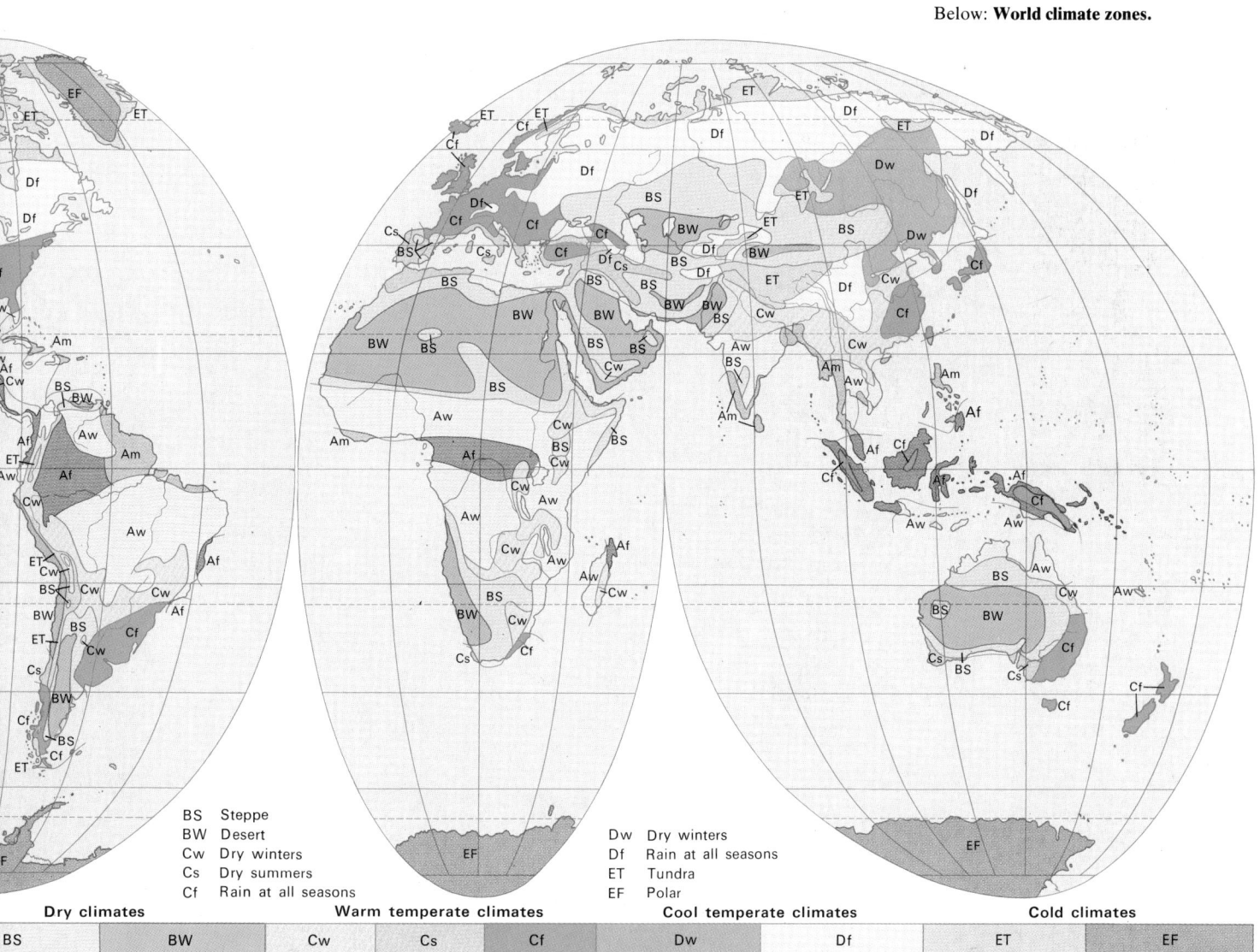

BS	Steppe		Dw	Dry winters
BW	Desert		Df	Rain at all seasons
Cw	Dry winters		ET	Tundra
Cs	Dry summers		EF	Polar
Cf	Rain at all seasons			

Dry climates		Warm temperate climates			Cool temperate climates		Cold climates	
BS	BW	Cw	Cs	Cf	Dw	Df	ET	EF

The Oceans

The oceans, which are interconnected, cover 70.8 per cent of the Earth's surface. The largest ocean, the Pacific, sprawls over the vast area of 165,236,000 square kilometres (63,798,000 square miles) — more than the combined area of all the continents. The oceans have an average depth of about 3.5 kilometres (2.2 miles), but the deepest known point is in Challenger Deep, part of the Mariana Trench in the Pacific, which is 11.033 kilometres (6.855 miles) deep.

The water in the oceans totals about 1,300 million cubic kilometres (312 million cubic miles) — more than 97 per cent of the world's total water. On average, seawater contains about 3.5 per cent by weight of dissolved substances. Nearly 3 per cent is composed of chlorine and sodium, which together form sodium chloride (common salt). Other substances, such as sulphur, magnesium, potassium and calcium, are present in abundance in seawater, and there are minute proportions of many other elements. In fact, seawater is a great treasure trove of valuable and useful minerals, but the extraction of most of them is extremely costly and, therefore, uneconomic. The only important substances currently obtained from seawater are common salt, magnesium and bromine. The extraction of other substances will probably not be undertaken until land reserves are nearly exhausted. Also present in seawater are various gases dissolved from the atmosphere. The most important is oxygen, on which marine organisms depend.

The salinity of seawater averages 35 parts per 1,000 (usually expressed as 35‰), but it varies from place to place. In the Red Sea, where the rate of evaporation is high, the salinity reaches 41‰. But, in the Baltic Sea, rivers supply large amounts of fresh water and the salinity is lowered to 7.2‰. Salinity and temperature affect the density of seawater, high salinity and low temperatures both causing the water to have a relatively high density. The temperature of ocean water varies between −2°C (28°F) — its approximate freezing point — and 29°C (84°F).

Density differences contribute to the continuous circulation of ocean waters, because dense water sinks beneath less dense water. However, the chief movements of ocean water are: tides, caused by the gravitational pull of the Moon and, to a lesser extent, the Sun; waves, which move water particles in a circular orbit, but not horizontally, except on shores; and ocean currents.

Surface ocean currents generally follow prevailing winds although, because of the Earth's spin, they swing to the right of the wind direction in the Northern Hemisphere and to the left in the Southern Hemisphere. Generally, currents cause the surface waters of the Northern Hemisphere to circulate in a clockwise direction. In the Southern Hemisphere, the circulation is anti-clockwise. Surface currents are classed as *cold* if they flow from polar regions towards the tropics, and *warm* if they flow polewards from the tropics. The temperature of offshore currents has a great effect on the climates of coastlands.

The effect of surface currents is hardly noticeable at about 350 metres (1,150 feet) below the surface. But the waters in the ocean depths are not still, and several deep, vigorous counter-currents have been found flowing in an opposite direction to those on the surface. Scientists have found that, even in the deepest parts of the oceans, the water is moving. They base this conclusion on the fact

Sea level

Transform fau

Mohorovičić discontinuity

Mantle

that fishes have been found at great depths. If the water were still, the oxygen dissolved from the air would have been used up long ago and no fishes could possibly survive.

The study of the ocean floor has been of tremendous importance in establishing how the oceans were formed and how the continents have drifted around the Earth's surface. The ocean floor consists of three main zones: the continental shelf, the continental slope and the abyss. The gently sloping continental shelves border the continents, extending outwards to a depth of about 180 metres (600 feet). They vary considerably in width. For example, the continental shelf off northwestern Europe extends about 300 kilometres (190 miles) west of Land's End. But, off the west coast of South America, there is practically no continental shelf. The shelves are, in fact, submerged parts of the continents. Islands that rise above water level are called continental islands to distinguish them from oceanic islands, which rise from the abyss.

The continental shelves end at the start of the continental slope, the true edge of the continents. The continental slope descends steeply down to the abyss.

The abyss contains large, sediment-covered plains, interrupted by lofty volcanic mountains, some of which surface as islands, and long, broad ridges, 2 to 4 kilometres (1.2 to 2.5 miles) high and up to 4,000 kilometres (2,500 miles) wide. One ridge runs the whole length of the Atlantic Ocean. These ridges, which surface in places such as Iceland, are centres of volcanic activity and earthquakes. Other important features of the abyss are yawning chasms called oceanic trenches.

Left: **Thor Heyerdahl's papyrus boat *Ra*, like those of ancient Egypt, was driven by winds and currents.**

Below: **A section through the Atlantic Ocean. In order to show the details clearly, the vertical scale has been exaggerated.**

rift

Crust (including sediments)

Asthenosphere

Formation of the Earth

The Restless Earth

The Earth was formed about 4,600 million years ago from a great cloud of gas, rock and dust that was orbiting around a new star, the Sun. Gradually, heavier materials, such as iron and nickel, sank towards the centre, while lighter materials rose to the surface. And parts of the molten surface hardened into a thin, solid crust of igneous rocks, probably consisting mostly of basalt.

But cracking and reheating often broke up the outer shell and, from remelting, even lighter granitic rocks separated out. When they hardened, these rocks formed the first parts of the continental crust. Gases and water vapour were released from the rocks by continuous volcanic eruptions. These gases formed the atmosphere. Great storms must have raged over the Earth and rains eroded the hardened igneous rock. Streams swept eroded fragments into primeval lakes and seas, where they accumulated to form the first sedimentary rocks.

The early atmosphere probably contained only a minute proportion of oxygen, because volcanic gases are deficient in this life-giving gas. But, after the evolution of oxygen-producing plants around 1,900 million years ago, the proportion of oxygen steadily increased.

The Earth today has an equatorial diameter of 12,756 kilometres (7,926 miles). Measured from pole to pole, however, the diameter is 43 kilometres (27 miles) less, because our planet is not a true sphere, being slightly flattened at the poles and bulging at the Equator. Our knowledge of the Earth's interior is based on the behaviour of seismic (earthquake) waves as they travel through the Earth. From a study of how these waves bend, scientists have concluded that the centre of the Earth's core is a solid sphere with a diameter of about 2,740 kilometres (1,700 miles). The rocks in the solid core are about three times as dense as those in the crust. Surrounding the inner core is a liquid outer core, which is about 2,100 kilometres (1,300 miles) thick. Temperatures in the outer core range from 2,000°C to 5,000°C (3,600°F to 9,000°F), and movements in this molten material

probably generate the electricity that gives the Earth its magnetic properties. Between the outer core and the crust is the dense mantle, which is about 2,900 kilometres (1,800 miles) thick. The mantle is mostly solid but, at its top, some rocks are molten or semi-solid. Heating causes these rocks to rise and spread beneath the crust in convection currents.

The Earth's crust beneath the oceanic abyss is only about 6 kilometres (3.7 miles) thick. But the continental crust is mostly 35 to 50 kilometres (22 to 25 miles) in thickness, reaching 60 kilometres (37 miles) under high mountain ranges. There are other contrasts between oceanic and continental crust. First, the basaltic oceanic crust is 3.0 times as dense as water, whereas granitic continental crust is only 2.7 times as dense as water. And all oceanic crust has been formed within the last 200 million years, whereas the continents contain rocks that are more than 3,500 million years old.

The study of the oceanic crust has contributed to the generally accepted theory of *plate tectonics,* or *continental drift.* Scientists now believe that the crust is cracked into a series of 'plates' which are moving around the Earth's surface. The continents are composed of light materials and they rest upon the moving plates.

Plate edges occur along the mid-oceanic ridges. Along these ridges, new crustal rock is being added as molten material wells up from below. For example, in the Atlantic Ocean, studies of rock samples reveal that rocks become progressively older east and west of the mid-Atlantic ridge. These rock samples often contain magnetized particles, which were aligned towards the Earth's magnetic poles when the rock hardened. But these particles have been twisted out of alignment — further evidence of movement.

As a result of this movement, the oceans are widening, or spreading, at 1 to 10 centimetres (0.4 to 4 inches) per year. But the Earth is not expanding, for the crust is being destroyed at other plate edges. These are the oceanic trenches. Here, one plate is pushed beneath another to about 700 kilometres (430 miles) below the surface, before it is finally melted and destroyed. Some

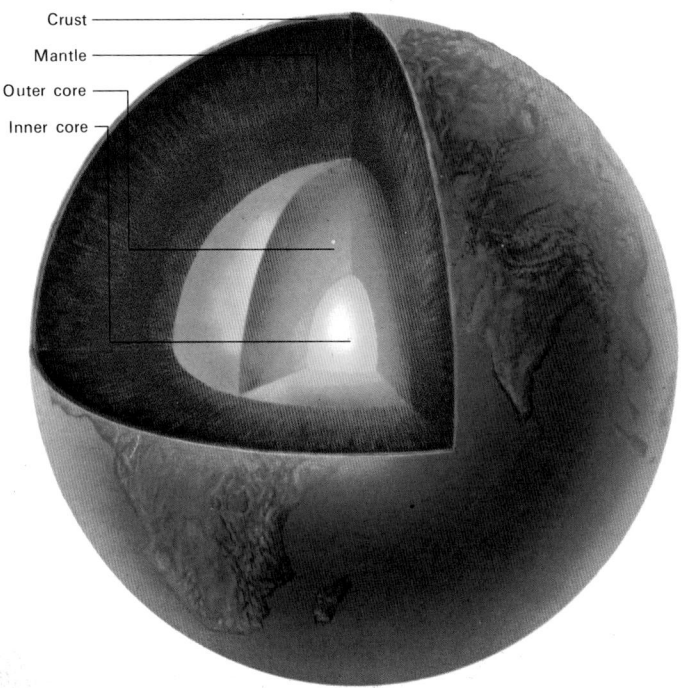

Crust
Mantle
Outer core
Inner core

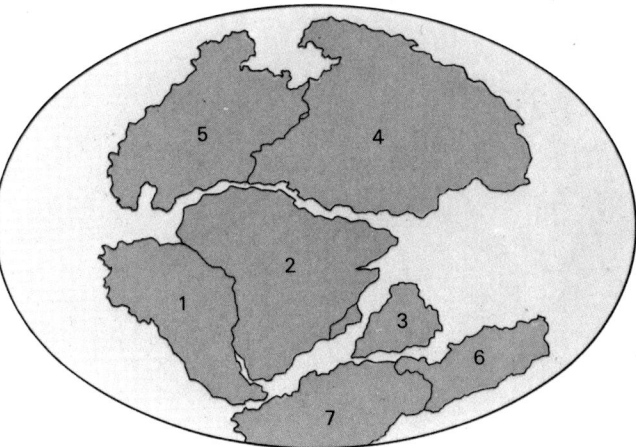

Left: **Zones within the Earth.**

Above: **A super-continent, called Pangaea, existed about 200 million years ago. Since then, the continents have broken away and drifted apart to their present positions.**

Right: **The volcanic island of Surtsey, on the mid-Atlantic ridge. This island appeared off the Icelandic coast in November, 1963 and grew rapidly. After three weeks, its crater had risen to 120 metres (390 feet) above sea level and was almost 1 kilometre (0.6 mile) across.**

of the melted rock may return to the surface through the overriding plate to form a chain of volcanic islands, roughly parallel to the trench. Another type of plate edge, a transform fault, occurs where plates move horizontally alongside each other.

Scientists now believe that, about 200 million years ago, all the continental land masses were grouped together in one super-continent, called Pangaea. The northern part of Pangaea, called Laurasia, consisted of North America and most of Eurasia. The southern part, Gondwanaland, consisted of South America, Africa, the Indian sub-continent, Australia and Antarctica. In the last 180 million years, Pangaea has split apart and the continents have drifted to their present positions. The Indian sub-continent, after separating from Gondwanaland, moved northward and eventually linked up with Asia.

Earthquakes

As plates drift apart, the movement occurs in sudden jerks, which cause earthquakes.

Earthquakes can occur anywhere. They are caused mostly by sudden movements along faults in rocks triggering off destructive vibrations. The most destructive earthquakes occur when the focus (point of origin) is within about 60 kilometres (37 miles) of the Earth's surface. The point on the Earth's surface directly above the focus is called the epicentre. About 10,000 earthquakes are recorded annually, although, on average, only 10 cause major destruction. By plotting the epicentres of all the earthquakes on a world map, it is evident that earthquakes predominate around the edges of the plates. They are much less common in areas away from plate edges.

The intensity of earthquakes is measured on a scale devised by C. F. Richter in 1935. An earthquake rated 2 on the Richter scale is hardly noticeable. But a magnitude of 5 causes some damage, and magnitude 7 is severe. One of the most intensive earthquakes in recent times had a magnitude of 8.9. It occurred in the Prince William Sound off Alaska on March 28, 1964.

This earthquake triggered off a so-called tidal wave — a misnomer because such waves have nothing to do with tides. Hence, scientists use the Japanese term *tsunami*. These fast waves travel through the water at speeds up to 800 kilometres per hour (500 m.p.h.). In the open sea, they may pass unnoticed, because the wave height (the vertical distance between the crest and the trough) is usually less than one metre (three feet). But the energy contained in a tsunami is tremendous, especially because, unlike a normal wave, it extends through the entire depth of the water. As tsunamis approach coasts, the wave height increases rapidly, and they batter the land with terrifying force. The Alaskan earthquake of March 1964 caused a tsunami that reached a height of 67 metres (220 feet). It is the highest yet recorded.

In recent times, scientists have been trying to find ways of alleviating the tension along faults and producing methods of reliable forecasting. One area of research is California in the United States. A long plate edge in California, called the San Andreas fault, is a transform fault. The jagged plate edges become jammed together until the pressure becomes so intense that the plates suddenly lurch forward. In 1906, the plates along the San Andreas fault, which is 960 kilometres (600 miles) long, moved violently. The ground shook with tremendous force and buildings in San Francisco swayed and collapsed. The shift along the fault near San Francisco was about 4.6 metres (15 feet). Broken gas pipes and overturned stoves caused raging fires.

Since 1906, many minor earthquakes have occurred around the San Andreas fault, and scientists now fear that San Francisco may again be threatened. They have, however, made some interesting discoveries. They have found that waste water pumped down disused wells lubricates faults, causing minor tremors. But, if water is pumped out of a well, the dry rocks become firmly locked together. Scientists have, therefore, suggested that they should

EARTHQUAKES
The most destructive earthquake occurred in September 1923, in Japan. After the earthquake, fires, caused mainly by overturned stoves, raged through Tokyo and Yokohama, and about 143,000 people lost their lives. The highest death toll caused by a single earthquake was 830,000. This disaster occurred in Shensi province, China, in 1556.

Right: **This building in the Philippines collapsed during an earthquake in August 1976.**

Below left: **Earthquake damage in Osoppo, Italy: a fireman inspects a house which is in danger of collapsing.**

Below: **World map showing continental plate boundaries, volcanoes and earthquake zones.**

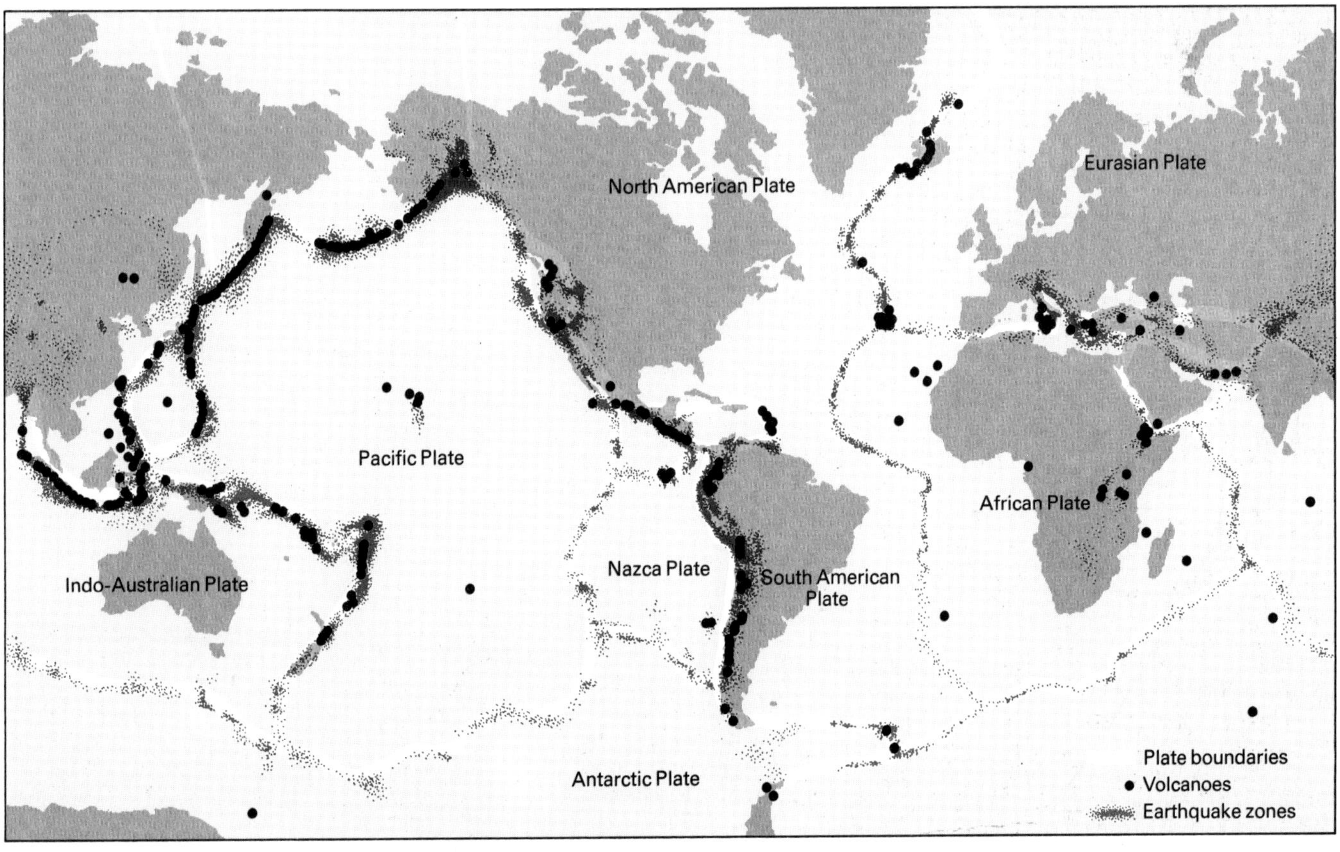

North American Plate

Eurasian Plate

Pacific Plate

Indo-Australian Plate

Nazca Plate

South American Plate

African Plate

Antarctic Plate

Plate boundaries
• Volcanoes
Earthquake zones

drill a series of wells along the San Andreas fault. If they pumped all the ground water from two wells, they would lock the fault at those points. Then, if they pumped water into a third well, between the two dry wells, they might set off a minor earthquake, which would relieve the pressure at that point. By leap-frogging along the fault in this way, they might induce many small quakes and avert a major tragedy. This method would be costly, though not as costly as the destruction of San Francisco.

Attempts at earthquake forecasting have been developing recently, especially in China, a country which has had more than its share of earthquake tragedies. Several methods have been proposed. One involves recording any slight tilting of the ground. Such tilting was noticed in the city of Haicheng in early 1975. About 100,000 people were evacuated two hours before a severe earthquake. But, despite this and other claimed successes, a severe earthquake at Tangshan in July, 1976 was not predicted.

Another possible method of forecasting is to record variations in the amount of a radioactive gas, radon, in well water. Radon, which results from the decay of radium, is normally trapped in rocks. But, if the rocks crack and open, the gas escapes and is dissolved in ground water. The onset of earthquakes may also be indicated by changes in the elasticity and electrical resistance of rocks. And, the Chinese claim, odd animal behaviour often precedes earthquakes.

Mountains and Volcanoes

The study of plate tectonics has not only helped us to understand better the causes and nature of earthquakes, it has also provided us with a much deeper understanding of how mountains are formed. There are three main kinds of mountains: fold mountains, block mountains and volcanoes.

Fold mountains are raised up when level layers of rock are squeezed together by tremendous lateral force. The rock layers are buckled upwards into large, complex folds. For example, it has been estimated that the folded Himalayas have been compressed by as much as 650 kilometres (400 miles). This process began about 120 million years ago, when a plate bearing the Indian sub-continent broke away from ancient Gondwanaland and began to drift towards Asia. About 50 million years ago, the Indian plate was pushing against Asia. The sediments that floored the intervening Tethys Sea and which contained the fossils of ancient sea creatures were squeezed upwards into the Himalayas.

Similarly, in the last 30 million years or so, the northward movement of the African plate rammed intervening, smaller plates in the Mediterranean area against Europe, causing the folded Alpine range to rise steadily upwards. It is possible that both the Himalayas and the Alps are still rising, but this cannot be measured because, even as mountains rise, so the forces of erosion plane them down.

The drifting plates create tension and tugging movements in the continental rocks they contain. Faults develop and blocks of land, such as the Vosges and Black Forest areas of Europe, are pushed upwards between roughly parallel faults. Sometimes, blocks of land slip downwards between parallel faults to form steep-sided rift valleys.

Fold and block mountains form slowly but, periodically, new volcanic mountains are created in a very short time. Volcanoes are formed from molten rock, called *magma,* which is erupted from large pockets beneath the Earth's crust. Magma occurs where one plate is forced beneath another and the descending rocks are melted by friction and pressure. Volcanoes occur also above radioactive heat sources within the Earth, such as those under the mid-oceanic ridges.

The magma is erupted to the surface under pressure in various forms, ranging from tiny fragments, such as volcanic dust and ash, to broad rivers of blazing molten lava. For example, in February

1943, a small hole opened up in a cornfield in Mexico, near the village of Parícutin. Hot ash erupted from the hole and piled up in a small cone. One day later, lava began to flow from the vent, and layer upon layer covered the surrounding land, continuously raising the new mountain's level. Two years later, the volcano, which had been christened Parícutin, stood about 500 metres (1,640 feet) above the level of the former cornfield, the greatest height it has yet attained. Parícutin was the first mountain whose birth and growth were witnessed and studied by scientists.

There are about 535 active volcanoes in the world, including 80 under the oceans. They are classified according to the way in which they erupt. Broadly, there are explosive, quiet and intermediate volcanoes. Explosive volcanoes contain magma that is highly charged with explosive gases. These gases expand and explode in the hot magma, shattering it into fragments of dust, ash, cinders and larger lumps called volcanic bombs. Explosive volcanoes are usually cone-shaped with steep sides. The greatest volcanic explosion in recent times destroyed the volcanic island of Krakatoa in 1883. The explosion set off a terrible tsunami, which killed 36,000 people in the nearby islands of Java and Sumatra.

Quiet volcanoes contain magma with little gas. They erupt by discharging streams of bubbling lava, which flows swiftly from the vent, often covering great distances before solidifying. Quiet volcanoes are flattened and shield-like in shape.

Many volcanoes are intermediate and combine both explosive and quiet eruptions. For example, the famous eruption of Vesuvius in AD 79 was explosive. Clouds of hot ash were flung into the air, burying the prosperous town of Pompeii. The nearby town of Herculaneum was engulfed by a mud-flow, consisting of hot ash mixed with rainwater. No lava streams appeared in AD 79, but they have accompanied most later eruptions. Scientific observatories have been set up around many active volcanoes in order to give warning of possible eruptions.

Hot springs and emissions of gas and steam are associated with dormant volcanoes. But the heat required for hot springs may also come from friction caused by earthquakes or from radioactivity. Geysers are spectacular kinds of hot springs, because they erupt tall columns of hot water and steam into the air. Some geyser eruptions are caused by steam pushing the water upwards. In other cases, gases in the heated water force it up.

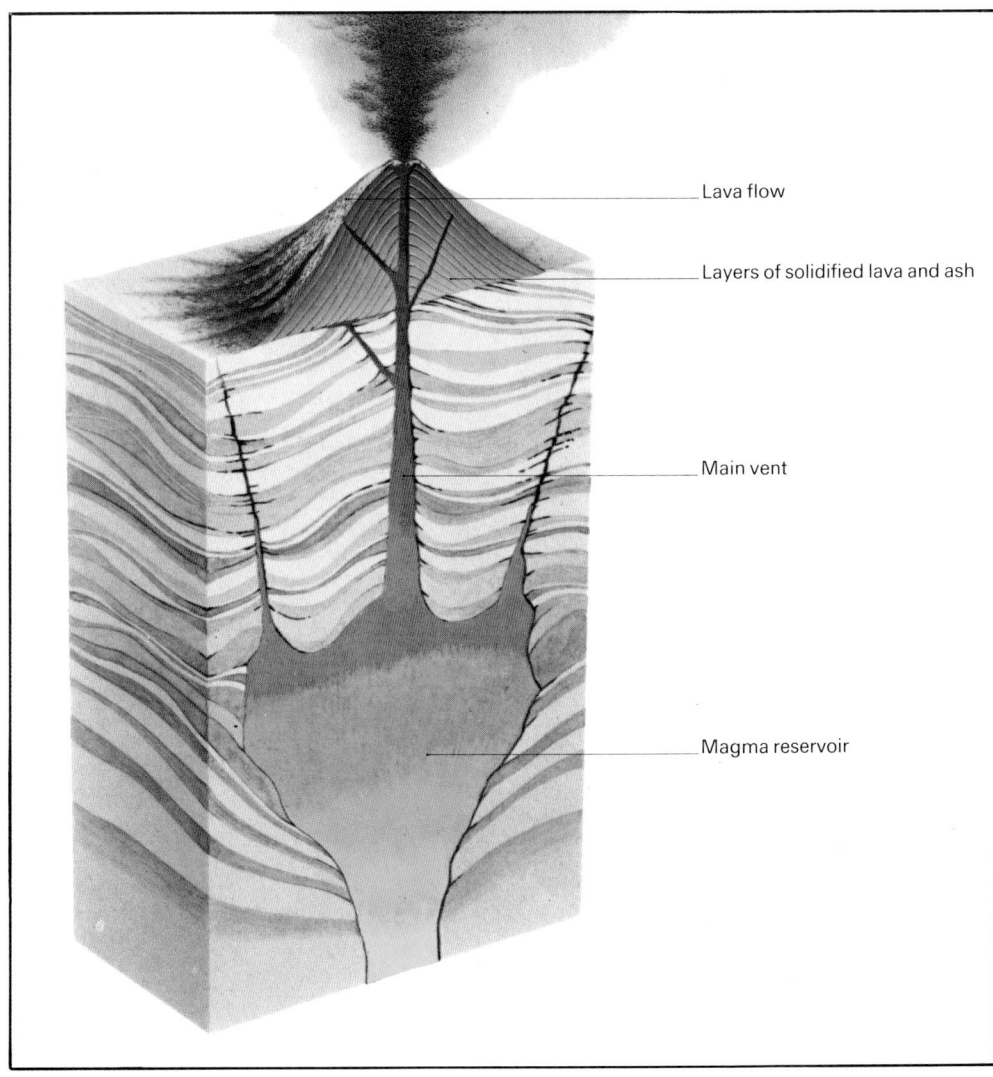

Lava flow

Layers of solidified lava and ash

Main vent

Magma reservoir

VOLCANIC ERUPTIONS
Scientists estimate that the greatest volcanic explosion in recorded history occurred in about 1470 BC, when the volcanic island of Santorini (now Thira), in the Aegean Sea, erupted with the power of 130 times the greatest H-bomb blast. The explosion removed about 62 square kilometres (15 cubic miles) of rock. Scientists also think that the eruption generated a tsunami, 50 metres (164 feet) high, which obliterated the Minoan civilization on Crete. The greatest eruption recently had only about one-fifth of the power of the Santorini eruption. It occurred in 1883 at Krakatoa, a volcanic island between Java and Sumatra. The sound of the explosion was heard more than 4,700 kilometres (2,900 miles) away.

Left: **Molten magma is forced upwards through the vent of a volcano, where it forms fine ash, rocky fragments or lava streams.**

Left: **The photograph of exposed rocks in Dyfed (formerly Pembrokeshire) in southwestern Wales shows how rock strata can be folded by Earth movements. In this case, the top part of the fold has been thrust over the bottom part along a fault in the rock.**

Right: **The Alps are a range of recently folded mountains. They were squeezed upwards as the Earth's plate bearing Africa moved towards the European plate. Smaller, intervening plates were rammed against the European mainland and the sedimentary rocks between were folded upwards. But, even as mountains rise, natural forces, such as weathering and valley glaciers, wear them down.**

Shaping of the Land

We tend to think of landscapes as unchanging and, in one person's lifetime, the land does not seem to alter, unless it is subject to human interference. But, in fact, the land is constantly changing, albeit slowly. Geologists estimate that, on average, about 3.4 centimetres (1.3 inches) of land is removed overall from North America every 1,000 years. Over millions of years, therefore, such erosion can remove the highest mountain ranges.

The rate of natural erosion varies considerably. It proceeds at its fastest rate in mountainous regions and is least effective on plains. Eroded material is broken down into smaller and smaller fragments during its transportation until it finally comes to rest, usually on the floors of seas or lakes. There, it accumulates in layers which become compacted together, possibly forming the building material for new mountain ranges which will arise millions of years later, only to be worn down in their turn.

A group of processes instrumental in the break up and decay of rocks are called weathering. Mechanical weathering occurs in hot deserts when rocks are rapidly heated and cooled. The widely alternating temperatures crack the outer shells of rocks, which peel away like layers of an onion — a process called *exfoliation*. And, in moist, temperate regions, water accumulates in rock crevices. But, when it freezes, the ice occupies nine per cent more space than the water. So it exerts such pressure on the rocks that it eventually prises them apart. Also included in mechanical weathering are the actions of plants and animals. For example, the downward-probing roots of trees can break boulders apart, and burrowing animals play a major role in the disintegration of rocks.

Chemical weathering involves the decay or dissolving of rocks. For example, *hydrolysis* is a process of rock decay caused by chemical reactions between water and minerals, such as the conversion of potash feldspar in granite into kaolin, a clay. The removal of rocks in solution results, for example, from a process called *carbonation*. Carbonation occurs in limestone rocks, which consist mostly of calcium carbonate and are insoluble in pure water. But rainwater, which contains carbon dioxide from the air, is a weak solution of carbonic acid. It reacts chemically with limestone to form soluble calcium bicarbonate.

Limestone plateaux are usually bleak areas. The exposed rocks are riven by vertical joints and horizontal bedding planes. Rainwater dissolves and widens the joints, giving the surface a paving-stone character. The surface is also pitted with deep fissures called swallow-holes, sink-holes or pot-holes. Some of these holes are dry, while others are entrances for streams, which plunge down into the subterranean world of limestone caves. These complex networks of passages and caverns were formed by water percolating through the joints and bedding planes. Many caves contain redeposited calcium carbonate in such features as hanging stalactites, pillar-like stalagmites and thin, wavy deposits resembling rock curtains.

One of the hazards of pot-holing (exploring limestone caves) is that heavy rainstorms can rapidly raise the level of subterranean rivers, trapping and drowning those within. These underground rivers usually return to the surface as a spring at the base of the limestone outcrop. Springs occur when any *aquifer* (water-bearing rock layer), such as limestone or sandstone, appears at the surface. Springs form the sources of streams and rivers.

Rivers are major agents of erosion, transportation and deposition. In their upper reaches, or youthful stage, they tumble down steep gradients, sweeping stones and, occasionally, boulders along their beds. As the loose fragments bump along the river beds they wear away more rock, causing downward erosion. This gives youthful rivers their characteristic steep-sided V-shaped

Below left: Rivers are agents of erosion and deposition. Oxbow lakes are formed when meandering rivers straighten their courses.
underground streams. Gorges occur when caves collapse. Stalactites and stalagmites are deposited in caves.

Below: This section through limestone shows a typical network of swallow holes, caves and
Right: Stalactites and stalagmites in a limestone cave at Divica, in Yugoslavia.

1. Youthful stage
2. Mature stage
3. Ox-bow
4. Old-age stage
5. Delta

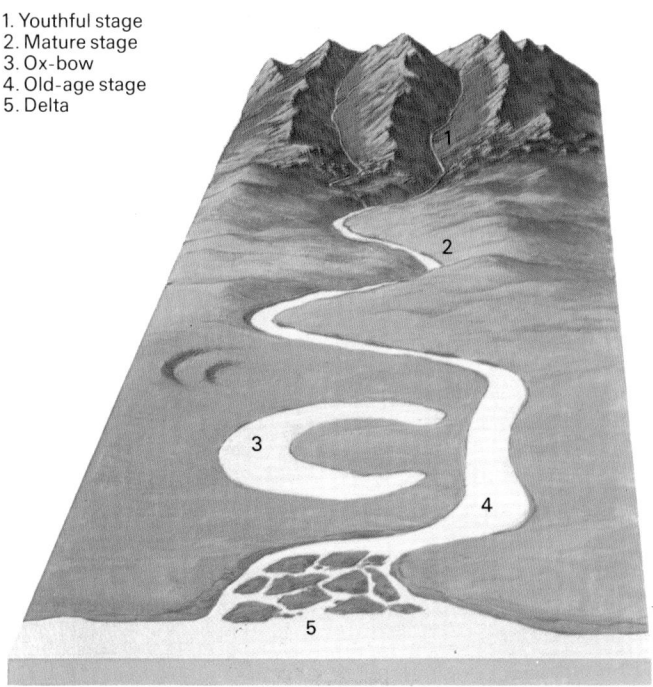

1. Swallow hole	4. Joints	7. Stalactites
2. Chimney	5. Pool	8. Roof fall
3. Chockstone	6. Stalagmites	9. Syphon

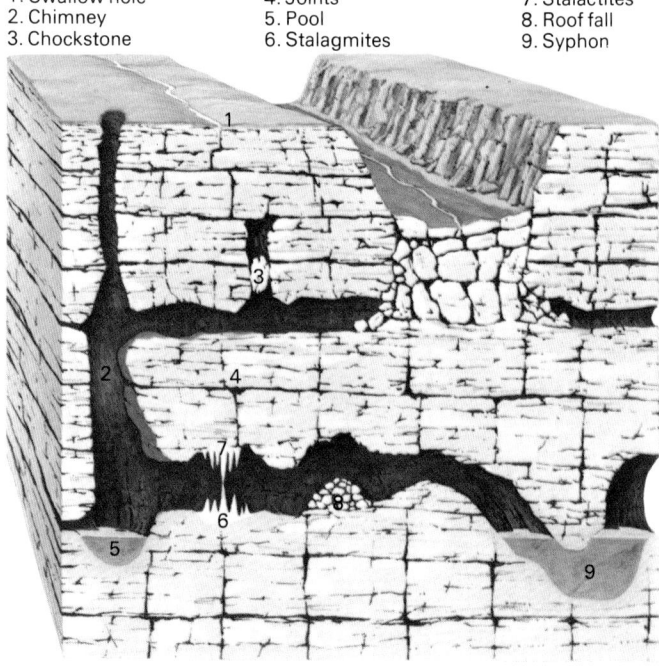

cross-section. But, when youthful rivers cross hard rocks, waterfalls and rapids occur.

In its mature stage, the river valley is broader, but erosion continues, especially as the outer bends are undercut. In old age, there is little river erosion, but sluggish, old-age rivers are major agents of transportation. The eroded material is mostly fine-grained silt or dissolved substances. When an old-age river floods, fertile silt is spread over the land. But most eroded material reaches the sea, at which point it may accumulate in deltas, if tides are weak, or be spread over the sea floor.

Occasionally, spectacular valleys result from the *rejuvenation* of old-age rivers. Rejuvenation occurred, for example, when a flat, coastal plain was uplifted to form the Colorado Plateau in the south-western United States. With a gradually increasing gradient, the Colorado River has etched the magnificent Grand Canyon into the plateau.

Ice sheets and glaciers in polar or mountain regions, the wind in arid and semi-arid areas, and the restless sea around coasts are other agents of erosion, transportation and deposition.

During the Pleistocene Ice Age, which began about 60,000 years ago and ended between 10,000 and 20,000 years ago, thick ice covered much of North America and northern Eurasia. The advance and retreat of the ice had a great effect on scenery.

In the world today, there are only two large ice sheets, one covering nearly all of Antarctica, and the other 85 per cent of Greenland. There are also smaller ice sheets in parts of northern Canada, Iceland, Norway and Spitzbergen. And valley glaciers occur above the permanent snowline in mountain regions in most parts of the world, even on the Equator. The total volume of land ice is the equivalent of 2.15 per cent of the world's total water supply. If all this ice were to melt, the sea level would rise by 60 to 90 metres (200 to 300 feet).

Large bodies of ice mould scenery as they slide downhill. Valley glaciers display the fastest movement, usually about one metre (three feet) per day, whereas the ice sheet of Antactica takes about a year to advance the same distance. Sometimes, the volume of a valley glacier is suddenly increased, for example, by an earthquake that dislodges snow and sends it crashing onto the glacier's source. This happened in 1936–7 on the Black Rapids glacier, Alaska, whose speed, as a result, reached a maximum of 60 metres (200 feet) in one day.

Glaciers transport weathered rock on their surfaces, within the ice or frozen in the base. Jagged rock fragments in the base of glaciers scrape over the land, eroding deep U-shaped valleys. Fiords are formerly glaciated valleys now filled by the sea. Near the source of valley glaciers, the ice freezes around projecting rocks and plucks them away. This action creates armchair-shaped basins called *cirques*. When two cirques are back to back, ice

erosion creates a knife-edge ridge, called an *arête,* between them. When three or more cirques occur back to back, a pyramidal peak, or *horn,* is formed.

Ice-eroded rock fragments, ranging in size from fine clay to boulders, are finally dumped as *moraine.* Around the snouts of glaciers, ridges of terminal moraine often accumulate. And streams issuing from glaciers transport the moraine for some distance. Large boulders composed of different rocks from the bedrock are sometimes dumped by the ice. Such boulders are called *erratics.*

Many land features in hot deserts were carved by water, either in the past, when the climate was different, or during occasional storms that occur every few years. But a major agent of desert erosion is wind-blown sand. Because sand particles are heavy, even the strongest winds cannot lift them much higher than an adult's shoulders. Erosion, therefore, occurs at low levels. But sandstorms can strip the paint off cars and frost their windscreens. Similarly, wind-blown sand can cut deeply into layers of softer rock or lines of weakness. And it can lead to the carving of mushroom rocks, which are supported by a narrow, precarious-looking pedestal. Wind-blown sand also scours rock surfaces, creating extensive depressions.

Sand covers only parts of the world's hot deserts. There are large areas of sandless *hammada* (bare rock) and *reg* (gravelly plains). Areas of sand are called *erg.* The sand accumulates in drifting dunes, some of which are crescent-shaped (*barchans*) and others are long ridges (*seif dunes*). Sand dunes are also features of some coasts.

Around coasts, the sea is constantly wearing away land, breaking up rocks into smaller particles and transporting debris out to sea or along the coast to create new land areas. Storm waves have great power. Hurled at cliffs, the waves trap and compress air in crevices. When the pressure is released, the air expands with explosive force, shattering the cliff rocks. Storm waves also lift up and bombard the shore with loose material, ranging from sand to boulders. The sea's weaponry undermines coastal rocks, cutting bays, caves, and natural arches through headlands. When natural arches collapse, rocky islets, or *stacks,* are left isolated in the sea.

Wave erosion is most effective on softer rocks. The Holderness coast of southeastern Yorkshire, England, is composed of glacial deposits. Since Roman times, the sea has removed a belt of around 4 to 5 kilometres (2.5 to 3 miles) of land from this coast.

Waves usually approach land at an oblique angle but, after the waves break, the water flows back at right angles to the shore. This means that the water and its load of sand and gravel move in a zig-zag path along the shore. When the direction of the coast changes, the loose material is dropped to form low ridges called *spits.* Some spits, called *tombolos,* link the mainland to an island.

Far left: **The Aletsch glacier in Switzerland is Europe's largest.**

Left: **Chesil Beach in Dorset, England has been formed by shingle deposited by the tides.**

Below: **This mushroom rock in Bahrain has been undercut by the abrasive action of wind-blown sand.**

Right: **This stretch of coastline in Northern Ireland is being steadily eroded by the sea. Wave action carves out bays. And caves, worn in headlands, meet to form natural arches. When the arches collapse, isolated stacks remain.**

Physical Statistics

The Earth

Dimensions: The Earth is flattened at the poles and bulges slightly at the Equator. Hence, the equatorial diameter and circumference are larger than the polar diameter and circumference.
Equatorial diameter: 12,756 kilometres (7,926 miles).
Equatorial circumference: 40,075 kilometres (24,901 miles).
Polar diameter: 12,713 kilometres (7,899 miles).
Polar circumference: 40,007 kilometres (24,859 miles).
Area: 510,061,938 square kilometres (196,936,480 square miles).
Land and water: Land covers 148,324,824 square kilometres (57,268,670 square miles) — about 29 per cent of the Earth's surface. Water covers 361,737,114 square kilometres (139,667,810 square miles) — about 71 per cent of the Earth's surface.
Mass: 5,976 million million metric tonnes (5,882 million million tons).

The Oceans

Size: Pacific Ocean 165,236,000 square kilometres (63,798,000 square miles); Atlantic Ocean 81,660,000 square kilometres (31,529,000 square miles); Indian Ocean 73,442,000 square kilometres (28,356,000 square miles); Arctic Ocean 14,351,000 square kilometres (5,541,000 square miles).
Volume of water: 1,300 million cubic kilometres (312 million cubic miles).
Deepest Point: 11.033 kilometres (6.856 miles), Challenger Deep in the Marianas Trench in the Pacific Ocean.
Highest wave in the open sea: 34 metres (112 feet) recorded in the Pacific by the U.S.S. *Ramapo* in 1933.
Largest islands: Greenland, 2,175,485 square kilometres (839,961 square miles); New Guinea 820,617 square kilometres (316,843 square miles); Borneo 743,211 square kilometres (286,956 square miles).
Highest oceanic mountain: Mauna Kea, Hawaii, rises 10,203 metres (33,474 feet) from the sea floor. (Mauna Kea is only 4,205 metres (13,796 feet) above sea level.)

Rivers

The World's Ten Largest Rivers

River	Continent	Length
Nile	Africa	6,670 km (4,145 miles)
Amazon	South America	6,448 km (4,007 miles)
Mississippi-Missouri	North America	6,270 km (3,896 miles)
Yangtze	Asia	4,990 km (3,101 miles)
Zaire	Africa	4,670 km (2,902 miles)
Amur	Asia	4,410 km (2,740 miles)
Hwang Ho	Asia	4,350 km (2,703 miles)
Lena	Asia	4,260 km (2,647 miles)
Mekong	Asia	4,180 km (2,597 miles)
Niger	Africa	4,180 km (2,597 miles)

The Amazon and its tributaries occupy the world's largest river basin, covering 7,045,000 square kilometres (2,720,000 square miles). One tributary, the Madeira, is the world's longest tributary. The Amazon also has the greatest flow of water, with an average discharge into the Atlantic of 120,000 cubic metres per second (4.2 million cubic feet per second).

Lakes

The largest lake, or inland sea, is the salty Caspian Sea, which is enclosed between Iran and the U.S.S.R. It covers 424,198 square kilometres (163,784 square miles). The largest freshwater lake, Lake Superior, lies between Canada and the United States. It has an area of 82,400 square kilometres (31,815 square miles). The highest large lake is Lake Titicaca, which is in the Andes range between Peru and Bolivia. Its surface is 3,812 metres (12,507 feet) above sea level. The lowest lake is the Dead Sea, whose shoreline is 395 metres (1,296 feet) below the mean sea level of the nearby Mediterranean Sea.

Mountains

World's highest mountains: Mount Everest 8,848 metres (29,029 feet) in the Himalayan range; K2 (Mount Godwin-Austen) 8,611 metres (28,251 feet) in the Karakoram range; Kanchenjunga 8,598 metres (28,209 feet) in the Himalayan range.
Highest in Africa: Mount Kilimanjaro 5,895 metres (19,341 feet).
Highest in North America: Mount McKinley 6,194 metres (20,320 feet)
Highest in South America: Mount Aconcagua 6,960 metres (22,835 feet).
Highest in Europe: Mount Elbrus 5,633 metres (18,481 feet).
Highest in Australia: Mount Kosciusko 2,230 metres (7,316 feet).
Highest in New Zealand: Mount Cook 3,764 metres (12,349 feet).

Above: **The River Amazon has a greater flow of water than any other river. It discolours the Atlantic Ocean for about 300 kilometres (190 miles) off the coast of Brazil.**

Right: **Mount Everest, in the Himalayas, is the world's highest peak. The first men to reach the summit were Sir Edmund Hillary and Tensing Norgay on May 29, 1953.**

The Living World

Vegetation

The natural vegetation of a place results from the interaction of soils, landforms and climate. Soils are complex substances, composed mostly of weathered particles, together with some humus (the decayed remains of plants and animals), water, air and countless micro-organisms. The nature of some soils depends on such factors as the bedrock or poor drainage. But the character of most soils is determined by climate. Such *zonal* soils are divided broadly into *pedalfers* in wet regions and *pedocals* in regions with much less rainfall.

For example, in rainy, tropical regions, soils are heavily leached — that is, soluble minerals are dissolved out of the top layer and removed completely or redeposited lower down. Characteristic wet tropical soils are the heavily-leached, reddish latosols, the top layer of which is laterite. This contains mostly insoluble substances, including iron, which colours the soil, bauxite and manganese. Other pedalfers include the greyish podzols of cold, snowy climates. Podzols are also heavily leached.

In regions with comparatively little rainfall, there is much less leaching and the top layers are coloured by humus. For example, the black chernozems of steppelands and the dark brown soils of prairies are pedocals coloured by decayed grass.

Soil and natural vegetation regions, therefore, follow a broadly similar pattern to climatic regions. When geographers talk of natural vegetation, they mean the climax vegetation — that is, the most flourishing vegetation that could occur in an area with particular soils and climate, providing it has not been altered by man. For example, the broadleaf forests of the eastern United States and western and central Europe have been mostly cut down. But, if man ceased to interfere with the natural plant life of these regions, broadleaf forests would probably reassert themselves before long.

Polar ice sheets, ice caps and adjacent areas that are permanently covered by snow are almost devoid of plant life. But the polar tundra has a short warm summer, when the top few centimetres of the soil thaw. Flat areas become marshes, and mosses, lichens and various flowering plants thrive. Beneath the surface layer, however, is permafrost — permanently frozen ground. This factor, together with the cold, prevents the growth of trees, other than dwarf shrubs.

Cold, snowy climates are characterized by vast forests of conifers. Conifers are especially well adapted to cold climates. Their narrow, conical shapes prevent over-loading by snow, their

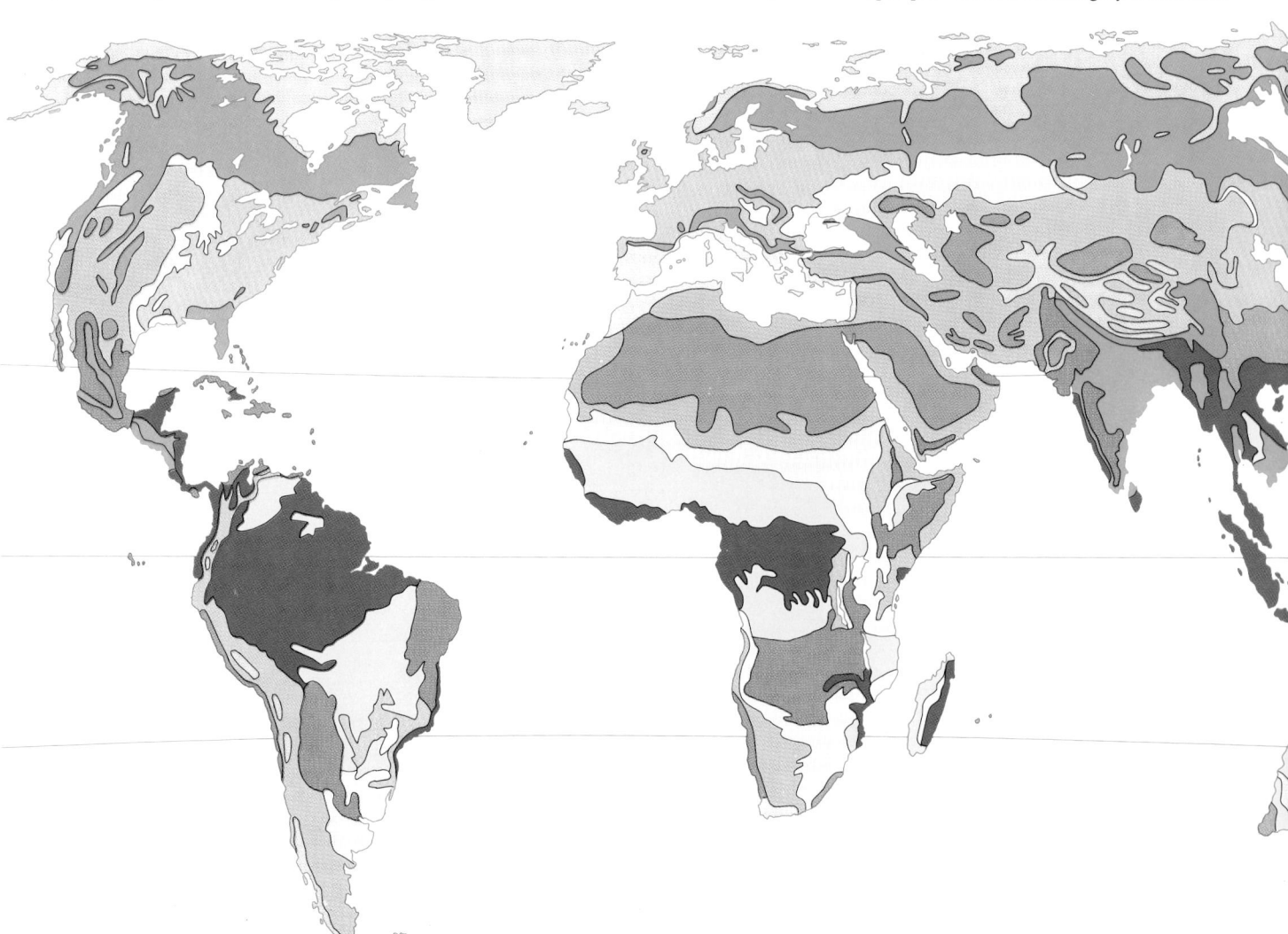

shallow roots absorb moisture, even when the subsoil freezes, and thick barks give protection against the cold. With the exception of larches, conifers are evergreens. Conifers also grow in Mediterranean regions, where their adaptations fit them to withstand the summer drought.

The boreal (northern) coniferous forests merge southwards into the broadleaf, or deciduous, forest belt. Deciduous trees are adapted to moist, temperate climates, with some rainfall throughout the year and temperatures above 6°C (43°F) for six months of the year. In autumn, deciduous trees shed their leaves, which form a thick carpet of humus on the forest floor. When the forests are cut down, their rich brown soils are very productive.

Grasslands are of two main kinds: the mid-latitude grasslands in continental interiors, including steppelands and prairies; and the tropical grasslands. In the mid-latitude grasslands, trees are rare, partly because of the aridity and partly because winters are extremely cold. Savanna is a term for tropical grassland, broken by scattered trees or patches of forest and merging into thorn forest and dry scrub. Tropical grasslands lie broadly between the equatorial forests and the sub-tropical deserts.

The world's hot deserts contain various xerophytes (drought-resistant plants). Adaptations include long, shallow roots, which absorb moisture from a large area; thick stems, which store water; and waxy coverings, which reduce loss of moisture by transpira-

tion. Some plants spring to life after the rare, infrequent rainstorms, and they may seed within two weeks of sprouting. The seeds may lie dormant for several years until the next rainstorm starts a new growth cycle.

The tropical forests include rain forests, with rain all the year round, and monsoon forests, where the rainfall is markedly seasonal. With abundant rainfall and high temperatures, tropical forests are luxuriant, and hundreds of species may occur in a small area. Trees grow to 30 to 40 metres (100 to 130 feet), with some protruding to more than 50 metres (160 feet). The thick canopy of leaves in the tree tops blocks out light from the forest floor, so few plants grow on the ground. Most of the other forest plants are climbers, such as vines, or epiphytes (parasitical plants).

Mountain regions have varying vegetation according to the altitude. Ascending some high mountains around the Equator is like taking a short trip to the poles. One can start in tropical forest, then climb through changing belts of vegetation and finally encounter tundra and polar conditions around the peak.

Natural vegetation

Tundra & ice
Coniferous forest
Broadleaf forest
Mediterranean scrub
Grassland
Savanna
Sub tropical forest
Dry tropical scrub & thorn forest
Monsoon forest
Tropical rain forest
Scrub, steppe and semidesert
Desert

Right: **Parts of the world's hot deserts are covered by barren shifting sands. Permanent settlement is possible only at oases.**

Below right: **The Himalayan foothills support luxuriant forests. But the vegetation gradually changes with altitude.**

Below: **The prairies of Alberta, in Canada, are part of the world's vast mid-latitude grasslands.**

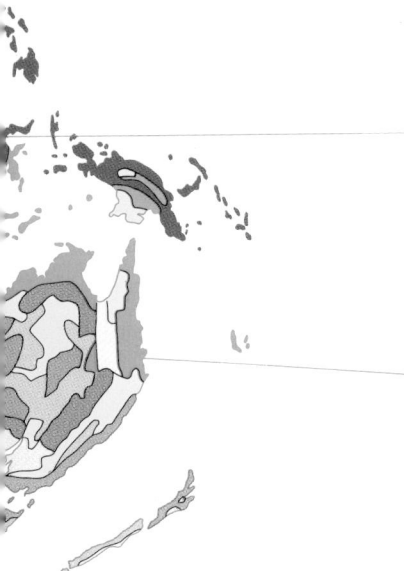

Evolution

Fossils, found in sedimentary rocks, are evidence of ancient life. Fast burial is a prerequisite for fossilization because, otherwise, plants and animals decay quickly. But, once buried, teeth, bones and other hard parts, such as shells and woody tissue, may be preserved. Many remains are petrified (turned to stone) by the replacement of each molecule of the organism by a molecule of a mineral. Some fossils are casts or moulds of organisms, while plant leaves and soft-bodied creatures, such as jellyfish, can be preserved as smears of carbon. Other fossils include animal droppings, footprints and holes bored by worms.

Ancient Greek scholars realized that most fossils were the remains of sea creatures and concluded that the rocks in which they occurred were once under the sea. But, when ancient Greece declined, this understanding was lost. For about 2,000 years, many fanciful ideas were advanced to explain fossils. Some people thought that they were the work of the Devil, who had put them in rocks to confuse us. Fossil belemnites, extinct creatures similar to cuttlefishes, are still sometimes called 'Devil's thunderbolts.'

In the 1700s, the Scottish geologist James Hutton deduced that sedimentary rocks were formed mostly on the floors of seas and

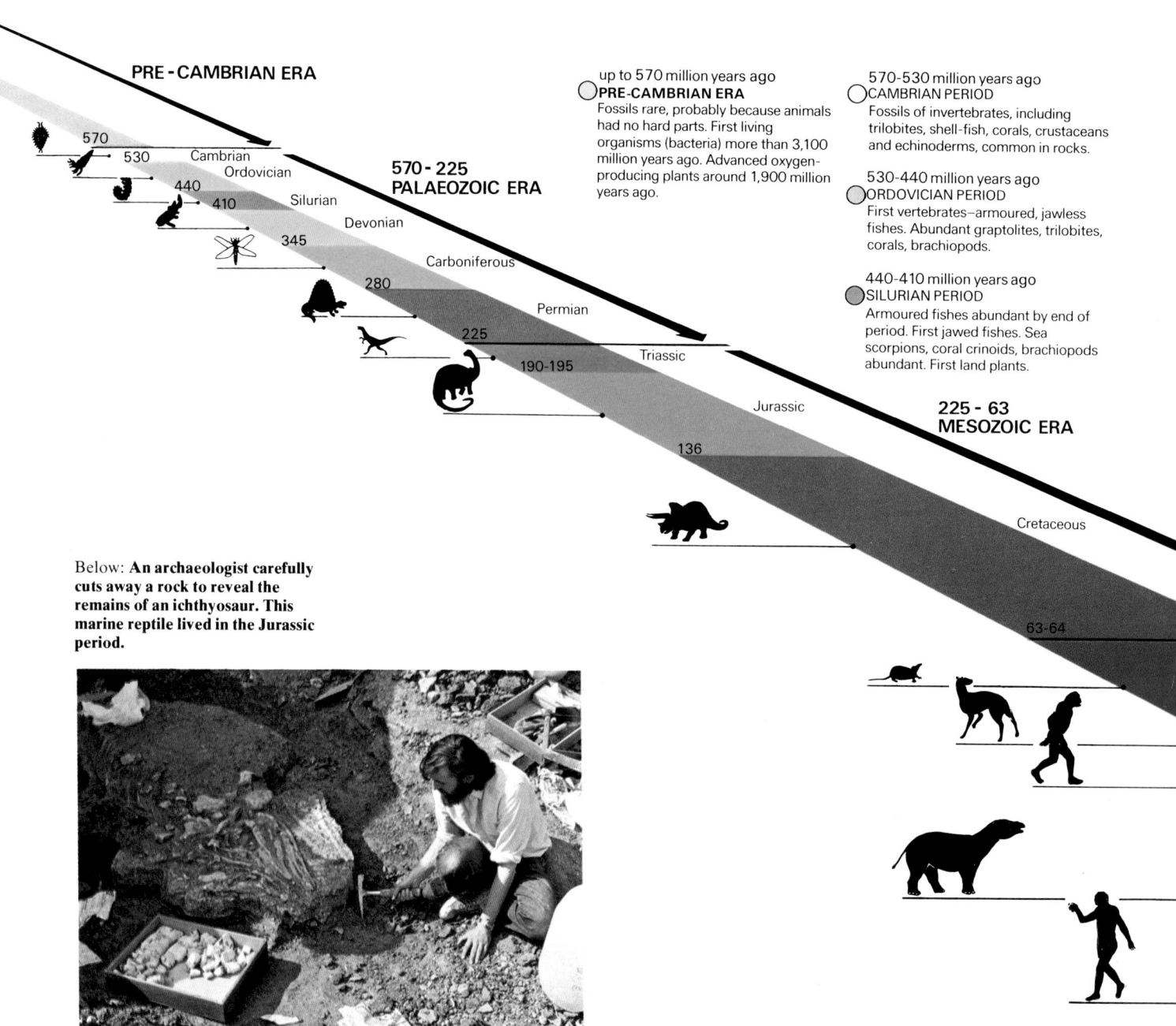

PRE-CAMBRIAN ERA

570
530   Cambrian
  Ordovician
440
410   Silurian
  Devonian
345
  Carboniferous
280
  Permian
225
190-195   Triassic
  Jurassic
136
  Cretaceous
63-64

**570 - 225
PALAEOZOIC ERA**

**225 - 63
MESOZOIC ERA**

up to 570 million years ago
PRE-CAMBRIAN ERA
Fossils rare, probably because animals had no hard parts. First living organisms (bacteria) more than 3,100 million years ago. Advanced oxygen-producing plants around 1,900 million years ago.

570-530 million years ago
CAMBRIAN PERIOD
Fossils of invertebrates, including trilobites, shell-fish, corals, crustaceans and echinoderms, common in rocks.

530-440 million years ago
ORDOVICIAN PERIOD
First vertebrates–armoured, jawless fishes. Abundant graptolites, trilobites, corals, brachiopods.

440-410 million years ago
SILURIAN PERIOD
Armoured fishes abundant by end of period. First jawed fishes. Sea scorpions, coral crinoids, brachiopods abundant. First land plants.

Below: **An archaeologist carefully cuts away a rock to reveal the remains of an ichthyosaur. This marine reptile lived in the Jurassic period.**

lakes. Their formation was slow, but they accumulated in great thicknesses before, eventually, they were raised up to form new land. The slow rate of sedimentation made Hutton and others appreciate that the Earth must be extremely old.

In the early 1800s, a British canal engineer William Smith collected fossils and began to classify rocks according to the fossils in them. He understood that, if two rock layers, however far apart, contained the same kind of fossils, then they were of the same age. Geologists were then able to work out the sequence, or relative ages, of sedimentary rocks, grouping them into eras, periods and epochs. The meaning of fossils was further clarified by the work of Charles Darwin, who advanced the theory of evolution by natural selection in his *Origin of the Species* (1859). In the early 1900s, the discovery that radioactive elements decay at specific rates

made it possible to provide absolute dates for rocks and their associated fossils.

Although many gaps occur in the fossil record, a clear pattern of evolutionary history has emerged. When a plant or animal group evolves from its ancestral form, such as the first reptiles from the amphibians in the Carboniferous period, the group first passes through a *divergence phase,* in which the group diverges from its ancestors by producing new features. *Improvement* follows as the group's new features are adapted by natural selection. Then, by a process called *adaptive radiation,* the group spreads to all available environments. For example, the reptiles evolved large and small species that lived on land, in the sea and in the air. Finally, however, comes *extinction.*

From a study of Earth history, extinction seems to be the fate of all species, even the most successful. Most large reptiles became extinct at the end of the Mesozoic era. Many theories have been advanced to explain what happened, including climatic changes, overpopulation, the bombardment of the Earth by cosmic rays, and the destruction of their eggs by mammals. But the extinction of species, whatever the reason, always seems to involve some change in the environment to which the group is unable to adapt.

410-345 million years ago
DEVONIAN PERIOD
Age of Fishes. Amphibians evolved near end of period. Plants spread on land. First insects. Graptolites died out.

345-280 million years ago
CARBONIFEROUS PERIOD
Amphibians increased. Reptiles evolved. Insects common. Many corals, brachiopods and fishes in seas.

280-225 million years ago
PERMIAN PERIOD
Reptiles spread on land. Ammonites in seas. But trilobites and many other sea creatures died out.

225-190 million years ago
TRIASSIC PERIOD
First dinosaurs and large sea reptiles. Ammonites abundant. First mammals evolved.

190-136 million years ago
JURASSIC PERIOD
Large reptiles, including dinosaurs and flying reptiles (pterosaurs) abundant. First bird (archaeopteryx) appeared. Ammonites and belemnites abundant in seas. Some mammals on land.

136-63 million years ago
CRETACEOUS PERIOD
Reptiles, including dinosaurs, dominated the land, but most died out at end of period, as did ammonites and many other sea creatures. Small mammals lived throughout period.

63-2 million years ago
TERTIARY
Palaeocene 63-44 million years ago
Rapid development of mammals.
Eocene 44-38 million years ago
First horses and elephants.
Oligocene 38-26 million years ago
Early apes; ancestors of many modern mammals.
Miocene 26-7 million years ago
Greatest variety of mammals.
Pliocene 7-2 million years ago
Man-apes in Africa. Many larger mammals died out.

2-0 million years ago
QUATERNARY PERIOD
Pleistocene 2-0.01 million years ago
Rise of man. Woolly mammoths and rhinos in cold northern hemisphere.
Recent 0.01-0 million years ago
Modern man.

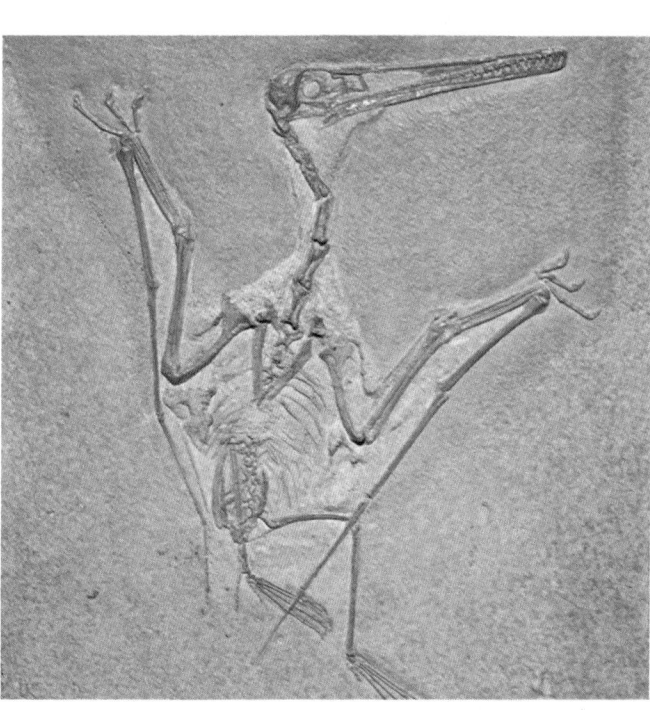

Above: **The petrified remains of a pterosaur (flying reptile), which lived in the Jurassic period.**

Eocene epoch

Oligocene epoch

Tertiary

**63 - 0
CENOZOIC ERA**

Pleistocene epoch

0.01

YEARS AGO (millions)   *Recent epoch*

Quaternary

Animal Life

Virtually every part of our planet is inhabited by animals. Only the icy wastes at the poles, the chill summits of the highest mountains and the thin air of the upper atmosphere are devoid of life — apart from human visitors. Elsewhere, animals exist in profusion and in great diversity.

There are two main reasons why the Earth possesses a wide range of animals. Physical barriers — mountain chains, oceans and seas, and deserts — separate the land into six zoogeographic regions, each containing its own particular kinds of animals. The barriers prevent the animals from intermixing, and distinct populations have evolved in each one. For example, the Australian region has monotreme animals, such as the duck-billed platypus, and many marsupials, including kangaroos. And the neo-tropical region contains most of the hummingbirds. Because islands in the ocean are isolated from the rest of the world, they often contain special kinds of animals not found elsewhere. In the oceans, different kinds of animals live at different depths.

The second factor that determines the kind of animals that live in a particular region is climate. Each of the climatic zones of the world has its own kind of animal life, because the animals have evolved to suit the conditions there. Similar environments tend to produce similar animals, even though they may be in different parts of the world and of different animal families. Desert animals, for example, are often very alike wherever they are found, having been shaped by the same harsh conditions. In considering the kinds of animals that inhabit the Earth, it is, therefore, better to look at them in the various climatic zones rather than the zoogeographic regions.

Animals of the Polar Regions

The polar regions are basically different from each other: the Arctic consists of a frozen sea surrounded by cold coasts, while the Antarctic is an ice-covered continent surrounded by cold seas. However, both regions are white with snow and ice. In the Arctic, many of the animals are also white so that they cannot easily be seen against their surroundings. In this way, they escape the attentions of other animals that hunt them or, if they are themselves hunters, they cannot easily be spotted by their prey. These white animals include the polar bear, arctic fox, arctic hare and snowy owl. In the Antarctic, few animals live on the ice cap because it is so cold, but many are found on the surrounding islands. Many of them, such as seals and penguins, and Arctic animals such as the polar bear and arctic fox, are large and have rounded bodies with small ears and short tails. All these features help to prevent heat escaping from their bodies, thus keeping them warm. The animals also have thick layers of fat and heavy coats of fur to retain their own heat. Some polar birds even have their feet covered with feathers.

Because the polar seas are so cold, they contain much dissolved oxygen, which supports a huge population of marine life. Feeding on the great shoals of fish and other sea creatures are seals and whales, and penguins and seabirds of several kinds, many of them adept at diving.

Animals of Coniferous Forests

Across Canada and the far north of Europe and Asia stretches a belt of coniferous forest. The needle-leaved evergreen trees stand tightly packed, their leaves cutting out the light all the year round so that little undergrowth surrounds their trunks. Many animals make their homes in this cold, forbidding place. Some feed on the trees. Beavers eat the bark and fell the trees to build their lodges;

grouse consume the leaves and buds, and crossbills can cut open the cones with their special crossing beaks to get at the seeds inside. Squirrels clamber about the trees, opening cones and storing the seeds for winter. Chipmunks also store seeds but hibernate for the winter, waking now and then when they get hungry. Insect-eating birds, such as woodpeckers and tits, work their way over the branches, pecking in crevices in the bark. Small mammals, such as voles and lemmings, wander over the ground eating plants and burrow beneath the snow in winter to find food. Other animals survive by preying on these creatures. Bears, lynxes and weasels hunt among the trees; hawks and falcons swoop from the air by day, and owls do so by night.

Animals of the Deciduous Forests

South of the coniferous forest, and also in the southernmost parts of the southern hemisphere, lies a broad belt of deciduous forest. Here the climate is mild and the trees shed their leaves in winter. Leaf mould builds up on the ground and light comes in, enabling a tangled undergrowth of shrubs and bushes to grow among the trees. Evergreen trees may be found too. Many different kinds of animals live in the forest. The leaves are easier to eat than the tough leaves of conifers, and caterpillars and aphids munch their way through plants, while deer browse among the trees. Birds, such as finches, and squirrels, mice and other small mammals take the seeds and buds. Other birds, including European warblers, and mammals, such as hedgehogs, seek insects in the forest. These insect eaters find food scarce in winter, so the birds migrate to warmer climes or rely on seeds, while the mammals may hibernate for the winter. Predators also hunt among the trees, as they do in coniferous forests. They include foxes, snakes, polecats, badgers, wild cats and birds of prey. However, their prey is not always defenceless — the skunk is famous for the way it squirts an evil-smelling liquid at predators, and many potential victims hide safely among the leaves and undergrowth.

Animals of Mountains

Because it gets colder as you go up a mountain, several different zones of life exist. There may be deciduous forest at the bottom, coniferous forest halfway up, and then a polar scene with scanty plants and snow at the top. Kinds of animals similar to those found in these climatic regions may, therefore, be found on the sides of a mountain, wherever in the world it is situated. However, polar animals will not be found, for they depend ultimately on the ocean for their food.

Some mountain animals have special features that help them to live on rocky slopes, where cold winds howl and few plants grow. Mountain goats have special feet that enable them to leap among the crags, and vicunas and yaks have woolly coats to keep out the cold. These animals can survive on poor plant food, but may have to descend to lower slopes for the winter. Mountain birds are mainly strong fliers, such as eagles, or small birds that nest and find food in rock crevices.

Animals of Grasslands

Between the forests and deserts of the world lie the grasslands, vast grassy plains dotted with a few stunted trees that manage to grow in the dry climate. These regions are known by several names, including steppes, prairies, savannas, pampas and veld. It is warm all the year round.

Great numbers of animals make their homes in grasslands. Many eat the grasses and other plants. They include: large

mammals, such as antelopes, zebras, gazelles, bison, elephants, giraffes, rhinoceroses, wild horses and kangaroos; small mammals, such as hares and rodents; flightless birds, such as emus and ostriches; and flocks of weaver birds that raid crops in the grasslands, as do locusts and other insects. Living on these animals in turn are insect eaters, like anteaters and armadillos, and the much-feared flesh eaters, including rattlesnakes and cobras, vultures, hyenas, wild dogs, lions and cheetahs.

Being in the open, the victims of these hunting animals cannot hide from danger. Many roam the grasslands in herds, finding safety in numbers, and the elephant is just too big to be worth attacking. Smaller animals, which may have to run for their lives, possess powerful legs and feet that enable them to sprint for long periods. The smallest animals retreat into their burrows when danger threatens.

Animals of Deserts

Desert regions occur on each side of the Equator. Little, if any, rain falls throughout the year, and it is usually very hot by day, though often cold by night. The stony or sandy ground supports little plant growth. Some animals do manage to survive in these harsh conditions, but they are faced with two main problems — how to keep cool and how to save water.

Many desert animals are small — a feature that helps them to lose heat — and live in burrows. Some, such as scorpions, avoid the daytime heat by staying in their burrows, seeking food only at night. Others, such as lizards, may prefer to hunt by day, but retire into their burrows or into shade during the hottest hours. The desert fox is one of several desert animals with large ears, which help to radiate excess body heat. And some animals hop or scurry over the hot sand to escape its heat. These adaptations also help the animals to hear and escape their predators. Many desert animals, including camels, are able to withstand high body temperatures and lack of water without harm. Their bodies may even be able to produce water from a diet of seeds or plants, so that they never need to drink. Gerbils survive in this way. And because they do not sweat, they retain as much water as possible inside their bodies. Some water is inevitably lost with body wastes, but desert animals reduce this amount to the minimum possible.

Animals of Tropical Forests

Along the Equator lies a belt of tropical forest. It is always hot and has frequent rain. Trees crowd together and fight for the light, producing a thick tangle of leaves and branches.

Many animals live among the leaves and branches of the forest. They are either able to fly or are good climbers. Toucans, parrots and other birds take fruit, hummingbirds seek nectar in flowers, and butterflies and moths flutter here and there. Many of these animals are brightly coloured, though the colours do not show up so vividly among the leaves. Sloths clamber among the branches, and monkeys swing to and fro, feeding from the trees. Chameleons seek insects in the leaves, changing colour to match their surroundings, and bats hunt insects in the air. Some animals, including several lizards and squirrels, have developed ways of gliding from one tree to another. On the ground, compact animals, such as pigs and rodents, push through the undergrowth, often eating ants and other insects that abound. Pheasants scratch about the forest floor, and lizards and snakes burrow in the litter of dead leaves. Feeding on the plant-eating and insect-eating animals are the hunters, such as tigers, leopards and jaguars, civets and snakes. They seek their victims in the trees and on the ground, often hunting by night.

Below: **A king penguin colony on the island of South Georgia.**

Far top left: **The Rocky Mountain goat lives among the high peaks of the Rocky Mountains in North America, easily scaling the rocky crags.**

Above left: **The red squirrel brings colour and life to the gloom and quiet of the coniferous forest.**

Below left: **The scorpion lives in the desert. It uses its claws to dig a burrow to escape the heat, and stings with its tail.**

Far bottom left: **A tube-nosed bat hangs upside-down from a branch. Bats can fly in the dark, using sound to navigate.**

Right: **A jay feeds its young. Jays are birds of deciduous forests. They collect acorns and bury them to form a winter food reserve.**

Below: **A herd of elephants heads for a water hole. Many elephants live on the grasslands of Africa, mostly in reserves, where they are protected from hunters and ivory poachers.**

Animals of Fresh Water

Rivers, ponds and lakes are home to many different kinds of animals. Fish sweep up food particles from the water, eating water plants, insects and other small water creatures, or even hunting other fish. Birds are a common sight, finding food in the water in several ways. Grebes, for example, dive for their food, while many ducks dabble at the surface. Kingfishers plunge into the water from the air, but herons stand or wade patiently in the shallows, waiting to make a catch. Insects abound, dragonflies hovering in the air, and pond skaters rowing themselves across the water surface. Amphibians breed in water, and many frogs, toads and newts remain in or around water all their lives. Reptiles and mammals are less common, for they feed and breed mostly away from water. However, crocodiles and turtles live in warm inland waters, and some snakes can swim. Otters and water voles can dive for food, and hippos rest in water, but come ashore to feed.

Fish can survive beneath the ice through a freezing winter, though such conditions make life hard for water birds.

Animals of the Seashore

Animals that live permanently on seashores where tides come and go every day face great problems of survival. One moment they are living in cool water and the next they may find themselves in the open air, being scorched by the sun. Only special kinds of animals can live in these conditions. On rocky shores, barnacles, mussels and other shellfish close their shells tightly as the tide goes down. Sea anemones pull in their stinging tentacles and close up, while small mobile animals, such as shrimps and crabs, take refuge in rock pools. On sandy and muddy shores, shellfish and worms burrow into the damp mud or sand to prevent their bodies drying up. Some have tubes that lead to the surface to obtain food and oxygen. These small shore dwellers feed on seaweeds, on minute creatures in the water, sand or mud, or on food particles that they sift from the water or sand. The seashore is also the home of larger animals. Birds wade in the shallows, peck in the sand or mud, or fly out to sea to find food. Seals and turtles come ashore in large numbers to breed.

Above: **Crocodiles live mostly in inland waters, where they often lie with their nostrils just above the surface. They capture other animals in their powerful jaws and drag them beneath the surface, where they tear apart and devour their victims.**

Right: **The common hippopotamus is the largest freshwater mammal. Common hippos live in African rivers, sleeping and resting by day and emerging at night to feed on plants near the water.**

Far right: **A sea anemone lies ready for a small fish or other creature to approach its stinging tentacles. It will then pull in its paralyzed victim and slowly digest it.**

Animals of the Oceans

The world's oceans contain a vast range of animals, from microscopic protozoans to the blue whale, the largest animal that has ever lived. In the oceans' surface layers drift huge numbers of minute plants and animals known as *plankton*. All other sea creatures depend on plankton for food, either by eating it directly or by consuming other plankton-eating animals.

Marine animals are classed into two groups — those that swim in the sea and those that live at the bottom. In waters near the shore, where light penetrates to the sea bed, an interesting array of creatures may be found. Flatfish swim over the sea floor, changing their body patterns to match the background, wherever they settle. This enables them to escape the attention of hunting animals. Lobsters and crabs, armed with a heavy shell and threatening pincers, scuttle about, and octopuses and cuttlefish wander or hide, squirting out a cloud of ink to confuse any enemy that appears. Starfish and sea urchins, and corals and sponges are among the many other strange animals of the seabed.

Fish of all kinds swim out in the open sea. Some live in great shoals, finding safety in numbers, and they are often coloured silvery-white, which makes them almost invisible in the water. Other creatures of the open sea include turtles, squids and sea mammals, such as whales and dolphins, which must continually rise to the surface to breathe air. The depths of the open sea are completely dark as light cannot penetrate very far. There, many animals are luminous and produce their own light to hunt or find a mate. The sea floor is often covered with mud, on which long-legged creatures walk and others lie.

Animal Movements

Not all creatures are content to remain in one place all their lives. Locusts, for example, wander in search of food, settling wherever they find enough to eat, and leaving when they have stripped everything bare. But many animals make regular journeys called migrations to find food and to raise their young.

The best-known migrations are those of birds. In spring, many fly to their breeding grounds, where there will be enough food to feed their young when they are born. This food supply disappears as the winter comes, and so the birds fly back to their winter quarters to find food until the spring arrives again. In the tropics, where there may be no real summer or winter, birds may migrate in the wet and dry seasons instead. Some mammals migrate too. Caribou walk long distances between breeding grounds and winter quarters, and whales may swim from one ocean to another.

Several fishes make extraordinary migrations that take years. Eels are born in mid-ocean and migrate to the rivers of surrounding lands, where they grow up before returning to the ocean to breed. Salmon migrate in the opposite direction, being born inland and then swimming out to sea. After several years, the adult salmon swim back to their birthplace to breed.

Below left: **The shark is one of the most feared animals of the sea, though not all sharks attack man.**

Below right: **A ray, one of the flatfishes, is related to the sharks. Like sharks, rays have cartilage,** not true bones. Most rays live on the sea bed, their colour matching their surroundings for camouflage.

Bottom: **The lobster lives on the sea bed close to the shore, feeding on plants and animals.**

Threats to Life

Animals are shaped by evolution to fit their environment — unlike man, who can change his environment to suit himself. If an animal cannot change to meet man's demands on nature, then it may find itself in danger. In clearing forests to create fields for farming, or in making space for houses, man destroys the habitats of particular animals and takes away their sources of food. His domestic animals may kill them, or man himself may hunt them for their meat or for valuable products such as ivory and furs.

Animals that live on islands uninhabited by man are highly vulnerable, as they have evolved to suit a special environment. For example, birds may have lost the power to fly because there are no predatory animals with which to contend. The arrival of man changes things so abruptly that these overspecialized animals may not survive for long. The flightless dodo of Mauritius, for example, was extinct less than two centuries after the arrival of Portuguese sailors there in the early 1500s. However, not only rare, defenceless creatures are threatened. In less than a century, man succeeded in wiping out the passenger pigeon, millions of which once lived in North America. The demise of the passenger pigeon is a warning that one should never be complacent about the conservation of wildlife.

Measures are now being organized on a world-wide scale to help save animals in danger of extinction. International conferences limit the number of whales that may be captured, and a vast campaign is under way to raise money to save the tiger. Many governments ban hunting and create national parks and nature reserves to shelter rare animals. But these measures are not always very effective, or may be too late. Whalers are beginning to find that their limits have been too high and that some species of whales have nearly vanished. A hunting ban is difficult to enforce in some countries, and hunters may even enter parks and reserves. Accidents may happen: the use of DDT as a pesticide has done wonders to control insect pests but also nearly succeeded in wiping out several birds of prey. Conservationists are, therefore, also conducting projects to save threatened animals directly by removing them from their endangered habitats to zoos or breeding centres. There, efforts are made to get the animals to breed in captivity. When numbers have increased, the animals are returned to the wild. This has often been successful; the nene, or Hawaiian goose — down to about 30 birds in 1950 — is now up to about 1,000, and many birds have been repatriated.

Wherever man spreads, the waste he creates causes pollution, which threatens life on this planet, including his own existence. Instead of being treated in sewage farms, human wastes are sometimes dumped into rivers and seas. This may be hazardous to health, for example, shellfish caught in a bay near a town may be contaminated with sewage. In addition, particularly in rivers, decomposition of the sewage by bacteria uses up oxygen needed by fish and other animals. Detergents from kitchen sinks make matters worse, and the water may lose virtually all its oxygen, resulting in the loss of its animal life. Industrial wastes are also dumped into rivers and seas, sometimes with harmful effects. At Minamata in Japan, people died in the 1950s from eating fish contaminated with mercury compounds discharged into the sea from a local plastics factory. However, increasing awareness of these dangers has led to anti-pollution measures that are cleaning up many rivers. Less rosy is the outlook for oil pollution, as supertankers carry crude oil about the world in ever-larger quantities, and undersea oil drilling becomes more common. Huge leaks of oil into the sea may now occur with any accident involving a tanker or oil rig, threatening all marine life in the area.

The atmosphere is liable to pollution in several ways too.

Burning fuel causes the release of gases into the air. Sulphur dioxide is among the most dangerous, for it dissolves in rain-water to produce a weak acid that can worsen breathing troubles and eat away the surfaces of buildings and statues. Furthermore, the pollutants may be blown long distances by winds and so affect places far away. In January 1974, all the winds in Europe converged on Norway for 12 days, depositing so much acid that fish were killed in lakes and rivers. Motor-cars emit lead compounds and oxides of nitrogen from their exhausts. Nitrogen oxides may contribute to breathing difficulties. In many places, air pollution has been reduced by banning the burning of coal and by treating fumes before they leave factory chimneys and the exhausts of motor-cars.

In the upper atmosphere, a layer of ozone gas prevents ultraviolet radiation from the Sun reaching the ground in harmful quantities. Scientists are worried that the ozone layer may be affected by pollution. Chemicals called fluorocarbons, released by aerosol sprays, and nitrogen oxides from jet aircraft (especially supersonic airliners, which fly very high) may be slowly destroying the ozone layer. Any resulting increase in ultraviolet rays reaching the ground could produce more skin cancer. So it may become necessary to ban aerosol sprays and there is a slight possibility that supersonic flight could be banned.

A third form of pollution, which may also affect future generations, is radioactivity. All waste from nuclear power stations produces harmful radiation, and some remains dangerous for centuries. At present, it is stored away so that no-one is harmed. But there is cause for alarm. A nuclear accident could release substantial amounts of radioactive material into the air. Nuclear installations have leaked to a small degree, and there are rumours that a nuclear accident killed many people in the U.S.S.R. several years ago. If governments build new 'fast' reactors to produce more energy, then there is a greater likelihood of a nuclear disaster because, unlike today's 'slow' reactors, fast reactors could possibly explode. Furthermore, there will be much greater amounts of long-lived radioactive waste to store, and the reactors will use plutonium, which is extremely poisonous as well as highly radioactive. For these reasons, many people are pressing governments to develop alternative energy supplies, such as wave power and solar energy, which are not polluting.

Left: **A seabird lies dead on the shore, smothered in oil.**

Above right: **In many parts of the world, waste products from factories are simply discharged into rivers and seas. As a result, fish may become contaminated with chemicals harmful to the fish or to anyone eating them.**

Right: **Oil pollution may threaten the livelihood of seaside resorts. Here a group of people clean up a beach in Brittany, France, after oil has been washed ashore.**

Far right: **A haze of pollution hangs over a town in Germany.**

Human Geography

The Human Race

Scientists consider that man and the apes are primates with a common, extinct ancestor. From fossil discoveries, we now know that various forms of man-like creatures evolved over the last 12 million years. The chief factors distinguishing man-like creatures from apes are man's larger brain and his ability to walk upright. Around 35,000 years ago, one species of man, *Homo sapiens,* became dominant, and all other forms, such as Neanderthal man, became extinct. *Homo sapiens* had been in existence for at least 70,000 years before that time.

All modern men and women, therefore, belong to the species *Homo sapiens*. And so, scientifically, all people belong to one race — the human race. But people display differing physical features, including skin colour, eye and hair colour, skull shapes, height and build. Anthropologists have devised various methods of classifying mankind, but it is generally accepted that there are three broad sub-groups. They are, in order of population size, the 'white-skinned' Caucasoids, the 'yellow-skinned' Mongoloids and the 'black-skinned' Negroids.

The term Caucasoid was first coined in the 1700s by the scientist J. F. Blumenbach, who used it to describe the people of the Caucasus mountain region between the Black Sea and the Caspian Sea — a region that was probably the original homeland of many of Europe's peoples. The term Caucasoid is now used to include a broad group of people who form the indigenous populations of Europe, southwestern Asia, India and northern and eastern Africa.

Caucasoids vary considerably. For example, skin colour ranges from white to dark brown, and eye colouring from light blue to dark brown. Hair varies from straight to curly, although body and facial hair is more abundant among Caucasoids than among other sub-groups. Caucasoids generally have narrow, prominent noses and thin lips, but all kinds of skull shapes occur, from long-headed to round-headed. The chief Caucasoid groups are the Mediterraneans, Alpines, Nordics, Lapps, East Baltics, Irano-Afghans, southern Indians, and northern and eastern Africans. However, intermixing has blurred the distinguishing features of these types in many areas.

Mediterraneans include the narrow-faced Basques of France and Spain, who are more properly called 'early Mediterraneans', because they are the purest descendants of the prehistoric inhabitants of Europe. The Mediterraneans proper are long-headed and dark-haired, with olive to light brown skins. They are found both north and south of the Mediterranean Sea and include Spaniards, Italians and Arabs. Alpine people are of medium height and they are sturdily built. Their round heads distinguish them from Mediterraneans and Nordics. The Nordics of Scandinavia are typically long-headed, tall people with blue eyes and blond hair.

The short Lapps have round heads, like the East Baltics of northeastern and eastern Europe and many Russians. On the otherhand, the Irano-Afghans of Afghanistan, Baluchistan, northwestern India and Iran are physically similar to Nordics, except for their darker hair and skin colouring. The Dinarics of southeastern Europe and the Armenians are similar to the Irano-Afghans.

The southern Indians are mostly of the Mediterranean type, except for their darker skins. African Caucasoids include the Berbers of northern Africa and some of the peoples of northeastern Africa, including some Ethiopians, Somalis and Sudanese. However, through intermixing, they have acquired some Negroid features. Mixed groups broadly included in the Caucasoid sub-group, include Polynesians, the Vedda of southern India and Australoids, including the Australian Aborigines. The Australoids, also called 'archaic whites', are sometimes considered to be a separate sub-group.

From the early 1500s, Europeans have spread around the world, exploring and colonizing the Americas, Africa and Australia. As a result, Caucasoids are the most widely spread of the three sub-groups.

Mongoloids are distinguished by their yellowish skin, straight black hair, flat faces and noses, high cheek bones and, in many cases, slanted eyes — caused by a skin fold of the upper eyelid. These features are displayed by the short-legged, thick-set Classic Mongoloids, including Eskimoes, Japanese, Koreans and northern Chinese.

The other Mongoloids do not have slanted eyes. They include: the broad-faced, rather thick-lipped Turkics of central Asia; the narrow-faced Tibetans, or Himalayans; the short and graceful Indonesian-Malays, including the Burmese, southern Chinese, Filipinos and Thais; and the American Indians, whose ancestors entered the Americas sometime between 20,000 and 10,000 years ago.

American Indians differ in various ways from typical Mongoloids. Their skin is often reddish or yellowish-brown, and their noses are prominent and seldom flat. But they have black hair, high cheek bones and little body hair.

The Negroids of Africa, south of the Sahara, mostly have very dark skins, thick, outward-turning lips, broad noses and narrow heads, with a protruding upper jaw. This sub-group includes some of the world's tallest people — the Nilotes — and the shortest — the Negrillos, or pygmies. Descendants of African slaves live in large numbers in the Americas, although they have intermixed considerably with Caucasoids. Asian Negroids include the Papuans of New Guinea and the Negritos, or pygmies, of Malaysia and many Pacific islands.

Left: **This woman from northern Thailand belongs to the Indonesian-Malay sub-group of the Mongoloid peoples. The Indonesian-Malays do not have the slanting eyes of the Classic Mongoloids.**

Above right: **Peoples of the world.**

Right: **This European mother and her children belong to the Caucasoid group of mankind. Within the Caucasoid group, there are many variations in the appearance of individuals.**

Far right: **The Hausa of northern Nigeria are essentially Negroid, although they speak a Hamitic tongue and they have intermixed to some extent with peoples from the north. As a result, they tend to be taller and often have narrower noses than the typical Negroes of the West African coastlands.**

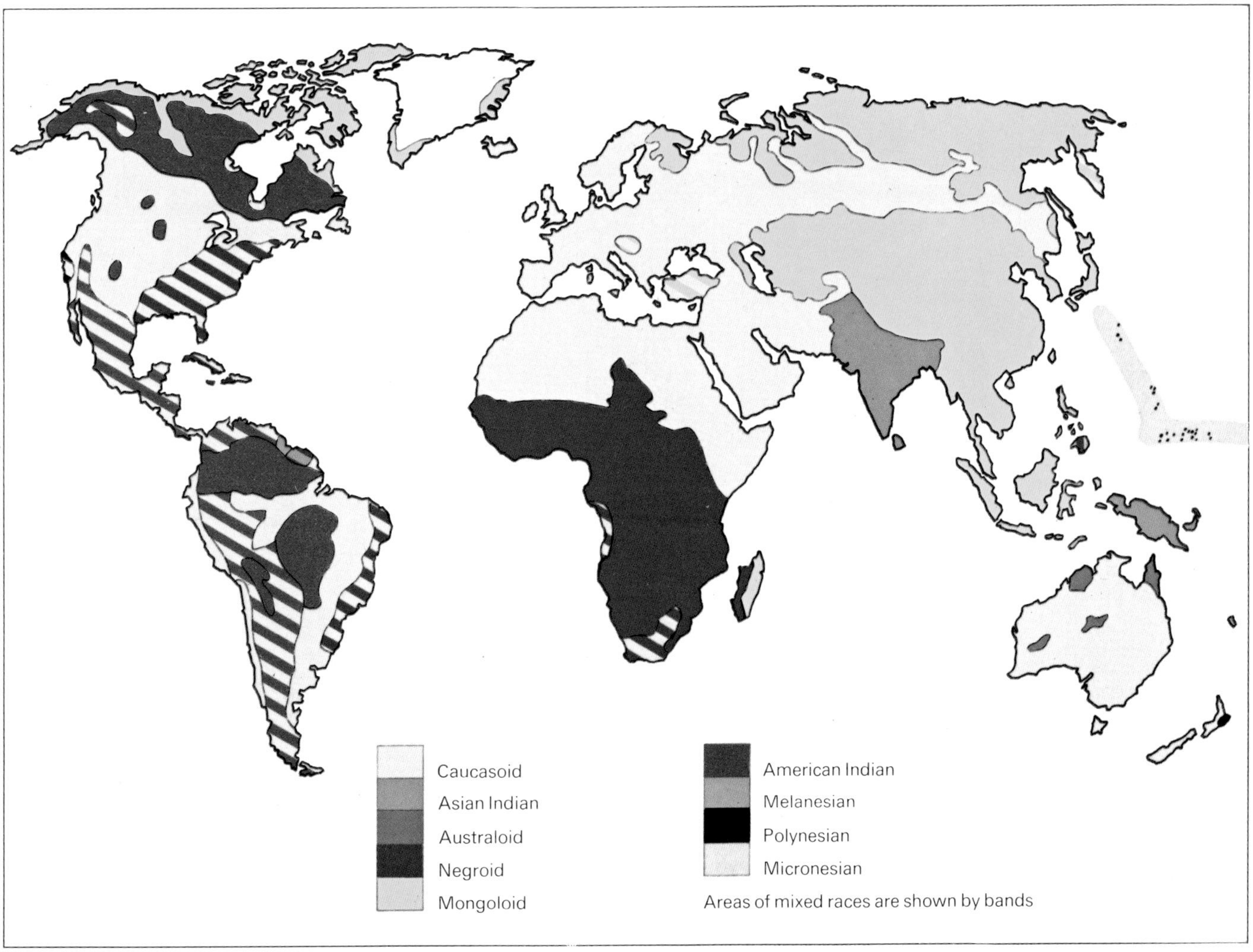

Caucasoid	American Indian
Asian Indian	Melanesian
Australoid	Polynesian
Negroid	Micronesian
Mongoloid	Areas of mixed races are shown by bands

Languages and Religions

The world's peoples are divided into many language and religious groups. These divisions have led to conflict between nations and divisions within nations.

Languages

There are nearly 2,800 languages, not including dialects. Some languages, such as those spoken by small groups in Africa and the Amazon basin, are spoken only by a few thousand people. Others, such as Chinese and English, are used by millions. A few languages have achieved international importance. The languages most used in international business are English, French and German, which together are used for about four-fifths of all business transactions. These languages have spread around the world, partly because of migration and colonization and partly because the countries in which these languages are spoken are among the world's foremost trading nations. Other languages that have spread widely from their original area are Spanish and Portuguese (throughout South America), Russian, Italian and Arabic. Chinese is of major importance in terms of the number of people who speak it, but this language is of minor importance in international business.

Of the great languages mentioned above, all except Arabic and Chinese belong to the world's largest single language family — the Indo-European. Languages of this family are used by about one-half of the world's population.

The Indo-European language family has several branches. The Balto-Slavic group includes Bulgarian, Czech, Latvian, Lithuanian, Polish, Russian, Serbo-Croat, Slovak, Slovenian and Ukrainian. The Germanic branch includes English, Dutch, Flemish (a Dutch dialect), German and the Scandinavian languages. Celtic languages include Breton, Gaelic (Irish and Scots) and Welsh. The Romance branch is based on Latin — the language of ancient Rome — and includes French, Italian, Portuguese, Romanian and Spanish. The Greek language forms a branch on its own, as does Albanian. The Iranian group includes Persian and Pushtu, the language of the Afghans. And the Indo-Aryan branch includes Bengali and Hindi.

The second largest language family is the Sino-Tibetan, which accounts for more than one-fifth of the world's population. It includes Burmese, Chinese (Sinitic), Thai and Tibetan. The other main language families are spoken by far fewer people. They include: the Semitic-Hamitic-Kushitic group, which includes Arabic and Hebrew; the Uralic and Altaic families, including Mongol, Finnish, and Turkish; the Japanese and Korean family; the Dravidian family of southern India; the Malayo-Polynesian family; the Mon-Khmer family of southeastern Asia; the languages of black Africa; and the American Indian languages.

Religions

Most religions combine the worship of one or several gods with ethical rules of conduct, although some are chiefly ethical and philosophical. There are 10 major religions: Christianity, Islam, Hinduism, Confucianism, Buddhism, Shinto, Taoism, Judaism, Sikhism and Jainism.

Hinduism is an ancient Indian religion, which is also followed by people in Malaysia, Mauritius, the Pacific islands and parts of eastern and southern Africa. Hinduism dates back to about 2500 BC. Hindus believe in one supreme power, Brahman, but they worship many gods, who are seen as reflections of Brahman. Incorporated in Hinduism are beliefs in reincarnation, the caste system and the sacredness of cattle. Buddhism developed from Hinduism. Its founder was Siddartha Gautama (560–480 BC),

who became the Buddha — the Enlightened One. Buddhists do not worship any god, but seek a state of complete peace and love called Nirvana. Although it began in India, Buddhism is now practised mostly in China, Japan, Tibet and southeastern Asia. Another religion developed from Hinduism is Jainism, which is practised in western India. Founded by Mahavira in the 500s BC, Jainism consists basically of ethical beliefs.

One of the earliest religions to embrace a belief in one God (monotheism) was Judaism, a religion based on the teachings in the Old Testament and the Talmud. Jews live in many parts of the world, but they regard Palestine as their spiritual home. Christianity incorporates most of the teachings of Judaism, together with the teachings of Jesus Christ in the New Testament. Today there are about 3,000 Christian denominations, but there are three major divisions — the Roman Catholic Church, the Eastern Orthodox Church and the Protestant denominations. Islam, a word generally taken to mean peace and submission to God, is a religion taught by Muhammad (AD 570–632). Islam retains much from Judaism and Christianity. Its holy book is the Koran. Islam has spread through northern Africa and southwestern Asia.

Sikhism, which is followed in northwestern India, was founded by Guru Nanak (AD 1469–1538). It combines Hindu and Islamic beliefs. The great religions of China are Buddhism, Confucianism (a philosophical religion founded by Confucius around 500 BC), and Taoism (a mystical religion, founded, according to tradition, by Lao Tzu in the 500s BC). Shinto is Japan's native religion. Dating back 2,500 years, Shinto involves the worship of many gods. In the past, Shintoists regarded the Japanese emperor as a descendant of the Sun God.

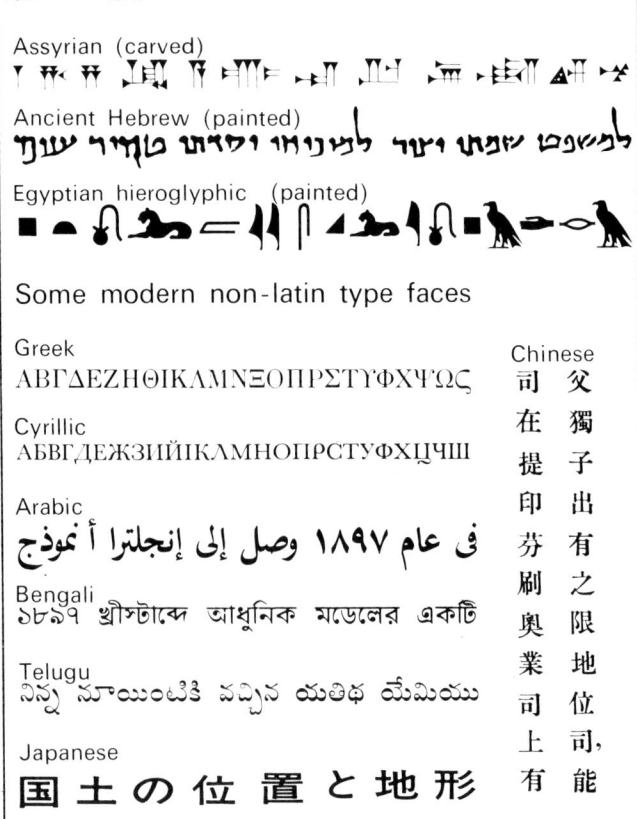

Above: **The Sultan Ahmet Mosque in Istanbul, one of the finest of Islamic buildings.**

Right: **A Christian church in Bavaria, in the southern part of West Germany.**

Below left: **Writing styles of ancient and modern times.**

Below: **Distribution of religious groups around the world.**

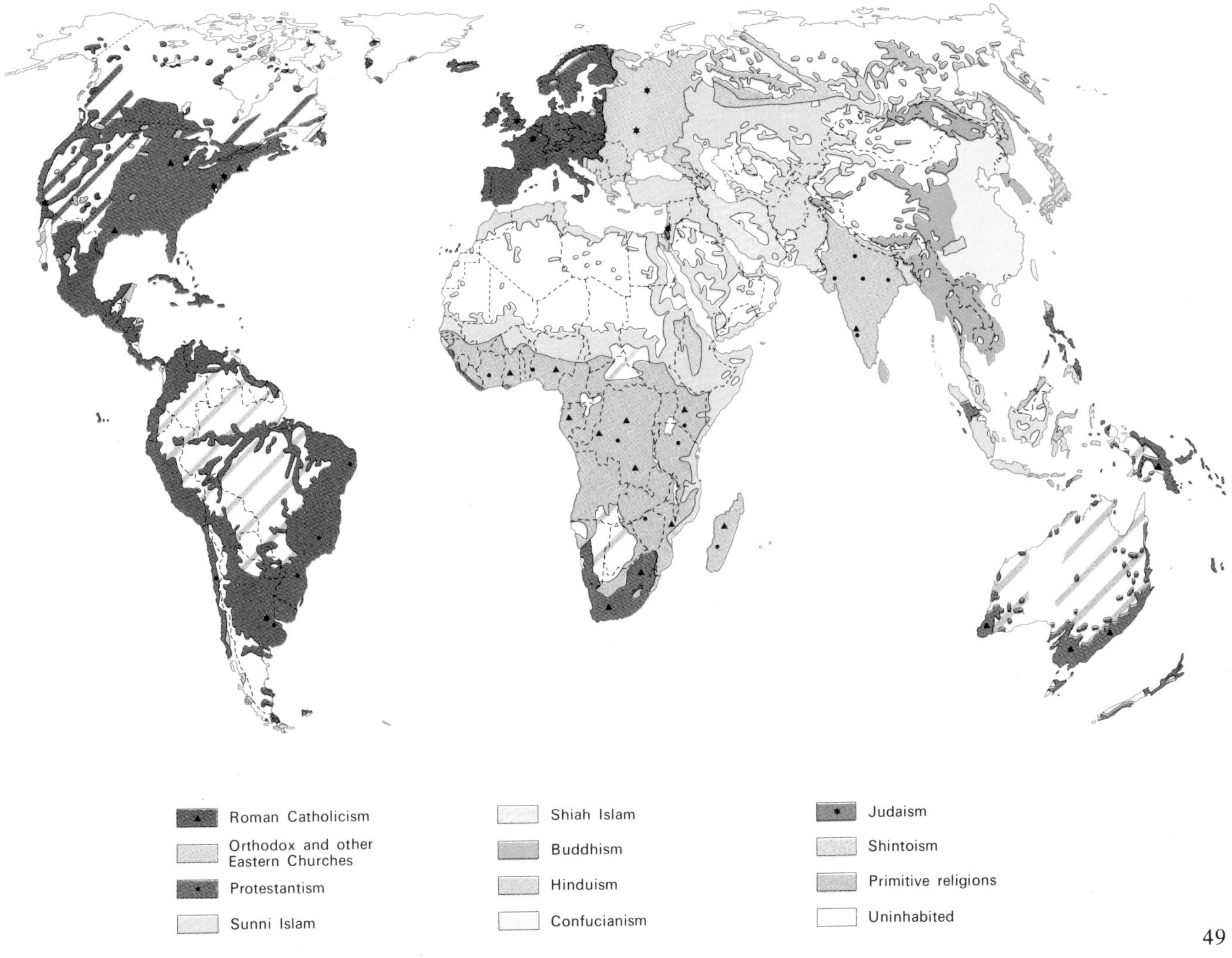

Roman Catholicism	Shiah Islam	Judaism
Orthodox and other Eastern Churches	Buddhism	Shintoism
Protestantism	Hinduism	Primitive religions
Sunni Islam	Confucianism	Uninhabited

Population

The world's population is very unevenly distributed. Vast tracts of land are too cold, too dry or too rugged and mountainous to support more than a few people. On the other hand, in parts of the farming belts, which total no more than 10 per cent of the Earth's land area, and in industrial zones, people are crowded together.

On average, in 1977, there were about 30 people to every square kilometre of land (78 per square mile), excluding the icy continent of Antarctica, which has no permanent population. But

Europe had a population density of 97 per square kilometre (251 per square mile) and Asia was second with 85 per square kilometre (220 per square mile). By contrast, Oceania, which includes Australia — two-thirds of which is virtually empty because it is desert — had only 2.7 people per square kilometre (7 per square mile), while the U.S.S.R. and North America had about 11.5 per square kilometre (30 per square mile).

The world's ten largest countries, by area, are the U.S.S.R.,

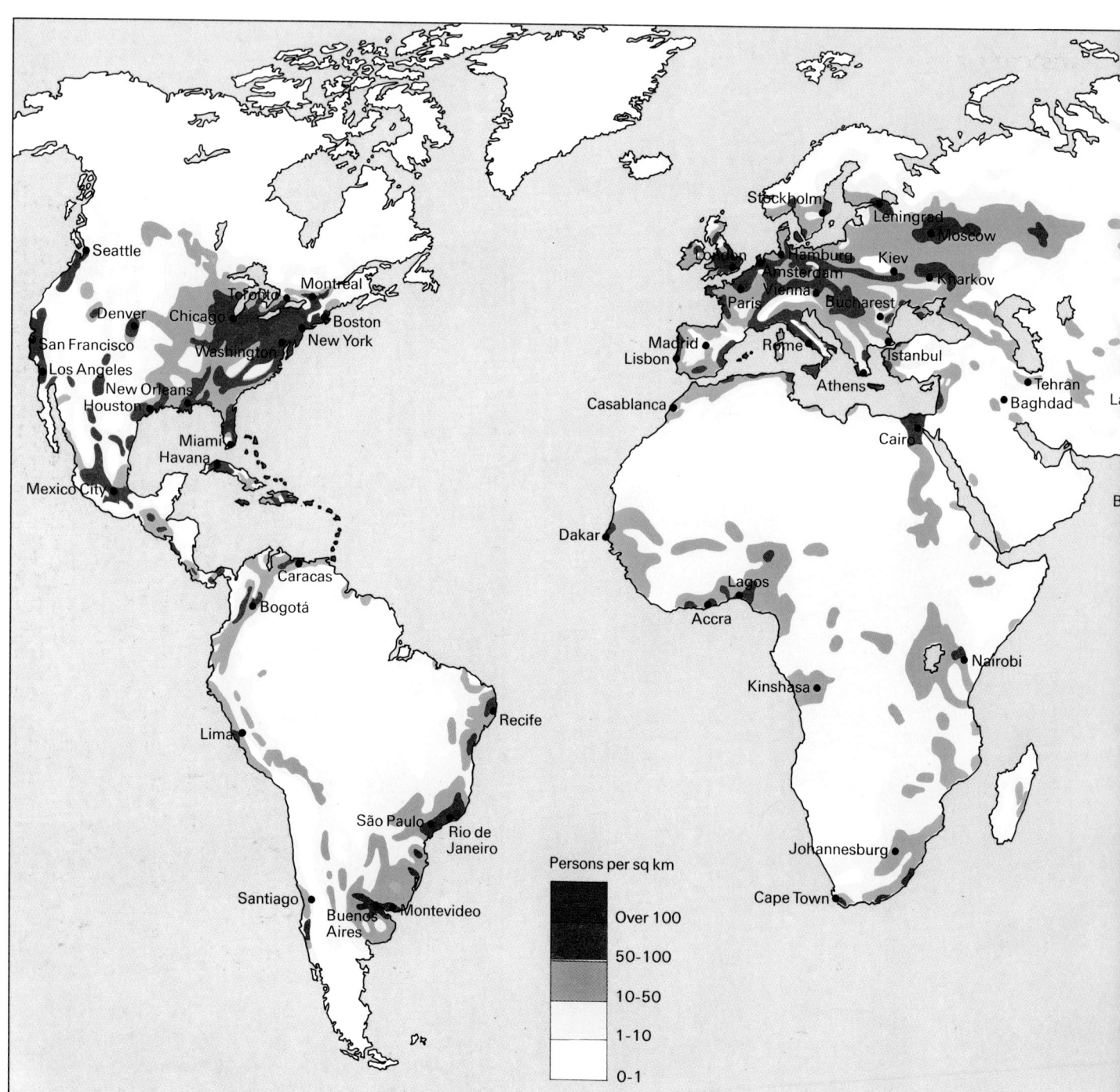

Persons per sq km

Over 100

50-100

10-50

1-10

0-1

Canada, China, the United States, Brazil, Australia, India, Argentina, Sudan and Algeria. But the ten most populated countries in 1977 were China (859 million), India (624 million) the U.S.S.R. (259 million), the United States (217 million), Indonesia (128 million), Japan (114 million), Brazil (113 million), Bangladesh (80 million), Pakistan (75 million) and Nigeria (66 million).

In 1977, the world had an estimated population of 4,116 million, and it was increasing by about 1.5 million per week. This is the fastest and most massive population increase in history. Around 6000 BC, the world had an estimated population of about 200 million. It then increased steadily until, in AD 1000, it had reached just over 300 million. After that, the rate of increase

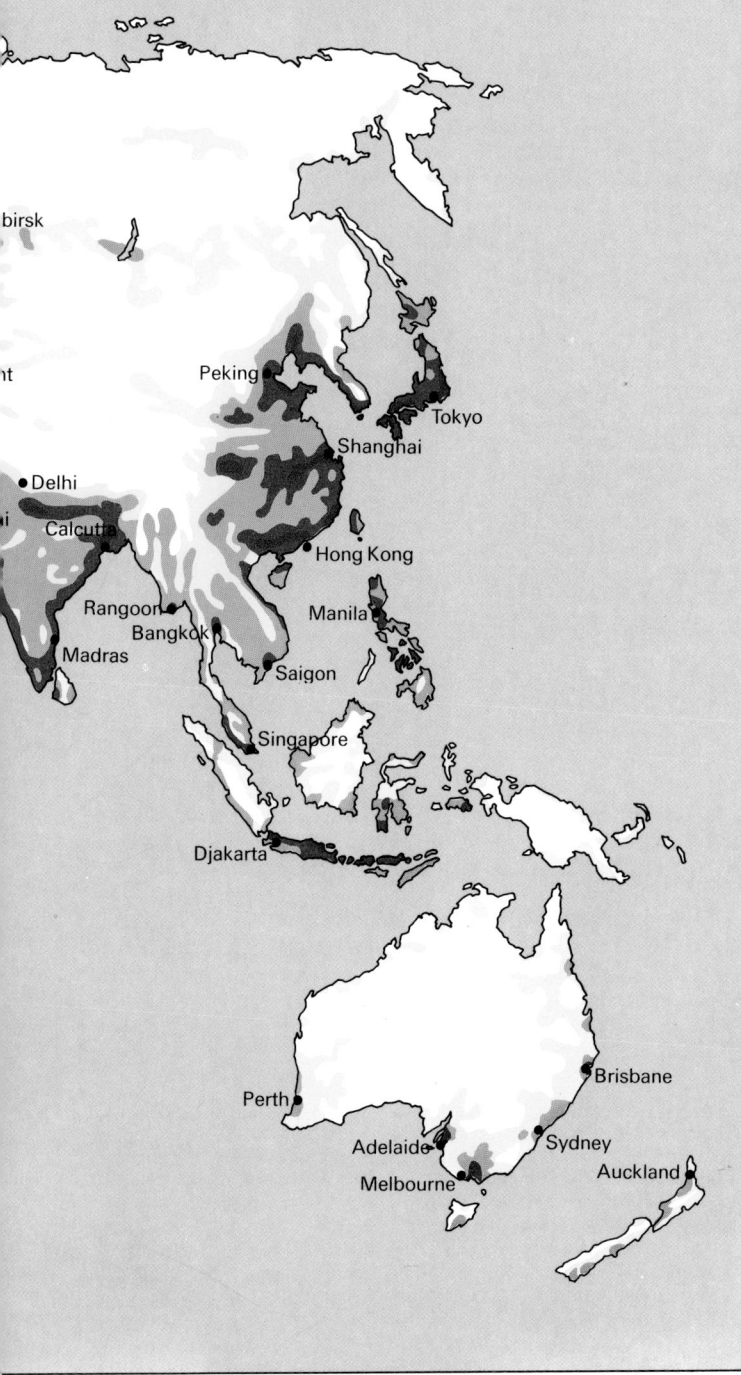

Top: **Mongolia contains large areas of bleak plateaux and mountains. Because of the severe and extreme climate, Mongolia is thinly-populated and most of the people are nomadic pastoralists.**

Above: **A crowded street in Tokyo, Japan's capital. Japan is densely populated but, in recent years, its annual rate of population growth has been reduced to only 1.3 per cent.**

51

began to accelerate, and the 1,000 million mark was passed in the 1800s. By the mid-1920s, it was nearly 2,000 million, and it doubled again in the following 50 years.

The explosion in world populations results from a net increase of births over deaths, mainly caused by a gradual decrease in infant mortality and longer average life spans. In the world as a whole, the average birth rate for the years 1965–74 was 33 per 1,000 people and the average death rate for the same period was 13 per 1,000. And, in 1970–4, there was a net increase in world population of about 1.9 per cent per year. If this rate continues, the world's population will double in the next 37 years.

There are considerable variations in population increases from country to country and from continent to continent. For example, the population of Pakistan has been estimated to be increasing by 3.3 per cent per year — an extremely fast rate that would double Pakistan's population in only 22 years. But, in West Germany, it would take more than 110 years for the population to double at the slow rate of 0.6 per cent per year.

Among the continents, the populations of Africa and Latin America (including Central America and Caribbean countries) are increasing at the fast rate of 2.7 per cent per year. This rate would double the population in only 26 years. Africa has the highest birth rate of all the continents — 47 per 1,000 people per year — but it also has the highest death rate — 21 per 1,000 people per year. Latin America has a lower birth rate at 38 per 1,000 per year, but its death rate is also much lower at 10 per 1,000 people. Asia's birth rate is almost as high as Latin America's at 37 per 1,000 people per year, but the death rate of 15 per 1,000 is considerably higher. Hence, the net average rate of population increase in Asia is lower at 2.1 per cent per year (1970–4 average) and it would take 34 years for the population to double at this rate.

By contrast, the populations of North America and the U.S.S.R. are increasing by 0.9 per cent per year, which means that it would take 78 years for their populations to double if this rate were maintained. And, in Europe, the average rate of increase is only 0.6 per cent per year. Europe and North America have the lowest birth rates at 17 per 1,000 people per year.

The highest population increases have thus been taking place in the developing world, and the lowest increases have occurred in the developed, industrialized world. In Asia, Japan is the only truly industrialized country and, significantly, its average rate of population increase is well below the average for Asia at 1.3 per cent per year. Part of the reason for this contrast is that, in developing countries, a high proportion of the people live at subsistence level. It is not surprising that many poor farmers may see their only hope for survival in old age as having enough sons to support them.

The average rate of population increase in the developed world is 1.1 per cent per year, whereas the rate in the developing world is more than twice as much, averaging 2.3 per cent. One of the most striking consequences of this difference is reflected in the age structures of the two worlds.

In Africa, Asia and Latin America, the populations are more youthful than in the developed world. On average, about 40 out of every 100 people are under 15 years of age; 56 are between 15 and 64; and only 4 out of every 100 are 65 or over. This contrasts with Europe, North America, Oceania and the U.S.S.R., where 27 out of every 100 people are under 15 years of age; 63 are between 15 and 64; and 10 are 65 or over.

The large and increasing school-age populations in developing countries already have too few educational facilities and teachers. Also, the developing world has a lower proportion of people of working age, and the average life expectation is much lower. The developed countries face different problems, such as the high and increasing proportion of older people, who do not contribute directly to the economy. For example, the average life expectation

for Canadian men and women in 1931 was 60 years and 62.1 years respectively. But, in the period 1965–7, it had risen to 68.75 for Canadian men and 75.18 for women.

The population explosion poses a threat to the Earth's resources. One vital resource is farmland, which is limited in extent by climate and topography. Today the world has about 1,440 million hectares (3,558 million acres) of farmland — that is, land under the plough or under permanent crops. In 1977, when the world's population stood at about 4,116 million, the average amount of farmland per person was just over one-third of a hectare (nearly nine-tenths of an acre). By the year 2000, the world's population will have increased to about 6,397 million at current rates of growth. The average amount of farmland per person will then be reduced to just over one-fifth of a hectare (slightly more than half an acre).

Crop yields must, therefore, rise if the world's increasing population is to be fed. But average figures conceal wide differences between the developed and developing worlds. Generally, crop yields per hectare are high in developed countries which have the lowest population growth rates, because farming is mostly highly mechanized and efficient. But, in developing countries, standards are generally low. For example, in Asia, rice is the staple food but, in 1970, average rice yields per hectare in Asia were less than half of those in Europe. Also the United States produces more food than it needs to feed its people, yet only about 7 out of every 200 people work on farms. In Asia, about 64 per cent of the people work on farms. And, in Africa, where 74 per cent of the people are farm workers, mostly at subsistence level, severe famines are all too frequent. In such poor African countries as Burundi, Malawi, Niger, Rwanda and Tanzania, more than 90 per cent of the people are farmers.

Fast-increasing populations, combined with a generally low level of economic production, are causing severe problems in many areas. A country's production is often expressed as its Gross Domestic Product (GDP). The GDP is the total value of a country's output of goods and services. For example, in 1973, the industrialized United States had a total GDP of $1,297,500 million, or $6,120 per person, whereas one of the poorest developing nations, Upper Volta, had a GDP of $320 million and a per capita GDP of $59. And, in Upper Volta, the per capita GDP has actually been declining in recent years because the population has been increasing at a faster rate than the GDP.

Population increase also threatens other resources, such as water supplies, mineral reserves and fossil fuel reserves. For example, it was estimated that the world's known petroleum resources in 1973 would be used up in only 27 years at the current rates of production. With increasing demand from an ever-growing population, oil wells will eventually run dry and many metals will be in short supply.

The problems posed by the population explosion are global in scale and must be treated globally, by a sensible distribution of food and other resources. Significantly, when countries develop and raise their per capita GDPs and standards of living, the rate of population increase starts to decline.

Opposite: **The diagram shows how the world's population has grown since 1650. At first, the increase was steady. But, after the 1,000 million mark had been passed in the 1800s, the rate of population increase accelerated. By the mid-1920s, the world had 2,000 million people, and the 4,000 million mark was passed in 1977 — the population having doubled in** just over 50 years. Today, the **average rate of population increase is estimated to be 1.9 per cent per year — a rate which, if it is maintained, will double the world's population in only 37 years. The diagram also shows that the fastest growing populations are in the developing, or poorer countries. The slowest rates of population growth occur in developed nations.**

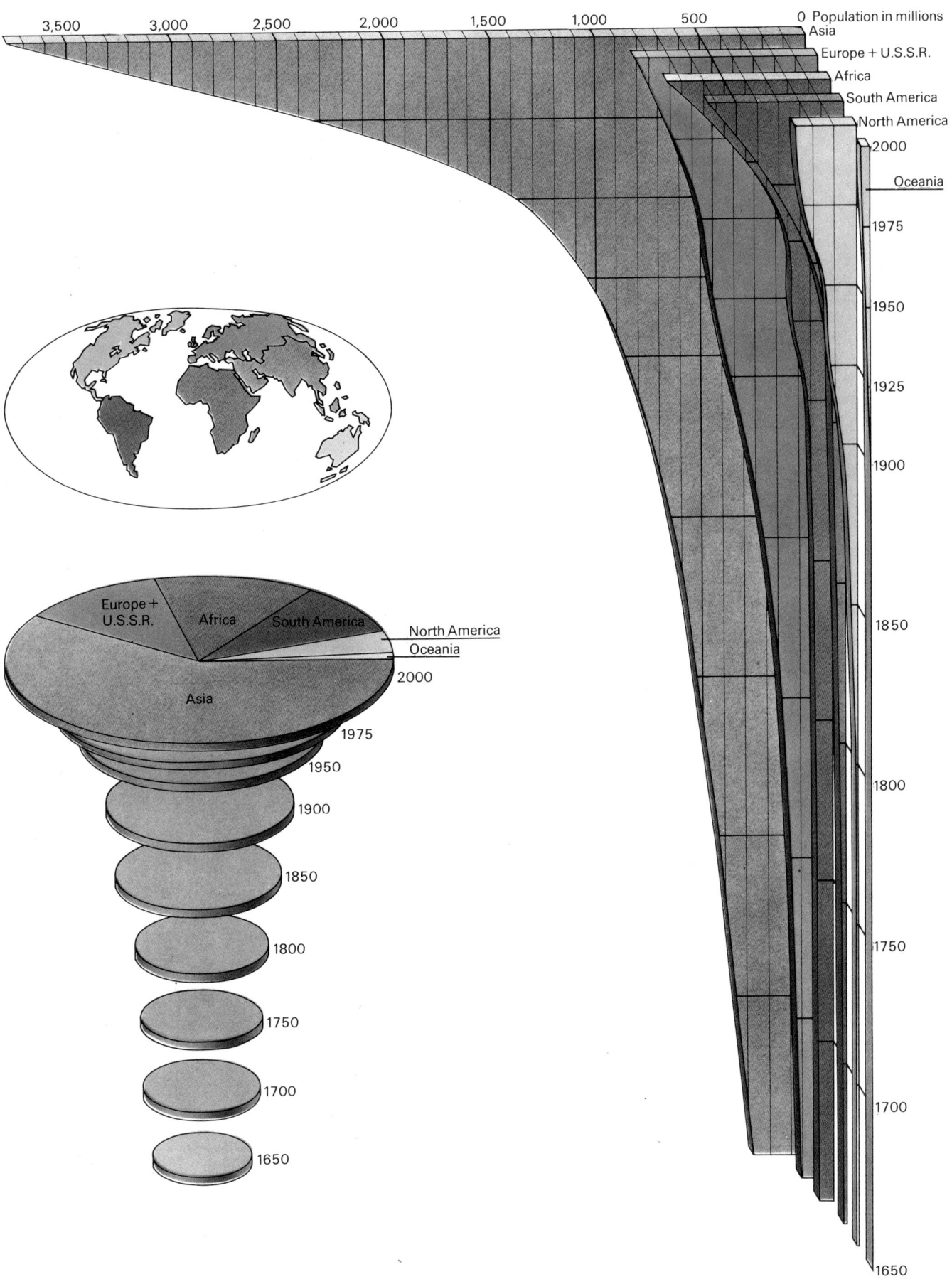

Population

Population in millions

3,500 3,000 2,500 2,000 1,500 1,000 500 0

Asia
Europe + U.S.S.R.
Africa
South America
North America

2000

Oceania

1975

1950

1925

1900

1850

1800

1750

1700

1650

Europe + U.S.S.R.   Africa   South America   North America   Oceania

Asia

2000
1975
1950
1900
1850
1800
1750
1700
1650

53

The Growth of Towns

One of the main features that distinguishes developed countries from their less fortunate developing neighbours is that developed countries have large manufacturing industries. On the other hand, the economies of most developing countries are based mainly on the production of primary products — food and raw materials, although such developing countries as Brazil and China do have important pockets of manufacturing industries.

Industrialization is the chief factor that has led to the rapid development of cities and towns since the late 1700s, when the Industrial Revolution began, at first in Britain, although rural manufacturing remains important in Norway and Switzerland. In the world as a whole, about one-third of the people live in urban areas. But, in the developed world, between two-thirds and nine-tenths of the people live and work in cities and towns. By contrast, in parts of Africa, only 10 per cent of the people are urbanized. In Asia, an average of only one-third of the people live in urban areas and, in Latin America, about half are town or city dwellers. However, as developing countries try to diversify their economies by establishing manufacturing industries and services, so more and more people are leaving the countryside for the towns and cities.

The earliest towns grew up in Mesopotamia following the start of agriculture and the production of food surpluses 6,000 years ago. By 3500 BC, there were many well-established towns in the area. Towns were later set up in Egypt and the Mediterranean area and, to the east, in India, central Asia and China. These early towns were essentially centres of trade and craft industries, but many of the sites were chosen because they were easily defended. In the towns, people had time to develop the arts and sciences, and so it was the towns that provided the stimulus for the development of the great early civilizations. But most towns remained small, although some ancient Chinese cities may have had about one million inhabitants.

The development of Paris is typical of many cities. It was first established as a settlement on an island in the River Seine. Because of the island, the settlement provided an easy bridging point of the river, and Paris developed as a communications centre. When it was taken by the Romans in 52 BC, it covered about 40 hectares (100 acres). As trade increased, Paris gradually expanded onto the north and south banks of the Seine and, by the Middle Ages, it covered nearly 8 square kilometres (3 square miles) and had a population of about 150,000. France began to industrialize in the early 1800s, and Paris grew quickly as factories sprang up in and around it. By the 1840s, industrial Paris covered 10 times the area of medieval Paris, and its population passed the 900,000 mark. Today, with its large suburbs, it sprawls over an area of 480 square kilometres (185 square miles) and has a population of 9,108,000.

In the early days of the Industrial Revolution, many new towns arose on coalfields, ironfields and other places where natural resources were to hand. But, as communications improved, so cities could be founded far from the resources they required for their people and industries. For example, ports handling imports and exports became industrial centres, and other cities were established on the expanding railway networks, especially at railway junctions.

Modern cities face many problems, including large-scale crime, noise, pollution, communications breakdowns, such as traffic jams, and a lack of community sense that may cause loneliness.

In the developing world, the lack of capital makes it difficult for governments to cope with the rapid expansion of their cities. Country people migrate to urban areas in search of better-paid jobs, higher standards of living and more amenities. The population of Brazil's cities, for example, will increase by an estimated 27 million people during the 1970s. This means that these cities will have to provide at least five million new family houses, otherwise ugly shanty towns with serious health hazards will arise. And, as most of the new arrivals are unskilled, there will be serious urban unemployment, unless the industrial expansion is fast enough to provide sufficient jobs. In one country, communist China, the government has been trying to reverse the world trend towards urbanization by diverting people back to rural communities, which they are trying to make self-sufficient.

The World's Largest 25 Cities*		
City	Country	Population
Tokyo	Japan	11,582,000
New York City	United States	11,571,000
Mexico City	Mexico	10,223,000
Paris	France	9,108,000
Buenos Aires	Argentina	8,353,000
Moscow	U.S.S.R.	7,410,000
London	United Kingdom	7,168,000
Los Angeles	United States	7,032,000
Calcutta	India	7,005,000
Shanghai	China	7,000,000
Chicago	United States	6,979,000
Bombay	India	5,968,000
Seoul	South Korea	5,536,000
Sao Paulo	Brazil	5,241,000
Peking	China	5,000,000
Cairo	Egypt	4,961,000
Philadelphia	United States	4,818,000
Djakarta	Indonesia	4,576,000
Rio de Janeiro	Brazil	4,316,000
Detroit	United States	4,200,000
Leningrad	U.S.S.R.	4,133,000
Tehran	Iran	3,858,000
Delhi	India	3,629,000
Tientsin	China	3,600,000
Karachi	Pakistan	3,469,000
*Including suburban areas		

Above left: **Italy, like most developed countries, suffers from traffic congestion in urban areas. The populations of urban areas in most parts of the world are increasing in size, partly as a result of natural population growth and partly because of rural depopulation.**

Above: **Land and housing are so limited in the crowded British colony of Hong Kong that many people have to live in boats.**

Right: **Many towns in Taiwan, like others in developing nations, are surrounded by shanty towns, where crime, disease and poverty are rife. Shanty towns develop when the urban building programmes cannot keep pace with the fast-increasing populations. Yet, in most countries, the exodus of people from the countryside continues, because the best-paid jobs are nearly all to be found in the towns.**

Health, Wealth and Poverty

Developed countries are distinguished from developing countries by their far higher per capita GDPs. For example, in the early 1970s, France had a per capita GDP of US$3,820; West Germany, $5,670; the Netherlands, $4,440; the United Kingdom, $2,470; and the United States, $6,120. People who live in these, or other developed countries can expect to live much longer, on average, than people in developing countries. For example, average life expectations in the late 1960s and early 1970s were as follows: France, men 68.5 years, women 76.1 years; West Germany, men 67.4, women 73.8; the Netherlands, men 70.8, women 76.8; the United Kingdom, men 67.8, women 73.8; and the United States, men 67.4, women 75.1.

Complete statistics are lacking in many developing countries. But the United Nations' latest available estimates of the average life expectations for both men and women are: in Ghana, 46 years; in India, 41; in Indonesia, 47½; and in Senegal, 41. The per capita GDPs in the early 1970s were: Ghana $230; India $99; Indonesia $124; and Senegal $250. Some African countries have even lower average life expectations and per capita GDPs.

Low economic production, poverty and short life expectations are all, therefore, inter-related. Experts estimate that 300 to 400 million people, mostly children in the developing world, are suffering from malnutrition. For good health, people need a balanced diet. They need carbohydrates and fats, which provide energy. They need proteins for the growth of bones, cells and muscles, and smaller amounts of mineral salts and vitamins, which enable the body to make use of foods consumed. But, in the developing world, many people suffer from deficiency diseases, caused by a lack of one or more of these essential elements.

Kwashiokor is a disorder caused by a lack of protein, although sufferers may be eating sufficient carbohydrates in the form of cereals. In fact, it is estimated that about half of the world's population obtain two-thirds or less of the proteins they require for good health. Survivors of deficiency diseases in childhood may be left with impaired mental powers and their bodies may be stunted. Yet these children are the adults of the future, on whose shoulders rests the responsibility for raising their countries' economic production.

In many developing countries, periodic droughts, attacks of pests, and various plant and animal diseases often cause terrible famines. For example, in the dry Sahelian savanna, south of the Sahara Desert, years of drought occurred in the late 1960s and early 1970s. Hundreds of thousands of cattle perished, crops failed and many people suffered great hardship and starvation.

The food that is available in many places is unevenly distributed. Even in developed countries, unequal distribution of wealth causes poverty and malnutrition in some areas. In some cases, in developing nations, the consumption of certain foods has been forbidden by ancient customs. In East Africa, in the early 1960s, many Masai people were starving as a result of drought, but they refused solid foods, such as maize meal, because their traditional diet consisted of milk and blood. Also, in developing countries, many people get poor-quality or inadequate food, which impairs their general health.

People whose general standard of health is low lack resistance to disease. Among such people, the infant mortality rate is also high, standards of hygiene are often low and medical facilities are extremely limited. In northern Nigeria, there was only one doctor for every 100,000 people in the mid-1960s, while the United States had about 150 per 100,000 people. In developing countries, money is lacking for medicines, hospitals and other health facilities. For example, in the mid-1960s, the United States had around 750 times as much money available to spend on health per person as Nigeria.

Much aid for developing countries is channelled through the U.N. For example, the World Health Organization has mounted a campaign in Africa to reduce the incidence of malaria by preventive medicine and the eradication of the mosquitoes' habitats. But new health hazards are sometimes created as developing countries progress. For example, hydro-electric stations at the Kariba Dam in southern Africa and the Aswan High Dam in Egypt provide cheap electricity for manufacturing industries. But, behind the dams, lakes Kariba and Nasser have provided vast breeding grounds for the parasite that communicates the dangerous disease bilharzia.

One interesting development in some countries has been the utilization of the limited cash available to train medical auxiliaries. These are not doctors, but they are given a short and, therefore, cheap training that enables them to diagnose illnesses, treat the simpler cases and educate people in hygiene and birth control. Patients they are unable to help are referred to the few hospitals, which are mostly in the towns. Medical auxiliaries have an especially important role in large developing countries, where the population is widely scattered.

Left: **Many nations have promoted campaigns to educate people in birth control methods in an attempt to slow down fast rates of population increase. Such measures should eventually lead to economic stability and a higher standard of general health. But many people oppose most birth control methods for religious reasons.**

Right: **Victims of the severe drought and famine that occurred in the Sahel region of West Africa in 1972-4.**

The Economic World

Vegetable Food Resources

Vegetable foods — that is, plants of all kinds — are the basis of all animal life, including Man. Even carnivores — flesh-eaters — depend for their food on animals that feed on plants. Man is an omnivore, with teeth adapted to eating either meat or vegetable foods. There are about as many domestic animals as people in the world, and they have to share the vegetable crop. But meat is an extravagant way of using food resources. A given amount of cereal food might provide the nutritional needs of, say, twenty people when eaten as cereal. But it would suffice for only two to eight people when fed to animals and eaten in the form of meat or other animal products.

The world's greatest crop-growing regions are not always those with the highest populations. As a result, many areas of the world are not self-sufficient in food supplies, and have to import a great deal of their needs. For example, Western Europe has to import a large amount of cereals, particularly maize (corn) and hard wheat. Many countries, particularly the poorest of the developing countries, do produce all their own food, but only to a very poor standard of nutrition.

In such countries, farming plays a major part in the lives of the people. For example, over large areas of West Africa, nine workers out of ten are engaged in agriculture. In Bangladesh, eight out of ten are farmers, yet the country still does not produce enough food for its needs. Some difficulties are caused by unreliable climate, poor soil, or a population too large for the available farming land. But generally, the shortage of food is due to old-fashioned and inefficient methods of cultivation.

For these countries, there is hope for the future in what has come to be called the Green Revolution, which has been taking place over the past 20 years. The men behind this revolution are the plant breeders. They are continually raising new varieties of plants that produce heavier crops than those formerly grown. During the late 1960s and early 1970s, yields of rice and wheat in many Asian countries increased by amounts ranging from 20 per cent to 100 per cent. This Green Revolution has also changed trading patterns. For example, Japan and the Philippines, which were big importers of rice in the early 1960s, have now become exporters of this crop.

The most important vegetable crops are the cereals, which provide the bulk of the world's food and the feed for its animals. The two leading cereals are rice, which is the staple food of Asia, and so of about half the world's population, and wheat. Wheat is grown in all parts of the world, including Asia. In the forms of bread, pasta, and breakfast cereals, it forms an important part of the diet in the northern hemisphere. Maize (corn), the third-ranking cereal, is used largely as animal feed.

Root crops are widely cultivated for human and animal consumption. Potatoes are a leading crop in Europe, North America, and the U.S.S.R.; sweet potatoes and yams are grown in China, Japan, and Korea; and cassava is grown in Africa, Asia and parts of South America. Pulses — beans, peas, lentils and chickpeas — form a vital part of the diet in many poor countries. Sugar, from sugar-beet and sugar-cane, is important as a high-energy food. Edible oils, obtained from olives, oilpalms, soybeans and groundnuts, are used in cooking and as an alternative to butter.

Leading Wheat Producers

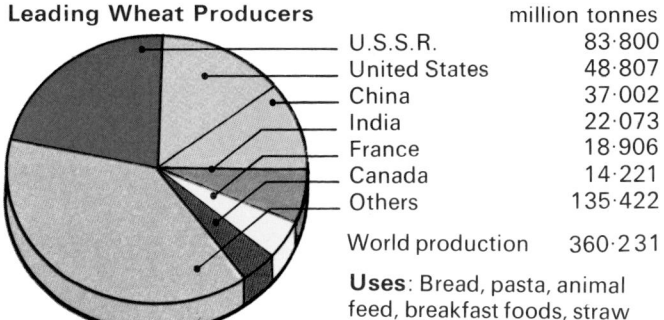

	million tonnes
U.S.S.R.	83·800
United States	48·807
China	37·002
India	22·073
France	18·906
Canada	14·221
Others	135·422
World production	360·231

Uses: Bread, pasta, animal feed, breakfast foods, straw

Leading Rye Producers

	million tonnes
U.S.S.R.	15·218
Poland	7·874
West Germany	2·559
East Germany	1·800
Czechoslovakia	0·750
Turkey	0·560
Others	3·850
World production	32·611

Uses: Bread, animal feed, alcoholic drinks, straw

Leading Millet and Sorghum Producers

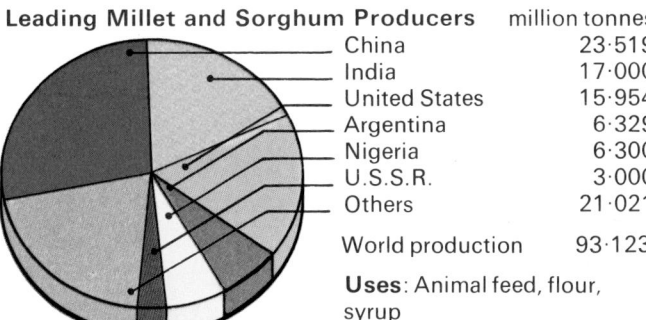

	million tonnes
China	23·519
India	17·000
United States	15·954
Argentina	6·329
Nigeria	6·300
U.S.S.R.	3·000
Others	21·021
World production	93·123

Uses: Animal feed, flour, syrup

Leading Maize (Corn) Producers

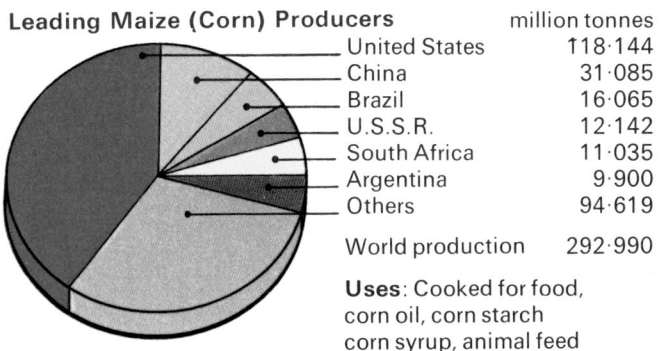

	million tonnes
United States	118·144
China	31·085
Brazil	16·065
U.S.S.R.	12·142
South Africa	11·035
Argentina	9·900
Others	94·619
World production	292·990

Uses: Cooked for food, corn oil, corn starch corn syrup, animal feed

Below left: **Much farm work in developing countries is done by hand, resulting in low production.**

Below: **Machinery like this combine harvester can greatly increase production.**

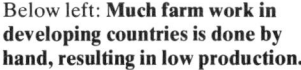

Vegetable Food Resources

Leading Rice Producers

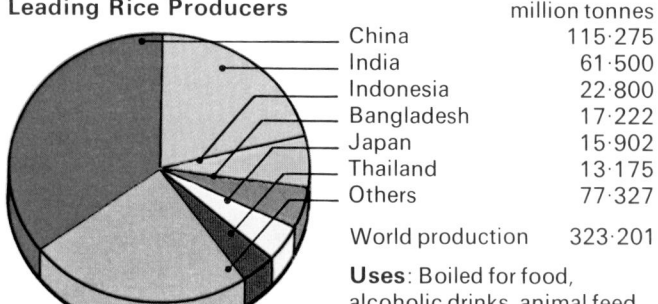

	million tonnes
China	115·275
India	61·500
Indonesia	22·800
Bangladesh	17·222
Japan	15·902
Thailand	13·175
Others	77·327
World production	323·201

Uses: Boiled for food, alcoholic drinks, animal feed, straw

Leading Sugar Producers

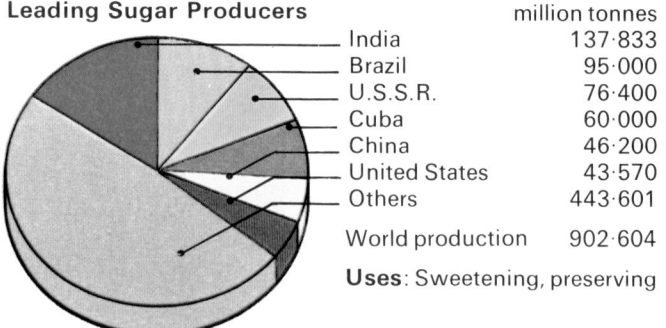

	million tonnes
India	137·833
Brazil	95·000
U.S.S.R.	76·400
Cuba	60·000
China	46·200
United States	43·570
Others	443·601
World production	902·604

Uses: Sweetening, preserving

Leading Barley Producers

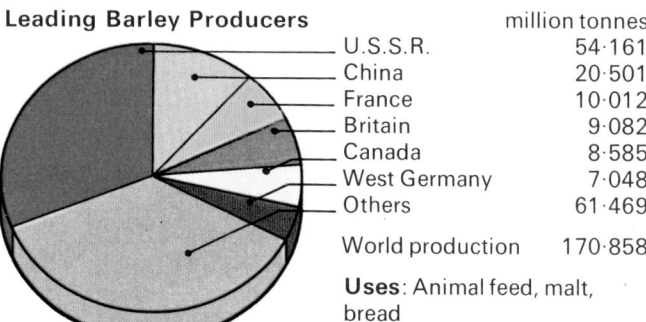

	million tonnes
U.S.S.R.	54·161
China	20·501
France	10·012
Britain	9·082
Canada	8·585
West Germany	7·048
Others	61·469
World production	170·858

Uses: Animal feed, malt, bread

Leading Cocoa Bean Producers

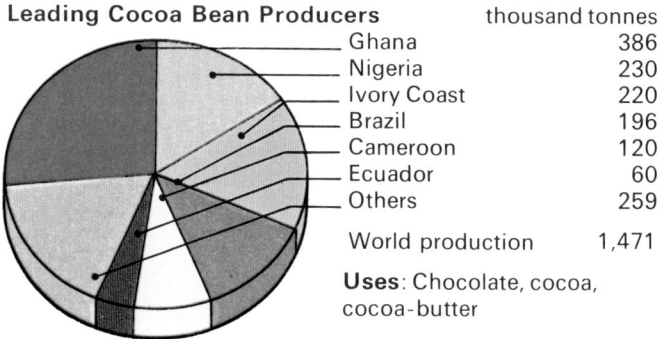

	thousand tonnes
Ghana	386
Nigeria	230
Ivory Coast	220
Brazil	196
Cameroon	120
Ecuador	60
Others	259
World production	1,471

Uses: Chocolate, cocoa, cocoa-butter

Leading Oats Producers

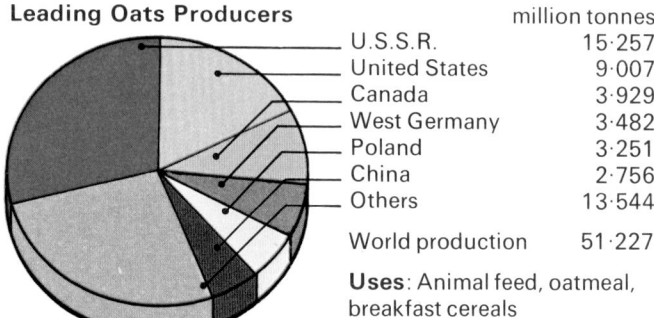

	million tonnes
U.S.S.R.	15·257
United States	9·007
Canada	3·929
West Germany	3·482
Poland	3·251
China	2·756
Others	13·544
World production	51·227

Uses: Animal feed, oatmeal, breakfast cereals

Leading Coffee Producers

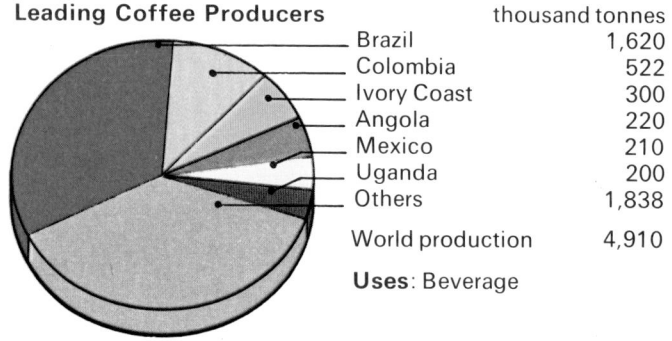

	thousand tonnes
Brazil	1,620
Colombia	522
Ivory Coast	300
Angola	220
Mexico	210
Uganda	200
Others	1,838
World production	4,910

Uses: Beverage

Leading Potato Producers

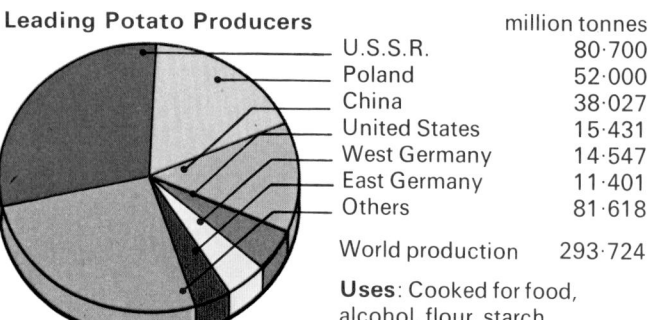

	million tonnes
U.S.S.R.	80·700
Poland	52·000
China	38·027
United States	15·431
West Germany	14·547
East Germany	11·401
Others	81·618
World production	293·724

Uses: Cooked for food, alcohol, flour, starch

Leading Tea Producers

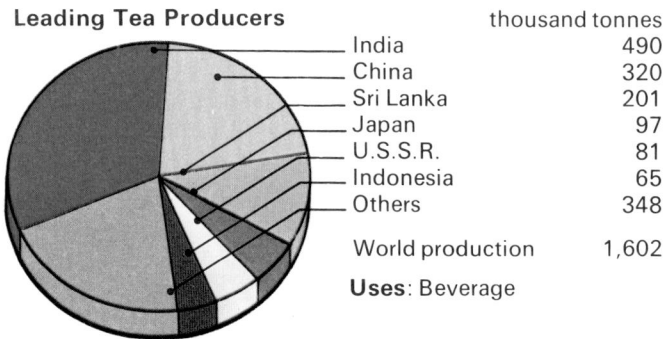

	thousand tonnes
India	490
China	320
Sri Lanka	201
Japan	97
U.S.S.R.	81
Indonesia	65
Others	348
World production	1,602

Uses: Beverage

Animal Food Resources

Although Man is largely a vegetable eater, meat and animal products form a valuable part of his diet. Meat provides a ready source of protein and fat — two essentials for health — and contains many vitamins. It also contains minerals such as iron, copper and phosphorus. The smell of cooked meat has been found to stimulate the digestive juices.

The main meats are beef, mutton and lamb, and pork. In some countries, particularly around the Mediterranean Sea, the flesh of goats is regularly eaten. In all parts of the world, people also eat the flesh of poultry and some other birds, such as ducks and geese.

Another valuable animal product is milk, usually from cows, though goat's milk and ewe's milk are also drunk in small quantities. Milk contains much the same nutrients as meat. A great deal of it is consumed in the form of butter and cheese, which contain a greater concentration of fats than plain milk.

Meat is raised largely in the grassland areas of the world; dairy cattle are kept mostly in the temperate zone countries, particularly in Europe, the United States, New Zealand and Australia. Sheep can be grazed on hilly land with poorer grass than required by cattle.

INDIA'S 'SACRED COWS'
Although India leads the world in the number of cattle produced, this can be misleading unless all the factors are known.

The cow is sacred to the Hindus, who form 85 per cent of India's people, and so they eat no beef — and the slaughter of cows, as distinct from bulls, is banned by the country's constitution. Although bullocks are the principal draft animals, India's huge cattle population includes a large number of useless beasts, and the milk yield from cows is among the world's lowest.

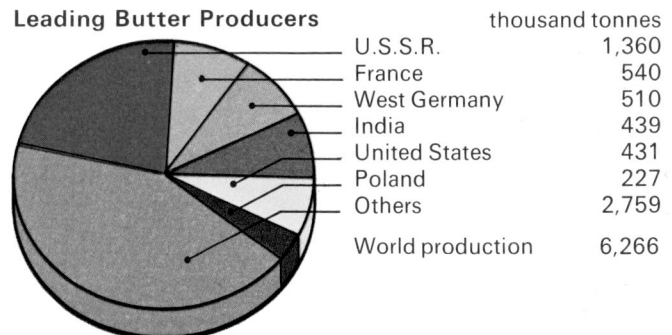

Leading Butter Producers — thousand tonnes

U.S.S.R.	1,360
France	540
West Germany	510
India	439
United States	431
Poland	227
Others	2,759
World production	6,266

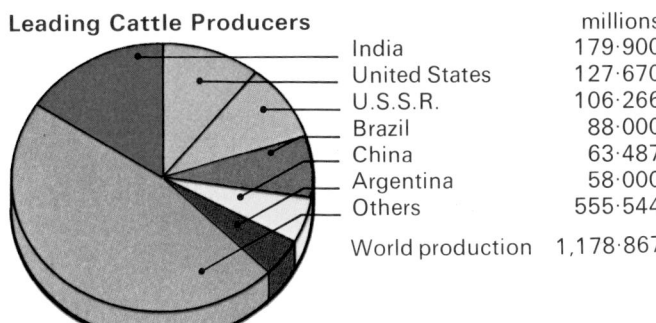

Leading Cattle Producers — millions

India	179·900
United States	127·670
U.S.S.R.	106·266
Brazil	88·000
China	63·487
Argentina	58·000
Others	555·544
World production	1,178·867

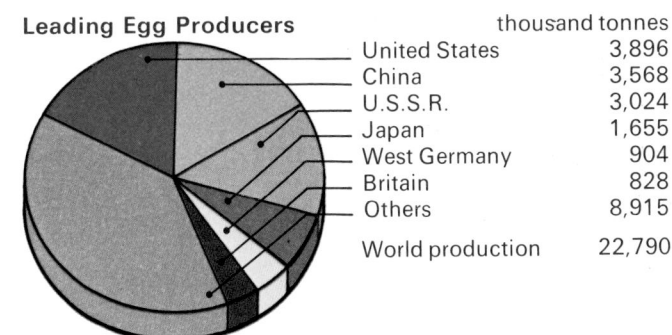

Leading Egg Producers — thousand tonnes

United States	3,896
China	3,568
U.S.S.R.	3,024
Japan	1,655
West Germany	904
Britain	828
Others	8,915
World production	22,790

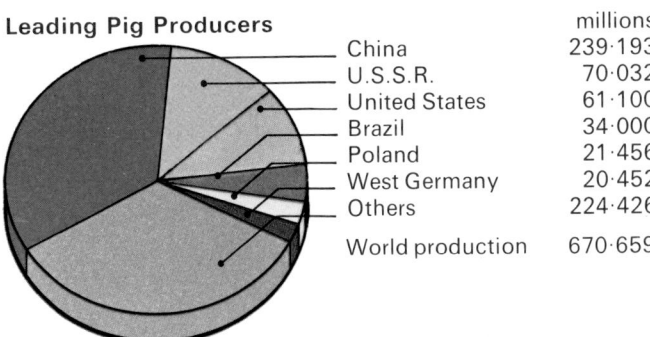

Leading Pig Producers — millions

China	239·193
U.S.S.R.	70·032
United States	61·100
Brazil	34·000
Poland	21·456
West Germany	20·452
Others	224·426
World production	670·659

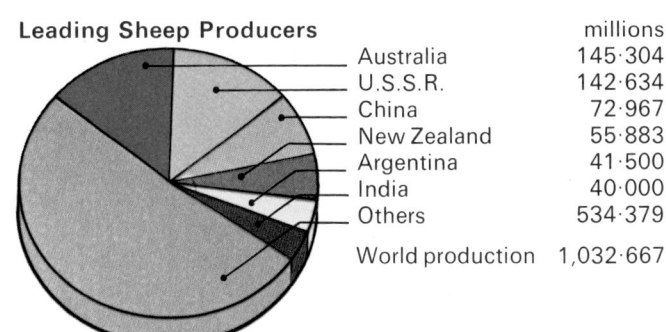

Leading Sheep Producers — millions

Australia	145·304
U.S.S.R.	142·634
China	72·967
New Zealand	55·883
Argentina	41·500
India	40·000
Others	534·379
World production	1,032·667

Leading Fish Producers

tonnes

Japan	10,702,000
U.S.S.R.	8,619,000
China	7,574,000
Norway	2,975,000
United States	2,670,000
Peru	2,299,000

WORLD FISHERIES
Fishing fleets of the world catch about 66 million tonnes of fish every year, and the total is constantly rising. There is a serious danger of over-fishing, and some traditional fishing grounds, such as those off Iceland, are already yielding significantly lower catches than they used to.

Fish are rich in protein and form an important part of the world diet. But some fish, and the waste of others, are used for other purposes. For example, fish-meal is used for chicken and livestock feed and as fertilizer. Other fish products include glue, isinglass, and oil for use in margarine, soap, candles, paints and linoleum.

WHALING
Whales are hunted largely for their oil, which is mostly made into margarine, but also for their flesh, which is esteemed in some countries, such as Japan. Overhunting has seriously reduced the world's whale population. Strenuous international efforts are now being made to limit whale catches.

The two main whaling countries are the U.S.S.R. and Japan, which take about 85 per cent of the total catch. Smaller whaling fleets are operated by Australia, Brazil, Canada, Chile, Denmark, Iceland, Norway, Peru, Portugal, South Africa and Spain. The world annual catch is about 32,350,000 tonnes.

Left: **Making cheese at Roquefort, France. The cheese, named after its place of origin, is made from the milk of goats and ewes.**

Right: **A worker tapping a rubber tree. Each tree yields about 18 litres (4 gallons) of latex a year, for up to 30 years.**

Leading Cheese Producers

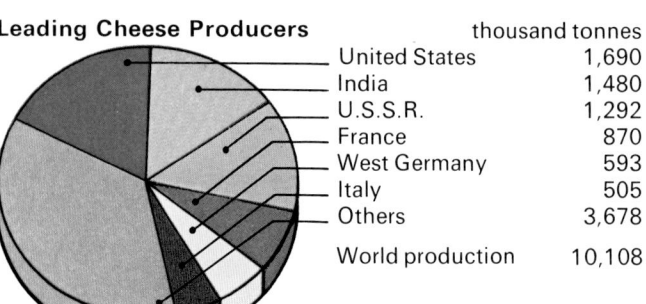

thousand tonnes

United States	1,690
India	1,480
U.S.S.R.	1,292
France	870
West Germany	593
Italy	505
Others	3,678
World production	10,108

Leading Milk Producers

thousand tonnes

U.S.S.R.	91,800
United States	52,352
France	29,600
West Germany	21,554
Poland	17,000
Britain	14,076
Others	160,536
World production	386,918

Natural Products for Manufacturing

Vegetable and animal products are used not only for food, but also as raw materials for manufacturing. Unlike mineral resources, animal and vegetable resources can be continually replenished, though reliance on wild crops has greatly reduced the world's timber stocks.

Before the advent of man-made fibres, people had to rely entirely on natural products for making fabrics and ropes. The most important vegetable fibre is cotton, which is used mostly for cloth. Flax is used for making linen and cord, and the leading producers are the U.S.S.R., Poland, France and Czechoslovakia. Hemp, used for carpeting, ropes, sailcloth and other coarse fabrics, comes mostly from the U.S.S.R., India, Romania and China. Jute, mainly used for sacking and hessian, is produced mostly in India, Bangladesh, China and Burma. Sisal, from which twine is made, comes mostly from East Africa.

The two main animal fibres are wool, produced mostly from sheep — though goats and rabbits also produce limited amounts — and silk, made by the silkworm moth, *Bombyx mori.*

Natural rubber, in great demand for motor-car tyres, is produced largely in southeastern Asia, though synthetic rubber is now made in even larger quantities. Most tobacco is grown for smoking, but it is used for numerous other products, including insecticides and drugs.

The world's forests yield many products. Forest lands have been greatly reduced in the past 2,000 years — for example, in Roman times, a large part of Britain was under forest. But today, careful management is ensuring that new growth is largely keeping up with demand, especially in the quick-growing softwoods.

Timber in its various forms is the most important forest product. Some of it is used as logs for telegraph poles and other items, while a great deal is turned into squared timber of various sections. Some timber is made into veneers, most of which is laminated to form plywood. Wood that is not suitable for such uses can be turned into chips, which are bonded with plastic glues into chipboards, or shredded into fibres for making into hardboards and similar products.

Newsprint is made from woodpulp, which is wood ground up in water. The many substances derived from wood include chemicals, such as acetone, methanol and glycerine, and such products as explosives, plastics and rayon.

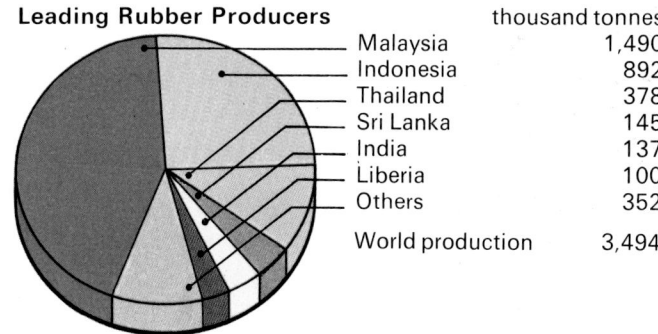

Leading Rubber Producers

	thousand tonnes
Malaysia	1,490
Indonesia	892
Thailand	378
Sri Lanka	145
India	137
Liberia	100
Others	352
World production	3,494

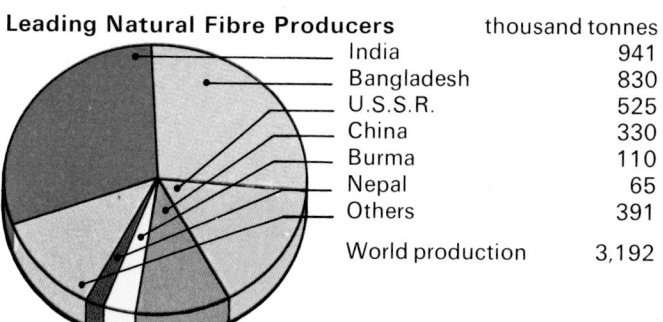

Leading Natural Fibre Producers

	thousand tonnes
India	941
Bangladesh	830
U.S.S.R.	525
China	330
Burma	110
Nepal	65
Others	391
World production	3,192

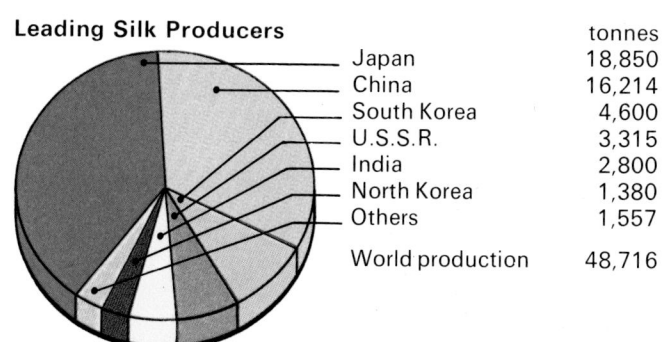

Leading Silk Producers

	tonnes
Japan	18,850
China	16,214
South Korea	4,600
U.S.S.R.	3,315
India	2,800
North Korea	1,380
Others	1,557
World production	48,716

Natural Products for Manufacturing

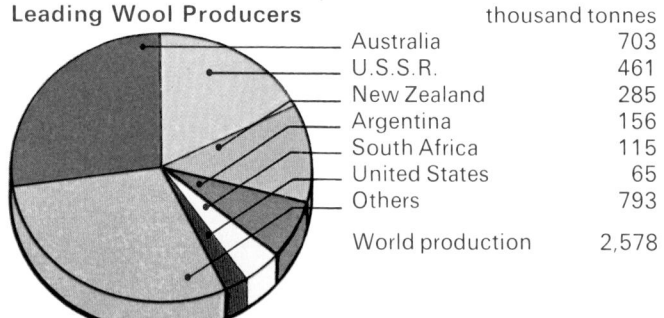

Leading Wool Producers

	thousand tonnes
Australia	703
U.S.S.R.	461
New Zealand	285
Argentina	156
South Africa	115
United States	65
Others	793
World production	2,578

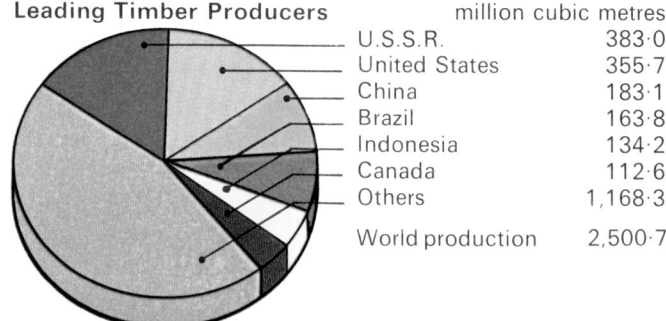

Leading Timber Producers

	million cubic metres
U.S.S.R.	383·0
United States	355·7
China	183·1
Brazil	163·8
Indonesia	134·2
Canada	112·6
Others	1,168·3
World production	2,500·7

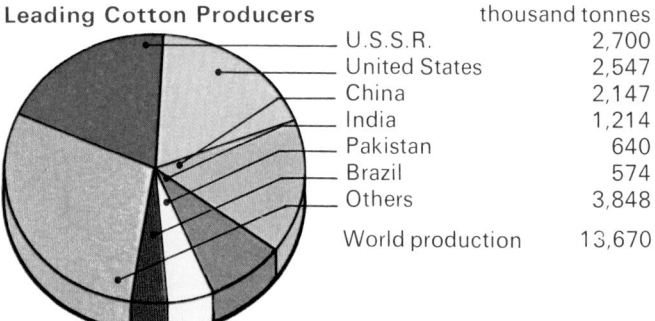

Leading Cotton Producers

	thousand tonnes
U.S.S.R.	2,700
United States	2,547
China	2,147
India	1,214
Pakistan	640
Brazil	574
Others	3,848
World production	13,670

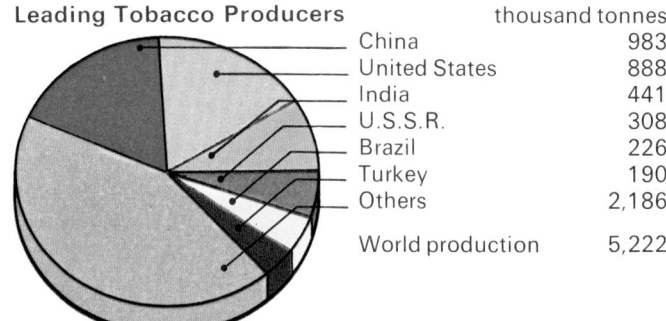

Leading Tobacco Producers

	thousand tonnes
China	983
United States	888
India	441
U.S.S.R.	308
Brazil	226
Turkey	190
Others	2,186
World production	5,222

Below: **This cotton picker is in Uzbekistan, in the U.S.S.R.**

Mineral Resources

The wealth of the world's industrialized countries is based on supplies of minerals, particularly the metals. When the Industrial Revolution began in the 1750s, and for many years afterwards, processing plants and factories that used metals were built near their sources. Today the industrialized countries import large quantities of minerals, often from many thousands of miles away, while modern technology demands the use of a great variety of metals and other substances that are found in different locations.

Iron is the most important of all metals, and a United Nations survey in the 1950s showed that the world supply of iron ore would last at least 800 years. The ore is distributed all over the globe, but some deposits, particularly those of Africa and the Americas, are especially rich, and it is cheaper to produce iron from these sources. Of the world's leading iron producers, the

U.S.S.R. has some of the richest deposits and has, therefore, no need to import iron ore.

Most iron is made into steel, an alloy that is harder and more useful than pure iron. All steel contains small quantities of carbon, a chemical element that is readily obtainable, but most steels have some other metal or metals mixed in to give them particular properties. For example, chromium, nickel and cobalt all help to make steel resistant to corrosion; tungsten and vanadium give it hardness; manganese gives it high tensile strength; and molybdenum gives it more elasticity.

These *ferro-alloys,* as they are called, come from much more limited sources than iron, so countries that have them possess a great strategic advantage in world politics. For example, the United States and Canada between them produce more than 75

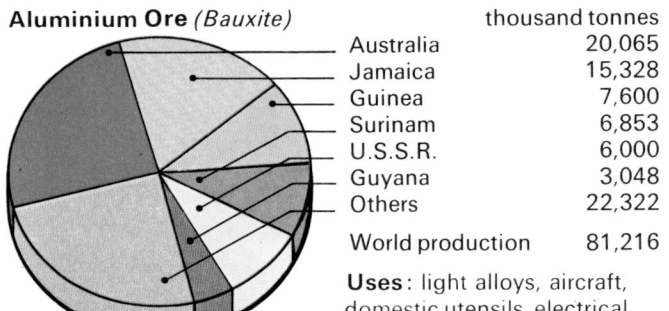

Aluminium Ore *(Bauxite)* — thousand tonnes

	thousand tonnes
Australia	20,065
Jamaica	15,328
Guinea	7,600
Surinam	6,853
U.S.S.R.	6,000
Guyana	3,048
Others	22,322
World production	81,216

Uses: light alloys, aircraft, domestic utensils, electrical apparatus

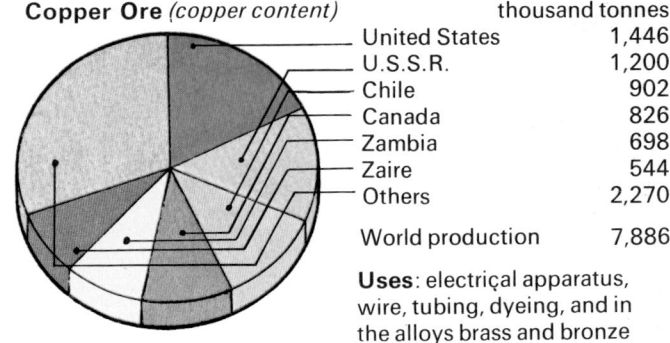

Copper Ore *(copper content)* — thousand tonnes

	thousand tonnes
United States	1,446
U.S.S.R.	1,200
Chile	902
Canada	826
Zambia	698
Zaire	544
Others	2,270
World production	7,886

Uses: electrical apparatus, wire, tubing, dyeing, and in the alloys brass and bronze

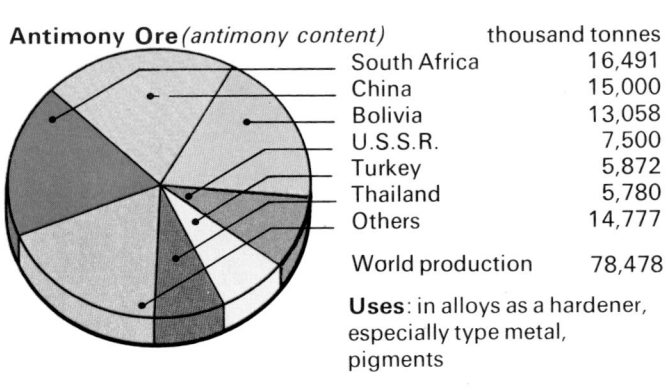

Antimony Ore *(antimony content)* — thousand tonnes

	thousand tonnes
South Africa	16,491
China	15,000
Bolivia	13,058
U.S.S.R.	7,500
Turkey	5,872
Thailand	5,780
Others	14,777
World production	78,478

Uses: in alloys as a hardener, especially type metal, pigments

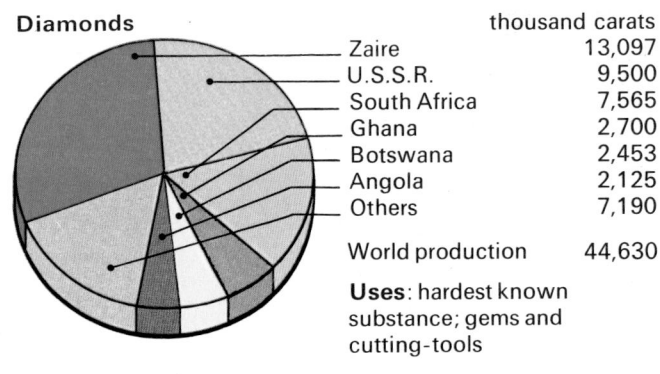

Diamonds — thousand carats

	thousand carats
Zaire	13,097
U.S.S.R.	9,500
South Africa	7,565
Ghana	2,700
Botswana	2,453
Angola	2,125
Others	7,190
World production	44,630

Uses: hardest known substance; gems and cutting-tools

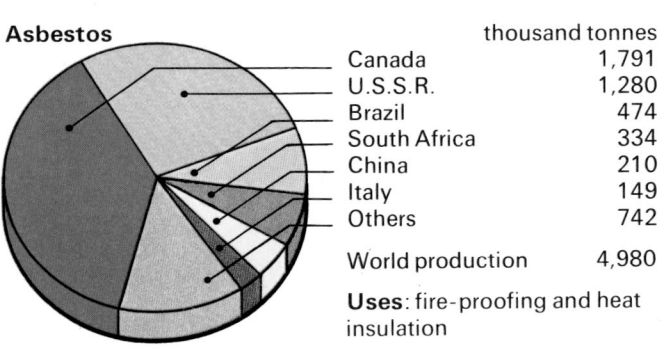

Asbestos — thousand tonnes

	thousand tonnes
Canada	1,791
U.S.S.R.	1,280
Brazil	474
South Africa	334
China	210
Italy	149
Others	742
World production	4,980

Uses: fire-proofing and heat insulation

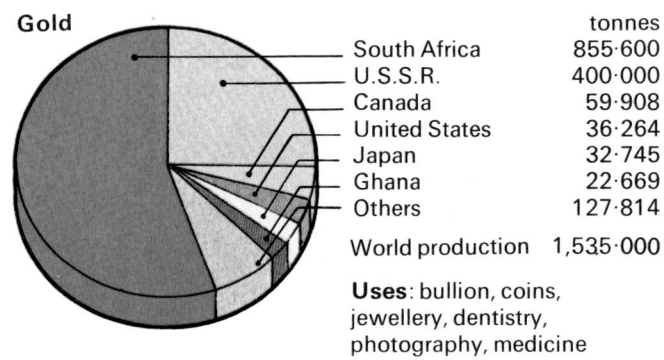

Gold — tonnes

	tonnes
South Africa	855·600
U.S.S.R.	400·000
Canada	59·908
United States	36·264
Japan	32·745
Ghana	22·669
Others	127·814
World production	1,535·000

Uses: bullion, coins, jewellery, dentistry, photography, medicine

per cent of the world's molybdenum; Canada, New Caledonia and the U.S.S.R. produce 71 per cent of the nickel; and Zaire produces 59 per cent of the cobalt.

Equally vital in modern industry are the non-ferrous metals — that is, those that are not used in alloys with iron. Among the most important of these metals is copper, which is widely used for electrical work and in plumbing. Outside North America and the U.S.S.R., main supplies occur in Zaire and Zambia in Africa, and in Chile and Peru in South America. A fall in the world price of copper caused these four countries to cut production in 1975. But their strategic importance remains, and they will have a considerable influence on world markets when prices are higher again.

Other important non-ferrous metals include aluminium, lead, zinc and tin. Aluminium is one of the most abundant chemical elements in the Earth's crust, and is certainly the most abundant of all metals. But it is difficult to extract, even from its best source, bauxite, which can be either a hard rock or soft mud. Australia and Jamaica head the world's sources of bauxite.

Tin, for which Cornwall in England was once famous as a source, now comes principally from Malaysia and Indonesia in southeastern Asia, and Bolivia. Lead is produced by the United States, the U.S.S.R. and Australia, while zinc has Canada as its principal supplier.

The precious metals — gold, silver and platinum and its related metals, such as palladium — are valued because of their natural beauty as much as for their industrial importance. Gold, of which South Africa has, by far, the largest supply, is used largely as a form of currency. Most of the gold mined goes straight into bank vaults or is used to make jewellery. Silver, less used today for money, has more industrial uses, and the U.S.S.R. and Canada lead in silver production. Platinum metals come from North America, South Africa, the U.S.S.R. and South America.

The world is using minerals, especially metals, at such a rate that scientists are forecasting serious shortages of some of them. Fortunately, pressure for supplies has stimulated research, so that known resources have actually increased. In 1965, for example, copper reserves were estimated at 140 million tonnes but, in 1973, nearly 300 million tonnes were known. But even with scrap copper providing half the world's needs, supplies are being used up at an alarming rate.

A report issued in 1975 by the United States National Academy of Sciences suggested that real shortages of five metals — chromium, gold, mercury, palladium, and tin — could occur during the 1980s. Other metals whose supply also seems to be in danger, though not so imminent, are antimony, silver, tungsten, vanadium and zinc.

Left: **A worker cuts a diamond for use as a gem-stone. This operator is at Martapura, in Indonesian Borneo; major centres of the industry are in the Netherlands and Israel.**

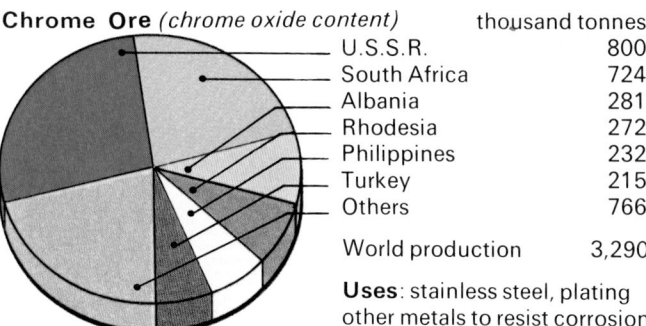

Chrome Ore (*chrome oxide content*)   thousand tonnes

U.S.S.R.	800
South Africa	724
Albania	281
Rhodesia	272
Philippines	232
Turkey	215
Others	766
World production	3,290

Uses: stainless steel, plating other metals to resist corrosion

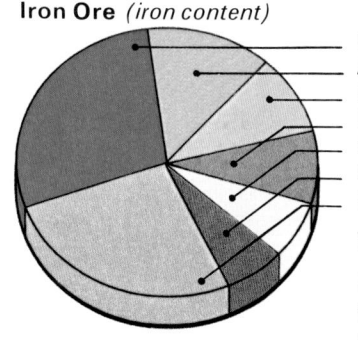

Iron Ore (*iron content*)   million tonnes

U.S.S.R.	135·000
Australia	59·623
United States	47·256
Brazil	40·408
China	39·000
Canada	30·000
Others	145·713
World production	497·000

Uses: machinery and structures of all kinds, mostly as steel

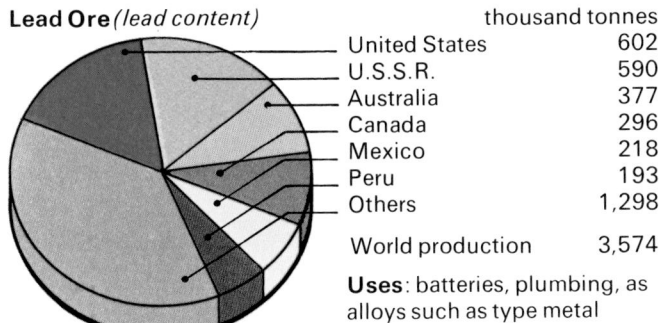

Lead Ore *(lead content)*

	thousand tonnes
United States	602
U.S.S.R.	590
Australia	377
Canada	296
Mexico	218
Peru	193
Others	1,298
World production	3,574

Uses: batteries, plumbing, as alloys such as type metal

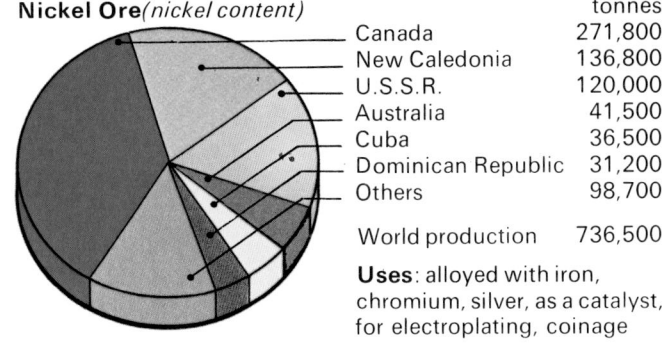

Nickel Ore *(nickel content)*

	tonnes
Canada	271,800
New Caledonia	136,800
U.S.S.R.	120,000
Australia	41,500
Cuba	36,500
Dominican Republic	31,200
Others	98,700
World production	736,500

Uses: alloyed with iron, chromium, silver, as a catalyst, for electroplating, coinage

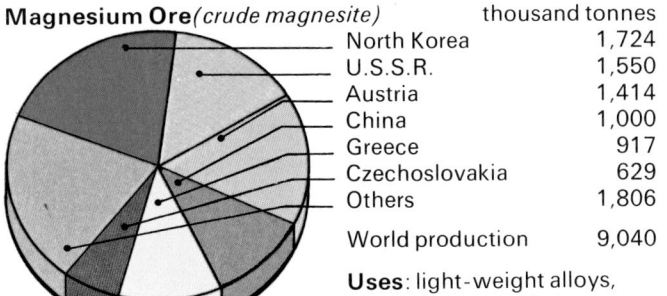

Magnesium Ore *(crude magnesite)*

	thousand tonnes
North Korea	1,724
U.S.S.R.	1,550
Austria	1,414
China	1,000
Greece	917
Czechoslovakia	629
Others	1,806
World production	9,040

Uses: light-weight alloys, photography, medicine, incendiary bombs

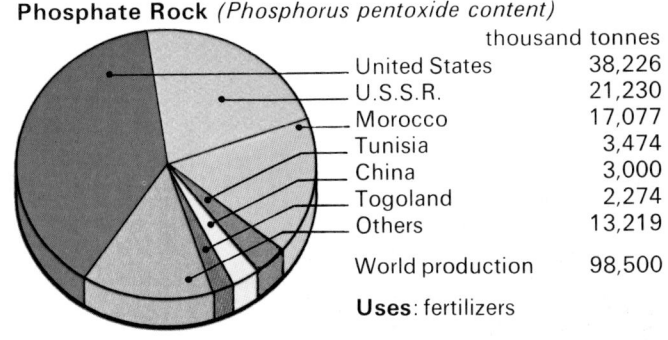

Phosphate Rock *(Phosphorus pentoxide content)*

	thousand tonnes
United States	38,226
U.S.S.R.	21,230
Morocco	17,077
Tunisia	3,474
China	3,000
Togoland	2,274
Others	13,219
World production	98,500

Uses: fertilizers

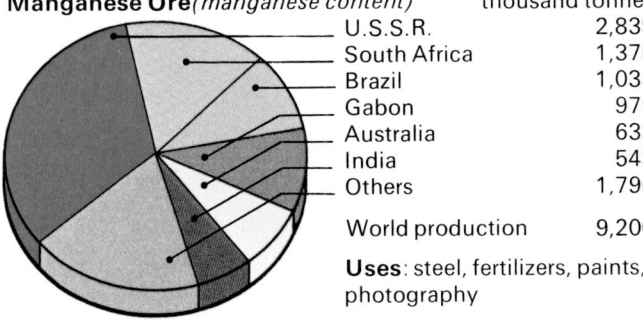

Manganese Ore *(manganese content)*

	thousand tonnes
U.S.S.R.	2,839
South Africa	1,375
Brazil	1,035
Gabon	979
Australia	633
India	543
Others	1,796
World production	9,200

Uses: steel, fertilizers, paints, photography

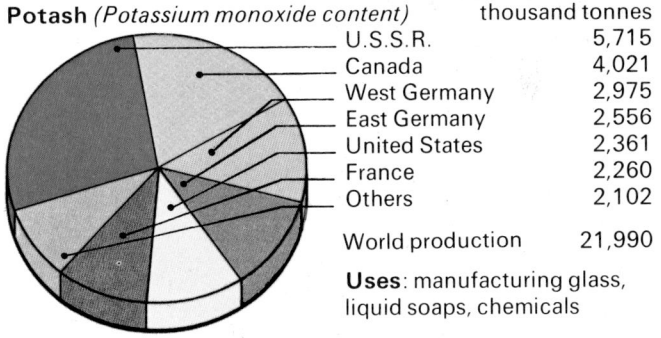

Potash *(Potassium monoxide content)*

	thousand tonnes
U.S.S.R.	5,715
Canada	4,021
West Germany	2,975
East Germany	2,556
United States	2,361
France	2,260
Others	2,102
World production	21,990

Uses: manufacturing glass, liquid soaps, chemicals

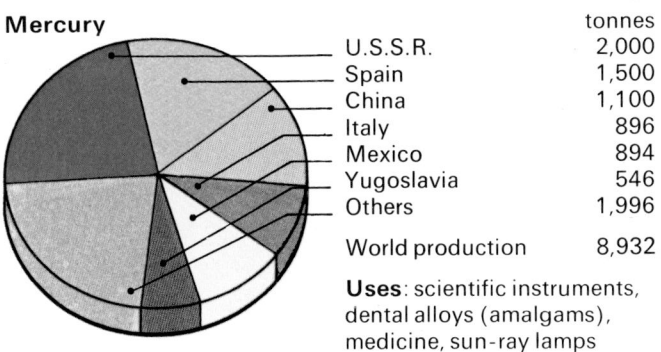

Mercury

	tonnes
U.S.S.R.	2,000
Spain	1,500
China	1,100
Italy	896
Mexico	894
Yugoslavia	546
Others	1,996
World production	8,932

Uses: scientific instruments, dental alloys (amalgams), medicine, sun-ray lamps

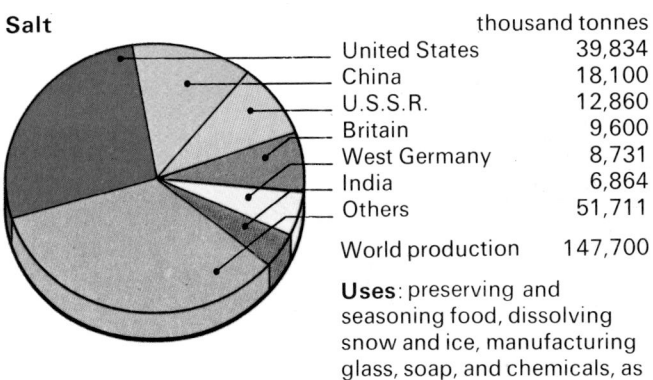

Salt

	thousand tonnes
United States	39,834
China	18,100
U.S.S.R.	12,860
Britain	9,600
West Germany	8,731
India	6,864
Others	51,711
World production	147,700

Uses: preserving and seasoning food, dissolving snow and ice, manufacturing glass, soap, and chemicals, as a flux in metallurgy

Mineral Resources

Silver Ore *(silver content)*

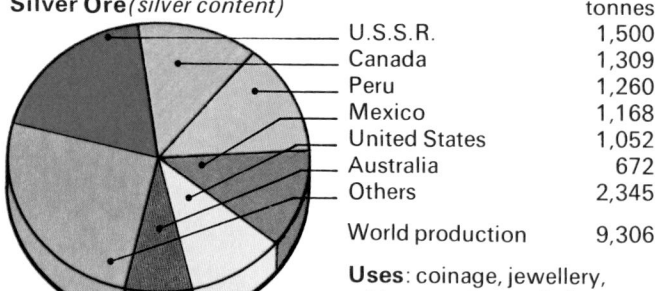

	tonnes
U.S.S.R.	1,500
Canada	1,309
Peru	1,260
Mexico	1,168
United States	1,052
Australia	672
Others	2,345
World production	9,306

Uses: coinage, jewellery, tablewear, electroplating, photography, mirrors

Uranium Ore *(uranium content)*

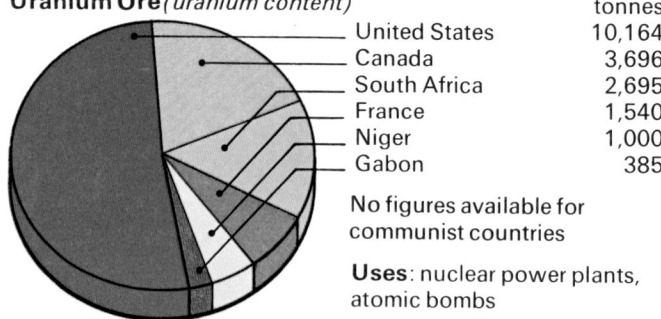

	tonnes
United States	10,164
Canada	3,696
South Africa	2,695
France	1,540
Niger	1,000
Gabon	385

No figures available for communist countries

Uses: nuclear power plants, atomic bombs

Sulphur *(unrefined)*

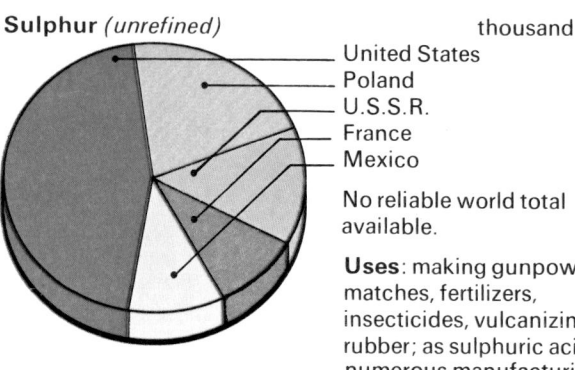

	thousand tonnes
United States	7,727
Poland	3,545
U.S.S.R.	2,300
France	1,841
Mexico	1,608

No reliable world total available.

Uses: making gunpowder, matches, fertilizers, insecticides, vulcanizing rubber; as sulphuric acid, in numerous manufacturing processes

Zinc Ore *(zinc content)*

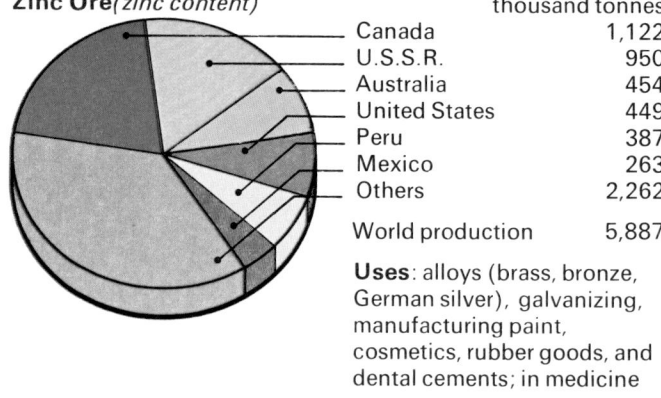

	thousand tonnes
Canada	1,122
U.S.S.R.	950
Australia	454
United States	449
Peru	387
Mexico	263
Others	2,262
World production	5,887

Uses: alloys (brass, bronze, German silver), galvanizing, manufacturing paint, cosmetics, rubber goods, and dental cements; in medicine

Tin Concentrates *(tin content)*

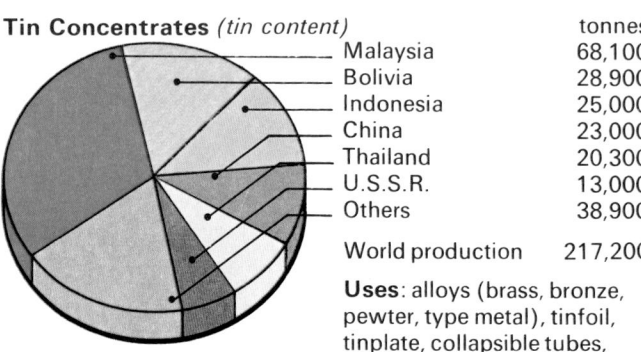

	tonnes
Malaysia	68,100
Bolivia	28,900
Indonesia	25,000
China	23,000
Thailand	20,300
U.S.S.R.	13,000
Others	38,900
World production	217,200

Uses: alloys (brass, bronze, pewter, type metal), tinfoil, tinplate, collapsible tubes, bearings, solder

Tungsten Ore *(tungstic acid content)*

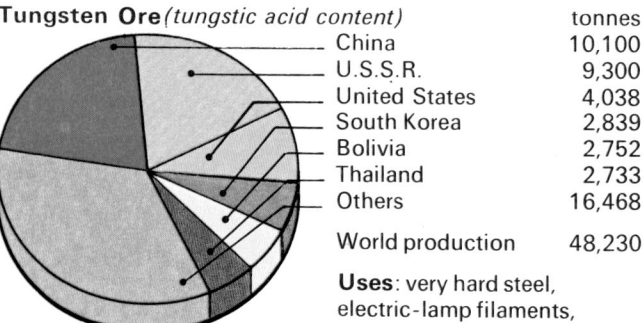

	tonnes
China	10,100
U.S.S.R.	9,300
United States	4,038
South Korea	2,839
Bolivia	2,752
Thailand	2,733
Others	16,468
World production	48,230

Uses: very hard steel, electric-lamp filaments, electronic apparatus, X-ray apparatus

Above: **Mining for gold at Elsburg, in the Witwatersrand of South Africa. Mines here vary in depth from 900 to 3,700 metres (3,000 to 12,000 feet), and are highly mechanized.**

Fuel and Energy

Modern civilization depends largely on plentiful sources of fuel to provide heat and power. The principal sources of heat and power today are provided by the *fossil fuels,* which were formed by decaying plant and animal life millions of years ago. The main fossil fuels are coal, oil and natural gas. In developed countries, all industry has been founded on these three fuels. Most of our electricity is produced in power stations, where coal or oil are used to turn water to steam. The steam drives turbines, which turn huge electricity generators. Coal, the most important fuel of the 1800s, has now taken third place to oil and natural gas.

The principal sources of oil, the most important fossil fuel, are the Middle East, North America, the North Sea, the U.S.S.R., Venezuela, Argentina, Indonesia, Libya and Nigeria. In the mid-1970s, the United States, although itself a big producer, was consuming about 30 per cent more oil than it produced, and relied heavily on imports from Venezuela, Canada and the Middle East. Western Europe produced very little oil and relied almost entirely on imports from the Middle East, Libya and Nigeria. Japan, another major user, also had to import nearly all its oil.

But the discovery and exploitation of new resources means that the pattern of the world's fuel supplies and distribution is changing all the time. The development of North Sea natural gas fields made Britain independent of gas imports in the mid-1970s. And Britain, Norway and the Netherlands were set to be independent in oil from the same source by the early 1980s. The ever-increasing cost of fuel from the Middle East has stimulated research for new sources.

Although the world's stocks of fossil fuels are vast, and more remain to be found and developed, there is already a serious threat of shortages — and, once exhausted, fossil fuels cannot be replaced. World coal stocks may last for about 800 years, but oil and gas are likely to be used up early next century. However, alternative sources of power are being developed.

An extremely important alternative to fossil fuels is hydro-

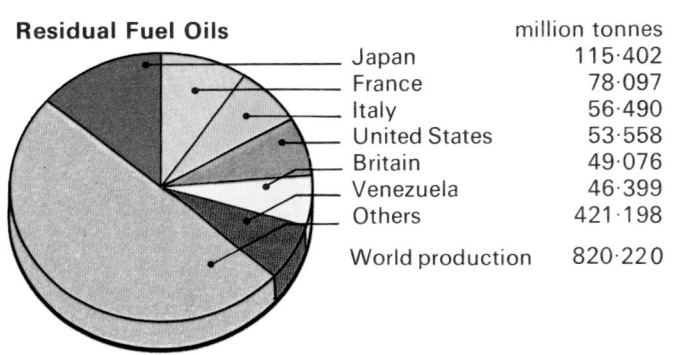

Residual Fuel Oils   million tonnes

Japan	115·402
France	78·097
Italy	56·490
United States	53·558
Britain	49·076
Venezuela	46·399
Others	421·198
World production	820·220

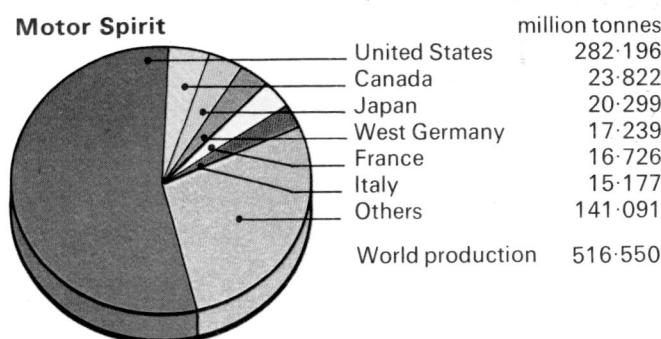

Motor Spirit   million tonnes

United States	282·196
Canada	23·822
Japan	20·299
West Germany	17·239
France	16·726
Italy	15·177
Others	141·091
World production	516·550

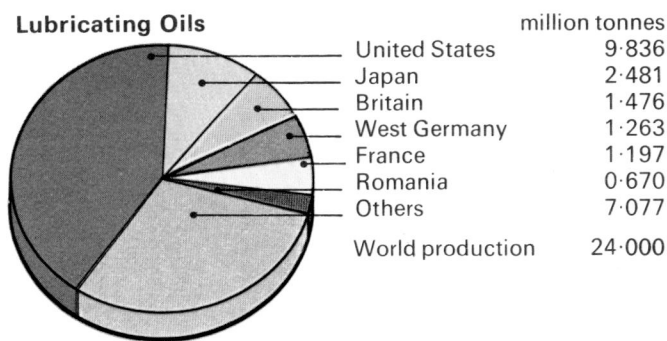

Lubricating Oils   million tonnes

United States	9·836
Japan	2·481
Britain	1·476
West Germany	1·263
France	1·197
Romania	0·670
Others	7·077
World production	24·000

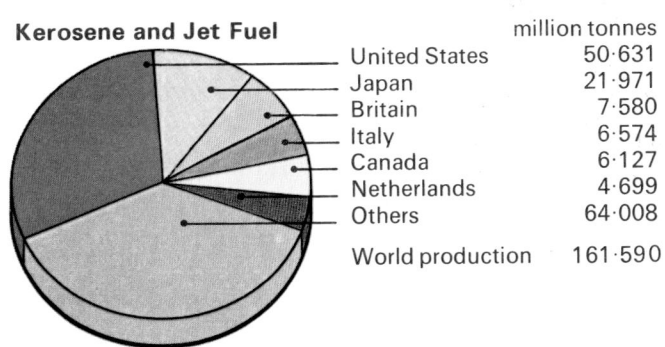

Kerosene and Jet Fuel   million tonnes

United States	50·631
Japan	21·971
Britain	7·580
Italy	6·574
Canada	6·127
Netherlands	4·699
Others	64·008
World production	161·590

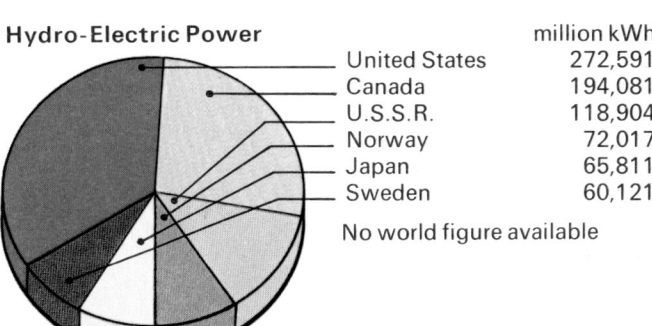

Hydro-Electric Power   million kWh

United States	272,591
Canada	194,081
U.S.S.R.	118,904
Norway	72,017
Japan	65,811
Sweden	60,121
No world figure available	

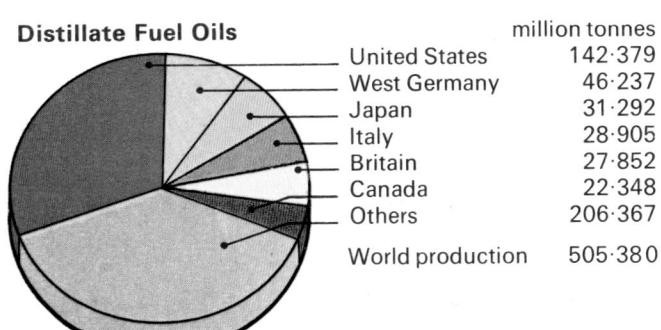

Distillate Fuel Oils   million tonnes

United States	142·379
West Germany	46·237
Japan	31·292
Italy	28·905
Britain	27·852
Canada	22·348
Others	206·367
World production	505·380

electric power, using the flow of rivers and the movement of the sea to drive generators. Many countries already make great use of hydro-electric power. Norway, for example, generates 99 per cent of its electricity this way.

Nuclear power, using the heat released by the fission (splitting up) of uranium atoms, is extremely important too. Britain is one of the leaders in this field, with about 10 per cent of its electricity coming from nuclear power stations. Uranium is, fortunately, in good supply, though high-grade ores — rocks from which the metal can easily be extracted — are less common. The main known reserves of uranium are in North America, Zaire, South Africa, Australia, France and Czechoslovakia. China and the U.S.S.R. have kept their resources of uranium secret, but it is thought they have substantial reserves. Modern breeder-reactors not only generate heat by nuclear fission, but also 'breed' more fuel at the same time.

A more useful long-term source of power is nuclear fusion. Fusion plants work on the same principle as the sun, fusing together atoms of hydrogen to form helium — a slightly heavier gas. In the process, great heat is released. Research on this process is likely to continue for several years, but success will solve fuel and energy problems for all time, because the hydrogen fuel can be readily extracted from water.

With the increasing use of nuclear power, conservationists are becoming more and more concerned about the possibility of pollution by waste products from nuclear power stations. Most of these products are radioactive and need to be stored extremely carefully in order to reduce the chance of pollution and the consequent endangering of life. Such waste products gradually decrease in radioactivity but, in some cases, it would take thousands of years for the radioactivity to decrease to a safe level.

Two other major sources of power are the heat of the Sun and the internal heat of the Earth. Various forms of solar cells have been devised to absorb the Sun's heat and convert it into electricity. But panels in which running water absorbs the Sun's heat are generally more successful. Even in climates where there is a fair amount of cloud, the use of heat collected by roof-mounted solar panels can considerably reduce fuel bills.

The Earth's heat is easiest to harness in places where there is volcanic activity, or where hot springs exist. Geothermal energy has been most successfully developed in Iceland, New Zealand and the southwestern part of the United States.

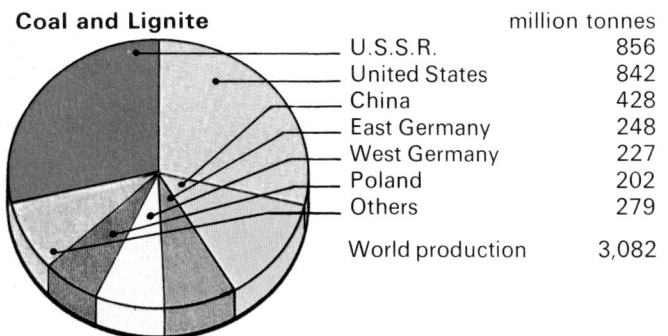

Coal and Lignite

	million tonnes
U.S.S.R.	856
United States	842
China	428
East Germany	248
West Germany	227
Poland	202
Others	279
World production	3,082

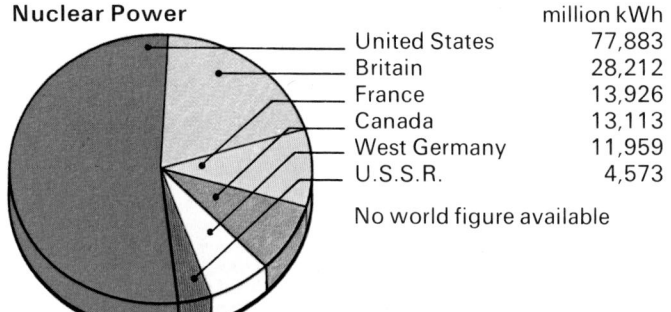

Nuclear Power

	million kWh
United States	77,883
Britain	28,212
France	13,926
Canada	13,113
West Germany	11,959
U.S.S.R.	4,573

No world figure available

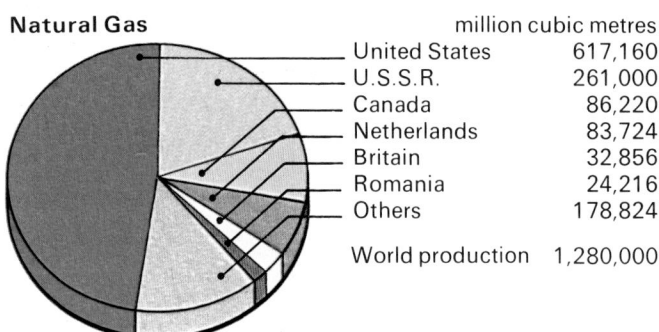

Natural Gas

	million cubic metres
United States	617,160
U.S.S.R.	261,000
Canada	86,220
Netherlands	83,724
Britain	32,856
Romania	24,216
Others	178,824
World production	1,280,000

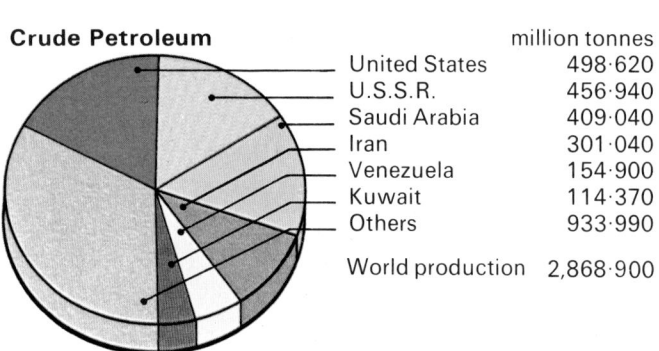

Crude Petroleum

	million tonnes
United States	498·620
U.S.S.R.	456·940
Saudi Arabia	409·040
Iran	301·040
Venezuela	154·900
Kuwait	114·370
Others	933·990
World production	2,868·900

Above: **Drilling for oil in Nigeria, which ranks seventh in world oil production.**

Right: **Modern coal-cutting machinery in a typical, highly mechanized British mine.**

Occupations, Manufacturing and Production

Basic requirements of all peoples are food and shelter, and for this reason the simplest economies are based on the provision of these two things. In parts of Africa and South America, primitive tribes practise subsistence farming, growing just enough food for themselves and their families. The production of a surplus, which can be sold to purchase other goods, is the first step towards development.

Subsistence farming is uneconomic because it requires enormous effort for comparatively little output. Even today, many important countries still have large parts of their working population engaged in agriculture, simply because they are using old-fashioned methods requiring a great deal of labour. For example, 70 per cent of India's workers are in agriculture, but India still has to import some food. In contrast, only 4.2 per cent of the workers are engaged in agriculture in the United States — a major food exporter. Other countries with high proportions of workers in agriculture are Bangladesh (85 per cent) and China (an estimated 80 per cent).

The major manufacturing countries are those of Western and Central Europe, where industrialization began, the United States, Canada and the U.S.S.R. The pattern is changing all the time.

Many of the developing nations, particularly former colonies, are increasing their industries by leaps and bounds, although they still have a long way to go before they catch up with the economies of the European countries.

A measure of a country's industrialization and prosperity is the proportion of its working population engaged in 'services' — non-productive occupations. These include communications, such as transport, press and television, many professional services, such as medicine and law, and the work of civil servants, bankers, shopkeepers, and many more. The United States, for example, has over 60 per cent of workers in services.

Another way of looking at a country's way of working is to consider its Gross Domestic Product — that is, the total value of all the goods and services its people produce in a year. India's 70 per cent engaged in farming contribute 44 per cent of the country's annual wealth, while 44 per cent of West Germany's GDP is produced by the 48.8 per cent working in industry. It is notable that, in developed countries heavily orientated towards agricultural production — such as Australia, Denmark and Argentina — the proportion of the GDP produced by it is small: 6 per cent, 8 per cent and 11 per cent respectively.

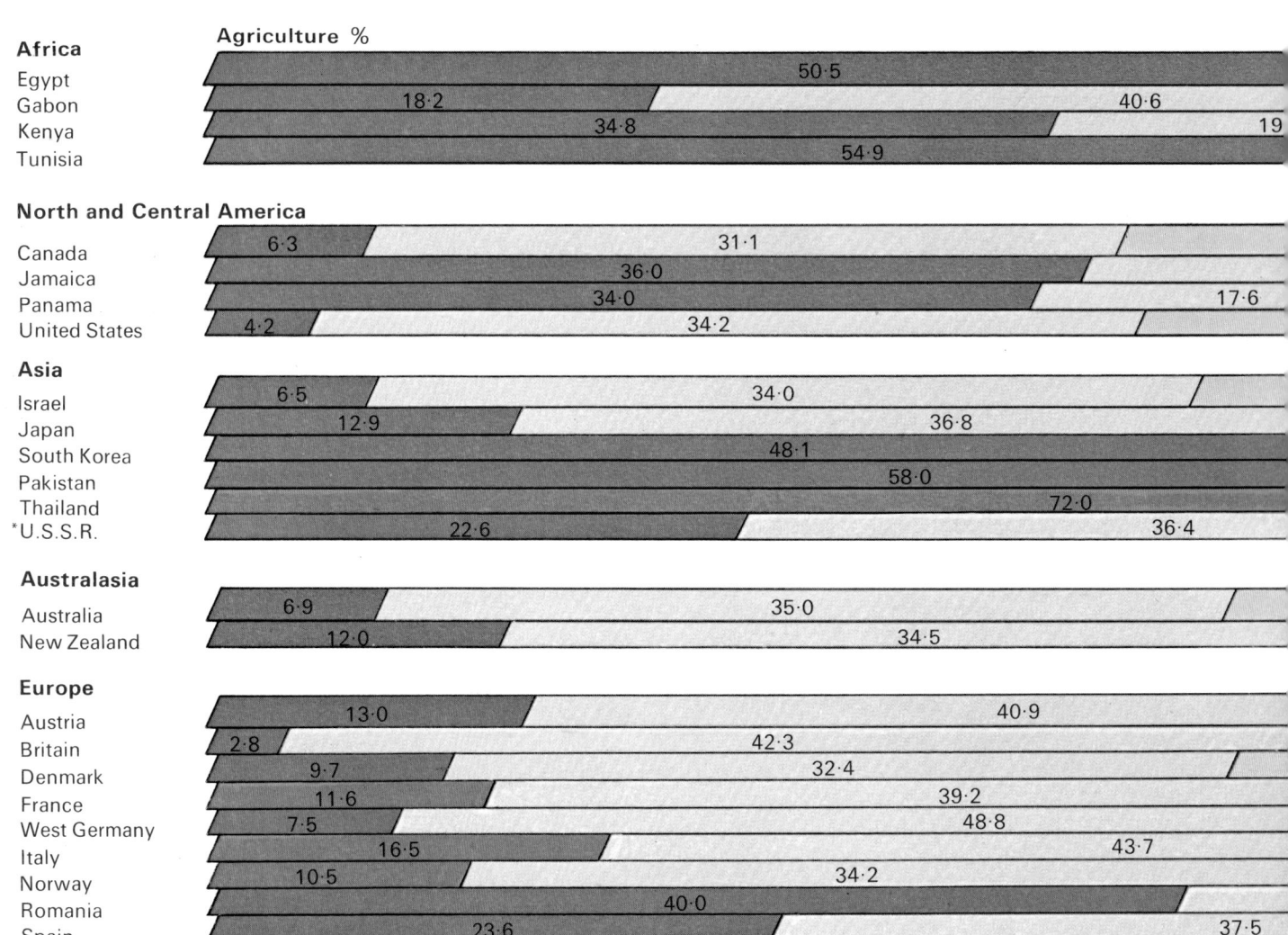

* Includes European part of the U.S.S.R.

Right: **A television cameraman at work during an outside broadcast. Most workers in radio and television are among those engaged in services – occupations that do not result in the production of goods.**

Below: **The chart shows the proportion of workers engaged in agriculture, industry and services in various countries.**

Industry %   Services %

17·4   32·1
41·2
46·2
20·2   24·9

62·6
2·2   41·8
48·4
61·6

59·5
50·3
22·0   29·9
16·4   25·6
9·5   18·5
41·0

58·1
53·5

46·1
54·9
57·9
49·2
43·7
39·8
55·3
37·7   22·3
38·9

Occupations, Manufacturing and Production

Leading Wheat Flour Manufacturers

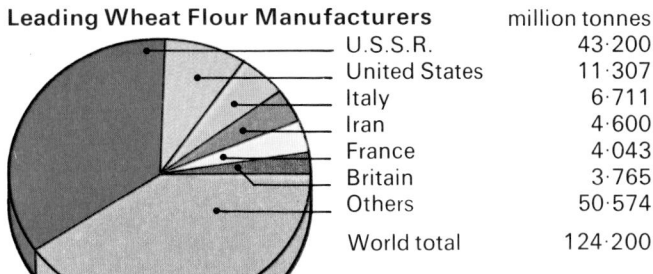

	million tonnes
U.S.S.R.	43·200
United States	11·307
Italy	6·711
Iran	4·600
France	4·043
Britain	3·765
Others	50·574
World total	124·200

Leading Mutton and Lamb Producers

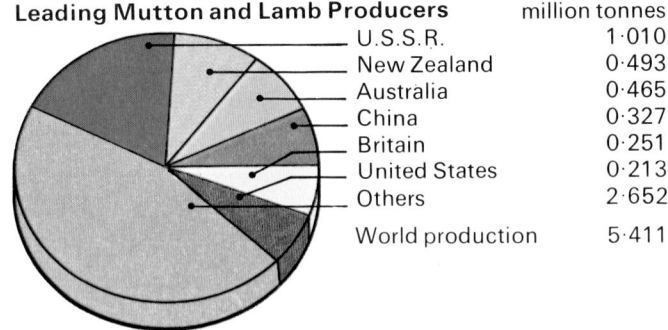

	million tonnes
U.S.S.R.	1·010
New Zealand	0·493
Australia	0·465
China	0·327
Britain	0·251
United States	0·213
Others	2·652
World production	5·411

Leading Raw Sugar Manufacturers

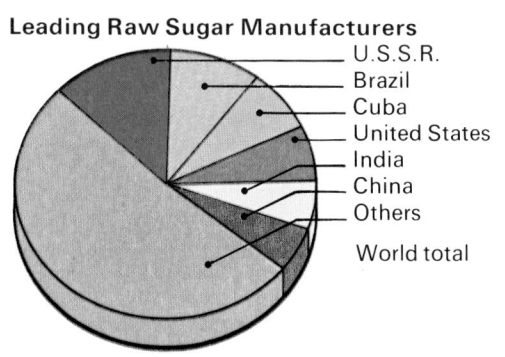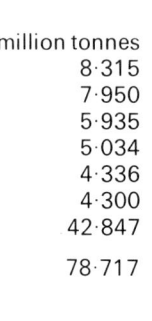

	million tonnes
U.S.S.R.	8·315
Brazil	7·950
Cuba	5·935
United States	5·034
India	4·336
China	4·300
Others	42·847
World total	78·717

Leading Pork Producers

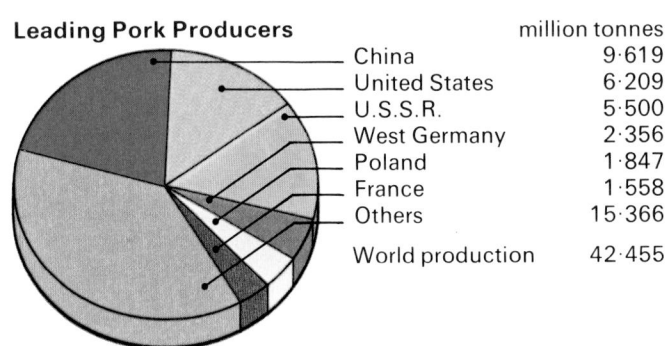

	million tonnes
China	9·619
United States	6·209
U.S.S.R.	5·500
West Germany	2·356
Poland	1·847
France	1·558
Others	15·366
World production	42·455

Leading Beef and Veal Producers

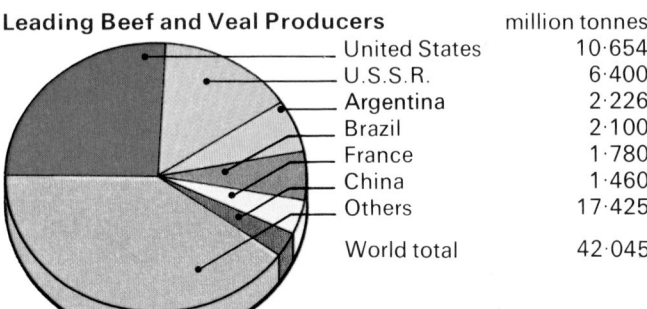

	million tonnes
United States	10·654
U.S.S.R.	6·400
Argentina	2·226
Brazil	2·100
France	1·780
China	1·460
Others	17·425
World total	42·045

Leading Commercial Vehicle Manufacturers

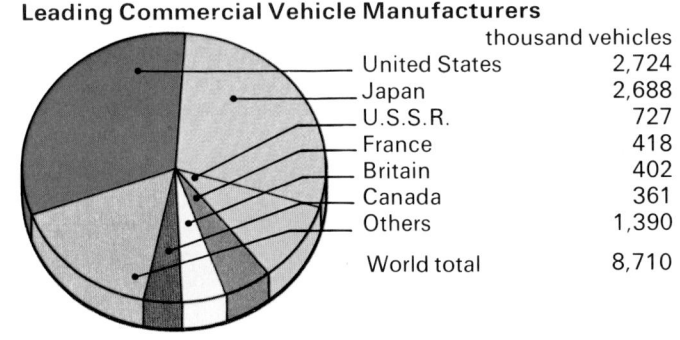

	thousand vehicles
United States	2,724
Japan	2,688
U.S.S.R.	727
France	418
Britain	402
Canada	361
Others	1,390
World total	8,710

Leading Motor-car Manufacturers

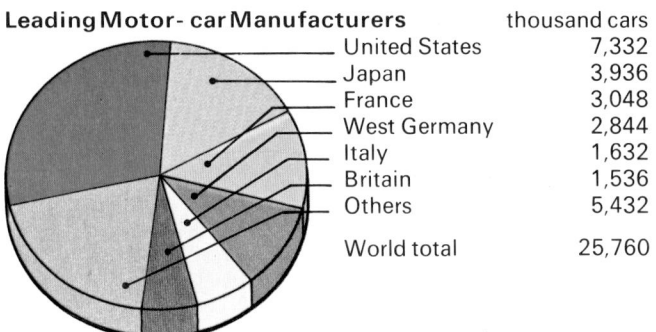

	thousand cars
United States	7,332
Japan	3,936
France	3,048
West Germany	2,844
Italy	1,632
Britain	1,536
Others	5,432
World total	25,760

Leading Merchant Ship Builders

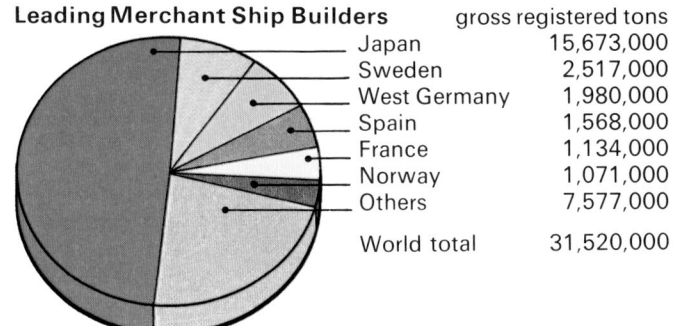

	gross registered tons
Japan	15,673,000
Sweden	2,517,000
West Germany	1,980,000
Spain	1,568,000
France	1,134,000
Norway	1,071,000
Others	7,577,000
World total	31,520,000

Leading Cotton Yarn Manufacturers   thousand tonnes

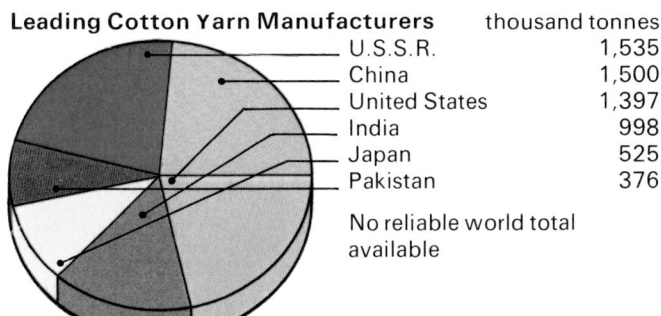

U.S.S.R.	1,535
China	1,500
United States	1,397
India	998
Japan	525
Pakistan	376

No reliable world total available

Leading Wood Pulp Manufacturers   million tonnes

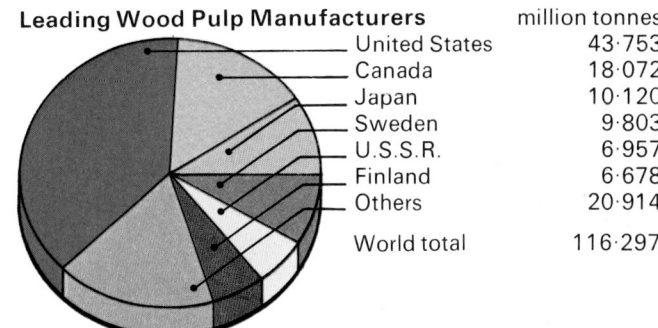

United States	43·753
Canada	18·072
Japan	10·120
Sweden	9·803
U.S.S.R.	6·957
Finland	6·678
Others	20·914
World total	116·297

Leading Wool Yarn Manufacturers   thousand tonnes

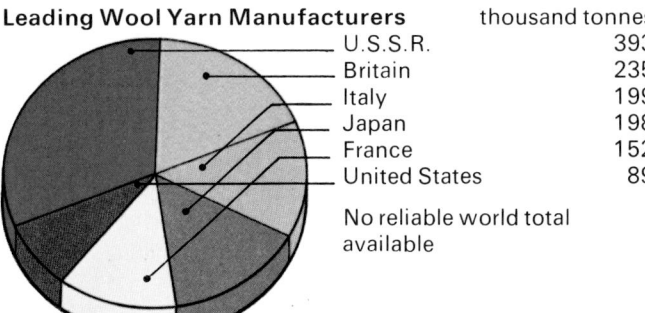

U.S.S.R.	393
Britain	235
Italy	199
Japan	198
France	152
United States	89

No reliable world total available

Leading Crude Steel Manufacturers   million tonnes

U.S.S.R.	135·996
United States	131·988
Japan	117·132
West Germany	53·232
China	28·000
France	27·024
Others	216·628
World total	710·000

Left: **Car bodies meeting their chassis on an assembly line at the Volkswagen factory in West Germany. Mass production methods were first introduced into the car industry in the United States by Ransom E. Olds in 1901. They have become the pattern for much industrial production of today.**

Transport

Good transport is the key to all industrial development and trade. It is essential to carry raw materials from their sources to where they are processed and turned into manufactured products, and also to carry those products to people who want to buy them. Transport is also needed to carry people from place to place.

The three basic kinds of transport are by land, sea and air. Patterns of transport change with the demands of traffic and the development of technology. Before World War II, most passenger traffic across the Atlantic Ocean was by sea; but, with the development of aviation, most transatlantic travellers now fly. Ships are still the cheapest and most efficient way of moving bulk cargoes from one place to another over long distances and, with the growth of fast highways and powerful trucks, road and sea transport are becoming more and more linked. Containers that can be carried by road and loaded straight onto ships are an increasingly popular way of carrying all but the bulkiest goods.

Liquids such as petroleum and natural gas are carried by a combination of giant, ocean-going tankers and overland pipelines. Major pipeline systems extend across North America, Western Europe and the U.S.S.R. The Russian system links with pipelines from the Arab oil states of the Middle East and also with Western Europe. All these networks are being continually extended as new supplies of oil and gas are developed.

Railways, the backbone of land transport in the late 1800s and for the first half of this century, are giving way in many parts of the world to road traffic, which is more economical to run and delivers goods from door to door. Inland waterways — rivers and canals — have maintained their importance in some parts of the world, particularly Western Europe, where there are many major navigable rivers.

PRINCIPAL MERCHANT FLEETS
It is difficult to say which country in the world actually has the largest merchant shipping fleet, because many shipping companies of other countries register their ships in Liberia and Panama. This is because these two countries charge lower taxes and enforce rules governing wages and safety regulations less severely. The table which follows gives an indication, in gross tonnage rather than numbers of vessels, of ship registrations.

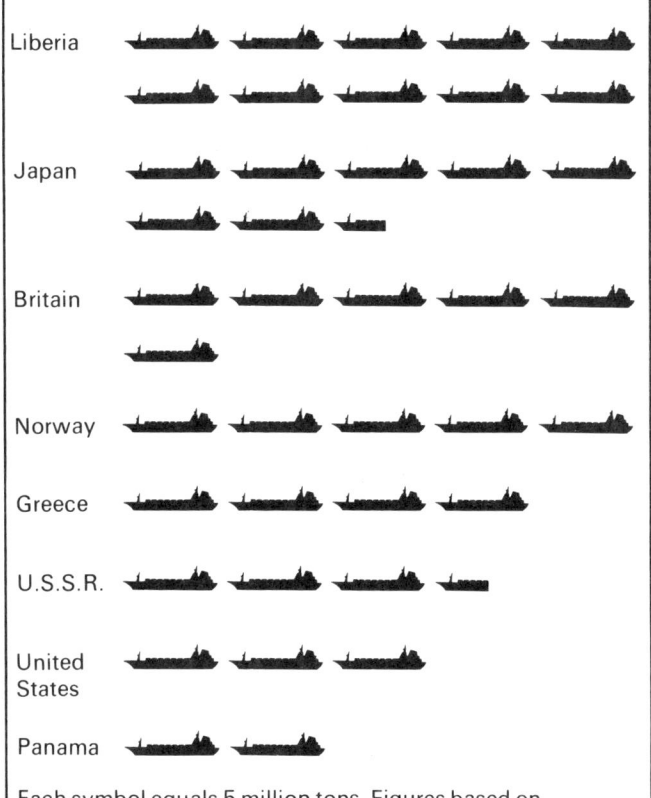

Each symbol equals 5 million tons. Figures based on Lloyd's Register of Shipping.

Each symbol equals 50 cars per 1000 people.

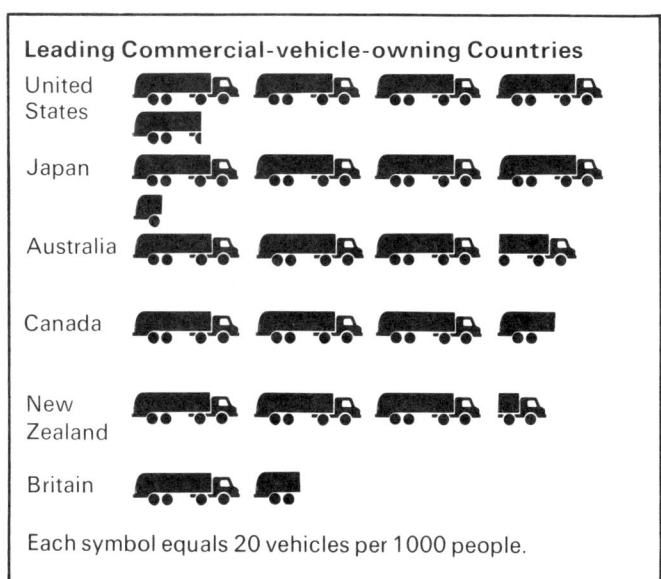

Each symbol equals 20 vehicles per 1000 people.

Below: **Sea transport remains the best and most economical method of carrying bulky cargo over long distances. Here, a bus is being loaded onto a ship at Miami Harbor in Florida.**

The volume of sea and air traffic has meant a great deal of international co-operation to ensure speedy and safe communication. Countries co-operate in providing up-to-date charts for shipping and weather forecasting. Some particularly busy sea routes, such as the English Channel, are 'policed' by the countries bordering them to make sure ships keep to recognized channels and so avoid collisions. Air transport comes under the control of a United Nations agency, the International Civil Aviation Organization, which has its headquarters in Montreal, Canada.

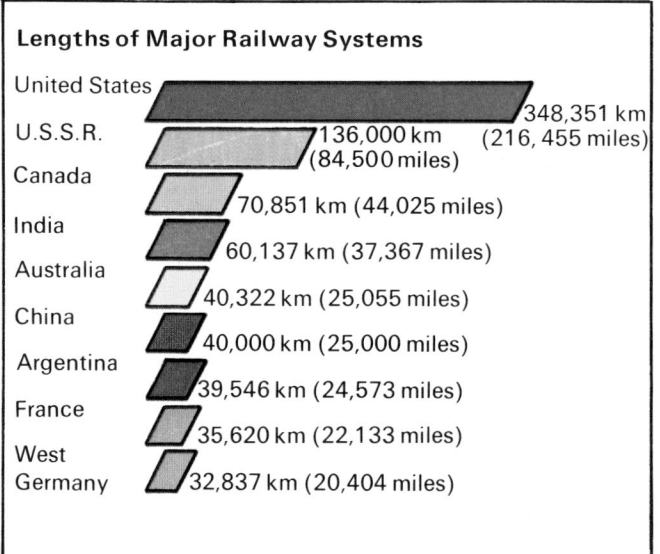

Lengths of Major Railway Systems

Country	Length
United States	348,351 km (216,455 miles)
U.S.S.R.	136,000 km (84,500 miles)
Canada	70,851 km (44,025 miles)
India	60,137 km (37,367 miles)
Australia	40,322 km (25,055 miles)
China	40,000 km (25,000 miles)
Argentina	39,546 km (24,573 miles)
France	35,620 km (22,133 miles)
West Germany	32,837 km (20,404 miles)

AVIATION FLEETS AND CONSTRUCTION
The world's airlines have around 10,000 passenger aircraft in service, but the numbers are constantly fluctuating. This is because new developments, such as faster and larger aircraft, make it possible to operate services efficiently with fewer planes, while developing countries, such as those of Africa, are building up their airlines.

The aircraft industry is concentrated in the United States, which has more than half the market, the U.S.S.R. with one-third, and the countries of Western Europe, particularly Britain, France, West Germany, Italy and the Netherlands. Canada also has a thriving construction industry. The enormous cost of development of new aircraft is tending to concentrate the industry into fewer and larger units, with several countries sharing the development and construction of new kinds of aircraft.

World Trade

World trade has developed over hundreds of years. Even back in medieval times, European countries used to export goods made by their craftsmen to other parts of the globe to pay for raw materials not available at home. With the growth of the Industrial Revolution from the 1750s onwards, this pattern of trade became intensified. Today, the countries of Europe are highly industrialized. Together with the United States, Canada and Japan, which have developed along European lines, they export manufactured goods and import mostly raw materials and food.

The developing countries of the world rely for their trade on minerals they can mine and food they can grow. To an extent, this even applies to the Europeanized countries, such as Australia, New Zealand and South Africa, whose industries still do not play a dominant part in their economies, even though they may absorb the bulk of the workforce.

However, clear-cut trading patterns in the style of the 1800s, when the industrialized countries produced all the world's goods, no longer exist. Most countries now have some industry and are developing more rapidly, while the biggest of all industrialized countries, the United States, is a major exporter of foodstuffs such as cereals. There is a growing tendency for countries to specialize in goods and services. For example, the Netherlands and Israel lead in cutting diamonds; Britain is a centre for banking and insurance; Japan is outstanding for photographic equipment; and Denmark and New Zealand are major producers of butter.

Financing international trade is a complicated business. Banks and other finance organizations, including the International Monetary Fund, operate the international finance market, through which traders can obtain currency to pay for the goods they buy. For example, a merchant in Brazil (currency, cruzeiros) may buy goods from India (rupees), which are carried in an American ship (dollars) and insured in Britain (pounds). Through the international banking network, the merchant can get the money he needs — even though Brazil may not possess any rupees. The necessary currency may well come through New York or London, two of the world's leading financial centres.

The Principal Food Importing and Exporting Countries

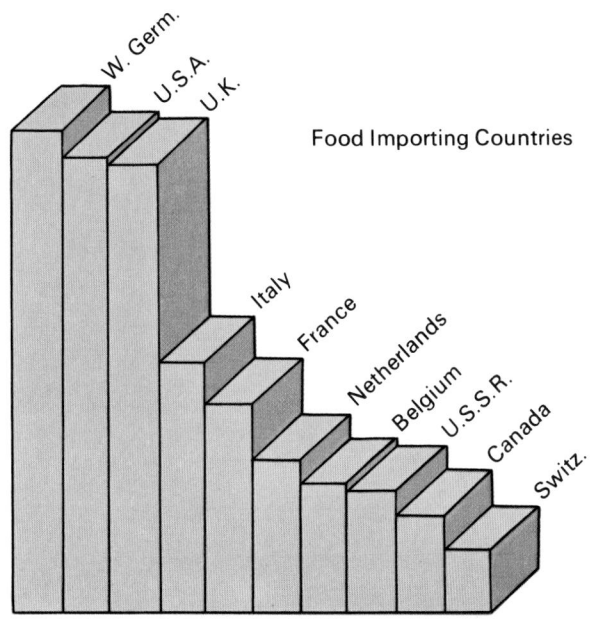

Food Importing Countries

W. Germ.
U.S.A.
U.K.
Italy
France
Netherlands
Belgium
U.S.S.R.
Canada
Switz.

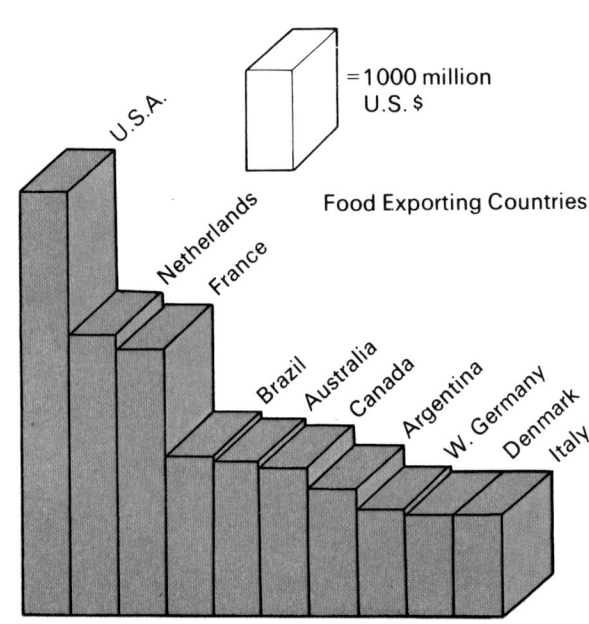

=1000 million U.S. $

Food Exporting Countries

U.S.A.
Netherlands
France
Brazil
Australia
Canada
Argentina
W. Germany
Denmark
Italy

INVISIBLE TRADE

Although most international trade consists of buying and selling goods, there is one form of trading that consists of selling and buying services. This is often called *invisible trade.* Some countries, particularly Britain, invariably import more goods than they export, but make up the difference in invisible exports.

Services under the heading of invisible exports include: freight charges by air and sea; banking; insurance; income from investments in other countries; spending by foreign visitors; and, to a lesser extent, payments of royalties or the transfer of money earned by citizens working abroad.

RESERVE CURRENCIES

Amounts of the world's currencies are held by other countries as part of their assets. Generally, only comparatively small sums of money are involved, but a number of currencies are held in great quantities; these are known as *reserve currencies.*

For many years, the two main reserve currencies have been the US $ and the £ sterling, though today West German Deutsche Marks are increasingly held as reserves. Other currencies play a lesser role.

Above left: **A million pounds in gold bullion, notes and coins photographed in the vaults of Hambros Bank in the City of London.**

Overleaf: **A busy dockyard scene at Dar-es-Salaam, Tanzania.**

Annual Imports and Exports of Leading Countries

Figures are in millions of US$.

Country	Imports	Exports	Country	Imports	Exports
Algeria	1,257	1,009	Iraq	713	87
Argentina	1,689	1,773	Ireland (Republic)	2,793	2,131
Austria	9,004	7,135	Israel	1,973	1,150
			Italy	40,712	30,300
Belgium with Luxembourg	28,378	28,034	Japan	62,035	55,598
Brazil	4,776	3,991	Kuwait	625	1,006
Britain	38,888	30,550	Malaysia	1,489	1,764
Canada	32,295	32,780	Mexico	2,935	1,844
Chile	1,119	1,234	Netherlands	23,803	24,043
China	2,300	2,200	New Zealand	1,524	1,796
Colombia	929	689	Nigeria	1,510	1,793
Cuba	1,385	859	Norway	8,418	6,274
Czechoslovakia	4,662	4,915	Philippines	1,319	1,116
Denmark	9,850	7,658	Poland	5,329	4,927
Finland	6,809	5,486	Portugal	4,583	2,276
France	48,068	41,563	Saudi Arabia	806	3,845
Germany (East)	5,905	6,183	Spain	15,329	7,077
Germany (West)	68,975	89,165	Sweden	10,543	12,072
Ghana	292	393	Switzerland	14,389	11,731
Greece	4,385	2,030	Turkey	1,508	885
Hungary	3,966	4,478	United States	100,972	97,143
India	2,406	2,043	Venezuela	1,913	3,114
Indonesia	1,104	1,199	Yugoslavia	7,520	3,805
Iran	2,593	3,812	Zaire	533	995

GENERAL REFERENCE

CONVERSION SCALE

Abbreviations of measures used — ft Feet; mm { Millimetres / Millimeters } cm { Centimetres / Centimeters } m { Metres / Meters } Km { Kilometres / Kilometers } mb Millibars

3386 ····· **Principal Shipping Routes** (Distances in Nautical Miles)

City and Town symbols in order of size

∴ Sites of Archæological or Historical Importance

——— International Boundaries

– – – International Boundaries (Undemarcated or Undefined)

········· Internal Boundaries

∿ Principal Roads

- - - Tracks, Seasonal and other Roads

⊣--⊢ Road Tunnels

∿ Principal Railways

∿ Other Railways

- - - Railways under construction

⊣--⊢ Railway Tunnels

⊥⊥⊥⊥ Principal Canals

—•—•— Principal Oil Pipelines

——— Principal Air Routes

☼ Principal Airports

∿ Perennial Streams

- - - Seasonal Streams

Seasonal Lakes, Salt Flats

Swamps, Marshes

Wells in Desert

Permanent Ice

≍ Passes

▲ 8848 Height above sea-level
▼ 8050 Depth below sea-level } in metres
1134 Height of lake-level

THE WORLD: Physical

1:150 000 000

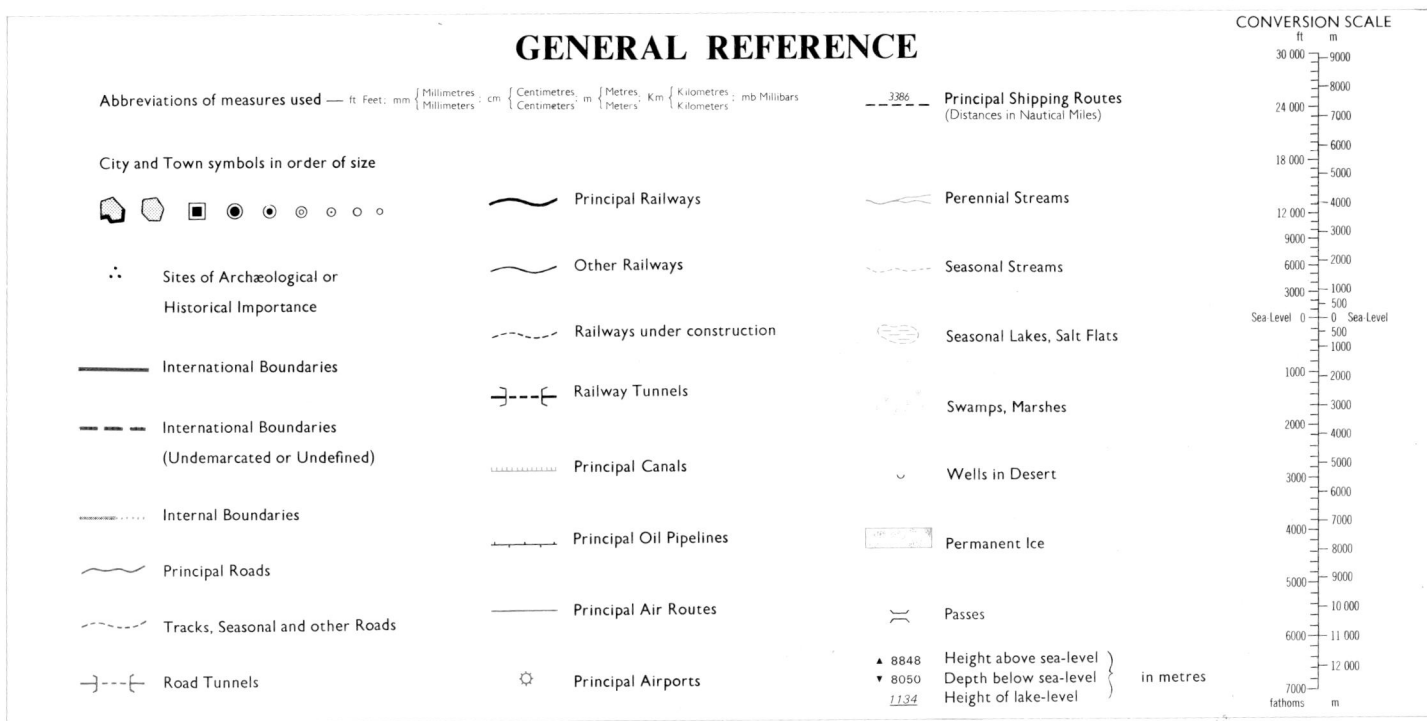

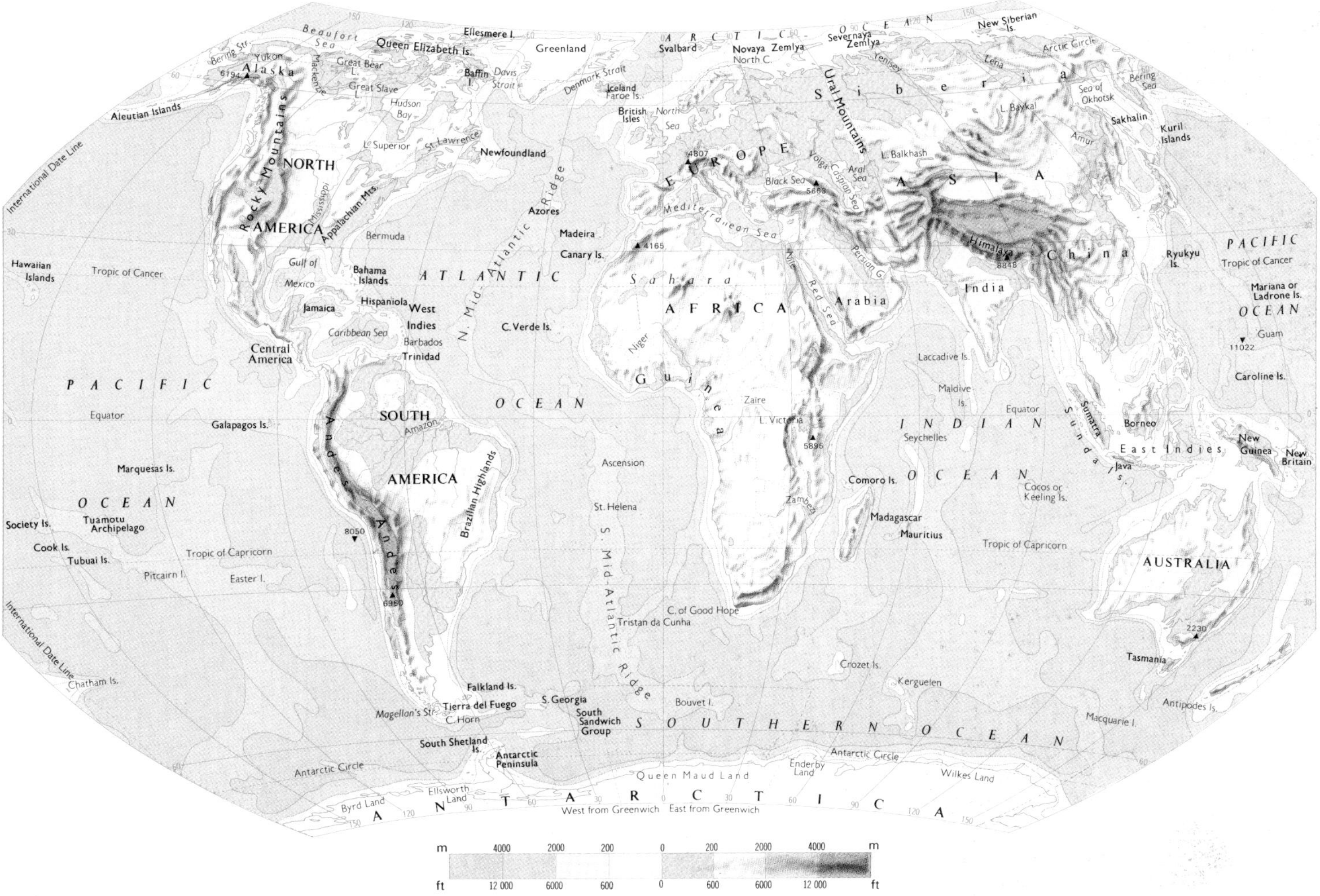

Projection: Hammer Equal Area

Projection: *Hammer Equal Area*

A R C T I C   O C E A N

Svalbard (Norway)

Barents Sea

Novaya Zemlya

Kara Sea

Franz Joseph Ld.

Severnaya Zemlya

Laptev Sea

New Siberian Is.

East Siberian Sea

S i b e r i a

UNION OF SOVIET SOCIALIST REPUBLICS

SOVIET FEDERAL SOCIALIST REPUBLIC

RUSSIAN

KAZAKHSTAN

UZBEKISTAN

TURKMENISTAN

KIRGIZIA

MONGOLIA

CHINA

Tibet

JAPAN

Tōkyō

PACIFIC

OCEAN

Sea of Okhotsk

Bering Sea

Kamchatka

Sakhalin

Kuril Islands

Tropic of Cancer

Mariana or Ladrone Is. (U.S.)

Wake I. (U.S.)

Guam (U.S.)

Marshall Is.

Caroline Is.

(U. S. Trust Territory)

Gilbert Is. (Br.)

Nauru

Truk

Ponape

Jaluit

Yap

Palau Is.

INDIA

PAKISTAN

AFGHANISTAN

IRAN

PERSIA

SAUDI ARABIA

IRAQ

TURKEY

Black Sea

Caspian Sea

Aral Sea

Arabian Sea

Bay of Bengal

SRI LANKA (CEYLON)

Maldive Is.

I N D I A N

O C E A N

Equator

Seychelles

Chagos Arch. (Br.)

Diego Garcia (Br.)

Amirante Is.

Aldabra

Comoro Is.

MADAGASCAR

MAURITIUS

Réunion (Fr.)

Rodriguez

Cargados Garajos (Br.)

Tropic of Capricorn

Amsterdam (Fr.) St. Paul (Fr.)

Kerguelen (Fr.)

Crozet Is. (Fr.)

Pr. Edward Is (South Africa)

Heard I. (Australia)

McDonald I. (Australia)

Bouvet I. (Norway)

MALAYSIA

INDONESIA

Sumatra

Borneo

Sulawesi

Java

PHILIPPINES

Manila

Quezon City

Cebu

South China Sea

VIET-NAM

CAMBODIA

THAILAND (SIAM)

BURMA

Bangkok

Saigon

Phnom Penh

Rangoon

Hainan

Hong Kong

TAIWAN

Taipei

East China Sea

Shanghai

PAPUA NEW GUINEA

Irian Jaya

New Guinea

New Britain

New Ireland

Admiralty Is.

Solomon Is.

New Caledonia

New Hebrides (Br.-Fr.)

Fiji Is.

Vanua Levu

Viti Levu Suva

Tuvalu (Ellice Is.)

Santa Cruz Is. (Br.)

Rotuma

Duff Is.

Louisiade Arch.

Arafura Sea

Timor Sea

Timor

Darwin

Christmas I. (Australia)

Cocos (Keeling) Is. (Australia)

AUSTRALIA

NORTHERN TERRITORY

WESTERN AUSTRALIA

SOUTH AUSTRALIA

QUEENSLAND

NEW SOUTH WALES

VICTORIA

TASMANIA

Perth

Adelaide

Melbourne

Sydney

Newcastle

Canberra

Brisbane

Townsville

Cairns

Rockhampton

Alice Springs

Kalgoorlie

Geraldton

Fremantle

Great Australian Bight

Tasman Sea

NEW ZEALAND

North I.

South I.

Auckland

Wellington

Christchurch

Dunedin

Lord Howe I. (Australia)

Norfolk I. (Australia)

Stewart I.

Antipodes Is. (N.Z.)

Bounty Is. (N.Z.)

Auckland I (N.Z.)

Campbell I. (N.Z.)

Macquarie I. (Australia)

S O U T H E R N   O C E A N

König Haakon VII Sea

Enderby Land

Antarctic Circle

Wilkes Land

S. Magnetic Pole 1965

Ross Sea

Balleny Is.

Maud Land

IAN DEPENDENCY

AUSTRALIAN DEPENDENCY

TERRE ADÉLIE

East from Greenwich

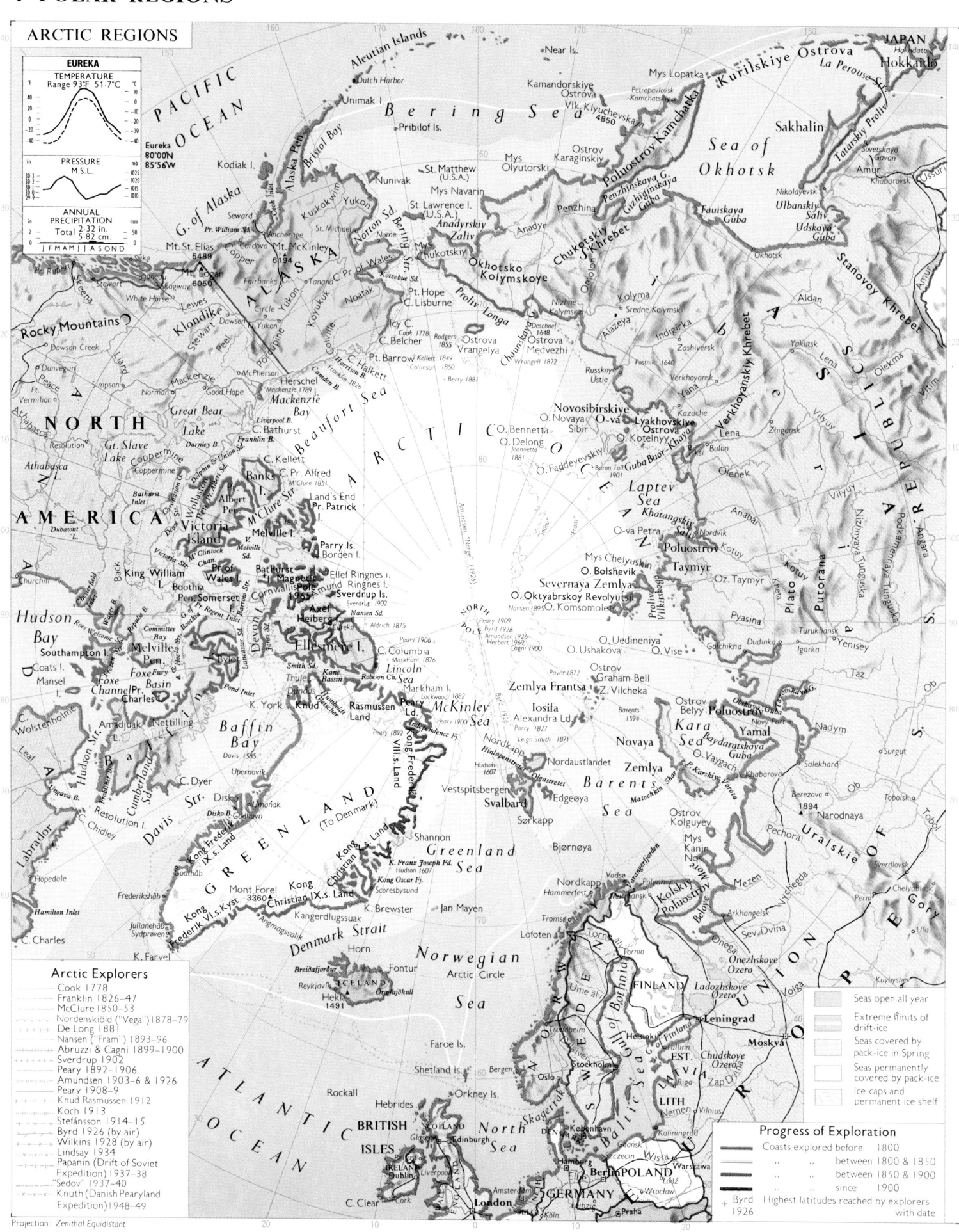

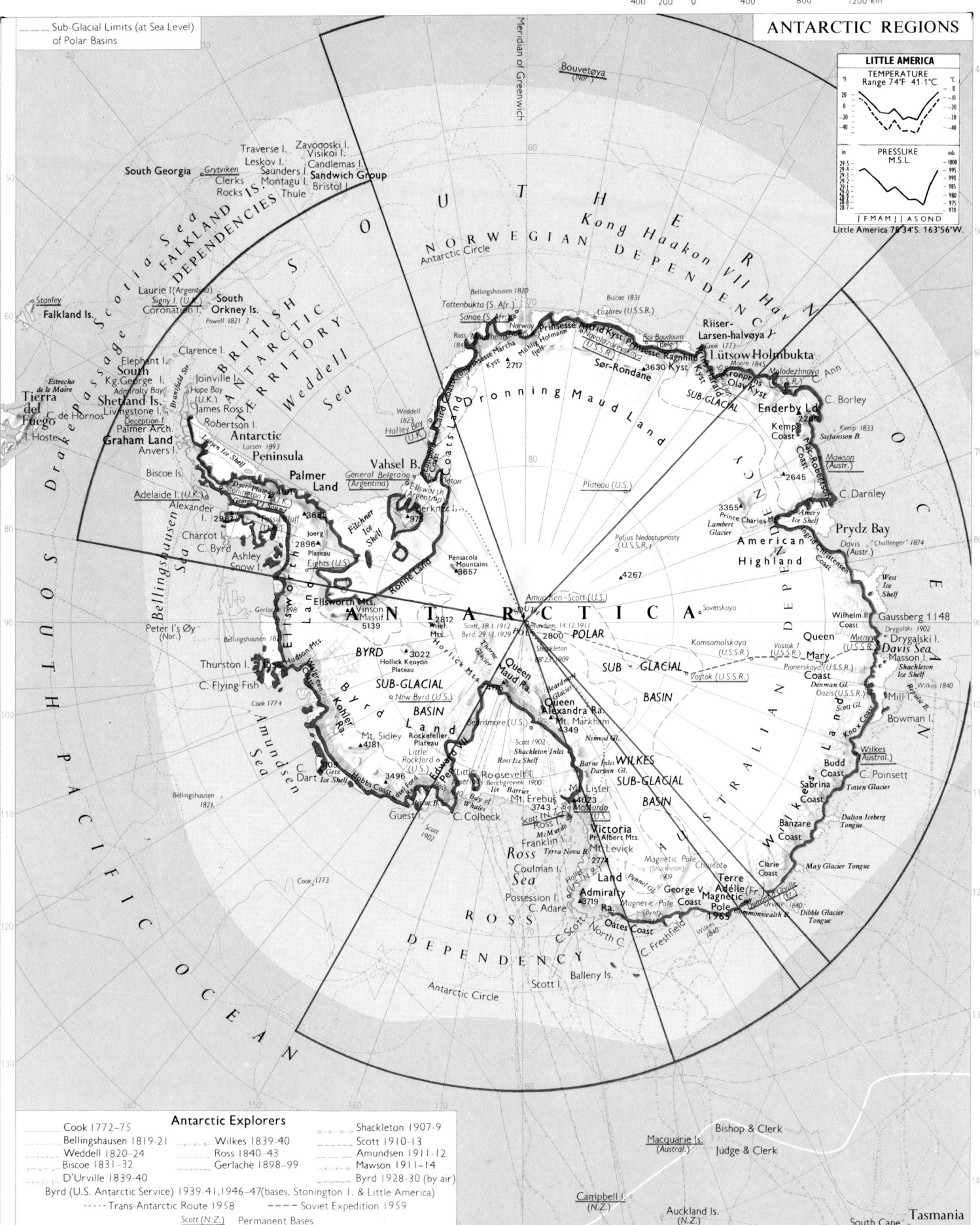

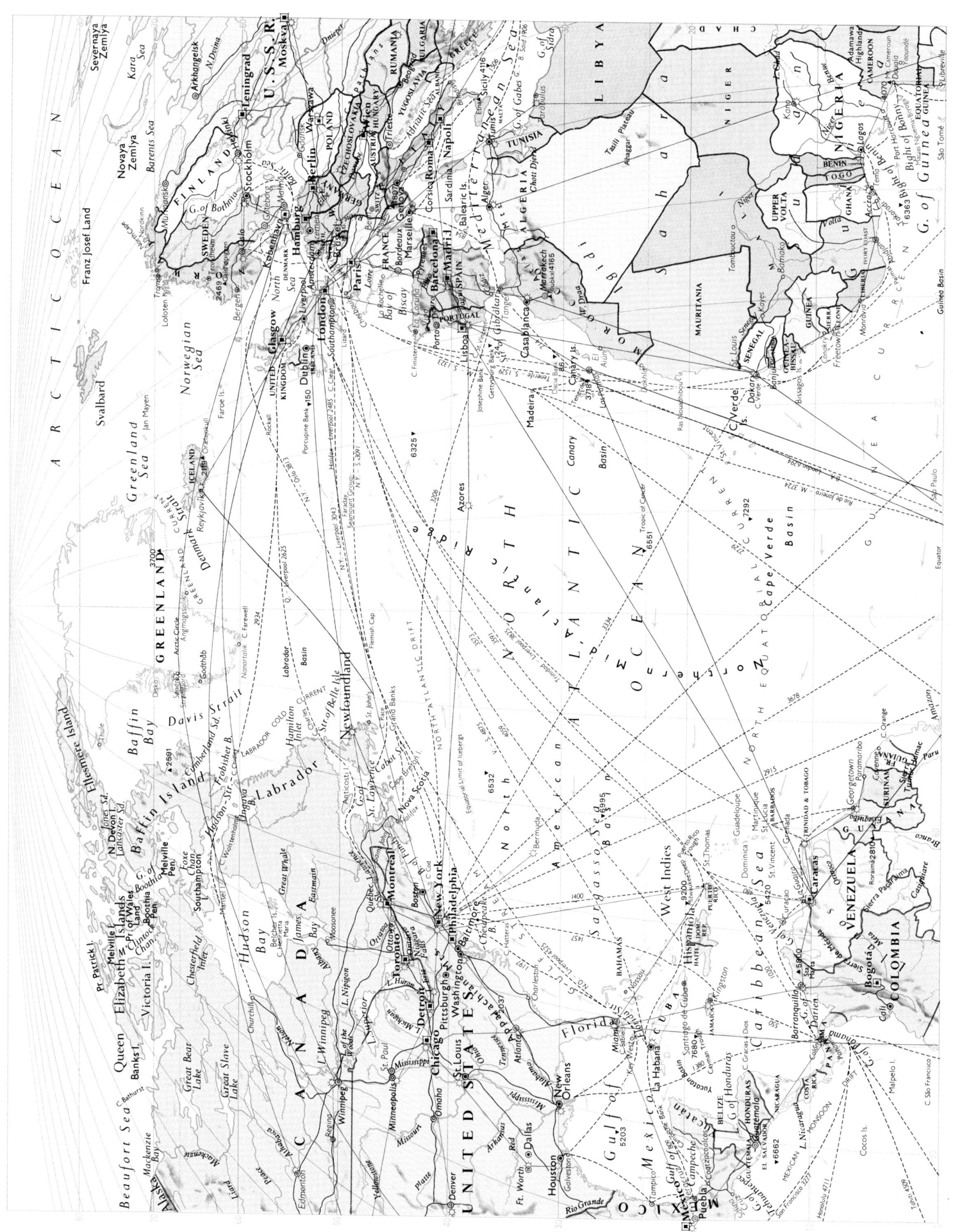

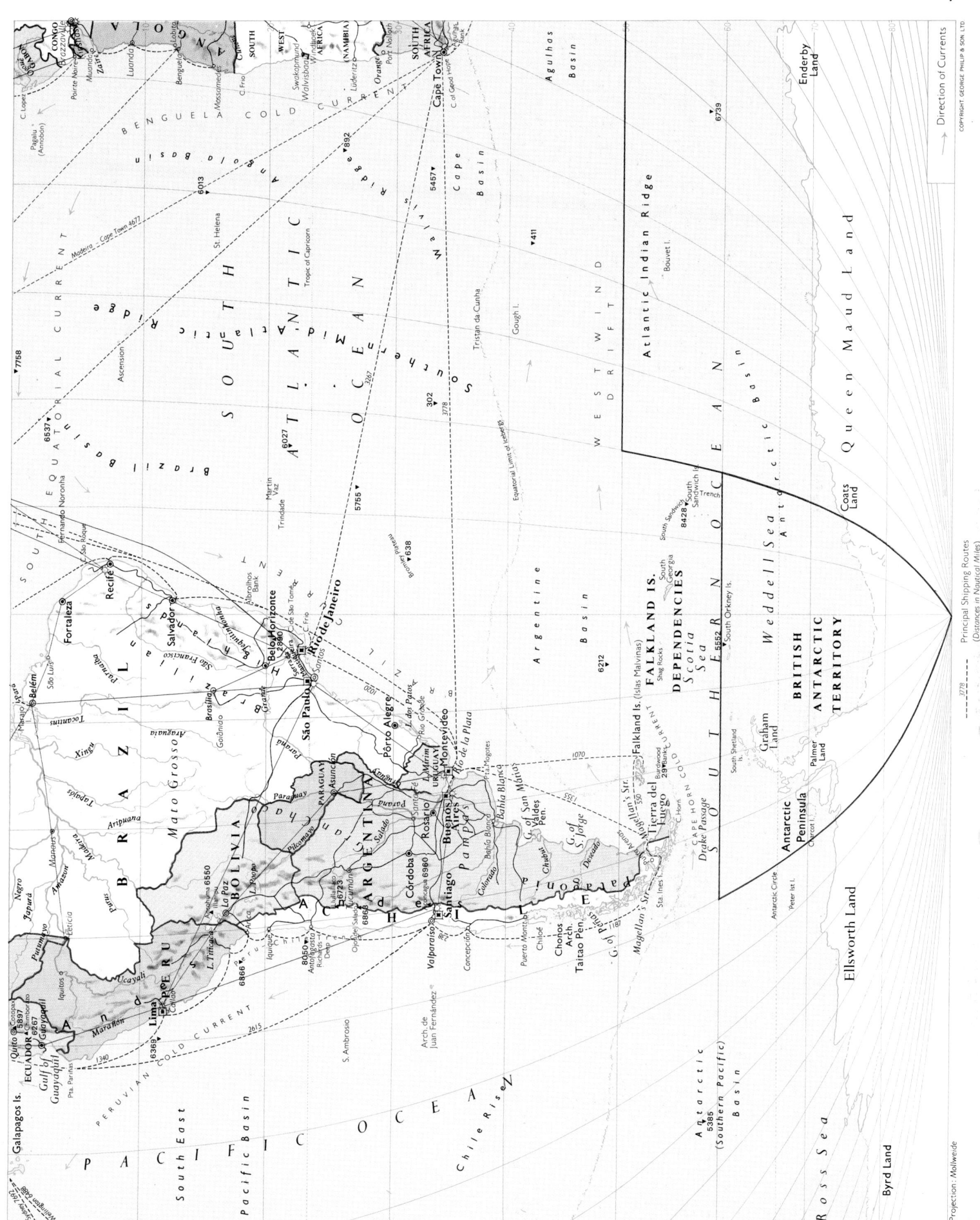

Direction of Currents

Principal Shipping Routes
(Distances in Nautical Miles)

COPYRIGHT. GEORGE PHILIP & SON, LTD.

Projection: Mollweide

8 EUROPE: Physical

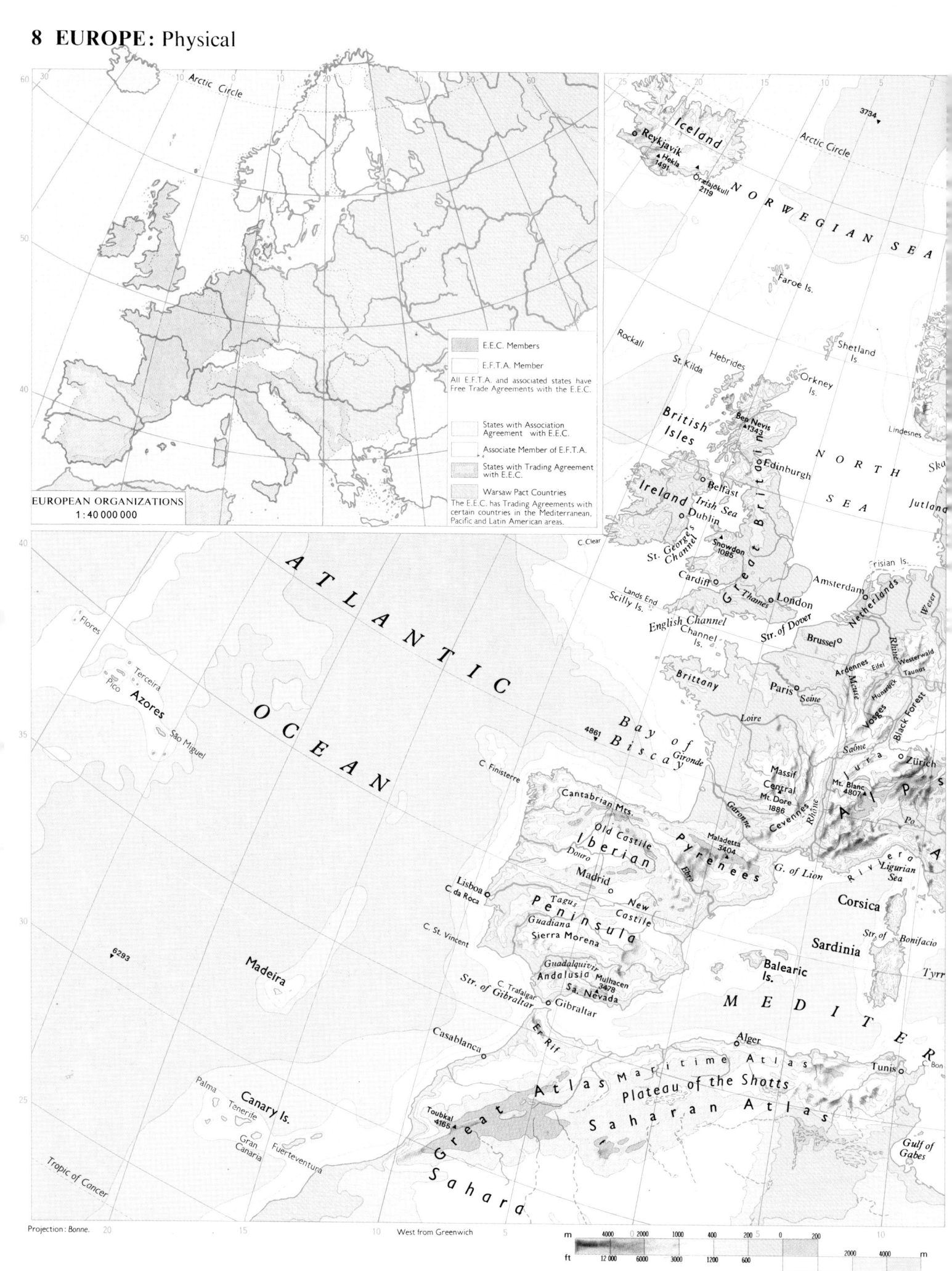

EUROPEAN ORGANIZATIONS
1 : 40 000 000

E.E.C. Members

E.F.T.A. Member

All E.F.T.A. and associated states have
Free Trade Agreements with the E.E.C.

States with Association
Agreement with E.E.C.

Associate Member of E.F.T.A.

States with Trading Agreement
with E.E.C.

Warsaw Pact Countries
The E.E.C. has Trading Agreements with
certain countries in the Mediterranean,
Pacific and Latin American areas.

Arctic Circle

NORWEGIAN SEA

Iceland
Reykjavik
Hekla 1491
Öraefajökull 2119

Faroe Is.

Rockall

St. Kilda
Hebrides

Shetland Is.

Orkney Is.

British Isles

Ben Nevis 1343
Edinburgh

NORTH SEA

Lindesnes

Jutland

Ireland
Belfast
Irish Sea
Dublin

Great Britain

St. George's Channel
Snowdon 1085

Cardiff
Thames
London

Amsterdam

Frisian Is.

Weser

Netherlands

Lands End
Scilly Is.

English Channel

Channel Is.

Str. of Dover

Brussel

Ardennes
Eifel
Westerwald
Taunus

C. Clear

Brittany

Paris
Seine

Rhine
Meuse
Hunsrück
Black Forest

Loire

Vosges
Saône
Jura

Zürich

ATLANTIC

OCEAN

Flores

Terceira
Pico
Azores
São Miguel

C. Finisterre

Bay of Biscay

4861
Gironde

Massif Central
Mt. Dore 1886

Mt. Blanc 4807

A L P S

Garonne

Cantabrian Mts.

Cévennes

Rhône

Riviera
Ligurian Sea

Old Castile
Iberian

Douro

Pyrenees

Maladetta 3404

G. of Lion

Corsica

Madrid

Ebro

Po

Lisboa
C. da Roca

New Castile

Sardinia

Str. of Bonifacio

6293

Madeira

Peninsula

Tagus
Guadiana
Sierra Morena

Balearic Is.

Tyrr

Guadalquivir
Andalusia
Sa. Nevada

Mulhacen 3478

MEDITER

C. St. Vincent

C. Trafalgar
Str. of Gibraltar

Gibraltar

Casablanca

Er Rif

Alger

Tunis

C. Bon

Palma

Canary Is.
Tenerife

Maritime Atlas

Plateau of the Shotts

Saharan Atlas

Gulf of Gabes

Great Atlas

Toubkal 4165

Gran Canaria
Fuerteventura

Tropic of Cancer

Sahara

Projection: Bonne.

West from Greenwich

m   4000   2000   1000   400   200   0   200
ft   12 000   6000   3000   1200   600
2000   4000   m
0   600   6000   12 000   ft

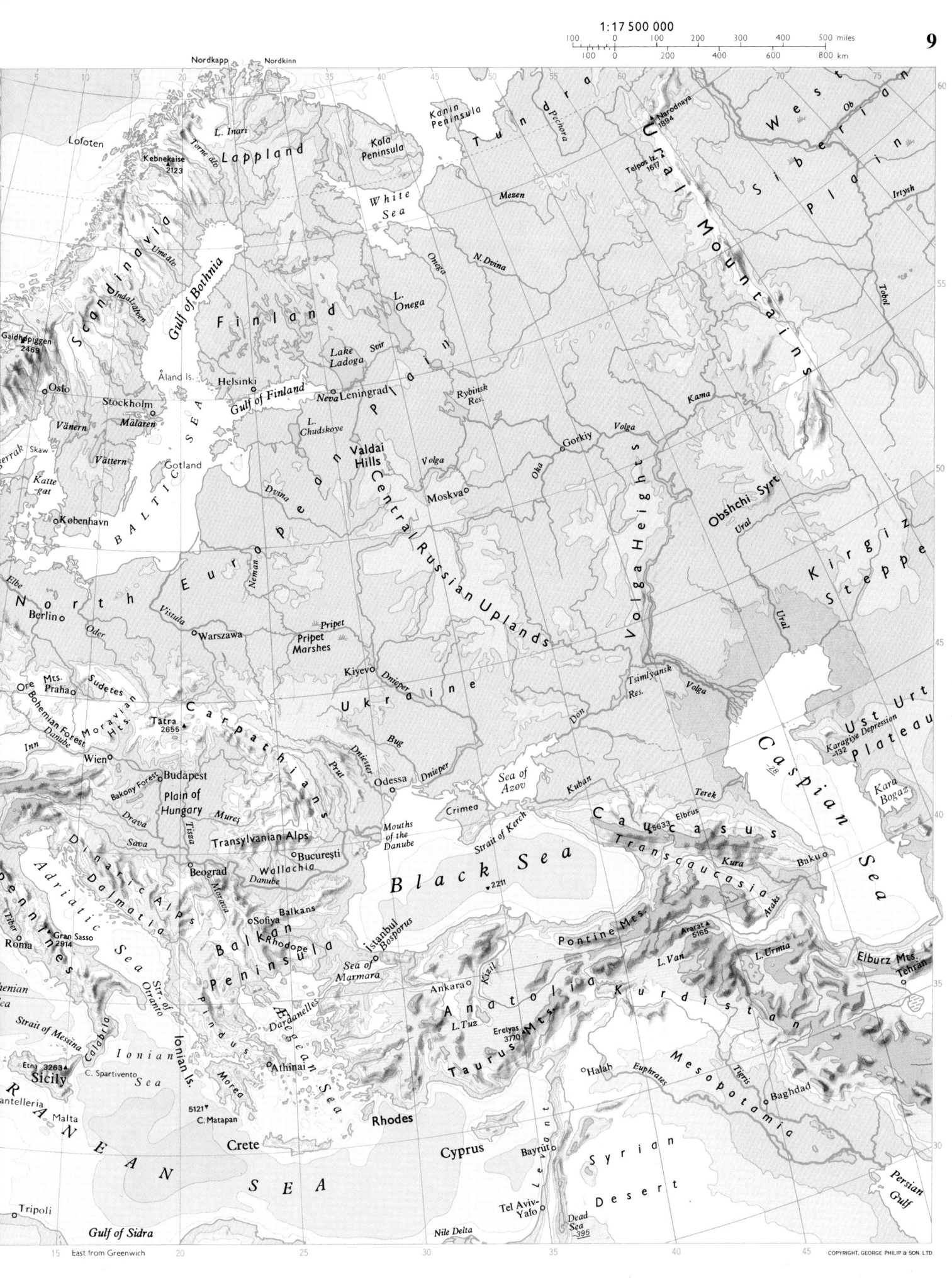

1:20 000 000

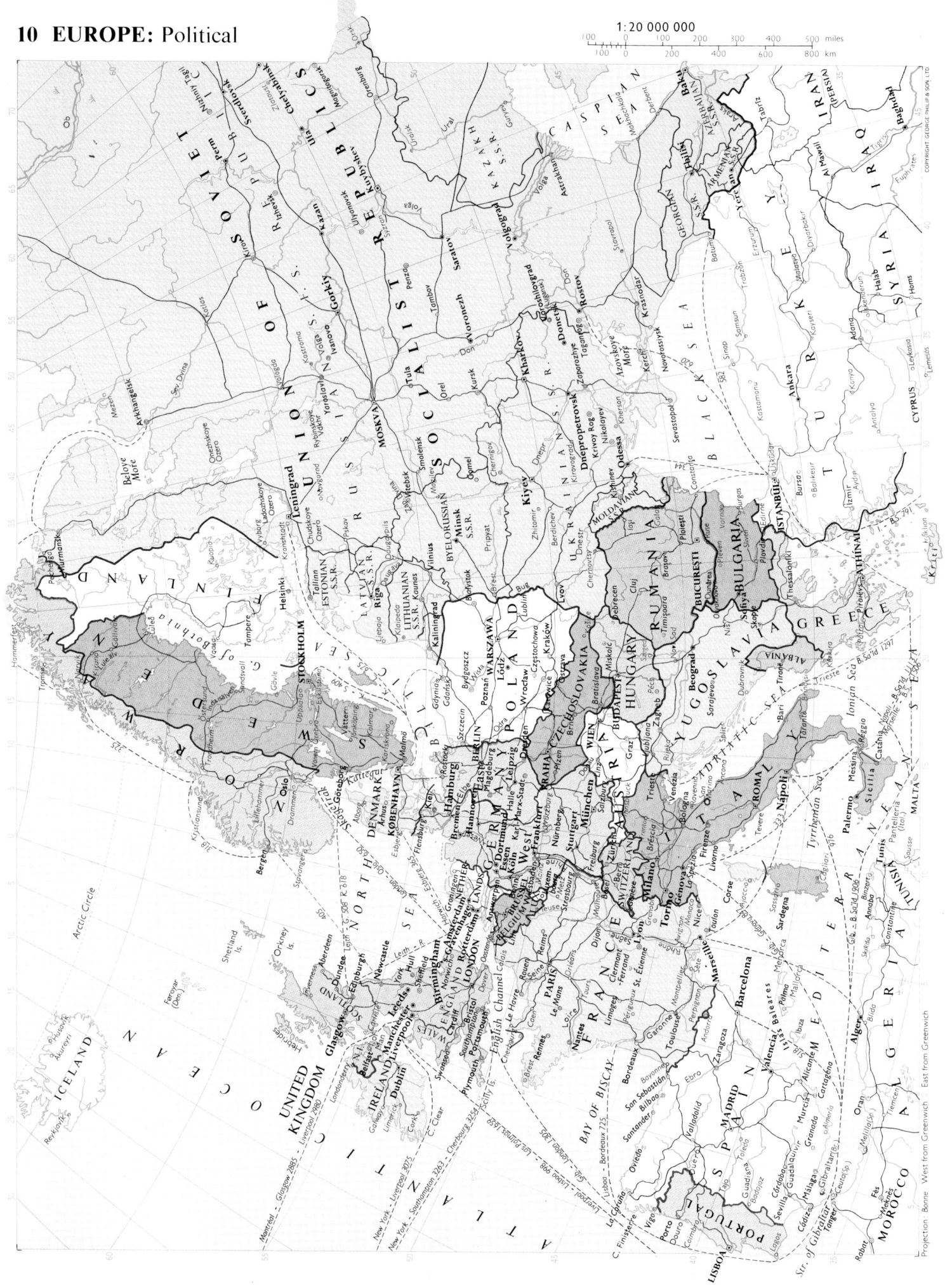

1 : 4 000 000

The DISTRICTS of Northern Ireland have been numbered and can be identified by reference to this table.

1	Londonderry	14	Craigavon
2	Limavady	15	Armagh
3	Coleraine	16	Newry & Mourne
4	Ballymoney	17	Banbridge
5	Moyle	18	Down
6	Larne	19	Lisburn
7	Ballymena	20	Antrim
8	Magherafelt	21	Newtownabbey
9	Cookstown	22	Carrickfergus
10	Strabane	23	North Down
11	Omagh	24	Ards
12	Fermanagh	25	Castlereagh
13	Dungannon	26	Belfast

1	Merseyside
2	Greater Manchester
3	West Yorkshire
4	South Yorkshire
5	West Glamorgan
6	Mid Glamorgan
7	South Glamorgan

Projection : Conical with two standard parallels

West from Greenwich   East from Greenwich

COPYRIGHT GEORGE PHILIP & SON LTD.

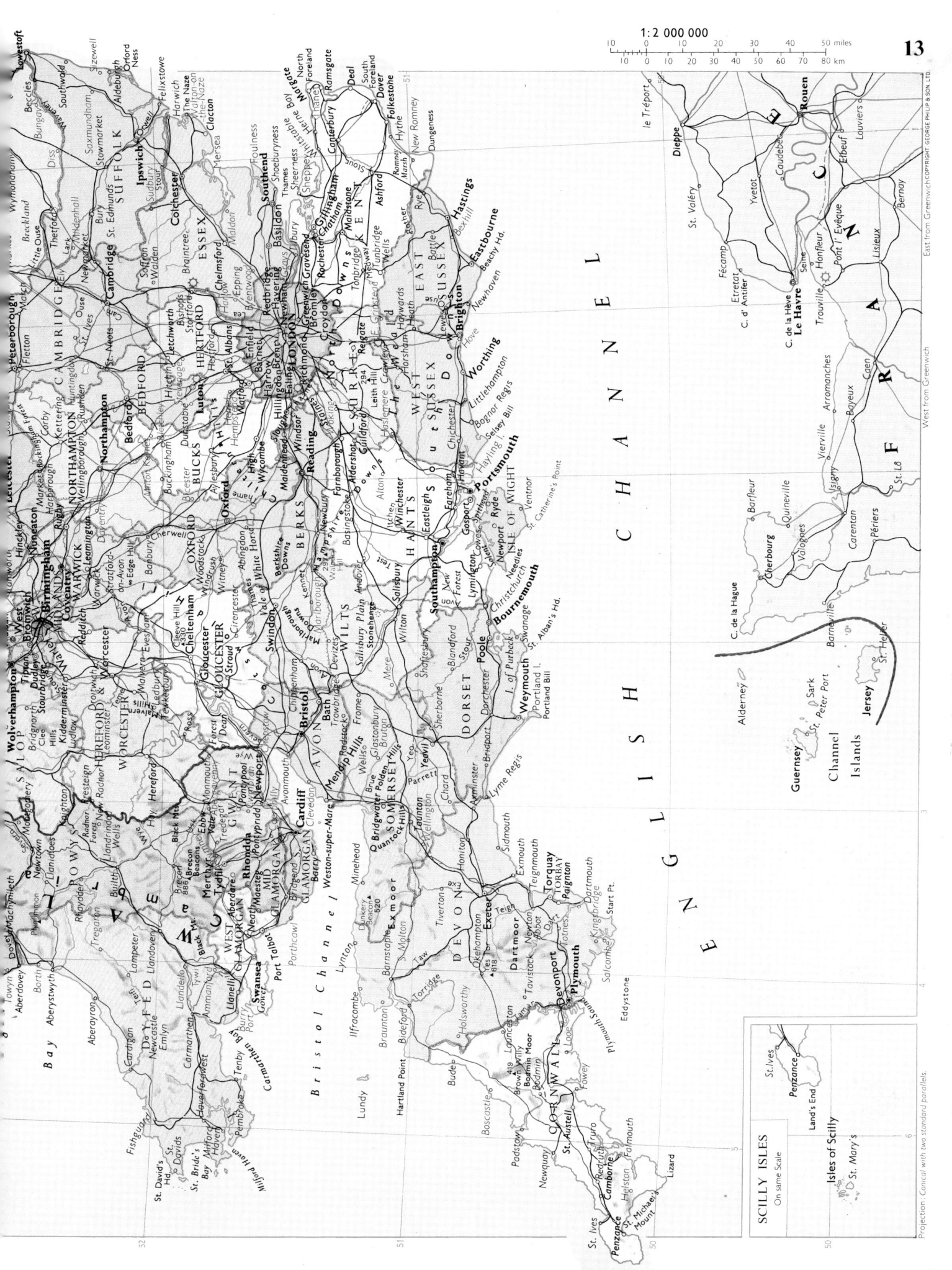

14 SCOTLAND

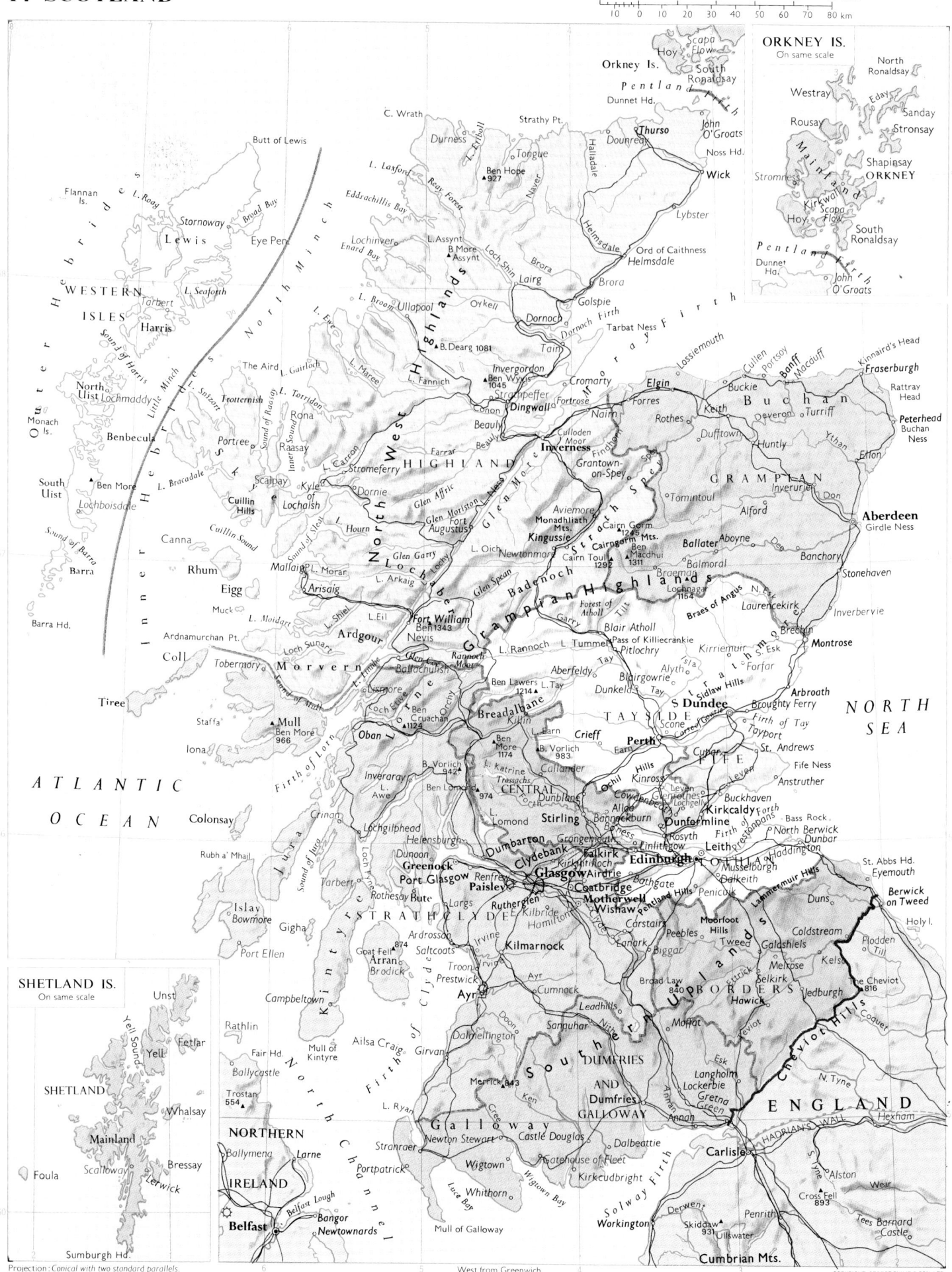

1 : 2 000 000

ORKNEY IS.
On same scale

SHETLAND IS.
On same scale

ATLANTIC OCEAN

NORTH SEA

WESTERN ISLES

ENGLAND

NORTHERN IRELAND

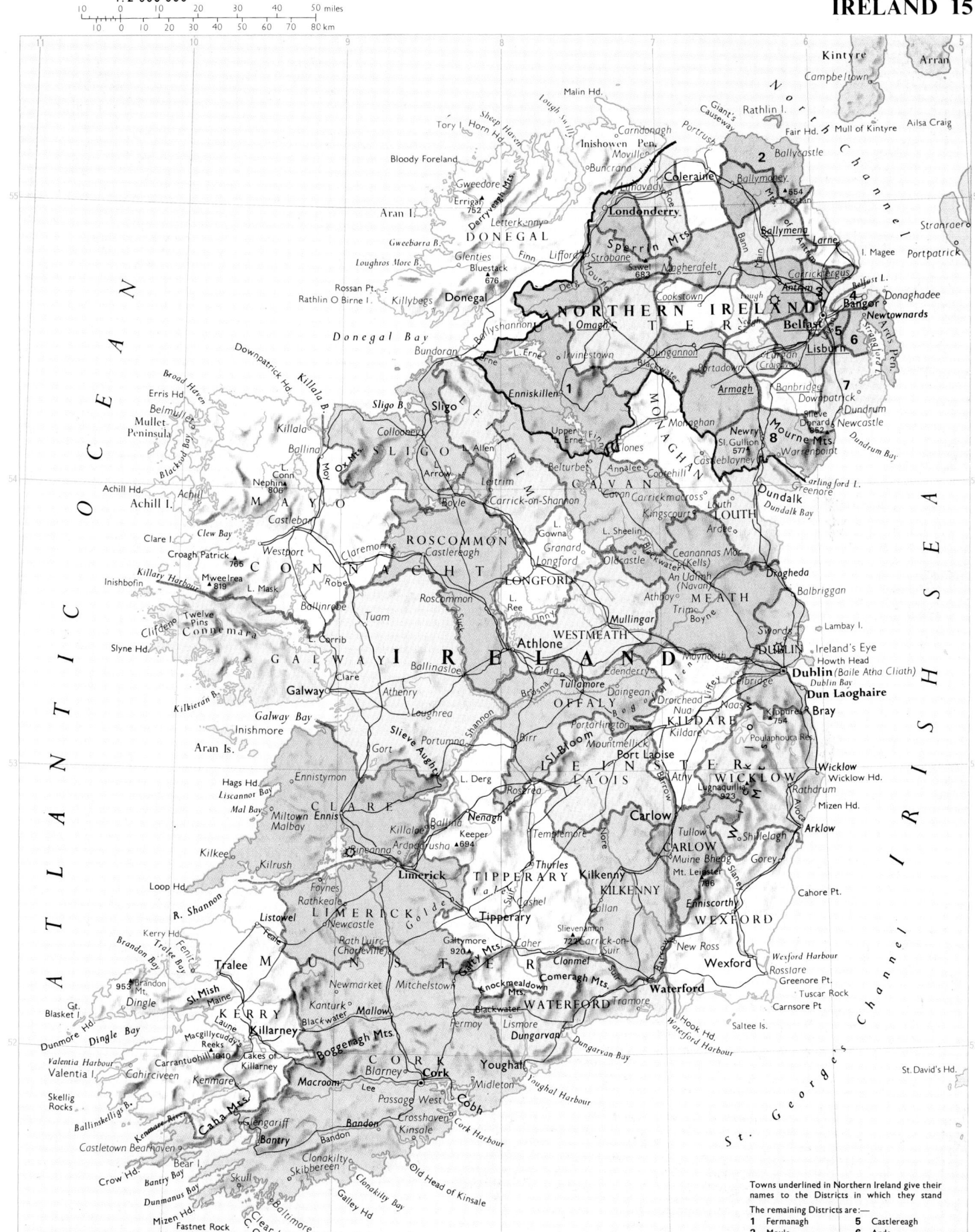

IRELAND 15

1 : 2 500 000

10   0   10   20   30   40   50 miles
10 0 10 20 30 40 50 60 70 80 km

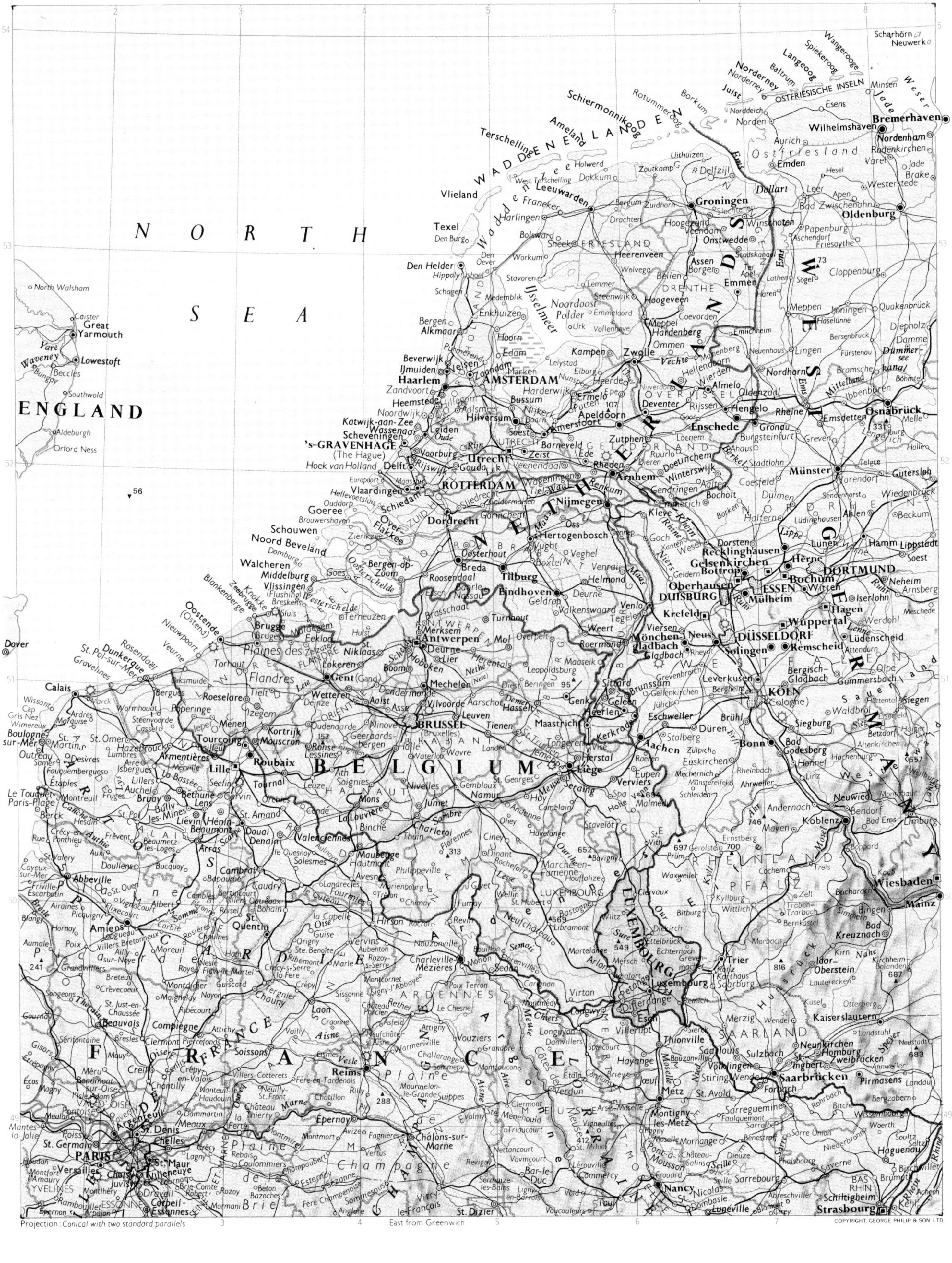

NORTH SEA

ENGLAND

NETHERLANDS

BELGIUM

LUXEMBOURG

FRANCE

GERMANY

OSTFRIESISCHE INSELN
Ostfriesland
WADDENEILANDEN

Major places:
Groningen, Leeuwarden, Den Helder, Haarlem, **AMSTERDAM**, Hilversum, Leiden, **'s-GRAVENHAGE** (The Hague), Delft, **ROTTERDAM**, Utrecht, Dordrecht, Nijmegen, Arnhem, Apeldoorn, Deventer, Enschede, Zwolle, Emmen, Breda, Tilburg, Eindhoven, Roosendaal, Middelburg, Vlissingen, Brugge (Bruges), Oostende (Ostend), Gent (Gand), **BRUSSEL** (Bruxelles), Antwerpen, Mechelen, Leuven, Hasselt, Liège, Namur, Mons, Charleroi, **Luxembourg**, Esch, Diekirch, Trier, Bremerhaven, Wilhelmshaven, Oldenburg, Osnabrück, Münster, Dortmund, Essen, Duisburg, Düsseldorf, Köln (Cologne), Bonn, Aachen, Mainz, Wiesbaden, Saarbrücken, Nancy, Strasbourg, Reims, Calais, Dunkerque, Boulogne-sur-Mer, Lille, Roubaix, Amiens, St Quentin, Abbeville, Arras, Valenciennes, Maubeuge, PARIS

Projection : Conical with two standard parallels

East from Greenwich

1:5 000 000

20 10 0 20 40 60 80 100 Statute Miles
40 20 0 40 80 120 160 Km

FRENCH DEPARTMENTS

A.	Ai.	01	Ain
A.	Ai.	02	Aisne
A.	Al.	03	Allier
A.H.P.		04	Alpes-de-Haute-Provence
A.	A.M.	06	Alpes-Maritimes
A.	Ard.	07	Ardèche
A.	Ard.	08	Ardennes
A.	Ari.	09	Ariège
A.	Aud.	11	Aude
Av.		12	Aveyron
B.R.		13	Bouches-du-Rhône
C.		14	Calvados
C.		15	Cantal
Cha.		16	Charente
Ch.M.		17	Charente-Maritime
Che.		18	Cher
Co.		19	Corrèze
C.Q.		20	Corse (Haute-Corse)
C.Q.		2A	Corse-du-Sud
C.N.		2B	Côtes-du-Nord
Cr.		23	Creuse
Do.		24	Dordogne
Do.		25	Doubs
Dr.		26	Drôme
E.L.		27	Eure-et-Loir
F.		28	Finistère (Nord et Sud)
G.		30	Gard
H.G.		31	Haute-Garonne
Ge.		32	Gers
Gi.		33	Gironde
H.		34	Hérault
I.V.		35	Ille-et-Vilaine
I.		36	Indre
I.L.		37	Indre-et-Loire
Is.		38	Isère
Ju.		39	Jura
La.		40	Landes
L.C.		41	Loir-et-Cher
Loi.		42	Loire
H.L.		43	Haute-Loire
L.A.		44	Loire-Atlantique
Loi.		45	Loiret
Lot		46	Lot
L.G.		47	Lot-et-Garonne
Loz.		48	Lozère
M.L.		49	Maine-et-Loire
Ma.		50	Manche
Mar.		51	Marne
H.M.		52	Haute-Marne
May.		53	Mayenne
M.M.		54	Meurthe-et-Moselle
Me.		55	Meuse
Mo.		56	Morbihan
Mos.		57	Moselle
N.		58	Nièvre
No.		59	Nord
O.		60	Oise
Or.		61	Orne
P.C.		62	Pas-de-Calais
P.D.		63	Puy-de-Dôme
P.A.		64	Pyrénées Atlantiques
H.P.		65	Hautes Pyrénées
P.O.		66	Pyrénées (Orientales)
B.R.		67	Bas Rhin
H.R.		68	Haut Rhin
Rh.		69	Rhône
H.S.		70	Haute Saône
S.L.		71	Saône-et-Loire
Sa.		72	Sarthe
Sa.		73	Savoie
H.Sa.		74	Haute-Savoie
		75	Paris
S.Me.		76	Seine-Maritime
S.M.		77	Seine-et-Marne
Y.		78	Yvelines
D.S.		79	Deux-Sèvres
So.		80	Somme
T.		81	Tarn
T.G.		82	Tarn-et-Garonne
Va.		83	Var
Va.		84	Vaucluse
Ve.		85	Vendée
Vi.		86	Vienne
H.V.		87	Haute Vienne
Vo.		88	Vosges
Y.		89	Yonne
B.		90	Belfort
E.		91	Essonne
H.S.		92	Hauts-de-Seine
S.St.D.		93	Seine-St-Denis
V.M.		94	Val-de-Marne
V.O.		95	Val-d'Oise

CORSICA
On same scale

Corse
Corse du Sud
Haute-Corse

COPYRIGHT GEORGE PHILIP & SON LTD

Projection: Conical with two standard parallels

East from Greenwich

West from Greenwich

MEDITERRANEAN SEA

BAY OF BISCAY

ENGLISH CHANNEL

GERMANY

SWITZERLAND

BELGIUM

Paris

FRANCE

ENGLAND

English Channel

E n g l i s h   C h a n n e l

CHANNEL
ISLANDS

Alderney
Guernsey
St. Peter Port
Herm
Sark
Jersey
St. Helier

Golfe de
St. Malo

Baie de la
Seine

NORMANDIE

CALVADOS

Le Havre
Rouen

BRETAGNE

Brest
Quimper
Lorient
Vannes

Rennes

Le Mans

MORBIHAN

ANJOU

Nantes

Angers

Tours

LOIRE

BAY   OF

BISCAY

Île de Noirmoutier

Île d'Yeu

Baie de Bourgneuf

la Roche-
sur-Yon

VENDÉE

DEUX-
SÈVRES

Poitiers

VIENNE

POITOU

la Rochelle

AUNIS

Rochefort

Île d'Oléron

Niort

ANGOUMOIS

CHARENTE

Cognac

Angoulême

Saintes

Limoges

HAUTE VIENNE

LIMOUSIN

Projection: Conical with two standard parallels

West from Greenwich   0   East from Greenwich

1:2 500 000

10   0   10   20   30   40   50 miles

10 0 10 20 30 40 50 60 70 80 km

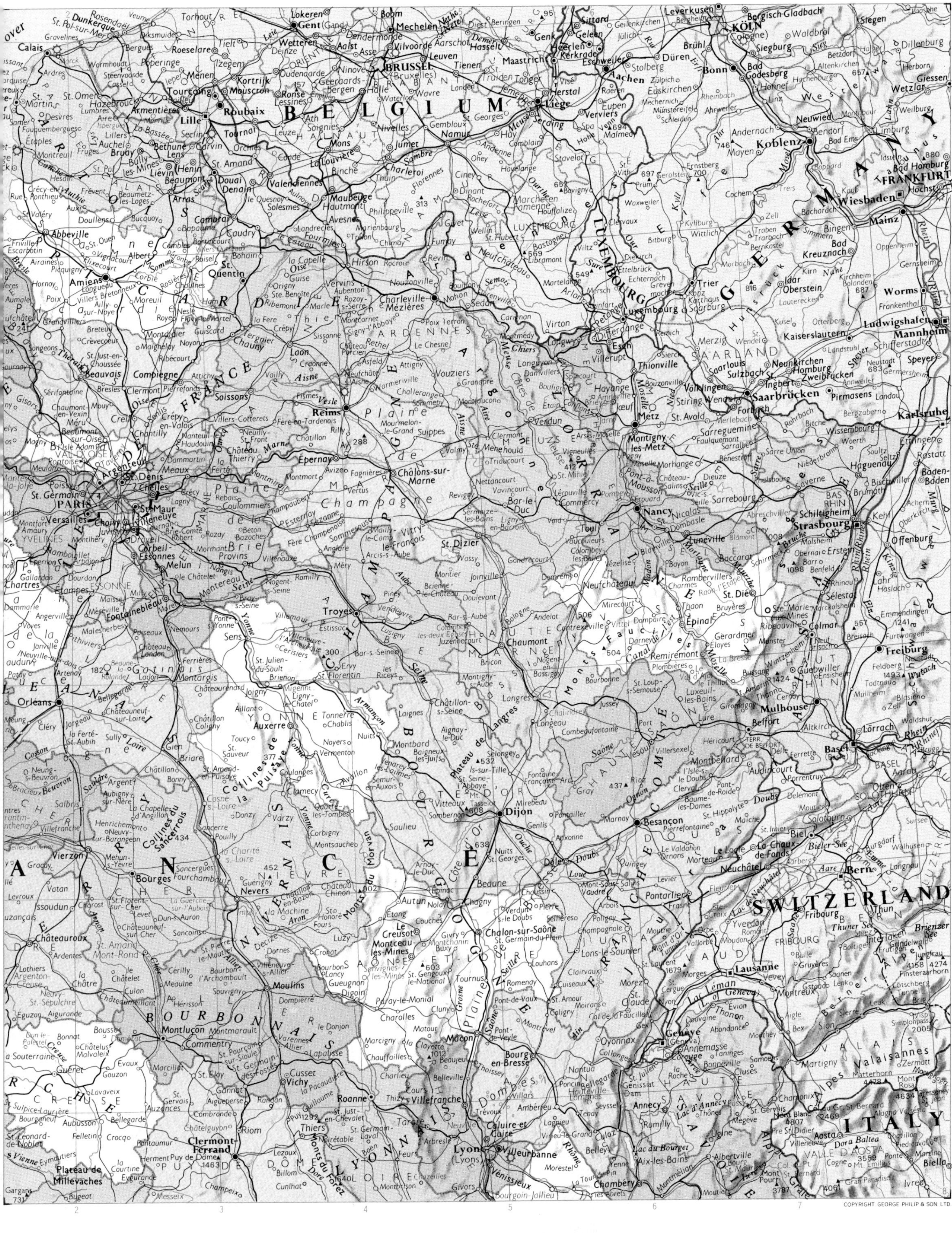

BELGIUM

GERMANY

FRANCE

SWITZERLAND

ITALY

LUXEMBOURG

ARDENNES

CHAMPAGNE

LORRAINE

SAARLAND

BOURGOGNE

FRANCHE-COMTÉ

PARIS

BRUSSEL (Bruxelles)

KÖLN (Cologne)

Bonn

Koblenz

FRANKFURT

Wiesbaden

Mainz

Worms

Mannheim

Ludwigshafen

Karlsruhe

Strasbourg

Saarbrücken

Metz

Nancy

Reims

Troyes

Dijon

Besançon

Mulhouse

Basel

Bern

Lausanne

Genève (Geneva)

Lyons (Lyon)

Orléans

Bourges

Clermont-Ferrand

Moulins

Nevers

Auxerre

Chaumont

Épinal

Colmar

Freiburg

Belfort

Neuchâtel

Liège

Namur

Charleroi

Mons

Lille

Roubaix

Amiens

Calais

Dunkerque

Maastricht

Aachen

Trier

Luxembourg

Verdun

Chalon-sur-Saône

Mâcon

Bourg-en-Bresse

Annecy

Chambéry

COPYRIGHT GEORGE PHILIP & SON. LTD

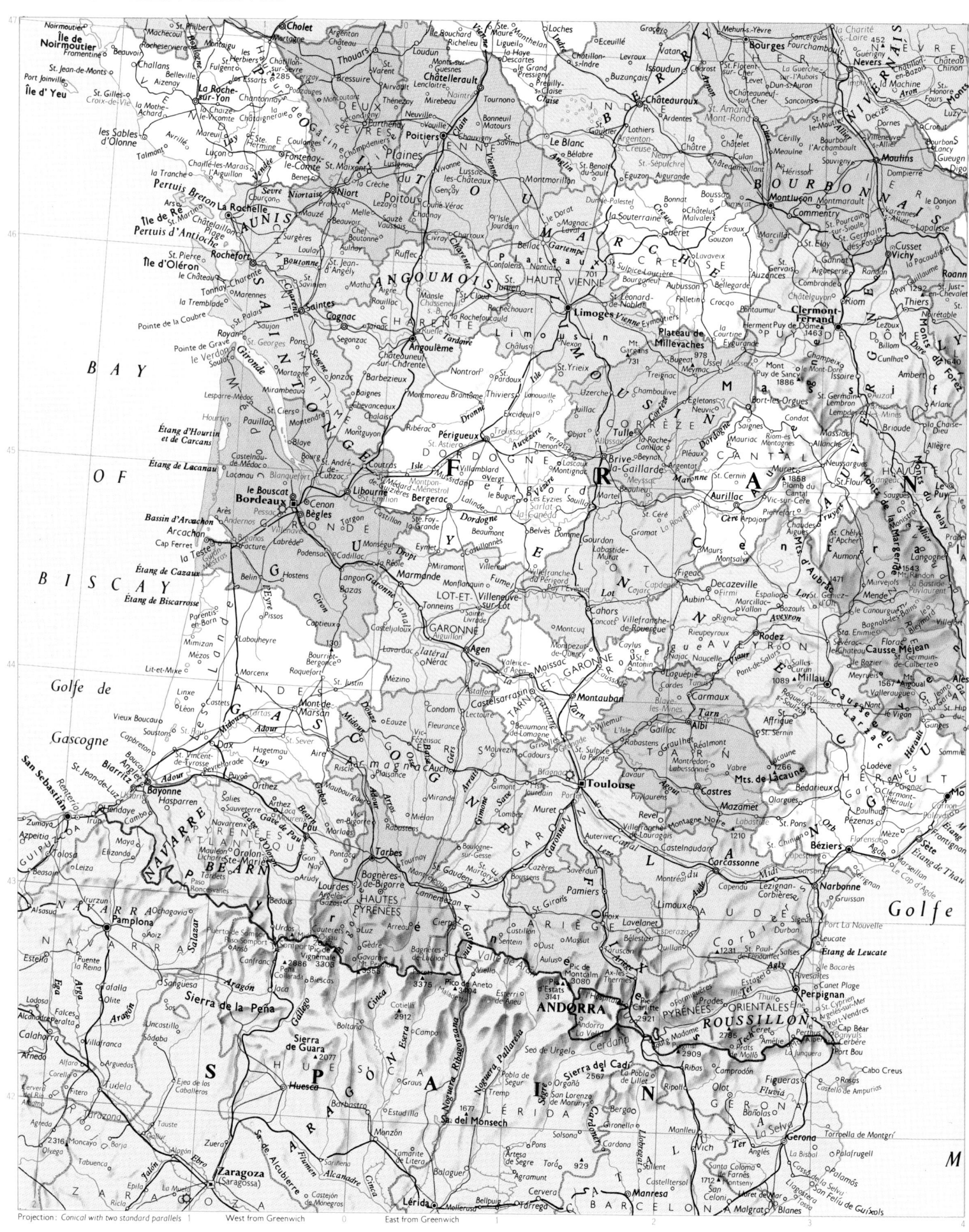

1 : 2 500 000

10   0   10   20   30   40   50 miles
10   0   10   20   30   40   50   60   70   80 km

SWITZERLAND

FRANCE

ITALY

CORSICA

HAUTE-CORSE

CORSE-DU-SUD

Golfo di Génova

LIGURIAN   SEA

MEDITERRANEAN   SEA

du Lion

COPYRIGHT. GEORGE PHILIP & SON. LTD.

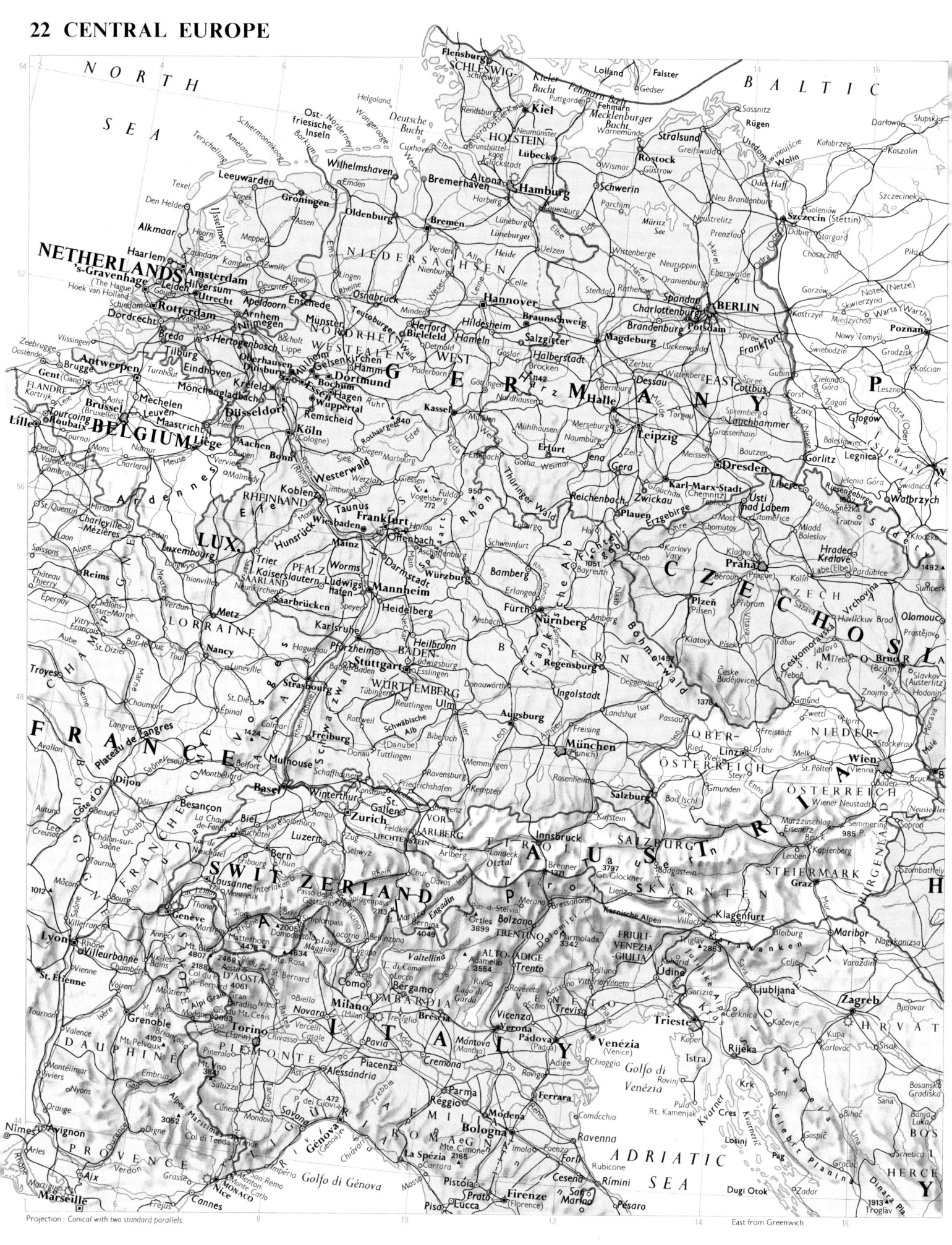

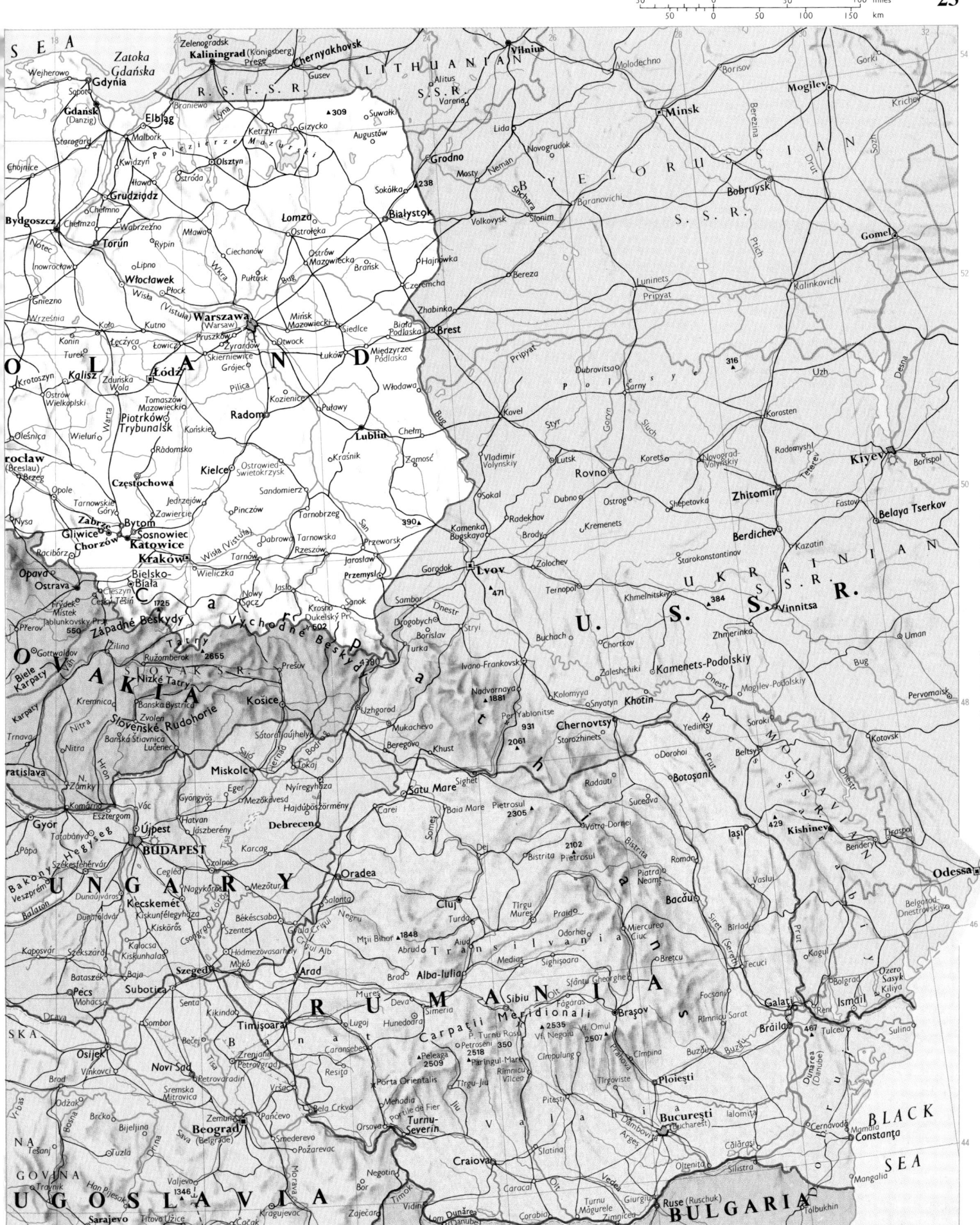

1:5 000 000

50   0   50   100 miles
50   0   50   100   150 km

SEA

Zatoka
Gdańska

Zelenogradsk
Kaliningrad (Königsberg)
Prege
Braniewo
Chernyakhovsk
Gusev

LITHUANIAN

Vilnius
Molodechno
Gorki

R. S. F. S. R.
S. S. R.

Alitus
Varena

Wejherowo
Sopot
Gdynia
Gdansk
(Danzig)
Starogard
Chojnice
Elbląg
Malbork
Kwidzyn
Lyna
Kętrzyn
Gizycko
▲309
Suwałki
Augustów
Sokółka
Grodno
Mosty
Neman
Sluchy
Lida
Novogrudok

Minsk
Borisov
Berezina
Mogilev
Krichev

BYELORUSSIAN

S. S. R.

Chelmno
Grudziądz
Chelmno
Toruń
Wabrzeźno
Rypin
Lipno
Inowrocław
Włocławek
Gniezno
Września
Konin
Turek
Koło
Kutno
Płock
Wisła
(Vistula)

Bydgoszcz
Notec

O L A N D

Łowicz
Łęczyca
Łódź
Zduńska
Wola
Pabianice

Ława
Mława
Ciechanów
Pułtusk
Bug
Warszawa
(Warsaw)
Pruszków
Żyrardów
Skierniewice
Grójec
Otwock
Mińsk
Mazowiecki
Siedlce
Łuków
Międzyrzec
Podlaski
Biała
Podlaska
Brest
Zhabinka

Ostrów
Mazowiecka
Brańsk
Hajnówka
Czeremcha
Bereza

Ostrołęka
Łomża
Białystok
Volkovysk
Slonim
Shchara
Baranovichi
Bobruysk
Ptich

Gomel

Luninets
Pripyat
Dubrovitsa
▲316
Kalinkovichi

Olesnica
rocław
(Breslau)
Brzeg
Opole
Nysa

Zabrze
Gliwice
Chorzów
Bytom
Sosnowiec
Katowice
Kraków

P o l e s y e

Sarny
Uzh

Pinsk
Pripyat
Korosten
Kovel
Styr
Goryn
Sluch
Radomyshl
Kiyev
Borispol

Wieliczka
Bielsko-
Biała
Cieszyn

Tarnów
Częstochowa
Kielce
Ostrowied
Świetokrzyski
Sandomierz
Tarnobrzeg
San
390▲
Przeworsk
Dąbrowa Tarnowska
Rzeszów
Jarosław
Przemyśl

Vladimir
Volynskiy
Lutsk
Rovno
Dubno
Ostrog
Korets
Novograd-
Volynskiy
Shepetovka
Zhitomir
Fastov
Berdichev
Belaya Tserkov
Kazatin

Radom
Puławy
Kozienice
Koński
Piotrków
Trybunalsk
Tomaszów
Mazowiecki
Radomsko
Jędrzejów
Pinczów
Opatów
Lublin
Chełm
Zamość
Kraśnik

Sokal
Brody
Kremenets
Starokonstantinov

Kalisz
Ostrów
Wielkopolski
Wieluń

Krotoszyn
Warta

Nowy
Sącz
Jasło
Krosno
Dukelský Pr.
Sanok
Lvov
Gorodok
471▲
Zolochev
Ternopol
Khmelnitskiy
384▲
Vinnitsa

U. S. S. R.

UKRAINIAN

S. S. R.

Opava
Ostrava
Přerov
550▲
Frýdek-
Místek
Jablunkovsky Pr.
Žilina
Ružomberok
2655▲
1725▲
Západné Beskydy
Tatry
Vychodné Beskyd
4780
C a r p a
Drohobych
Borislav
Stryi
Jurka
Dnestr
Buchach
Chortkov
Zaleshchiki
Zhmerinka
Uman
Gottwaldov
Biele
Karpaty
Gvan
Nízké Tatry
Kremnica
Banská Bystrica
Zvolen
Slovenské Rudohorie
Banská Štiavnica
Lučenec
Košice
Prešov
502▲
Ivano-Frankovsk
Nadvornaya
1881▲
931▲
Kolomyya
Snyatyn
Kamenets-Podolskiy
Khotin
Maglev-Podolskiy
Dnestr
Pervomaisk
Bug

O V A K I A

SLOVAKIA

Nitra
Trnava
N.
Zámky
Hron
Salg
Sátoraljaújhely
Uzhgorod
Mukachevo
Beregovo
Khust
Tokaj
Bod
2061▲
Per Yablonitse
t
Chernovtsy
Storozhinets
Yedintsy
Soroki
Kotovsk

ratislava
Komárno
Gyor
Győr
Pápa
Tokaj
Miskolc
Eger
Mezőkövesd
Nyíregyháza
Hajdúböszörmény
Satu Mare
Sighet
Carei
Baia Mare
Pietrosul
2305▲
Radauti
Suceava
Vatra-Dornei
Dorohoi
Botoşani
Beltsy
Kishinev
429▲
Tiraspol
Benderi
MOLDAVIAN

Bakony
Veszprém
BUDAPEST
Újpest
Vác
Esztergom
Tatabánya
Hegyalja
Székesfehérvár
Hatvan
Jászberény
Gyöngyös
Szolnok
Karcag
Debrecen
Somes
Dej
Bistrita
2102▲
Pietrosul
Piatra-
Neamţ
Roman
Bîrlad
Vaslui
Iaşi
Prut
Kagul
Bolgrad
Belgorod-
Dnestrovskiy

Odessa

Balaton
Dunaújváros
Kecskemét
Kiskunfélegyháza
Cegléd
Nagykőrös
Mezőtúr
Oradea
Salonta
Negru
Cluj
Turda
Aiud
Tirgu
Mures
Praid
Odorhei
Miercurea
Ciuc
Bacău
Bretcu
Focşani
Tecuci
Galati
Brăila
467▲

U N G A R Y

HUNGARY

Kaposvár
Kalocsa
Kiskunhalas
Szeged
Mikó
Arad
Békéscsaba
Szentes
Hódmezővásárhely
Gyula
Crisul
Mţii Bihor
1848▲
Abrud
Brad
Sul Alb
Alba-Iulia
Medias
Sighişoara
Sfântu Gheorghe
Rîmnicu Sarat
Buzău
Buzau
Tulcea

T r a n s i l v a n i a

Pécs
Mohács
Batacsék
Baja
Subotica
Senta
Kikinda
Timişoara
Zrenjanin
(Petrovgrad)
Lugoj
Deva
Hunedoara
Simeria
Sibiu
Deva
Fǎgǎraş
Olt
Carpaţii   Meridionali
2535▲
Vf. Negoiu
Vl. Omul
2507▲
Braşov
Cîmpina
Ploieşti
Tîrgovişte
Ialomita
Cernavodă
Constanţa

SKA

Osijek
Drava
Novi Sad
Petrovaradin
Sremska
Mitrovica
Vrsac
Bečej
Bela Crkva
Caransebes
Reşita
Porta Orientalis
2509▲
2518▲
Peleaga
Parîngul Mare
Petroseni
350▲
P. Turnu Roşu
Câmpulung
Rîmnicu
Vîlcea
Pitesti
Arges
Dambovita
Bucureşti
(Bucharest)
Călăraşi
Silistra

R U M A N I A
RUMANIA

Brod
Odžak
Bosna
Bijeljina
Brčko
Tuzla
Zemun
Beograd
(Belgrade)
Pančevo
Smederevo
Požarevac
Orsova
Porțile de Fier
Mehadia
Turnu-
Severin
Jiu
Tirgu-Jiu
Slatina
Olt
Olteniţa
Giurgiu

NA
Tešanj
GOVINA
Travnik
Han Pijesak
1346▲
Valjevo
Bor
Timok
Negotin
Craiova
Caracal
Turnu
Măgurele
Zimnicea
Ruse (Ruschuk)

SEA

Mangalia

BLACK

SEA

UGOSLAVIA
YUGOSLAVIA
Sarajevo
Titova Užice
Čačak
Kragujevac
Ježevac
Vidin
Lom
Dunărea
(Danube)
Corabia

BULGARIA

Tolbukhin

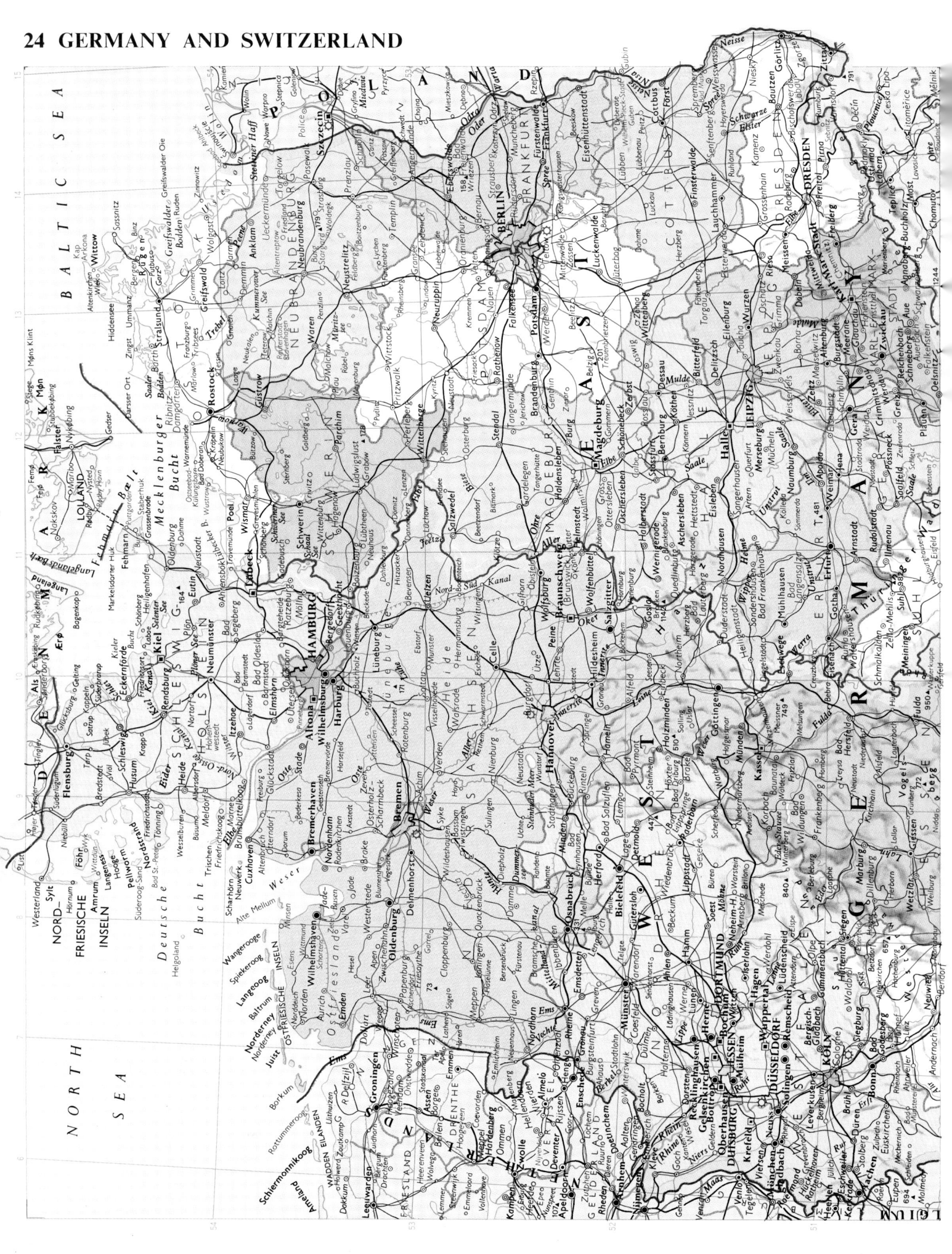

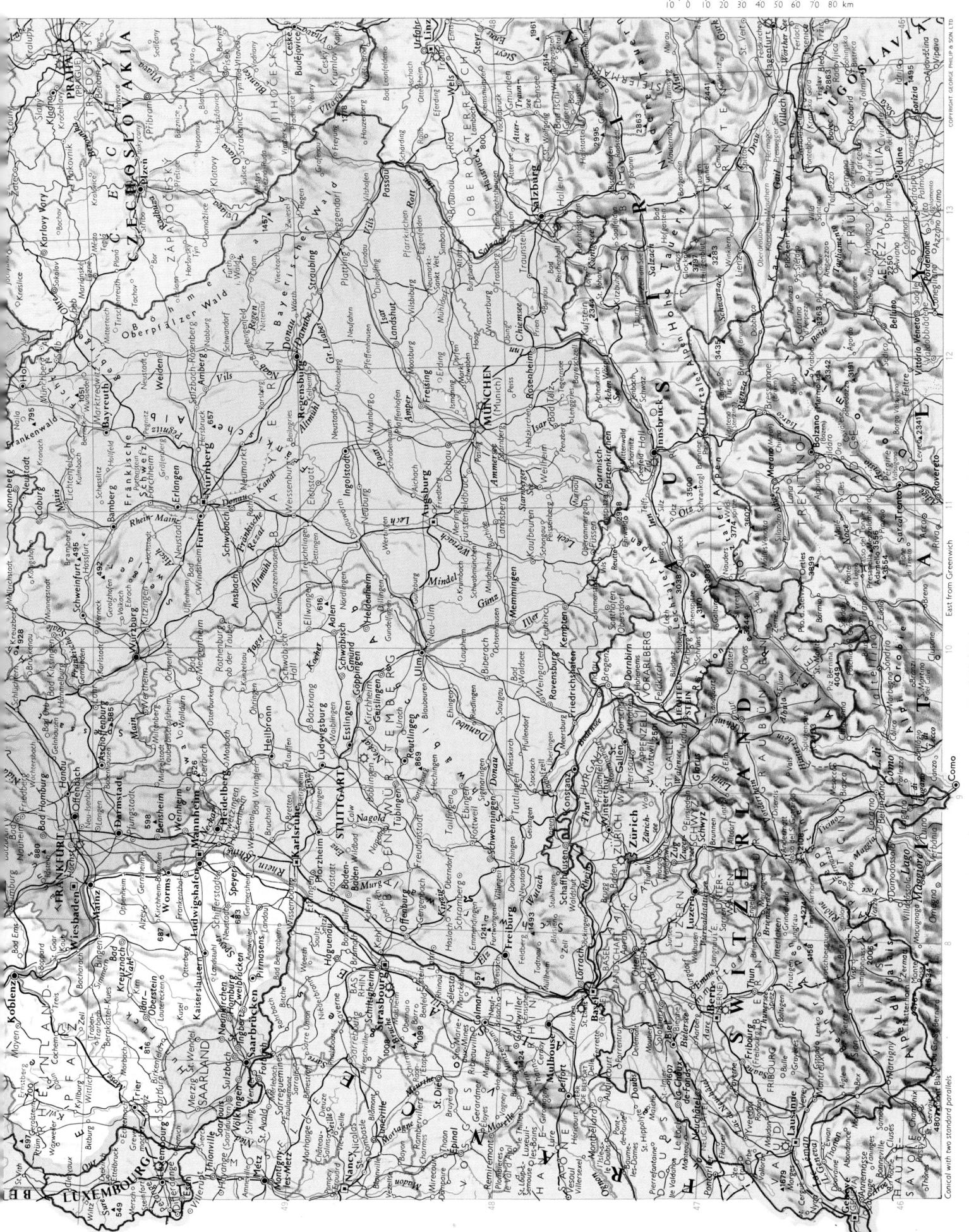

1:2 500 000

Conical with two standard parallels

East from Greenwich

1 : 2 500 000

```
10   0      10    20   30    40      50 miles
10  0  10  20  30  40  50  60  70  80 km
```

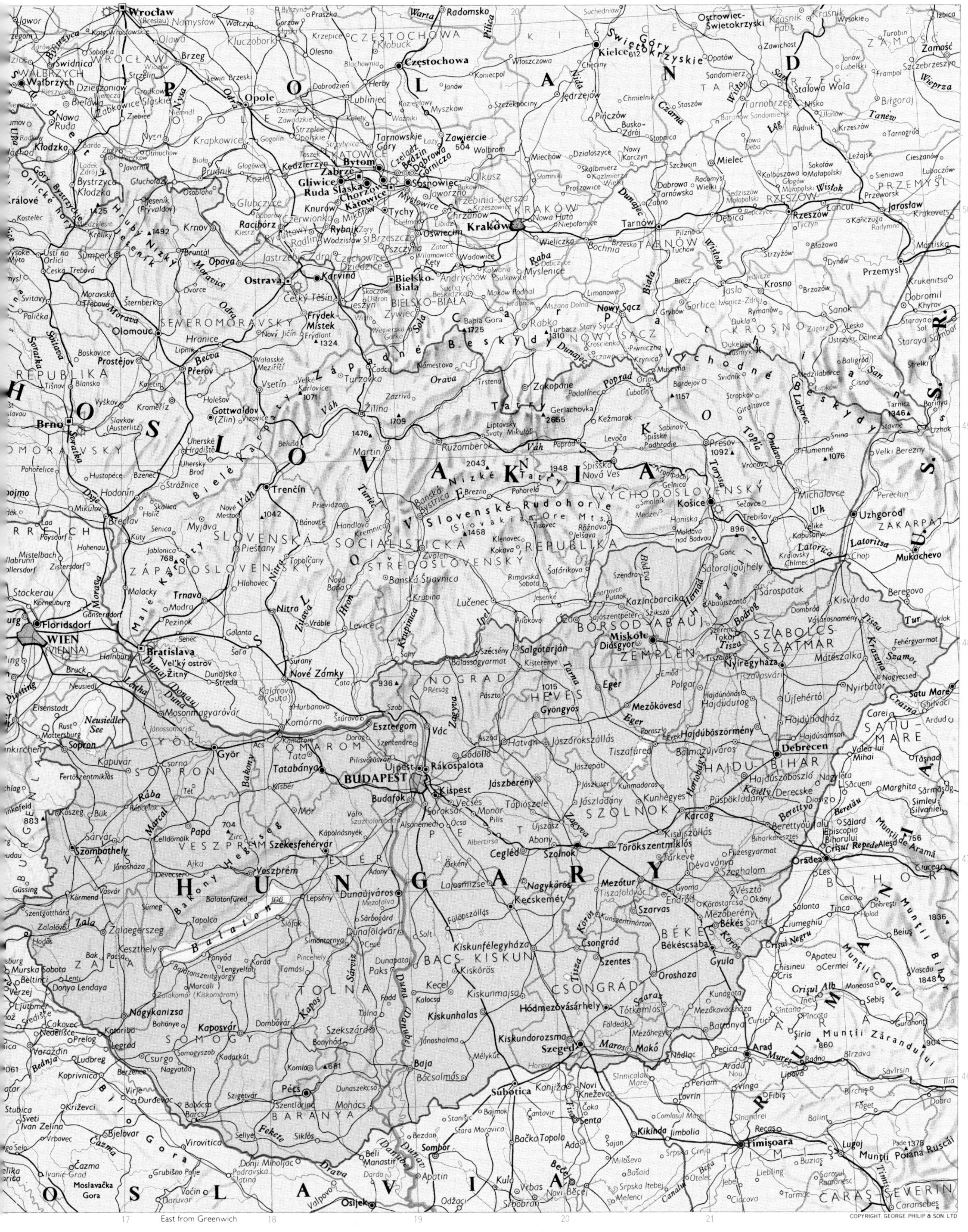

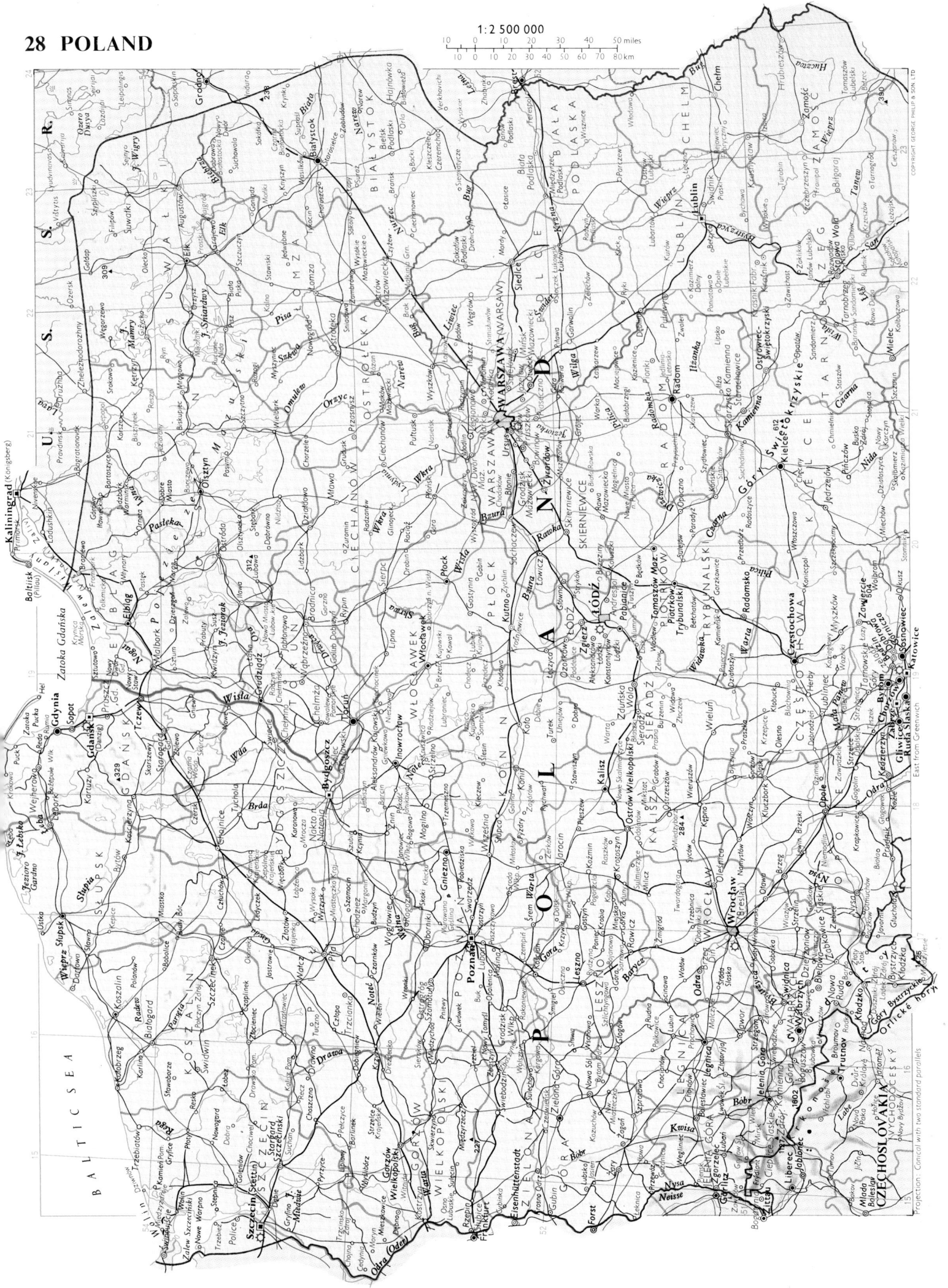

28 POLAND

1:5,000,000

50 0 50 100 miles

50 0 50 100 150 km

East from Greenwich

West from Greenwich

Projection: Conical with two standard parallels

FRANCE

ANDORRA

Pyrenees

SPAIN

PORTUGAL

ALGERIA

MOROCCO

GALICIA ASTURIAS VASCONGADAS NAVARRA ARAGON CATALUÑA CASTILLA LA VIEJA CASTILLA LA NUEVA MURCIA ANDALUCIA ESTREMADURA

MINHO TRAS OS MONTES ALTO DOURO DOURO LITORAL BEIRA ALTA BEIRA BAIXA BEIRA LITORAL RIBATEJO ESTREMADURA ALTO ALENTEJO BAIXO ALENTEJO ALGARVE

BAY of BISCAY

ATLANTIC OCEAN

MEDITERRANEAN SEA

Golfe du Lion

Golfo de Rosas

Golfo de Valencia

Golfo de San Jorge

Golfo de Cádiz

Islas Baleares Menorca Mallorca Ibiza Formentera Cabrera

Strait of Gibraltar

Sierra Nevada 3478

Cordillera Cantábrica

Sierra de la Demanda 2262

Sierra de Gredos 2592

Sierra Morena

Montes de Toledo

Mts. del Maestrazgo

Serranía de Cuenca

Sa. de Albarracín 2019

Toulouse Montpellier Béziers Narbonne Perpignan Bayonne Biarritz Pau Foix

Montpellier

San Sebastián Bilbao Vitoria Pamplona Logroño Soria Zaragoza Huesca Lérida Gerona Barcelona Badalona Sabadell Tarrasa Hospitalet Tarragona Tortosa Castellón de la Plana Valencia Alicante Elche Murcia Cartagena Lorca Almería Granada Guadix Jaén Linares Ciudad Real Albacete Cuenca Guadalajara MADRID Toledo Segovia Ávila Salamanca Valladolid Palencia Burgos León Zamora Oviedo Gijón Santander La Coruña Lugo Orense Pontevedra Vigo Santiago de Compostela El Ferrol

Córdoba Sevilla Jerez Cádiz Huelva Badajoz Cáceres Málaga La Línea de la Concepción Gibraltar (Br.) Ceuta (Sp.) Tanger Tetouán

Braga Porto Coímbra Lisboa Setúbal Évora Santarém Lagos Palma

Alger Boufarik Koléa Blida Khemis Miliana El Asnam Oran Mostaganem

C. Creus C. de Tortosa C. Nao C. de la Nao C. de Palos C. de Gata C. Finisterre C. Ortegal C. de Peñas C. de S. Vicente C. de S. Marfa Pta. de Europa C. Trafalgar C. Espichel

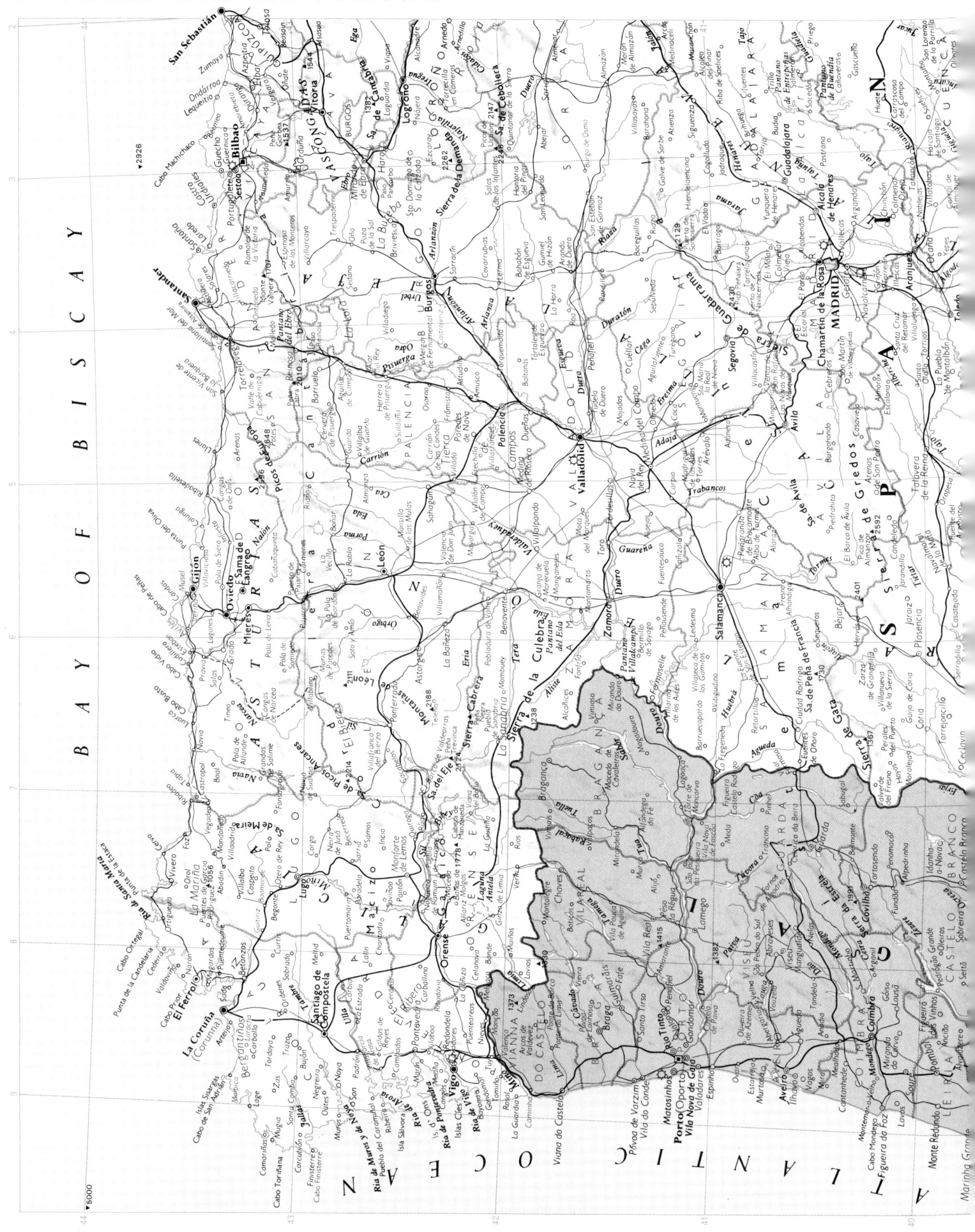

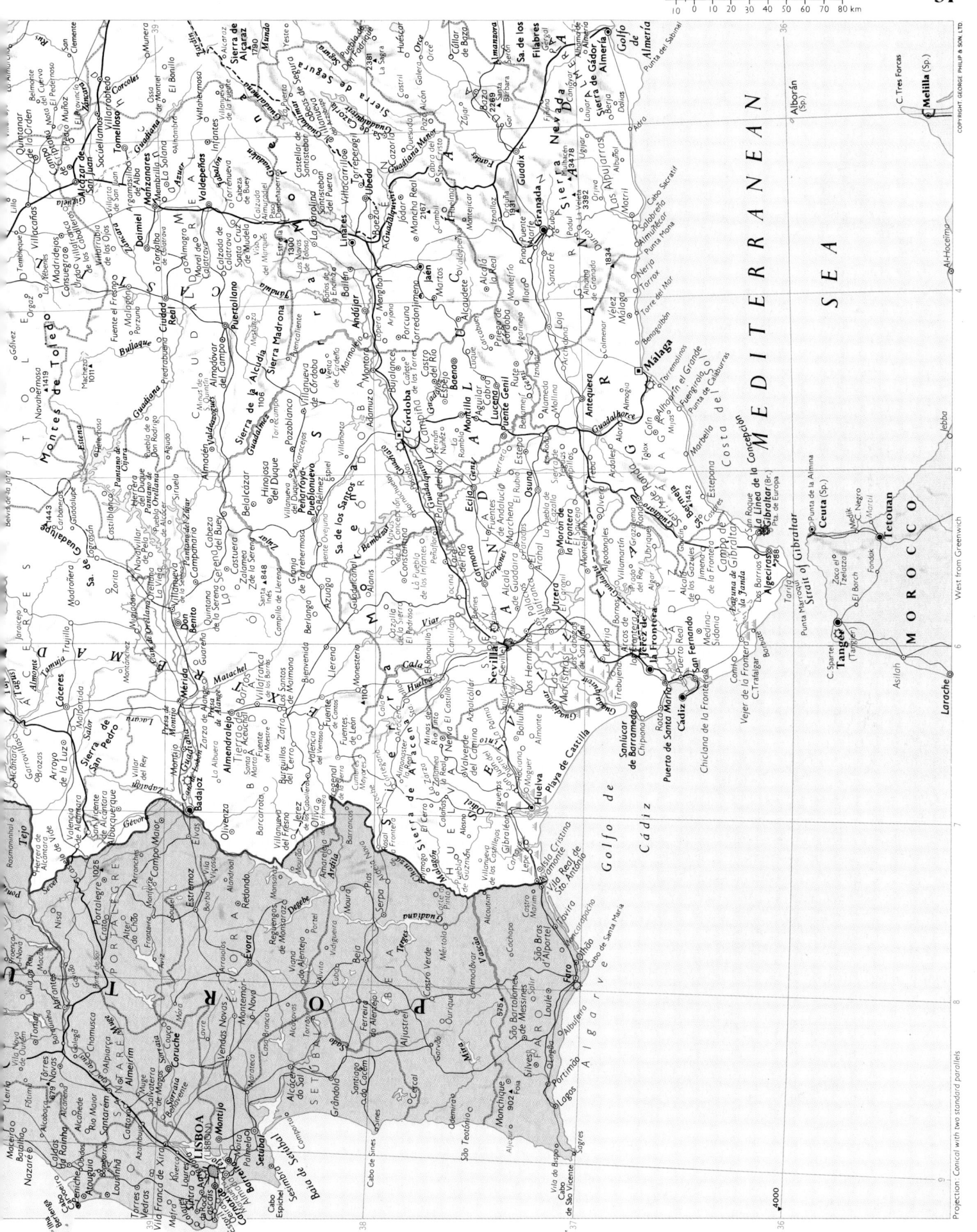

1:2 500 000

MEDITERRANEAN SEA

MOROCCO

Projection Conical with two standard parallels

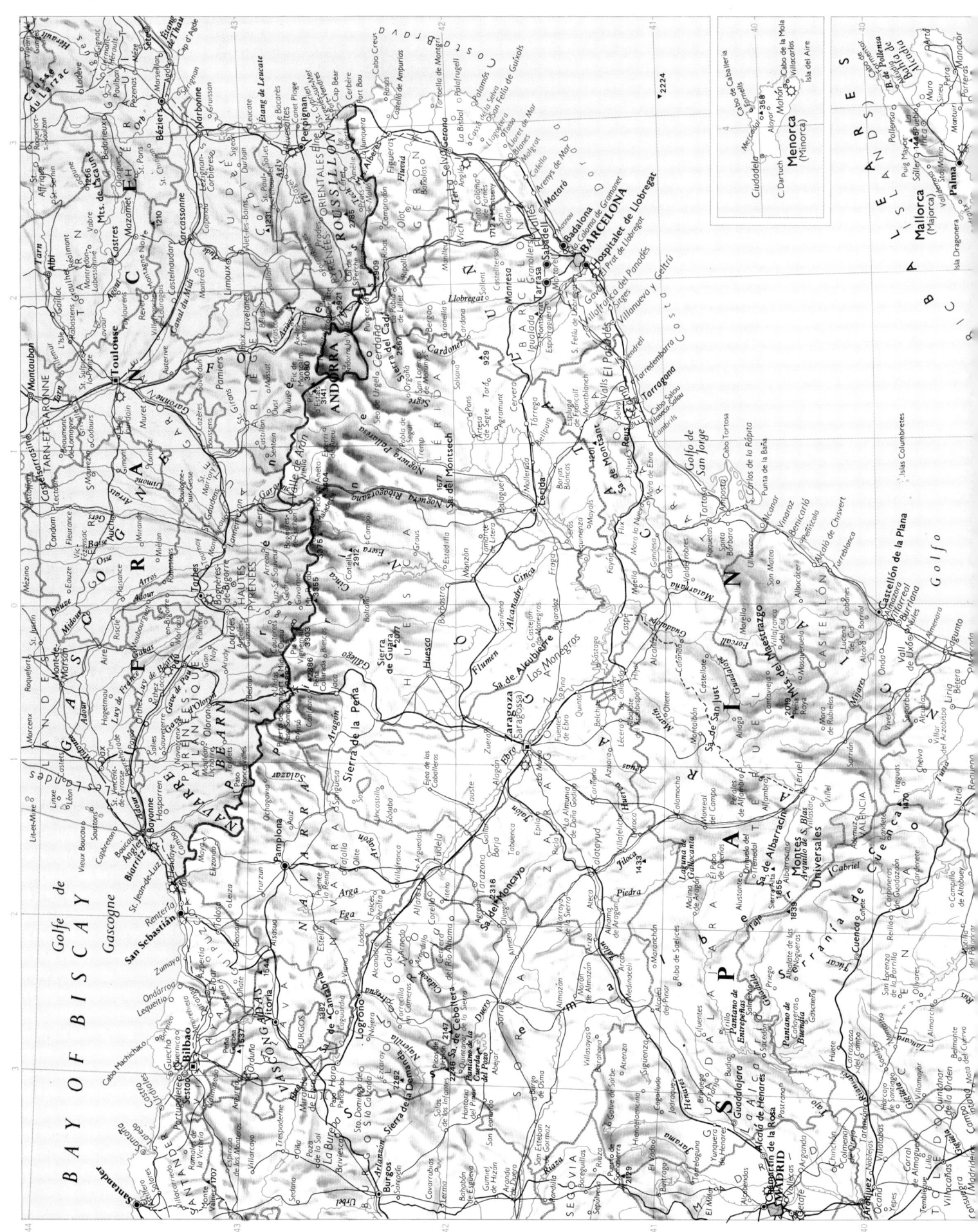

1 : 2 500 000

10   0   10   20   30   40   50 miles
10 0 10 20 30 40 50 60 70 80 km

COPYRIGHT GEORGE PHILIP & SON, LTD

East from Greenwich

West from Greenwich

Projection: Conical with two standard parallels

M E D I T E R R A N E A N   S E A

A L G E R I A

MOROCCO

ALGER (Algiers)
Boufarik
Blida
Koléa
Bou Ismail
El Arba
Médéa
Berrouaghia
Khemis Miliana
Miliana
Cherchel
Gouraya
El Asnam
Ténès
C. Kramis
Ain Tédelès
Tissemsilt
Zemmora
Ighil Izane
Tiaret
Mostaganem
Arzew
Mohammadia
Sig
Mascara
ORAN
Sidi-Bel-Abbès
Ain Témouchent
C. Caxine
C. Falcon
Misserghin
Beni Saf
Nedroma
Ghazzaouet
Nador
Melilla (Sp.)
Berkane
Kabr el Boukhari
Ksar-Chellala
Chabounia
Hamadia
Bir Toguine
Guelt es Stel
Tarfa
Sebou
Saïdia

VALENCIA
Valencia
Albufera de Valencia
Torrent
Alcira
Sueca
Cullera
Tabernes de Valldigna
Gandía
Oliva
Denia
Cabo de San Antonio
Jávea
Cabo de la Nao
Calpe
Benisa
Benidorm
Villajoyosa
Alcoy
Sa. de Alcoy
Alicante
Elche
Santa Pola
Isla de Tabarca
Elda
Petrel
Novelda
Aspe
Crevillente
Orihuela
Murcia
Cartagena
Cabo de Palos
Mar Menor
La Unión
San Pedro del Pinatar
Torrevieja
Guardamar del Segura
Cabo Cervera
Lorca
Totana
Aguilas
Golfo de Mazarrón
Puerto Mazarrón
Mazarrón
Cabo Cope
Cabo Tiñoso
Albacete
Yecla
Jumilla
Hellín
Chinchilla de Monte Aragón
La Roda
La Gineta
Montealegre
Almansa
Villena
Sax
Monóvar
Pinoso
Fortuna
Archena
Cieza
Calasparra
Caravaca
Cehegín
Mula
Bullas
Moratalla
Lorca
Cehegín
Tobarra
Sierra de Segura
Sierra de Alcaraz
Alcaraz
El Bonillo
Munera
Ossa de Montiel
Villarrobledo
Socuéllamos
Tomelloso
Argamasilla de Alba
Manzanares
Valdepeñas
Daimiel
Alcázar de San Juan
Villarrobledo
Villanueva de los Infantes
Ciudad Real
Puertollano
Sierra de Cazorla
Úbeda
Baeza
Jaén
Linares
Guadix
Granada
Sierra Nevada
Sierra de los Filabres
Sierra de Gádor
Almería
Golfo de Almería
Cabo de Gata
Adra
Motril
Albox
Cuevas del Almanzora
Vera
Garrucha
Mojácar
Huércal Overa
Baza
Huéscar
Orce
Vélez Rubio
Vélez Blanco

Ibiza (Iviza)
San Antonio Abad
San José
San Juan Bautista
San Miguel
Isla de Tagomago
Santa Eulalia
Isla del Espardell
Formentera
Punta de Cala Codolar
Cabo Berberia
San Francisco Javier
Isla del Vedra

B A L E A R E S

Bahía de Palma
Campos del Puerto
Cabo de Salinas
Cabo Blanco
Cabo de Berberia
Isla Conejera
Cabrera
Santany

2850

509
475
192
1985
1558
2167
3478
3392
1931
1125
1371
1204
2381
2043
2269
1884
1790

1:10 000 000

50   0   50   100   150   200 miles
50   0   100   200   300 km

BLACK SEA

MEDITERRANEAN SEA

AEGEAN SEA

Ionian Sea

Adriatic Sea

POLAND
Warszawa
Poznań
Łódź
Radom
Legnica
Wrocław
Lublin
Brest
Pinsk
Chorzów
Kraków
Kielce
Lvov
Przemyśl

CZECHOSLOVAKIA
Ostrava
Brno
Bratislava
Wien
Graz
Košice
Miskolc
Budapest

HUNGARY
Kecskemét
Pécs
Szeged
Debrecen
Oradea
Cluj
Arad

RUMANIA
Bucureşti
Ploieşti
Craiova
Braşov
Galaţi
Brăila
Constanţa

YUGOSLAVIA
Zagreb
Beograd
Novi Sad
Sarajevo
Niš
Skopje

BULGARIA
Sofiya
Plovdiv
Varna
Burgas

GREECE
Athínai
Thessaloníki
Pátrai
Piraievs

ALBANIA
Tirana
Durrës

TURKEY
İstanbul
Ankara
İzmir
Bursa
Konya
Adana
Kayseri
Antalya

CYPRUS
Lefkosia (Nicosia)

SYRIA
Halab
Hamā
Homs
Dimashq (Damascus)

LEBANON
Bayrût (Beirut)

ISRAEL
Tel Aviv-Yafo
Jerusalem
Haifa

JORDAN
Ammān

EGYPT
El Qâhira
El Iskandariya
Bûr Saîd
El Suweis

LIBYA
Banghâzi
Tobruq

U.S.S.R.
Kiyev
Kharkov
Rostov
Odessa
Volgograd
Krasnodar
Sevastopol
Simferopol

MOLDAVIAN
S.S.R.
Kishinev

COPYRIGHT. GEORGE PHILIP & SON. LTD.

1 : 2 500 000

CORSE

CORSICA

Iles Sanguinaires
G. d'Ajaccio
Petreto
Tartaro
Tinaudine
Zonza
2136
Levie
Favone
Solenzara
G. de Valinco
Propriano
Sartène
Porto-Vecchio
CORSE-DU-SUD
Iles Cerbicales
Bonifacio
I. de Cavallo
Bouches de Bonifacio
Maddalena
Santa Teresa Gallura
La Maddalena
Caprera
Punta dello Scorno
Pto. Cervo
Costa
Arzachena
Smeralda
Asinara
Golfo dell'
Asinara
Golfo Aranci
Coghinas
Aggius
Calangianus
G. di Olbia
Porto Torres
Tempio Pausania
1362
Tavolara
C. dell'Argentiera
Sorso
Sennori
M. Limbara
Olbia
Sassari
Osilo
L. di Coghinas
Fertilia
Ittiri
Oschiri
Posada
Alghero
Ozieri
Tanaunella
Villanova
Pattada
Buddusò
Monteleone
Borrova
1259
1150
Siniscola
Bosa
Bitti
C. Comino
Temo
Macomer
Orune
Dorgali
Nuoro
Oliena
Golfo di
Orosei
SARDEGNA
Ghilarza
L. del Tirso
Fonni
Baunei
C. Mannu
Sorgono
Monti del
C. di Monte Santu
SARDEGNA
Gennargentu
1834
Cabras
Tirso
Arbatax
Oristano
M. Arci
Laconi
Lanusei
Golfo di
812
Mannu
Jerzu
Oristano
Arborea
Terralba
Nurri
SARDINIA
Mandas
Flumendosa
Guspini
S. Gavino
Sanluri
Senorbì
C. Pécora
Monreale
Arbus
1236
Villacidro
S. Vitão
Villaputzu
Fluminimaggiore
M. Linas
Gonnosfanadiga
Serramanna
Muravera
Iglesias
Serbi
Dolianova
C. Ferrato
Portoscuso
Gonnesa
Siliqua
Sinnai
1069
Carloforte
Assemini
Sestu
Pta. Serpeddì
San Pietro
Carbonia
1116
Selargius
Quartu Sant'Elena
Sant'Antioco
Santadi
Cagliari
Serpentara
Sant'
Porto Botte
Golfo di
Antioco
Pula
Cagliari
C. Carbonara
G. di Palmas
Teulada
C. Spartivento

TYRRHENIAN

SEA

3719

3589

ROMA
(Rome)
Vatican City
Tivoli
Sabioco
Conca
del Fucino
Fregene
Palestrina
Trevi
Lido di Ostia
(Lido di Roma)
Alatri
Véroli
228
Prática
di Mare
Frascati
Ferentino
Arpino
Monte S. Giovanni
Albano
Anagni
Cisterna di Latina
Ceccano
Priverno
Frosinone
Aprilia
Sezze
Sonnino
Pontecorvo
Anzio
Latina
Cassino
Nettuno
Pontinia
Fondi
1533
Sabáudia
Formia
Sess
Monte Circeo
Terracina
Aurun
541
Gaeta
Minturno
Golfo di
Cariglia
Zannone
Gariglia
Mondragone
Palmarola
Ponza
Gaeta
Volturno
Isole
283
Casal di
Ponziane
Giuglian
Ventotene
788
Poz
Proci
Ischia
(Naples)

Ustica

Golfo
del Golfo
C. San Vito
C. Gallo
di Castellammare
Favarotta
PALERMO
Monreale
Terrasini
Levanzo
Trapani
1110
G. di Carini
Bagheria
Isole Egadi
Erice
Partinico
Misilmeri
Alcamo
S. Giuseppe
Maréttimo
Paceco
Jato
Marineo
Favignana
Calatafimi
Comparesle
Belsito
Favignana
Salemi
Corleone
1613
Mado
Stagnone
Gibellina
Lercara
Alia
Marsala
Partanna
Prizzi
Frido
Bisacquino
Castelvetrano
Sambuca
SICIL
Mazara
di Sicilia
Caterin
del Vallo
Burgio
Mussomeli
Villalem
Menfi
Campobello di
Belice
Sciacca
Platani
San Cataldo
Sicilian Channel
Cattolica Eraclea
Ribera
Racalmuto
Caltanis
Roffadali
Siculiana
Canicatti
Porto Empédocle
Agrigento
Favara
Nara
Son
Palma di Montechiaro
Campobello di Licata
Licato
Ravanus

Iles de la
Galite

Bizerte
(Binzert)
C. Blanc
Cani
C. Serrat
Menzel-Bourguiba
Plane
Mateur
Zembra
Golfe de Tunis
C. Bon
El Kala
Tébourba
TUNIS
Kelibia
Tabarka
Halq el Oued
(La Goulette)
ALGERIA
Bou Salem
Béja
Medjerda
Menzel
Temime
Mejier
Soliman
Pantelleria
Pantelleria
Nabeul
Melléq
Téboursouk
836 (lt.)
Hammamet
TUNISIA
Zaghouan
MEDITE

1319

Malte

1:2 500 000

10 0 10 20 30 40 50 miles

10 0 10 20 30 40 50 60 70 80 km

A D R I A T I C

S E A

I O N I A N

S E A

Golfo di Táranto

Strait of Otranto

ABRUZZI

MOLISE

I T A L I A

BASILICATA

CALABRIA

SICILIA

NAPOLI

G. di Napoli

G. di Salerno

G. di Policastro

Golfo di Sant'Eufémia

Golfo di Squillace

G. di Gióia

Golfo di Gela

Isole Eólie o Lípari (Æolian Is.)

L. di Lésina

G. di Manfredónia

Bari

Taranto

Brindisi

Lecce

Cosenza

Catanzaro

Réggio di Calábria

Messina

Catánia

Siracusa

ALBANIA

TIRANA

DURRĒSI

ELBASANI

BERATI

VLORA

Tirana (Tiranë)

Durrēs (Durazzo)

Vlora (Valona)

Kérkira (Corfu)

M E D I T E R R A N E A N   S E A

Malta Channel

COPYRIGHT GEORGE PHILIP & SON LTD

1:2 500 000

10 0 10 20 30 40 50 miles
10 0 10 20 30 40 50 60 70 80 km

R A N S I L V A N I A

CLUJ

Turda · Ludus · Band · Tîrgu Mures · Sovata · Praid · Frumoasa · Bacău · Moinești · Pîrjinea · Crasna · Vutcani · Leova · Volintirovka

Ariès · Turzii · Mures · Corund · Muntii Harghita · 1523 · Muntii Vrancei · Vaslui · Komrat

Mtii Trăscău · Micăsasa · Mures · Miercurea Ciuc · Nemira 1648 · Tîrgu Ocna · Adjud · Bîrlad · Murgeni · Fălciu

1438 · Aiud · Tîrnava Mare · Sighișoara · Odorhei · Sînmartin · Gheorghe Gheorghiu-Dej · Chadyr-Lunga

ALBA · Alba-Iulia · Blaj · Medias · Dumbrăveni · COVASNA · Cîmpuri · Panciu · Tecuci · UKRAINIAN S.S.R.

Sebeș · Seica Mare · Soars · Sfîntu Gheorghe · Vidra · Mărăsești · Cudalbi · Bolgrad · Ozero Yalpukh · Ozero Kitai · Ozero Sasyk

Mercurea · Nocrich · Agnita · 1105 · VRANCEA · Focșani · Liești · Reni · Kiliya · Vilkovo

Sibiu · Olt · Făgăraș · 1783 · Odobești · Siret · Galați · Dunay (Danube) · Bratul Chilia · Ostrov Letea

Muntii Făgăraș · Negoiu 2535 · Moldoveanu · Rîmna · Rîmnicu Sărat · Buzău · Brăila · Măcin · 467 · Tulcea · Bratul Sulina · Sulina

Cîmpulung · Omul 2507 · Sinaia · 1956 · BRĂILA · Dunăvătu de Sus · Sfîntu Gheorghe

R O M Â N I A · PRAHOVA · Buzău · DOBROGEA · Babadag · Lacul Razelm · Ostrov Dranov

Rîmnicu Vîlcea · Tîrgoviste · Ploiesti · Buzău · Hîrsova · Lacul Sinoe

VÎLCEA · ARGES · DÎMBOVITA · IALOMITA · Cernavoda

Pitesti · **V A L A H I A (W A L A C H I A)** · **BUCURESTI (Bucharest)** · Călărasi · Dunărea (Danube) · Medgidia · Siut Ghiol · Constanța

Craiova · ILFOV · Silistra · Eforie Sud

DOLJ · TELEORMAN · Alexandria · Giurgiu · Ruse (Ruschuk) · Tutrakan · DOBRUDJA · Mangalia

Lom · Turnu Măgurele · Zimnicea · Razgrad · Tolbukhin (Dobrich Bazargic) · Shabla (Šabla)

Nikopol · Svishtov · Dve Mogili · Kolarovgrad (Šumen) · Novi Pazar · Balchik · Kavarna (Carvana)

Pleven · Byala · Popovo · Tûrgovishte · Provadiya · Varna

B U L G A R I A · Lovech · Sevlievo · Tûrnovo · Preslavska Planina · Golyama Kamchiya · **B L A C K**

Vratsa · Troyan · Gabrovo · Elena · Kotlenska Pl. · Stara Planina (Balkan) · Obzor · **S E A**

Sofiya (Sofia) · Sredna Gora · Kazanlûk · Sliven · Burgaski Zaliv · Burgas

Plovdiv (Philippopolis) · Stara Zagora · Nova Zagora · Yambol · Sozopol

Velingrad · Asenovgrad · Khaskovo · Maritsa · Topolovgrad · Michurin (Tsarevo)

Smolyan · Rodopi · Kûrdzhali · Istranca Daglari · Rezovo

Iztochni Rodopi · Momchilgrad · Edirne (Adrianople) · KIRKLARELI · Midye

DRAMA · Nestos · Xanthi · Komotini · **T U R K E Y** · Saray · TEKIRDAĞ · İSTANBUL · Üsküdar

G R E E C E · SERRAI · Lüleburgaz · Çorlu · Karadeniz Boğazı (Bosporus)

U.S.S.R. · IZMAIL · Ismail · Kagul

COPYRIGHT GEORGE PHILIP & SON LTD

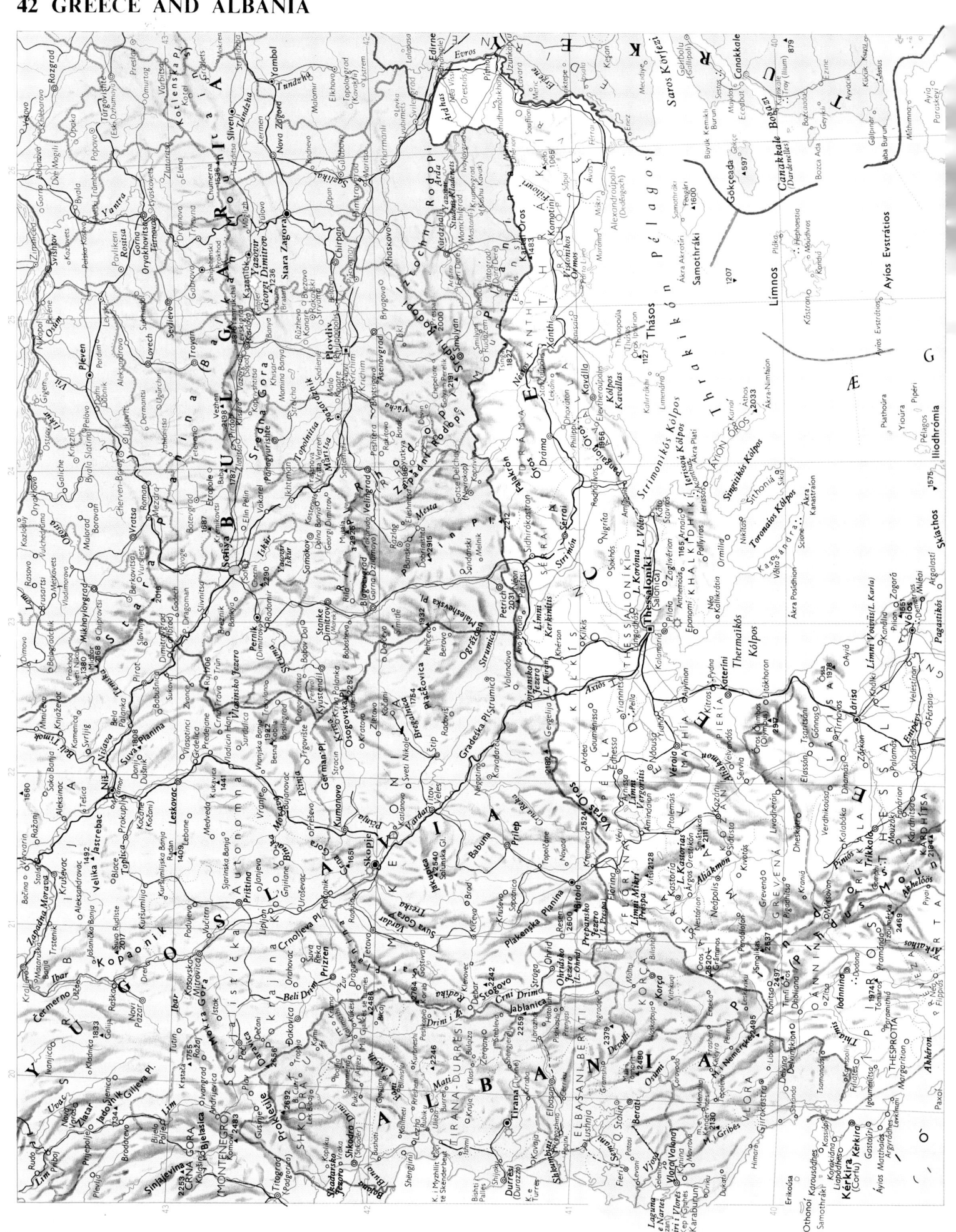

1:2 500 000

10   0   10   20   30   40   50 miles

10   0   10   20   30   40   50   60   70   80 km

Mitilíni
Pýrrha
Ayiásos
968 1212
Plomárion
Kólpos Kallonís
(Lesbos)
Eressós
Kara Burun
Oinousa
Kardhámila 1297
Volissós
Khíos (Chios)
Ákra Mastikho
Psará

Ikaría
Foúrnoi
Áyios Kirikos
Fódhele
1262
Melíssa 951
822
Dhenoúsa
Amorgós
Astipálaia
Astipálaia
Khamilonísion

S E A

Andípsara
Skópelos
Kaloyeroi

Mikonos
Dhragonísi
Dhilos
Ríni
Náxos
Náxos 1001
Íos
Íos
Koronís
Skhoinoúsa
Káros
Koufonísia
Anídhros
Anáfi
Makrá

Ándros
Ándros

Tinos
Tínos

Síros
Síros (Ermoúpolis)
Páros
Páros 706
Andíparos
Dhespotikó
Síkinos
Folégandros
Thíra
Thirasía
Khristianá

Skíros
Skíros 792
Valáxa

Megálo Petáli
Kéa
Kéa 560
Kíthnos
Kíthnos
Dhirós
Sérifos
Sérifos
Sífnos
Sífnos
Kímolos
Kímolos
Polaíogos
Mílos
Mílos 751
Andímilos
Andínes

S E A   O F   C R E T E
(Sea of Candia)

Iráklion (Candia)
Día
Knossós

K R I T I   (C R E T E)

Khersónisos
Akrotíri
Kólpos Soúdhas
Khaniá
Réthimnon
2456
Ídhi Oros 2453
Spíli
Timbákion
Kólpos Mesarás
Ákra Líthinon
Paximádhia
Gávdhopoúla
Gávdhos

Ierápetra

Sitía

1476

N O R T H E R N   S P O R A D H E S

Vóriai Sporádhes (Northern Sporades)
Perístera
Skántzoúra

Skópelos
Skópelos
Ayía Anna
Mandoúdhion
Límni

Khalkís (Chalcis)
1743
Kími
Oxílithos
Alivérion
Okhi Oros 1398
Káristos
Ákra Kafiréis

Lamía
Límni Xinías
Dhomokós
Sperkhiós
Stilís
Lárimna
Atalándi
Livanátai
Livadhiá
Orkhomenós
Thívai (Thebes)
Erithraí
Mégara
Elevsís
Pendelikón
ATHÍNAI (ATHENS)
Piraiévs (Piraeus)
Kallithéa
Salamís
Aíyina
Saronikós Kólpos
Mégalo
Markoúpoulon
Lávrion
Kératea
Soúnion
Ákra Soúnion

B O I O T I A

A T T I K I

Pátrai
Aíyion
Kórinthos (Corinth)
Corinth Canal
Nemea
Mikínai (Mycenae)
Árgos
Návplion
Argolikós Kólpos

Néa Epídhavros
Palaiá Epídhavros
Méthana
Póros
Galatás
Ídhra
Ídhra
Ermióni
Dhokós
Spétsai
Spétsai

P E L O P O N N I S O S

Olimbía
Pírgos
Alfeós
Megalópolis
Parnon Oros 1935
Taíyetos Oros 2407
Spárti (Sparta)
Evrótas
Lakonía
Lakonikós Kólpos
Ákra Maléa

Kíthira (Cérigo)
Kíthira
Ákra Kapéllo
Potamós

A R K A D H I A

Kiparissiakós Kólpos
Kiparissía
Pílos
Methóni
Sapiéntza
Messíni
Kalámai
Messiniakós Kólpos
Koróni
Ákra Akrítas
Venétiko

M E S S I N I A

Ithaki (Ithaca)
Ákra Skinári
Zákinthos (Zante)
Zákinthos

Kefallinía (Cephalonia)
Argostólion
Póros
Lixoúrion

Levkás (Santa Maura)
Préveza
Nicópolis
Actium

I O N I A N   I S L A N D S

I O N I A N   S E A

A I T O L I A
A K A R N A N I A
Agrínion
Mesolóngion
Pátraikós Kólpos

Andíparos
Stroffádhes

Continuation Eastwards on same scale

S A M O S
Sámos
Marathókambos
Foúrnoi

Kuşadası
Kuşadası Körfezi
Samsun Dağı
Ephesus
Söke
1229
Aydın
Aydın Dağı
Bozdoğan
Besparmak Dağı 1367

T W O D I N
B O Z D A Ğ

1412
Yatağan
Oren
Muğla
1175
Marmaris
1215
Ródhos (Rhodes)
Ródhos
Atávíros 1215

M U Ğ L A

Kerme Körfezi

Bodrum (Halicarnassus)
Kara
1175
Sími
Sími
Mandalya Körfezi
Mílas
Akköy

Pátmos
Léros
Kálimnos
Kálimnos
Kos
Kos 846
Yalí
Nísiros
Tílos (Piscopi)
Alimniá
Khálki

D H E K A N I S O S (D O D E C A N E S E)

Léros
Lipsoí
Farmakonísi
Myrtiás
Kálolímnos

Astipálaia
Sírna
Livítha

Megálo Khorió
Nísiros

Stenón Karpáthos

Kárpathos
Kárpathos
Sária
1215
Pigádhia
Posídion
Ákra Kastéllou

Kásos
Kásos

Stenón Kásos

East from Greenwich

1 : 2 500 000

10   0   10   20   30   40   50 miles
10 0 10 20 30 40 50 60 70 80 km

BALTIC SEA

POLAND

GERMANY

Gotland
Visby

KALMAR LÄN
Kalmar
Öland
Oskarshamn
Nybro

Norrköping
Linköping
Mjölby
Motala
ÖSTERGÖTLAND

JÖNKÖPINGS LÄN
Jönköping
Nässjö
Huskvarna
Värnamo
Växjö
KRONOBERGS LÄN

BLEKINGE LÄN
Karlskrona
Karlshamn
Ronneby

KRISTIANSTADS L.
Kristianstad

MALMÖHUS L.
Malmö
Lund
Landskrona
Helsingborg
Trelleborg
Ystad

Bornholm
Rønne

SKARABORGS LÄN
Skövde
Lidköping
Falköping
Mariestad

ÄLVSBORGS LÄN
Borås
Alingsås
Vänersborg
Trollhättan
Uddevalla

GÖTEBORGS OCH BOHUS
Göteborg
Mölndal
Kungsbacka

HALLANDS LÄN
Halmstad
Falkenberg
Varberg

Vänern

Vättern

Kattegat

Skagerrak

Skagen
Frederikshavn
Sæby

Ålborg
NORDJYLLANDS AMT
Hjørring
Thisted
Nykøbing
Brønderslev

Ålborg Bugt

Læsø
Anholt

VIBORG AMT
Viborg
Skive
Struer
Holstebro

RINGKØBING AMT
Ringkøbing
Herning
Ikast

ÅRHUS AMT
Århus
Randers
Silkeborg
Djursland
Grenå

VEJLE AMT
Vejle
Kolding
Horsens
Fredericia

RIBE AMT
Esbjerg
Varde

SØNDERJYLLANDS AMT
Haderslev
Åbenrå
Sønderborg
Tønder

FYN
Odense
Svendborg
Nyborg
Middelfart
Fåborg

SJÆLLAND
København
Roskilde
Helsingør
Hillerød
Frederikssund
Køge
Næstved
Slagelse
Ringsted
Holbæk
Kalundborg

STORSTRØMS AMT
Vordingborg
Nykøbing
Nakskov

LOLLAND
FALSTER
Maribo

VESTSJÆLLANDS AMT

DENMARK

Store Bælt

Øresund

Limfjorden

Flensburg
Schleswig
Husum
Kiel
Rendsburg

Kieler Bucht
Fehmarn

Rügen
Hiddensee

Stralsund
Rostock

Slupsk
Słupsk

Norge

Nyköping
Oxelösund

Finspång

East from Greenwich

Projection Conical with two standard parallels

COPYRIGHT GEORGE PHILIP & SON, LTD.

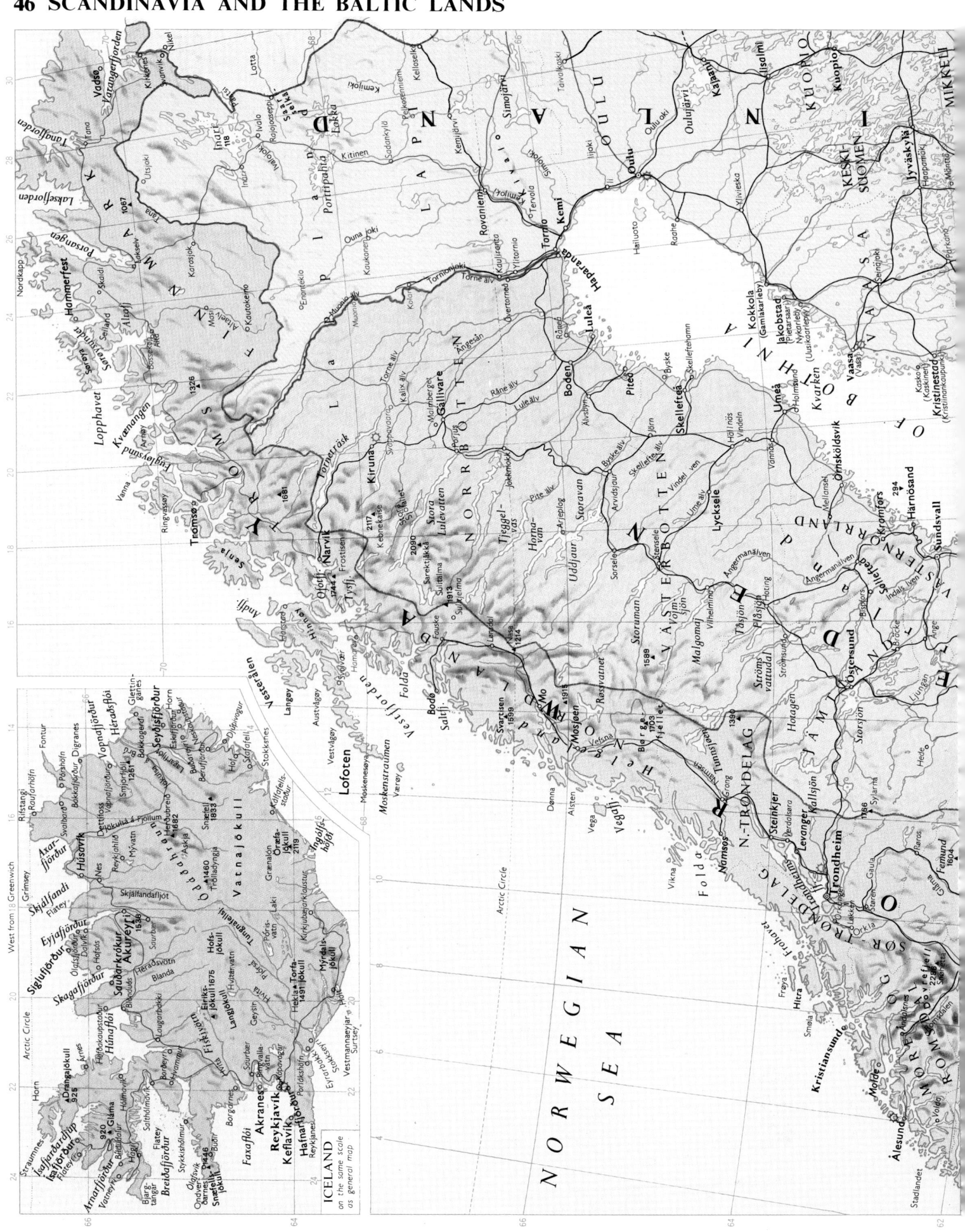

NORWEGIAN SEA

ICELAND
on the same scale
as general map

1:5 000 000

20 10 0   40   60   80   100 miles
40   20   0   40   80   120   160 km

COPYRIGHT GEORGE PHILIP & SON, LTD.

BALTIC SEA

GULF OF FINLAND

GULF OF BOTHNIA

FINLAND

Mikkeli Heinola Lahti Kotka Loviisa Kouvola
Hämeenlinna Tampere HELSINKI (Helsingfors)
TURUN JA PORIN HÄME Pori Rauma Uusikaupunki
Turku (Åbo) Hangö (Hanko) Tallinn

ESTONIA S.S.R.
Rakvere Valga Haapsalu Pärnu Viljandi Valmiera Cēsis
Hiiumaa (Dagö) Saaremaa (Ösel) Kingisepp Kärdla

LATVIA S.S.R.
Riga Rīgas Jūras Līcis (Gulf of Riga) Jelgava Ainaži
Ventspils Kuldīga Liepāja Tukums

LITHUANIA S.S.R.
Vilnius Kaunas Klaipėda Telšiai Šiauliai
Sovetsk Kaliningrad Chernyakhovsk

R.S.F.S.R.

POLAND
Grodno Białystok Łomża Ostrołęka Suwałki Olsztyn
Elbląg Gdańsk Gdynia Grudziądz Toruń Bydgoszcz
Zatoka Gdańska Malbork Chełmno Chojnice Słupsk
Koszalin Kołobrzeg Szczecin (Stettin)

SWEDEN
Hudiksvall Söderhamn Bollnäs Gävle Sandviken
Mora Falun Borlänge Hedemora Avesta Fagersta
STOCKHOLM Uppsala Västerås Eskilstuna Södertälje
Nyköping Norrköping Oxelösund Örebro Kumla
Karlstad Arvika Filipstad Kristinehamn Karlskoga
Motala Linköping Mjölby Skövde Falköping
Jönköping Nässjö Huskvarna Tranås Vetlanda
Västervik Oskarshamn Kalmar Nybro Växjö Ljungby
Karlskrona Karlshamn Kristianstad Simrishamn
Ängelholm Helsingborg Landskrona Malmö Lund
Trelleborg Ystad Halmstad Varberg Falkenberg
Borås Mölndal Göteborg Alingsås Trollhättan
Vänersborg Lidköping Mariestad Uddevalla Strömstad

Gotland Visby Gotska Sandön Fårö Öland Borgholm

NORWAY
Bergen Haugesund Kopervik Stavanger Sandnes
Egersund Flekkefjord Farsund Kristiansand Mandal
Lillesand Grimstad Arendal Risør Kragerø Skien
Larvik Sandefjord Tønsberg Horten Moss OSLO
Drammen Kongsberg Hønefoss Gjøvik Hamar
Lillehammer Kongsvinger Halden Fredrikstad Sarpsborg

SOGN OG FJORDANE HORDALAND ROGALAND VEST-AGDER
AUST-AGDER TELEMARK BUSKERUD OPPLAND HEDMARK
AKERSHUS ØSTFOLD VESTFOLD

Galdhøpiggen 2468 Glittertind 2481 Jotunheimen

DENMARK
Hjørring Ålborg Frederikshavn Thisted Viborg
Randers Århus Silkeborg Herning Holstebro
Ringkøbing Esbjerg Ribe Vejle Horsens Fredericia
Kolding Åbenrå Haderslev Sønderborg Odense
Svendborg Nyborg Korsør Slagelse Roskilde
KØBENHAVN Helsingør Nykøbing Nakskov Maribo

Sjælland Fyn Lolland Falster Møn Bornholm Rønne

Limfjorden Skagerrak Kattegat The Sound Store Bælt
Lille Bælt Anholt Læsø

GERMANY
Flensburg Kiel Lübeck Hamburg Rostock Schwerin
Wismar Stralsund Greifswald Bremen Bremerhaven
Wilhelmshaven Oldenburg Verden Lüneburg Itzehoe
Rügen Usedom Wolin

NETHERLANDS
Groningen Emden

East from Greenwich
Projection Conical with two standard parallels

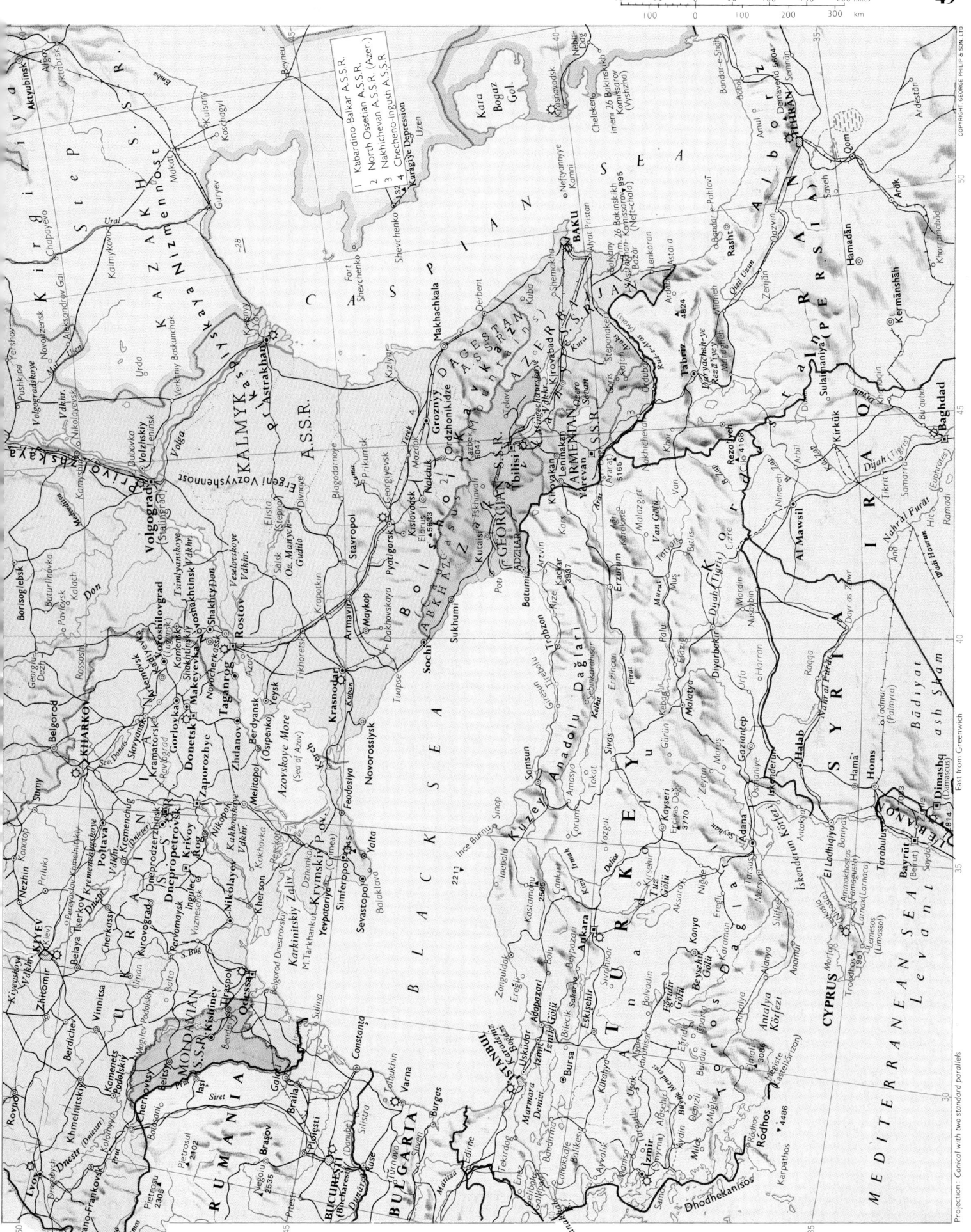

1:10 000 000

49

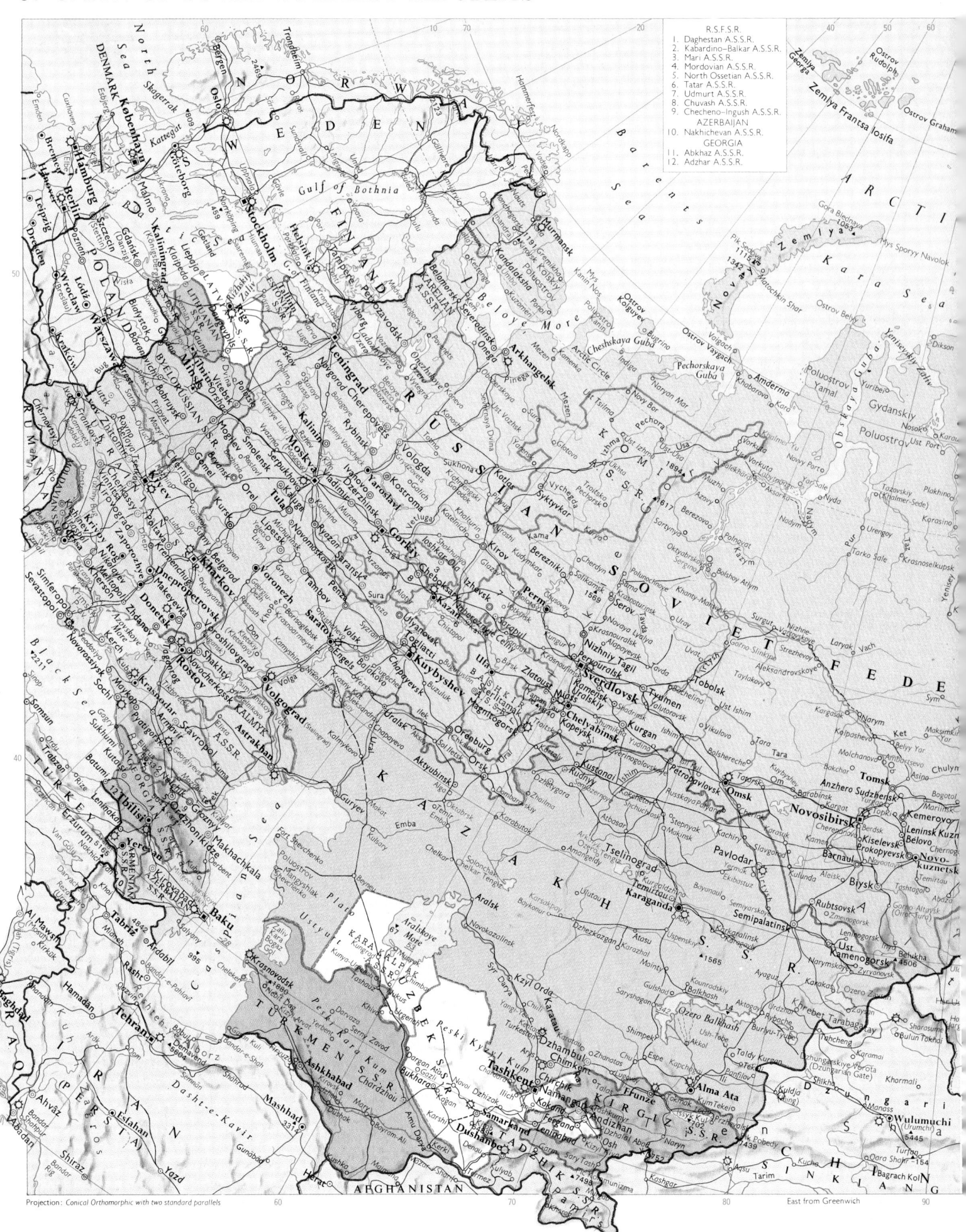

R.S.F.S.R.
1. Daghestan A.S.S.R.
2. Kabardino–Balkar A.S.S.R.
3. Mari A.S.S.R.
4. Mordovian A.S.S.R.
5. North Ossetian A.S.S.R.
6. Tatar A.S.S.R.
7. Udmurt A.S.S.R.
8. Chuvash A.S.S.R.
9. Checheno–Ingush A.S.S.R.
AZERBAIJAN
10. Nakhichevan A.S.S.R.
GEORGIA
11. Abkhaz A.S.S.R.
12. Adzhar A.S.S.R.

Projection: Conical Orthomorphic with two standard parallels

East from Greenwich

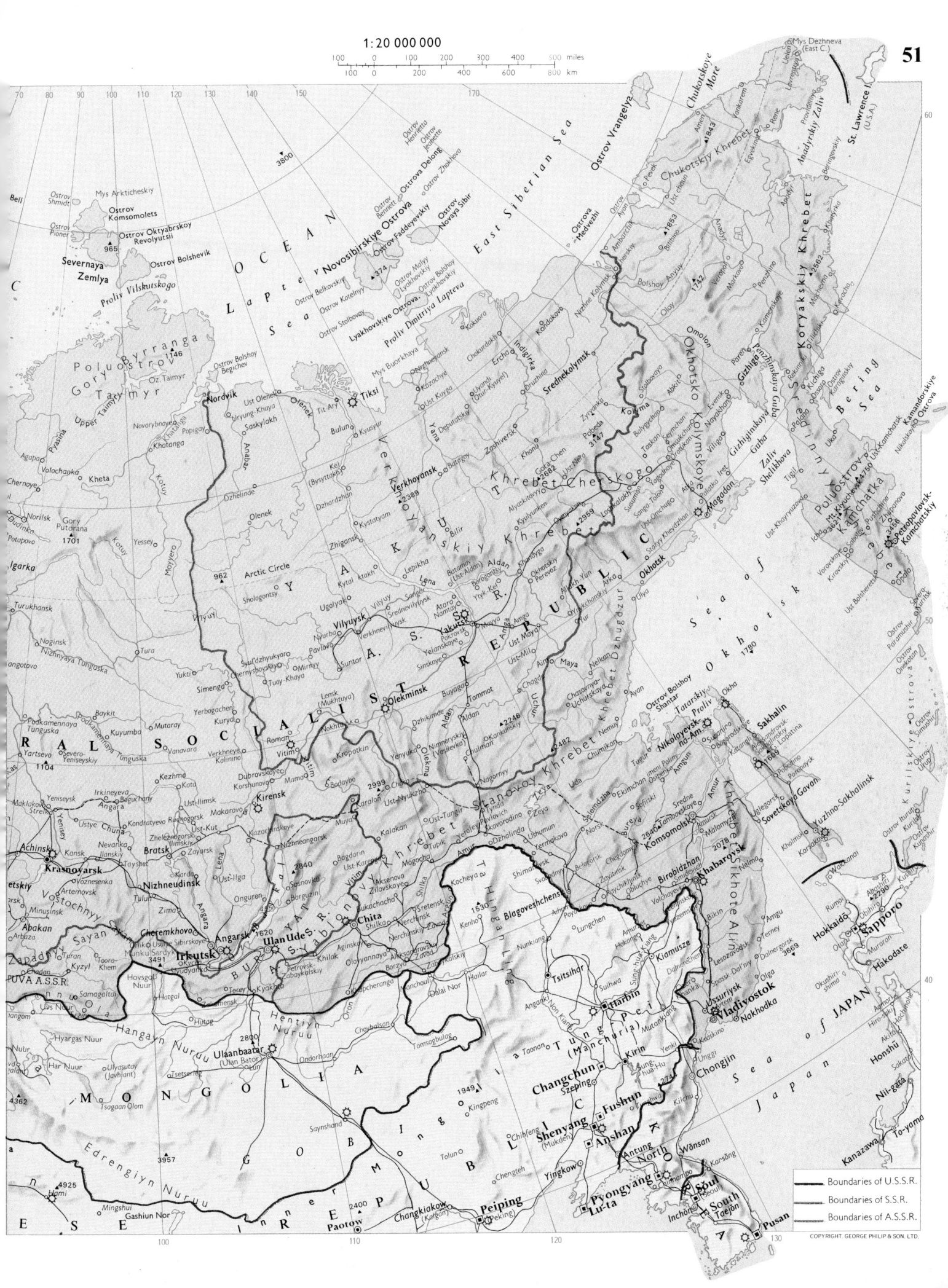

1:50 000 000

250   0   250   500   750   1000 miles
250   0   500   1000   1500   km

PACIFIC OCEAN

ARCTIC OCEAN

INDIAN OCEAN

Aleutians
Bering Sea
Kamchatka Peninsula
Gydan Ra. (Kolyma)
Kolyma
Indigirka
New Siberian Is.
Verkhoyansk Range
Lena
Olenek
Central Siberian Plateau
Taimyr Peninsula
Khatanga
Yenisei
Lower Tunguska
Angara
Severnaya Zemlya
Laptev Sea
Chelyuskin
Kara Sea
Novaya Zemlya
Barents Sea
Kolguyev
Kola Pen.
White Sea
North Cape
N. Dvina
Scandinavia
Finland
Baltic Sea
Svalbard
Greenland
Iceland
British Isles
North Sea
Rhine
Elbe
Oder
Vistula
Danube
Carpathians
North European Plain
Central Russian Uplands
Dnepr
Don
Volga
Ural
Ural Mountains 1640
West Siberian Plain
Ob
Irtysh
Tobol
Narodnaya 1894
Obskaya
Altai
Bukhtarma 4506
Sayan Mts
Selenga
Baikal
Yablonovy Ra.
Stanovoy Ra.
Amur
Manchurian Plain
Great Khingan Mts
Plateau of Mongolia
Koko Nor
Tarim
Takla Makan
Turfan Basin
Tien Shan
Pamirs 7495
Kommunizm Pk.
Hindu Kush
Karakoram Ra. 8611
Kunlun Shan
Plateau of Tibet
Everest 8882
Himalaya
Tsangpo
Brahmaputra
Ganga
Yamuna
Thar
Sulaiman Ra.
Indus
Helmand
Hari Rud
Plateau of Iran
Turan Plain
Amu Darya
Syr Darya
Chu
Ili
L. Balkhash
Aral Sea
Caspian Sea
Elburz Mts.
Demavend
Great Salt Desert
Zagros
Tigris
Euphrates
Mesopotamia
Persian Gulf
G. of Oman
Arabian Sea
Rub al Khali
Arabia
Arabian Peninsula
Red Sea
G. of Aden
Socotra
C. Guardafui
Somali Peninsula
Ras Asir
Caucasus 5633
Elbruz
Black Sea
Bosporus
Ararat 5165
Anatolia Plat.
Taurus Mts.
Cyprus
Mediterranean Sea
Adriatic Sea
Dead Sea
Syrian Desert
Sinai Pen.
Suez Canal
Nile
Libyan Desert
Lake Tsana
Amirantes
Seychelles
Chagos Arch.
Equator
Maldive Is.
Laccadive Is.
C. Comorin
Ceylon
Polk Strait
Gulf of Mannar
Western Ghats
Eastern Ghats
Deccan
Narmada
Godavari
Krishna
India
Bay of Bengal
Andaman Is.
Nicobar Is.
Irrawaddy
Salween
Menam
G. of Siam
Malay Peninsula
Str. of Malacca
Sumatra
Sunda Is.
Sunda Str.
Java
Java Sea
Java Sea
Borneo
Kinabalu 4101
Sulu Sea
Palawan
South China Sea
Hainan
Si-kiang
Tong-king
G. of Tonkin
Mekong
Hong (Red)
Yangtze
Great Plain of China
Hwang
Si Chuan
China
Yellow Sea
Korea
Korea Str.
Sea of Japan
Japan
Hokkaido
Honshu
Shikoku
Kyushu
East China Sea
Ryukyu Is.
Formosa
Tropic of Cancer
Luzon
Mindanao 10 497
Philippine Is.
Palew Is.
Caroline Is. 11 022
Guam Is.
Cape Johnson
Bonin Is.
Kurili Is. 10 542
Sakhalin
Okhotsk
Sea of Okhotsk
La perouse Str.
Sikhote Alin Ra.
Sredneru Ra.
Bering Str.
C. Dezhnev
Wrangel I.
Molucca
Halmahera
Celebes
Celebes Sea
Makasar Strait
Moluccas
Ceram
Banda Sea
Flores
Timor
Bali
Arafura Sea
New Guinea
Australia
Menam
m / ft elevation legend

1 : 50 000 000

250   0   250   500   750   1000 miles
250   0   500   1000   1500   km

COPYRIGHT GEORGE PHILIP & SON LTD.

Projection Bonne

East from Greenwich

PACIFIC OCEAN

ARCTIC OCEAN

INDIAN OCEAN

U. S. S. R.

CHINESE REPUBLIC

INNER MONGOLIA

MONGOLIA

SINKIANG UIGUR

TIBET

INDIA

PAKISTAN

AFGHANISTAN

IRAN (PERSIA)

IRAQ

SAUDI ARABIA

TURKEY

SYRIA

ISRAEL

JORDAN

EGYPT

LIBYA

SUDAN

ETHIOPIA

SOMALI REP

KENYA

TANZANIA

ZAIRE

ZAMBIA

MALAWI

BURMA

THAILAND (SIAM)

VIETNAM

CAMBODIA

LAOS

MALAYA

INDONESIA

PHILIPPINES

AUSTRALIA

JAPAN

KOREA

N. KOREA

S. KOREA

NEPAL

BANGLADESH

BHUTAN

SRI LANKA (CEYLON)

KASHMIR

OMAN

UNITED ARAB EMIRATES

QATAR

BAHRAIN

KUWAIT

YEMEN

SOUTH YEMEN

SINGAPORE

BRUNEI

SABAH

SARAWAK

TIMOR

MANCHURIA

UNITED KINGDOM

ICELAND

E U R O P E

A F R I C A

Cities: London, Paris, Roma, Berlin, Warszawa, Wien, Beograd, Thessaloniki, Istanbul, Ankara, Izmir, Bursa, Athinai, Leningrad, Moskva, Odessa, Rostov, Arkhangelsk, Murmansk, Volgograd, Astrakhan, Orenburg, Sverdlovsk, Chelyabinsk, Magnitogorsk, Omsk, Novosibirsk, Barnaul, Semipalatinsk, Tomsk, Krasnoyarsk, Irkutsk, Chita, Kyakhta, Ulaanbaatar (Ulan Bator), Yakutsk, Khabarovsk, Vladivostok, Komsomolsk, Nikolayevsk, Petropavlovsk, Sapporo, Hakodate, Hokkaido, Tokyo, Yokohama, Nagoya, Kyoto, Osaka, Kobe, Kitakyushu, Kyushu, Nagasaki, Pusan, Seoul, Pyongyang, Dairen, Peiping, Tientsin, Tsingtao, Shenyang (Mukden), Changchun, Harbin, Nanking, Shanghai, Wuhan, Soochow, Foochow, Canton, Hong Kong, Macau, Hainan, Chengtu, Chungking, Siangtan, Sian, Lanchow, Lhasa, Kashgar, Khotan, Yarkand, Urumchi (Wulumuchi), Hovd, Tashkent, Samarkand, Bukhara, Khiva, Alma Ata, Ashkhabad, Krasnovodsk, Baku, Tbilisi, Yerevan, Tabriz, Tehran, Esfahan, Shiraz, Mashhad, Herat, Kabul, Kandahar, Quetta, Peshawar, Karachi, Hyderabad, Ahmadabad, Bombay, Goa, Madras, Pondicherry, Calcutta, Hyderabad, Lahore, Delhi, Agra, Kanpur, Lucknow, Allahabad, Varanasi, Simla, Calicut, Colombo, Baghdad, Al Basrah, Kuwait, Damascus (Dimashq), Bayrut, Tripoli (Tarabulus), Halab, Jerusalem, Al Madinah, Makkah (Mecca), Muscat, Bandar e Bushehr, Zahedan, Gwadar, El Qahira, El Iskandariya, Aswan, El Khartum, El Obeid, Suakin, Djibouti, Zeila, Berbera, Hargeisa, Mogadishu, Obbia, Addis Abeba, Harer, Nairobi, Mombasa, Dar es Salaam, Rangoon, Mandalay, Myitkyina, Hanoi, Hue, Vientiane, Saigon, Phnom Penh, Bangkok, Kuala Lumpur, George Town, Kuching, Manila, Davao, Zamboanga, Jakarta

Seas and water bodies: Bering Sea, Sea of Okhotsk, Laptev Sea, Kara Sea, Barents Sea, Baltic Sea, Black Sea, Caspian Sea, Aral Sea, Mediterranean Sea, Red Sea, Arabian Sea, Bay of Bengal, Persian Gulf, G. of Oman, G. of Aden, South China Sea, Yellow Sea, East China Sea, Sea of Japan, Java Sea, Celebes Sea, Sulu Sea, Banda Sea, Molucca Sea, North Sea

Islands: Svalbard, Novaya Zemlya, Severnaya Zemlya, Franz Josef Land, Wrangel I., Aleutian Is., Kuril Is., Sakhalin, Ryukyu-retto, Taiwan (Formosa), Hainan, Luzon, Mindanao, Palawan, Borneo, Sumatra, Java, Sulawesi, Ceram, Halmahera, Maluku (Moluccas), New Guinea, Irian Jaya, Caroline Is., Guam, Andaman Is. (India), Nicobar Is. (India), Lakshadweep (India), Maldive Is., Amirantes, Seychelles, Socotra

Rivers: Lena, Ob, Yenisey, Amur, Aldan, Angara, Irtysh, Tobol, Ural, Volga, Don, Dnieper, Danube, Rhine, Syr Darya, Amu Darya, Tigris, Euphrates, Nile, Indus, Ganges, Brahmaputra, Godavari, Narmada, Mekong, Irrawaddy, Tarim, Yangtze Kiang, Hwang Ho

Tropic of Cancer

Equator

Arctic Circle

Limit of ice (Spring)

1:1 000 000

10   10   20 miles
10   0   10   20   30 km

1949–1967 Armistice lines between
Israel and the Arab States.

LEBANON

SYRIA

Sūr (Tyre)

Qiryat Shemona

BIRKET RAM
Massada
Under
Israeli
Occupation

An-Nāqūrah
Kefar Rosh Haniqra
Sulam Tsor
Bezet
Hanita
Shomera

Nahariyya
Ben 'Ammi
1208
Zimri
Kefar Szold
Qiryat Bialik

HAIFA
Qiryat Yam
Qiryat Ata
Tirat Karmel

Hag alil (Galilee)

TEL HAZOR

KEFAR NAHUM (CAPERNAUM)

Yam Kinneret (Sea of Galilee)
Tiberias -209

'ATLIT
546

Nazareth

Degania

4515

El Hamma
Um Qeis

MEGIDDO
'Afula

Irbid

QESARI (CAESAREA)
Or 'Aqiva

Jenin

Emeq Dotan

1198

Netanya

Shomron (Samaria)

SAMARIA
940
Nabulus
SHECHEM
JACOB'S WELL
888

1247
Suf
Jarash
Al Madwar
Al Mafraq

TEL ARSHAF
Herzliyya
Ramat HaSharon

Under
Israeli
JORDAN

Er Rumman
Az-Zarqa'

TEL AVIV-YAFO (Jaffa)
Ramat Gan
Petah Tiqwa
Bat Yam
Holon
Rishon Le Zion
Nes Ziyyona
Ramla
Rehovot

SHILO
1113

Occupation
As Salt
'AMMAN

Ashdod

Rām Allāh
El Arīhā (Jericho)

TEL GEZER

JERUSALEM (Yerushalayim, Al Quds)
Bayt Lahm (Bethlehem)
BURAK SULAYMAN (SOLOMON'S POOLS)
QUMRAN

Ashqelon

Qiryat Gat
BET GUVRIN
TEL LAKHISH

1020
Hebron

Gaza Strip
Gaza
Khān Yūnis

Be'er Sheva'

MESADA

EGYPT

Projection: Conical with two standard parallels

East from Greenwich

MEDITERRANEAN SEA

(DEAD SEA) YAM HAMMELAH

Continuation Southwards
1:2 500 000

Gaza Strip
Gaza
Khān Yūnis

Hebron
Be'er Sheva'
Dimona
SHIVTA

ISRAEL

H a   n e g e v

1035
Mizpe Ramon
Makhtesh Ramon

Under
Israeli

PETRA
1727

EGYPT

Occupation
Elat
Al 'Aqaba

0   10   20 miles
0   10   20   30 km

COPYRIGHT. GEORGE PHILIP & SON. LTD.

1:15 000 000

100   0   100   200   300   400 miles
100   0   100   200   300   400   500   600 km

LEBANON   SYRIA
Bayrūt   Dimashq (Damascus)
Haifa
ISRAEL
Tel Aviv-Yafo
Jerusalem   Amman
Gaza
Bûr Sa'îd
El 'Arîsh
El Qantara
Ismâ'ilîya
El Suweis   Under Israeli
(Suez)   Occupation   Gebel el Tîh
Es Sinâ
2637   2578
JORDAN
Ma'ān
'Aqaban   Elat
Tabūk
1128   ash Shâm
TRANS ARABIAN
Turayf
Rutba
IRAQ
Baghdad
Al Jazîra
Al Hadîtha
Al Hilla
Karbalâ   Kut Dujra
An Nâsirîya
An Nafûd
Dûmat al Jandal (Al Jawf)
Rafhâon
OIL PIPELINE (TAPLINE)
Badanah
Hafar al Bâtin
Al Wari'ah
Abu Hadrîya
KUWAIT
AL Kuwayt (Kuwait)
Al Fao
Bubiyan
Failaka
Umm Qasr
Al Basrah
Abadan
Ahvāz
Bandar-e Mashur
Esfahān   4548
Yazd
IRAN (PERSIA)
Dasht-e Lūt
Kermān
Zābol
AFGHANISTAN
Shīrāz   4419   Kuh-e Hazār
Bam
Bāft   Zābol

Dezfūl   Masjed Soleymān
Borūjerd
Kāshān
Ardestān
Khvar
Shahrizā

EGYPT
Aswân
Esnā
Idfu
Kôm Ombo
(Luxor) El Uqsur
Qenā
Sadd el Aalî   1st Cataract
Buheiret en Naser (Lake Nasser)
2nd Cataract
Wadi Halfa
Es Sahrâ en Nûbiya
(Nubian Desert)
3rd Cataract   El Kab
Argo   Abu Dis
Delgo
Abri
Kareima
Merowe
Korti
Dongola
4th Cataract
Berber
Atbara
Ed Dâmer
Shendi
Omdurmân   El Khartûm Bahrî
El Khartûm (Khartoum)
Wâd Hamid
5th Cataract
Kassala
El Geteina
El Kamlin
Wâd Medanî
Sennar
Singa
Gedaref
SUDAN
KORDOFAN
El Obeid
Er Rahad
Rashad
Kaka
Kôsti
Ed Dueim
Umm Dam
Renk
Gelhak
Melut
Tungaru
Kodok
Malakal
A'ÂLÂ EN NÎL
Abwong
Fangak
Kongor
Pibor P.
Nasir
Bôr
Yirol
Tali P.
EL ISTWÂ'YA
Jûba
Kaju Kaji
Torit
ZAIRE   Nimule
UGANDA

RED SEA
Rās Bânâs
Qulan
Bîr Shalatein
Hā'il
Halaib   2216
Rās Hadarba
Rās Abu Shagara
Muhammad Qôl
Bûr Sûdân (Port Sudan)
2635
Suakin
Sinkat
Trinkitat
Tokar
Derudub
Musmar
Karora   2780
Adarama
Nakfa
Akordat
Keren
Barentu
Asmera (Asmara)
Adwa
Aksum
Mekele
Adigrat
Ras Dashen 4620
Debark
Gonder
Metema
Gallabat
L. Tana
Debre Tabor
Dase (Dessye)
Debre Markos
Debre Sina
4154   Mota
Denbecha
Talo

SAUDI-ARABIA
Taimâ
Al Muwaylih
Qal'at al Akhdar
Madâ'in Sâlih
Tābah
Buraidah
'Unaizah
Az Zilfi
Al Majma'ah
Shaqra'
Ar Riyad (Riyadh)
Duwadami
Dafina
Hariq
Sulaimiya
Hilla
1143   Ghail
Laila
Al Ubailah
Ar Rab' al Khâlî
Al Ayn al Mugshin
W. Hamdh
Hodiya
Umm Lajj
Al Madînah
Yanbu' al Bahr
1814
Rabigh
Mastura
Jiddah
Makkah (Mecca)   2565
At Ta'if
Turaba
Al Lith
Dhurm
Khurm
Ad Dam
Tamra
Qasr Hamam
Na'ifah

TRANS ARABIAN
HIJAZ
'ASIR
Al Qunfidha
Hali
Abhā
Dhahran
Aba Saud
Jazâ'ir Farasân
Qizân
Sa'dah   3200
Khamir
Al Matamma
Marib
3600   Sana
Dhamar
Ibb   Ta'izz
Zabid
Hodeida
Hanish
Loheia
Kamaran
Mukeiras
3200
Mukha

YEMEN
SOUTH YEMEN
Shibâm
Al Houta
Inat al Milah
Dhula   2469
Saihut
Mukalla
Ras al Kalb
5143
Haura
Shuqra
Zinjibar
Ahwar
Al 'Adan (Aden)
Madînat al Shaab
Perim
Bâb al Mândeb

HADHRAMAWT
W. Masila
Ghubbat al Qamar
Shisur   1678
Marbat
Salâlah
Jazâ'ir Khūryān Mūryān

OMAN
ZUFÂR
Al Juwara
Al Jazir
Al Khalaf
Al Masîrah
Masqat (Muscat)   2151
Sūr   3019
Matrah
Wudhūm
Miskin
Al Khābūrah
Sohar
Al Buraimi
Abu Dhabi
UNITED ARAB EMIRATES
TRUCIAL STATES
Dubai
Sharjah
Kalbā
2057   Oman
Gābrik
Bandar 'Abbās
Minab
Khāmir
Band-e Nakhilu
Jāsk
Bampūr

PERSIAN GULF
BAHRAIN   102
QATAR
Doha
Musay'id
Ad Dammam
Dhahran
Al Hufūf
Al Uqair
Hofuf
Umm az Zamul
Yibal
Al Hasa
Safaniya
Manifa
Ra's al Khafji
Qatif

Gulf of Oman

Tropic of Cancer

ETHIOPIA
Addis Abeba (Addis Ababa)
Gimbi
Nekemte
Sire
Gedo
Dembi Dolo
Gore
Majji
L. Zwai
Asela
3381   Harar
Dire Dawa
Awash
Harer
Shala
Gobā   4307
Ginir
L. Abaya
Chencha
Soda
Arba Minch
L. Shamo
Gidole
Burji
Negele
Yabelo
Arero
El Niybo
Chew Bahir
L. Stefanie
Mega
Moyale
Dolo
Lugh Ganana
Bulo Burti

SOMALI REPUBLIC
Burao
Hargeisa
Berbera
Borama
Zeila
Djibouti
DJIBOUTI
Tendaho
Tadjoura
Erigavo   2406
Bosaso (Bender Cassim)
El Gal
Alula
Bereda
Ras Asir (C. Guardafui)
Bargal
Candala
Las Khoreh
Karin
Bulhar
'Abd al Kūrī   1503
Socotra (South Yemen)   Hadibu
Las Anod
Degeh-Bur
Sasabeneh
Warandab
Imi
Kebri Dehar
Geriogubi
Werder
Gelladi
Galcaio
Ghelinsor   5824
Iddan
Domo
Wardere
Welwel
Galladi
Obbia
Wabi Shebele
Kelafo
Ferfer
Dusa Mareb
Sinadogo
Harardera
Belet Uen
El Dere
Mahaddei Uen
Afgoi
Warsciek
Mogadiscio (Mogadishu)
Merca
Bardera
Brava
Bur Acaba
Isha Baidoa
Adale

INDIAN OCEAN

Gulf of Aden

KENYA
L. Turkana
North Horr
Marsabit
Wajir
Habaswein
Dif
El Wak
Buna

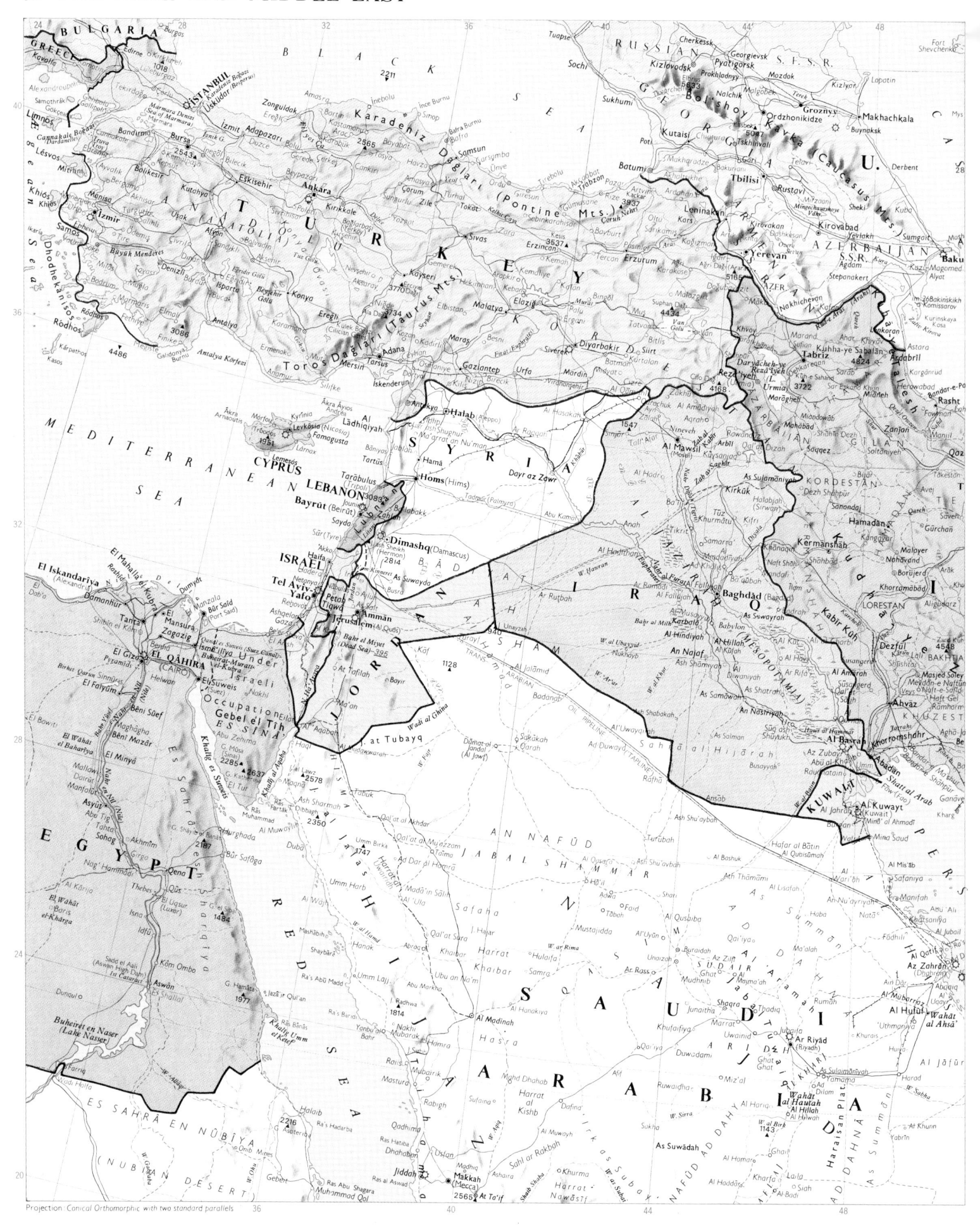

Projection: Conical Orthomorphic with two standard parallels

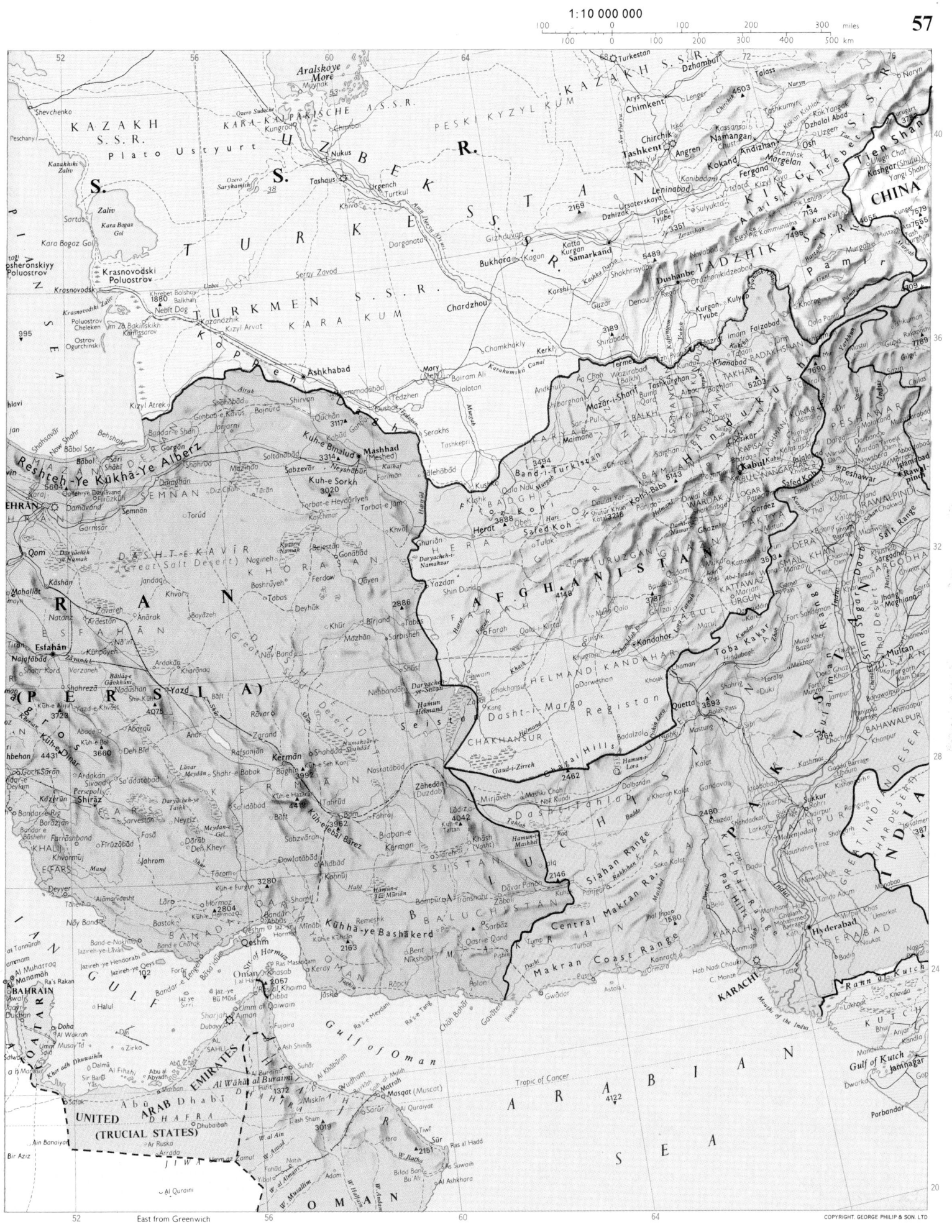

1:10 000 000

100   100   0   100   200   300   miles
100   0   100   200   300   400   500 km

KAZAKH S.S.R.

S.   U Z B E K   S. S. R.

Plato Ustyurt

Peschany

Kazakhski Zaliv

Sortas

Kara Bogaz Gol

Aralskoye More
Muynak

KARA-KALPAKISCHE A.S.S.R.

Nukus

Tashaus

PESKI KYZYL KUM

KAZAKH S.S.R.

Turkestan

Chimkent

Chirchik   Tashkent   Angren   Namangan

Arys

Lenger

KIRGIZ S.S.R.

Talass

Naryn

TIEN SHAN

CHINA

Kashgar (Shufu)
Yangi Shahr

T U R K M E N   S. S. R.

K A R A   K U M

Ashkhabad

I R A N   (P E R S I A)

A F G H A N I S T A N

Kabul

P A K I S T A N

I N D I A

A R A B I A N   S E A

P E R S I A N   G U L F

Gulf of Oman

OMAN

UNITED ARAB EMIRATES
(TRUCIAL STATES)

BAHRAIN

QATAR

East from Greenwich

COPYRIGHT GEORGE PHILIP & SON LTD

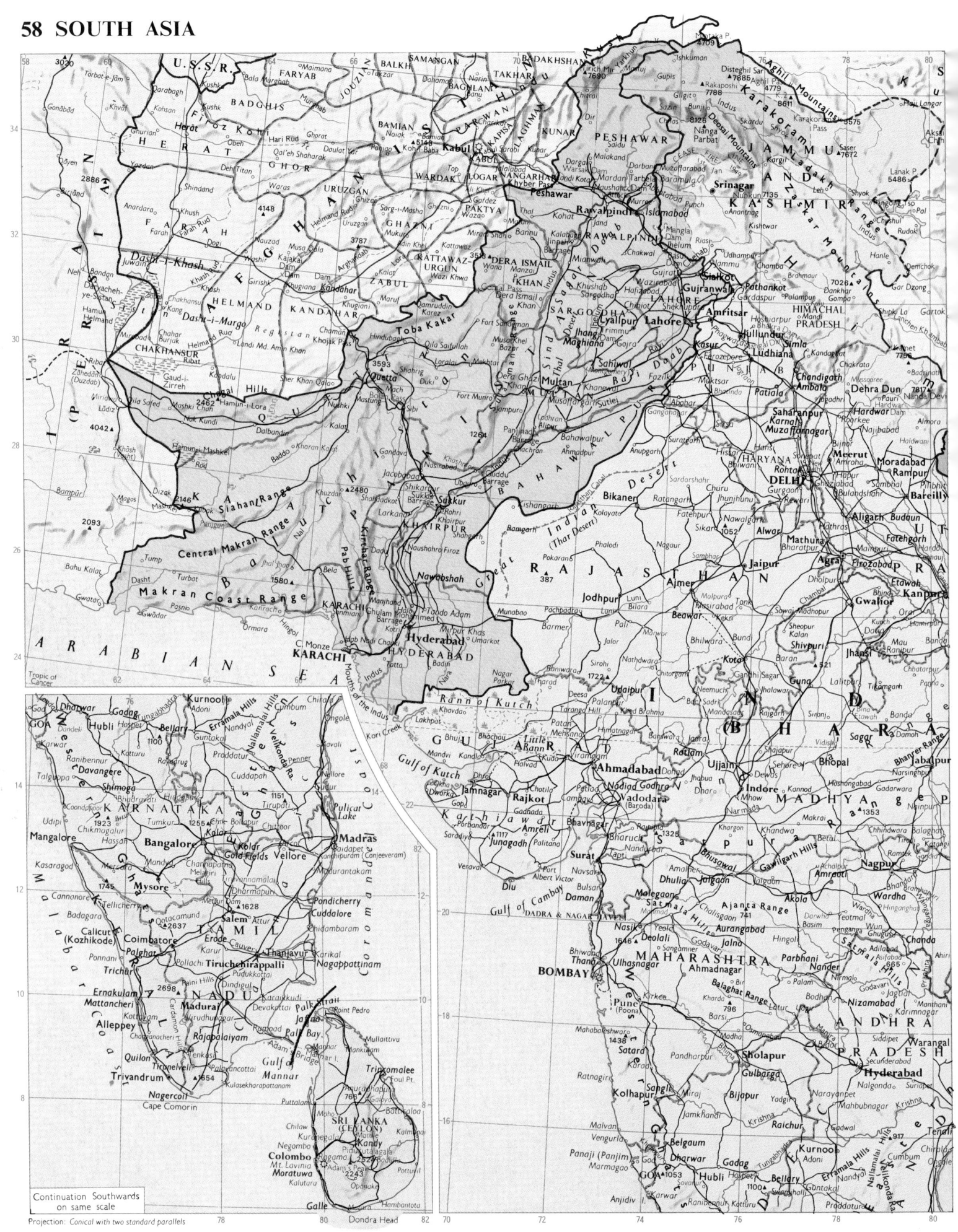

1:10 000 000

50   0   50   100   150   200 miles

50   0   50   100   150   200   250   300 km

I N K I A N G - n J u i g U R S h a n

K o k o S h i l i

T S I N G H A I

Sumpa Kangri
6300

Ngoring Nor

Amne Machin Shan
6094

Polur

Shazidu

C H I N E S E   R E P U B L I C

Mantekomu Hu

Khetinsiring

Tengko

Chatsam La
4593

Jf Chabubrun La
4526

Doyung

Kashum Tso

Mani

Joma
6800

Achok Gomba

Iyekundo
(Yushu)

Tsanga

C H I N E S E   R E P U B L I C

Kansze

Aling Kangri
7315

T I B E T

Nagrong

T a n g l h a

Tang La
5180

Dungbuya La
4930

Ed Dzong

S h a n

Angenong

Denchin

Lantsien

Paiyu

Tungbo

A T i n g

Senge Khambab

K a n g r i

Shaba Gomba

Züling Tso

Nagchu Dzong

Lolungchunglka

Tapsing Chu (Salween)

Ningtsin

Shugden Gomba

Bum La

Chamdo

Paan

Ningtsin Lan Tsang Ru

SZECHWAN

4959

Lihwa

Yaking

Kangtiss Nagari Shan

Jiachan (Indus)
5425

Selipuk Gompa

Sangchen La

Tangra Tso

Wampo

Kyaring Tso

Nam Tso

Gioring La
5940

N y e n c h e n   T a n g l h a   S h a n

Nagchu Dzong

Chiali (Lhariguo)

Giomda Dzong

Pondo Dzong

Tsanga

Ol Weiss

Chungtien

Yangpring

(Sutlej)

Laka Chih

Mayum La

Mendong Gompa

Shentsa

Tsangpo (Brahmaputra)

Kani

7756

Rima

Longdam

Tzuchien

Mula

B A Y   O F   B E N G A L

I N D I A N   O C E A N

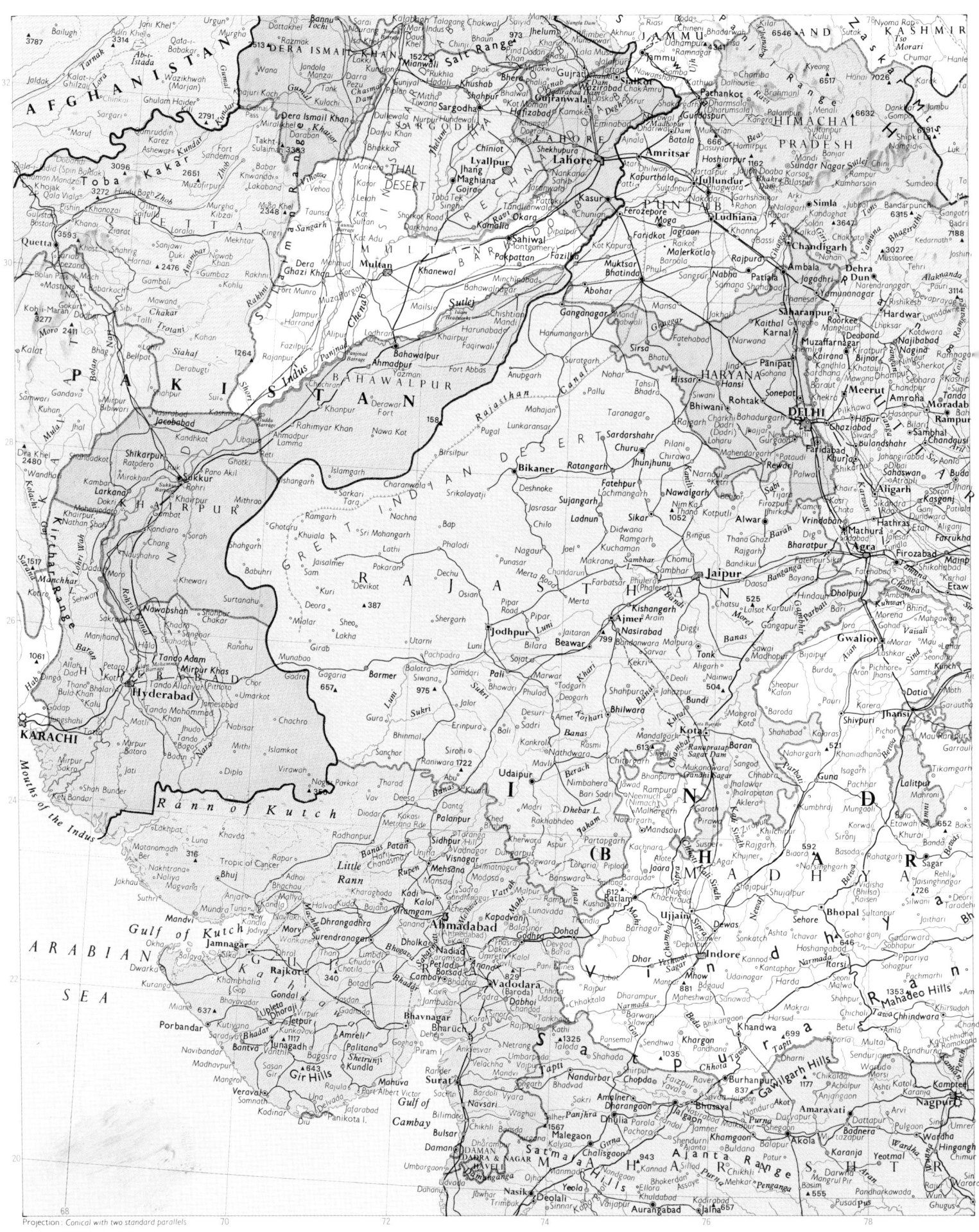

Projection: Conical with two standard parallels

1:6 000 000

50   0   50   100   150 miles

50   0   50   100   150   200   250 km

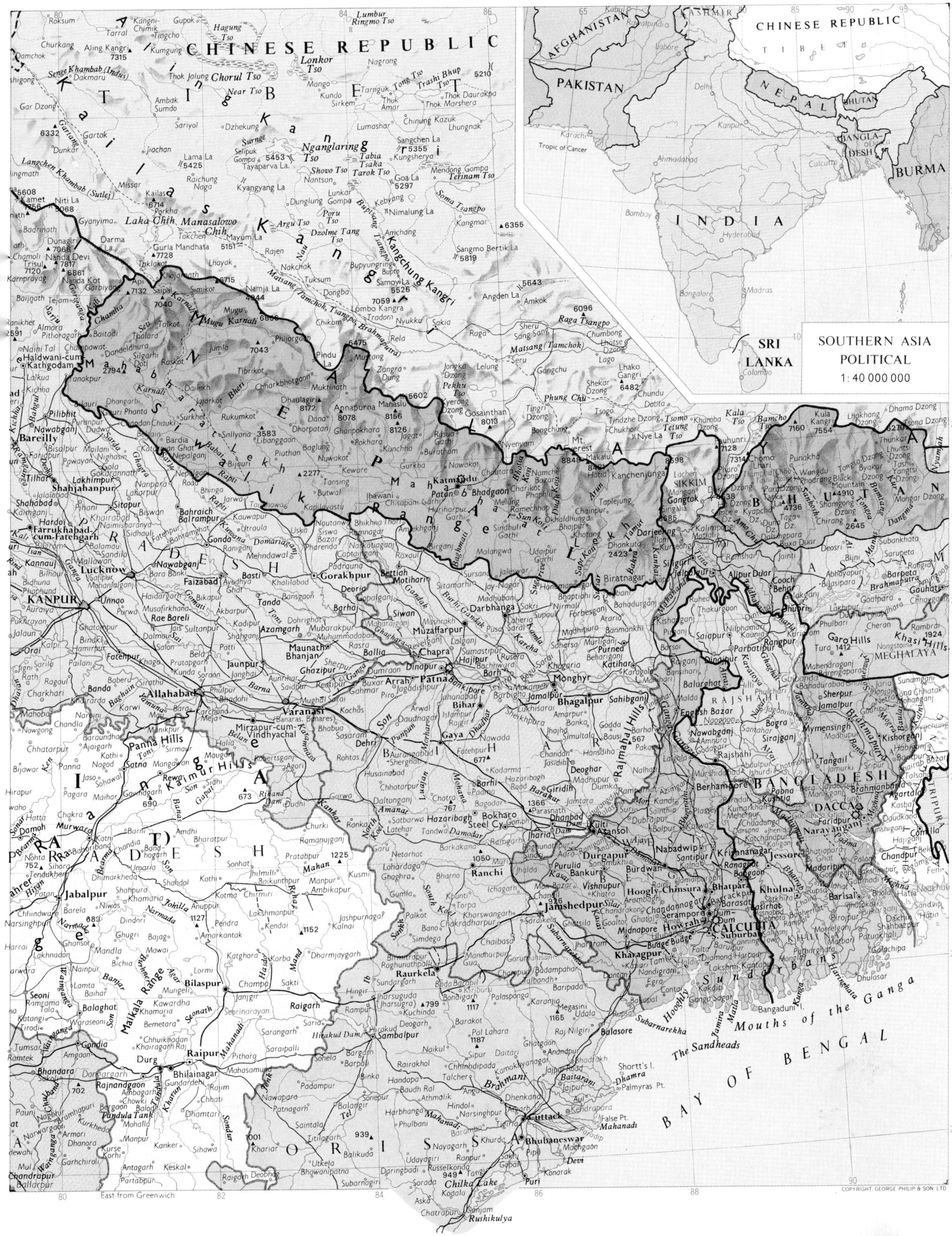

CHINESE REPUBLIC

T I B E T

SOUTHERN ASIA POLITICAL
1:40 000 000

AFGHANISTAN
PAKISTAN
CHINESE REPUBLIC
TIBET
NEPAL
BHUTAN
BANGLA-DESH
BURMA
INDIA
SRI LANKA
Tropic of Cancer

Karachi · Delhi · Kanpur · Calcutta
Ahmadabad · Bombay · Hyderabad
Bangalore · Madras · Colombo

Kailas
Kangri

N E P A L

Mahabharat Range
Siwalik
Pangra Lekh
Mahalangur

Dhaulagiri 8172
Annapurna 8078
Manaslu 8156
Gosainthan 8013
Mt. Everest 8848
Makalu
Kanchenjunga 8598

Katmandu
Bhadgaon

SIKKIM
Gangtok
Darjeeling

B H U T A N

U T T A R   P R A D E S H

Bareilly · Shahjahanpur · Sitapur
Lucknow · KANPUR · Faizabad
Gorakhpur · Allahabad · Varanasi
Mirzapur-cum-Vindhyachal

B I H A R

Patna · Muzaffarpur · Darbhanga
Bhagalpur · Monghyr · Gaya
Ranchi · Jamshedpur · Dhanbad
Hazaribagh

M A D H Y A   P R A D E S H

Panna Hills · Kaimur Hills · Maikala Range
Jabalpur · Bilaspur · Raipur · Durg
Bhilainagar · Raigarh · Sambalpur

O R I S S A

Raurkela · Cuttack · Bhubaneswar
Puri · Chilka Lake

M E G H A L A Y A
Garo Hills · Khasi Hills · Shillong

A S S A M
Gauhati · Brahmaputra

B A N G L A D E S H
DACCA · Mymensingh · Narayanganj
Faridpur · Barisal · Chandpur · Comilla
Khulna · Jessore · Rajshahi · Bogra
English Bazar · Berhampore

W E S T   B E N G A L
CALCUTTA · Howrah · Asansol
Durgapur · Burdwan · Kharagpur
Midnapore · Hooghly-Chinsura

Mouths of the Ganga
The Sandheads
Sunderbans

BAY OF BENGAL

East from Greenwich

COPYRIGHT GEORGE PHILIP & SON LTD

1:6 000 000

50 ... 0 ... 50 ... 100 ... 150 miles
50 ... 0 ... 50 ... 100 ... 150 ... 200 ... 250 km

MAHARASHTRA

MADHYA PRADESH

ORISSA

EASTERN GHATS

BOMBAY

Ahmadnagar

Nasik

Aurangabad

Poona (Pune)

HYDERABAD
Secunderabad

ANDHRA PRADESH

Warangal

Sholapur

Gulbarga

Bijapur

Kolhapur

Sangli

Belgaum

GOA

Panaji (Panjim)
Marmagao

KARNATAKA

Hubli
Dharwar

Raichur

Bellary

Kurnool

Rajahmundry

Vishakhapatnam

Vijayawada (Bezawada)

Guntur

Machilipatnam (Bandar)

BAY OF BENGAL

Nellore

Anantapur

Cuddapah

Tirupati

Chittoor

MADRAS

Bangalore

Mysore

Mangalore

Tiruvottiyur

Vellore

Arkonam

Kanchipuram (Conjeeveram)

Pondicherry

Cuddalore

Coimbatore

Salem

TAMIL NADU

Tiruchchirappalli

Thanjavur (Tanjore)

Nagappattinam (Negapatam)

Madurai

KERALA

Calicut (Kozhikode)

Cochin
Ernakulam

Alleppey

Quilon

Trivandrum

C. Comorin

ARABIAN SEA

Gulf of Manaar (Mannar)

Coromandel Coast

SRI LANKA (CEYLON)

SRI LANKA
On same scale

Palk Strait

Palk Bay

Jaffna

Trincomalee

Anuradhapura

Kandy

COLOMBO
Dehiwala
Moratuwa

Negombo

Galle
Matara
Dondra Head

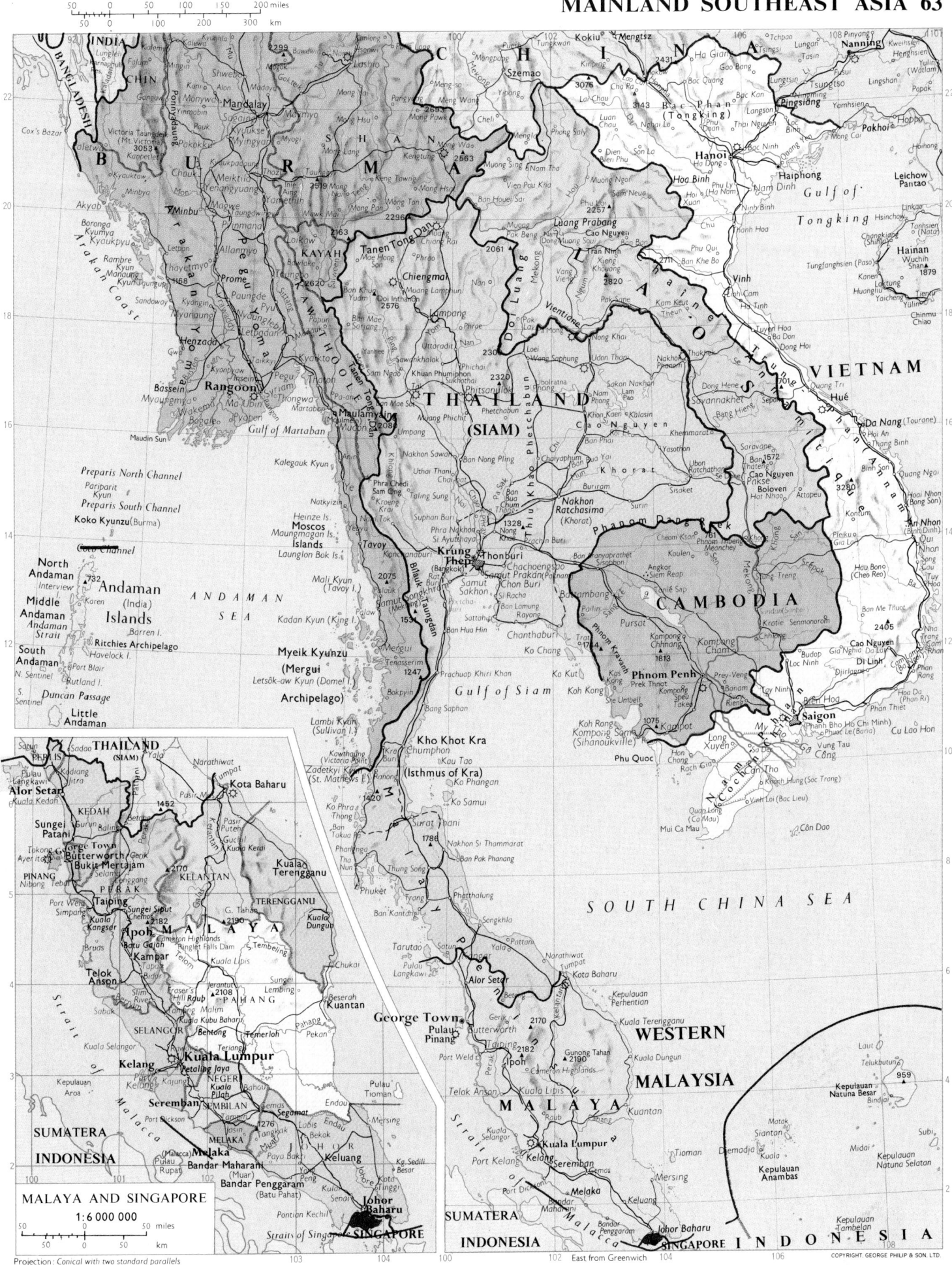

1:10 000 000

50   0   100   150   200 miles
50   0   100   200   300 km

MALAYA AND SINGAPORE
1:6 000 000

50   0   50 miles
50   0   km

Projection: Conical with two standard parallels

East from Greenwich

COPYRIGHT. GEORGE PHILIP & SON, LTD.

East from Greenwich

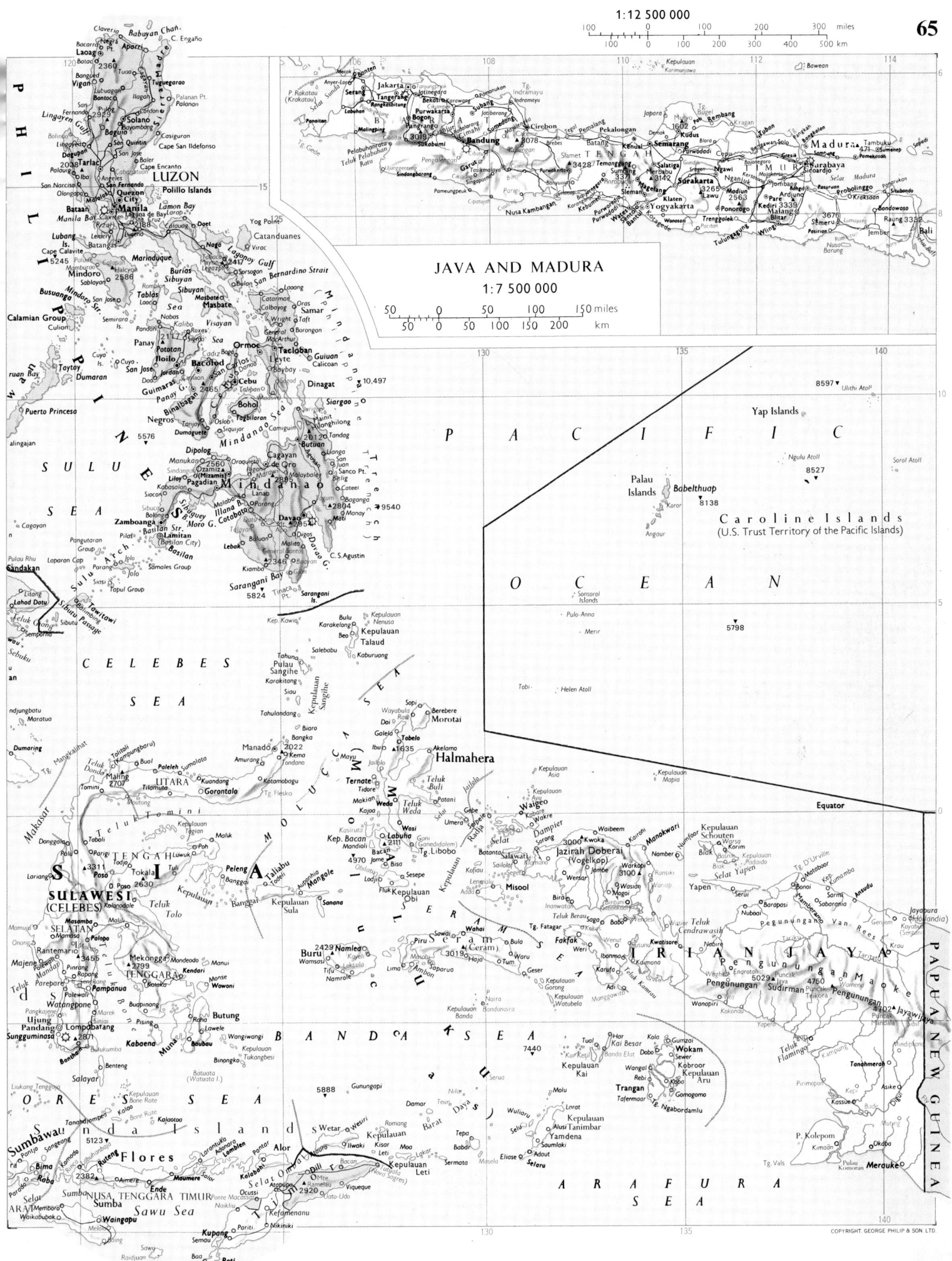

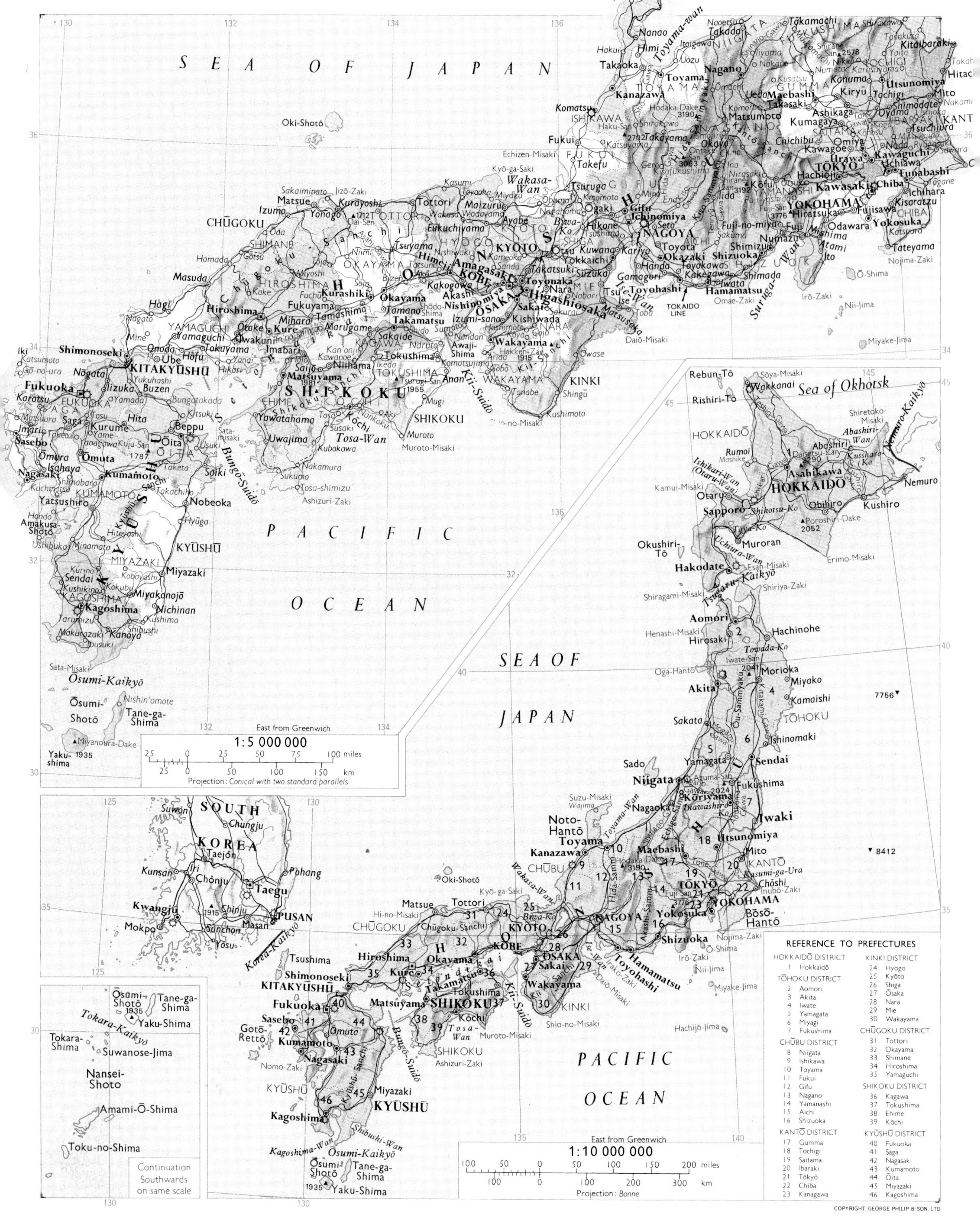

SEA OF JAPAN
PACIFIC OCEAN
SEA OF JAPAN
PACIFIC OCEAN
Sea of Okhotsk
East from Greenwich
1:5 000 000
25 0 25 50 75 100 miles
25 0 50 100 150 km
Projection: Conical with two standard parallels
East from Greenwich
1:10 000 000
100 50 0 50 100 150 200 miles
100 0 100 200 300 km
Projection: Bonne
HOKKAIDŌ
HONSHU
SHIKOKU
KYŪSHŪ
CHŪGOKU
KINKI
CHŪBU
KANTŌ
TŌHOKU
SOUTH KOREA
Sapporo
Hakodate
Asahikawa
Kushiro
Aomori
Akita
Morioka
Sendai
Niigata
Fukushima
Toyama
Kanazawa
Nagano
Maebashi
Utsunomiya
Mito
TŌKYŌ
YOKOHAMA
Kawasaki
Chiba
NAGOYA
Shizuoka
Hamamatsu
Toyohashi
Gifu
Fukui
KYOTO
ŌSAKA
KOBE
Nara
Wakayama
Himeji
Okayama
Hiroshima
Tottori
Matsue
Yamaguchi
Shimonoseki
KITAKYŪSHŪ
Fukuoka
Saga
Nagasaki
Kumamoto
Ōita
Miyazaki
Kagoshima
Takamatsu
Matsuyama
Tokushima
Kōchi
Sado
Oki-Shotō
Tsushima
Ōsumi-Shotō
Tane-ga-Shima
Yaku-Shima
Tokara-Kaikyō
Tokara-Shima
Suwanose-Jima
Nansei-Shoto
Amami-Ō-Shima
Toku-no-Shima
Continuation Southwards on same scale
TOKAIDO LINE
REFERENCE TO PREFECTURES
HOKKAIDŌ DISTRICT
1 Hokkaidō
TŌHOKU DISTRICT
2 Aomori
3 Akita
4 Iwate
5 Yamagata
6 Miyagi
7 Fukushima
CHŪBU DISTRICT
8 Niigata
9 Ishikawa
10 Toyama
11 Fukui
12 Gifu
13 Nagano
14 Yamanashi
15 Aichi
16 Shizuoka
KANTŌ DISTRICT
17 Gumma
18 Tochigi
19 Saitama
20 Ibaraki
21 Tōkyō
22 Chiba
23 Kanagawa
KINKI DISTRICT
24 Hyogo
25 Kyōto
26 Shiga
27 Ōsaka
28 Nara
29 Mie
30 Wakayama
CHŪGOKU DISTRICT
31 Tottori
32 Okayama
33 Shimane
34 Hiroshima
35 Yamaguchi
SHIKOKU DISTRICT
36 Kagawa
37 Tokushima
38 Ehime
39 Kōchi
KYŪSHŪ DISTRICT
40 Fukuoka
41 Saga
42 Nagasaki
43 Kumamoto
44 Ōita
45 Miyazaki
46 Kagoshima

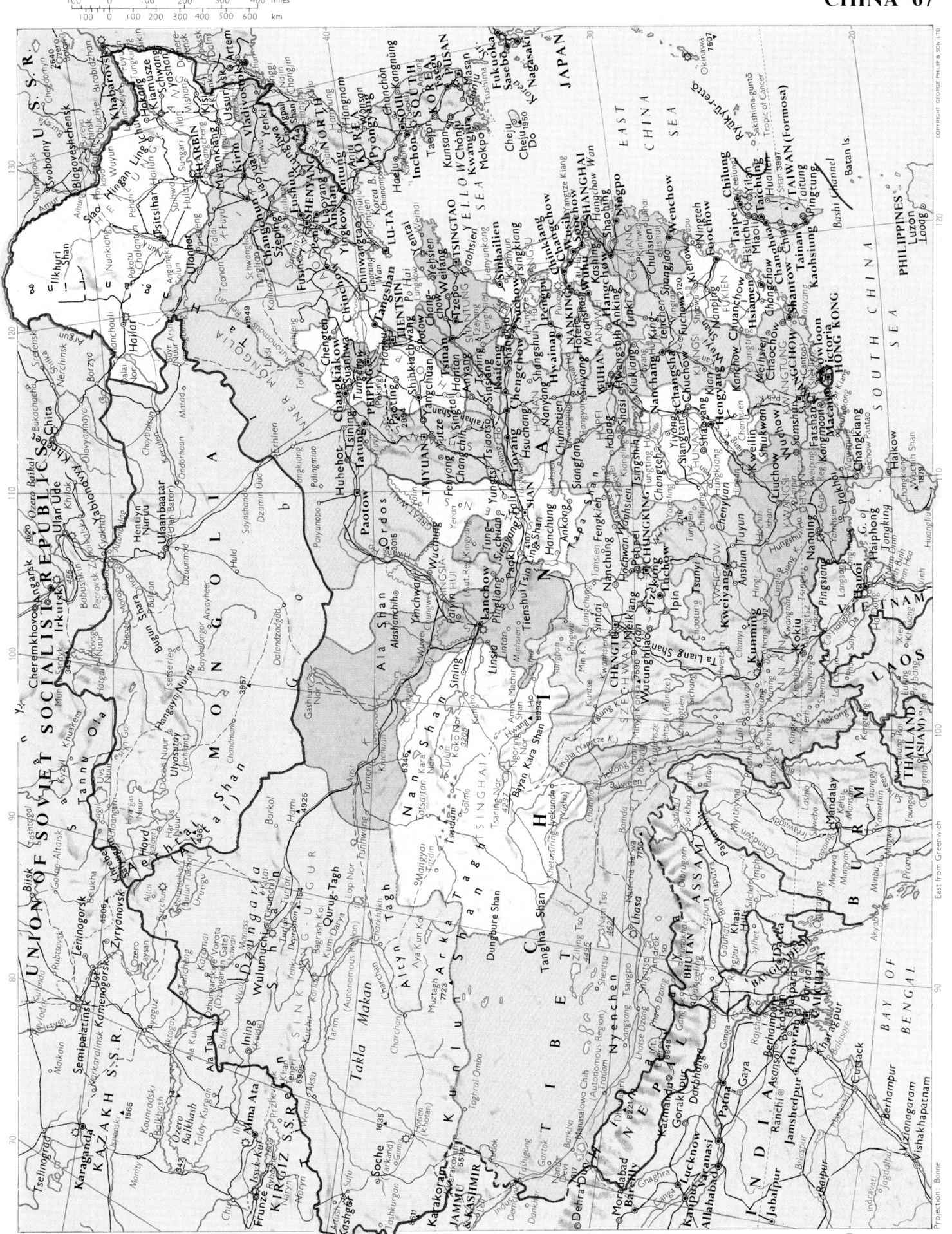

1:20 000 000

Projection: Bonne

East from Greenwich

COPYRIGHT GEORGE PHILIP & SON LTD

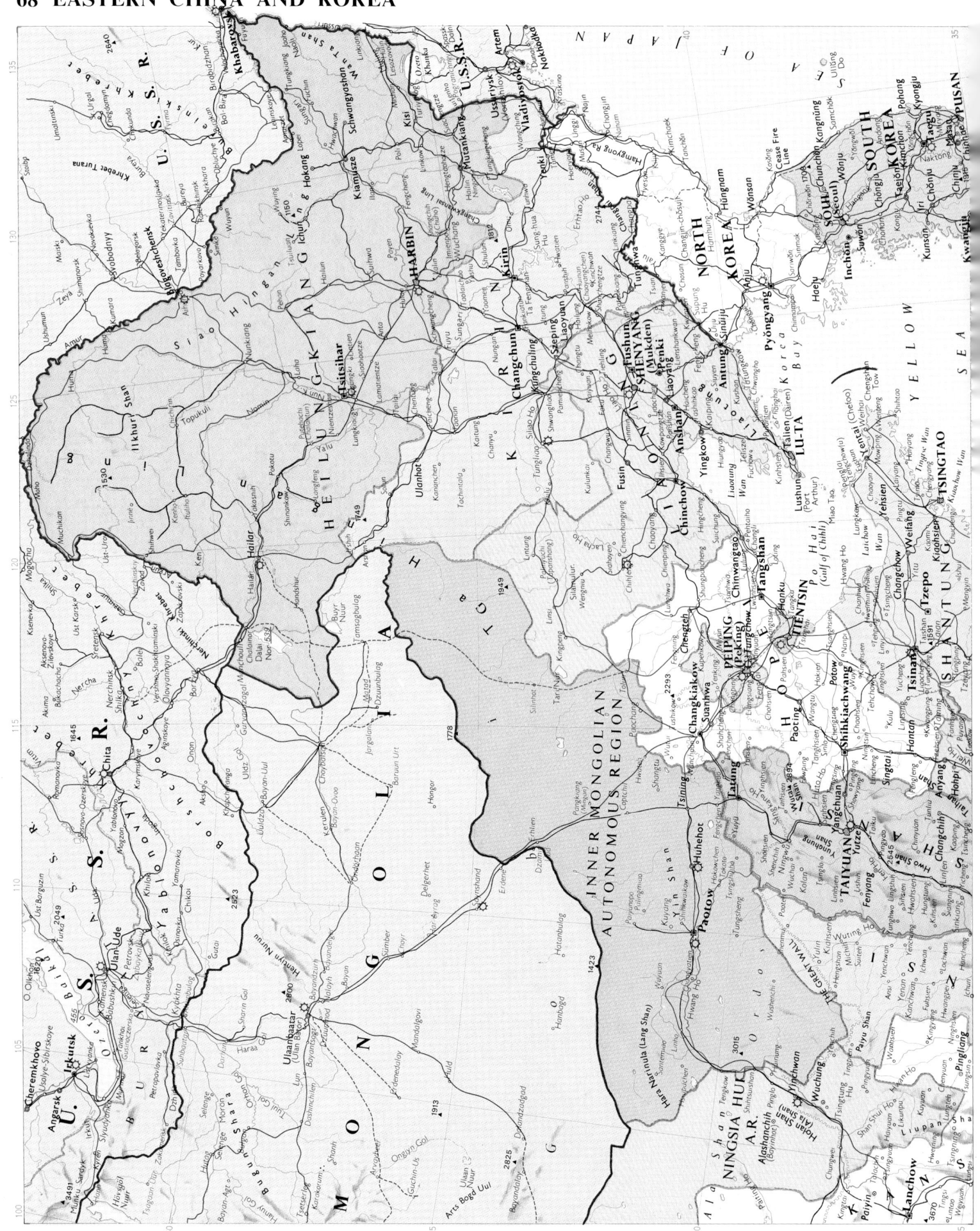

1:10 000 000

50   50   100   150   200   250 miles
50   0   50 100 150 200 250 300 350 400 km

PACIFIC OCEAN

Tropic of Cancer

EAST CHINA SEA

JAPAN
KITAKYŪSHŪ
Fukuoka
Kurume
Sasebo Ōmuta
Nagasaki
Amakusa
Makurazaki
Kagoshima

Nansei-shotō

Tokara-guntō

Amami
Amami guntō

Tokuno-erabu-shima
Okino erabu-shima
Oku
Okinawa
Okinawa-wa-guntō
Naha

Sakishima-guntō
Miyako rettō
Ishigaki guntō
Iriomote
Yaeyama-rettō

Senkaku guntō

Mokpo
Cheju
Cheju Do
(Quelpart)

RYUKYU

TAIWAN
(FORMOSA)

Chilung (Keelung)
Tanshui
Taipei
Taoyuan
Hsinchu
Yilan
Miaoli
Taichung
Changhua
Nantou
Hualien
Yunlin
Chiai
Taitung
Tainan
Anping
Kongshan
Kaohsiung
Pingtung
Tungkang

Lan Yu
Lu Tao

Batan Is.
Babuyan Is.
Calayan
Babuyan
Camiguin
Dalupiri
Fuga

PHILIPPINES
LUZON
Laoag
Aparri
Vigan
Bangued
Tuguegarao

C. Bojeador
C. Engaño
Aubarede Pt.

SOUTH CHINA SEA

Tungsha Tao
(Pratas)

SHANGHAI
Tsungming Tao
Yangtze Kiang
Nantung

KIANGSU

CHEKIANG
Hangchow
Ningpo
Shaohing
Wenchow
Nanchang

KIANGSI

FUKIEN
Foochow (Minhow)
Nanping
Kienow
Chuanchow
Tsuamen (Amoy)
Kinmen (Quemoy)

Chungking
CHUNGKING
SZECHWAN

KWEICHOW
Kweiyang
Anshun

HUNAN
Changsha
Hengyang
Shaoyang

KWANGSI - CHUANG
Nanning (A.D.)
Liuchow
Kweilin

KWANGTUNG
Canton KWANGCHOW (Canton)
Fatshan
Shiukwan
Swatow
Shantow
Chaochow
Meihsien

HONGKONG (Br.)
Kowloon
Victoria

Macau
(Port)

Hainan
Haikow
Leichow Pantao

Gulf of Tongking

VIETNAM
HANOI
Haiphong

WUHAN
Hankow
Hanyang
Wuchang
HUPEH

HONAN
Loyang
Kaifeng

SHANSI

ANHWEI
Hofei
Wuhu

NANKING
Chinkiang
Soochow
Wusih
Changchow

East from Greenwich

Projection: Lambert's Equivalent Azimuthal

1:40 000 000

200   0   200   400   600   800   1000 miles
200   0   200 400 600 800 1000 1200 1400 1600 km

British Isles

ATLANTIC OCEAN

Bay of Biscay

A L P S

Carpathians

Caucasus   Elburus 5633

Caspian Sea

Aral Sea

Iberian Peninsula

Pyrenees   Mt Blanc 4807

Apennines   Dinaric Alps   Adriatic Sea

Corsica

Sardinia

Black Sea

Anatolia

6578

Madeira

Str. of Gibraltar

High Plateaus   Saharan Atlas

Middle Atlas   High Atlas

Anti Atlas   Toubkal   Dra   4165

Canary Is.   3718

Tenerife

C. Bon   Sicily
Malta   5121   Crete   Cyprus

Mediterranean Sea

Levant

Mesopotamia   Tigris

Euphrates

Persian G.

Bahrain I.

B a r b a r y

Tripolitania   Cyrenaica

G. of Gabes   Chott Djerid

G. of Sidra

Siwa

Libyan Desert

Egypt

Nile

Arabian Desert

Sinai 2285

Red Sea

H e j a z

A r a b i a

Tropic of Cancer

C. Blanc

I g i d i

S el Juf

S a h a r a

Adrar

Air

Bilma

Tasili Plateau

Hoggar

Tibesti   3415

Kufra   El Kharga   1st Cat.

Nubian Desert

3rd Cat.   4th Cat.   5th Cat.

6th Cat.

N u b i a

Rub' al Khali

Perim I.   Gulf of Aden
Str. of Bab el Mandeb   Ras Asir

Socotra

C. Vert

Senegal   Senegambia   Gambia

Fouta Djalon

Niger (Joliba)   Volta   Niger

S u d

Benue

G u i n e a

Gold Coast   Slave Coast
Grain Coast   Ivory Coast   C. Palmas

6363

Bight of Benin   Macias Nguema Biyoga

Cameroon Peak   4070

Adamawa Highlands

Gulf of Guinea

São Tomé   Príncipe

Pagalu

C. Lopez

Ogowe

L. Chad

Chari

Wadai   Darfur

Dar Banda

Kordofan

White Nile   Blue Nile   Atbara

Ras Dashan 4620   L. Tana

Ethiopian Highlands

Somali Peninsula

Shabelle

Bahr el Ghazal   Bahr el Ghazal   Bahr el Jebel

Uele

Ubangi   Zaire

C o n g o

Basin

Congo   Kasai   Sankuru   Kasai

L. Mobutu Sese Seko   Chutes Boyoma   Ruwenzori 5109

L. Idi Amin Dada   L. Kivu   Lualaba

Eigon 4321   Kenya 5199

L. Victoria

Kilimanjaro 5895

Turkana

Juba   Shibeli   Tana

Equator

INDIAN OCEAN

Pemba   Zanzibar

Aldabra Is.

Ascension

ATLANTIC OCEAN

St. Helena

Cuanza

Cuango   Cuango   Lovua

L. Tanganyika

L. Mweru   Rungwe 2961   L. Nyasa   C. Delgado

Katanga   Luapula   L. Bangweulu   Malawi   Ruvuma

Comoro Is.

Bié Plateau

Cuando   Zambezi   Mlanje 3000

Cunene

C. Fria

Namib Desert

Walvis Bay

Cubango   Cubango

Victoria Falls

Kalahari

Limpopo

Matopo

Mozambique Channel

Madagascar   2643

Mauritius   Réunion

Tropic of Capricorn

Delagoa Bay

Orange   Vaal

Highveld   3482   Drakensberg

Compass B. 2505   Gt. Karoo   Swartberg
Nieuweveldberge

C. of Good Hope   C. Agulhas

Algoa Bay

Agulhas Bank

West from Greenwich   East from Greenwich

Projection: Zenithal Equidistant.

m   4000 3000 2000 1500 1000 400 200
ft   12 000 9000 6000 4500 3000 1200 600

1000 2000 4000 6000 m
0   600 3000 6000 12 000 18 000 ft

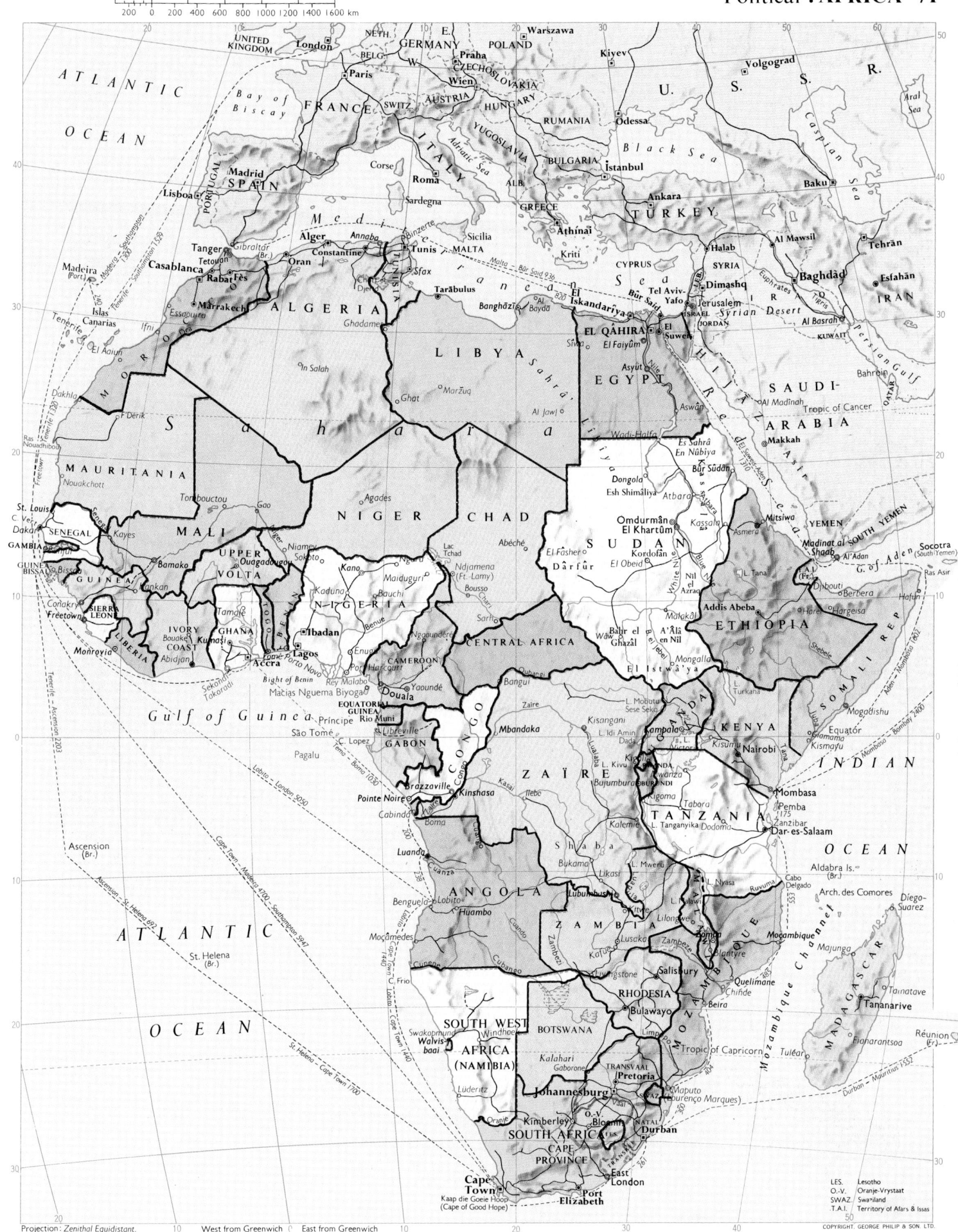

1:40 000 000

200   0   200   400   600   800   1000 miles
200   0   200 400 600 800 1000 1200 1400 1600 km

ATLANTIC

OCEAN

UNITED
KINGDOM
London   NETH.
BELG.   GERMANY   POLAND   Warszawa
Paris   W.   Praha   Kiyev
FRANCE   SWITZ.   Wien   CZECHOSLOVAKIA
AUSTRIA   HUNGARY   RUMANIA   Odessa   U.   S.   S.   R.
Bay of   Volgograd
Biscay
Corse   Adriatic Sea   YUGOSLAVIA   Black Sea
Roma   BULGARIA   İstanbul   Ankara   Baku   Aral Sea
Sardegna   GREECE   TURKEY
Madrid   ITALY   Athínai   Caspian Sea
SPAIN   Kriti   CYPRUS   SYRIA   Halab   Al Mawsil   Tehrān
Lisboa   Sicilia   MALTA   Tel Aviv-   Dimashq   Esfahān
Madeira   Tanger   Gibraltar   Tunis   Malta-Bûr Said 936   Yafo   JORDAN   Baghdād   IRAN
Casablanca   Alger   Annaba   Bizerte   El   Bûr Said   ISRAEL   Syrian   Al Basrah
Rabat Fès   Oran   Constantine   Sfax   Iskandarîya   Desert   KUWAIT   Persian Gulf
Marrakech   Djerba   EL QÂHIRA   El Suweis   Bahrein   QATAR
ALGERIA   LIBYA   El Faiyûm   SAUDI-
El Aaiun   In Salah   Siwa   EGYPT   Al Madînah   ARABIA
Dakhla   Ghadames   Tropic of Cancer   Makkah
Marzuq   Aswân   Es Sahrâ
Ghat   Al Jawf   Wadi-Halfa   En Nûbiya   YEMEN   SOUTH YEMEN
MAURITANIA   S a h a r a   Dongola   Esh Shimâliya   Mitsiwa   Madînat al   Socotra
Nouakchott   Esh Shimâliya   Asmera   Shaab   Al Adan   (South Yemen)
Tombouctou   Agades   Omdurmân   Djibouti   G. of Aden   Ras Asir
St. Louis   Gao   NIGER   CHAD   El Khartûm   Kassala   Berbera
Dakar   Kayes   MALI   Abéché   SUDAN   Kordofân   Hargeisa   Hafun
SENEGAL   Niamey   El Fâsher   El Obeid   ETHIOPIA   Harer   SOMALI REP
GAMBIA   Bamako   UPPER   Sokoto   Dârfûr   Addis Abeba   Shebele
GUINEA BISSAU   Ouagadougou   VOLTA   Kano   Ndjamena   Malakâl   A'Âlâ
GUINEA   Kankan   NIGERIA   Kaduna   (Ft.-Lamy)   Bahr el   en Nil   Mongalla
SIERRA LEONE   Bauchi   Maiduguri   Bousso   Ghazal   El Istwâ'iya
Freetown   Tamale   IVORY   GHANA   Ngaoundéré   Sarh   CENTRAL AFRICA   Turkana
LIBERIA   Bouaké   Ibadan   Benue   Bangui   UGANDA   KENYA
Monrovia   COAST   Kumasi   Enugu   CAMEROON   Kisangani   Kampala   Nairobi
Abidjan   Accra   Porto Novo   Port   Yaoundé   L. Victoria   Mombasa
Sekondi   Lagos   Harcourt   Douala   ZAÏRE   L. Kivu   INDIAN
Takoradi   EQUATORIAL   Libreville   CONGO   Kisumu   Kismayu   Equator
Macias Nguema Biyogoa   GUINEA   Rio Muni   Brazzaville   Kinshasa   TANZANIA   Mogadishu
São Tomé   GABON   Pointe Noire   ZAMBIA   Dar-es-Salaam
Gulf of Guinea   Príncipe   Cabinda   Boma   Shaba   Pemba   OCEAN
Pagalu   Luanda   Kalemie   Zanzibar
ATLANTIC   Ascension   ANGOLA   Lubumbashi   L. Nyasa   Arch. des Comores
Ascension (Br.)   Huambo   ZAMBIA   L. Malawi   Diego-Suárez
St. Helena (Br.)   Benguela-Lobito   Lusaka   Lilongwe   Moçambique
Moçâmedes   Zambezi   Zomba   Quelimane   MADAGASCAR
OCEAN   SOUTH WEST   Salisbury   Blantyre   Tananarive
AFRICA (NAMIBIA)   BOTSWANA   RHODESIA   Beira   Réunion (Fr.)
Walvis-baai   Windhoek   Bulawayo   Chinde   Fianarantsoa
Swakopmund   Kalahari   Gaborone   Tropic of Capricorn   Tuléar
Lüderitz   TRANSVAAL   Pretoria   Maputo   Majunga
Johannesburg   Lourenço Marques   Tamatave
Kimberley   Bloemfontein   Durban
SOUTH AFRICA   Natal
CAPE PROVINCE   East London
Cape Town   Port Elizabeth
Kaap die Goeie Hoop (Cape of Good Hope)

LES.   Lesotho
O.-V.   Oranje-Vrystaat
SWAZ.   Swaziland
T.A.I.   Territory of Afars & Issas

Projection: Zenithal Equidistant.   West from Greenwich   East from Greenwich
COPYRIGHT. GEORGE PHILIP & SON. LTD.

NORTH ATLANTIC

OCEAN

SPAIN · Málaga · Almería

Cabo de São Vicente

Str. of Gibraltar
Gibraltar (Br.)
Tanger · Ceuta (Sp.)
Tetouan · Melilla
Larache · Al Hoceima
Kenitra (Port-Lyautey)
Salé · Fès · Taza
Rabat · Meknès
Casablanca
El Jadida · Berrechid
Settat · Khouribga
Safi
Essaouira
Marrakech
C. Cantin
C. Rhir · Toubkal ▲ 4165
Agadir · Anti Atlas
Sidi Ifni
Tarfaya (Villa Bens)
El Aaiún
Bu Craa
C. Bojador
Smara
Dakhla
Pta. Durnford

Madeira (Port.) · Funchal · Pto. Santo · 6578

Islas Canarias (Sp.)
La Palma · Lanzarote · Arrecife
Tenerife · Fuerteventura
Gomera · Sta. Cruz · Puerto del Rosario
Hierro · Gran Canaria · Las Palmas
C. Juby

ALGERIA
Plateau du Tademait
Erg · Tanezrouft
Ahaggar · Tahat ▲ 2918
Tamanrasset
Adrar des Iforas
Poste Maurice Cortier (Bidon 5)

Alger (Algiers) · Tizi-Ouzou
Blida · Constantine · Guelma
Sétif · Batna · Biskra
Tunis · Tabarka
TUNISIA · Gabès
Chott el Djerid
Ghardaïa · Hassi Messaoud
Ft. Lallemand · Hassi el Gassi
Ghudāmes · Daraj

MAURITANIA
El Djouf
Nouadhibou (Port Étienne)
Ras Nouadhibou · Cité de Cansado
Atar · Chinguetti · Ouadane
Akjoujt · Nouakchott
Boutilimit · Tidjikdja · Tichit
Rachid · Yagba · Kidal
Mederdra · Aleg · Tamchaket
Kiffa · Néma · Oualata
Timbédra · Bassikounou · Nioro

MALI
Taoudenni · Tessalit
Araouane · Bou Djebeha · Mabrouk
El Ouïga · Etelia
Tombouctou · Bamba · Gao
Goundam · Kabara · Gourma-Rharous
Diré · Bourem · Ansongo · Ménaka
Mopti · Douentza · Hombori

NIGER
Aïr (Azbine)
Iférouane · Monts Tamgak 1900
Agadez · In-Gall · Fachi
Tanout · Gangara · Zinder

St. Louis · Dakar · SENEGAL
GAMBIA · Banjul (Bathurst)
GUINEA-BISSAU · Bissau
Conakry · GUINEA
Fouta Djalon
SIERRA LEONE · Freetown
LIBERIA · Monrovia
IVORY COAST · Abidjan
GHANA · Accra · Kumasi · Lake Volta
UPPER VOLTA · Ouagadougou · Bobo-Dioulasso
TOGO · Lomé
BENIN · Porto-Novo · Cotonou
NIGERIA · Lagos · Ibadan · Kano · Kaduna · Zaria
Niamey · Sokoto · Katsina
CAMEROON · Yaoundé

Bight of Benin

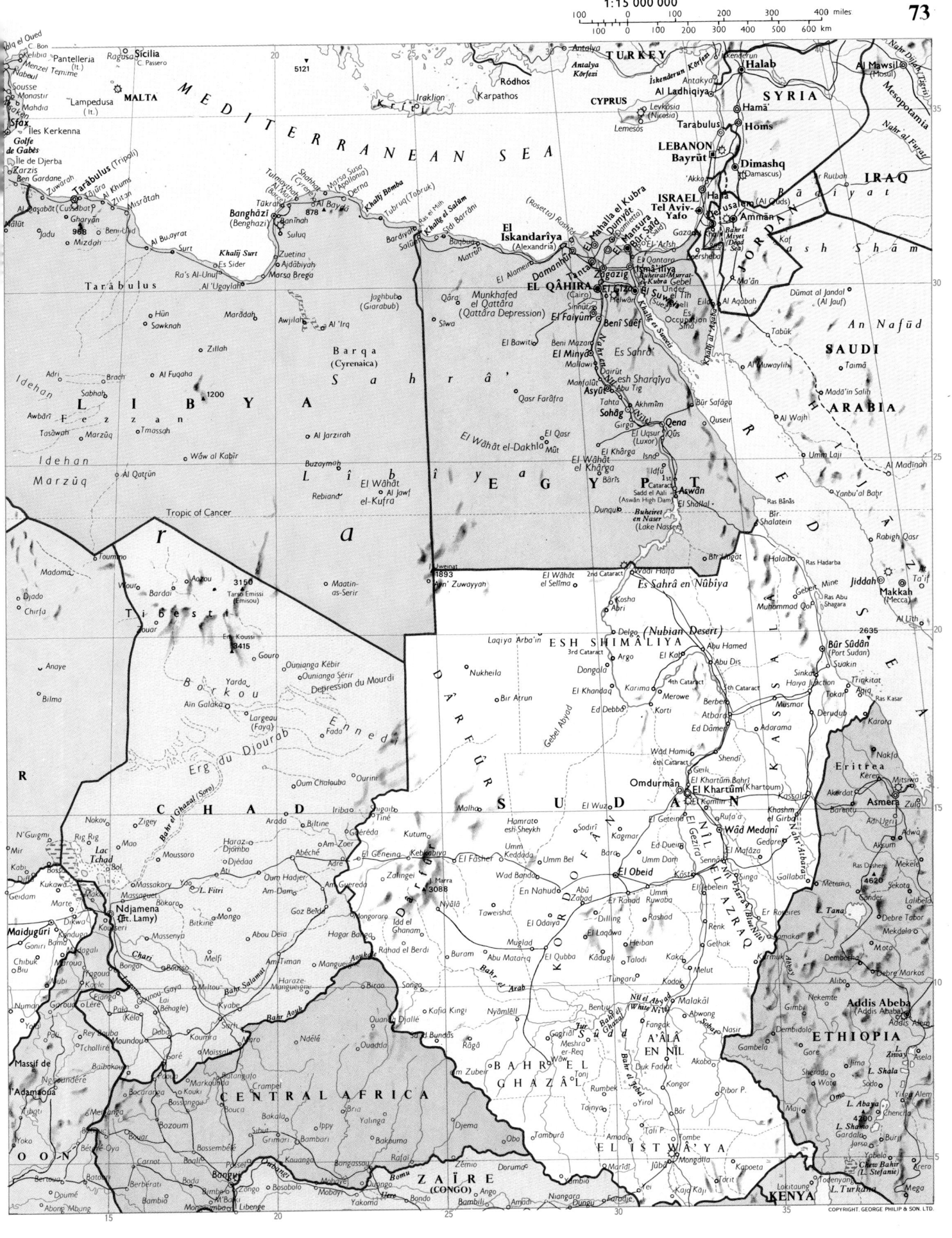

1:15 000 000

100   100   200   300   400 miles
100   0   100   200   300   400   500   600 km

MEDITERRANEAN SEA

TURKEY

Antalya
Antalya Körfezi
Ródhos
Karpathos

İskenderun Körfezi
İskenderun
Al Iskenderun

Halab

SYRIA

CYPRUS
Leykosía
(Nicosia)
Lemesós

Al Ladhiqiya
Hamā

Tarabulus
Homs

Al Mawsil
(Mosul)

Mesopotamia

LEBANON
Bayrūt

Dimashq
(Damascus)

Nahr Dijla (Tigris)

MALTA
Sicilia
Ragusa
C. Bon
Kélibia
Menzel Temime
Pantelleria (It.)
C. Passero

Nabeul
Sousse
Monastir
Mahdia
Sfax
Îles Kerkenna
Golfe de Gabès
Île de Djerba
Zarzis
Ben Gardane

Lampedusa (It.)

Kríti
Iráklion

Krétikó

IRAQ

Bādiyat
ash Shām

ISRAEL
Tel Aviv-
Yafo
Haifa
'Akko
Jerusalem
(Al Quds)
Amman

JORDAN

Dumat al Jandal
(Al Jauf)

Ma'ān
Tabūk

Ras
Dra'
el Milh

El Iskandarîya
(Alexandria)

(Rosetta) Rashid
Dumyât
(Damietta)
Pôrt Said

El Mahalla el Kubra
Mansura
Ismâ'îliya

El Qāhira
(Cairo)

El Gīza
Helwân

Gazaza
Bahr el Miyet
(Dead Sea)

Eilat
Al 'Aqabah

Khalīj el 'Aqaba

SAUDI

An Nafūd

Al Muwaylih

Zuwarah
Tarabulus (Tripoli)
Al Khums
Misrātah

Al Khalīj
(Cussabat)
Jadu
Gharyān
Mizdah
968
Beni-Ulid

Banghâzî
(Benghazi)
Ajdâbiyah
Marsa Brega

878

Tulmaythah
(Cyrene)
Shahhat
Marsa Susa
(Apollonia)
Tūkrah
Al Bayḍā

Derna

Khalīj Bomba
Tubruq (Tobruk)

Bardiyah
Sallūm
Buqbuq
Sîdi Barrâni

Matrûh

El Alamein
Damanhûr
Tanta
Zagazig

El Suweis
(Suez)

El 'Arîsh
El Qantara
Kubra
Gebel
Er-Rummânah-Murrat-el-
Es Suweis

Khalīj es Suweis

Es
Occupation
Sinai

TURKEY

Qâra
Siwa

Munkhafed
el Qattâra
(Qattâra Depression)

El Faiyûm
Sinnûris
Beni Suêf

En Nakhl

Mad'in Salih

Taimā

Al Wajh

HIJAZ

ARABIA

Tarâbulus

Es Sider
Ra's Al 'Unuf
Zuetina

Khalīj Surt

Surt

Al 'Ugaylah

Hūn
Sawknah

Marādah

Barqa
(Cyrenaica)

Awjilah
Al 'Irq

Jaghbub
(Giarabub)

Sahrâ'

Beni Mazar
El Minya
Mallawi

El Bawiti

Qasr Farâfra

Dairût
Manfalût
Asyût

Esh Sharqiya
Es Sahrâ'

Nahr en Nîl

Bûr Safâga

Umm Laji

Al Madînah

Idehan
Adri
Sabhat
Awbâri
Fezzan
Tasawah
Marzûq

LIBYA

1200

Al Fuqaha

Zillah

Brach
Al Jarzirah

Tmassah

Al Qatrûn

Wâw al Kabîr

Lî b

î y e g

Rebiana

Tahta
Akhmîm
Sohâg
Girga

Qena

El Wâhât el-Dakhla
Mût

El Qasr

El Wâhât
el Khârga

El Khârga

Bâris

Qasr
El Uqsur
(Luxor)
Qûs
Qusêir

Jiddah
Makkah
(Mecca)

Idehan
Marzûq

Toummo

Madama

Djado
Chirfa

Anaye

Bilma

Aozou
Bardai

3150
Tarso Emissi
(Emisou)

Tibesti

Emi Koussi
3415

Gouro

Ounianga Kébir
Ounianga Sérir
Depression du Mourdi
Fada

Borkou

Yarda
Largeau
(Faya)
Aïn Galaka

Erg du Djourab (Soro)

Ourini

Oum Chalouba

ENNEDI

Tropic of Cancer

r
a

Buzaymah

Aïn Zuwayyah
1893

'Uweinat

El Wâhât
el Selîma

Es Sahrâ en Nûbîya

2nd Cataract
Wadi Halfa

Kosha
Abri

Delgo

Laqiya Arba'in

Nukheila

Bir Atrun

DA'R FU'R

ESH SHIMÂLIYA

3rd Cataract
Argo
Dongola
El Kurru
El Khandaq
Karima
Merowe
Korti

Abu Hamed
El Kab
Abu Dis

4th Cataract
5th Cataract

Berber
Atbara
Ed Dâmer
Adarama

Aswân
Sadd el Ali
(Aswân High Dam)
El Shallal
1st
Cataract

Buheiret
en Naser
(Lake Nasser)

Dunqul

Bîr
Ugât

Halaib

Ras Bânâs

Bîr
Shalatein
Ras Hadarba

Gebel Mine
Ras Abu
Shagara

Muhammad Qol

Sinkat
Haiya Junction

2635

Bûr Sûdân
(Port Sudan)
Suakin
Derudub

Trinkitat
Tokar
Aqiq
Ras Kasar

Karora

Rabigh Qasr

Yanbu'al Bahr

RED

SEA

Al Lith

Al Madînah

KASSALA

Nakfa
Karora
Eritrea
Kerén

Mitsiwa
Asmera
Zula

(Nubian Desert)

R

N'Guigmi

Kabi
Duff

Mao
Moussoro
Bol

Rig Rig
Kukawa
Geidam
Marte

Maidugúri
Goniri
Chibuk
Biu
Numan

Gambar
Kusseri
Makari

Ndjamena
(Ft. Lamy)

Kinderku
Magala
Pagoua
Maroua

Bongor
Goundi
Kélo
Lère
Pala
Rey Bouba
Tcholliré
Baïbokoum

Massif de
Nghaoundéré
l'Adamaoua

Yoko
N'Gaoundéré
Bétaré-Oya

Bertoua
Doumé
Abong Mbang

Lac
Tchad

Chari

CHAD

Zigey
Massakory
Yao
Bokoro
Massaguet

L. Fitri

Bitkine
Mongo
Melfi

Bousso
Bongor
Miltou
Massenya

Bahr
Salamat

Guélengdeng

Bahr el Ghazal

Djédaa
Ati

Haraz-Djombo

Moundou

Doba

Koumra
Kyabé

Bahr Aouk

Sarh

Maltou

Gounou-Gaya

Lai
(Behagle)

Nokou
Biltine
Arada

Iriba
Guéréda

Am-Zoer
Kutum
Abéché
Adré

Am Guereda
Goz Beïda
Am Dam

Oum Hadjer

Abou Deia
Hagar Banga

Aouk

Birao
Ndélé
Ouandja
Ouadda

Sah
Bundâs

Ouanda Djallé

Tiné

Kebkabiya
El Geneina

Zalingei

Jebel Marra
3088

Nyâlâ

Idd el Ghanam

Rahad el Berdi

Buram

Abu Matariq

Radom

Tawisha

Shiqaïb

El Fasher

Umm
Keddada

Wad Banda

En Nahud

Abû
Zabad

Malha

Hamrato
esh Sheykh

Sodirî

Umm
Dam

Umm Ruwaba

El Obeid

Sennar

Ed Dueim
Kôsti

Ed Damazin
Er Roseires

Dilling
Kadugli
Talodi
Heiban
Rashad

El Lagowa
El Odaiya
El Quba

Tungaru

Muglad

Gelhak
Melut

Kodok

Renk

Wâd Medanî

Kamlin
El Geteina

Rufa'a

Kagmar

Khashm
el Girba

Gallabat
Métema
Gedaref

El Mafâza
Singa

Sennar

Kassala

Ar Rahad

Ed Dueim

SUDAN

KORDOFAN

DARFUR

EL GEZIRA

NAHR EL AZRAQ (Blue Nile)

El Khartûm Bahrî
(Khartoum)
Omdurmân
El Khartûm

6th Cataract
Geili
Shendi

Gebel Abyad

Ed Debba

Khashm
el Girba

L. Tana

Gonder
Debre Tabor

4620
Sekota

Mekele
Adwa
Aksum

Dese

Lalibela

Mota

Alibo
Dembecha
Debre Markos

ERITREA

Akordat
Adi Ugri
Barentu
Adi Ugri

Mersa Fatma

Aksum

CENTRAL AFRICA

Baïbokoum
Gore
Baboua
Bossangoa
Bossembélé
Bozoum
Carnot
Boda
Bossel
Boali
Bangui

Berbérati
Nola

Batouri

BAHR EL GHAZAL

Raga
Deim Zubeir
Wau
Bo
Tonj
Rumbek

Meshra
er-Req
Jur

Bahr el Ghazal

Bahr el 'Arab

A'ÂLÂ
EN NIL

Fangak
Abwong
Sobat

Nasir

Malakal
Nil el Abyad
(White Nile)

Bentiu

Nilel Ghazal

Kodok

Bor
Kongor
Pibor P.

Amadi
Tombe
Tali P.
Tamburâ

Bangasou
Rafaï
Zémio

Obo

Djema
Bakouma
Yalinga
Bria

Ippy
Bambari
Grimari

Sibut
Kouki

Markounda

EL ISTWÂ'IYA

Maridi
Jûba
Mongalla

Kapoeta

Torit

Lokitaung

Todenyang

L. Turkana

Chew Bahir
(L. Stefanie)

Mega

ETHIOPIA

Addis Abeba
(Addis Ababa)
Addis Alem

Nekemte
Gimbi
Dembidolo
Gambela

L. Ziway
Jima

Shashemene
L. Abaya
Soddo
L. Shala
4200
Chencha
L. Shamo
Gardula
Jinka

Yirga Alem
Asela

Yabelo

Moyale

KENYA

ZAÏRE
(CONGO)

Bondo
Ango
Doruma
Niangara
Dungu
Faradje

Yakoma
Libenge
Yambio

Mobaye
Abumombazi

COPYRIGHT. GEORGE PHILIP & SON. LTD.

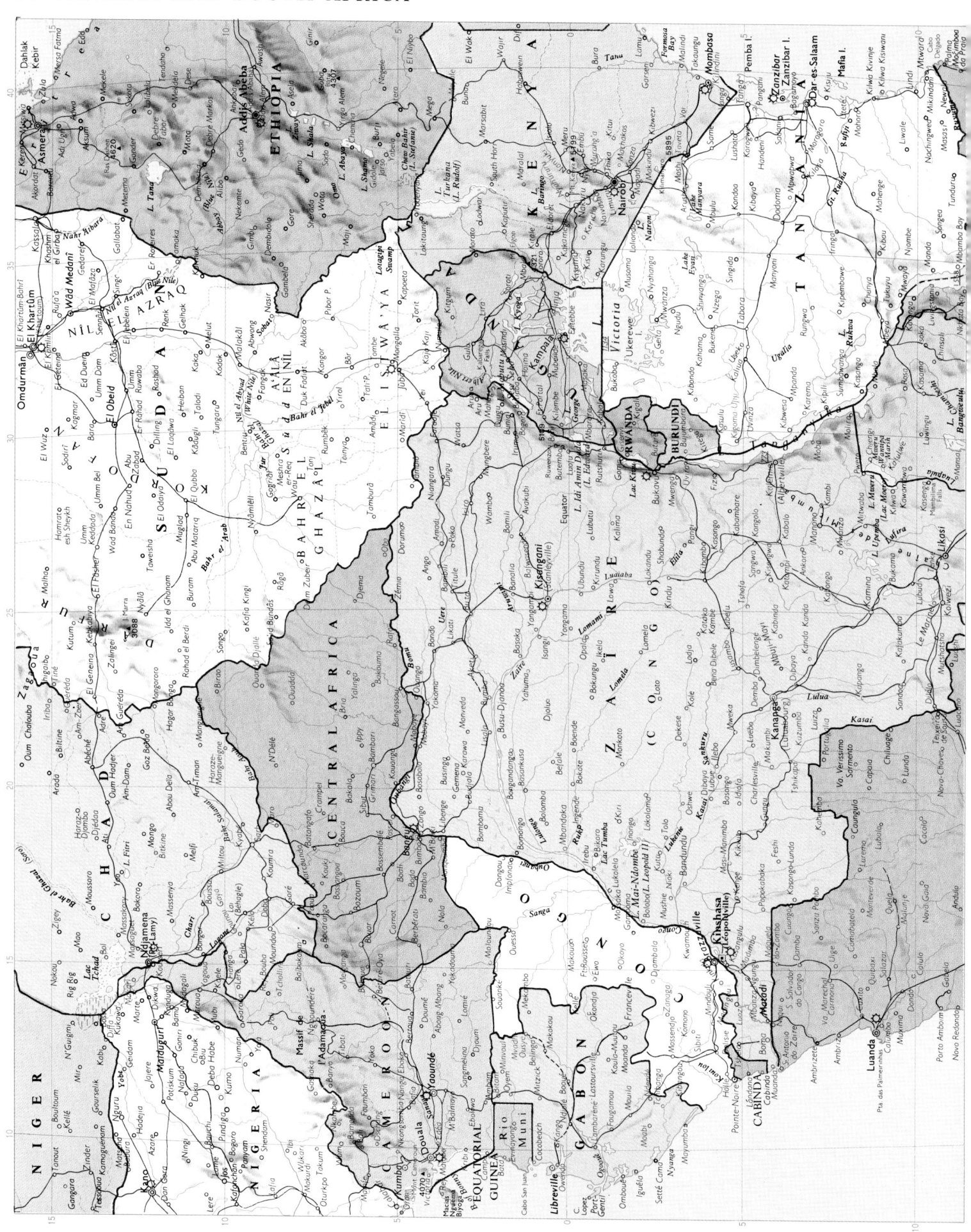

1:15 000 000

| 100 | | 100 | 200 | 300 | 400 miles |

| 100 | 0 | 100 | 200 | 300 | 400 | 500 | 600 km |

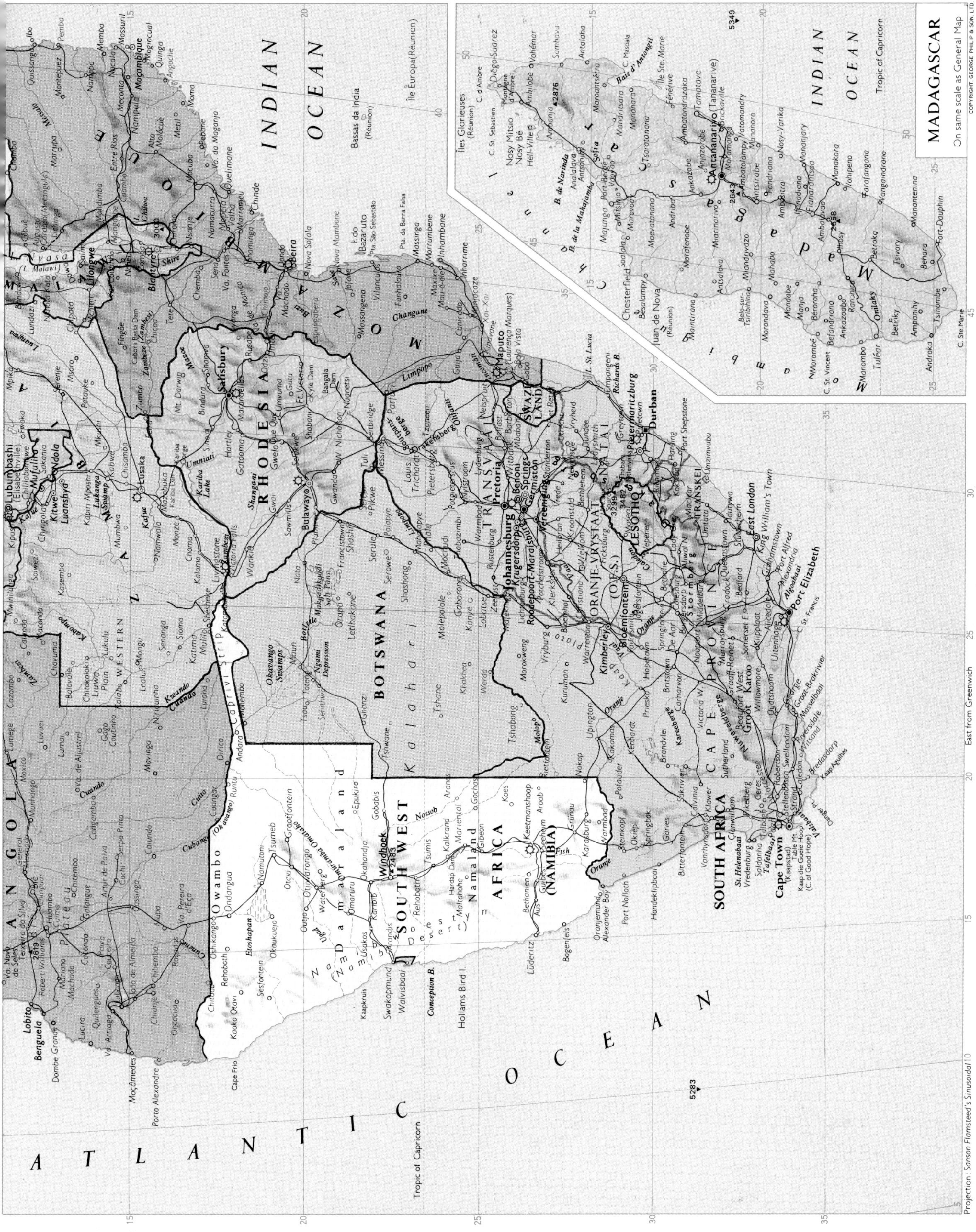

MADAGASCAR

On same scale as General Map

COPYRIGHT GEORGE PHILIP & SON LTD

Projection: Sanson Flamsteed's Sinusoidal

East from Greenwich

I N D I A N   O C E A N

A T L A N T I C   O C E A N

Tropic of Capricorn

A N G O L A

Z A M B I A

RHODESIA

BOTSWANA

SOUTH WEST AFRICA (NAMIBIA)

SOUTH AFRICA

CAPE PROVINCE

TRANSVAAL

NATAL

ORANJE-VRYSTAAT (O.F.S.)

LESOTHO

SWAZILAND

TRANSKEI

M O Z A M B I Q U E

Kalahari

East from Greenwich

5615 Principal Shipping Routes
(Distances in Nautical Miles)

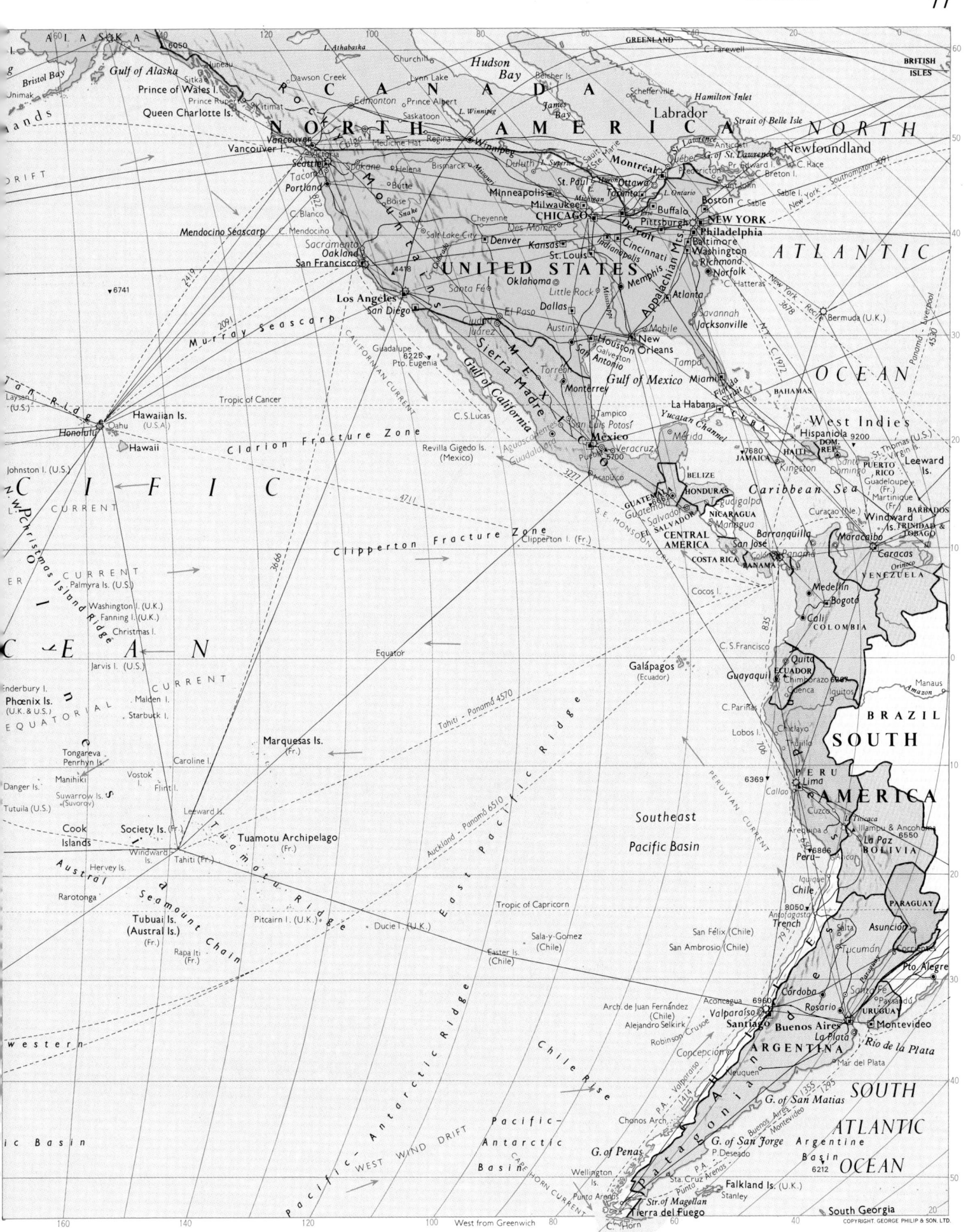

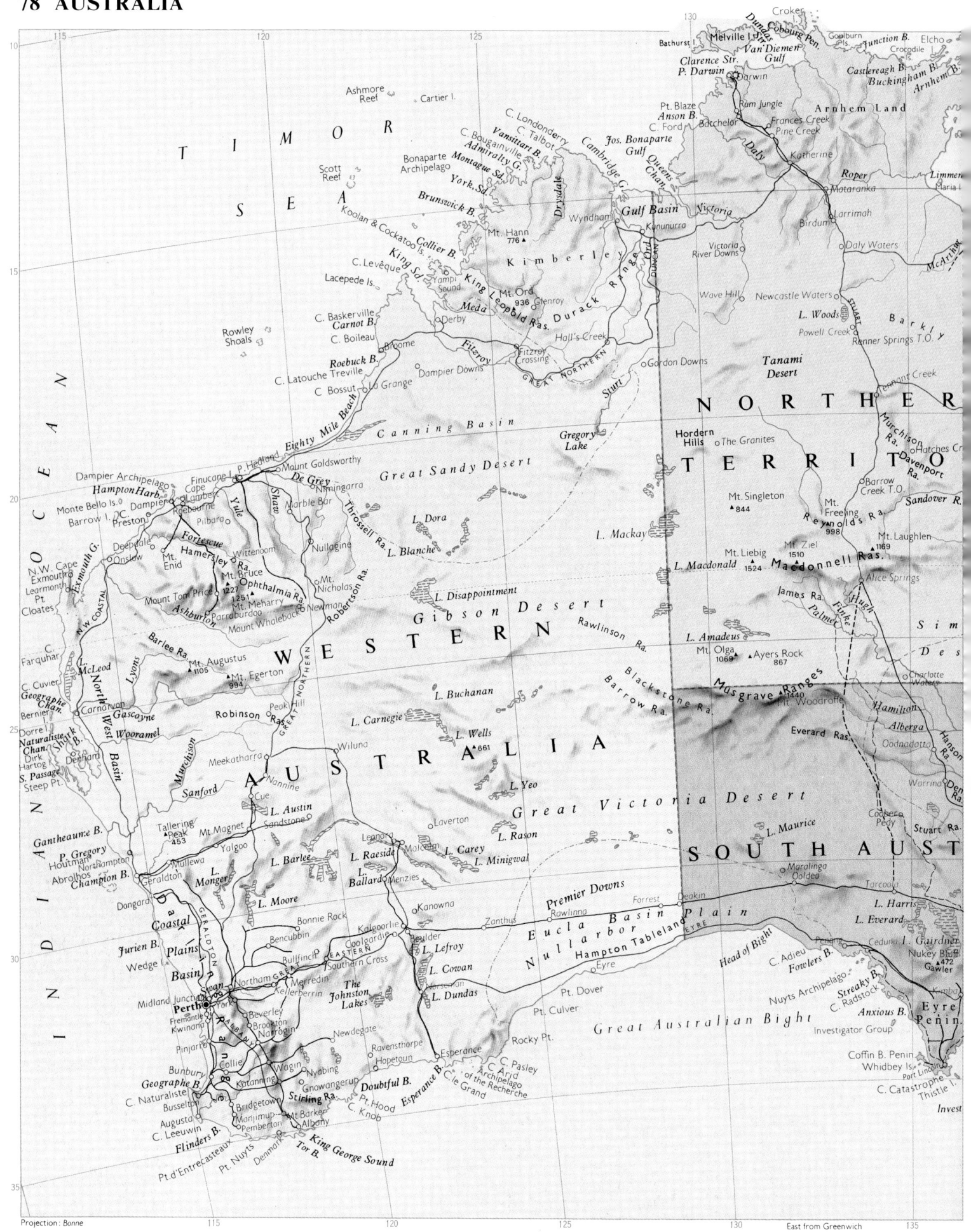

TIMOR SEA

INDIAN OCEAN

Ashmore Reef
Cartier I.

Scott Reef
Rowley Shoals

Croker
Dundas
Cobourg Pen.
Melville I.
Van Diemen Gulf
Bathurst I.
Clarence Str.
P. Darwin
Darwin
Pt. Blaze
Anson B.
C. Ford
Batchelor
Rum Jungle
Frances Creek
Pine Creek
Katherine
Goulburn
Junction B.
Crocodile
Elcho
Castlereagh B.
Buckingham B.
Arnhem B.
Arnhem Land
Roper
Matarnka
Larrimah
Birdum
Daly Waters
Limmen
Maria I.
McArthur

C. Londonderry
C. Talbot
Vansittart B.
C. Bougainville
Admiralty G.
Montague Sd.
York Sd.
Brunswick B.
Bonaparte Archipelago
Cambridge G.
Jos. Bonaparte Gulf
Queens Chan.
Wyndham
Kununurra
Gulf Basin
Victoria
Victoria River Downs
Wave Hill
Newcastle Waters
L. Woods
Barkly
Powell Creek
Renner Springs T.O.

Koolan & Cockato Is.
King Sd.
C. Levêque
Lacepede Is.
C. Baskerville
Carnot B.
C. Boileau
Yampi Sound
Meda
Derby
Broome
Roebuck B.
C. Latouche Treville
C. Bossut
La Grange
Dampier Downs

Mt. Hann 776
Kimberley
King Leopold Ras.
Mt. Ord 936
Glenroy
Hall's Creek
Fitzroy Crossing
Fitzroy
Drysdale
Durack Range
Gordon Downs
Sturt
GREAT NORTHERN

Gregory Lake
Hordern Hills
The Granites
Tanami Desert
Mt. Singleton 844
Mt. Freeling 998
Reynolds Ra.
Barrow Creek T.O.
Sandover R.
Davenport Ra.
Murchison Ra.
Hatches Cr.

NORTHERN TERRITORY

Eighty Mile Beach
Canning Basin
Great Sandy Desert
L. Dora
L. Blanche
L. Mackay
Mt. Liebig 1510
Mt. Ziel 1510
L. Macdonald 1524
Macdonnell Ras.
Mt. Laughlen 1169
Alice Springs
James Ra.
Hugh
Finke
Palmer
Sim
Des

Dampier Archipelago
Finucane I.
P. Hedland
Cape
Lambert
Roebourne
Monte Bello Is.
Barrow I.
Dampier
Preston
Pilbara
De Grey
Nimingarra
Marble Bar
Nullagine
Throssell Ra.
Mount Goldsworthy
Shaw
Yule
L. Disappointment
Gibson Desert
Rawlinson Ra.
L. Amadeus
Mt. Olga 1069
Ayers Rock 867
Charlotte Waters

N.W. Cape
Exmouth G.
Learmonth
Pt. Cloates
Deepdale
Onslow
Mt. Enid
Hamersley Ra.
Wittenoom
Mt. Bruce 1227
Ophthalmia Ra.
Mt. Meharry 1251
Ashburton
Mount Tom Price
Parraburdoo
Mount Whaleback
Newman
Mt. Nicholas
Robertson Ra.
WESTERN

Blackstone Ra.
Barrow Ra.
Musgrave Ranges
Mt. Woodroffe 1440
Everard Ras.
Hamilton
Alberga
Oodnadatta
Hanson Ra.
Warrina
Den Ra.

C. Farquhar
C. Cuvier
Geographe Chan.
Bernier I.
Dorre I.
Dirk Hartog I.
Shark B.
Denham
S. Passage
Steep Pt.
McLeod
North West
Gascoyne
Wooramel
West Basin
Murchison
Barlee Ra.
Mt. Augustus 1105
Mt. Egerton 994
Lyons
Peak Hill
Robinson
GREAT NORTHERN
AUSTRALIA
L. Buchanan
L. Carnegie
L. Wells 661
L. Yeo
Great Victoria Desert
L. Rason
L. Maurice
Coober Pedy
Stuart Ra.
SOUTH AUST

Gantheaume B.
P. Gregory
Houtman Abrolhos
Northampton
Champion B.
Geraldton
Dongara
Mullewa
Yalgoo
Meekatharra
Nannine
Cue
Sanford
Tallering Peak 453
Mt. Magnet
Sandstone
L. Austin
L. Barlee
L. Moore
L. Monger
L. Raeside
L. Ballard
Menzies
Wiluna
Leonora
Malcolm
L. Carey
L. Minigwal
Laverton
Kanowna
Kalgoorlie
Boulder
L. Lefroy
L. Cowan
Coolgardie
Southern Cross
Premier Downs
Rawlinna
Forrest
Deakin
Maralinga
Oldea
Tarcoola
L. Harris
L. Everard
L. Gairdner
Nukey Bluff 472
Gawler
Cedunna
Penong

Jurien B.
Wedge
Coastal Plains Basin
Dongara
Swan
Northam
York
Midland Junction
Perth
Fremantle
Kwinana
Pinjarra
Beverley
Brookton
Narrogin
Bunbury
Collie
Newdegate
Ravensthorpe
Hopetoun
Bencubbin
Bullfinch
Merredin
Kellerberrin
The Johnston Lakes
Bonnie Rock
L. Dundas
Zanthus
Eucla Basin
Nullarbor Plain
Hampton Tableland
Eyre
Pt. Dover
Pt. Culver
Rocky Pt.
Head of Bight
C. Adieu
Fowlers B.
Nuyts Archipelago
Streaky B.
Anxious B.
Investigator Group
Coffin B. Penin
Whidbey Is.
Port Lincoln
C. Catastrophe
Thistle I.
Eyre Penin.
Kimba
Radstock

Geographe B.
C. Naturaliste
Busselton
Augusta
C. Leeuwin
Flinders B.
Pt. d'Entrecasteaux
Bridgetown
Manjimup
Pemberton
Katanning
Wagin
Nyabing
Gnowangerup
Stirling Ra.
Mt. Barker
Albany
Denmark
Tor B.
King George Sound
Pt. Hood
Doubtful B.
C. Knob
Esperance B.
Esperance
C. Arid
Archipelago of the Recherche
C. Pasley
C. le Grand
Great Australian Bight

115   120   125   130   135

Boundaries of the artesian basins -------

1:12 000 000

AUSTRALASIA
PHYSICAL
1:80 000 000

TASMANIA

on same scale

COPYRIGHT. GEORGE PHILIP & SON. LTD.

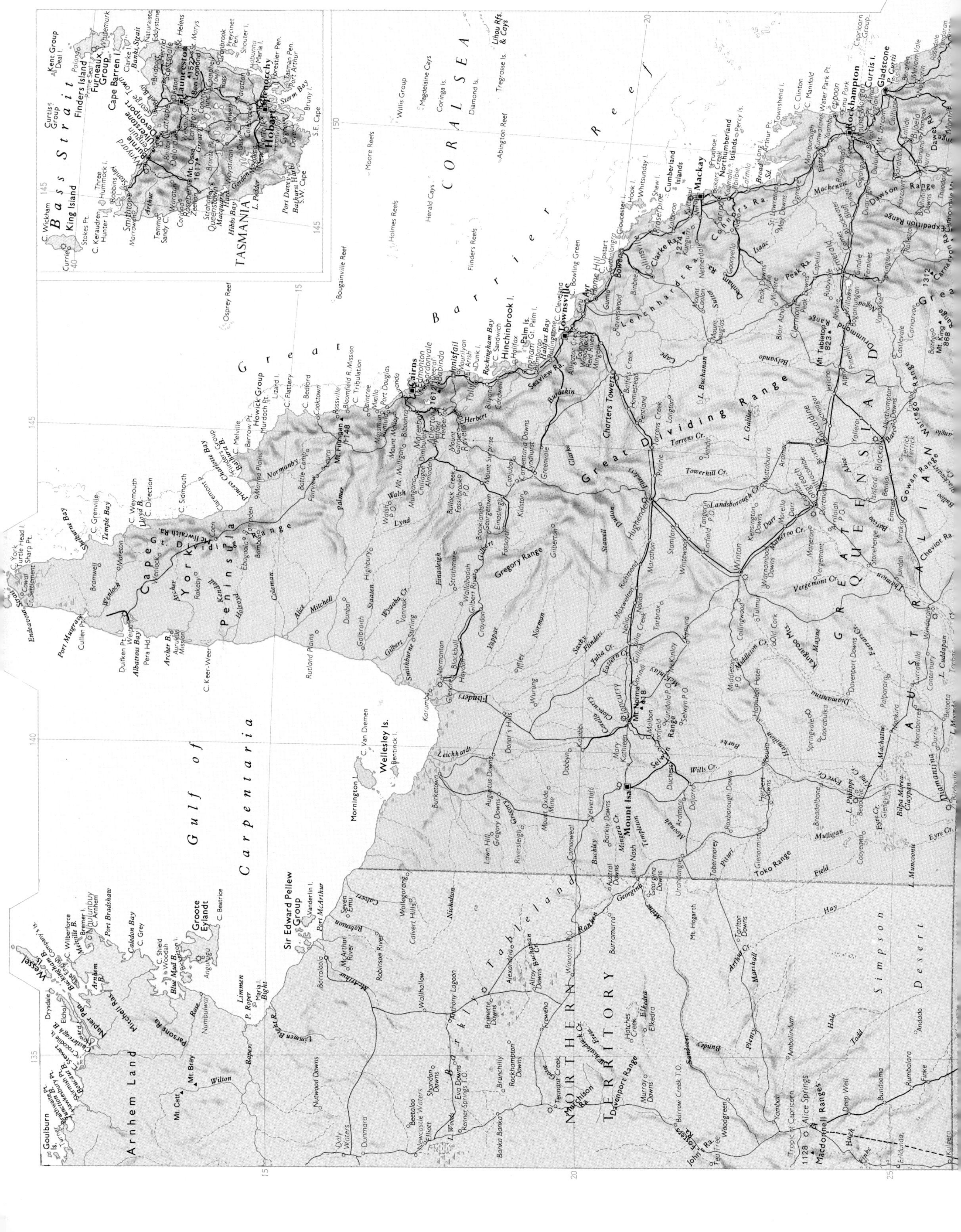

Inset: TASMANIA

Bass Strait

Kent Group — Deal I.
King Island
Curtis Group
Furneaux Group
Cape Barren I.
Finders Island
Flinders Island

TASMANIA
Hobart
Launceston
Devonport
Burnie
Queenstown
Strahan
Cradle Mt. 1617
S.E. Cape

Main Map

CORAL SEA

Great Barrier Reef

Gulf of Carpentaria

Arnhem Land

Cape York Peninsula

Gt. Dividing Range

Great Dividing Range

QUEENSLAND

NORTHERN TERRITORY

GREAT AUSTRALIAN RANGE

Simpson Desert

Barkly Tableland

Macdonnell Ranges

Tropic of Capricorn

Coastal cities and towns

Rockhampton
Gladstone
Mackay
Townsville
Cairns
Bowen
Ayr
Ingham
Innisfail
Cooktown
Charters Towers
Cloncurry
Mount Isa
Alice Springs
Tennant Creek

Seas and gulfs

Gulf of Carpentaria
Coral Sea
Bass Strait

Islands and reefs

Groote Eylandt
Wellesley Is.
Mornington I.
Hinchinbrook I.
Cumberland Islands
Northumberland Islands
Whitsunday I.
Curtis I.
Wessel Is.
Sir Edward Pellew Group
Osprey Reef
Bougainville Reef
Willis Group
Herald Cays
Magdelaine Cays
Coringa Is.
Diamond Is.
Lihou Rfs. & Cays
Tregrosse Is.
Holmes Reefs
Flinders Reefs
Moore Reefs

1 : 8 000 000

50   100   150   200 miles
50   0   100   200   300 km

T A S M A N

S E A

B A S I N

Great Dividing Range

Darling Downs

Great Artesian Basin

Grey Range

BRISBANE

Toowoomba

Ipswich

NEW SOUTH WALES

Darling

SYDNEY

Newcastle

Wollongong

Dubbo

Broken Hill

CANBERRA

COMMONWEALTH TERR.

Flinders Ranges

SOUTH AUSTRALIA

Lake Eyre North

Lake Eyre South

Lake Torrens

Lake Gairdner

Eyre Peninsula

Spencer Gulf

ADELAIDE

Kangaroo I.

Mildura

VICTORIA

The Grampians

MELBOURNE

Ballarat

Bendigo

Geelong

Warrnambool

Mount Gambier

Bass Strait

King Island

Furneaux Group

Flinders Island

Cape Barren I.

East from Greenwich

Projection Bonne

COPYRIGHT GEORGE PHILIP & SON Ltd

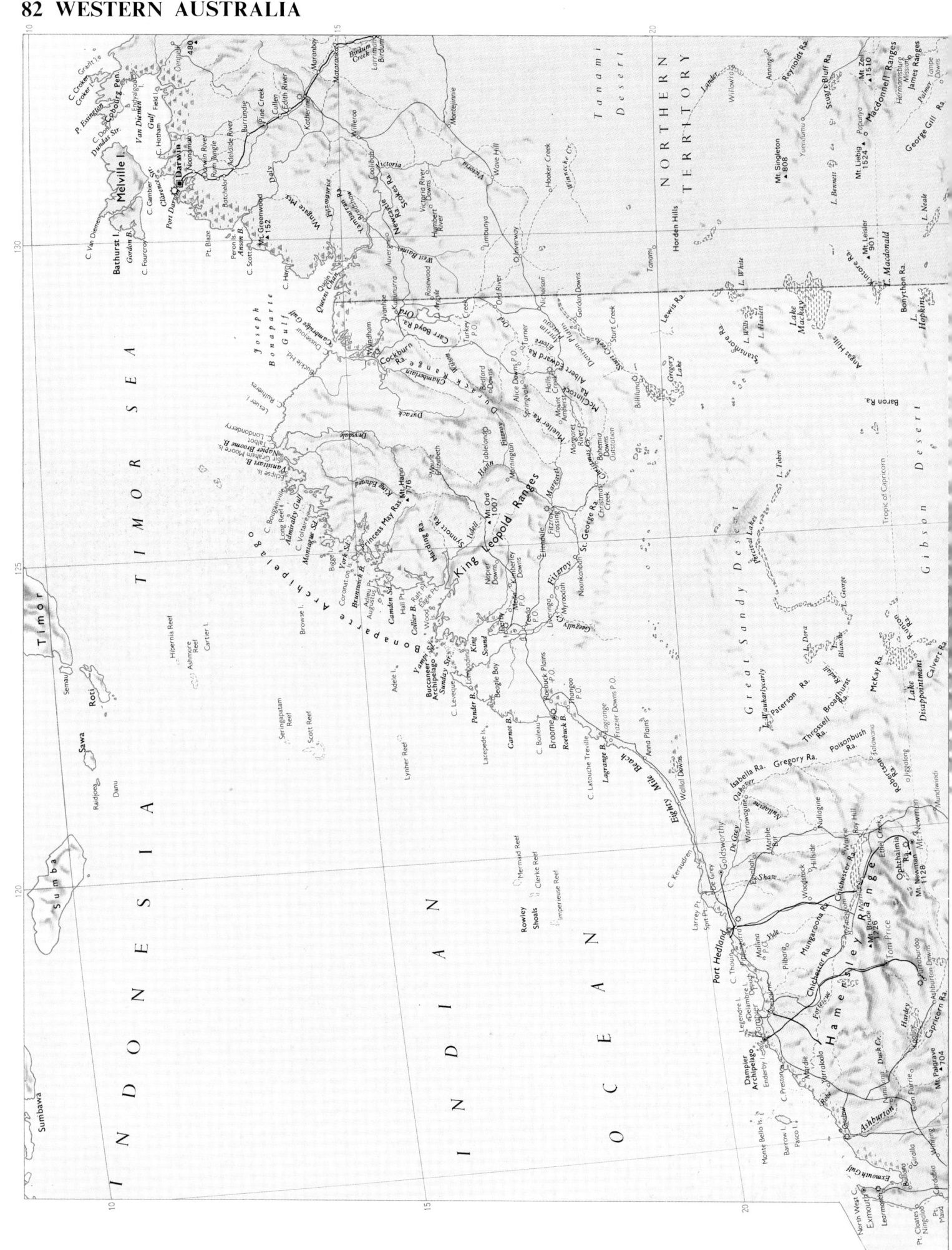

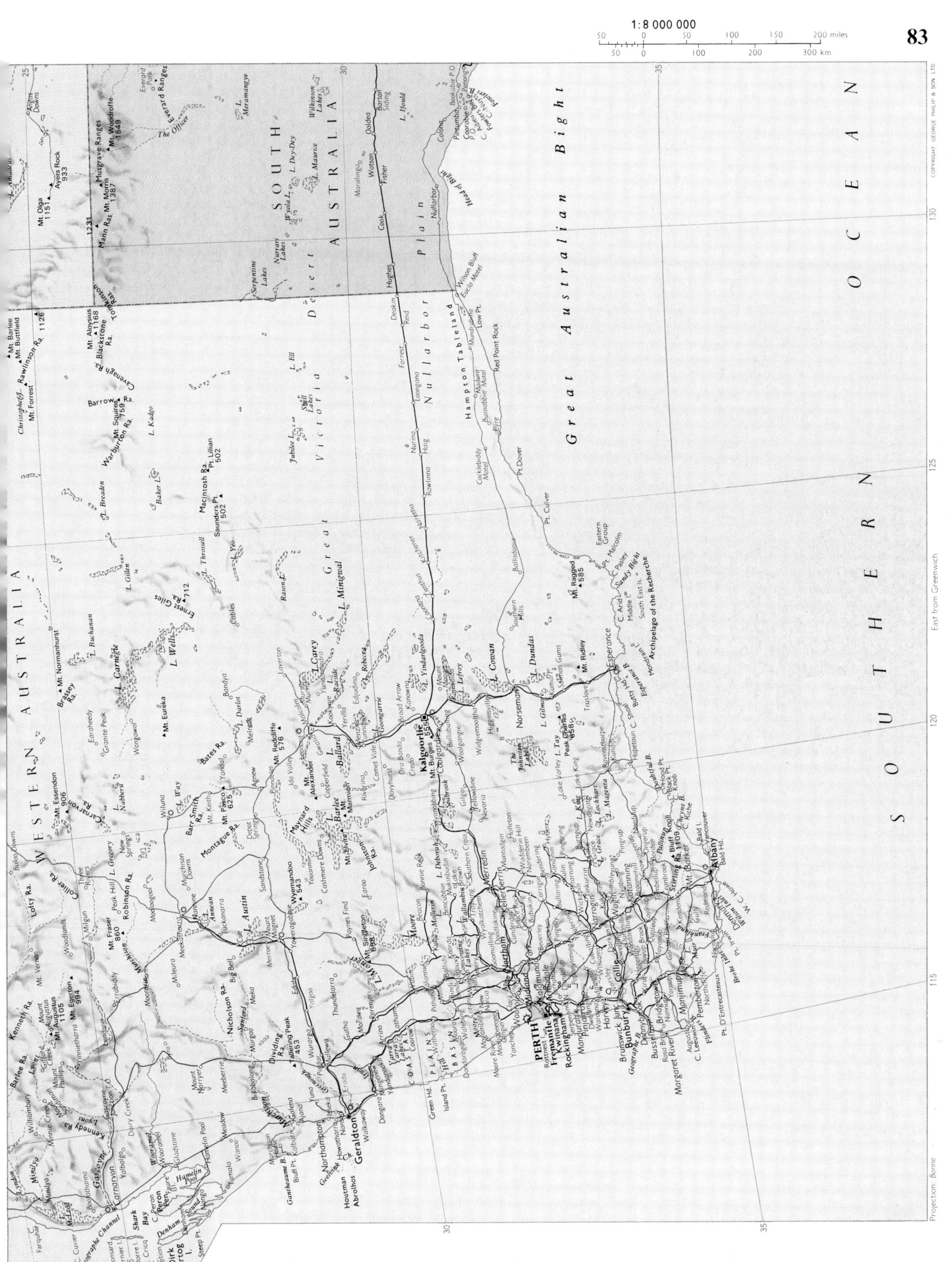

1:4 500 000

Projection: Albers' Equal Area with two standard parallels

East from Greenwich

COPYRIGHT GEORGE PHILIP & SON LTD

TASMAN SEA

NEW SOUTH WALES

VICTORIA

SOUTH AUSTRALIA

SYDNEY

MELBOURNE

Newcastle

Canberra

AUSTRALIAN CAPITAL TERRITORY

Wollongong

Broken Hill

Geelong

Ballarat

Bendigo

Albury

Wagga Wagga

Goulburn

Bathurst

Orange

Dubbo

Queanbeyan

Katoomba (Blue Mts.)

Mildura

Warrnambool

Mount Gambier

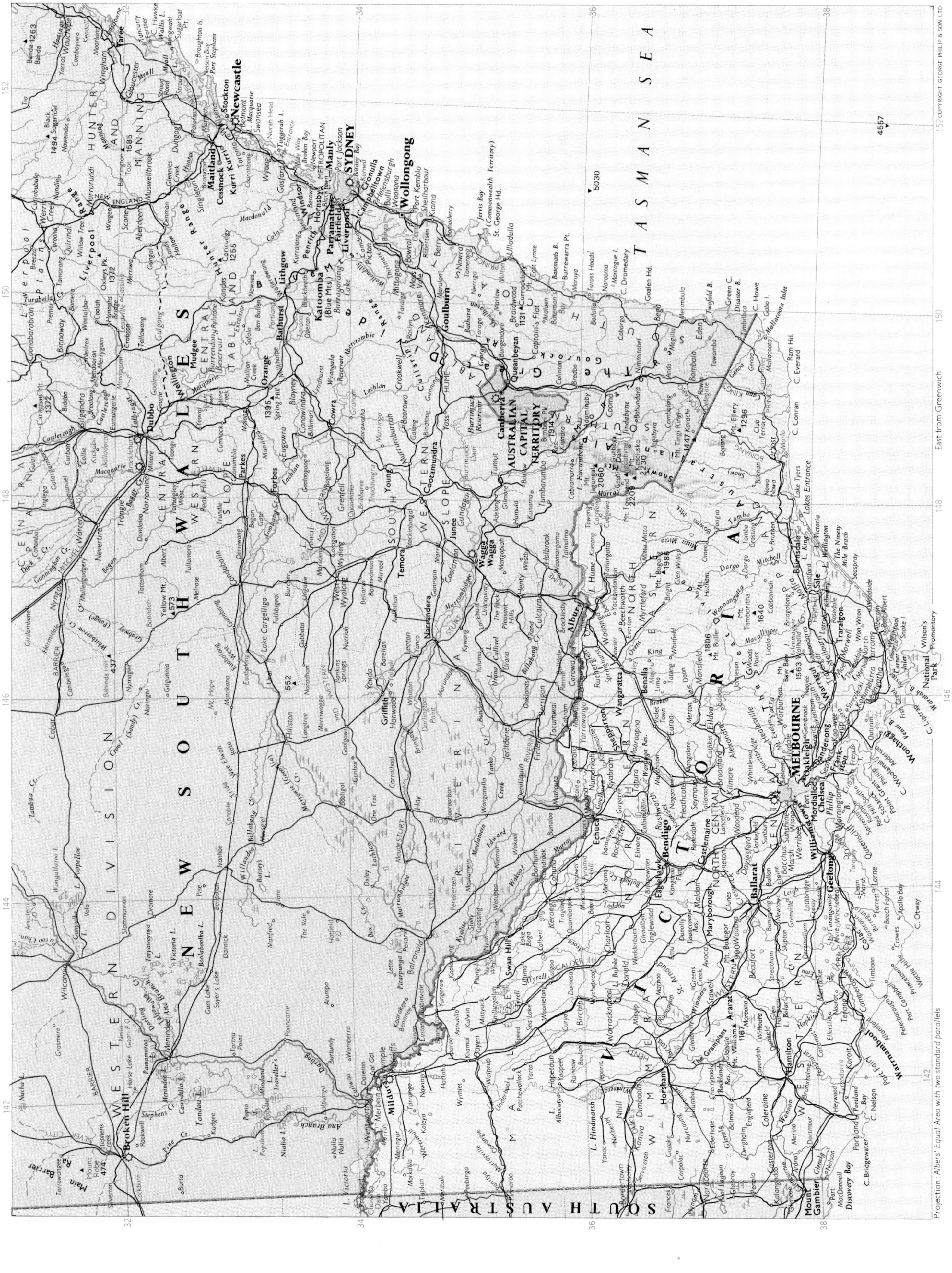

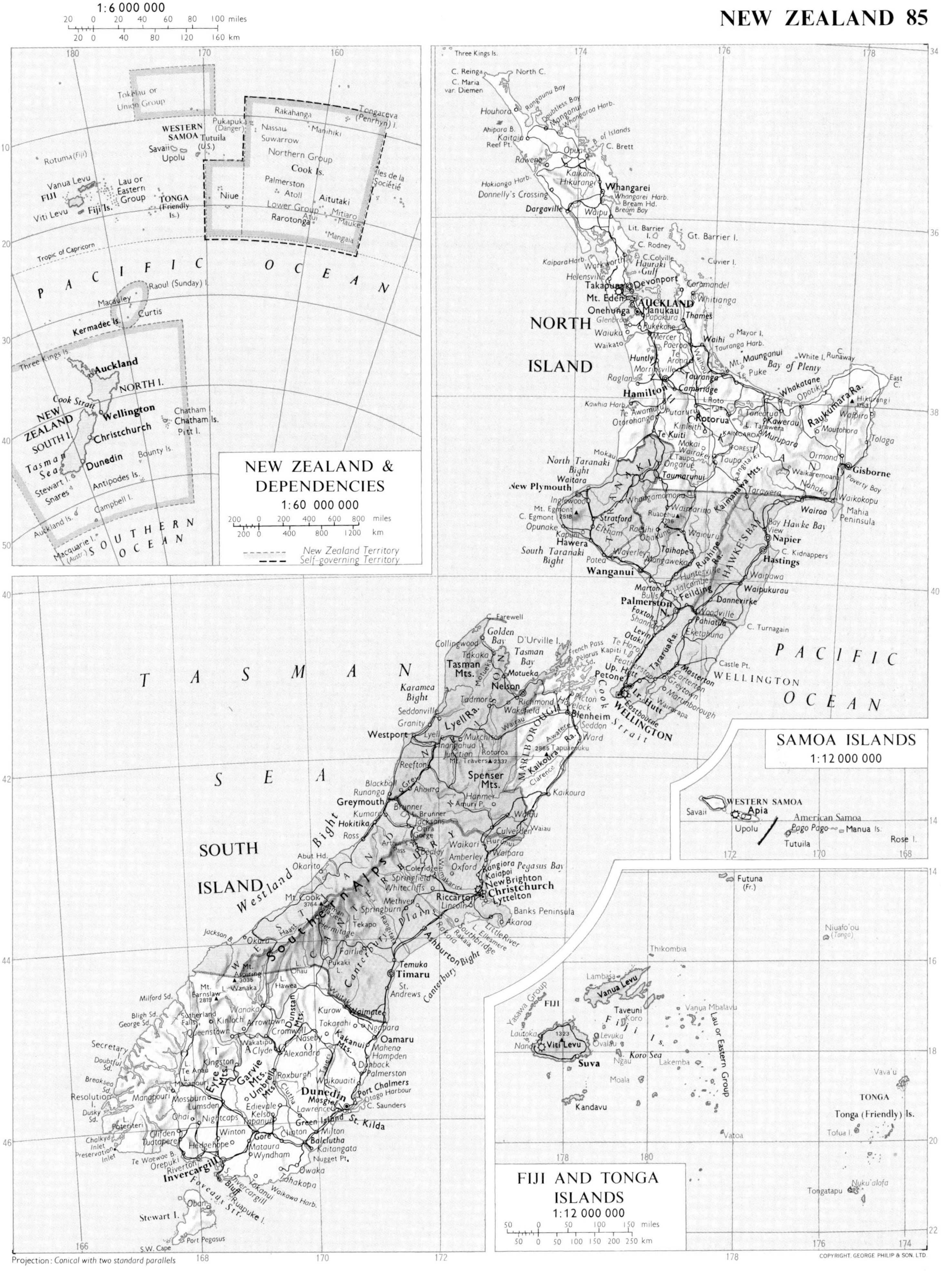

1:6 000 000
20 0 20 40 60 80 100 miles
20 0 40 80 120 160 km

NEW ZEALAND & DEPENDENCIES
1:60 000 000
200 0 200 400 600 800 miles
200 0 400 800 1200 km

New Zealand Territory
Self-governing Territory

NORTH ISLAND

SOUTH ISLAND

TASMAN SEA

PACIFIC OCEAN

SOUTHERN OCEAN

Tropic of Capricorn

SAMOA ISLANDS
1:12 000 000

WESTERN SAMOA
Apia
Savaii
Upolu
American Samoa
Pago Pago
Tutuila
Manua Is.
Rose I.

FIJI AND TONGA ISLANDS
1:12 000 000
50 0 50 100 150 miles
50 0 50 100 200 250 km

FIJI
Vanua Levu
Taveuni
Viti Levu
Suva
Koro Sea
Lau or Eastern Group
TONGA
Tonga (Friendly) Is.
Tongatapu
Nuku'alofa

Projection: Conical with two standard parallels

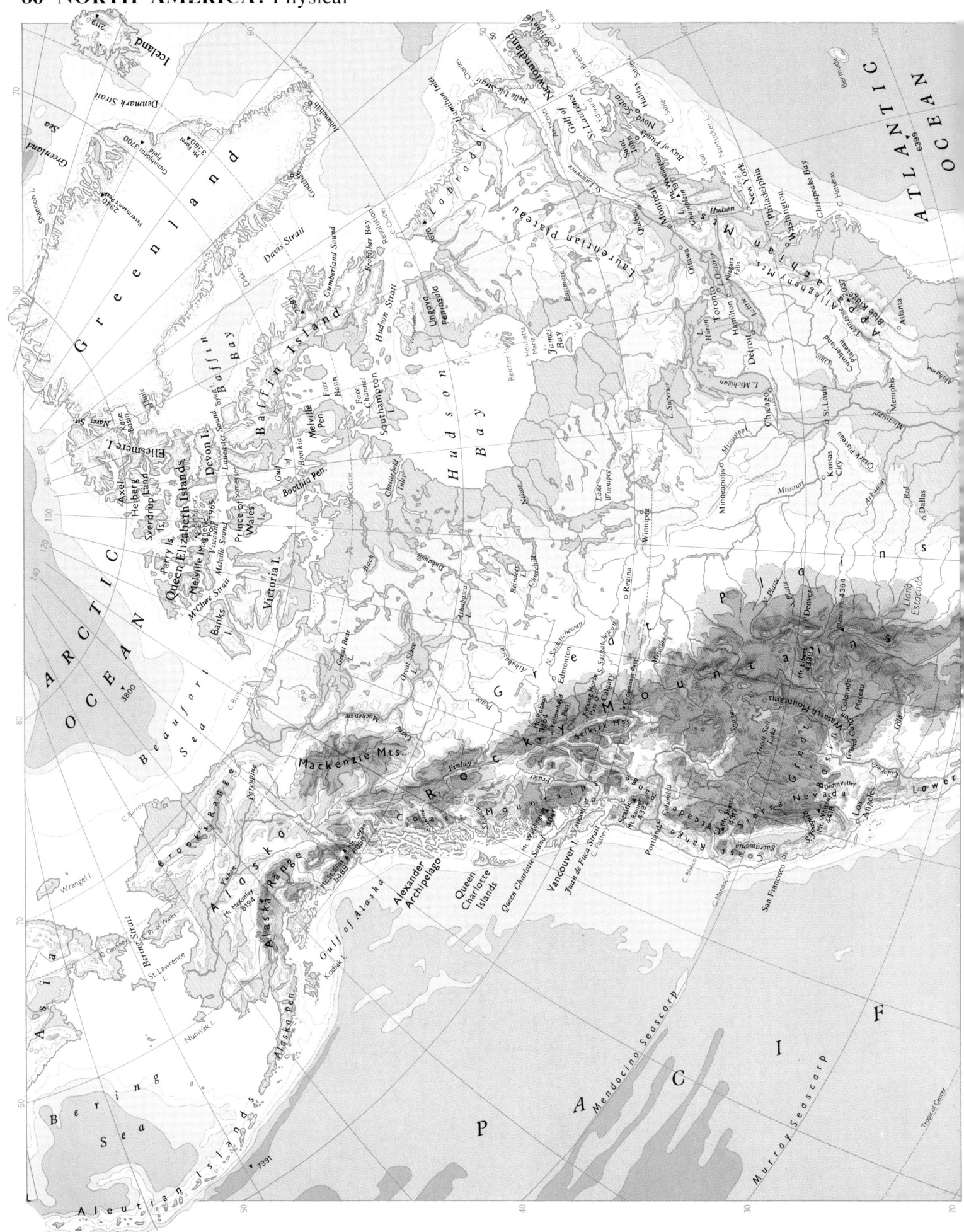

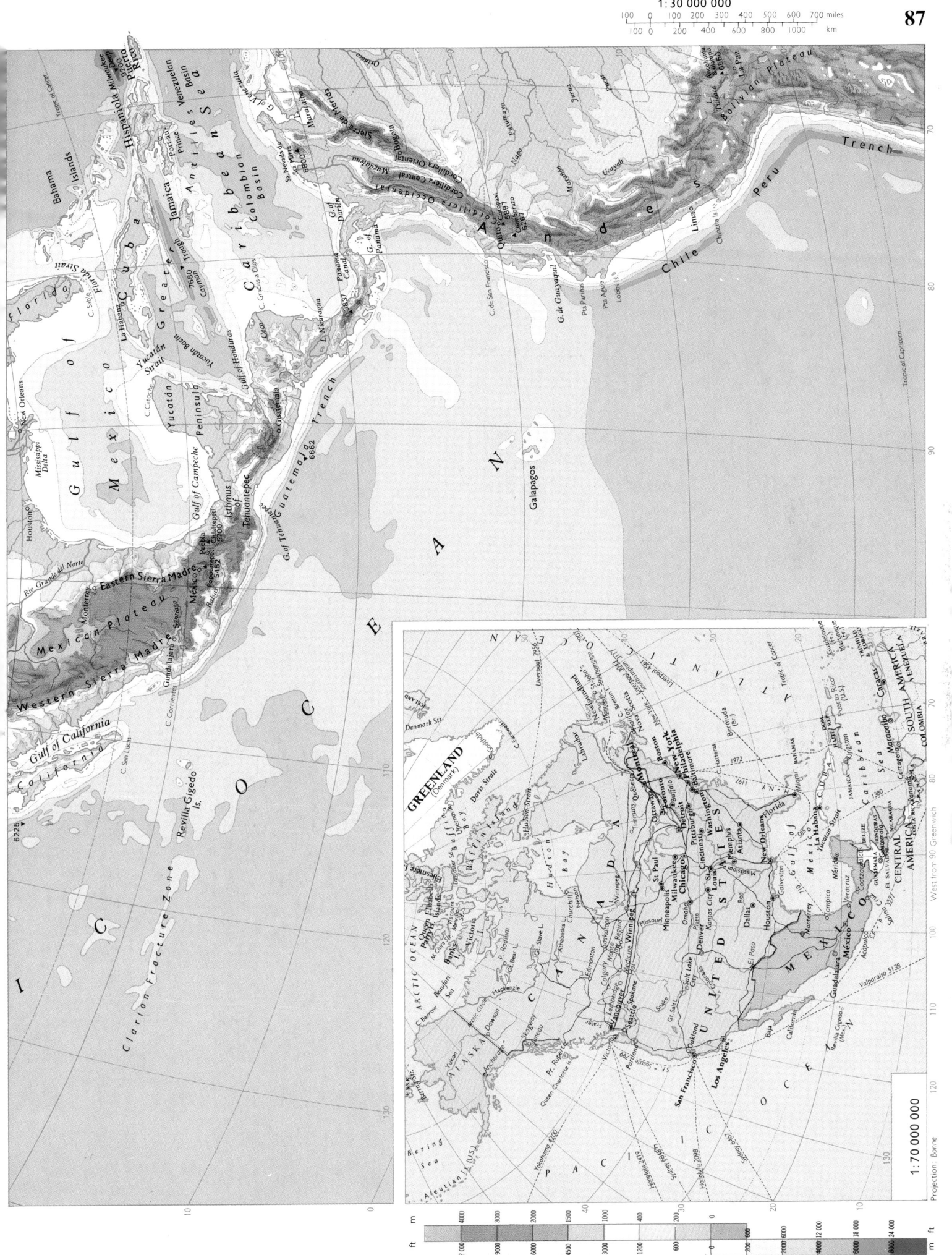

1 : 30 000 000

100 0 100 200 300 400 500 600 700 miles

100 0 200 400 600 800 1000 km

87

Bahama Islands

Florida Strait

Tropic of Cancer

New Orleans

Mississippi Delta

Houston

G u l f   o f   M e x i c o

Rio Grande del Norte

Monterrey Eastern Sierra Madre

Mexican Plateau

Western Sierra Madre

Guadalajara México Puebla

Bajio Popocatepetl 5452 Citlaltepetl 5700

Isthmus of Tehuantepec

Gulf of Campeche

C. Catoche

Yucatán Strait

Yucatán Peninsula

Yucatán Basin

Gulf of Honduras

Guatemala

Caribbean   S e a

G r e a t e r   A n t i l l e s

Cuba

La Habana

Jamaica

C. Sable

7680 Cayman Trough

Casco

G. de Gracias a Dios

L. Nicaragua

Guatemala Trench 6662

G. of Tehuantepec

Puerto Rico 9200 Milwaukee Deep

Hispaniola

Puerto Rico

S. Nevada de S. Marta

5800

Sierra de Merida

Maracaibo

G. of Venezuela

Orinoco

Lesser Antilles

Venezuelan Basin

Colombian Basin

G. of Darién

G. of Panamá

Panamá Canal

3837

Cordillera Occidental

Cordillera Central

Cordillera Oriental

Quito 5897

Chimborazo 6267

Napo

Marañón

Ucayali

Huallaga

Pichincha

Jurua

Bolivian Plateau

La Paz

L. Titicaca

Illampu 6550

C. San Francisco

G. de Guayaquil

Pta Parinas

Lobos Is.

Chincha Is.

Lima

A   n   d   e   s

Chile

Peru Trench

Tropic of Capricorn

P   A   C   I   F   I   C

O   C   E   A   N

Galapagos

Gulf of California

California

C. San Lucas

C. Corrientes

Revilla Gigedo Is.

6225

Clarion Fracture Zone

Projection: Bonne

1 : 70 000 000

ARCTIC OCEAN

GREENLAND (Denmark)

Denmark Str.

C. Farewell

Baffin Island

Baffin Bay

Davis Strait

Ellesmere I.

Parry Islands

Victoria I.

Banks I.

M'Clure Str.

Gt Bear L.

F. Radium

Mackenzie

Gt Slave L.

Athabasca L.

C. Barrow

Beaufort Sea

Yukon

ALASKA (U.S.)

Anchorage

Skagway

Pr. Rupert

Queen Charlotte Is.

Vancouver

Victoria

Fraser

Seattle

Portland

Spokane

San Francisco

Oakland

Los Angeles

Baja California

C A N A D A

Edmonton

Calgary

Lethbridge

Regina

Winnipeg

Churchill

Hudson Bay

Labrador

Quebec

Montreal

Ottawa

Toronto

Buffalo

Detroit

Pittsburgh

New York

Boston

Philadelphia

Baltimore

Washington

Cincinnati

Chicago

Milwaukee

Minneapolis

St Paul

Omaha

Kansas City

St Louis

Memphis

Atlanta

New Orleans

Dallas

Houston

Galveston

El Paso

Denver

Salt Lake City

Platte

Missouri

Mississippi

Red

U N I T E D   S T A T E S

M E X I C O

Monterrey

Guadalajara México

Veracruz

Tampico

Mérida

Acapulco

Gulf of Mexico

Florida

Miami

CUBA

La Habana

Yucatán Strait

BAHAMAS

Bermuda (Br.)

C. Hatteras

C. Race

Nova Scotia

Newfoundland

Hudson Strait

ATLANTIC OCEAN

Tropic of Cancer

HAITI

JAMAICA

Caribbean Sea

Kingston

PUERTO RICO (U.S.)

Maracaibo

Caracas

VENEZUELA

COLOMBIA

SOUTH AMERICA

CENTRAL AMERICA

BELIZE

GUATEMALA

HONDURAS

EL SALVADOR

NICARAGUA

COSTA RICA

PANAMA

TRINIDAD

Guadeloupe (Fr.)

Martinique (Fr.)

Revilla Gigedo (Mex.)

PACIFIC OCEAN

Bering Sea

Aleutian Is. (U.S.)

West from 90 Greenwich

m ft

12 000 4000

9000 3000

6000 2000

4500 1500

3000 1000

1200 400

600 200

0 0

200 600

2000 6000

4000 12 000

6000 18 000

8000 24 000

ft m

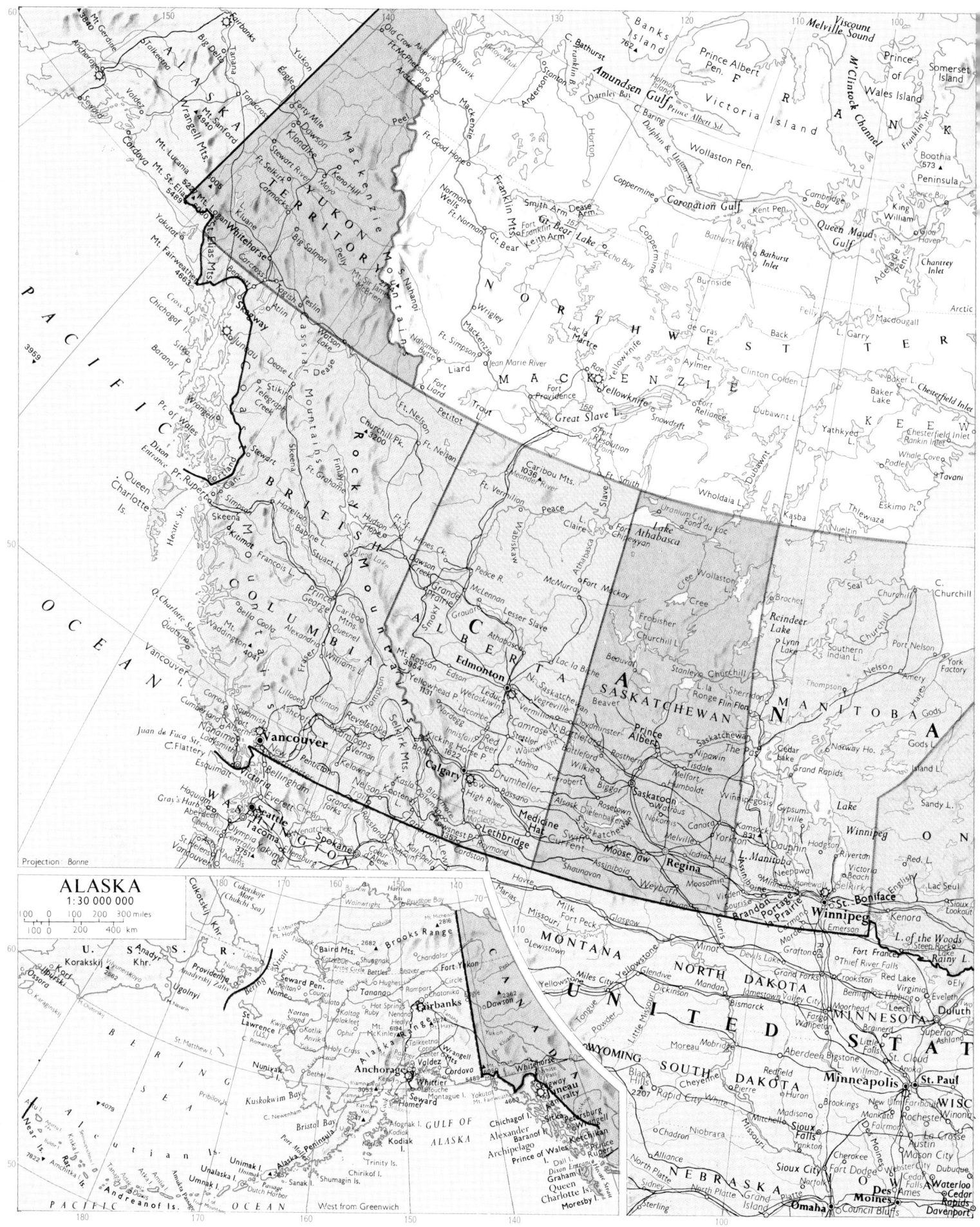

ALASKA
1:30 000 000

Projection: Bonne

1:15 000 000

100 50 0 100 200 300 400 miles
100 0 100 200 300 400 500 600 km

Devon Island
Lancaster Sound
Arctic Bay 1890 Bylot I. Pond Inlet
Brodeur Milne Inlet Pond Inlet
Peninsula Scott I.
Gulf of Boothia 2136 Baffin Bay
Svartenhuk Halvø Angmagssalik

GREENLAND

Kong Frederik VI's Kyst
2850
Godthåb
Frederikshåb
Ivigtut
Julianehåb
Nanortalik Kap Farvel

ATLANTIC OCEAN

Disko B.
Disko
Davis Strait
Holsteinsborg
Sukkertoppen
Søndre Strømfjord
Sondre

C. Hewett
Clyde
Home B.
Broughton Island
Padloping Island
C. Dyer
Cape Dyer
2591 Cumberland Peninsula
Pangnirtung
Hoare B.
C. Mercy
Cumberland Sd.

Fury & Hecla Str.
Igloolik Island
Hall Lake
Prince Charles I.
Foxe Basin
Melville Peninsula
Nettilling L.

Pelly Bay
Rae Isthmus
Repulse Bay
Circle

Foxe Channel
C. Dorchester
Foxe Penin.
Amadjuak L.
Amadjuak
Cape Dorset
Lake Harbour
Frobisher B.
Frobisher Bay
Resolution I.

Rae's Welcome Sd.
Wager B.
Wager Bay
Southampton I.
Coral Harbour
Bell Pen.
Coats I.
Mansel I.
Digges Is.

Hudson Strait
C. Chidley
3809

Hudson Bay

Ottawa Is.
▼257
Sleeper Is.
King George Is.
Baker's Dozen
Belcher Is.

C. Tatnam
Winisk
Big Trout L.
Attawapiskat
Ft. Severn
Severn
Fort Albany
Albany
Moosonee

Saglouc (Sugluk)
Ivugivik (Notre Dame d'Ivugivic)
Notre Dame de Koartac
Koartac
Maricourt (Wakeham Bay)
Akpatok I.
Payne (Payne Bay)
Bellin
Ungava Bay
Payne
Ungava

Portland Promontory
Inoucdjouac (Port Harrison)
Leaf
Koksoak
Ft. Chimo
George
Port Nouveau Québec (George R.)
Hebron
Nutak
Nain
1676

PENINSULA

L. Minto
Lower Seal L.
Whale
Koksoak
Kaniapiskau

Port de la Baleine (Great Whale River)
Gr. de Whale
Clearwater
Lac Bienville
Petitsikapau L.
Schefferville
Michikamau
Indian Harbour
C. Harrison
Hopedale
Rigolet

NEWFOUNDLAND
LABRADOR
North West R.
Churchill Falls
Churchill
Goose Bay
L. Melville
Cartwright
Battle Harb.
Belle Isle

James Bay
Akimiski I.
Nouveau Comptoir (Paint Hills)
Ft. George
Fort George
C. Jone

QUEBEC

1128
Gagnon
Wabush City
Moisie
Ashuanipi
L. Romaine
St. Augustin
Str. of Belle Isle

C. Henrietta Maria
East Main
Eastmain
Fort Rupert
Rupert
Charlton I.
Ft. Albany

L. Mistassini
L. Albanel
Waswanipi
La Grande
Nemiscau

L. St. Joseph
Armstrong
Nakina
Kenogami
Nipigon
L. Nipigon
Longlac
Hearst
Cochrane
Timmins
Kirkland Lake
Cobalt

Twillingate
Lewisporte
Grand Falls
Gander
Bonavista
Trinity B.
Carbonear
St. John's
Placentia
Trepassey
C. Race
814
Port aux Basques
C. Ray
Corner Brook
Deer Lake

Anticosti I.
Mingan
Sept Iles
Port Cartier
Moisie
R. St. Lawrence
Gaspé
Gaspé Pen.
Matane
Rimouski
Campbellton

Gulf of St. Lawrence
Magdalen Is.
P.R. EDWARD I.
Summerside
Charlottetown
C. North
Cape Breton I.
Glace Bay
Sydney
Port Hawkesbury
Mulgrave
C. Canso
St. PIERRE et MIQUELON (Fr.)

Baie Comeau
Betsiamites
Chibougamau
Gouin Reservoir
La Tuque
Weymont
Senneterre
Doucet
Val d'Or
Rouyn
Amos

Dolbeau
L. St. John
Roberval
Jonquière
Chicoutimi
1190
Saguenay
Tadoussac
Rivière du Loup
Edmundston
St. Leonard
Bathurst
Newcastle
Chatham
Moncton
Amherst
Springhill
Windsor
Truro
New Glasgow
Dartmouth
Halifax
Bridgewater
Liverpool
Shelburne
C. Sable
Sable I. (Nova Scotia)
6309 ▼

NEW BRUNSWICK
NOVA SCOTIA
Saint John
Fredericton
Woodstock
St. Stephen
B. of Fundy
Digby
Kentville
Yarmouth

Haileybury
Timiskaming L.
Cabonga Reservoir
Shawinigan
Trois Rivières
Québec
Lévis
Thetford Mines
Victoriaville
St. Hyacinthe
Sorel
Drummondville
Sherbrooke
Lennoxville
Lewiston
Portland
MAINE
Bangor
Augusta
Lewiston

Thunder Bay (Ft. William)
Michipicoten
Heron Bay
Oba
Franz
Sault Ste. Marie
Sudbury
Coppercliff
North Bay
Pembroke
Arnprior
Ottawa
Hull
MONTRÉAL
Lachine
Cornwall
L. Champlain
1917
Burlington
VERMONT
NEW HAMPSHIRE
Concord
Manchester
Lowell
MASS.
Boston
C. Cod
Worcester
Providence
R.I.
CONN.
New Haven
Bridgeport
New York
NEW JERSEY
Trenton

ONTARIO
Georgian Bay
Parry Sound
Orillia
Barrie
Owen Sound
Lake Huron
Collingwood
Midland
Peterborough
Belleville
Kingston
Watertown
NEW YORK
Utica
Syracuse
Rochester
Albany
Schenectady
Springfield
Waterbury
Hartford

Lake Superior
Marquette
Houghton
Keweenaw Bay
L'Anse
Iron Mt.
Menominee
Green Bay
Manitowoc
Sheboygan
Milwaukee
Racine
Kenosha
Madison
WISCONSIN
Appleton
Oshkosh
Wausau
Rhinelander
Antigo
Muskegon
Grand Rapids
Lansing
Flint
Saginaw
Bay City
Port Huron
Sarnia
Detroit
Windsor
Toledo
OHIO
Cleveland
Akron
Youngstown
Erie
PENNSYLVANIA
Williamsport
Scranton
Binghamton
Elmira
Ithaca
Jamestown
Buffalo
Niagara Falls
Hamilton
Toronto
Guelph
Kitchener
Stratford
London
Brantford
Chatham
St. Thomas
Lake Erie
Lake Ontario
Lake Michigan

CHICAGO
Evanston
Gary
South Bend
ILLINOIS
INDIANA
Rockford
MILWAUKEE

West from Greenwich
COPYRIGHT GEORGE PHILIP & SON LTD

60 50 40 30 40 50 60 70 80 90

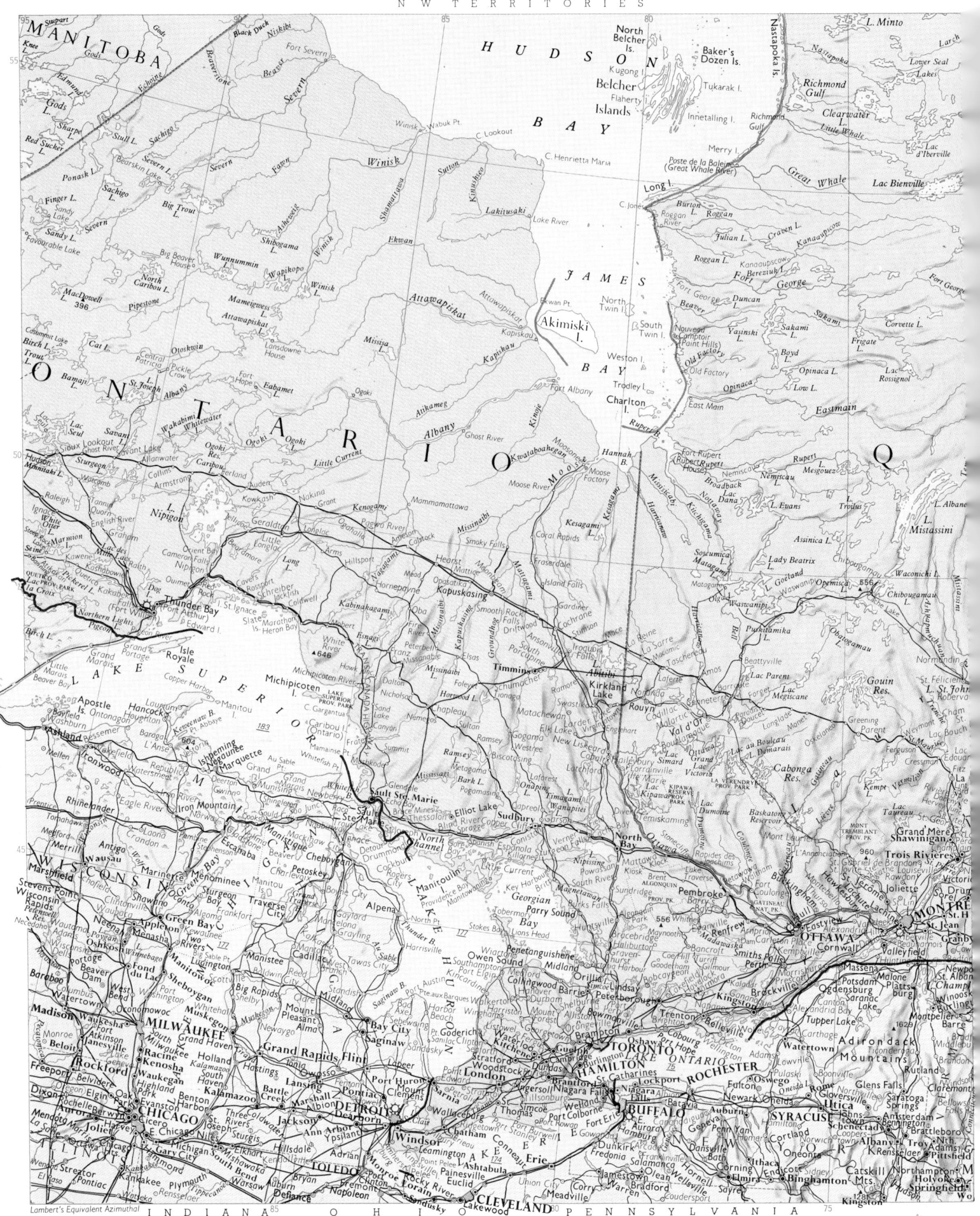

1 : 7 000 000

50   0   50   100   150   200 miles
50   0   50   100   150   200   300 km

COAST OF LABRADOR

QUEBEC

NEWFOUNDLAND

GULF OF ST. LAWRENCE

Anticosti I.

Gaspé Peninsula

NEW BRUNSWICK

PRINCE EDWARD ISLAND

NOVA SCOTIA

Cape Breton Island

SAINT-PIERRE ET MIQUELON (Fr.)

Avalon Peninsula

St. John's

MAINE

BOSTON

ATLANTIC OCEAN

Sable I. (Nova Scotia)

West from Greenwich

Projection: Lambert's Equivalent Azimuthal   West from Greenwich

1 : 7 000 000

50 0 50 100 150 200 miles
50 0 50 100 150 200 250 300 km

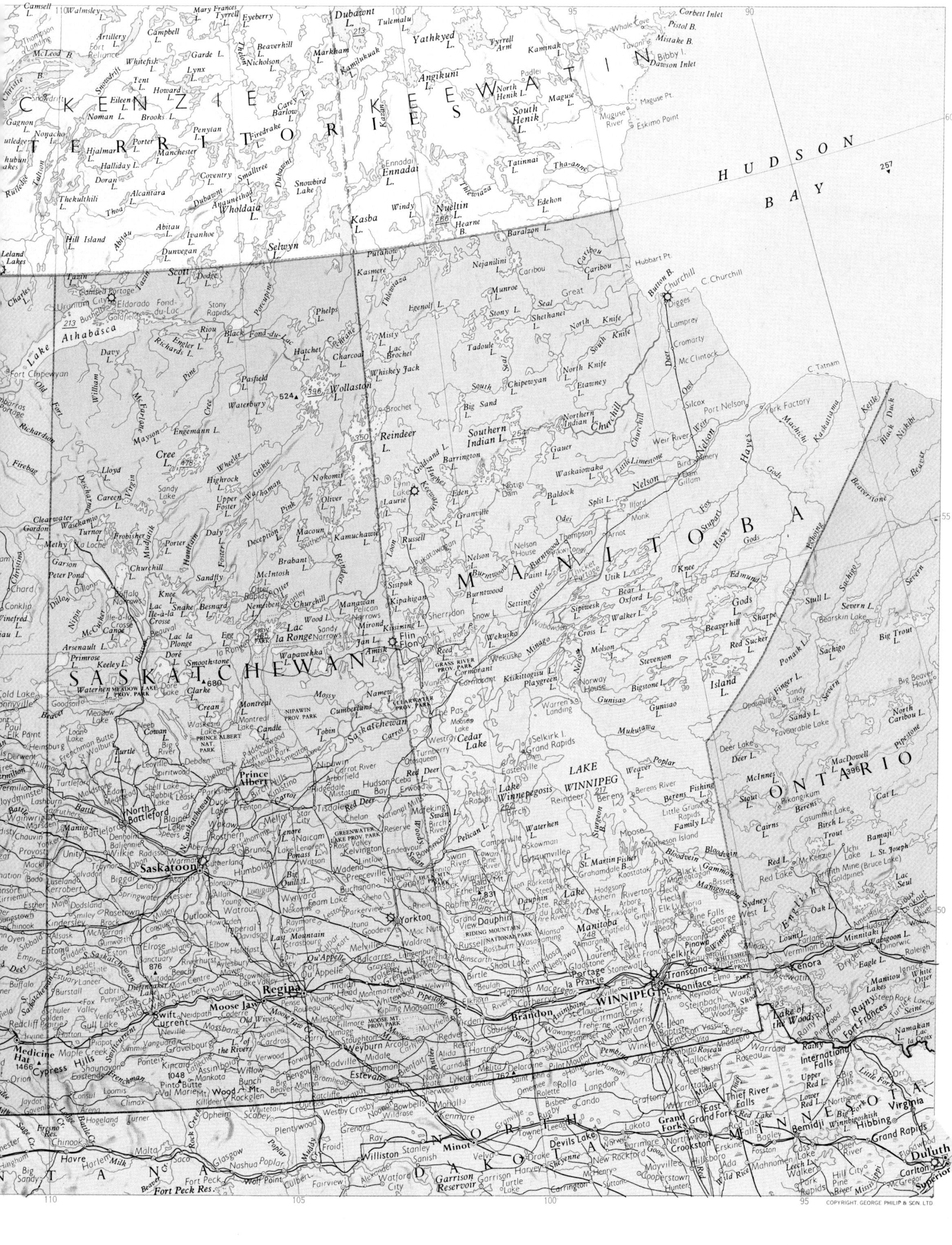

MACKENZIE

TERRITORIES KEEWATIN

HUDSON BAY

SASKATCHEWAN

MANITOBA

ONTARIO

Lake Athabasca

Cree L.

Reindeer L.

Wollaston L.

Southern Indian L.

Lac la Ronge

Churchill

Nelson

LAKE WINNIPEG

Lake Winnipegosis

Lake Manitoba

Cedar Lake

RIDING MOUNTAIN NATIONAL PARK

PRINCE ALBERT NATIONAL PARK

Prince Albert

Saskatoon

North Battleford

Yorkton

Regina

Moose Jaw

Swift Current

Medicine Hat

Cypress Hills

Weyburn

Estevan

Brandon

WINNIPEG

Portage la Prairie

Selkirk

Kenora

Lake of the Woods

NORTH DAKOTA

MINNESOTA

MONTANA

Fort Peck Res.

Havre

Williston

Minot

Devils Lake

Grand Forks

Bemidji

Duluth

Lake Superior

COPYRIGHT. GEORGE PHILIP & SON. LTD

110 105 100 95

1:12 000 000

50   0   50   100   150   200   250   300 miles
50 0 50 100 150 200 250 300 350 400 450 km

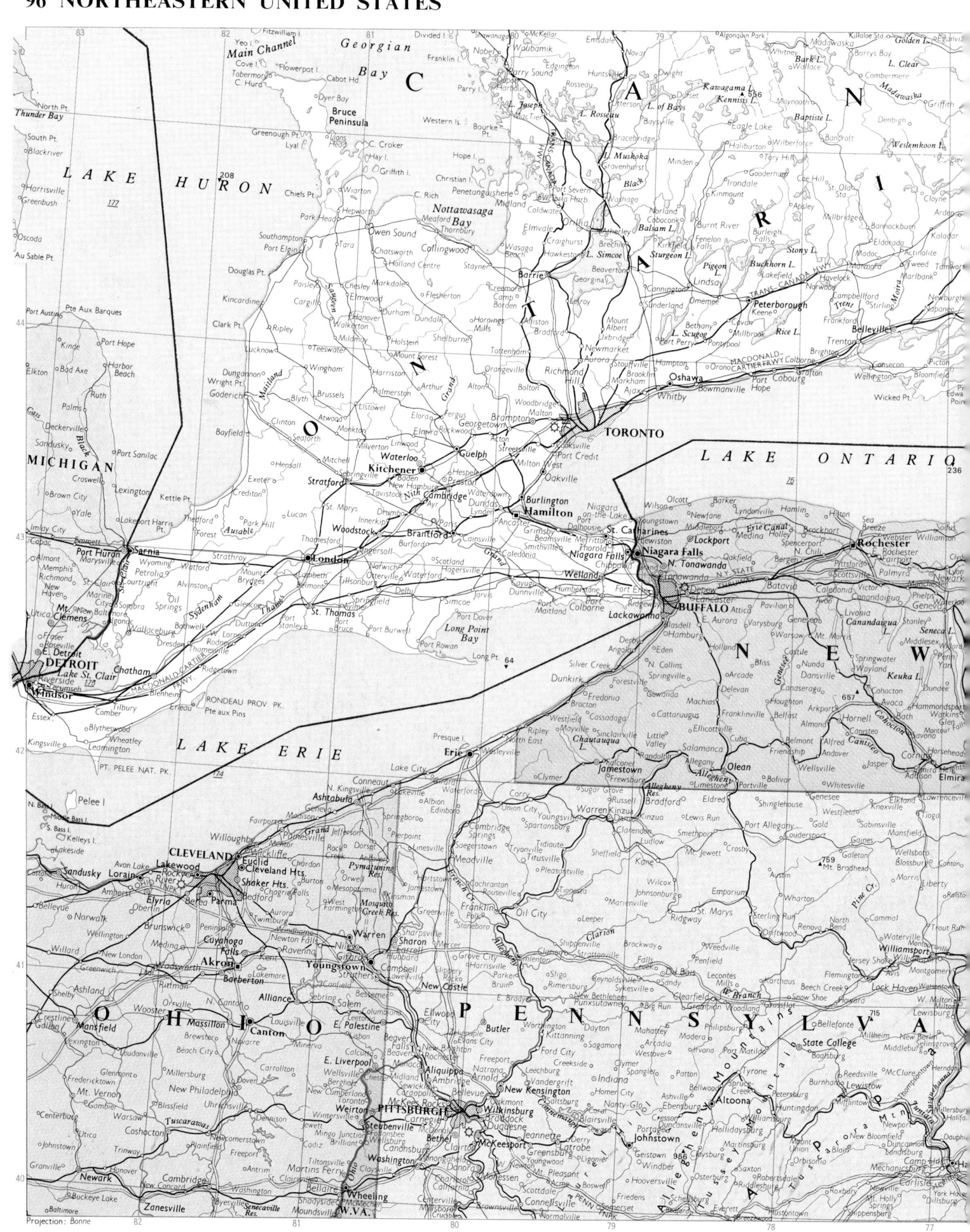

Projection: Bonne

====== Interstate Highways (U.S.A.), Superhighways (Canada)
===== Interstate Highways and Superhighways under Construction

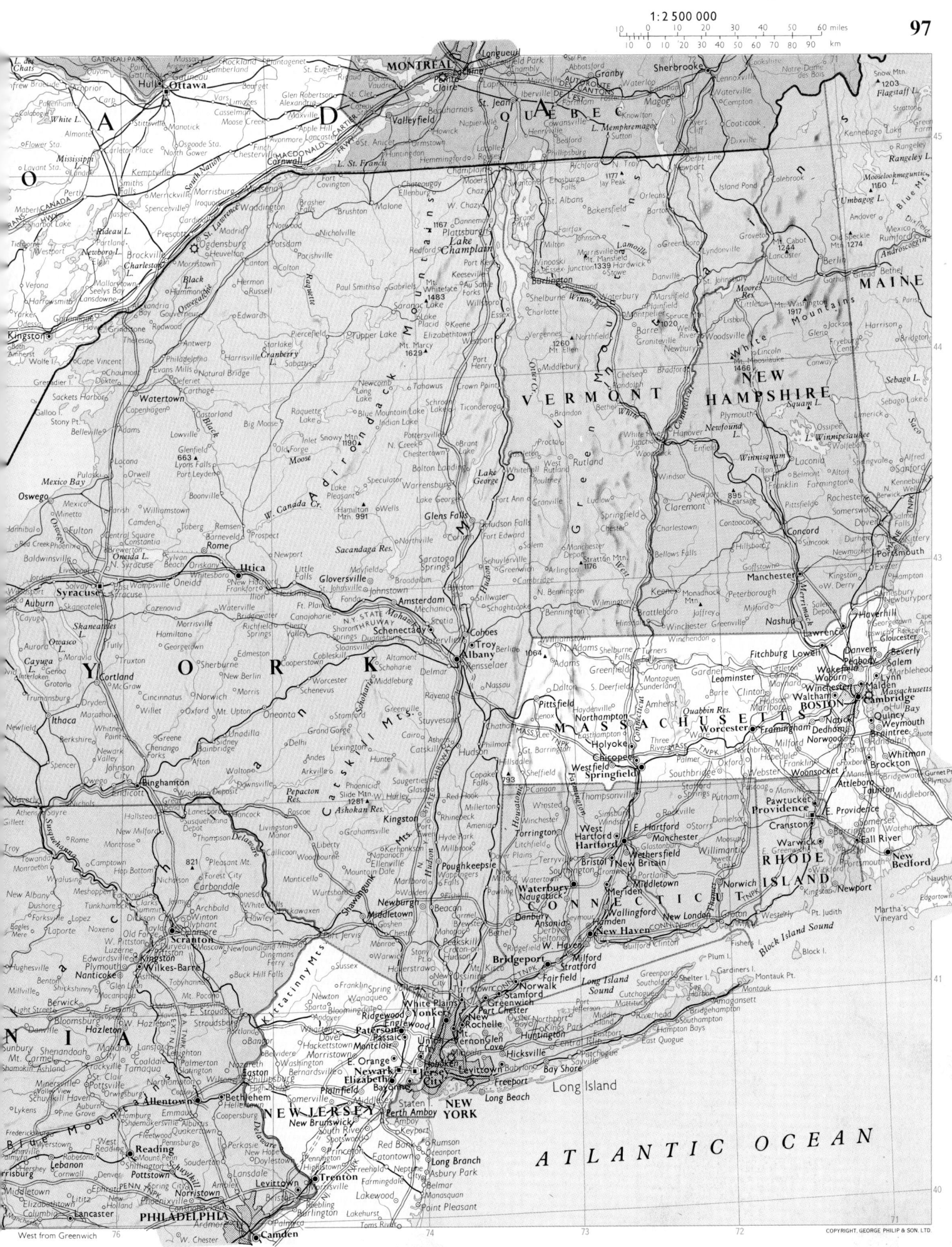

1 : 2 500 000

10   0   10 20   30   40   50   60 miles
10 0 10 20 30 40 50 60 70 80 90 km

QUEBEC

MONTREAL

MAINE

VERMONT

NEW HAMPSHIRE

Lake Champlain

Mt Marcy 1629

Adirondack Mountains

Green Mountains

White Mountains

NEW YORK

Watertown

Utica

Syracuse

Auburn

Oswego

Ithaca

Cortland

Binghamton

Schenectady

Albany

Troy

Catskill Mts.

Kingston

Poughkeepsie

MASSACHUSETTS

BOSTON

Cambridge

Worcester

Springfield

Pittsfield

Holyoke

Chicopee

RHODE ISLAND

Providence

Pawtucket

Fall River

New Bedford

CONNECTICUT

Hartford

New Haven

Bridgeport

Waterbury

Stamford

Norwich

New London

Long Island Sound

Block Island Sound

Block I.

Montauk Pt.

Long Island

New Rochelle

Yonkers

White Plains

NEW YORK

Newark

Jersey City

Elizabeth

Paterson

NEW JERSEY

New Brunswick

Trenton

Perth Amboy

Long Branch

Asbury Park

ATLANTIC OCEAN

PHILADELPHIA

Camden

Reading

Allentown

Bethlehem

Scranton

Wilkes-Barre

Hazleton

Easton

Kittatinny Mts.

Blue Mountains

NIA (PENNSYLVANIA)

Lancaster

Pottstown

Norristown

Levittown

Q U E B E C
O N T A R I O
LAKE SUPERIOR
LAKE HURON
LAKE ERIE
LAKE ONTARIO
Georgian Bay
MONTREAL
Ottawa
Quebec
TORONTO
Hamilton
BOSTON
NEW YORK
PHILADELPHIA
BALTIMORE
WASHINGTON D.C.
PITTSBURGH
CLEVELAND
DETROIT
CHICAGO
MILWAUKEE
CINCINNATI
BUFFALO
Indianapolis
Columbus
Louisville
Richmond
Norfolk
NEW YORK
PENNSYLVANIA
OHIO
INDIANA
MICHIGAN
ILLINOIS
KENTUCKY
VIRGINIA
WEST VIRGINIA
MARYLAND
DELAWARE
NEW JERSEY
W I S C O N S I N
Chesapeake Bay

1:6 000 000

50   0   50   100 miles

50   0   50   150 km

Continuation
Eastwards
On same scale

COPYRIGHT GEORGE PHILIP & SON, LTD

MAINE

NEW HAMPSHIRE

BAHAMAS

ATLANTIC OCEAN

NORTH CAROLINA

SOUTH CAROLINA

TENNESSEE

GEORGIA

ALABAMA

MISSISSIPPI

FLORIDA

GULF OF MEXICO

EVERGLADES NAT. PARK

West from Greenwich

Projection. Alber's Equal Area with two standard parallels

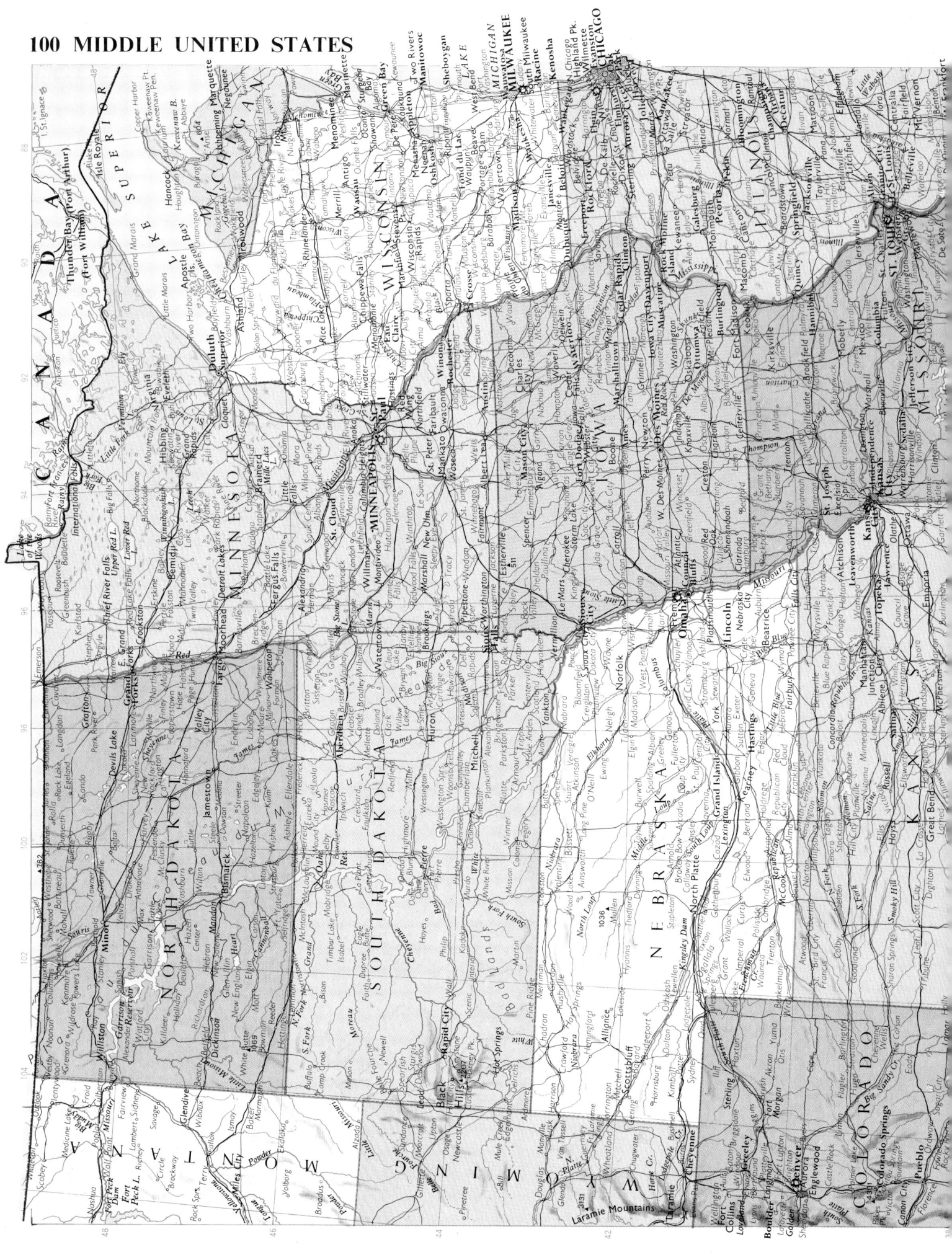

1:6 000 000

miles

km

West from Greenwich

Projection: Albers Equal Area with two standard parallels

COPYRIGHT GEORGE PHILIP & SON LTD.

Continuation Southwards on same scale

GULF OF MEXICO

TENNESSEE

MISSISSIPPI

LOUISIANA

ARKANSAS

OKLAHOMA

TEXAS

NEW MEXICO

COAHUILA

CHIHUAHUA

MEXICO

NEW ORLEANS

Memphis

Little Rock

Tulsa

Oklahoma City

Wichita

Fort Worth

Dallas

Houston

San Antonio

Galveston

Corpus Christi

Baton Rouge

Shreveport

Amarillo

Lubbock

Odessa

Midland

Brownsville

Laredo

Nuevo Laredo

Sangre de Cristo Mts.

1:6 000 000

West from Greenwich

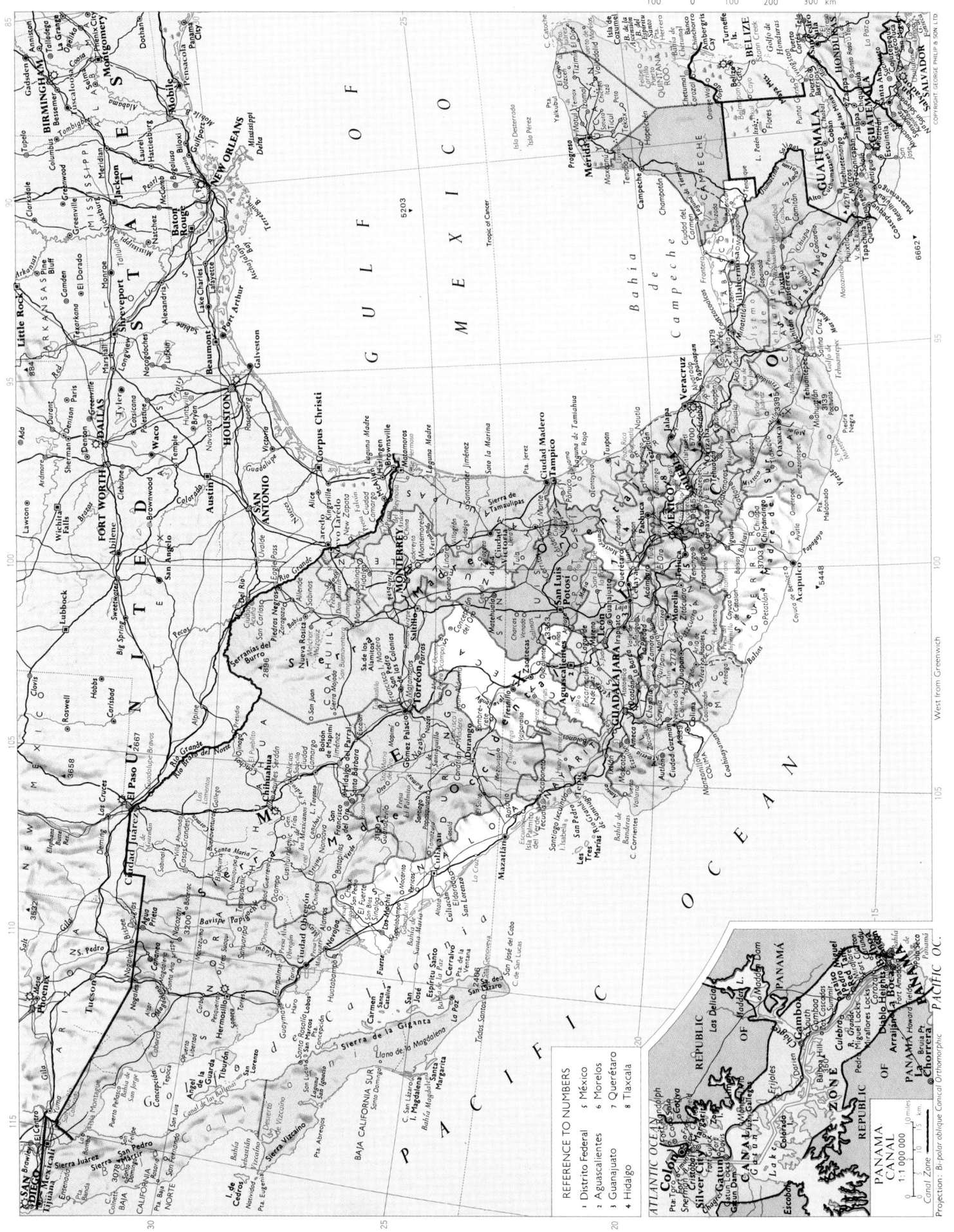

1:12 000 000

REFERENCE TO NUMBERS

1 Distrito Federal   5 México
2 Aguascalientes   6 Morelos
3 Guanajuato   7 Querétaro
4 Hidalgo   8 Tlaxcala

PANAMA CANAL
1:1 000 000

Projection: Bi-polar oblique Conical Orthomorphic

West from Greenwich

COPYRIGHT GEORGE PHILIP & SON, LTD.

1:12 000 000

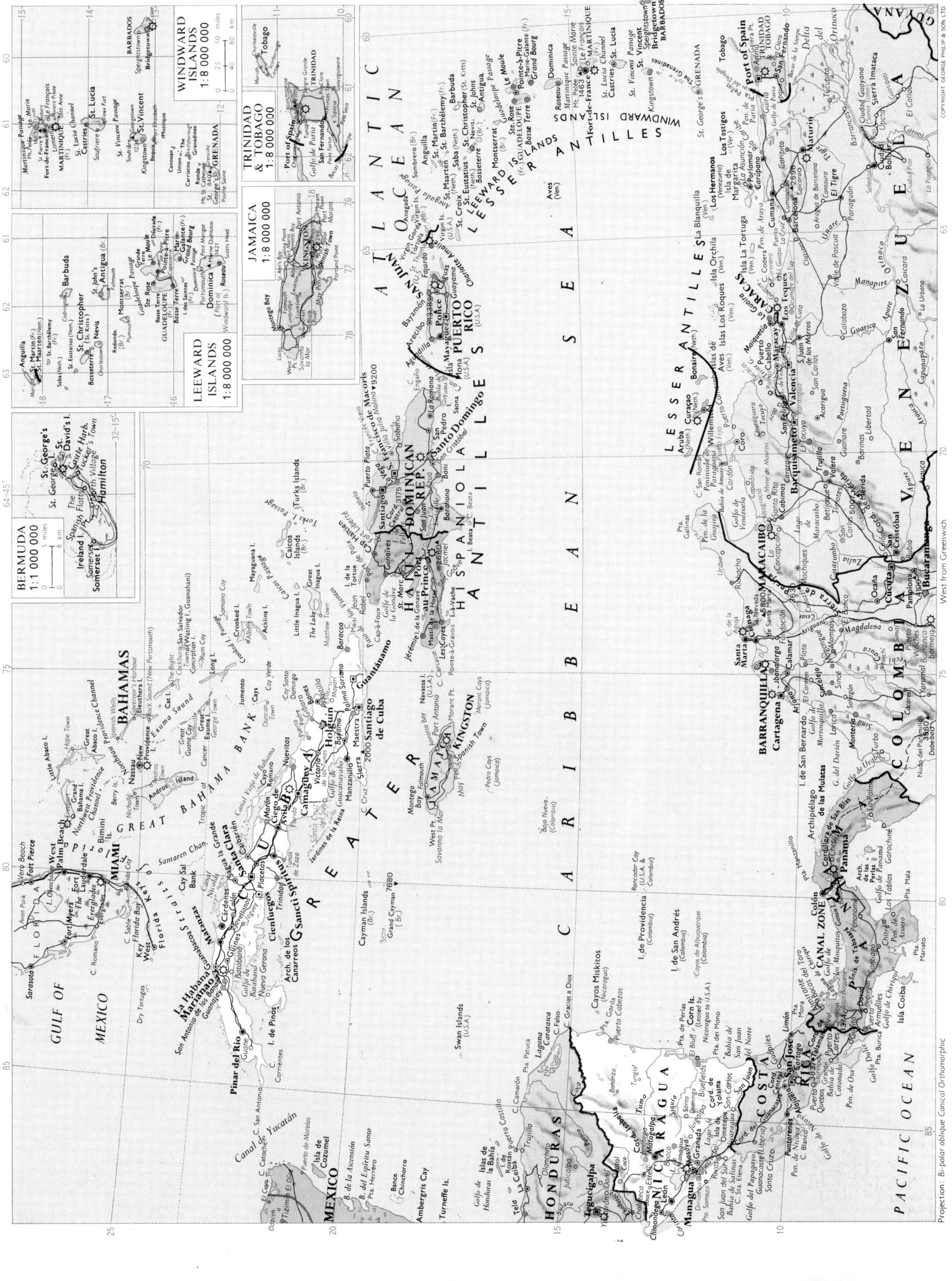

100   0   100   200 miles
100   0   100   200   300 km

WINDWARD ISLANDS
1:8 000 000

TRINIDAD & TOBAGO
1:8 000 000

JAMAICA
1:8 000 000

LEEWARD ISLANDS
1:8 000 000

BERMUDA
1:1 000 000

COPYRIGHT GEORGE PHILIP & SON LTD

West from Greenwich

Projection: Bi-polar oblique Conical Orthomorphic

ATLANTIC OCEAN

CARIBBEAN SEA

GULF OF MEXICO

PACIFIC OCEAN

GREATER ANTILLES

LESSER ANTILLES

BAHAMAS

CUBA

JAMAICA

HAITI

DOMINICAN REP.

PUERTO RICO

HISPANIOLA

MEXICO

HONDURAS

NICARAGUA

COSTA RICA

PANAMA

CANAL ZONE

COLOMBIA

VENEZUELA

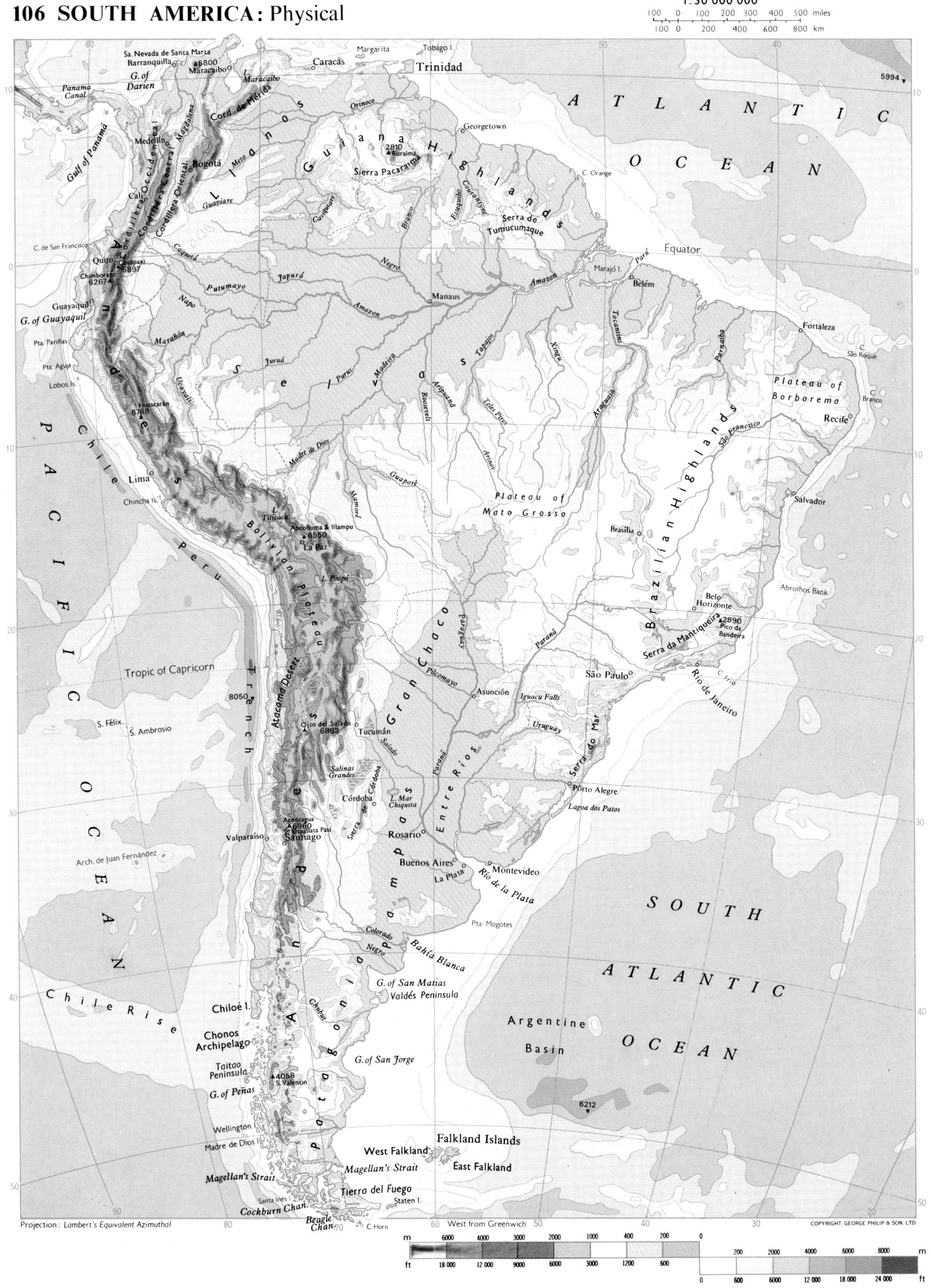

1:30 000 000

100 0 100 200 300 400 500 miles
100 0 200 400 600 800 km

Projection: Lambert's Equivalent Azimuthal

West from Greenwich

COPYRIGHT. GEORGE PHILIP & SON. LTD.

| m | 6000 | 4000 | 3000 | 2000 | 1000 | 400 | 200 | 0 |
| ft | 18 000 | 12 000 | 9000 | 6000 | 3000 | 1200 | 600 | |

| | 200 | 2000 | 4000 | 6000 | 8000 | m |
| | 600 | 6000 | 12 000 | 18 000 | 24 000 | ft |

1:30 000 000

100   0   100 200 300 400 500 miles
100   0   200   400   600   800 km

NORTH ATLANTIC OCEAN

COSTA RICA
CANAL ZONE (U.S.)
PANAMA
Golfo de Darién
Golfo de Panamá
S.F. 3277
Honolulu 4683

Punto Fijo
Isla de Margarita
Port of Spain
TRINIDAD AND TOBAGO
Trinidad
Tobago

Barranquilla
Cartagena
Ciénaga
Maracaibo
Cabimas
Barquisimeto
Caracas
Cumaná
Maturín

San José
Wellington 6483, Sydney 7673
Panamá
Medellín
Manizales
Pereira
Ibagué
Buenaventura
Cali
Popayán
Pasto
Montería
Cúcuta
Bucaramanga
Bogotá
San Cristóbal
Mérida
Valencia
San Fernando
Orinoco
Ciudad Guayana
Ciudad Bolívar

VENEZUELA
Pto. Ayacucho
Orinoco

Georgetown
New Amsterdam
Paramaribo
Cayenne
C. Orange

GUYANA
SURINAM
FRENCH GUIANA

COLOMBIA

C. de San Francisco

Quito
ECUADOR
Guayaquil
Riobamba
Cuenca
G. de Guayaquil
Honolulu 4854
Santa Cruz 2010
San Francisco 5980
Pta. Aguja

Napo
Putumayo
Caquetá
Japurá
Iquitos
Marañón

Negro
Branco
Macapá

Equator

Amazonas (Amazon)
Ilha de Marajó
Belém (Pará)
Santarém

Manaus
Tefé
Benjamim Constant

São Luís
Bacabal
Teresina

Fortaleza (Ceara)
C. de São Roque
Natal
João Pessoa (Paraíba)

Juruá
Cruzeiro do Sul
Purus
Madeira
Manicoré
Tapajós
Xingu
Tocantins
Araguaia
Parnaíba

Juazeiro do Norte
Recife (Pernambuco)
Maceió

Honolulu 5132
Islas de Chincha

PERU
Callao
Lima
Huancayo
Ayacucho
Cuzco

Pôrto Velho
Rio Branca
Guajará-Mirim
Madre de Dios
Guaporé
Mamoré

Aracaju

BRAZIL

Wellington 5718

Chiclayo
Trujillo
Pucallpa
Ucayali

Iquique
Juliaca
Titicaca
Arequipa
La Paz
Mollendo
Tacna
Arica
Oruro
Uyuni
Sucre
Tarija

BOLIVIA
Cochabamba
Santa Cruz
Corumbá

São Francisco
Salvador (Bahia)

Cuiabá
Brasília
Goiânia
Jataí
Montes Claros
Gov. Valadares
Uberaba
Belo Horizonte
Vitória
Campos
Niterói
RIO DE JANEIRO

Wellington 5116
Yokohama 9330

Honolulu 5916

Tropic of Capricorn

Isla San Félix (Chile)
Isla San Ambrosio (Chile)

Antofagasta
Salta
San Miguel de Tucumán
Santiago del Estero

Campo Grande
PARAGUAY
Pedra Juan Caballero
Asunción
Pilcomayo
Paraguay
Ponta Porã
Pres Prudente
Bauru
Londrina
SÃO PAULO
Campinas
Santos
Curitiba

Ribeirão Prêto
Paraná
Juiz de Fora

PARANÁ

Honolulu 5044, Sydney 6257

San Francisco 5138

Resistencia
Corrientes
Uruguay
Santa Maria
Pôrto Alegre
Florianópolis

ARGENTINA
Córdoba
Santa Fe
Paraná
Rosario
Mendoza
San Rafael
Mercedes
Salado

URUGUAY
Uruguaiana
Salto
Lagoa dos Patos
Pelotas

Valparaíso
Santiago
Arch de Juan Fernández (Chile)

Buenos Aires
La Plata
Río de la Plata
Montevideo

SOUTH ATLANTIC OCEAN

Talca
Concepción
Valdivia

Santa Rosa
Bahía Blanca
Colorado
Negro
Tandil
Mar del Plata

Montevideo – Cape Town 3649

Puerto Montt
Isla de Chiloé

Zapala
Viedma

Buenos Aires – Adelaide 8885, Melbourne 9090, Sydney 9564

PACIFIC OCEAN

Archipiélago de los Chonos

San Carlos de Bariloche
Chubut
Trelew

Peninsula Valdés

Golfo Comodoro Rivadavia
San Jorge

Buenos Aires – Rio de Janeiro 1910

G. de Penas

I. Wellington
Santa Cruz
Río Gallegos

FALKLAND ISLANDS (ISLAS MALVINAS) (U.K.)
West Falkland
Stanley
East Falkland

Punta Arenas – Cape Town 4036

Estrecho de Magallanes
Punta Arenas
Isla Grande de Tierra del Fuego
Strait of Magellan

Wellington – Rio de Janeiro 6815

Cabo de Hornos (Cape Horn)

West from Greenwich

Projection: Lambert's Equivalent Azimuthal

COPYRIGHT. GEORGE PHILIP & SON. LTD.

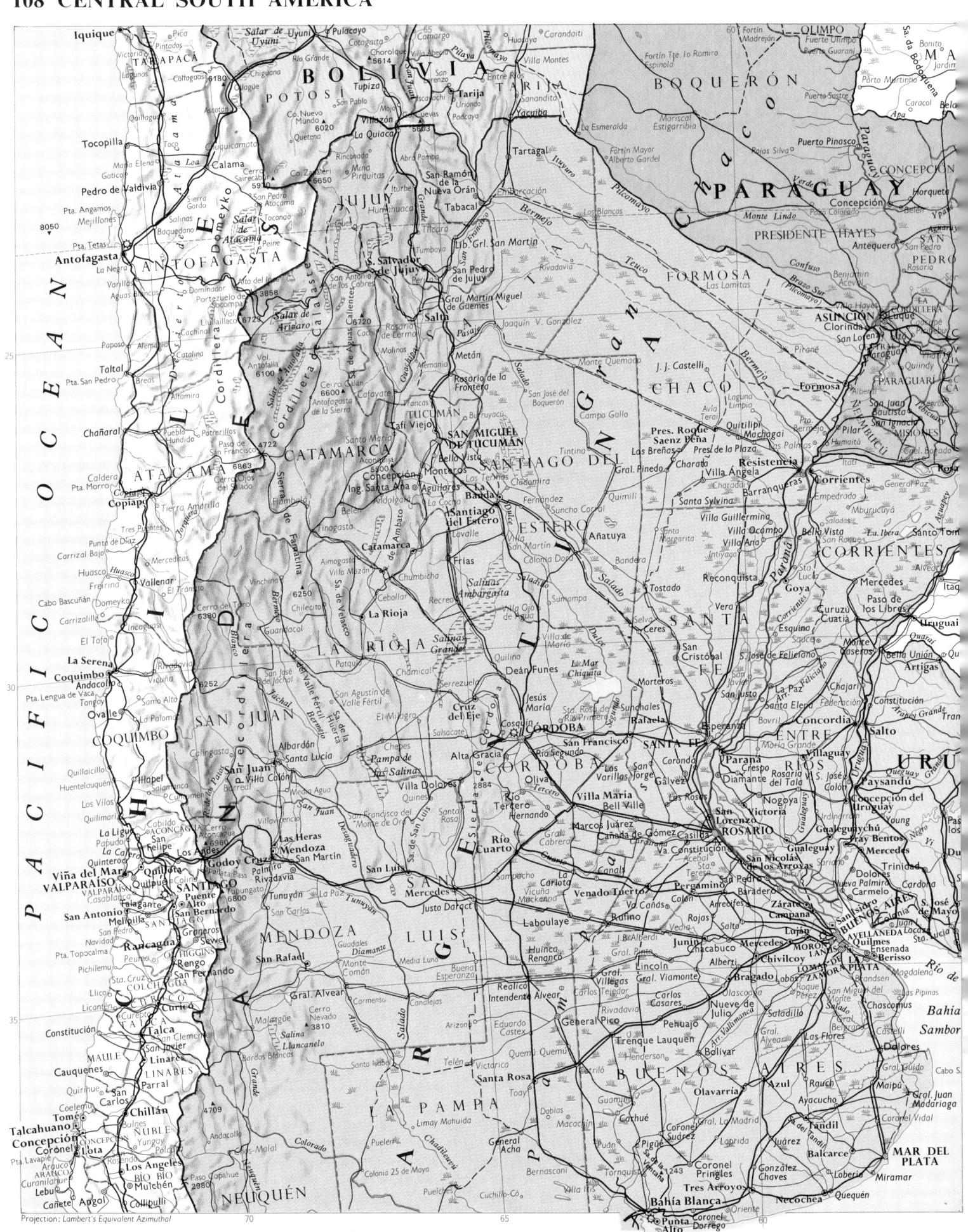

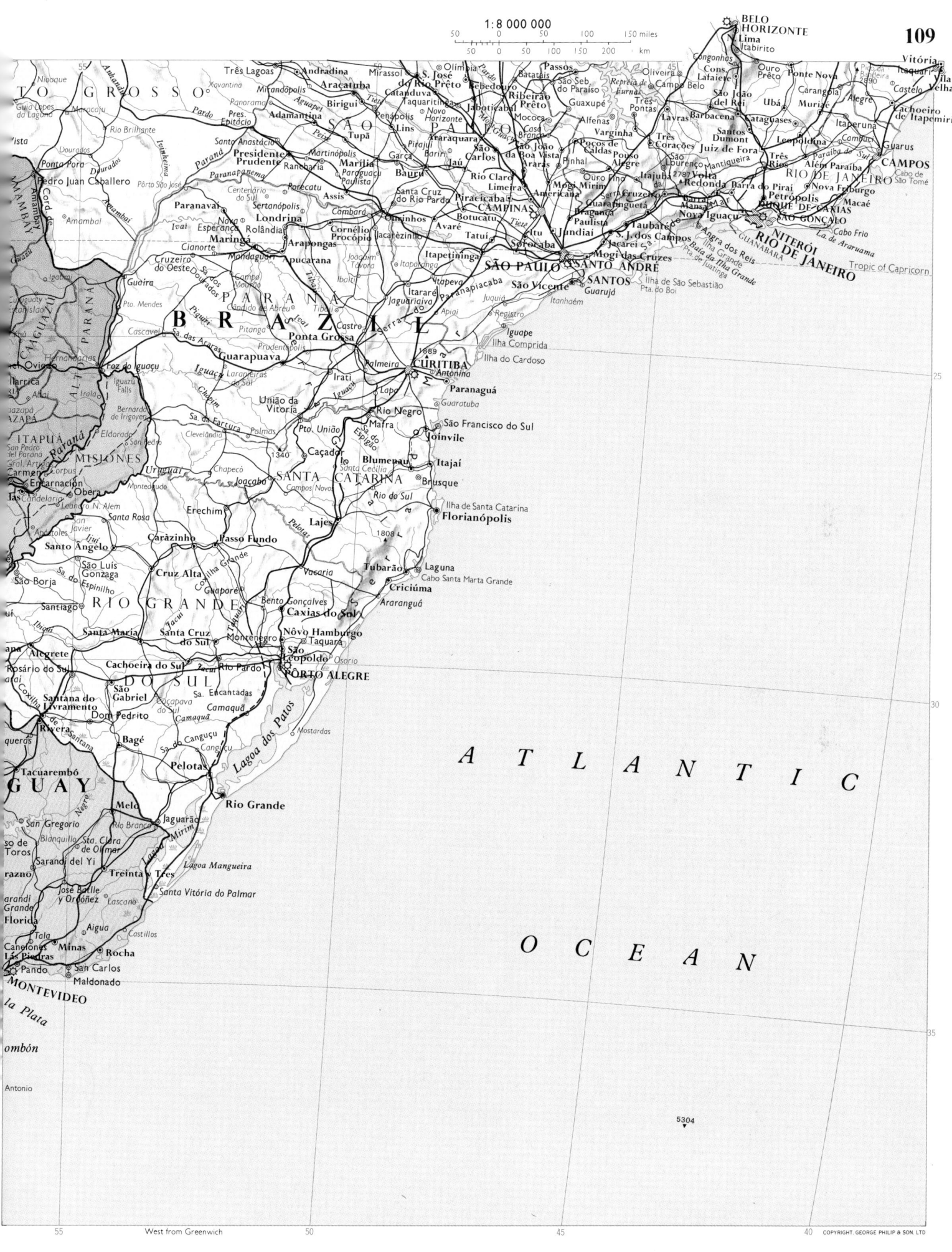

1:8 000 000

50   0   50   100   150 miles

50   0   50   100   150   200   km

BELO HORIZONTE

VITÓRIA

A T L A N T I C

O C E A N

5304

1:16 000 000

100   0   100   200   300   400   500 miles
100 0 100 200 300 400 500 600 700 800 km

A T L A N T I C

O C E A N

wn
Amsterdam
Nieuw Nickerie
Totness
Paramaribo
Nieuw Amsterdam
Kwakoegron
Albina
Moengo
Mana
St. Laurent
Iracouba
Sinnamary
Kourou
Cayenne
C. Orange
St. Georges
Oiapoque
SURINAM
FR.
GUIANA
Serra
Tumucumaque
Merirumã
Camopi
Contpi
Approuague
Kaw

AMAPÁ
Amapá
Araguari
C. do Norte
Ilha de Maracá
Estuário do
Rio Amazonas
Ilha Caviana
Macapá
Ilha Mexiana

Equator

Mazagão
Afuá
Ilha de
Marajó
Chaves
Soure
C. Maguarinho
Curuçá
Salinópolis
Vigia
Igarapé Açu
Bragança
Viseu
I. Grande
de Gurupá
Breves
Muaná
Belém (Pará)
Abaetetuba
Acará
Turiaçu
Sururupu
Guimarães
B. de São Marcos
São Luís (Maranhão)

PARÁ
Santarém
Belterra
Almeirim
Porto de Móz
Gurupá
Cametá
Baião
Tucuruí
Turiaçu
Alcântara
Rosário
Viana
Itapecuru-
Mirim
Barreirinhas
Tutóia
Luís Correia
Parnaíba
Camocim
Granja
Fortaleza (Ceará)
Maranguape
Rocas
Fernando de Noronha
(Braz.)

MARANHÃO
Marabá
São João
do Araguaia
Imperatriz
Grajaú
Barra do
Corda
Caxias
Timon
Teresina
Bacabal
Coroatá
Codó
Arareiras
Piripiri
Campo Maior
Baturité
Quixadá
Sobral
Crateús
Ipu
Aracati
Areia Branca
Macau
Mossoró
Russas
Ceará Mirim
C. de São Roque
Natal

CEARÁ
RIO GRANDE
DO NORTE
Senador Pompeu
Iguatú
Oros
Icó
Caicó
Nova Cruz
Canguaretama

PIAUÍ
Carolina
Loreto
Riachão
Floriano
Novalorque
Oeiras
Amarante
Valença do
Piauí
Colinas
Uruçuí
São João
do Piauí
Paulistana
Crato
Juàzeiro do
Norte
Sousa
Patos
Pombal
Alagoa
Grande
Campina Grande
João Pessoa
(Paraíba)
PARAÍBA
Caruaru
RECIFE
(Pernambuco)
B. de Santo Antão

PERNAMBUCO
Conceição do
Araguaia
Araguacema
Pedro Afonso
Sta. Filomena
Caracol
Remanso
Petrolina
Juàzeiro
Casa Nova
Paulo Afonso
Garanhuns
Palmares
Pal. dos Índios
Rio Largo
Barreiros
Maceió
ALAGOAS

GOIÁS
Natividade
Peixe
Manuel Alves
Paranã
Campos Belos
São Domingos
Porto Nacional
Barra
Xique-Xique
Parnaguá
Campo
Formoso
Senhor do
Bonfim
Queimadas
Propriá
SERGIPE
Penedo
6059

BAHIA
Aruanã
Niquelândia
Uruaçu
Posse
Carinhanha
Sta. Maria
da Vitória
Bom Jesus
da Lapa
Caetité
Barra do
Mendes
Irecê
Paratinga
Itaberaba
Jacobina
Serrinha
Feira de
Santana
Santo Amaro
São Cristóvão
Estância
Aracajú
Alagoinhas
Santo Amaro
Salvador (Bahia)
B. de Todos os Santos

TO GROSSO
Pouso Alegre
Diamantino
Cuiabá
Antônio
Rondonópolis
Baliza

Planalto do
Mato Grosso
Mortes
Araguaiana

MATO GROSSO
Itaberaba
Valença
Jequié
Brumado
Ituaçu
Itacaré
Vitória da
Conquista
Ubaitaba
Itabuna
Ilhéus
Januária
Canavieiras
Monte Azul
Belmonte
Condeúba
Porto Seguro

DIST.
FED.
Brasília
Formoso
Corumbá
Anápolis
Goiás
Vianópolis
Luziânia
Goiânia
São Francisco
Montes
Claros
Salinas
Jequitinhonha
Pedra Azul
Jequitinhonha
Prado
Caravelas
Banca
Abrolhos
Mucuri

Alto
Araguaia
Rio Verde
Jataí
Morrinhos
Itumbiara
Catalão
Paracatú
Pirapora
Bocaiúva
Diamantina
Teófilo Otoni
Nanuque
Mucuri
Conceição da Barra
São Mateus

Campo
Grande
Agua Clara
Nova Granada
Araguari
Uberlândia
Patrocínio
Araxá
Formiga
Divinópolis
Gov. Valadares
Aimorés
Nova
Venécia
Linhares

Aquidauana
Três Lagoas
Nova
Andradina
Prata
Uberaba
Belo Horizonte
Caratinga
Manhuaçu
Vitória

MINAS GERAIS

PAULO
Araçatuba
São
José do
Rio Preto
Ribeirão Preto
Franco
Passos
Poços de
Caldas
São João del Rei
Lavras
São
Lourenço
Campos

Marília
Bauru
Piracicaba
Campinas
São Carlos
Botucatú
Petrópolis
RIO DE JANEIRO
Niterói
RIO DE JANEIRO
GUANABARA
Cabo Frio

Trindade
(Braz.)

Greenwich

1:16 000 000

100 50 0   100   200   300 miles
100   0   100   200   300   400 km

PARAGUAY

PARANÁ

BRAZIL

SANTA CATARINA

RIO GRANDE DO SUL

URUGUAY

SÃO PAULO

RIO DE JANEIRO

Santos

Curitiba

Paranaguá

Florianópolis

Pôrto Alegre

Pelotas

MONTEVIDEO

BUENOS AIRES

Asunción

Antofagasta

Tropic of Capricorn

San Miguel de Tucumán

Salta

Córdoba

Santa Fe

Rosario

Mendoza

SANTIAGO

Valparaíso

Viña del Mar

Concepción

Talcahuano

Valdivia

Osorno

Pto. Varas

Puerto Montt

I. de Chiloé

Archipiélago de los Chonos

Comodoro Rivadavia

Golfo San Jorge

Trelew

Peninsula Valdés

Golfo San Matías

Golfo Nuevo

Bahía Blanca

Mar del Plata

La Plata

Avellaneda

Neuquén

Río Gallegos

Punta Arenas

Estrecho de Magallanes (Magellan's Str.)

Tierra del Fuego

Cabo de Hornos (C. Horn)

Canal Beagle

Islas Diego Ramírez

SOUTH ATLANTIC OCEAN

FALKLAND ISLANDS (ISLAS MALVINAS) (Br.)

West Falkland

East Falkland

Stanley

South Georgia (Br.)

Peru–Chile Trench

Richard's I.

La Serena

Coquimbo

Ovalle

Chaco Boreal

Chaco Central

Chaco Austral

Santiago del Estero

Catamarca

La Rioja

San Juan

San Luis

Concepción

Resistencia

Corrientes

Posadas

Encarnación

Concordia

Paysandú

Rivera

Caxias do Sul

Santa Maria

Lagoa dos Patos

Río Grande

Projection: Sanson-Flamsteed's Sinusoidal

60 West from Greenwich 55

The number in bold type which precedes each name in the index refers to the number of the page where that feature or place will be found.

The geographical co-ordinates which follow the place name are sometimes only approximate but are close enough for the place name to be located.

An open square □ signifies that the name refers to an administrative division of a country while a solid square ■ follows the name of a country.

Rivers have been indexed to their mouth or to their confluence.

The alphabetical order of names composed of two or more words is governed primarily by the first word and then by the second. This is an example of the rule:

> *West Wyalong*
> *West Yorkshire*
> *Westbrook*
> *Westbury*
> *Westerland*
> *Western Australia*

Names composed of a proper name (Gibraltar) and a description (Strait of) are positioned alphabetically by the proper name. All river names are followed by R. If the same word occurs in the name of a town and a geographical feature, the town name is listed first followed by the name or names of the geographical features.

Names beginning with M', Mc are all indexed as if they were spelled Mac.

If the same place name occurs two or more times in the index and all are in the same country, each is followed by the name of the administrative subdivision in which it is located. The names are placed in the alphabetical order of the subdivisions. For example:

> *Stour, R., Dorset*
> *Stour, R., Hereford and Worcester*
> *Stour, R., Kent*
> *Stour, R., Suffolk*

If the same place name occurs twice or more in the index and the places are in different countries they will be followed by the country names and the latter in alphabetical order.

> *Sheffield, U.K.*
> *Sheffield, U.S.A.*

If there is a mixture of these situations, the primary order is fixed by the alphabetical sequence of the countries and the secondary order by that of the country subdivisions. In the latter case the country names are omitted.

> *Rochester, U.K.*
> *Rochester, Minn.* (U.S.A.) are omitted from
> *Rochester, N.H.* (U.S.A.) the index
> *Rochester, N.Y.* (U.S.A.)
> *Rochester, Pa.* (U.S.A.)

The following is a list of abbreviations used in the index

A.S.S.R. – *Autonomous Soviet Socialist Republic*
Ala. – *Alabama*
Alas. – *Alaska*
Ang. – *Angola*
Arch. – *Archipelago*
Arg. – *Argentina*
Ariz. – *Arizona*
Ark. – *Arkansas*
B. – *Baie, Bahia, Bay, Boca, Bucht, Bugt*
B.C. – *British Columbia*
Br. – *British*
C. – *Cabo, Cap, Cape*
C.A.R. – *Central African Republic*
C. Prov. – *Cape Province*
Calif. – *California*
Chan. – *Channel*
Col. – *Colombia*
Colo. – *Colorado*
Conn. – *Connecticut*
Cord. – *Cordillera*
D.C. – *District of Columbia*
Del. – *Delaware*
Dep. – *Dependency*
Des. – *Desert*
Dist. – *District*
Dom. Rep. – *Dominican Republic*
E. – *East*
Eng. – *England*

Fd. – *Fjord*
Fed. – *Federal, Federation*
Fla. – *Florida*
Fr. – *France, French*
G. – *Golfe, Golfo, Gulf, Guba*
Ga. – *Georgia*
Gt. – *Great*
Hants. – *Hampshire*
Hd. – *Head*
Hts. – *Heights*
I.(s) – *Ile, Ilha, Insel, Isla, Island (s)*
Id. – *Idaho*
Ill. – *Illinois*
Ind. – *Indiana*
J. – *Jezero (L.)*
K. – *Kap, Kapp*
Kans. – *Kansas*
Kep. – *Kepulauan (I.)*
Kól. – *Kólpos (B.)*
Ky. – *Kentucky*
L. – *Lac, Lacul, Lago, Lagoa, Lake, Limni, Loch, Lough*
La. – *Louisana*
Ld. – *Land*
Mad. P. – *Madhya Pradesh*
Man. – *Manitoba*
Mass. – *Massachusetts*
Md. – *Maryland*
Me. – *Maine*
Mich. – *Michigan*
Minn. – *Minnesota*

Miss. – *Mississippi*
Mo. – *Missouri*
Mont. – *Montana*
Mt.(s) – *Mont, Monte, Monti, Muntii, Montaña, Mountain (s)*
Mys. – *Mysore*
N. – *North, Northern*
N.B. – *New Brunswick*
N.C. – *North Carolina*
N.D. – *North Dakota*
N.H. – *New Hampshire*
N. Ire. – *Northern Ireland*
N.J. – *New Jersey*
N. Mex. – *New Mexico*
N.S.W. – *New South Wales*
N.Y. – *New York*
N.Z. – *New Zealand*
Nat. Park – *National Park*
Nebr. – *Nebraska*
Neth. – *Netherlands*
Nev. – *Nevada*
Newf. – *Newfoundland*
Nic. – *Nicaragua*
Nig. – *Nigeria*
O.F.S. – *Orange Free State*
Okla. – *Oklahoma*
Ont. – *Ontario*
Oreg. – *Oregon*
Os. – *Ostrov (I.)*
Oz – *Ozero (L.)*
P. – *Pass, Passo, Pasul*

P.N.G. – *Papua New Guinea*
Pa. – *Pennsylvania*
Pak. – *Pakistan*
Pass. – *Passage*
Pen. – *Peninsula*
Pk. – *Peak*
Plat. – *Plateau*
Pol. – *Poluostrov*
Port. – *Portugal, Portuguese*
Prov. – *Province, Provincial*
Pt. – *Point*
Pta. – *Ponta, Punta*
Pte. – *Pointe*
Que. – *Quebec*
Queens. – *Queensland*
R. – *Rio, River*
R.S.F.S.R. – *Russian Soviet Federal Socialist Republic*
Ra.(s) – *Range(s)*
Reg. – *Region*
Rep. – *Republic*
Res. – *Reserve, Reservoir*
S. – *South*
S. Africa – *South Africa*
S.C. – *S. Carolina*
S.D. – *South Dakota*
S. Leone – *Sierra Leone*
S.S.R. – *Soviet Socialist Republic*
Sa. – *Serra, Sierra*
Sask. – *Saskatchewan*
Scot. – *Scotland*

Sd. – *Sound*
Sp. – *Spain, Spanish*
St. – *Saint*
Str. – *Strait, Stretto*
Switz. – *Switzerland*
Tanz. – *Tanzania*
Tas. – *Tasmania*
Tenn. – *Tennessee*
Terr. – *Territory*
Tex. – *Texas*
U.K. – *United Kingdom*
U.S.A. – *United States of America*
U.S.S.R. – *Union of Soviet Socialist Republics*
Ut. P. – *Uttar Pradesh*
Va. – *Virginia*
Vdkhr. – *Vodokhranilishche (Res.)*
Ven. – *Venezuela*
Vic. – *Victoria*
Vt. – *Vermont*
W. – *West*
W. Va. – *West Virginia*
Wis. – *Wisconsin*
Wyo. – *Wyoming*
Yorks. – *Yorkshire*
Yug. – *Yugoslavia*

Aachen Albany, R.

A

24 Aachen 50 47N 6 4E
73 A'Âlâ en Nîl □ 8 50N 29 55E
25 Aalen 48 49N 10 6E
16 Aalsmeer 52 17N 4 43E
16 Aalst 50 56N 4 2E
16 Aalten 51 56N 6 35E
25 Aarau 47 23N 8 4E
25 Aare, R. 47 37N 8 13E
25 Aargau □ 47 26N 8 10E
45 Aarhus □ 56 15N 10 15E
16 Aarschot 50 59N 4 49E
72 Aba 5 10N 7 19E
55 Abā Saud 17 15N 43 55E
56 Abadan 30 22N 48 20E
30 Abadin 43 21N 7 29W
109 Abai 25 58S 55 54W
51 Abakan 53 40N 91 10E
32 Abanilla 38 12N 1 3W
57 Abarqu 31 10N 53 20E
54 Abasan 31 19N 34 21E
66 Abashiri 44 0N 144 15E
66 Abashiri-Wan, G. 44 0N 144 30E
50 Abay 49 38N 72 53E
74 Abaya, L. 6 30N 37 50E
50 Abaza 52 39N 90 6E
54 Abba Hillēl 31 42N 34 38E
19 Abbeville, Fr. 50 6N 1 49E
99 Abbeville, U.S.A. 30 0N 92 7W
36 Abbiategrasso 45 23N 8 55E
58 Abbottabad 34 10N 73 15E
73 Abéché 13 50N 20 35E
30 Abejar 41 48N 2 47W
45 Åbenrå 55 3N 9 25E
72 Abeokuta 7 3N 3 19E
13 Aberayron 52 15N 4 16W
13 Aberdare 51 43N 3 27W
84 Aberdeen, Australia 32 9S 150 56E
14 Aberdeen, U.K. 57 9N 2 6W
102 Aberdeen, Id. 42 57N 112 50W
99 Aberdeen, Miss. 33 49N 88 13W
100 Aberdeen, S.D. 45 28N 98 29W
102 Aberdeen, Wash. 46 59N 123 50W
13 Aberdovey 52 33N 4 3W
14 Aberfeldy 56 37N 3 50W
30 Abergaria-a-Velha 40 41N 8 32W
13 Abergavenny 51 49N 3 1W
13 Aberystwyth 52 25N 4 6W
55 Abhā 18 0N 42 34E
72 Abidjan 5 26N 3 58W
100 Abilene, Kans. 39 0N 97 16W
101 Abilene, Tex. 32 22N 99 40W
13 Abingdon 51 40N 1 17W
49 Abkhaz A.S.S.R. 43 0N 41 0E
51 Abkit 64 10N 157 10E
60 Abohar 30 10N 74 10E
72 Abomey 7 10N 2 5E
74 Abong Mbang 4 0N 13 8E
27 Abony 47 12N 20 3E
73 Abou Deïa 11 20N 19 20E
14 Aboyne 57 4N 2 48W
56 Abqaiq 26 0N 49 45E
31 Abrantes 39 24N 8 7W
30 Abraveses 40 41N 7 55E
19 Abreschviller 48 39N 7 6E
37 Abruzzi □ 42 15N 14 0E
102 Absaroka Ra. 44 40N 110 0W
56 Abū al Khasib 30 25N 48 0E
55 Abu Arish 16 53N 42 48E
73 Abu Dis 19 12N 33 38E
54 Abū Ghōsh 31 48N 35 6E
73 Abu Hamed 19 32N 33 13E
73 Abu Tig 27 4N 31 15E
73 Abū Zabad 12 25N 29 10E
57 Abū Zabī 24 28N 54 36E
73 Abyad, Gebel Reg. 17 30N 28 0E
104 Acajutla 13 36N 89 50W
104 Acámbaro 20 0N 100 40W
104 Acaponeta 22 30N 105 20W
104 Acapulco 16 51N 99 56W
111 Acará 1 57S 48 11W
104 Acatlan 18 10N 98 3W
104 Acayucan 17 59N 94 58W
36 Accéglio 44 28N 6 59E
72 Accra 5 35N 0 6W
12 Accrington 53 46N 2 22W
64 Aceh □ 4 50N 96 0E
39 Acerra 40 57N 14 22E
31 Aceuchal 38 39N 6 30W
60 Achalpur 21 22N 77 32E
26 Achenkirch 47 32N 11 45E
26 Achensee, L. 47 26N 11 45E
60 Acher 23 10N 72 32E
15 Achill 53 56N 9 55W
15 Achill, I. 53 58N 10 5W
51 Achinsk 56 20N 90 20E
39 Acireale 37 37N 15 9E
105 Acklins I. 22 30N 74 0W
92 Acme 51 33N 113 30W
108 Aconcagua, Cerro, Mt. 32 39S 70 0W
108 Aconcagua □ 32 15S 70 30W
39 Acquaviva delle Fonti 40 53N 16 50E
36 Acqui 44 40N 8 28E
110 Acre □ 9 1S 71 0W
39 Acri 39 29N 16 23E
27 Acs 47 42N 18 0E
55 Ad Dam 20 33N 44 45E
56 Ad Dammam 26 20N 50 5E
56 Ad Khālis 33 40N 44 55E
101 Ada, U.S.A. 34 50N 96 45W
40 Ada, Yug. 45 49N 20 9E
30 Adaja, R. 41 32N 4 52W
55 Adale 2 58N 46 27E
109 Adamantina 21 42S 51 4W
73 Adamaoua, Massif de l' 7 20N 12 20E
36 Adamello, Mt. 46 10N 10 34E
97 Adams, Mass. 42 38N 73 8W
100 Adams, Wis. 43 59N 89 50W
102 Adams, Mt. 46 10N 121 28W
62 Adam's Bridge 9 15N 79 40E
62 Adam's Pk. 6 55N 80 45E
31 Adamuz 38 2N 4 32W
56 Adana 37 0N 35 16E
30 Adanero 40 56N 4 36W
65 Adaut 8 8S 131 7E
36 Adda, R. 45 8N 9 53E
73 Addis Ababa= Addis Abeba 9 2N 38 42E
73 Addis Abeba 9 2N 38 42E
81 Adelaide 34 52S 138 30E
5 Adelaide I. 67 15S 68 30W
88 Adelaide Pen. 67 40N 98 0W
82 Adelaide River 13 15S 131 7E
32 Ademuz 40 5N 1 13W
55 Aden= Al 'Adan 12 50N 45 0E
55 Aden, G. of 13 0N 50 0E
36 Adige, R. 45 10N 12 20E
62 Adilabad 19 33N 78 35E
62 Adirampattinam 10 28N 79 20E
97 Adirondack Mts. 44 0N 74 15W
41 Adjud 46 7N 27 10E
82 Admiralty, G. 14 20S 125 55E
102 Admiralty Inlet 48 0N 122 40W
92 Admiralty I. 57 50N 134 30W
76 Admiralty Is. 2 0S 147 0E
62 Adoni 15 33N 77 18E
27 Adony 47 6N 18 52E
20 Adour, R. 43 32N 1 32W
61 Adra, India 23 30N 86 42E
33 Adra, Sp. 36 43N 3 3W
39 Adrano 37 40N 14 19E
72 Adrar des Iforas, Mts. 19 40N 1 40E
37 Ádria 45 4N 12 3E
98 Adrian 41 55N 84 0W
62 Adur 9 8N 76 40E
49 Adzhar A.S.S.R. 42 0N 42 0E
43 Ægean Sea 37 0N 25 0E
67 Aerhtai Shan, Mts. 48 0N 90 0E
45 Ærø, I. 54 53N 10 20E
45 Ærøskøbing 54 53N 10 20E
57 Afghanistan ■ 33 0N 65 0E
55 Afgoi 2 7N 44 59E
39 Afragola 40 54N 14 15E
1 Africa 5 0N 20 0E
111 Afuá 0 15S 50 10W
54 Afula 32 37N 35 17E
56 Afyon 38 20N 30 15E
72 Agadez 16 58N 7 59E
72 Agadir 30 28N 9 25W
51 Agapa 71 27N 89 15E
61 Agartala 23 50N 91 23E
41 Agăş 46 28N 26 15E
62 Agashi 19 32N 72 47E
65 Agats 5 34S 138 5E
72 Agboville 5 55N 4 15W
20 Agde 43 19N 3 28E
20 Agen 44 12N 0 38E
45 Agger 56 47N 8 13E
39 Agira 37 40N 14 30E
20 Agly, R. 42 47N 3 2E
83 Agnew 28 1S 120 30E
20 Agout, R. 43 47N 1 41E
60 Agra 27 17N 77 58E
32 Agreda 41 51N 1 55W
38 Agrigento 37 19N 13 33E
43 Agrinion 38 37N 21 27E
39 Agrópoli 40 23N 14 59E
111 Agua Clara 20 25S 52 45W
104 Agua Prieta 31 20N 109 32W
110 Aguadas 5 40N 75 38W
105 Aguadilla 18 27N 67 10W
91 Aguanish 50 14N 62 2W
104 Aguascalientes 22 0N 102 12W
104 Aguascalientes □ 22 0N 102 20W
30 Agueda 40 34N 8 27W
31 Aguilar 37 31N 4 40W
30 Aguilar de Campóo 42 47N 4 15W
108 Aguilares 27 26S 65 35W
33 Aguilas 37 23N 1 35W
75 Agulhas, K. 34 52S 20 0E
54 Agur 31 42N 34 55E
72 Ahaggar, Reg. 23 0N 6 30E
85 Ahaura 42 20S 171 32E
24 Ahaus 52 4N 7 1E
24 Ahlen 51 45N 7 52E
60 Ahmadabad 23 0N 72 40E
62 Ahmadnagar 19 7N 74 46E
60 Ahmadpur 29 12N 71 10E
24 Ahrensbök 54 0N 10 34E
104 Ahuachapán 13 54N 89 52W
56 Ahvāz 31 20N 48 40E
47 Ahvenanmaa= Åland, I. 60 15N 20 0E
55 Ahwar 13 31N 46 42E
57 Aibaq 36 15N 68 5E
66 Aichi □ 35 0N 137 15E
39 Aidone 37 26N 14 26E
19 Aignay-le-Duc 47 40N 4 43E
109 Aigua 34 12S 54 45W
20 Aigueperse 46 3N 3 13E
21 Aigues-Mortes 43 35N 4 2E
21 Aigues-Mortes, G. d' 43 31N 4 3E
20 Aiguillon 44 18N 0 21E
68 Aihun 49 55N 127 30E
59 Aijal 23 40N 92 44E
99 Aiken 33 44N 81 50W
14 Ailsa Craig, I. 55 15N 5 7W
51 Aim 59 0N 133 55E
111 Aimorés 19 30S 41 4W
21 Ain □ 46 5N 5 20E
72 Aïn Beida 35 50N 7 35E
56 Ain Dār 25 55N 49 10E
55 Ainabo 9 0N 46 25E
43 Aínos Óros 38 10N 20 35E
72 Aïr 18 0N 8 0E
14 Airdrie 55 53N 3 57W
20 Aire, Landes 43 40N 0 20W
19 Aire, Pas-de-Calais 50 37N 2 22E
19 Aire, R., Fr. 49 19N 4 49E
12 Aire, R., U.K. 53 44N 0 44W
20 Airvault 46 50N 0 8W
19 Aisne, R. 49 26N 2 50E
19 Aisne □ 49 42N 3 40E
33 Aitana, Sa. de 38 35N 0 24W
43 Aitolía kai Akarnanía □ 38 45N 21 18E
43 Aitolikón 38 26N 21 21E
67 Aitush 39 54N 75 40E
41 Aiud 46 19N 23 44E
21 Aix-en-Provence 43 32N 5 27E
21 Aix-les-Bains 45 41N 5 53E
20 Aix-les-Thermes 42 43N 1 51E
43 Aíyina, I. 37 45N 23 26E
42 Aiyínion 40 28N 22 28E
43 Aiyion 38 15N 22 5E
18 Aizenay 46 44N 1 38W
21 Ajaccio 41 55N 8 40E
21 Ajaccio, G. d' 41 52N 8 40E
83 Ajana 27 56S 114 35E
96 Ajax 43 50N 79 1W
73 Ajdabiyah 30 54N 20 4E
54 'Ajlun 32 18N 35 47E
57 Ajman 25 25N 55 30E
60 Ajmer 26 28N 74 37E
103 Ajo 32 18N 112 54W
62 Akalkot 17 32N 76 12E
85 Akaroa 43 49S 172 59E
66 Akashi 34 45N 135 0E
44 Akershus □ 60 10N 11 15E
74 Aketi 2 38N 23 47E
43 Akhaïa □ 38 5N 21 45E
43 Akharnaí 38 5N 23 44E
56 Akhisar 38 56N 27 48E
43 Akhladhókambos 37 31N 22 35E
73 Akhmîm 26 31N 31 47E
90 Akimiski I. 52 50N 81 30W
66 Akita 39 45N 140 0E
66 Akita □ 39 40N 140 30E
72 Akjoujt 19 45N 14 15W
54 Akko 32 35N 35 4E
60 Akkol 43 36N 70 45E
88 Aklavik 68 25N 135 0W
66 Akō 34 45N 134 24E
60 Akola 20 42N 77 2E
73 Akordat 15 30N 37 40E
60 Akot 21 10N 77 10E
89 Akpatok I. 60 30N 68 0W
46 Akranes 64 19N 22 6W
96 Akron 41 7N 81 31W
50 Aksarka 66 31N 67 50E
56 Aksehir 38 18N 31 30E
51 Aksenovo Zilovskoye 53 20N 117 40E
67 Aksu 41 4N 80 5E
73 Aksum 14 5N 38 40E
50 Aktogay 44 25N 76 44E
50 Aktyubinsk 50 10N 57 3E
72 Aku 6 40N 7 18E
72 Akure 7 15N 5 5E
46 Akureyri 65 40N 18 5W
59 Akyab 20 15N 92 45E
55 Al 'Adan 12 50N 45 0E
56 Al Amārah 31 55N 47 15E
56 Al 'Aqabah 29 37N 35 0E
54 Al Barah 31 55N 35 12E
56 Al Basrah 30 30N 47 55E
73 Al Baydā 32 30N 21 40E
57 Al Buraimi 24 15N 55 53E
56 Al Hadithan 34 0N 41 13E
56 Al Hadr 35 35N 42 44E
56 Al Hasa, Reg. 25 40N 50 0E
56 Al Hasakah 36 35N 40 45E
55 Al Hauta 16 5N 48 20E
55 Al Hawra 13 49N 47 37E
56 Al Hillah, Iraq 32 30N 44 25E
56 Al Hillah, Saudi Arabia 23 35N 46 50E
23 Al Hilwah 23 24N 46 48E
56 Al Hindiyah 32 30N 44 10E
72 Al-Hoceïma 35 15N 3 58W
56 Al Hufūf 25 25N 49 45E
56 Al Jahrah 29 25N 47 40E
56 Al Jalāmid 31 20N 39 45E
55 Al Jazir 18 30N 56 31N
56 Al Jazirah, Reg. 26 10N 21 20E
56 Al Jubail 27 0N 49 50E
55 Al Juwara 19 0N 57 13E
57 Al Khābūrah 23 57N 57 5E
55 Al Khalaf 20 30N 57 56E
73 Al Khums 32 40N 14 17E
56 Al Kūt 32 30N 46 0E
56 Al Kuwayt 29 20N 48 0E
56 Al Ladhiqiyah 35 30N 35 45E
55 Al Līth 20 9N 40 15E
56 Al Madīnah 24 35N 39 52E
54 Al Mafraq 32 17N 36 14E
57 Al Manamāh 26 10N 50 30E
73 Al Marj 32 25N 20 30E
55 Al Masīrah 20 25N 58 50E
55 Al Matamma 16 43N 33 22E
56 Al Mawsil 36 15N 43 5E
54 Al Mazra' 31 18N 35 32E
56 Al Miqdadiyah 34 0N 45 0E
56 Al Mubarraz 25 30N 49 40E
57 Al Muharraq 26 15N 50 40E
55 Al Mukha 13 18N 43 15E
56 Al Qamishli 37 10N 41 10E
56 Al Qatif 26 35N 50 0E
73 Al-Qatrūn 24 56N 15 3E
55 Al Qunfidha 19 3N 41 4E
55 Al Ubailah 21 59N 50 57E
73 Al 'Ugaylah 30 12N 19 10E
57 Al Wakrah 25 10N 51 40E
56 Al Wari 'ah 27 50N 47 30E
36 Ala 45 46N 11 0E
68 Ala Shan, Reg. 40 0N 104 0E
99 Alabama, R. 31 8N 87 57W
99 Alabama □ 31 0N 87 0W
111 Alagôa Grande 7 3S 35 35W
111 Alagôas □ 9 0S 36 0W
111 Alagoinhas 12 0S 38 20W
32 Alagón 41 46N 1 12W
30 Alagón, R. 39 44N 6 53W
105 Alajuela 10 2N 84 8W
48 Alakurtti 67 0N 30 30E
103 Alameda 35 10N 106 43W
103 Alamogordo 32 59N 106 0W
103 Alamosa 37 30N 106 0W
62 Aland 17 36N 76 35E
47 Åland, I. 60 15N 20 0E
31 Alandroal 38 41N 7 24W
31 Alanis 38 3N 5 43W
50 Alapayevsk 57 52N 61 42E
30 Alar del Rey 42 38N 4 20W
30 Alaraz 40 45N 5 17W
68 Alashanchih 38 58N 105 14E
88 Alaska □ 65 0N 150 0W
88 Alaska, G. of 58 0N 145 0W
88 Alaska Pen. 56 0N 160 0W
88 Alaska Ra. 62 50N 151 0W
38 Alatri 41 44N 13 21E
48 Alatyr 54 45N 46 35E
110 Alausi 2 0S 78 50W
30 Álava □ 42 48N 2 28W
81 Alawoona 34 45S 140 30E
36 Alba 44 41N 8 1E
30 Alba de Tormes 40 50N 5 30W
40 Albac 46 28N 23 1E
33 Albacete 39 0N 1 50W
33 Albacete □ 38 50N 2 0W
45 Ålbæk 57 14N 10 26E
33 Albaida 38 51N 0 31W
32 Albalate del Arzobispo 41 6N 0 31W
41 Alba-Iulia 46 4N 23 35E
42 Albania ■ 41 0N 20 0E
38 Albano Laziale 41 44N 12 40E
83 Albany, Australia 35 1S 117 58E
99 Albany, Ga. 31 40N 84 10W
97 Albany, N.Y. 42 40N 73 47W
102 Albany, Oreg. 44 41N 123 0W
90 Albany, R. 52 17N 81 31W

3

Árgos Ayre, Pt. of

43 Árgos 37 40N 22 43E
43 Argostólion 38 12N 20 33E
103 Arguello, Pt. 34 34N 120 40W
51 Argun, R. 43 22N 45 55E
82 Argyle, L. 16 20S 128 40E
45 Århus 56 8N 10 11E
39 Ariano Irpino 41 10N 15 4E
110 Arica, Chile 18 32S 70 20W
110 Arica, Col. 1 30S 75 30W
83 Arid, C. 34 1S 123 10E
66 Arida 33 29N 135 44E
20 Ariège, R. 43 31N 1 32E
20 Ariège □ 42 56N 1 30E
105 Arima 10 38N 61 17W
14 Arisaig 56 50N 5 40W
62 Ariyalur 11 8N 79 8E
32 Ariza 41 19N 2 3W
103 Arizona □ 34 20N 111 30W
110 Arjona 10 14N 75 22W
51 Arka 60 15N 142 0E
67 Arka Tagh, Mts. 36 30N 90 0E
101 Arkadelphia 34 5N 93 0W
43 Arkadhía □ 38 48N 21 3E
14 Arkaig, L. 56 58N 5 10W
101 Arkansas, R. 33 48N 91 4W
101 Arkansas □ 35 0N 92 30W
101 Arkansas City 37 4N 97 3W
48 Arkhangelsk 64 40N 41 0E
15 Arklow 52 48N 6 10W
24 Arkona, C. 54 41N 13 26E
62 Arkonam 13 7N 79 43E
20 Arlanc 45 25N 3 42E
30 Arlanza, R. 42 6N 4 9W
30 Arlanzón, R. 42 3N 4 17W
26 Arlberg P. 49 9N 10 12E
21 Arles 43 41N 4 40E
101 Arlington 44 25N 97 4W
16 Arlon 49 42N 5 49E
45 Arlöy 55 38N 13 5E
83 Armadale 32 12S 116 0E
15 Armagh 54 22N 6 40W
15 Armagh □ 54 16N 6 35W
20 Armagnac, Reg. 43 44N 0 10E
19 Armançon, R. 47 57N 3 30E
49 Armavir 45 2N 41 7E
110 Armenia 4 35N 75 45W
49 Armenian S.S.R. □ 40 0N 41 10E
40 Armeniş 45 13N 22 17E
19 Armentières 50 40N 2 50E
81 Armidale 30 30S 151 40E
92 Armstrong, B.C. 50 25N 119 10W
90 Armstrong, Ont. 50 20N 89 0W
62 Armur 18 48N 78 16E
19 Arnay-le-Duc 47 10N 4 27E
32 Arnedo 42 12N 2 5W
16 Arnhem 51 58N 5 55E
80 Arnhem, B. 12 20S 136 10E
62 Arni 12 43N 79 19E
36 Arno, R. 43 31N 10 17E
96 Arnold 40 36N 79 44W
26 Arnoldstein 46 33N 13 43E
90 Arnprior 45 23N 76 25W
24 Arnsberg 51 25N 8 10E
24 Arnstadt 50 50N 10 56E
31 Aroche 37 56N 6 57E
30 Arosa, Ria de 42 28N 8 57W
41 Arpaşu de Jos 45 45N 24 38E
38 Arpino 41 40N 13 35E
81 Arrabury 26 45S 141 0E
61 Arrah 25 35N 84 32E
31 Arraiolos 38 44N 7 59W
14 Arran, I. 55 34N 5 12W
19 Arras 50 17N 2 46E
20 Arreau 42 54N 0 22E
20 Arrats, R. 44 6N 0 52E
72 Arrecife 28 59N 13 40W
108 Arrecifes 34 5S 60 5N
18 Arrée, Mts. d' 48 26N 3 55W
83 Arrino 29 30S 115 40E
18 Arromanches 49 20N 0 38W
31 Arronches 39 8N 7 16W
20 Arros, R. 43 30N 0 2W
18 Arrou 48 6N 1 8E
92 Arrowhead 50 40N 117 55W
85 Arrowtown 44 57S 168 50E
31 Arroyo de la Luz 39 30N 6 38W
20 Ars 46 13N 1 30W
41 Arsache 43 47N 25 45E
68 Arshan 46 59N 120 0E
37 Arsiero 45 49N 11 22E
62 Arsikere 13 15N 76 15E
19 Ars-sur-Moselle 49 5N 6 4E
32 Artá 39 40N 3 20E
43 Árta 39 8N 21 2E
89 Artemovsk 48 35N 37 55E
19 Artenay 48 5N 1 50E
32 Artesa de Segre 41 54N 1 3E
101 Artesia 32 55N 104 25W
80 Arthur, Pt. 22 7S 150 3E
108 Artigas 30 20S 56 30W
19 Artois, Reg. 50 20N 2 30E
56 Artvin 41 14N 41 44E
65 Aru, Kep. 6 0S 134 30E
74 Arua 3 1N 30 58E
111 Aruanã 15 0S 51 10W
105 Aruba, I. 12 30N 70 0W
59 Arunachal Pradesh □ 28 0N 95 0E
62 Aruppukottai 9 31N 78 8E
74 Arusha 3 20S 36 40E
102 Arvada 44 43N 106 6W
68 Arvayheer 46 15N 102 48E
21 Arve, R. 46 12N 6 8E
60 Arvi 20 59N 78 16E
91 Arvida 48 16N 71 14W
46 Arvidsjaur 65 35N 19 10E
44 Arvika 59 40N 12 36E
50 Arys 42 26N 68 48E
48 Arzamas 55 27N 43 55E
72 Arzew 35 50N 0 23W
37 Arzignano 45 30N 11 20E
26 Aš 50 13N 12 12E
54 As Salt 32 2N 35 43E
56 As Samāwah 31 15N 45 15E
56 As Sulaimānīyah 24 8N 47 10E
56 As Sulamānīyah 35 35N 45 29E
57 As Suwaih 22 10N 59 33E
56 As Suwayda 32 40N 36 30E
56 As Suwayrah 32 55N 45 0E
66 Asahikawa 43 45N 142 30E
61 Asansol 23 40N 87 1E
91 Asbestos 45 47N 71 58W
97 Asbury Park 40 15N 74 1W
104 Ascensión, B. de la 19 50N 87 20W
71 Ascension, I. 8 0S 14 15W
26 Aschach 48 23N 14 0E
25 Aschaffenburg 49 58N 9 8E
24 Aschersleben 51 45N 11 28E
37 Ascoli Piceno 42 51N 13 34E
39 Áscoli Satriano 41 11N 15 32E
55 Aseb 13 0N 42 40E
45 Aseda 57 10N 15 20E
41 Asenovgrad 42 1N 24 51E
103 Ash Fork 35 14N 112 32W
56 Ash Shāmiyah 31 55N 44 35E
56 Ash Sharma 28 1N 35 18E
54 Ash Shuna 32 32N 35 34E
48 Asha 35 10N 33 38E
85 Ashburton 43 53S 171 48E
82 Ashburton, R. 37 52S 145 5E
82 Ashburton Downs 23 25S 117 4E
12 Ashby-de-la-Zouch 52 45N 1 29W
54 Ashdod 31 39N 34 35E
54 Ashdot Yaaqov 32 39N 35 35E
99 Asheboro 35 43N 79 46W
99 Asheville 35 39N 82 30W
13 Ashford 51 8N 0 53E
66 Ashikaga 36 28N 139 29E
12 Ashington 55 12N 1 35W
50 Ashkhabad 38 0N 57 50E
98 Ashland, Ky. 38 25N 82 40W
96 Ashland, Ohio 40 52N 82 20W
102 Ashland, Oreg. 42 10N 122 38W
97 Ashland, Pa. 40 45N 76 22W
100 Ashland, Wis. 46 40N 90 52W
97 Ashley 41 12N 75 55W
54 Ashquelon 31 42N 34 55E
96 Ashtabula 41 52N 80 50W
102 Ashton 44 6N 111 30W
12 Ashton-under-Lyne 53 30N 2 8W
1 Asia 45 0N 75 0E
72 Asilah 35 29N 6 0W
38 Asinara, G. dell' 41 0N 8 30E
38 Asinara, I. 41 5N 8 15E
50 Asino 57 0N 86 0E
55 Asir, Ras 11 55N 51 0E
55 Asir, Reg. 18 40N 42 30E
54 Asira esh Shamaliya 32 16N 35 16E
44 Askim 59 35N 11 10E
57 Asmar 35 10N 71 27E
73 Asmera 15 19N 38 55E
45 Asnen, L. 56 35N 15 45E
36 Ásola 45 12N 10 25E
33 Aspe 38 20N 0 40W
85 Aspiring, Mt. 44 23S 168 46W
21 Aspres 44 32N 5 44E
59 Assam □ 25 45N 92 30E
16 Asse 50 54N 4 6E
16 Assen 53 0N 6 35E
93 Assiniboia 49 40N 106 0W
92 Assiniboine, Mt. 50 52N 115 39W
93 Assiniboine, R. 49 53N 97 8W
109 Assis 22 40S 50 20W
37 Assisi 43 4N 12 36E
14 Assynt, L. 58 25N 5 10W
49 Astara 38 30N 48 50E
36 Asti 44 54N 8 11E
43 Astipálaia, I. 36 32N 26 22E
30 Astorga 42 29N 6 8W
102 Astoria 46 16N 123 50W
45 Astorp 56 6N 12 55E
49 Astrakhan 46 25N 48 5E
30 Asturias, Reg. 43 15N 6 0W
108 Asunción 25 21S 57 30W
73 Aswân 24 4N 32 57E
73 Aswân High Dam 24 5N 32 54E
73 Asyût 27 11N 31 4E
56 At Ta'if 21 5N 40 27E
106 Atacama Des. 24 0S 69 20W
108 Atacama, Salar de 24 0S 68 20W
108 Atacama □ 27 30S 70 0W
72 Atakpamé 7 31N 1 13E
43 Atalándi 38 39N 22 58E
66 Atami 35 0N 139 55E
72 Atar 20 30N 13 5W
51 Atara 63 10N 129 10E
31 Atarfe 37 13N 3 40W
50 Atasu 48 30N 71 0E
73 Atbara 17 42N 33 59E
73 'Atbara, Nahr, R 17 40N 33 56E
50 Atbasar 51 48N 68 20E
100 Atchison 39 40N 95 0W
32 Ateca 41 20N 1 49W
37 Atessa 42 5N 14 27E
16 Ath 50 38N 3 47E
92 Athabasca 54 45N 113 20W
93 Athabasca, L. 59 10N 109 30W
93 Athabasca, R. 58 40N 110 50W
15 Athboy 53 37N 6 55W
15 Athenry 53 18N 8 45W
99 Athens, Ala. 34 49N 86 58W
99 Athens, Ga. 33 56N 83 24W
98 Athens, Ohio 39 52N 82 64W
101 Athens, Tex. 32 11N 95 48W
43 Athens=Athínai 37 58N 23 46E
80 Atherton 17 17S 145 30E
43 Athínai 37 58N 23 46E
15 Athlone 53 26N 7 57W
62 Athni 16 44N 75 6E
14 Atholl, Forest of 56 51N 3 50W
91 Atholville 48 5N 67 5W
42 Athos, Mt. 40 9N 24 22E
15 Athy 53 0N 7 0W
51 Atka 60 50N 151 48E
88 Atka I. 52 15N 174 30W
99 Atlanta 33 50N 84 24W
100 Atlantic 41 25N 95 0W
98 Atlantic City 39 25N 74 25W
1 Atlantic Ocean 0 0 30 0W
72 Atlas, Anti, Mts. 30 0N 8 0W
72 Atlas, Moyen, Mts. 37 0N 5 0W
72 Atlas Saharien, Mts. 34 10N 3 30E
92 Atlin 59 31N 133 41W
54 Atlit 32 42N 34 56E
62 Atmakur 14 37N 79 40E
99 Atmore 31 2N 87 30W
104 Atotonilco 20 20N 98 40W
31 Atouguia 39 20N 9 20W
37 Atri 42 35N 14 0E
90 Attawapiskat 53 0N 82 30W
90 Attawapiskat L. 52 20N 88 0W
90 Attawapiskat, R. 52 57N 82 18W
26 Attersee 47 55N 13 31E
26 Attersee, L. 47 52N 13 33E
19 Attigny 49 28N 4 35E
43 Attikí □ 38 10N 23 40E
54 Attil 32 23N 35 4E
97 Attleboro 41 56N 71 18W
58 Attock 33 52N 72 20E
88 Attu I. 52 55N 173 0E
62 Attur 11 35N 78 30E
45 Atvidaberg 58 12N 16 0E
100 Atwood 39 52N 101 3W
21 Aubagne 43 17N 5 37E
19 Aube, R. 48 34N 3 43E
19 Aube □ 48 15N 4 0E
21 Aubenas 44 37N 4 24E
19 Aubigny-sur-Nère 47 30N 2 24E
20 Aubrac, Mts. d' 44 38N 2 58E
99 Auburn, Ala. 32 57N 85 30W
102 Auburn, Calif. 38 50N 121 10W
99 Auburn, Me. 44 6N 70 14W
97 Auburn, N.Y. 42 57N 76 39W
20 Aubusson 45 57N 2 11E
20 Auch 43 39N 0 36E
19 Auchel 50 30N 2 39E
85 Auckland 36 52S 174 46E
76 Auckland Is. 51 0S 166 0E
20 Aude □ 44 13N 3 15E
90 Auden 50 17N 87 54W
18 Auderville 49 43N 1 57W
18 Audierne 48 1N 4 34W
19 Audincourt 47 30N 6 50E
24 Aue 50 34N 12 43E
24 Auerbach 50 30N 12 25E
18 Auffay 49 43N 1 7E
81 Augathella 25 48S 146 35E
25 Augsburg 48 22N 10 54E
83 Augusta, Australia 34 22S 115 10E
39 Augusta, Italy 37 14N 15 12E
99 Augusta, U.S.A. 33 29N 81 59W
99 Augusta 44 20N 69 46W
75 Augusto Cardoso 12 44S 34 50E
28 Augustów 53 51N 23 0E
83 Augustus, Mt. 24 20S 116 50E
80 Augustus Downs 18 35S 139 55E
18 Aulne, R. 48 17N 4 16W
19 Aulnoye 46 2N 0 22W
20 Aunis, Reg. 46 0N 0 50W
61 Aurangabad, Bihar 24 25N 84 18E
60 Aurangabad, Maharashtra 19 50N 75 23E
18 Auray 47 40N 3 0W
24 Aurich 53 28N 7 30E
20 Aurillac 44 55N 2 26E
100 Aurora, Colo. 39 44N 104 55W
98 Aurora, Ill. 41 42N 88 20W
96 Aurora, Ohio 41 21N 81 20W
47 Aust-Agde □ 58 55N 7 40E
100 Austin, Minn. 43 37N 92 59W
102 Austin, Nev. 39 30N 117 1W
101 Austin, Tex. 30 20N 97 45W
78 Australia ■ 23 0S 135 0E
84 Australian Alps, Mts. 36 30S 148 8E
84 Australian Capital Terr. □ 35 15S 149 8E
5 Australian Dependency □ 73 0S 90 0E
26 Austria ■ 47 0N 14 0E
19 Authie, R. 50 21N 1 38E
104 Autlán 19 40N 104 30W
21 Autun 46 58N 4 17E
82 Auvergne 15 39S 130 1E
20 Auvergne, Mts. 45 20N 2 45E
20 Auvergne, Reg. 45 30N 3 20E
20 Auvézère, R. 45 12N 0 51E
19 Auxerre 47 48N 3 32E
21 Auxonne 47 10N 5 20E
20 Auzances 46 2N 2 30E
20 Auzat 45 27N 3 19E
19 Avallon 47 30N 3 53E
91 Avalon Pen. 47 0N 53 20W
62 Avanigadda 16 0N 80 56E
109 Avaré 23 5S 48 55W
42 Ávas 40 57N 25 56E
111 Aveiro, Brazil 3 10S 55 5W
30 Aveiro, Port. 40 37N 8 38W
30 Aveiro □ 40 40N 8 35W
108 Avellaneda 34 50S 58 10W
39 Avellino 40 54N 14 46E
44 Averøya, I. 63 0N 7 35E
39 Aversa 40 58N 14 11E
110 Aves, Is. de 12 0N 67 40W
19 Avesnes 50 8N 3 55E
44 Avesta 60 9N 16 10E
20 Aveyron, R. 44 5N 1 16E
20 Aveyron □ 44 22N 2 45E
37 Avezzano 42 2N 13 24E
14 Aviemore 57 11N 3 50W
39 Avigliano 40 44N 15 41E
21 Avignon 43 57N 4 50E
30 Ávila 40 39N 4 43W
30 Ávila, Sa. de 40 40N 5 0W
30 Ávila □ 40 30N 5 0W
30 Avilés 43 35N 5 57W
84 Avoca 37 5S 143 28E
15 Avoca, R. 52 48N 6 10W
92 Avola, Canada 51 45N 119 30W
39 Avola, Italy 36 56N 15 7E
39 Avola 36 56N 15 7E
83 Avon, R, Australia 31 40S 116 7E
13 Avon, R., Avon 51 30N 2 43W
13 Avon, R., Dorset 50 43N 1 46W
13 Avon, R., Gloucester 51 59N 2 10W
13 Avon □ 51 30N 2 40W
97 Avonmore 45 11N 74 57W
13 Avonmouth 51 30N 2 42W
18 Avranches 48 40N 1 20W
41 Avrig 45 43N 24 21E
66 Awaji-Shima, I. 34 30N 134 50E
57 Awali 26 0N 50 30E
74 Awash 9 1N 40 10E
85 Awatere, R. 41 37S 174 10E
14 Awe, L. 56 15N 5 15W
73 Awjilah 29 8N 21 7E
86 Axel Heiberg Ld. 80 0N 90 0W
20 Ax-les-Thermes 42 44N 1 50E
13 Axminster 50 47N 3 1W
19 Ay 49 3N 4 0E
66 Ayabe 35 20N 135 20E
110 Ayacucho, Arg. 37 5S 58 20W
108 Ayacucho, Peru 13 0S 74 0W
50 Ayaguz 48 10N 80 0E
31 Ayamonte 37 12N 7 24W
51 Ayan 56 30N 138 16E
63 Ayer Itam 1 55N 103 11E
42 Ayía Paraskevi 39 14N 26 16E
42 Ayíos Evstrátios 39 34N 24 58E
48 Aykin 62 20N 49 56E
93 Aylesbury, Canada 50 55N 105 53W
13 Aylesbury, U.K. 51 48N 0 49W
88 Aylmer, L. 64 0N 109 0W
80 Ayr, Australia 19 35S 147 25E
14 Ayr, U.K. 55 28N 4 37W
14 Ayr, R. 55 29N 4 28W
12 Ayre, Pt. of 54 27N 4 21W

6

Barat □, Kalimantan — Belmonte, Port.

64 Barat, □ Kalimantan 0 0s 111 0E
64 Barat, Sumatera 1 0s 101 0E
Sumatera 1 0s 101 0E
65 Barat Daja, Kep. 7 30s 128 0E
109 Barbacena 21 15s 43 56w
110 Barbacoas 1 45N 78 0w
105 Barbados ■ 13 0N 59 30w
32 Barbastro 42 2N 0 5E
31 Barbate 36 13N 5 56w
75 Barberton, S. Africa 25 42s 31 2E
96 Barberton, U.S.A. 41 0N 81 40w
105 Barbuda, I. 17 30N 61 40w
80 Barcaldine 22 33s 145 13E
73 Barce=Al Marj 32 25N 20 40E
32 Barcelona, Sp. 41 21N 2 10E
110 Barcelona, Ven. 10 10N 64 40w
32 Barcelona □ 41 30N 2 0E
39 Barcellona Pozzo di Gotto 38 8N 15 15E
21 Barcelonnette 44 23N 6 40E
110 Barcelos 1 0s 63 0w
73 Bardaî 21 25N 17 0E
55 Bardera 2 20N 42 0s
73 Bardiyah 31 45N 25 0E
12 Bardsey I. 52 46N 4 47w
61 Bareilly 28 22N 79 27E
18 Barentin 49 33N 0 58E
4 Barents Sea 73 0N 39 0E
18 Barfleur 49 40N 1 17w
18 Barfleur, Pte. de 49 42N 1 17w
36 Barga 44 5N 10 30E
55 Bargal 11 25N 51 0E
80 Bargara 24 50s 152 25E
51 Barguzin 53 37N 109 37E
61 Barh 25 29N 85 46E
61 Barhaj 26 18N 83 44E
61 Barhi 24 15N 85 25E
60 Bari, India 26 39N 77 39E
39 Bari, Italy 41 6N 16 52E
60 Bari Doab, Reg. 30 20N 73 0E
110 Barinas 8 36N 70 15w
88 Baring, C. 70 0N 116 30w
73 Bârîs 24 42N 30 31E
61 Barisal 22 30N 90 20E
64 Barisan, Bukit, Mts. 3 30s 102 15E
64 Barito, R. 4 0s 114 50E
57 Barkah 24 30N 58 0E
67 Barkha 31 0N 81 45E
80 Barkly Tableland 19 50s 138 40E
19 Bar-le-Duc 48 47N 5 10E
83 Barlee, L. 29 15s 119 30E
39 Barletta 41 20N 16 17E
84 Barmedman 34 9s 147 21E
60 Barmer 25 45N 71 20E
81 Barmera 34 15s 140 28E
12 Barmouth 52 44N 4 3w
60 Barnagar 23 7N 75 19E
12 Barnard Castle 54 33N 1 55w
50 Barnaul 53 20N 83 40E
100 Barnesville 33 6N 84 9w
13 Barnet 51 37N 0 15w
16 Barneveld 52 7N 5 36E
18 Barneville 49 23N 1 46w
12 Barnsley 53 33N 1 29w
13 Barnstaple 51 5N 4 3w
60 Baroda=Vadodara 22 20N 73 10E
73 Barqa 27 0N 20 0E
31 Barquinha 39 28N 8 25w
110 Barquisimeto 9 58N 69 13w
111 Barra 11 5s 43 10w
14 Barra, I. 57 0N 7 30w
111 Barra de Corda 5 30s 45 10w
109 Barra do Piraí 22 30s 43 50w
109 Barra Mansa 22 35s 44 12w
81 Barraba 30 21s 150 35E
61 Barrackpur 22 44N 88 30E
39 Barrafranca 37 22N 14 10E
110 Barranca 10 45s 77 50w
110 Barrancabermeja 7 0N 73 50w
110 Barrancas 8 55N 62 5w
31 Barrancos 38 10N 6 58w
108 Barranqueras 27 30s 59 0w
110 Barranquilla 11 0N 74 50w
111 Barras 1 45s 73 13w
90 Barraute 47 30N 76 50w
97 Barre 44 15N 73 30w
111 Barreiras 12 8s 45 0w
111 Barreirinhas 2 30s 42 50w
31 Barreiro 38 40N 9 6w
111 Barreiros 8 49s 35 12w
111 Barretos 20 30s 48 35w
92 Barrhead 54 10N 114 30w
90 Barrie 44 25N 79 45w
97 Barrington 41 43N 71 20w
12 Barrow, U.K. 54 8N 3 15w
88 Barrow, U.S.A. 71 16N 156 50w
82 Barrow, I. 20 45s 115 20E
15 Barrow, R. 52 46N 7 0w
80 Barrow Creek 21 30s 133 55E
30 Barruecopardo 41 4N 6 40w
30 Barruelo 42 54N 4 17w
13 Barry 51 23N 3 19w
90 Barry's Bay 45 30N 77 40w
62 Barsi 18 10N 75 50E
103 Barstow 34 58N 117 2w
19 Bar-sur-Aube 48 14N 4 40E
110 Bartica 6 25N 58 40w
101 Bartlesville 36 50N 95 58w
83 Barton Siding 30 31s 132 39E
12 Barton-upon-Humber 53 41N 0 27w
28 Bartoszyce 54 15N 20 55E
99 Bartow 27 53N 81 49w
68 Baruun Urt 46 46N 113 15E
60 Barwani 22 2N 74 57E
19 Bas Rhin □ 48 40N 7 30E
41 Basarabi 44 10N 28 26E
108 Bascuñan, C. 28 52s 71 35w
25 Basel 47 35N 7 35E
25 Basel Landschaft □ 47 26N 7 45E
39 Basento, R. 40 25N 16 40E
48 Bashkir A.S.S.R. □ 54 0N 57 0E
65 Basilan, I. 6 35N 122 0E
65 Basilan City=Lamitan 6 37N 122 0E
65 Basilan Str. 13 10s 122 0E
13 Basildon 51 34N 0 29E
39 Basilicata □ 40 30N 16 0E
13 Basingstoke 51 15N 1 5w
61 Basirhat 22 40N 88 54E
90 Baskatong Res. 46 46N 75 50w
25 Basle=Basel 47 35N 7 35E
62 Basmat 19 15N 77 12E
74 Basoka 1 16N 23 40E
14 Bass Rock 56 5N 2 40w
80 Bass, Str. 39 15s 146 30E
37 Bassano del Grappa 45 45N 11 45E
75 Bassas da India, I. 22 0s 39 0E
105 Basse Terre 16 0N 61 40w
59 Bassein, Burma 16 45N 94 30E
62 Bassein, India 19 26N 72 48E
105 Basseterre 17 17N 62 43w
100 Bassett 42 37N 99 30w
60 Bassi 30 44N 76 21E
19 Bassigny, Reg. 48 0N 5 10E
57 Bastak 27 15N 54 25E
61 Basti 26 52N 82 55E
21 Bastia 42 40N 9 30E
16 Bastogne 50 1N 5 43E
54 Bat Yam 32 2N 34 44E
74 Bata 1 57N 9 50E
65 Bataan, Pen. 14 38N 120 30E
105 Barabanó, G. de 22 30N 82 30w
51 Batagoy 67 38N 134 38E
51 Batamay 63 30N 129 15E
69 Batan Is. 20 25N 121 59E
65 Batang 6 55s 109 40E
65 Batangas 13 35N 121 10E
109 Batatais 20 54s 47 37w
96 Batavia 43 0N 78 10w
82 Batchelor 13 4s 131 1E
101 Batesville 35 48N 91 40w
13 Bath, U.K. 51 22N 2 22w
96 Bath, Me. 43 50N 69 49w
99 Bath, N.Y. 42 20N 77 17w
14 Bathgate 55 54N 3 38w
72 Bathurst=Banjul 13 28N 16 40w
84 Bathurst, Australia 33 25s 149 31E
91 Bathurst, Canada 47 37N 65 43w
88 Bathurst, C. 70 30N 128 30w
82 Bathurst, I., Australia 11 30s 130 10E
86 Bathurst I., Canada 76 30N 130 10w
88 Bathurst Inlet 67 15N 108 30w
91 Bathurst Mines 47 30N 65 47w
57 Batinah, Reg. 24 0N 57 0E
72 Batna 35 34N 6 15E
101 Baton Rouge 30 30N 91 5w
74 Batouri 4 30N 14 25E
63 Battambang 13 7N 103 12E
62 Batticaloa 7 43N 81 45E
39 Battipáglia 40 38N 15 0E
54 Battir 31 44N 35 8E
13 Battle 50 55N 0 30E
93 Battle, R. 52 45N 108 15w
98 Battle Creek 42 20N 85 10w
91 Battle Harbour 52 13N 55 42w
102 Battle Mountain 40 45N 117 0w
93 Battleford 52 45N 108 15w
27 Battonya 46 16N 21 03E
64 Batu, Kep. 0 30s 98 25E
63 Batu Gajah 4 28N 101 3E
63 Batu Pahat=Bandar Penggaram 1 50N 102 56E
49 Batumi 41 30N 41 30E
64 Baturadja 4 11s 104 15E
111 Baturité 4 28s 38 45w
65 Baubau 5 25s 123 50E
72 Bauchi 10 22N 9 48E
18 Baud 47 52N 3 1w
31 Bauer, C. 32 44N 134 4E
18 Baugé 47 31N 0 8w
80 Bauhinia Downs 24 35s 149 18E
24 Baunatal 51 19N 9 15E
109 Bauru 22 10s 49 0w
111 Baus 18 22s 52 47½
24 Bautzen 51 11N 14 25w
59 Bawdwin 23 5N 97 50E
64 Bawean, I. 5 46s 112 35E
59 Bawlake 19 11N 97 21E
98 Bay City, Mich. 43 35N 83 51w
101 Bay City, Tex. 28 59N 95 55w
97 Bay Shore 40 44N 73 15w
85 Bay View 39 25s 176 50E
105 Bayamón 18 24N 66 10w
68 Bayan 47 20N 107 55E
67 Bayan Kara Shan, Mts. 34 0N 98 0E
68 Bayan-Uul 49 6N 112 12E
50 Bayanaul 50 45N 75 45E
68 Bayantsogt 47 58N 105 1E
25 Bayerischer Wald, Reg. 49 0N 13 0E
25 Bayern □ 49 7N 11 30E
18 Bayeux 49 17N 0 42w
51 Baykal, Oz. 53 0N 108 0E
51 Baykal, L.=Baykal, Oz. 53 0N 108 0s
51 Baykir 61 50N 95 50E
50 Baykonur 47 48N 65 50E
19 Bayon 48 30N 6 20E
20 Bayonne, Fr. 43 30N 1 28E
97 Bayonne, U.S.A. 40 40N 74 5w
25 Bayreuth 49 56N 11 35E
56 Bayrūt 33 53N 35 31E
54 Bayt Aula 31 37N 35 2E
54 Bayt Jālā 31 43N 35 11E
54 Bayt Lahm 31 43N 35 12E
54 Bayt Sāhūr 31 42N 35 13E
54 Baytin 31 56N 35 14E
101 Baytown 29 42N 94 57w
33 Baza 37 30N 2 47w
75 Bazaruto, I. do 21 40s 35 28E
20 Bazas 44 27N 0 13w
93 Beach 46 57N 104 0w
13 Beachy Hd. 50 44N 0 16E
83 Beacon, Australia 30 20s 117 55E
97 Beacon, U.S.A. 41 32N 73 58w
112 Beagle, Can. 55 0s 68 30w
85 Bealey 43 2s 171 36E
90 Beardmore 49 36N 87 59w
100 Beardstown 40 0N 90 25w
20 Béarn, Reg 43 28N 0 36w
20 Béarn, R. 43 40N 0 47w
33 Beas de Segura 38 15N 2 53w
32 Beasain 43 3N 2 11w
100 Beatrice 40 20N 96 40w
21 Beaucaire 43 48N 4 39E
91 Beauceville 46 13N 70 46w
81 Beaudesert 27 59s 153 0E
64 Beaufort, Malaysia 5 30N 115 40E
84 Beaufort, Australia 37 25s 143 25E
99 Beaufort, U.S.A. 34 45N 76 40w
86 Beaufort Sea 70 30N 146 0w
75 Beaufort West 32 18s 22 36E
90 Beauharnois 45 20N 73 20w
21 Beaujolais, Reg. 46 0N 4 25E
21 Beaulieu 43 45N 7 20E
14 Beauly 57 29N 4 27w
12 Beaumaris 53 16N 4 7w
18 Beaumont, Fr. 44 45N 0 46E
101 Beaumont, U.S.A. 30 5N 94 8w
19 Beaumont-sur-Oise 49 9N 2 17E
21 Beaune 47 2N 4 50E
93 Beausejour 50 5N 96 35E
19 Beauvais 49 25N 2 8E
93 Beauval 55 9N 107 35w
20 Beauvoir 46 12N 0 30w
20 Beauvoir-sur-Mer 46 55N 2 1w
96 Beaver, Canada 40 40N 80 18w
88 Beaver, U.S.A. 66 40N 147 50w
100 Beaver Dam 43 28N 88 50w
96 Beaver Falls 40 44N 80 20w
60 Beawar 26 3N 74 18E
109 Bebedouro 21 0s 48 25w
13 Beccles 52 2N 1 33E
40 Bečej 45 36N 20 3E
30 Becerreá 42 51N 7 10w
72 Béchar 31 38N 2 18E
98 Beckley 37 50N 81 8w
24 Beckum 51 47N 8 5E
18 Bécon 47 30N 0 50w
33 Bédar 37 11N 1 59w
20 Bédarieux 43 37N 3 10E
90 Bedford, Canada 45 10N 73 0w
75 Bedford, S. Africa 32 40s 26 10E
13 Bedford, U.K. 52 8N 0 29w
96 Bedford, Pa. 40 1N 78 30w
98 Bedford, Ind. 38 50N 86 30w
13 Bedford □ 52 4N 0 28w
92 Bednesti 53 50N 123 10w
80 Bedourie 24 30s 139 30E
27 Bedzin 50 19N 19 7E
24 Beelitz 52 14N 12 58E
81 Beenleigh 27 43s 153 10E
54 Be'er Sheva 31 15N 34 48E
54 Be'erotayim 32 19N 34 59E
12 Beeston 52 55N 1 11w
24 Beetzendorf 52 42N 11 6E
101 Beeville 28 27N 97 44w
84 Bega 36 41s 149 51E
40 Bega, Canalul 45 37N 20 46E
18 Bégard 48 38N 3 18w
30 Begonte 43 10N 7 40w
61 Begu-Sarai 25 24N 86 9E
56 Behbehan 30 30N 50 15E
57 Behshahr 36 45N 53 35E
16 Beilen 52 52N 6 27E
25 Beilngries 49 1N 11 27E
75 Beira 19 50s 34 52E
29 Beira-Alta, Reg. 41 0N 7 20w
29 Beira-Baixa, Reg. 40 0N 7 30w
29 Beira Litoral, Reg. 40 0N 7 30w
56 Beirut=Bayrut 33 53N 35 31E
54 Beit Hanun 31 32N 34 32E
54 Beit'Ur et Tahta 31 54N 35 5E
75 Beitbridge 22 12s 30 0E
54 Beituniya 31 54N 35 10E
31 Beja, Port. 38 2N 7 53w
72 Béja, Tunisia 36 10N 9 0E
31 Beja □ 37 55N 7 55w
72 Béjaïa 36 42N 5 2E
30 Béjar 40 23N 5 46w
27 Békés 46 47N 21 9E
27 Bekes □ 46 45N 21 0E
27 Békéscsaba 46 40N 21 10E
63 Bekok 2 20N 103 7E
61 Bela, India 25 50N 82 0E
58 Bela, Pak. 26 12N 66 20E
40 Bela Crkva 44 55N 21 27E
40 Bela Palanka 43 13N 22 17E
64 Belawan 3 33N 98 32E
49 Belaya Tserkov 49 45N 30 10E
90 Belcher Is. 56 20N 79 20w
32 Belchite 41 18N 0 43w
48 Belebey 54 72N 54 7E
111 Belém 1 20s 48 30w
108 Belén 27 40s 67 5w
103 Belen 34 40N 106 50w
41 Belene 43 39N 25 10E
55 Belet Uen 4 30N 45 5E
15 Belfast, U.K. 54 35N 5 56w
99 Belfast, U.S.A. 44 30N 69 0w
15 Belfast, L. 54 40N 5 50w
15 Belfast □ 54 35N 5 56w
19 Belfort 47 38N 6 50E
19 Belfort, Terr. de □ 47 38N 6 52E
62 Belgaum 15 55N 74 35E
16 Belgium ■ 51 30N 5 0E
15 Belgooly 51 44N 8 30w
49 Belgorod 50 35N 36 35E
49 Belgorod-Dnestrovskiy 46 11N 30 23E
40 Belgrade=Beograd 44 50N 20 37E
64 Belitung, Pulau, I. 3 10s 107 50E
104 Belize ■ 17 0N 88 30w
104 Belize City 17 25N 88 0w
108 Bell Ville 32 40s 62 40w
92 Bella Coola 52 25N 126 40w
108 Bella Unión 30 15s 57 40w
108 Bella Vista 28 33s 59 0w
36 Bellágio 45 59N 9 15E
96 Bellaire 40 1N 80 46w
62 Bellary 15 10N 76 56E
81 Bellata 29 53s 149 46E
18 Belle I. 47 20N 3 10w
91 Belle I, Str. of 51 30N 56 30w
100 Belle Fourche 44 43N 103 52w
99 Belle Glade 26 43N 80 38w
21 Belledonne, Mts. 45 11N 6 0E
98 Bellefontaine 40 20N 83 45E
21 Bellegarde 46 4N 3 49E
21 Belleville, Fr. 46 7N 4 45E
100 Belleville, Ill. 38 30N 90 0w
96 Belleville, N.Y. 43 46N 76 10w
96 Bellevue, Can. 46 35N 84 10w
96 Bellevue, U.S.A. 40 29N 80 3w
21 Belley 45 46N 5 41E
89 Bellin 60 0N 70 0w
81 Bellingen 30 25s 152 50E
102 Bellingham 48 45N 122 27w
5 Bellingshausen Sea 66 0s 80 0w
25 Bellinzona 46 11N 9 1E
97 Bellows Falls 43 10N 72 30w
32 Bellpuig 41 37N 1 1E
37 Belluno 46 8N 12 6E
97 Belmar 40 10N 74 2w
31 Bélmez 38 17N 5 17w
84 Belmont 33 4s 151 42E
111 Belmonte, Brazil 16 0s 39 0w
30 Belmonte, Port. 40 21N 7 20w

Belmopan Bischofshofen

104 Belmopan 17 18N 88 30W
15 Belmullet 54 13N 9 58W
109 Belo Horizonte 19 55S 43 56W
51 Belogorsk 51 0N 128 20E
40 Belogradchik 43 37N 22 40E
100 Beloit 42 35N 89 0W
48 Belomorsk 64 35N 34 30E
48 Beloretsk 53 58N 58 24E
50 Belovo 54 30N 86 0E
48 Beloye, Oz. 60 10N 37 35E
48 Beloye More 66 0N 38 0E
48 Belozersk 60 0N 37 30E
39 Belpasso 37 37N 15 0E
38 Belsito 37 50N 13 47E
49 Belsty 47 48N 28 0E
81 Beltana 30 48S 138 25E
111 Belterra 2 45S 55 0W
101 Belton 31 4N 97 30W
15 Belturbet 54 6N 7 28W
39 Belvedere Marittimo 39 37N 15 52E
100 Belvidere 42 15N 88 55W
50 Belyy Os. 73 30N 71 0E
50 Belyy Yar 58 26N 84 30E
24 Belzig 52 8N 12 36E
31 Bembézar, R. 38 0N 5 20W
100 Bemidji 47 30N 94 50W
14 Ben Cruachan, Mt. 56 26N 5 8W
73 Ben Gardane 33 11N 11 11E
14 Ben Hope, Mt. 58 24N 4 36W
14 Ben Lawers, Mt. 56 33N 4 13W
81 Ben Lomond, Mt., Australia 30 1S 151 43E
14 Ben Lomond, Mt., U.K. 56 12N 4 39W
14 Ben Macdhui, Mt. 57 4N 3 40W
14 Ben More, Mt. 56 26N 6 2W
14 Ben More Assynt, Mt. 58 7N 4 51W
14 Ben Nevis, Mt. 56 48N 5 0W
14 Ben Wyvis, Mt. 57 40N 4 35W
74 Bena Dibele 4 4S 22 50E
31 Benagalbón 36 45N 4 15W
84 Benalla 36 30S 146 0E
61 Benares=Varanasi 25 22N 83 8E
30 Benavente 38 59N 8 49W
30 Benavides 42 30N 5 54W
14 Benbecula, I. 57 26N 7 20W
81 Benbonyathe Hill 30 25S 139 11E
83 Bencubbin 30 48S 117 52E
102 Bend 44 2N 121 15W
55 Bender Beila 9 30N 50 48E
83 Bendering 32 23S 118 18E
49 Bendery 46 50N 29 50E
84 Bendigo 36 40S 144 15E
54 Bene Beraq 32 5N 34 50E
26 Benešóv 49 46N 14 41E
19 Bénestroff 48 54N 6 45E
39 Benevento 41 7N 14 45E
19 Benfeld 48 22N 7 34E
73 Benghazi=Banghazī 32 11N 20 3E
64 Bengkalis 1 30N 102 10E
64 Bengkulu 3 50S 102 12E
64 Bengkulu □ 3 50S 102 10E
93 Bengough 49 25N 105 10W
75 Benguela 12 37S 13 25E
74 Beni 32 11S 148 43E
73 Beni Mazar 28 32N 30 44E
72 Beni Mellal 32 21N 6 21W
73 Benî Suêf 29 5N 31 6E
32 Benicarló 40 23N 0 23E
33 Benidorm 38 33N 0 9W
72 Benin, B. of 5 0N 3 0E
72 Benin City 6 20N 5 31E
33 Benisa 38 43N 0 3E
108 Benjamin Aceval 24 58S 57 34W
110 Benjamin Constant 4 40S 70 15W
80 Benlidi 24 35S 144 50E
99 Bennettsville 34 38N 79 39W
97 Bennington 42 52N 73 12W
18 Bénodet 47 53N 4 7W
75 Benoni 26 11S 28 18E
25 Bensheim 49 40N 8 38E
103 Benson 31 59N 110 19W
65 Benteng 6 10S 120 30E
101 Benton, Ark. 34 30N 92 35W
100 Benton, Ill. 38 0N 88 55W
98 Benton Harbor 42 10N 86 28W
63 Bentong 3 31N 101 55S
72 Benue, R. 7 47N 6 45E
40 Beograd 44 50N 20 37E
66 Beppu 33 15N 131 30E
54 Ber Dagan 32 1N 34 49E
42 Berati 40 43N 19 59E
73 Berber 18 0N 34 0E
55 Berbera 10 30N 45 2E
74 Berbérati 4 15N 15 40E
33 Berberia, C. 38 39N 1 24E
36 Berceto 44 30N 10 0E
25 Berchtesgaden 47 37N 13 1E
19 Berck 50 25N 1 36E
49 Berdicher 49 57N 28 30E
50 Berdsk 54 47N 83 2E
49 Berdyansk 46 45N 36 50E
55 Bereda 11 45N 51 0E
72 Berekum 7 29N 2 34W
93 Berens River 52 25N 97 0W
27 Berettyóújfalu 47 13N 21 33E
48 Berezniki 59 24N 56 46E
50 Berezovo 64 0N 65 0E
32 Berga 42 6N 1 48E
36 Bergamo 45 42N 9 40E
30 Bergantiños 43 20N 8 40W
24 Bergedorf 53 28N 10 12E
24 Bergen, E. Germany 50 24N 13 26E
16 Bergen, Neth. 52 40N 4 42E
47 Bergen, Norway 60 23N 5 27E
16 Bergen-op-Zoom 51 30N 4 18E
20 Bergerac 44 51N 0 30E
24 Bergheim 50 57N 6 38E
24 Bergisch-Gladbach 50 59N 7 9E
19 Bergues 50 58N 2 24E
16 Bergum 53 13N 5 59E
61 Berhampore 24 2N 88 27E
62 Berhampur 19 15N 84 54E
88 Bering Sea 66 0N 170 0W
4 Bering Str. 65 0N 168 0W
16 Beringen 51 3N 5 14E
51 Beringovskiy 63 3N 179 19E
108 Berisso 34 40S 58 0W
33 Berja 36 50N 2 56W
102 Berkeley 38 0N 122 20W
5 Berkner I. 79 30S 50 0W
41 Berkovitsa 43 16N 23 8E
13 Berkshire □ 51 30N 1 20W
31 Berlanga 38 17N 5 50W
24 Berleburg 51 3N 8 22E
31 Berlenga, I. 39 25N 9 30W
24 Berlin, Germany 52 32N 13 24W
97 Berlin, U.S.A. 44 29N 71 10W
31 Bermeja, Sa. 36 45N 5 11W
32 Bermeo 43 25N 2 47W
105 Bermuda, I. 32 45N 65 0W
25 Bern 46 57N 7 28E
25 Bern □ 46 45N 7 40E
39 Bernalda 40 24N 16 44E
103 Bernalilo 35 17N 106 37W
109 Bernardo de Irigoyen 26 15S 53 40W
24 Bernau 47 53N 12 20E
18 Bernay 49 5N 0 35E
26 Berndorf 47 59N 16 1E
25 Berne=Bern 46 57N 7 28E
25 Berner Alpen, Mts. 46 27N 7 35E
83 Bernier, I. 24 50S 113 12E
25 Bernina, Piz 46 20N 9 54E
26 Beroun 49 57N 14 5E
26 Berounka, R. 50 0N 13 47E
84 Berowra 33 35S 151 12E
21 Berre 43 28N 5 11E
21 Berre, Étang de 43 27N 5 5E
72 Berrechid 33 18N 7 36W
81 Berri 34 14S 140 35E
84 Berrigan 35 38S 145 49E
19 Berry, Reg. 47 0N 2 0E
24 Bersenbrück 52 33N 7 56E
19 Bertincourt 50 5N 2 58E
74 Bertoua 4 30N 13 45E
97 Berwick 41 4N 76 17W
12 Berwick-upon-Tweed 55 47N 2 0W
12 Berwyn Mts. 52 54N 3 26W
27 Berzence 46 12N 17 11E
19 Besançon 47 9N 6 0E
21 Bessèges 44 18N 4 8E
99 Bessemer 46 27N 90 0W
18 Bessin, Reg. 49 21N 1 0W
18 Bessines-sur-Gartempe 46 6N 1 22E
54 Bet Ha 'Emeq 32 58N 35 8E
54 Bet Ha Shitta 32 31N 35 27E
54 Bet Ha'tmeq 32 58N 35 8E
54 Bet Oren 32 43N 34 59E
54 Bet Qeshet 32 41N 35 21E
54 Be't She'an 32 30N 35 30E
54 Bet Shemesh 31 45N 35 0E
54 Bet Yosef 32 34N 35 33E
30 Betanzos 43 15N 8 12W
74 Bétaré-Oya 5 40N 14 5E
32 Betera 39 35N 0 28W
75 Bethanien 26 31S 17 8E
54 Bethany=Eizariya 31 47N 35 15E
97 Bethel, Conn. 41 22N 73 25W
96 Bethel, Pa. 40 20N 80 2W
97 Bethel, Vt. 43 50N 72 37W
54 Bethlehem, Jordan=Bayt Lahm 31 43N 35 12E
75 Bethlehem, S. Africa 28 14S 28 18E
97 Bethlehem, U.S.A. 40 39N 75 24W
75 Bethulie 30 30S 25 29E
19 Béthune 50 30N 2 38E
18 Béthune, R. 49 56N 1 5E
19 Betan Bazoches 48 42N 3 15E
80 Betoota 25 40S 140 42E
61 Bettiah 26 48N 84 33E
36 Bèttola 44 46N 9 35E
66 Betung 2 0S 103 10E
41 Beuca 44 14N 24 56E
21 Beuil 44 6N 7 0E
84 Beulah, Australia 35 58S 142 29E
93 Beulah, Canada 50 16N 101 2W
24 Bevensen 53 5N 10 34E
83 Beverley, Australia 32 9S 116 56E
12 Beverley, U.K. 53 52N 0 26W
92 Beverly, Canada 53 36N 113 21W
97 Beverly, U.S.A. 42 32N 70 50W
103 Beverly Hills 34 4N 118 29W
16 Beverwijk 52 28N 4 38E
25 Bex 46 15N 7 0E
72 Beyla 8 30N 8 38W
13 Bexhill 50 51N 0 29E
50 Beyneu 45 10N 55 3E
56 Beypazari 40 10N 31 48E
56 Beyşehir Gólú, L. 37 40N 31 45E
62 Bezawada=Vijayawada 16 31N 80 39E
40 Bezdan 45 28N 18 57E
54 Bezet 33 4N 35 8E
48 Bezhitsa 53 19N 34 17E
20 Béziers 43 20N 3 12E
61 Bhadrakh 21 10N 86 30E
62 Bhadravati 13 49N 76 15E
61 Bhagalpur 25 10N 87 0E
62 Bhaisa 19 10N 77 58E
60 Bhakkar 31 40N 71 5E
61 Bhakra Dam 31 30N 76 45E
59 Bhamo 24 15N 97 15E
62 Bhamragarh 19 30N 80 40E
62 Bhandara 21 5N 79 42E
61 Bhanrer Ra. 23 40N 79 45E
58 Bharūch 21 47N 73 0E
60 Bharatpur 27 15N 77 30E
60 Bhatinda 30 15N 74 57E
62 Bhatkal 13 58N 74 35E
61 Bhatpara 22 50N 88 25E
62 Bhattiprolu 16 7N 80 45E
60 Bhaun 32 55N 72 40E
62 Bhavani 11 27N 77 43E
60 Bhavnagar 21 45N 72 10E
60 Bhera 32 29N 72 57E
60 Bhilwara 25 25N 74 38E
62 Bhima, R. 17 20N 76 30E
62 Bhimavaram 16 30N 81 30E
60 Bhind 26 30N 78 46E
62 Bhiwandi 19 15N 73 0E
60 Bhiwani 28 50N 76 9E
62 Bhiwndi 19 15N 73 0E
62 Bhongir 17 30N 78 56E
60 Bhopal 23 20N 77 53E
62 Bhor 18 12N 73 53E
61 Bhubaneswar 20 15N 85 50E
60 Bhuj 23 15N 69 49E
60 Bhusaval 21 15N 69 49E
61 Bhutan ■ 27 25N 89 50E
27 Biała, R 49 46N 17 40E
28 Biała Piska 53 37N 22 5E
28 Biała Podlaska 52 4N 23 6E
28 Biela Podlaska □ 52 0N 23 0S
28 Białogard 54 2N 15 58E
28 Białystok 53 10N 23 10E
28 Białystok □ 52 50N 23 10E
39 Biancaville 37 39N 14 50E
20 Biarritz 43 29N 1 33W
25 Biasca 46 22N 18 58E
25 Biberach 48 5N 9 49E
30 Bibey, R. 42 24N 7 13W
72 Bibiani 6 30N 2 8W
91 Bic 48 20N 68 41W
39 Biccari 41 23N 15 12E
72 Bida 9 3N 5 58E
13 Bicester 51 53N 1 9W
62 Bidar 17 55N 77 35E
99 Biddeford 43 30N 70 28E
13 Bideford 51 1N 4 13W
63 Bidor 4 6N 101 15E
75 Bié 12 22S 16 55E
75 Bié Plat. 12 0S 16 0E
102 Bieber 41 4N 121 6W
25 Biel 47 8N 7 14E
28 Bielawa 50 43N 16 37E
27 Bielé Karpaty, Mts. 49 5N 18 0E
24 Bielefeld 52 2N 8 31E
36 Biella 45 33N 8 3E
28 Bielsk Podlaski 52 47N 23 12E
27 Bielsko-Biała 49 50N 19 8E
27 Bielsko Biała 49 45N 19 10E
63 Biên Hoa 10 57N 106 49E
25 Bienne=Biel 47 8N 7 14E
31 Bienvenida 38 18N 6 12W
32 Biescas 42 37N 0 20W
39 Biferno, R. 41 40N 14 38E
90 Big Beaver House 52 59N 89 50W
101 Big Bend Nat. Park 29 15N 103 15W
88 Big Delta 64 15N 145 0W
97 Big Moose 43 49N 74 58W
98 Big Rapids 43 42N 85 27W
93 Big River 53 50N 107 0W
88 Big Salmon 61 50N 136 0W
101 Big Spring 32 10N 101 25W
99 Big Stone Gap 36 52N 82 45W
90 Big Trout L. 53 40N 90 0W
20 Biganos 44 39N 0 59W
93 Biggar, Canada 52 10N 108 0W
14 Biggar, U.K. 55 38N 3 31W
82 Bigge, I. 14 35S 125 10E
81 Biggenden 25 31S 152 4E
102 Bighorn Mts. 44 30N 107 20W
20 Bigorre, Reg. 43 5N 0 2E
102 Bigtimber 45 33N 110 0W
37 Biháć 44 49N 15 57E
61 Bihar 25 5N 85 40E
61 Bihar □ 25 0N 86 0E
27 Bihor □ 47 0N 22 10E
72 Bijagos, Arquipélago dos 11 15N 16 10W
62 Bijapur 26 2N 77 36E
40 Bijeljina 44 46N 19 17E
60 Bijnor 29 27N 78 11E
60 Bikaner 28 2N 73 18E
51 Bikin 46 50N 134 20E
76 Bikini Atoll, I. 12 0N 167 30E
60 Bilara 26 14N 73 53E
61 Bilaspur, Mad. P. 22 2N 82 15E
60 Bilaspur, Punjab 31 19N 76 50E
63 Bilauk Taungdan, Ra. 13 0N 99 0E
30 Bilbao 43 16N 2 56W
40 Bileća 42 53N 18 27E
56 Bilecik 40 5N 30 5E
51 Bilibino 68 3N 166 20E
51 Bilir 65 40N 131 20E
42 Bilishti 40 37N 20 59E
83 Billabalong 27 25S 115 49E
82 Billiluna 19 37S 127 41E
12 Billingham 54 36N 1 18W
102 Billings 45 43N 108 29W
44 Billingsfors 58 59N 12 15E
20 Billom 45 43N 3 20E
73 Bilma 18 50N 13 30E
40 Bilo Gora 45 53N 17 15E
80 Biloela 24 34S 150 31E
101 Biloxi 30 30N 89 0W
73 Biltine 14 40N 20 50E
80 Bilyana 18 5S 145 50E
65 Bima 8 22S 118 49E
60 Bina-Etawah 24 13N 78 14E
65 Binalbagan 10 12N 122 50E
64 Binatang 2 10N 111 40E
80 Binbee 20 19S 147 56E
16 Binche 50 26N 4 10E
83 Bindi Bindi 30 37S 116 22E
75 Bindura 17 18S 31 18E
81 Bingara, N.S.W. 29 40S 150 40E
81 Bingara, Queens. 28 10S 144 37E
25 Bingen 49 57N 7 53E
102 Bingham Canyon 40 31N 112 10W
97 Binghamton 42 9N 75 54W
63 Binh Dinh=An Nhon 13 55N 109 7E
63 Binh Son 15 20N 104 40E
64 Binjai 3 50N 98 30E
54 Binyamina 32 32N 34 56E
72 Binzerte 37 15N 9 50E
108 Bío Bío □ 37 35S 72 0W
37 Biograd 43 56N 15 29E
40 Biokovo 43 23N 17 0E
62 Bir 19 0N 75 54E
73 Bir Atrun 18 15N 26 40E
54 Bir Nabala 31 52N 35 12E
73 Bîr Shalatein 23 5N 35 25E
54 Bir Zeit 31 59N 35 11E
61 Biratnagar 26 18N 87 17E
93 Birch Hills 53 10N 105 10W
84 Birchip 35 52S 143 0E
79 Bird, I. 22 20S 155 20E
80 Birdsville 25 51S 139 20E
82 Birdum 15 50S 133 0E
64 Bireuen 5 14N 96 39E
109 Birigui 21 18S 50 16W
57 Birjand 32 57N 59 10E
12 Birkenhead 53 24N 3 1W
26 Birkfeld 47 21N 15 45E
41 Bîrlad 46 15N 27 38E
13 Birmingham, U.K. 52 30N 1 55W
99 Birmingham, U.S.A. 33 31N 86 50W
72 Birnin-Kebbi 12 32N 4 12E
51 Birobidzhan 48 50N 132 50E
15 Birr 53 7N 7 55W
93 Birtle 50 30N 101 5W
61 Bisalpur 28 14N 79 48E
103 Bisbee 31 30N 110 0W
20 Biscarrosse, Étang de 44 22N 1 10W
29 Biscay, B. of 45 0N 2 0W
39 Biscéglie 41 14N 16 30E
26 Bischofshofen 47 26N 13 14E

Braşov Bzenec

41 Braşov 45 7N 25 39 E
16 Brasschaat 51 19N 4 27 E
27 Bratislava 48 10N 17 7 E
51 Bratsk 56 10N 101 3 E
97 Brattleboro 42 53N 72 37W
41 Braţul Chilia, R. 45 25N 29 20 E
41 Braţul Sfîntu Gheorghe 45 0N 29 20 E
41 Braţul Sulina, R. 45 10N 29 20 E
26 Braunau 48 15N 13 3 E
24 Braunschweig 52 17N 10 28 E
13 Braunton 51 6N 4 9W
55 Brava 1 20N 44 8 E
103 Brawley 32 58N 115 30W
15 Bray 53 12N 6 6W
19 Bray, Reg. 49 40N 1 40 E
19 Bray-sur-Seine 48 25N 3 14 E
107 Brazil ■ 10 0S 50 0W
98 Brazil 39 30N 87 8W
106 Brazilian Highlands, Mts. 18 0S 46 30W
101 Brazol, R. 30 30N 96 20W
74 Brazzaville 4 9S 15 12 E
40 Brčko 44 54N 18 46 E
80 Breadalbane 23 48S 139 33 E
14 Breadalbane, Reg. 56 30N 4 15W
85 Bream, B. 35 56S 174 35 E
85 Bream Head 35 51S 174 36 E
65 Brebes 6 52S 109 3 E
14 Brechin 56 44N 2 40W
101 Breckenridge 32 48N 98 55W
13 Breckland, Reg. 52 30N 0 40 E
27 Breclav 48 46N 16 53 E
13 Brecon 51 57N 3 23W
13 Brecon Beacons, Mts. 51 53N 3 27W
16 Breda 51 35N 4 45 E
75 Bredasdorp 34 33S 20 2 E
84 Bredbo 35 38S 149 10 E
26 Bregenz 47 30N 9 45 E
46 Breidafjördur 65 20N 23 0W
21 Breil 43 56N 7 31 E
111 Brejo 3 41S 42 50W
24 Bremen 53 4N 8 47 E
24 Bremerhaven 53 34N 8 35 E
102 Bremerton 47 30N 122 48W
31 Brenes 37 32N 5 54W
101 Brenham 30 5N 96 27W
26 Brenner P. 47 0N 11 30 E
90 Brent, Canada 46 0N 78 30W
13 Brent, U.K. 51 33N 0 18W
13 Brentwood 51 37N 0 19W
36 Bréscia 45 33N 10 13 E
28 Breslau=Wrocław 51 5N 17 5 E
19 Bresles 49 25N 2 13 E
37 Bressanone 46 43N 11 40 E
14 Bressay, I. 60 10N 1 5W
21 Bresse, Plaine de 46 20N 5 10 E
20 Bressuire 46 51N 0 30W
18 Brest, Fr. 48 24N 4 31W
48 Brest, U.S.S.R. 52 10N 23 40 E
18 Bretagne, Reg. 48 0N 3 0W
41 Bretçu 46 7N 26 18 E
19 Breteuil 49 38N 2 18 E
20 Breton, Pertuis 46 16N 1 22W
85 Brett, C. 35 10S 174 20 E
111 Breves 1 38S 50 25W
81 Brewarrina 30 0S 146 51 E
99 Brewer 44 43N 68 50W
97 Brewster 41 23N 73 37W
99 Brewton 31 9N 87 2W
27 Brezno 48 50N 19 40 E
74 Bria 6 30N 21 58 E
21 Briançon 44 54N 6 39 E
19 Briare 47 38N 2 45 E
19 Bricon 48 5N 5 0 E
18 Bricquebec 49 29N 1 39W
13 Bridgend 51 30N 3 35W
97 Bridgeport 41 12N 73 12W
98 Bridgeton 39 29N 75 10W
83 Bridgetown, Australia 33 58S 116 7 E
105 Bridgetown, Barbados 13 0N 59 30W
91 Bridgetown, Canada 44 55N 65 12W
84 Bridgewater, Australia 36 36S 143 59 E
91 Bridgewater, Canada 44 25N 64 31W
13 Bridgnorth 52 33N 2 25W
13 Bridgwater 51 7N 3 0W
12 Bridlington 54 4N 0 10W
13 Bridport 50 43N 2 45W
19 Brie, Plaine de la 48 35N 3 10 E
19 Brie-Comte Robert 48 40N 2 35 E
19 Brienon 48 0N 3 35 E
25 Brienzersee, L. 46 44N 7 53 E
25 Brig 46 18N 7 59 E
12 Brigg 53 33N 0 30W
102 Brigham City 41 30N 112 1W
81 Brighton, Australia 35 1S 138 30 E
90 Brighton, Canada 44 3N 77 44W
13 Brighton, U.K. 50 50N 0 9W
18 Brignogan-Plages 48 40N 4 20W
21 Brignoles 43 25N 6 5 E
39 Bríndisi 40 39N 17 55 E
20 Brioude 45 18N 3 23 E
81 Brisbane 27 25S 152 54 E
37 Brisighella 44 13N 11 46 E
13 Bristol, U.K. 51 26N 2 35W
97 Bristol, Conn. 41 44N 72 37W
97 Bristol, Mass. 41 40N 71 15W
97 Bristol, Pa. 40 7N 74 52W
88 Bristol B. 58 0N 159 0W
13 Bristol Chan. 51 18N 3 30W
101 Bristow 35 5N 96 28W
5 British Antarctic Terr. 66 0S 45 0W
92 British Columbia □ 55 0N 125 15W
11 British Is. 55 0N 4 0W
75 Britstown 30 37S 23 30 E
90 Britt 45 46N 80 35W
100 Britton 45 50N 97 47W
20 Brive-la-Gaillarde 45 10N 1 32 E
30 Briviesca 42 32N 3 19W
80 Brixton 23 32S 144 52 E
27 Brno 49 10N 16 35 E
60 Broach 21 47N 73 0 E
83 Broad Arrow 30 23S 121 15 E
14 Broad Law, Mt. 55 30N 3 22W
84 Broadford 37 14S 145 4 E
12 Broads, The 52 30N 1 15 E
93 Brock 51 27N 108 42W
96 Brockport 43 12N 77 56W
97 Brockton 42 8N 71 2W
90 Brockville 44 37N 75 38W
89 Brodeur Pen. 72 0N 88 0W
14 Brodick 55 34N 5 9W
28 Brodnica 53 15N 19 25 E
100 Broken Bow 41 25N 99 35W
84 Broken Hill 31 58S 141 29 E
13 Bromley 51 20N 0 5 E
45 Bromölla 56 5N 14 25 E
45 Brönderslev 57 17N 9 55 E
39 Bronte 37 48N 14 49 E
80 Bronte Pk. 42 8S 146 30 E
100 Brookfield 39 50N 92 50W
101 Brookhaven 31 40N 90 25W
100 Brookings 44 19N 96 48W
88 Brooks Ra. 68 40N 147 0W
83 Brookton 32 22N 116 57 E
14 Broom, L. 57 55N 5 15W
82 Broome 18 0S 122 15W
83 Broomehill 33 40S 117 36 E
14 Brora 58 0N 3 50W
45 Brösarp 55 44N 14 8 E
15 Brosna, R. 53 8N 8 0W
40 Broşteni 47 14N 25 43 E
89 Broughton I. 67 35N 63 50W
14 Broughty Ferry 56 29N 2 50W
13 Brown Willy, Mt. 50 35N 4 34W
101 Brownfield 33 10N 102 15W
102 Browning 48 35N 113 10W
93 Brownlee 50 43N 105 59N
101 Brownsville 25 54N 97 30W
101 Brownwood 31 45N 99 0W
19 Bruay 50 29N 2 33 E
82 Bruce, Mt. 22 31S 118 6 E
90 Bruce Mines 46 20N 83 45W
96 Bruce Pen. 45 0N 81 15W
83 Bruce Rock 31 51S 118 2 E
25 Bruchsal 49 9N 8 39 E
26 Bruck 47 24N 15 16 E
13 Brue, R. 51 10N 2 50W
25 Brugg 47 29N 8 11 E
16 Brugge 51 13N 3 13 E
92 Brule 53 15N 117 38W
111 Brumado 14 13S 41 40W
19 Brumath 48 43N 7 40 E
64 Brunei ■ 4 52N 115 0 E
80 Brunette Downs 18 38S 135 57 E
44 Brunflo 63 4N 14 50 E
37 Brunico 46 48N 11 56 E
44 Brunkeberg 59 25N 8 30 E
85 Brunner 42 27S 171 20 E
93 Bruno 52 20N 105 30W
24 Brunsbüttelkoog 53 52N 9 13 E
16 Brunssum 50 57N 5 59 E
24 Brunswick, W. Germany= Braunschweig 52 17N 10 28 E
99 Brunswick, Ga. 31 10N 81 30W
99 Brunswick, Me. 43 53N 69 50W
96 Brunswick, Ohio 41 15N 81 50W
112 Brunswick, Pen. 53 30S 71 30W
83 Brunswick Junction 33 15S 115 50 E
40 Brusartsi 43 40N 23 5 E
109 Brusque 27 5S 49 0W
16 Brussel 50 51N 4 21 E
84 Bruthen 37 43S 147 48 E
16 Bruxelles= Brussel 50 51N 4 21 E
19 Bruyères 48 10N 6 40 E
28 Brwinow 52 9N 20 40 E
98 Bryan, Ohio 41 30N 84 30W
101 Bryan, Tex. 30 40N 96 27W
48 Bryansk 53 13N 34 25 E
47 Bryne 58 45N 5 36 E
40 Brzava, R. 45 21N 20 45 E
27 Brzeg 50 52N 17 30 E
28 Brzeg Din 51 16N 16 41 E
56 Bucak 37 28N 30 36 E
110 Bucaramanga 7 0N 73 0W
14 Buchan, Reg. 57 32N 2 8W
14 Buchan Ness, Pt. 57 29N 1 48W
93 Buchanan, Canada 51 40N 102 45W
72 Buchanan, Liberia 5 57N 10 2W
91 Buchans 49 0N 57 2W
24 Buchholz 53 19N 9 51 E
24 Bückeburg 52 16N 9 2 E
103 Buckeye 33 28N 112 40W
98 Buckhannon 39 2N 80 10W
14 Buckie 57 40N 2 58W
13 Buckingham, U.K. 52 0N 0 59W
90 Buckingham, U.S.A. 45 37N 75 24W
62 Buckingham Canal 14 0N 80 5 E
13 Buckinghamshire □ 51 50N 0 55W
91 Buctouche 46 30N 64 45W
41 Bucureşti 44 27N 26 10 E
98 Bucyrus 40 48N 83 0W
27 Budafok 47 26N 19 2 E
59 Budalin 22 20N 95 10 E
27 Budapest 47 29N 19 5 E
60 Budaun 28 5N 79 10 E
13 Bude 50 49N 4 33W
41 Budeşti 44 13N 26 30 E
61 Budge Budge 22 30N 88 25 E
37 Búdrio 44 31N 11 31 E
40 Budva 42 17N 18 50 E
110 Buenaventura 29 15S 69 40W
32 Buendia, Pantano de 40 25N 2 43W
108 Buenos Aires 34 30S 58 20W
112 Buenos Aires, L. 46 35S 72 30W
108 Buenos Aires □ 34 30 58 20W
93 Buffalo, Canada 50 49N 110 42W
96 Buffalo, U.S.A. 42 55N 78 50W
93 Buffalo Narrows 55 52N 108 28W
28 Bug, R. 51 20N 23 40 E
110 Buga 4 0N 77 0W
40 Bugojno 44 2N 17 25 E
48 Bugulma 54 38N 52 40 E
68 Bugun Shara, Mts. 48 30N 102 0 E
48 Buturuslan 53 39N 52 26 E
48 Bui 58 23N 41 27 E
13 Builth Wells 52 10N 3 26W
30 Buitrago 41 0N 3 38W
31 Bujalance 37 54N 4 23W
40 Bujanovac 42 27N 21 46 E
32 Bujaraloz 41 29N 0 10W
74 Bujumbura 3 16S 29 18 E
51 Bukachacha 52 55N 116 50 E
74 Bukavu 2 20S 28 52 E
74 Bukene 4 15S 32 48 E
50 Bukhara 39 50N 64 10 E
63 Bukit Mertajam 5 22N 100 28 E
64 Bukittinggi 0 20S 100 20 E
62 Bukkapatnam 14 14N 77 46 E
74 Bukoba 1 20S 31 49 E
67 Bulak 45 2N 82 5 E
60 Bulandshahr 28 28N 77 58 E
75 Bulawayo 20 7S 28 32 E
41 Bulgaria ■ 42 35N 25 30 E
55 Bulhar 10 25N 44 30 E
83 Bullabulling 31 0S 120 55 E
31 Bullaque, R. 39 26N 4 13W
81 Bullara 22 30S 114 2 E
83 Bullaring 32 28S 117 40 E
33 Bullas 38 2N 1 40W
80 Bullock Creek 17 40S 144 30 E
85 Bulls 40 10S 175 24 E
19 Bully-les-Mines 50 27N 2 44 E
55 Bulo Burti 3 50N 45 33 E
60 Bulsar 20 40N 72 58 E
51 Bulun 70 37N 127 30 E
74 Bumba 2 13N 22 30 E
41 Bumbeşti Jiu 45 10N 23 22 E
59 Bumhpa Bum, Mt. 26 40N 97 20 E
83 Bunbury 33 20S 115 35 E
15 Buncrana 55 8N 7 28W
81 Bundaberg 24 54S 152 22 E
60 Bundi 25 30N 75 35 E
80 Bundooma 24 54S 134 16 E
12 Bure, R. 52 38N 1 38 E
24 Burg 54 25N 11 10 E
41 Burgas 42 33N 27 29 E
41 Burgaski Zaliv, B. 42 30N 27 39 E
25 Burgdorf, Switz. 47 3N 7 37 E
24 Burgdorf, W. Germany 52 27N 10 0 E
27 Burgenland □ 47 20N 16 20 E
91 Burgeo 47 36N 57 34W
75 Burgersdorp 31 0S 26 20 E
30 Burgo de Osma 41 35N 3 4W
30 Burgos 42 21N 3 41W
30 Burgos □ 42 21N 3 41W
24 Burgstädt 50 55N 12 49 E
24 Burgsteinfurt 52 9N 7 23 E
31 Burguillos del Cerro 38 23N 6 35W
60 Burhanpur 21 18N 76 20 E
65 Burias, I. 13 5N 122 55 E
105 Burica, Pta 8 3N 82 51W
54 Burin 32 11N 35 15 E
63 Buriram 15 0N 103 0 E
80 Burketown 17 45S 139 33 E
90 Burks Falls 45 37N 79 10W
102 Burley 42 37N 113 55W
96 Burlington, Canada 43 25N 79 45W
100 Burlington, Colo. 39 21N 102 18W
100 Burlington, Iowa 40 50N 91 5W
100 Burlington, Kans. 38 15N 95 47W
99 Burlington, N.C. 36 7N 79 27W
97 Burlington, N.J. 40 5N 74 50W
102 Burlington, Wash. 48 29N 122 19W
50 Burlyu-Tyube 46 30N 79 10 E
59 Burma ■ 21 0N 96 30 E
83 Burngup 33 0S 118 35 E
80 Burnie 41 4S 145 56 E
12 Burnley 53 47N 2 15W
102 Burns 43 40N 119 4W
92 Burns Lake 54 20N 125 45W
96 Burnt River 44 40N 78 42 E
93 Burntwood, L. 55 35N 99 40W
54 Burqa 32 18N 35 11 E
81 Burra 33 40S 138 55 E
84 Burrendong Res. 32 45S 149 10 E
32 Burriana 39 50N 0 4W
13 Burry Port 51 41N 4 17W
56 Bursa 40 15N 29 5 E
12 Burton-on-Trent 52 48N 1 39W
65 Buru, I. 3 30S 126 30 E
74 Burundi ■ 3 15S 30 0 E
64 Burung 0 21N 108 25 E
72 Burutu 5 20N 5 29 E
12 Bury 53 36N 2 19W
13 Bury St. Edmunds 52 15N 0 42 E
51 Buryat A.S.S.R. □ 53 0N 110 0 E
44 Buskerud □ 60 20N 9 0 E
40 Busovača 44 6N 17 53 E
19 Bussang 47 50N 6 50 E
83 Busselton 33 42S 115 15 E
16 Bussum 52 16N 5 10 E
30 Busto, C. 43 34N 6 28W
36 Busto Arsizio 45 38N 8 50 E
74 Busu-Djanoa 1 50N 21 5 E
65 Busuanga, I. 12 10N 120 0 E
24 Büsum 54 7N 8 50 E
74 Buta 2 50N 24 53 E
74 Butare 2 31S 29 52 E
14 Bute, I. 55 48N 5 2W
74 Butembo 0 9N 29 18 E
39 Butera 37 10N 14 10 E
74 Butiaba 1 50N 31 20 E
96 Butler 40 52N 79 52W
14 Butt of Lewis, Pt. 58 30N 6 20W
102 Butte, Mont. 46 0N 112 31W
100 Butte, Neb. 42 56N 98 54W
63 Butterworth 5 24N 100 23 E
65 Butuan 8 52N 125 36 E
65 Butung, I. 5 0S 122 45 E
49 Buturlinovka 50 50N 40 35 E
24 Butzbach 50 24N 8 40 E
61 Buxar 25 34N 83 58 E
12 Buxton 53 16N 1 54W
51 Buyaga 59 50N 127 0 E
68 Buyr Nuur, L. 47 50N 117 35 E
41 Buzău 45 10N 26 50 E
41 Buzău, R. 45 10N 27 20 E
66 Buzen 33 35N 131 5 E
37 Buzet 45 24N 13 58 E
48 Buzuluk 52 48N 52 12 E
97 Buzzards Bay 41 45N 70 38W
41 Byala, Bulgaria 42 53N 27 55 E
41 Byala, Bulgaria 43 28N 25 44 E
41 Byala Slatina 43 26N 23 55 E
28 Bydgoszcz 53 10N 18 0 E
28 Bydgoszcz □ 53 16N 18 0 E
48 Byelorussian S.S.R. □ 53 30N 27 0 E
103 Bylas 33 11N 110 9W
45 Bylderup 54 58N 9 8 E
89 Bylot I. 73 0N 78 0W
75 Byrd Ld. 79 30S 125 0W
5 Byrd Sub-Glacial Basin 82 0S 120 0W
81 Byrock 30 40S 146 27 E
81 Byron Bay 28 30S 153 30 E
46 Byske 64 59N 21 17 E
51 Byrranga, Gory 75 0N 100 0 E
27 Bystrzyca Kłodzka 50 19N 16 39 E
27 Bytom 50 25N 19 0 E
28 Bytów 54 10N 17 30 E
27 Bzenec 48 58N 17 18 E

Ca Mau, Mui, Pt. Carmen, Paraguay

C

63 Ca Mau, Mui, Pt. . . 8 35N 104 42 E
108 Caacupé . . . 25 23N 57 5W
109 Caaguazú □ . . . 25 0N 55 45W
109 Caazapá □ . . . 26 10S 56 0W
108 Caazapá . . . 26 9S 56 24W
32 Caballeria, C. . . . 40 5N 4 5 E
91 Cabana . . . 8 25S 78 5W
65 Cabanatuan . . . 15 30N 121 5 E
32 Cabanes . . . 40 9N 0 2 E
111 Cabedelo . . . 7 0S 34 50W
31 Cabeza del Buey . . 38 38N 3 12W
110 Cabimas . . . 10 30N 71 25W
74 Cabinda . . . 5 40S 12 11 E
102 Cabinet Mts. . . . 48 8N 115 46W
112 Cabo Blanco . . . 47 56S 65 47W
109 Cabo Frio . . . 22 51S 42 3W
90 Cabonga Res. . . . 47 35N 76 40W
81 Caboolture . . . 27 5S 152 47 E
75 Cabora Bassa
Dam . . . 15 30S 32 40 E
104 Caborca . . . 30 40N 112 10W
91 Cabot Str. . . . 47 15N 59 40W
31 Cabra . . . 37 30N 4 28W
33 Cabra del Santó.
Cristo . . . 37 42N 3 16W
33 Cabrera, I. . . . 39 6N 2 59 E
30 Cabrera, Sa. . . . 42 12N 6 40W
93 Cabri . . . 50 35N 108 25W
33 Cabriel, R. . . . 39 14N 1 3W
110 Cabruta . . . 7 50N 66 10W
109 Caçador . . . 26 47S 51 0W
40 Čačak . . . 43 54N 20 20 E
109 Caçapava do Sul . . 30 30S 53 30W
31 Cáceres □ . . . 39 45N 6 0W
31 Cáceres . . . 39 26N 6 23W
90 Cache Bay . . . 46 26N 80 0W
90 Cache Lake . . . 49 55N 74 35W
111 Cachoeira . . . 12 30S 39 0W
109 Cachoeira do Sul . . 30 3S 52 53W
109 Cachoeiro de
Itapemirim . . . 20 51S 41 7W
75 Caconda . . . 13 48S 15 8 E
27 Čadca . . . 49 26N 18 45 E
32 Cadí, Sa. del . . . 42 17N 1 42 E
90 Cadillac, Canada . . 49 45N 108 0W
98 Cadillac, U.S.A. . . . 44 16N 85 25W
65 Cadiz, Philippines . 11 30N 123 15 E
31 Cádiz, Sp. . . . 36 30N 6 20W
31 Cádiz □ . . . 36 35N 5 50W
31 Cádiz, G. of . . . 36 35N 6 20W
92 Cadomin . . . 52 59N 117 28W
83 Cadoux . . . 30 47S 117 8 E
18 Caen . . . 49 10N 0 22W
12 Caernarfon . . . 53 8N 4 17W
12 Caernarfon B. . . . 53 4N 4 40W
13 Caerphilly . . . 51 34N 3 13W
54 Caesarea=Qesari . . 32 30N 34 53 E
111 Caetité . . . 13 50S 42 50W
65 Cagayan de Oro . . . 8 30N 124 40 E
37 Cagli . . . 43 32N 12 38 E
38 Cágliari . . . 39 15N 9 6 E
38 Cágliari, G. di . . . 39 8N 9 10 E
21 Cagnes-sur-Mer . . . 43 40N 7 9 E
105 Caguas . . . 18 14N 66 4W
15 Caher . . . 52 23N 7 56W
15 Cahirciveen . . . 51 57N 10 13W
15 Cahore Pt. . . . 52 34N 6 11W
20 Cahors . . . 44 27N 1 27 E
105 Caibarién . . . 22 30N 79 30W
110 Caicara . . . 7 50N 66 10W
111 Caicó . . . 6 20S 37 0W
105 Caicos Is. . . . 21 40N 71 40W
5 Caird Coast . . . 75 0S 25 0W
14 Cairn Gorm, Mt. . . 57 7N 3 40W
14 Cairngorm Mts. . . . 57 6N 3 42W
80 Cairns . . . 16 55S 145 51 E
73 Cairo, Egypt=
El Qâhira . . . 30 1N 31 14 E
99 Cairo, Ga. . . . 30 52N 84 12W
101 Cairo, Mo. . . . 37 0N 89 10W
36 Cairo Montenotte . 44 23N 8 16 E
110 Cajamarca . . . 7 5S 78 28W
111 Cajazeiras . . . 7 0S 38 30W
72 Calabar . . . 4 57N 8 20 E
110 Calaboza . . . 9 0N 67 20W
39 Calabria □ . . . 39 4N 16 30 E
31 Calaburras,
Pta. de . . . 36 31N 4 38W
112 Calafate . . . 50 25S 72 25W
32 Calahorra . . . 42 18N 1 59W
19 Calais . . . 50 57N 1 56 E
108 Calalaste,
Cord. de . . . 25 0S 67 0W
108 Calama . . . 22 30S 68 55W
110 Calamar . . . 10 15N 74 55W
65 Calamian Group,
Is. . . . 11 50N 119 55 E
32 Calamocha . . . 40 50N 1 17W
31 Calañas . . . 37 40N 6 53W
32 Calanda . . . 40 56N 0 15W
41 Călăraşi . . . 44 14N 27 23 E
33 Calasparra . . . 38 14N 1 41W
38 Calatafimi . . . 37 56N 12 50 E
32 Calatayud . . . 41 20N 1 40W
65 Calauag . . . 13 55N 122 15 E
31 Caldas da Rainha . 39 24N 9 8W
30 Caldas de Reyes . . 42 36N 8 39W
12 Calder R. . . . 53 44N 1 21W
102 Caldwell . . . 43 45N 116 42W
75 Caledon . . . 34 14S 19 26 E
75 Caledon, R. . . . 30 31S 26 5 E
12 Calf of Man, I. . . . 54 4N 4 48W
92 Calgary . . . 51 0N 114 10W
110 Cali . . . 3 25N 76 35W
62 Calicut . . . 11 15N 75 43 E
103 Caliente . . . 37 43N 114 34W
96 California . . . 40 4N 79 55W
103 California □ . . . 37 25N 120 0W
104 California, G. de . . 27 0N 111 0W
104 California,
Baja, Reg. . . . 30 0N 115 0W
41 Călineşti . . . 45 21N 24 18 E
103 Calipatria . . . 33 8N 115 30W
18 Callac . . . 48 25N 3 27W
15 Callan . . . 52 33N 7 25W
110 Callao . . . 12 0S 77 0W
80 Callide . . . 24 23S 150 33 E
80 Calliope . . . 24 0S 151 16 E
33 Callosa de
Ensarriá . . . 38 40N 0 8W
33 Callosa de Segura . 38 1N 0 53W
81 Caloundra . . . 26 45S 153 10 E
33 Calpe . . . 38 39N 0 3 E
39 Calatagirone . . . 37 13N 14 30 E
39 Caltanissetta . . . 37 30N 14 3 E
21 Caluire-et-Cuire . . . 45 49N 4 51 E
18 Calvados □ . . . 49 5N 0 15W
21 Calvi . . . 42 34N 8 45 E
75 Calvinia . . . 31 28S 19 45 E
13 Cam, R. . . . 52 21N 0 15 E
63 Cam Lam . . . 5 0N 109 10 E
63 Cam Rhan . . . 11 54N 109 12 E
105 Camagüey . . . 21 20N 78 0W
36 Camaiore . . . 43 57N 10 18 E
21 Camarat, C. . . . 43 12N 6 41 E
21 Camargue, Reg. . . . 43 20N 4 38 E
112 Camarones . . . 44 50S 66 0W
30 Cambados . . . 42 31N 8 49W
109 Cambará . . . 23 2S 53 5W
60 Cambay . . . 22 23N 72 33 E
60 Cambay, G. of . . . 20 45N 72 30 E
63 Cambodia ■ . . . 12 15N 105 0 E
13 Camborne . . . 50 13N 5 18W
19 Cambrai . . . 50 11N 3 14 E
13 Cambrian Mts. . . . 52 10N 3 52W
96 Cambridge, Canada 43 20N 80 20W
85 Cambridge, N.Z. . . 37 54S 175 29 E
13 Cambridge, U.K. . . 52 13N 0 8 E
97 Cambridge, Mass. . 42 20N 71 8W
97 Cambridge, N.Y. . . 43 2N 73 22W
96 Cambridge, Ohio . . 40 1N 81 22W
13 Cambridge □ . . . 52 21N 0 5 E
88 Cambridge B. . . . 69 10N 105 0W
82 Cambridge, G. . . . 14 45S 128 0 E
32 Cambrils . . . 41 8N 1 3 E
109 Cambuci . . . 21 34S 41 55W
84 Camden, Australia 34 5S 150 38 E
99 Camden, Ala. . . . 31 59N 87 15W
101 Camden, Ark. . . . 33 30N 92 50W
97 Camden, N.J. . . . 39 57N 75 1W
99 Camden, S.C. . . . 34 17N 80 34W
37 Camerino . . . 43 10N 13 4 E
101 Cameron . . . 30 53N 97 0W
63 Cameron
Highlands, Mts. . 4 27N 101 22 E
73 Cameroon ■ . . . 3 30N 12 30 E
72 Cameroun, Mt. . . . 4 45N 8 55 E
111 Cametá . . . 2 0S 49 30W
81 Camira Creek . . . 29 15S 153 10 E
111 Camocim . . . 2 55S 40 50W
80 Camooweal . . . 19 56S 138 7 E
111 Camopi . . . 3 45N 52 50W
39 Campagna . . . 40 40N 15 5 E
31 Campahario . . . 38 52N 5 36W
108 Campana . . . 34 10S 58 55W
39 Campania □ . . . 40 50N 14 45 E
112 Campana, I. . . . 48 20S 75 10W
96 Campbell . . . 41 5N 80 36W
76 Campbell I. . . . 52 30S 169 0 E
92 Campbell River . . . 50 1N 125 15W
80 Campbell Town . . . 41 52S 147 30 E
84 Campbelltown,
Australia . . . 34 5S 150 48 E
91 Campbellton, N.B. 47 57N 66 43W
92 Campbellton, Alta. 53 32N 113 15W
14 Campbeltown . . . 55 25N 5 36W
104 Campeche . . . 19 50N 90 32W
104 Campeche □ . . . 19 50N 90 32W
104 Campeche, B. de . . 19 30N 93 0W
84 Camperdown . . . 38 4S 143 12 E
38 Campidano . . . 39 30N 8 40 E
32 Campillo de
Altobuey . . . 39 36N 1 49W
111 Campino Grande . . 7 20S 35 47W
109 Campinas . . . 22 50S 47 0W
37 Campli . . . 42 44N 13 40 E
109 Campo Belo . . . 21 0S 45 30W
33 Campo de
Criptana . . . 39 25N 3 7W
31 Campo de
Gibraltar . . . 36 15N 5 25W
111 Campo Formoso . . 10 30S 40 20W
111 Campo Grande . . . 20 25S 54 40W
111 Campo Maior,
Brazil . . . 4 50S 42 12W
31 Campo Maior,
Port. . . . 38 59N 7 7W
109 Campo Mourão . . . 24 3S 52 22W
110 Campalegre . . . 2 48N 75 20W
39 Campobasso . . . 41 34N 14 40 E
38 Campobello di
Licata . . . 37 16N 13 55 E
38 Campobello di
Mazara . . . 37 38N 12 45 E
109 Campos . . . 21 50S 41 20W
111 Campos Belos . . . 13 10S 46 45W
33 Campos del
Puerto . . . 39 26N 3 1 E
92 Camrose . . . 53 0N 112 50W
63 Can Tho . . . 10 2N 105 46 E
88 Canada ■ . . . 60 0N 100 0W
108 Cañada de
Gómez . . . 32 55S 61 30W
101 Canadian, R. . . . 35 27N 95 3W
104 Canal Zone . . . 9 10N 79 48W
33 Canáls, Sp. . . . 38 58N 0 35W
108 Canáls, Arg. . . . 33 35S 62 40W
96 Canandaigua . . . 42 55N 77 18W
104 Cananea . . . 31 0N 110 20W
72 Canarias, Is. . . . 29 30N 17 0W
105 Canarreos, Arch.
de los . . . 21 35N 81 40W
72 Canary Is.=
Canarias, Is. . . . 29 30N 17 0W
99 Canaveral, C. . . . 28 28N 80 31W
111 Canavieiras . . . 15 45S 39 0W
84 Canberra . . . 35 15S 149 8 E
18 Cancale . . . 48 40N 1 50W
19 Canche, R. . . . 50 31N 1 39 E
30 Candas . . . 43 35N 5 45W
109 Candelaria . . . 27 29S 55 44W
30 Candelaria, Pta.
de la . . . 43 45N 8 0W
30 Candeleda . . . 40 10N 5 14W
109 Cândido de Abreu . 24 35S 51 20W
88 Candle . . . 65 55N 161 56W
108 Canelones . . . 34 32S 56 10W
108 Cañete . . . 37 50S 73 10W
20 Canet Plage . . . 42 42N 3 3 E
32 Canfranc . . . 42 42N 0 31W
75 Cangamba . . . 13 40S 19 54W
30 Cangas de Narcea . 43 10N 6 32W
111 Canguaretama . . . 6 20S 35 5W
109 Canguçu . . . 31 22S 52 43W
38 Canicatti . . . 37 21N 13 50 E
64 Canipaan . . . 8 33N 117 15 E
30 Cañizal . . . 41 20N 5 22W
33 Canjáyar . . . 37 1N 2 44W
92 Canmore . . . 51 7N 115 18W
84 Cann River . . . 37 35S 149 6 E
14 Canna, I. . . . 57 3N 6 33W
56 Cannakale . . . 40 5N 27 20 E
56 Cannakale Boğazi=
Dardenelles, Str. 40 10N 27 20 E
62 Cannanore . . . 11 53N 75 27 E
21 Cannes . . . 43 32N 7 0 E
12 Cannock . . . 52 42N 2 2W
100 Canon City . . . 39 30N 105 20W
96 Canonsburg . . . 40 15N 80 11W
93 Canora . . . 51 40N 102 30W
39 Canosa di Púglia . . 41 13N 16 4 E
91 Canso . . . 45 20N 61 0W
32 Cantabria, Sa. . . . 42 40N 2 30W
29 Cantábrica
Cord. . . . 43 0N 5 10W
20 Cantal □ . . . 45 4N 2 45 E
30 Cantanhede . . . 40 20N 8 36W
85 Canterbury □ . . . 43 45S 117 19 E
80 Canterbury,
Australia . . . 33 55S 151 7 E
13 Canterbury, U.K. . . 51 17N 1 5 E
85 Canterbury Bight . . 44 16S 171 55 E
85 Canterbury Plain . . 43 55S 171 22 E
69 Canton, China=
Kwangchow . . . 23 10N 133 10 E
100 Canton, Mo. . . . 40 10N 91 33W
97 Canton, N.Y. . . . 44 32N 75 3W
96 Canton, Ohio . . . 40 47N 81 22W
76 Canton I. . . . 36 12N 98 40W
36 Cantù . . . 45 44N 9 8 E
103 Canutillo . . . 31 55N 106 36W
102 Canyon . . . 44 43N 110 36W
103 Canyonlands
Nat. Park . . . 38 25N 109 30W
37 Cáorle . . . 45 36N 12 51 E
91 Cap Breton, I. . . . 46 0N 61 0W
91 Cap Chat . . . 49 6N 66 40W
105 Cap Haïtien . . . 19 40N 72 20W
6 Cap Verde Is. . . . 16 0N 24 0W
20 Capbreton . . . 43 39N 1 26W
80 Cape Barren, I. . . . 40 25S 184 15 E
72 Cape Coast . . . 5 5N 1 15W
89 Cape Dorset . . . 64 30N 77 0W
89 Cape Dyer . . . 66 30N 61 0W
101 Cape Girardeau . . . 37 20N 89 30W
75 Cape Province □ . . 32 0S 23 0 E
75 Cape Town . . . 33 55S 18 22 E
80 Cape York Pen. . . . 13 30S 142 30 E
111 Capela . . . 10 15S 37 0W
80 Capella . . . 23 2S 148 1 E
20 Capendu . . . 43 11N 2 31 E
40 Čapljina . . . 43 35N 17 43 E
36 Capraia, I. . . . 43 2N 9 50 E
90 Capreol . . . 46 40N 80 50W
39 Capri, I. . . . 40 34N 14 15 E
75 Caprivi Strip, Reg. 18 0S 23 0 E
39 Capua . . . 41 7N 14 5 E
110 Caquetá, R. . . . 3 8S 64 46W
41 Caracal . . . 44 8N 24 22 E
110 Caracas . . . 10 30N 66 50W
111 Caracol . . . 9 15S 64 20W
84 Caragabal . . . 33 54S 147 50 E
109 Carangola . . . 20 50S 42 5W
83 Carani . . . 30 57S 116 28 E
40 Caransebeş . . . 45 28N 22 18 E
18 Carantec . . . 48 40N 3 55W
105 Caratasca, L. . . . 15 30N 83 40W
111 Caratinga . . . 19 50S 42 10W
111 Caraúbas . . . 5 50S 37 25W
33 Caravaca . . . 38 8N 1 52W
36 Caravaggio . . . 45 30N 9 39 E
111 Caravelas . . . 17 50S 39 20W
109 Caràzinho . . . 28 0S 53 0W
30 Carballino . . . 42 26N 8 5W
30 Carballo . . . 43 13N 8 41W
93 Carberry . . . 49 50N 99 25W
30 Carbia . . . 42 48N 8 14W
38 Carbonara, C. . . . 39 8N 9 30 E
102 Carbondale, Colo. . 39 30N 107 10W
101 Carbondale, Ill. . . . 37 45N 89 10W
97 Carbondale, Pa. . . . 41 37N 75 30W
91 Carbonear . . . 47 42N 53 13W
33 Carboneras . . . 37 0N 1 53W
32 Carboneras de
Guadazaón . . . 39 54N 1 50 E
38 Carbonia . . . 39 10N 8 30 E
33 Carcagente . . . 39 8N 0 28W
20 Carcans,
Étang de, L. . . . 45 8N 1 8 E
20 Carcassonne . . . 43 13N 2 20 E
92 Carcross . . . 60 20N 134 40W
82 Cardabia . . . 23 2S 113 55 E
62 Cardamon Hills . . . 9 30N 77 15 E
105 Cárdenas, Cuba . . . 23 0N 81 30W
104 Cárdenas, Mexico . 22 0N 99 41W
32 Cardenete . . . 39 42N 1 41W
13 Cardiff . . . 51 28N 3 11W
13 Cardigan . . . 52 6N 4 41W
13 Cardigan Bay . . . 52 30N 4 30W
108 Cardona . . . 33 53S 57 18W
32 Cardoner, R. . . . 41 41N 1 51 E
109 Cardoso, I. do . . . 25 5S 48 0W
93 Cardross . . . 49 50N 105 40W
92 Cardston . . . 49 15N 113 20W
80 Cardwell . . . 18 14S 146 2 E
27 Carei . . . 47 40N 22 29 E
18 Carentan . . . 49 19N 1 15W
83 Carey, L. . . . 29 0S 122 15 E
20 Carnon . . . 43 32N 3 59 E
3 Cargados
Garajos, Is. . . . 17 0S 59 0 E
21 Cargèse . . . 42 7N 8 35 E
108 Carhué . . . 37 10S 62 50W
105 Caribbean Sea . . . 15 0N 75 0W
92 Cariboo Mts. . . . 53 0N 121 0W
19 Carignan . . . 49 38N 5 10 E
32 Cariñena . . . 41 20N 1 13W
111 Carinhanha . . . 14 15S 44 0W
38 Carinola . . . 41 11N 13 58 E
110 Caripito . . . 10 2N 63 0W
39 Carlentini . . . 37 15N 15 2 E
90 Carleton Place . . . 45 8N 76 11W
102 Carlin . . . 40 50N 116 5W
15 Carlingford L. . . . 54 0N 6 5W
100 Carlinville . . . 39 20N 89 55W
12 Carlisle, U.K. . . . 54 54N 2 55W
96 Carlisle, U.S.A. . . . 40 12N 77 10W
20 Carlitte, Pic. . . . 42 35N 1 54 E
108 Carlos Casares . . . 35 53S 61 20W
15 Carlow . . . 52 50N 6 58W
15 Carlow □ . . . 52 43N 6 50W
101 Carlsbad . . . 32 20N 104 7W
88 Carmacks . . . 62 0N 136 0W
36 Carmagnola . . . 44 50N 7 42 E
93 Carman . . . 49 30N 98 0W
13 Carmarthen . . . 51 52N 4 20W
20 Carmaux . . . 44 3N 2 10 E
54 Carmel, Mt. . . . 32 45N 35 3 E
108 Carmelo . . . 34 0S 58 10W
110 Carmen, Col. . . . 9 43N 75 6W
109 Carmen, Paraguay . 27 13S 56 12W

Chao Phraya, R. Circle

63 Chao Phraya, R. 13 32N 100 36E
69 Chaoan 23 45N 117 11E
69 Chaochow 23 45N 116 32E
69 Chaohwa 32 16N 105 41E
67 Chaotung 27 30N 103 40E
68 Chaoyang 41 46N 120 16E
104 Chapata, L. 20 10N 103 20W
50 Chapayevo 50 25N 51 10E
48 Chapayevsk 53 0N 49 40E
109 Chapecó 27 14S 52 41W
99 Chapel Hill 35 53N 79 3W
90 Chapleau 47 45N 83 30W
61 Chapra 25 48N 84 50E
110 Charagua 19 45S 63 10W
110 Charambira, Pta. 4 20N 77 30W
110 Charaña 17 30S 69 35W
108 Charata 27 13S 61 14W
67 Charchan 38 4N 85 16E
67 Charchan, R. 39 0N 86 0E
13 Chard, U.K. 50 52N 2 59W
93 Chard, U.S.A. 55 55N 111 10W
50 Chardara 41 16N 67 59E
50 Chardzhou 39 0N 63 20E
20 Charente □ 45 50N 0 36W
20 Charente, R. 45 57N 1 5W
20 Charente-Maritime □ 45 50N 0 35W
73 Chari, R. 12 58N 14 31E
57 Charikar 35 0N 69 10E
67 Charkhlikh 39 16N 88 17E
16 Charleroi 50 24N 4 27E
98 Charles, C. 37 10N 75 52W
100 Charles City 43 2N 92 41W
101 Charleston, Mass. 34 2N 90 3W
99 Charleston, S.C. 32 47N 79 56W
98 Charleston, W. Va. 38 24N 81 36W
105 Charlestown, Nevis 17 8N 62 37W
97 Charlestown, U.S.A. 38 29N 85 40W
81 Charleville, Australia 26 24S 146 15E
15 Charleville, Eire= Rath Luire 52 21N 8 40W
19 Charleville-Mézières 49 44N 4 40E
99 Charlotte 35 16N 80 46W
105 Charlotte Amalie 18 22N 64 56W
98 Charlottesville 38 1N 78 30W
91 Charlottetown 46 19N 63 3W
84 Charlton 36 16S 143 24E
100 Charlton 40 59N 93 20W
90 Charlton I. 52 0N 79 20W
91 Charny 46 43N 71 15W
21 Charolles 46 27N 4 16E
20 Charroux 46 9N 0 25E
80 Charters Towers 20 5S 146 13E
18 Chartres 48 29N 1 30E
108 Chascomús 35 30S 58 0W
41 Chatal Balkan= Udvoy, Mts. 42 50N 26 50E
88 Chatanika 65 7N 147 31W
20 Château Chinon 47 4N 3 56E
18 Château-du-Loir 47 40N 0 25E
18 Château Gontier 47 50N 0 42W
19 Château Porcien 49 31N 4 13E
18 Château Renault 47 36N 0 56E
19 Château Thierry 49 3N 3 20E
18 Château-la-Vallière 47 30N 0 20E
18 Châteaubourg 48 7N 1 25W
18 Châteaubriant 47 43N 1 23W
18 Châteaudun 48 3N 1 20E
18 Châteaulin 48 11N 4 8W
20 Châteaumeillant 46 35N 2 12E
20 Châteaunuef-sur-Charente 45 36N 0 3W
19 Châteauneuf-sur-Loire 47 52N 2 13E
20 Châteauroux 46 50N 1 40E
20 Châtelaillon Plage 46 5N 1 5W
20 Châtelguyon 45 55N 3 4E
20 Châtellerault 46 50N 0 30E
13 Chatham, U.K. 51 22N 0 32E
91 Chatham, N.B. 47 2N 65 28W
96 Chatham, Ont. 42 23N 82 15W
98 Chatham, Alas. 57 30N 135 0W
97 Chatham, N.Y. 42 21N 73 32W
76 Chatham Is. 44 0S 176 40W
92 Chatham Str. 57 0N 134 40W
20 Châtillon-en-Bazois 47 3N 3 39E
21 Châtillon-en-Diois 44 41N 5 29E
20 Châtillon-sur-Indre 46 48N 1 10E
19 Châtillon-sur-Seine 47 50N 4 33E
20 Châtillon-sur-Sèvre 46 56N 0 45W
99 Chattahoochee 30 43N 84 51W
99 Chattanooga 35 2N 85 17W
19 Chaulnes 49 48N 2 47E
19 Chaumont 48 7N 5 8E
19 Chauny 49 37N 3 12E
21 Chaussin 46 59N 5 22E
20 Chauvigny 46 34N 0 39E
111 Chaves, Brazil 0 15S 49 55W
30 Chaves, Port. 41 45N 7 32W
26 Cheb 50 9N 12 20E
48 Cheboksary 56 8N 47 30E
98 Cheboygan 45 38N 84 29W
68 Chefoo=Yentai 37 30N 121 21E
51 Chegdomyn 51 7N 132 52E
102 Chehallis 46 44N 122 59W
69 Cheju 33 28N 126 30E
69 Cheju Do, I. 33 29N 126 34E
69 Chekiang □ 29 30N 120 0E
112 Chelforó 39 0S 66 40W
50 Chelkar 47 40N 59 32E
50 Chelkar Tengiz Solonchak 48 0N 62 30E
19 Chelles 48 52N 2 33E
28 Chełm 51 8N 23 30E
28 Chełm □ 51 20N 23 20E
28 Chełmno 53 20N 18 30E
13 Chelmsford 51 44N 0 29E
28 Chełmno 53 20N 18 30E
84 Chelsea 38 5S 145 8E
13 Cheltenham 51 55N 2 5W
50 Chelyabinsk 55 10N 61 35E
92 Chemainus 48 54N 123 41W
75 Chemba 17 11S 34 53E
48 Chemikovsk 54 58N 56 0W
18 Chemillé 47 14N 0 45W
63 Chemor 4 44N 101 6E
102 Chemult 43 14N 121 54W
60 Chenab, R. 29 23N 71 2E
69 Chengchow 34 47N 113 46E
67 Chengkiang 24 58N 102 59E
68 Chengteh 41 0N 117 55E
68 Chengting 38 8N 114 37E
67 Chengtu 30 45N 104 0E
68 Chengyang 36 20N 120 16E
69 Chenhsien 25 45N 112 37E
69 Chenning 25 57N 105 51E
68 Chentung 46 2N 123 1E
69 Chenyuan 27 0N 108 20E
41 Chepelare 41 44N 24 40E
105 Chepo 9 10N 79 6W
13 Chepstow 51 39N 2 41W
100 Chequamegon B. 46 40N 90 30W
19 Cher □ 47 10N 2 30E
18 Cherbourg 49 39N 1 40W
72 Cherchell 36 35N 21 63E
48 Cherdyn 60 20N 56 20E
51 Cheremkhovo 53 32N 102 40E
50 Cherepanovo 54 15N 83 30E
49 Cherkassy 49 30N 32 0E
41 Cherni, Mt. 42 35N 23 28E
48 Chernigov 51 28N 31 20E
49 Chernovtsy 48 0N 26 0E
51 Chernoye 70 30N 89 10E
100 Cherokee 42 40N 95 30W
48 Cheropovets 59 5N 37 55E
112 Cherquenco 38 35S 72 0W
51 Cherskogo Khrebet 65 0N 143 0E
41 Cherven-Bryag 43 17N 24 7E
13 Cherwell, R. 51 44N 1 15W
98 Chesapeake B. 38 0N 76 12W
12 Cheshire □ 53 14N 2 30W
33 Cheste 39 30N 0 41W
12 Chester, U.K. 53 12N 2 53W
98 Chester, Pa. 39 54N 75 20W
99 Chester, S.C. 34 44N 81 13W
12 Chesterfield 53 14N 1 26W
88 Chesterfield Inlet 63 30N 91 0W
76 Chesterfield Is. 19 52S 158 15E
104 Chetumal 18 30N 88 20W
104 Chetumal, B. de 18 40N 88 10W
20 Chevanceaux 45 18N 0 14W
12 Cheviot, The, Mt. 55 28N 2 8W
12 Cheviot Hills 55 20N 2 30W
74 Chew Bahir, L. 4 40N 30 50E
102 Chewelah 48 25N 117 56W
100 Cheyenne 41 9N 104 49W
100 Cheyenne, R. 44 40N 101 15W
60 Chhindwara 22 2N 78 59E
63 Chi, R. 15 13N 104 45E
69 Chiai 23 29N 120 25E
75 Chianje 15 35S 13 40E
104 Chiapas □ 17 0N 92 45W
39 Chiaramonte Gulfi 37 1N 14 41E
36 Chiari 45 31N 9 55E
36 Chiávari 44 20N 9 20E
36 Chiavenna 46 18N 9 23E
66 Chiba 35 30N 140 7E
66 Chiba □ 35 30N 140 20E
75 Chibemba 15 48S 14 8E
90 Chibougamau 49 56N 74 24W
98 Chicago 41 45N 87 40W
98 Chicago Heights 41 29N 87 37W
92 Chichagof I. 58 0N 136 0W
13 Chichester 50 50N 0 47W
104 Chichén Itzá 20 40N 88 34W
66 Chichibu 36 5N 139 10E
68 Chichirin 50 35N 123 45E
101 Chickasha 35 0N 98 0W
31 Chiclana de la Frontera 36 26N 6 9W
110 Chiclayo 6 42S 79 50W
102 Chico 39 45N 121 54W
112 Chico, R. 43 50S 66 25W
97 Chicopee 42 6N 72 37W
91 Chicoutimi 48 28N 71 5W
62 Chidambaram 11 20N 79 45E
89 Chidley, C. 60 30N 64 15W
25 Chiemsee, L. 47 53N 12 27E
74 Chiengi 8 38S 29 10E
63 Chiengmai 18 55N 98 55E
37 Chienti, R. 43 18N 13 45E
36 Chieri 45 0N 7 50E
19 Chiers, R. 49 39N 5 0E
37 Chieti 42 22N 14 10E
68 Chihfeng 42 10N 118 56E
69 Chihing 25 2N 113 45E
69 Chihkiang 27 21N 109 45E
68 Chihli, G. of= Po Hai, G. 38 30N 119 0E
69 Chihsien 35 29N 114 1E
104 Chihuahua 28 40N 106 3W
104 Chihuahua □ 28 40N 106 3W
50 Chiilí 44 10N 66 55E
62 Chik Ballapur 13 25N 77 45E
62 Chikmagalur 13 15N 75 45E
62 Chikodi 16 26N 74 38E
58 Chilas 35 25N 74 5E
81 Childers 25 15S 152 17E
101 Childress 34 30N 100 50W
107 Chile ■ 35 0S 71 15W
110 Chilete 7 10S 78 50W
75 Chililabombwe 12 18S 27 43E
61 Chilka L. 19 40N 85 25E
108 Chillán 36 40S 72 10W
100 Chillicothe, Mo. 39 45N 93 30W
98 Chillicothe, Ohio. 39 53N 82 58W
92 Chilliwack 49 10N 122 0W
112 Chiloé, I. de 42 50S 73 45W
104 Chilpancingo 17 30N 99 40W
84 Chiltern 36 10S 146 36E
13 Chiltern Hills 51 44N 0 42W
69 Chilung 25 3N 121 45E
75 Chilwa, L. 15 15S 35 40E
67 Chimai 34 0N 101 39E
110 Chimborazo, Mt. 1 20S 78 55W
110 Chimbote 9 0S 78 35W
50 Chimkent 42 40N 69 25E
59 Chin □ 22 0N 93 0E
67 China ■ 35 0N 100 0E
105 Chinandega 12 30N 87 0W
110 Chincha Alta 13 20S 76 0W
81 Chinchilla 26 45S 150 38E
33 Chinchilla de Monte Aragón 38 53N 1 40W
68 Chinchow 41 10N 121 2E
75 Chinde 18 45S 36 30E
59 Chindwin, R. 21 26N 95 15E
69 Ching Ho, R. 34 20N 109 0E
62 Chingleput 12 42N 79 58E
75 Chingola 12 31S 27 53E
75 Chingole 13 4S 34 17E
68 Chinhae 35 9N 128 58E
60 Chiniot 31 45N 73 0E
68 Chinju 35 12N 128 2E
69 Chinkiang 32 2N 119 29E
103 Chino Valley 34 54N 112 28W
18 Chinon 47 10N 0 15E
93 Chinook, Canada 51 28N 110 59W
102 Chinook, U.S.A. 48 35N 109 19W
61 Chinsura 22 53N 88 27E
62 Chintamani 13 26N 78 3E
68 Chinwangtao 40 0N 119 31E
37 Chióggia 45 13N 12 15E
92 Chip Lake 53 35N 115 35W
75 Chipata 13 38S 32 28E
31 Chipiona 36 44N 6 26W
62 Chiplun 17 31N 73 34E
96 Chippawa 43 5N 79 10W
13 Chippenham 51 27N 2 7W
100 Chippewa, R. 44 25N 92 10W
100 Chippewa Falls 44 56N 91 24W
104 Chiquimula 14 51N 89 37W
110 Chiquinquira 5 37N 73 50W
62 Chirala 15 50N 80 20E
60 Chirawa 28 14N 75 42E
62 Chirayinkil 8 41N 76 49E
50 Chirchik 81 58N 69 15E
88 Chirikof I. 55 50N 155 35W
105 Chiriquí, G. de 8 0N 82 10W
105 Chiriquí, L. de 9 10N 82 0W
105 Chiriqui, Mt. 8 55N 82 35W
75 Chiromo 16 30S 35 7E
41 Chirpan 42 10N 25 19E
75 Chisamba 14 55S 28 20E
60 Christian Mandi 29 50N 72 55E
51 Chita 52 0N 113 25E
62 Chitapur 17 10N 76 50E
75 Chitembo 13 30S 16 50E
60 Chitorgarh 24 52N 74 43E
62 Chitradurga 14 15N 76 28E
105 Chitré 7 59N 80 27W
59 Chittagong 22 19N 91 55E
61 Chittagong □ 24 5N 91 25E
62 Chittoor 13 15N 79 5E
62 Chittur 10 40N 76 45E
33 Chiva 39 27N 0 41W
36 Chivasso 45 10N 7 52E
108 Chivilcoy 35 0S 60 0W
26 Chlumec 50 9N 15 29E
28 Chodziez 52 58N 17 0E
62 Chodavaram 17 40N 82 50E
112 Choele Choel 39 11S 65 40W
19 Choisy 48 45N 2 24E
28 Choinice 53 42N 17 40E
20 Cholet 47 4N 0 52W
105 Choluteca 13 20N 87 14W
75 Choma 16 48S 26 59E
60 Chomu 27 15N 75 40E
26 Chomutov 50 28N 13 23E
63 Chon Buri 13 21N 101 1E
68 Chonan 36 56N 127 3E
110 Chone 0 40S 80 0W
68 Chongjin 41 51N 129 58E
68 Chŏngju, N. Korea 39 41N 125 13E
68 Chŏngju, S. Korea 36 39N 127 27E
68 Chŏnju 35 50N 127 4E
112 Chonos, Arch. de los 45 0S 75 0W
60 Chopda 21 20N 75 15E
12 Chorley 53 39N 2 39W
27 Chorzow 50 18N 19 0E
66 Chōshi 35 45N 140 45E
28 Choszczno 53 7N 15 25E
102 Choteau 47 50N 112 10W
68 Choybalsan 48 3N 114 28E
85 Christchurch, N.Z. 43 33S 172 47W
13 Christchurch, U.K. 50 44N 1 47W
75 Christiana 27 52S 25 8E
82 Christmas Creek 18 29S 125 23E
77 Christmas I. 1 58N 157 27W
26 Chrudim 49 58N 15 43E
27 Chrzanów 50 10N 19 21E
50 Chu 43 36N 73 42E
69 Chu Kiang, R. 24 50N 113 37E
69 Chuanchow 24 57N 118 31E
69 Chuanhsien 25 50N 111 12E
66 Chūbu □ 36 45N 137 0E
112 Chubut, R. 43 20S 65 5W
68 Chucheng 36 0N 119 16E
69 Chuchow 27 56N 113 3E
48 Chudskoye, Oz. 58 13N 27 30E
88 Chugiak 61 25N 149 30W
66 Chūgoku □ 35 0N 133 0E
66 Chūgoku-Sanchi, Mts. 35 0N 133 0E
69 Chuhsien 30 51N 107 1E
63 Chukai 4 13N 103 25E
51 Chukotskiy Khrebet 68 0N 175 0E
51 Chukotskoye More 68 0N 175 0W
103 Chula Vista 33 44N 117 8W
69 Chumatien 33 0N 114 4E
51 Chumikan 54 40N 135 10E
63 Chumphon 10 35N 99 14E
68 Chuncho E9n 37 58N 127 44E
69 Chunghsien 30 17N 108 4E
69 Chungking 29 30N 106 30E
67 Chungtien 28 0N 99 30E
68 Chungwei 37 35N 105 10E
60 Chunian 31 10N 74 0E
74 Chunya 8 30S 33 27E
25 Chur 46 52N 9 32E
93 Churchill 58 45N 94 5W
93 Churchill, R., Man. 58 47N 94 12W
91 Churchill, R., Newf. 53 30N 60 10W
92 Churchill Pk. 58 10N 125 10W
60 Churu 28 20N 75 0E
69 Chusan, I. 30 0N 122 20E
48 Chuvash A.S.S.R. □ 53 30N 48 0E
48 Chuvovoy 58 15N 57 40E
65 Cianjur 6 81S 107 7E
109 Cianorte 23 37S 52 37W
65 Cibatu 7 8S 107 59E
98 Cicero 41 48N 87 48W
28 Ciechanów 52 52N 20 38E
28 Ciechanów □ 53 0N 20 0E
105 Ciego de Avila 21 50N 78 50W
110 Ciénaga 11 0N 74 10W
105 Cienfuegos 22 10N 80 30W
26 Cieplice Slaskie Zdrój 50 50N 15 40E
20 Cierp 42 55N 0 40E
27 Cieszyn 49 45N 18 35E
33 Cieza 38 17N 1 23W
32 Cifuentes 40 47N 2 37W
31 Cijara, Pantano, Res. 39 18N 4 52W
65 Cilacap 7 43S 109 0E
101 Cimarron, R. 36 10N 96 17W
65 Cimahi 6 53S 107 33E
36 Cimone, Mte. 44 12N 10 42E
41 Cîmpina 45 10N 25 45E
41 Cîmpulung 45 17N 25 3E
32 Cinca, R. 41 26N 0 21E
98 Cincinnati 39 10N 84 26W
37 Cîngoli 43 23N 13 10E
21 Cinto, Mt. 42 24N 8 54E
38 Circéo, Mte. 41 14N 13 3E
88 Circle 47 26N 105 35W

Circleville, Ohio Coonamble

98 Circleville, Ohio ... 39 35N 82 57W
103 Circleville, Utah ... 38 12N 112 24W
65 Cirebon ... 6 45S 108 32E
13 Cirencester ... 51 43N 1 59W
101 Cisco ... 32 25N 99 0W
41 Cislău ... 45 14N 26 33E
39 Cisternino ... 40 45N 17 26E
38 Cisterna di Latina ... 41 35N 12 50E
104 Citlaltepetl, Mt. ... 19 0N 97 20W
37 Città di Castello ... 43 27N 12 14E
37 Città Sant'Angelo ... 42 32N 14 5E
37 Cittadella ... 45 39N 11 48E
39 Cittanova ... 38 22N 16 0E
41 Ciuc, Mt. ... 45 31N 25 55E
104 Ciudad Acuña ... 29 20N 101 10W
110 Ciudad Bolívar ... 8 5N 63 30W
104 Ciudad Camargo ... 27 41N 105 10W
104 Ciudad de Valles ... 22 0N 98 30W
104 Ciudad del Carmen ... 18 20N 97 50W
110 Ciudad Guayana ... 8 20N 62 35W
104 Ciudad Guzmán ... 19 40N 103 30W
104 Ciudad, Juárez ... 31 40N 106 28W
104 Ciudad Madero ... 22 19N 97 50W
104 Ciudad Mante ... 22 50N 99 0W
104 Ciudad Obregón ... 27 28N 109 59W
110 Ciudad Piar ... 7 27N 63 19W
31 Ciudad Real ... 38 59N 3 55W
31 Ciudad Real □ ... 38 50N 4 0W
30 Ciudad Rodrigo ... 40 35N 6 32W
104 Ciudad Victoria ... 23 41N 99 9W
32 Ciudadela ... 40 0N 3 50E
41 Ciulniţa ... 44 26N 27 22E
37 Cividale del Friuli ... 46 6N 13 25E
37 Civita Castellana ... 42 18N 12 24E
37 Civitanova Marche ... 43 18N 13 41E
37 Civitavécchia ... 42 6N 11 46E
56 Çivril ... 38 20N 29 55E
83 Clackline ... 31 40S 116 32E
13 Clacton ... 51 47N 1 10E
20 Clain, R. ... 46 47N 0 32E
96 Clairton ... 40 18N 79 54W
19 Clamecy ... 47 28N 3 30E
15 Clara ... 53 20N 7 38W
81 Clare ... 33 20S 143 50E
15 Clare □ ... 52 52N 8 55W
15 Clare, R. ... 53 20N 9 3W
97 Claremont ... 43 23N 72 20W
101 Claremore ... 36 20N 95 20W
15 Claremorris ... 53 45N 9 0W
112 Clarence, I. ... 54 0S 72 0W
82 Clarence, Str. ... 12 0S 131 0E
85 Clarence, R. ... 42 10S 173 56E
101 Clarendon ... 34 41N 91 20W
91 Clarenville ... 48 10N 54 1W
92 Claresholm ... 50 0N 113 45W
100 Clarinda ... 40 45N 95 0W
102 Clark Fork, R. ... 48 9N 116 15W
103 Clarkdale ... 34 53N 112 3W
91 Clarke City ... 50 12N 66 38W
91 Clarkes Harbour ... 43 25N 65 38W
98 Clarksburg ... 39 18N 80 21W
101 Clarksdale ... 34 12N 90 33W
102 Clarkston ... 46 28N 117 2W
99 Clarksville ... 36 32N 87 20W
15 Clear, I. ... 51 26N 9 30W
96 Clearfield ... 41 0N 78 27W
92 Clearwater, Canada ... 51 38N 120 2W
99 Clearwater, U.S.A. ... 27 58N 82 45W
90 Clearwater L. ... 56 10N 75 0W
101 Cleburne ... 32 18N 97 25W
13 Clee Hills ... 55 25N 2 35W
12 Cleethorpes ... 53 33N 0 2W
21 Clelles ... 44 50N 5 38E
80 Clermont, Australia ... 22 46S 147 38E
19 Clermont, Meuse ... 49 5N 5 4E
19 Clermont, Oise ... 49 22N 2 24E
20 Clermont-Ferrand ... 45 46N 3 4E
20 Clermont-l'Hérault ... 43 38N 3 26E
19 Clerval ... 47 25N 6 30E
19 Cléry ... 47 50N 1 46E
13 Clevedon ... 51 27N 2 51W
81 Cleveland, Australia ... 27 31S 153 3E
101 Cleveland, Miss. ... 33 34N 90 43W
96 Cleveland, Ohio ... 41 28N 81 43W
99 Cleveland, Tenn. ... 35 9N 84 52W
101 Cleveland, Tex. ... 30 18N 95 0W
12 Cleveland □ ... 54 30N 1 12W
102 Cleveland, Mt. ... 48 56N 113 51W
96 Cleveland Hts. ... 41 32N 81 30W
12 Cleveleys ... 53 53N 3 3W
15 Clew B. ... 53 54N 9 50W
15 Clifden, Eire ... 53 30N 10 2W
85 Clifden, N.Z. ... 46 1S 167 42E
103 Clifton ... 33 8N 109 23W
98 Clifton Forge ... 37 49N 79 51W
99 Clingmans Dome, Mt. ... 35 35N 83 30W
92 Clinton, B.C. ... 51 0N 121 40W
90 Clinton, Ont. ... 43 38N 81 33W
85 Clinton, N.Z. ... 46 12S 169 23E
100 Clinton, Ark. ... 35 37N 92 30W
99 Clinton, Ill. ... 40 8N 89 0W
100 Clinton, Iowa ... 41 50N 90 18W
97 Clinton, Mass. ... 42 26N 71 40W
100 Clinton, Mo. ... 38 20N 93 40W
101 Clinton, N.C. ... 35 5N 78 15W
88 Clinton Colden L. ... 64 0N 107 0W
77 Clipperton I. ... 10 18N 109 13W
15 Clonakilty ... 51 37N 8 53W
80 Cloncurry ... 20 40S 140 28E
105 Clones ... 54 10N 7 13W
15 Clonmel ... 52 22N 7 42W
24 Cloppenburg ... 52 50N 8 3E
100 Cloquet ... 46 40N 92 30W
108 Clorinda ... 25 16S 57 45W
101 Clovis, Calif. ... 36 54N 119 45W
103 Clovis, N.Mex ... 34 20N 103 10W
21 Cluses ... 46 5N 6 35E
85 Clutha, R. ... 46 20S 169 49E
12 Clwyd □ ... 53 0N 3 15W
12 Clwyd, R. ... 53 20N 3 30W
89 Clyde, Canada ... 70 30N 68 30W
85 Clyde, N.Z. ... 45 12S 169 20E
14 Clyde, R. ... 55 56N 4 29W
14 Clyde, Firth of ... 55 42N 5 0W
14 Clydebank ... 55 54N 4 25W
30 Côa, R. ... 41 5N 7 6W
103 Coachella ... 33 44N 116 13W
91 Coachman's Cove ... 50 6N 56 20W
104 Coahuila □ ... 27 0N 112 30W
92 Coaldale, Canada ... 49 45N 112 35W
97 Coaldale, U.S.A. ... 40 50N 75 54W
103 Coalinga ... 36 10N 120 21W
12 Coalville ... 52 43N 1 21W
92 Coast Mts. ... 52 0N 126 0W
102 Coast Ra. ... 40 0N 124 0W
83 Coastal Plains Basin ... 30 10S 115 30E
14 Coatbridge ... 55 52N 4 2W
104 Coatepeque ... 14 46N 91 55W
91 Coaticook ... 45 10N 71 46W
89 Coats I. ... 62 30N 82 0W
5 Coats Ld. ... 77 0S 25 0W
104 Coatzalcoalcos ... 18 7N 94 35W
41 Cobadin ... 44 5N 28 13E
90 Cobalt ... 47 25N 79 42W
104 Coban ... 15 30N 90 21W
84 Cobar ... 31 27S 145 48E
15 Cobh ... 51 50N 8 18W
81 Cobham ... 30 10S 142 0E
90 Cobourg ... 44 0N 78 20W
25 Coburg ... 50 15N 10 58E
30 Coca ... 41 13N 4 32W
62 Cocanada = Kakinada ... 16 55N 82 20E
33 Cocentaina ... 38 45N 0 27W
110 Cochabamba ... 17 15S 66 20W
62 Cochin ... 9 55N 76 22E
63 Cochin-China, Reg. = Nam-Phan, Reg. ... 10 30N 106 0E
92 Cochrane, Alta. ... 51 20N 114 30W
90 Cochrane, Ont. ... 49 0N 81 0W
112 Cochrane, L. ... 47 10S 72 0W
84 Cockburn, Australia ... 32 5S 141 2E
112 Cockburn, Canada ... 54 30S 72 0W
105 Coco, R. ... 15 0N 83 8W
63 Coco Chan. ... 13 45N 93 0E
77 Cocos I. ... 5 25N 87 55W
3 Cocos Is. ... 12 12S 96 54E
86 Cod, C. ... 42 8N 70 10W
110 Codajás ... 3 40S 62 0W
37 Codigoro ... 44 50N 12 5E
111 Codó ... 4 30S 43 55W
36 Codogno ... 45 10N 9 42E
37 Codróipo ... 45 57N 13 0E
105 Codrington ... 17 43N 61 49W
102 Cody ... 44 35N 109 0W
80 Coen ... 13 52S 143 12E
24 Coesfeld ... 51 56N 7 10E
102 Coeur d'Alene ... 47 45N 116 51W
101 Coffeyville ... 37 0N 95 40W
31 Coffin, B. ... 34 20S 135 10E
81 Coffs Harbour ... 30 16S 153 5E
41 Cogealac ... 44 36N 28 36E
38 Coghinas, L. di ... 40 35S 9 2E
20 Cognac ... 45 41N 0 20W
97 Cohoes ... 42 47N 73 42W
84 Cohuna ... 35 45S 144 15E
105 Coiba, I. ... 7 30N 81 40W
112 Coig, R. ... 51 0S 69 10W
112 Coihaique ... 45 35S 72 8W
62 Coimbatore ... 11 2N 76 59E
30 Coimbra ... 40 15N 8 27W
30 Coimbra □ ... 40 15N 8 27W
31 Coín ... 36 40N 4 48W
110 Cojimies ... 0 20N 80 0W
104 Cojutepeque ... 13 41N 88 54W
84 Colac ... 38 10S 143 30E
62 Colachel ... 8 10N 77 15E
31 Colares ... 38 48N 9 30W
100 Colby ... 39 27N 101 2W
108 Colchagua □ ... 34 30S 71 0W
13 Colchester ... 51 54N 0 55E
93 Cold Lake ... 54 27N 110 10W
14 Coldstream ... 55 39N 2 14W
90 Coldwell ... 48 45N 86 30W
101 Coleman ... 31 52N 99 30W
84 Coleraine, Australia ... 37 36S 141 40E
15 Coleraine, U.K. ... 55 8N 6 40W
15 Coleraine □ ... 55 8N 6 40W
62 Coleroon, R. ... 11 22N 79 51E
75 Colesburg ... 30 45S 25 5E
112 Colhué Huapí, L. ... 45 30S 69 0W
104 Colima ... 19 10N 103 50W
104 Colima □ ... 19 10N 103 40W
111 Colinas ... 6 0S 44 10W
84 Colinton ... 35 50S 149 10E
14 Coll, I. ... 56 40N 6 35W
31 Collarenebri ... 29 33S 148 35E
36 Colle Salvetti ... 43 34N 10 27E
99 College Park ... 33 42N 84 27W
83 Collie ... 33 25S 116 30E
82 Collier, B. ... 16 0S 124 0E
36 Colline Metallifere, Mts. ... 43 10N 11 0E
80 Collingwood, Australia ... 22 20S 142 31E
90 Collingwood, Canada ... 44 30N 80 20W
85 Collingwood, N.Z. ... 40 42S 172 40E
80 Collinsville ... 20 30S 147 56E
108 Collipulli ... 37 55S 72 30W
15 Collooney ... 54 11N 8 28W
19 Colmar ... 48 5N 7 20E
31 Colmenar ... 36 54N 4 20W
30 Colmenar de Oreja ... 40 6N 3 25W
30 Colmenar Viejo ... 40 39N 3 47W
12 Colne ... 53 51N 2 11W
84 Colo, R. ... 33 20S 150 40E
37 Cologna Veneta ... 45 19N 11 21E
24 Cologne=Köln ... 50 56N 9 58E
19 Colombey-les-deux Églises ... 48 20N 4 50E
110 Colombia ■ ... 3 45N 73 0W
111 Colombia ... 3 24N 79 49W
62 Colombo ... 6 56N 79 58E
108 Colón, Buenos Aires ... 32 55S 61 5W
108 Colón, Entre Ríos ... 32 12S 58 30W
104 Colón, Panama ... 9 20N 80 0W
83 Colona ... 31 38S 132 5E
37 Colonèlla ... 42 52N 13 50E
108 Colonia ... 34 25S 57 50W
14 Colonsay, I. ... 56 4N 6 12W
103 Colorado □ ... 37 40N 106 0W
112 Colorado, R., Arg. ... 39 50S 62 8W
103 Colorado, R. Mex.–U.S.A. ... 31 45N 114 40W
101 Colorado, R., U.S.A. ... 28 36N 95 58W
103 Colorado Aqueduct ... 34 0N 115 20W
101 Colorado City ... 32 25N 100 50W
103 Colorado Plat. ... 36 40N 110 30W
100 Colorado Springs ... 38 55N 104 50W
101 Columbia, La. ... 32 7N 92 5W
100 Columbia, Mo. ... 38 58N 92 20W
97 Columbia, Pa. ... 40 2N 76 30W
99 Columbia, S.C. ... 34 0N 81 0W
99 Columbia, Tenn. ... 35 40N 87 0W
98 Columbia, District of □ ... 38 55N 77 0W
92 Columbia, Mt. ... 52 20N 117 30W
102 Columbia, R. ... 45 49N 120 0W
102 Columbia Falls ... 48 25N 114 16W
100 Columbia Heights ... 45 5N 93 10W
102 Columbia Plat. ... 47 30N 118 30W
32 Columbretes, I. ... 39 50N 0 50E
99 Columbus, Ga. ... 32 30N 84 58W
98 Columbus, Ind. ... 39 14N 85 55W
99 Columbus, Miss. ... 33 30N 88 26W
100 Columbus, N.D. ... 48 52N 102 48W
98 Columbus, Ohio ... 39 57N 83 1W
30 Colunga ... 43 29N 5 16W
85 Colville, C. ... 36 29S 175 21E
88 Colville, R. ... 70 25N 150 30W
12 Colwyn Bay ... 53 17N 3 44W
37 Comácchio ... 44 41N 12 10E
37 Comácchio, Valli di, L. ... 44 40N 12 10E
112 Comallo ... 41 0S 70 5W
41 Comana ... 44 10N 26 10E
19 Combeaufontaine ... 47 43N 5 45E
19 Combles ... 50 0N 2 50E
80 Comet ... 23 36S 148 38E
61 Comilla ... 23 22N 91 18E
38 Comino, C. ... 40 28N 9 47E
39 Cómiso ... 36 57N 14 35E
104 Comitán ... 16 18N 92 9W
89 Committee B. ... 68 0N 87 0W
20 Commentry ... 46 20N 2 46E
101 Commerce ... 33 15N 95 50W
19 Commercy ... 48 46N 5 34E
36 Como ... 45 48N 9 5E
36 Como, L. di ... 46 5N 9 17E
112 Comodoro Rivadavia ... 45 50S 67 40W
62 Comorin, C. ... 8 3N 77 40E
40 Comorişte ... 45 10N 21 35E
70 Comoro Is. ... 12 10S 44 15E
92 Comox ... 49 42N 125 0W
19 Compiègne ... 49 24N 2 50E
109 Comprida, I. ... 25 0S 80 50W
72 Conakry ... 9 29N 13 49W
80 Conard Junction ... 41 48S 143 70E
18 Concarneau ... 47 52N 3 56W
111 Conceição do Araguaia ... 8 0S 49 2W
111 Conceiçao do Barra ... 18 50S 39 50W
108 Concepción, Arg. ... 27 20S 65 35W
108 Concepción, Chile ... 36 50S 73 0W
108 Concepción, Paraguay ... 23 30S 57 20W
108 Concepción □ ... 37 0S 72 30W
112 Concepción, Canal. ... 50 50S 75 0W
103 Concepcion, Pt. ... 34 30N 120 34W
104 Concepción del Oro ... 24 40N 101 30W
108 Concepción del Uruguay ... 32 35S 58 20W
18 Conches ... 48 58N 0 58E
99 Concord, N.C. ... 35 28N 80 35W
97 Concord, N.H. ... 43 5N 71 30W
108 Concordia, Arg. ... 31 20S 58 2W
100 Concordia, U.S.A. ... 39 35N 97 40W
81 Condamine ... 26 55S 150 3E
19 Condé ... 50 26N 3 34E
84 Condobolin ... 33 4S 147 6E
20 Condom ... 43 57N 0 22E
37 Conegliano ... 45 53N 12 18E
19 Conflans ... 49 10N 5 52E
20 Confolens ... 46 2N 0 40E
12 Congleton ... 53 10N 2 12W
74 Congo ■ ... 1 0S 16 0E
74 Congo (Kinshasa) ■ = Zaïre ■ ... 3 0S 22 0E
74 Congo, R. = Zaïre, R. ... 6 4S 12 24E
103 Congress ... 34 11N 112 56W
31 Conil ... 36 17N 6 10W
90 Coniston ... 46 32N 80 51W
62 Conjeeveram = Kanchipuram ... 12 52N 79 45E
80 Conjuboy ... 18 35S 144 45E
15 Connaucht □ ... 53 23N 8 40W
96 Conneaut ... 41 55N 80 32W
97 Connecticut □ ... 41 40N 72 40W
97 Connecticut, R. ... 41 17N 72 21W
96 Connellsville ... 40 5N 79 32W
15 Connemara ... 53 29N 9 45W
98 Connersville ... 39 40N 85 10W
93 Conquest ... 53 35N 107 0W
101 Conroe ... 30 15N 95 28W
12 Consett ... 54 51N 1 49W
97 Conshohocken ... 40 5N 75 18W
93 Consort ... 52 1N 110 46W
41 Constanţa ... 44 14N 28 38E
31 Constantina ... 37 51N 5 40W
72 Constantine ... 36 25N 6 42E
108 Constitución, Chile ... 35 20S 72 30W
108 Constitución, Uruguay ... 31 0S 58 10W
31 Consuegra ... 39 28N 3 43W
37 Contarina ... 45 2N 12 13E
19 Contrexéville ... 48 10N 5 53E
39 Conversano ... 40 57N 17 8E
101 Conway, Ark. ... 35 5N 92 30W
97 Conway, N.H. ... 43 58N 71 8W
99 Conway, S.C. ... 33 49N 79 2W
12 Conwy ... 53 17N 3 50W
12 Conwy R. ... 53 17N 3 50W
31 Coober Pedy ... 28 56S 134 45E
61 Cooch Behar ... 26 22N 89 29E
83 Cook ... 30 42S 130 48E
112 Cook, B. ... 55 10S 70 0W
88 Cook Inlet ... 59 0N 151 0W
77 Cook Is. ... 22 0S 157 0W
85 Cook, Mt. ... 43 36S 170 9E
85 Cook, Str. ... 41 15S 174 29E
99 Cookeville ... 36 12N 85 30W
80 Cooktown ... 15 30S 145 16E
15 Cookstown □ ... 54 40N 6 43W
81 Coolabah ... 31 0S 146 15E
81 Coolangatta ... 28 11S 153 29E
83 Coolgardie ... 30 55S 121 8E
103 Coolidge ... 33 1N 111 35W
103 Coolidge Dam ... 33 10N 110 30W
84 Cooma ... 36 12S 149 8E
84 Coonabarabran ... 31 14S 149 18E
81 Coonamble ... 30 56S 148 27E

Coonana Dalkeith

83 Coonana 31 0s 123 0E
62 Coondapoor 13 42N 74 40E
81 Coongoola 27 43s 145 47E
62 Coonoor 11 10N 76 45E
99 Cooper.......... 39 57N 75 7W
81 Cooper Creek, R., L. ... 28 0s 139 0E
81 Coorong, The 35 50s 139 20E
83 Coorow 29 50s 115 59E
81 Cooroy 26 22s 152 54E
102 Coos Bay 43 26N 124 7W
84 Cootamundra 34 36s 148 1E
15 Cootehill 54 5N 7 5W
33 Cope, C. 37 26N 1 28W
45 Copenhagen= København 55 41N 12 34E
39 Copertino 40 17N 18 2W
108 Copiapó 27 15s 70 20E
37 Copparo 44 52N 11 49E
88 Copper Center 62 10N 145 25W
90 Copper Cliff 46 30N 81 4W
92 Copper Mountain . 49 20N 120 30W
88 Coppermine 68 0N 116 0W
41 Copşa Mică 46 6N 24 15E
12 Coquet, R. 55 22N 1 37W
74 Coquilhatville= Mbandaka 0 1N 18 18E
108 Coquimbo 30 0s 71 20W
108 Coquimbo □ 30 0s 71 0W
41 Corabia 43 48N 24 30E
110 Coracora 15 5s 73 45W
89 Coral Harbour 64 0N 83 0W
90 Coral Rapids 50 20N 81 40W
76 Coral Sea 15 0s 150 0E
96 Coraopolis 40 30N 80 10W
39 Corato 41 12N 16 22E
19 Corbeil-Essonnes 48 36N 2 25E
20 Corbières, Mts. ... 42 55N 2 35E
98 Corbin 37 0N 84 3W
31 Corbones, R. 37 36N 5 39W
13 Corby 52 29N 0 41W
33 Corcoles, R. 39 12N 2 40W
103 Corcoran 36 6N 119 35W
30 Corcubión 42 56N 9 12W
99 Cordele 31 55N 83 49W
108 Córdoba, Arg. 31 20s 64 10W
108 Córdoba, Arg. □ .. 31 22s 64 15W
104 Córdoba, Mexico .. 26 20N 103 20W
31 Córdoba, Sp. 37 50N 4 50W
108 Córdoba □, Arg. .. 31 22s 64 15W
31 Córdoba □, Sp. ... 38 5N 5 0W
65 Cordon 16 42N 121 32E
88 Cordova 60 36N 145 45W
80 Corfield 21 40s 143 21E
42 Corfu, I.= Kérkira, I. 39 38N 19 50E
30 Corgo 42 56N 7 25W
30 Coria 40 0N 6 33W
39 Corigliano Cálabro 39 36N 16 31E
43 Corinth, Greece= Kórinthos 37 56N 22 55E
99 Corinth, U.S.A. ... 34 54N 88 30W
43 Corinth Canal 37 48N 23 0E
111 Corinto, Brazil 18 20s 44 30W
105 Corinto, Nic. 12 30N 87 10W
15 Cork 51 54N 8 30W
15 Cork □ 51 54N 8 30W
38 Corleone 37 48N 13 16E
56 Çorlu 41 11N 27 49E
93 Cormorant 54 5N 100 45W
105 Corn Is. 12 0N 83 0W
109 Cornélio Procópio . 23 7s 50 40W
91 Corner Brook 49 0N 58 0W
102 Corning, Calif. 39 56N 122 9W
96 Corning, N.Y. 42 10N 77 3W
90 Cornwall 45 5N 74 45W
13 Cornwall □ 50 26N 4 40W
110 Coro 11 30N 69 45W
111 Coroatá 4 20s 44 0W
110 Corocoro 17 15s 69 19W
85 Coromandel 36 45s 175 31E
62 Coromandel Coast Reg. 12 30N 81 0E
103 Corona 33 49N 117 36W
103 Coronado 32 45N 117 9W
105 Coronado, B. de .. 9 0N 83 40W
88 Coronation G. 68 0N 114 0W
108 Coronda 31 58s 60 56W
108 Coronel 37 0s 73 10W
108 Coronel Bogado ... 27 11s 56 18W
108 Coronel Dorrego .. 38 40s 61 10W
108 Coronel Oviedo ... 25 24s 56 30W
108 Coronel Pringles .. 38 0s 61 30W
108 Coronel Suárez ... 37 30s 62 0W
109 Corpus 27 10s 55 30W
101 Corpus Christi 27 50N 97 28W
30 Corral de Almaguer 39 45N 3 10W
36 Corréggio 44 46N 10 47E
20 Corrèze □ 45 20N 1 50E
15 Corrib, L. 53 25N 9 10W
108 Corrientes 27 30s 58 45W
108 Corrientes □ 28 0s 57 0W
105 Corrientes, C., Cuba 21 43N 84 30W
110 Corrientes, C., Col. 5 30N 77 34W
83 Corrigin 32 18s 117 45E
96 Corry 41 55N 79 39W
21 Corse, C. 43 1N 9 25E
21 Corse, I. 42 0N 9 0E
21 Corsica, I.= Corse, I. 42 0N 9 0E
101 Corsicana 32 5N 96 30W
21 Corte 42 19N 9 11E
31 Cortegana 37 52N 6 49W
103 Cortez 37 24N 108 35W
37 Cortina d'Ampezzo 46 32N 12 9E
97 Cortland 42 35N 76 11W
37 Cortona 43 16N 12 0E
31 Coruche 38 57N 8 30W
56 Çorum 40 30N 35 5E
110 Corumbá 19 0s 57 30W
102 Corvallis 44 36N 123 15W
104 Cosamalopan 18 23N 95 50W
39 Cosenza 39 17N 16 14E
41 Coşereni 44 38N 26 35E
96 Coshocton 40 17N 81 51W
19 Cosne-sur-Loire ... 47 24N 2 54E
108 Cosquín 31 15s 64 30W
36 Cossato 45 34N 8 10E
33 Costa Blanca, Reg. 38 25N 0 10W
32 Costa Brava, Reg. . 41 30N 3 0E
31 Costa del Sol, Reg. 36 30N 4 30W
32 Costa Dorada, Reg. 40 45N 1 15E
105 Costa Rica ■ 10 0N 84 0W
41 Costeşti 44 40N 24 53E
38 Cost Smeralda 41 5N 9 35E
25 Coswig 51 52N 12 31E
65 Cotabato 7 8N 124 13E
21 Côte d'Azur, Reg. . 43 25N 6 50E
19 Côte d'Or □ 47 30N 4 50E
21 Côte d'Or, Reg. ... 47 10N 4 50E
18 Cotentin, Reg. 49 30N 1 30W
19 Côtes de Meuse, Reg. 49 15N 5 22E
18 Côtes-du-Nord □ .. 48 28N 2 50W
72 Cotonou 6 20N 2 25E
110 Cotopaxi, Mt. 0 30s 78 30W
13 Cotswold Hills 51 42N 2 10W
102 Cottage Grove 43 48N 123 2W
24 Cottbus 51 44N 14 20E
24 Cottbus □ 51 43N 13 30E
103 Cottonwood 34 48N 112 1W
31 Couço 38 59N 8 17W
102 Coulee City 47 44N 119 12W
19 Coulommiers 48 50N 3 3E
21 Coulon, R. 43 51N 5 0E
88 Council, Alas. 64 55N 163 45W
102 Council, Id. 44 45N 116 30W
100 Council Bluffs 41 20N 95 50W
21 Couronne, C. 43 19N 5 3E
18 Courseulles 49 20N 0 29W
21 Cours 46 7N 4 19E
92 Courtenay 49 45N 125 0W
18 Courville 48 28N 1 15E
18 Coutances 49 3N 1 28W
20 Coutras 45 3N 0 8W
30 Covilhã 40 17N 7 31W
99 Covington, Ga. 33 36N 83 50W
98 Covington, Ky. 39 5N 84 30W
93 Cowan 52 5N 100 45W
83 Cowan, L. 31 45s 121 45E
84 Cowangie 35 12s 141 26E
90 Cowansville 45 14N 72 46W
14 Cowdenbeath 56 7N 3 20W
81 Cowell 33 38s 136 40E
13 Cowes 50 45N 1 18W
84 Cowra 33 49s 148 42E
111 Coxim 18 30s 54 55W
59 Cox's Bazar 21 25N 92 3E
104 Cozumel, I. de 20 30N 86 40W
75 Cradock 32 8s 25 36E
102 Craig 40 32N 107 44W
15 Craigavon □ 54 27N 6 26W
41 Craiova 44 21N 23 48E
74 Crampel 7 8N 19 8E
93 Cranberry Portage . 54 36N 101 22W
80 Cranbrook, Tas. 42 0s 148 5E
83 Cranbrook, W. Australia 34 20s 117 35E
92 Cranbrook Canada 49 30N 115 55W
97 Cranston 41 47N 71 27W
41 Crasna 46 32N 27 51E
111 Crateús 5 10s 40 50W
111 Crato, Brazil 7 10s 39 25W
31 Crato, Port. 39 16N 7 39W
21 Crau, Reg. 43 32N 4 40E
98 Crawfordsville 40 2N 86 51W
13 Crawley 51 7N 0 10W
19 Crécy 48 50N 2 53E
93 Cree L. 57 30N 107 0W
19 Creil 49 15N 2 34E
36 Crema 45 21N 9 40E
36 Cremona 45 8N 10 2E
19 Crépy 49 37N 3 32E
19 Crépy-en-Valois ... 49 14N 2 54E
37 Cres, I. 44 58N 14 25E
102 Crescent City 41 45N 124 12W
108 Crespo 32 2s 60 20W
90 Cressman 47 40N 72 55W
21 Crest 44 44N 5 2E
92 Creston, Canada .. 49 10N 116 40W
100 Creston, U.S.A. ... 41 0N 94 20W
99 Crestview 30 45N 86 35W
43 Crete=Kriti, I. 35 10N 25 0E
43 Crete, Sea of 26 0N 25 0E
32 Creus, C. 42 20N 3 19E
20 Creuse □ 46 0N 2 0E
20 Creuse, R. 47 0N 0 34E
37 Crevalcore 44 41N 11 10E
33 Crevillente 38 12N 0 48W
12 Crewe 53 6N 2 28W
109 Criciúma 28 40s 49 23W
14 Crieff 56 22N 3 50W
37 Crikvenica 45 11N 14 40E
49 Crimea= Krymskaya, Reg. 45 0N 34 0E
24 Crimmitschau 50 48N 12 23E
14 Crinan 56 4N 5 30W
104 Cristóbal 9 10N 80 0W
101 Crockett 31 20N 95 30W
21 Croisette, C. 43 13N 5 20E
82 Croker, I. 11 12s 132 32E
14 Cromarty 57 40N 4 2W
12 Cromer 52 56N 1 18E
85 Cromwell 45 3s 169 14E
84 Cronulla 34 3s 151 8E
105 Crooked I. 22 50N 74 10W
100 Crookston 47 50N 96 40W
12 Cross Fell, Mt. 54 44N 2 29W
15 Crosshaven 51 48N 8 19W
97 Croton-on-Hudson 41 19N 73 55W
39 Crotone 39 5N 17 6E
102 Crow Agency 45 40N 107 30W
15 Crow Hd. 51 34N 10 9W
101 Crowley 30 15N 92 20W
97 Crown Point 41 24N 87 23W
92 Crowsnest P. 49 40N 114 40W
80 Croydon, Australia 18 15s 142 14E
13 Croydon, U.K. 51 18N 0 5W
18 Crozon 48 15N 4 30W
109 Cruz Alta 28 40s 53 32W
108 Cruz del Eje 30 45s 64 50W
109 Cruzeiro 22 50s 45 0W
109 Cruzeiro do Oeste . 23 46s 53 4W
110 Cruzeiro do Sul ... 7 35s 72 35W
81 Crystal Brook 33 21s 138 13E
101 Crystal City 38 15N 90 23W
27 Csongrád 46 43N 20 12E
27 Csongrád □ 46 32N 20 15E
27 Csurgo 46 16N 17 9E
75 Cuamba 14 45s 36 22E
75 Cuando, R. 14 0s 19 30E
31 Cuba 38 10N 7 54W
105 Cuba ■ 22 0N 79 0W
83 Cuballing 32 50s 117 15E
110 Cucui 1 10N 66 50W
110 Cúcuta 7 54N 72 31W
62 Cuddalore 11 46N 79 45E
62 Cuddapah 14 30N 78 47E
30 Cudillero 43 33N 6 9W
83 Cue 27 20s 117 55E
30 Cuéllar 41 23N 4 21E
32 Cuenca, Sp. 40 5N 2 10W
110 Cuenca, Ecuador .. 2 50s 79 9W
32 Cuenca, Sp. □ 40 0N 2 0W
32 Cuenca, Sa. de 39 55N 1 50W
104 Cuernavaca 18 50N 99 20W
101 Cuero 29 5N 97 17W
111 Cuiabá 15 30s 56 0W
14 Cuillin Hills 57 14N 6 15W
21 Cuiseaux 46 30N 5 22E
104 Cuitzeo, L. 19 55N 101 5W
20 Culan 46 34N 2 20E
84 Culcairn 35 41s 147 3E
30 Culebra, Sa. de la . 41 55N 6 20W
104 Culiacán 24 50N 107 40W
33 Cúllar de Baza 37 35N 2 34W
14 Cullen 57 45N 2 50W
82 Cullen, Pt. 11 50s 141 47E
33 Cullera 39 9N 0 17W
14 Culloden Moor 57 29N 4 7W
21 Culoz 45 47N 5 46E
85 Culverden 42 47s 172 49E
110 Cumaná 10 30N 64 5W
92 Cumberland, Canada 49 40N 125 0W
98 Cumberland, U.S.A. 39 40N 78 43W
89 Cumberland Pen. .. 67 0N 65 0W
86 Cumberland Plat. .. 36 0N 84 30W
89 Cumberland Sd. ... 65 30N 66 0W
31 Cumbres Mayores . 38 4N 6 39W
12 Cumbria □ 54 44N 2 55W
12 Cumbrian, Mts. ... 54 30N 3 0W
31 Cummins 34 16s 135 44E
83 Cunderdin 31 39s 117 15E
75 Cunene, R. 17 20s 11 50E
36 Cúneo 44 23N 7 32E
81 Cunnamulla 28 4s 145 41E
93 Cupar, Canada 51 0N 104 10W
14 Cupar, U.K. 56 20N 3 0W
110 Cupica, G. de 6 25N 77 30W
40 Ćuprija 34 57N 21 26E
105 Curaçao 12 10N 69 0W
19 Cure, R. 47 40N 3 41E
110 Curiapo 8 33N 61 5W
108 Curicó 34 55s 71 20W
108 Curicó □ 34 50s 71 15W
109 Curitiba 25 20s 49 10W
111 Currais Novos 6 13s 36 30W
111 Curralinho 1 35s 49 30W
80 Currawilla 25 10s 141 20E
102 Currie 40 16N 114 45W
80 Curtis, I. 23 40s 151 15E
111 Curuçá 0 35s 47 50W
111 Cururupu 1 50s 44 50W
108 Curuzú Cuatiá 29 50s 58 5W
111 Curvelo 18 45s 44 27W
84 Curya 35 53s 142 54E
101 Cushing 31 43N 94 50W
36 Cusna, Mte. 44 17N 10 23E
20 Cusset 46 8N 3 28E
100 Custer 43 45N 103 38W
102 Cut Bank 48 40N 112 15W
39 Cutro 39 1N 16 58E
61 Cuttack 20 25N 85 57E
83 Cuvier, C. 23 14s 113 22E
24 Cuxhaven 53 51N 8 41E
96 Cuyahoga Falls 41 8N 81 30W
110 Cuzco, Mt. 20 0s 66 50W
110 Cuzco 13 32s 72 0W
80 Cygnet 43 8s 147 1E
56 Cyprus ■ 35 0N 33 0E
73 Cyrenaica=Barqa Reg. 27 0N 20 0E
73 Cyrene=Shahhat .. 32 39N 21 18E
27 Czechoslovakia ■ . 49 0N 17 0E
27 Czechowice Dziedzice 49 54N 18 59E
27 Czeladz 50 16N 19 2E
28 Czempiń 52 9N 16 33E
27 Czerwionka 50 7N 18 37E
27 Częstochowa 50 49N 19 7E
28 Czestichowa □ 50 50N 19 0E
28 Człuchów 53 41N 17 22E

D

63 Da, R. 16 0N 107 0E
63 Da Lat 12 3N 108 32E
63 Da Nang 16 10N 108 7E
72 Dabakala 8 15N 4 20W
60 Dabhoi 22 10N 73 20E
28 Dąbie 53 27N 14 45E
72 Dabola 10 50N 11 5W
27 Dabrowa Gornieza 50 15N 19 10E
27 Dabrowa Tarnówska 50 10N 21 0E
61 Dacca 23 43N 90 26E
61 Dacca □ 24 0N 90 0E
25 Dachau 48 16N 11 27E
110 Dadanawa 3 0N 59 30W
60 Dadau 26 45N 67 45E
49 Dagesta A.S.S.R. □ 42 30N 47 0E
65 Dagupan 16 3N 120 33E
72 Dahomey ■= Benin ■ 8 0N 2 0E
31 Daimiel 39 5N 3 35W
15 Daingean 53 18N 7 15W
68 Dairen=Talien 39 0N 121 31E
73 Dairût 27 34N 30 43E
83 Dairy Creek 25 12s 115 48E
66 Daisetsu-Zan, Mt. . 43 30N 142 57E
80 Dajarra 21 42s 139 30E
72 Dakar 14 34N 17 29W
72 Dakhla 23 50N 15 53W
49 Dakhovskaya 44 13N 40 13E
60 Dakor 22 45N 73 11E
40 Dakovica 42 22N 20 26E
40 Dakovo 45 19N 18 24E
68 Dalai Nor, L. 49 0N 117 50E
44 Dalälven, R. 60 38N 17 27E
68 Dalandzadgad 43 35N 104 30E
58 Dalbandin 28 53N 64 25E
14 Dalbeattie 54 56N 3 49W
81 Dalby 27 11s 151 16E
101 Dalhart 36 4N 102 31W
91 Dalhousie 48 0N 66 26W
54 Daliyat el Karmel . 32 41N 35 3E
40 Dalj 45 29N 18 59E
14 Dalkeith 55 54N 3 4W

Dinard Eagle Pass

Page	Name	Lat.	Long.
18	Dinard	48 38N	2 4W
9	Dinaric Alps, Mts.	43 50N	16 35W
62	Dindigul	10 21N	77 58E
15	Dingle	52 8N	10 15W
15	Dingle, B.	52 5N	10 15W
80	Dingo	23 39S	149 20E
72	Dinguiraye	11 18N	10 43W
14	Dingwall	57 35N	4 29W
102	Dinosaur Nat. Mon.	40 32N	108 58W
103	Dinuba	36 32N	119 23W
27	Diósgyör	48 7N	20 43E
72	Diourbel	14 40N	16 15W
65	Dipolog	8 36N	123 20E
55	Dire Dawa	9 37N	41 52E
105	Diriamba	11 53N	86 15W
83	Dirk Hartog, I.	25 48S	113 0E
81	Dirranbandi	28 35S	148 14E
102	Disappointment.C.	46 18N	124 3W
82	Disappointment, L.	23 30S	122 50E
88	Discovery	63 0N	115 0W
84	Discovery, B.	38 12S	141 7E
4	Disko, I.	69 50N	53 30W
13	Diss	52 23N	1 6E
58	Disteghil Sar, Mt.	36 22N	75 12E
111	Districto Federal □	15 45S	47 45W
104	Distrito Federal □	19 15N	99 10W
60	Diu	20 43N	70 69E
18	Dives	49 18N	0 8W
18	Dives, R.	48 55N	0 5W
49	Divnoye	45 55N	43 27E
100	Dixon	41 50N	89 29W
92	Dixon Entrance	54 25N	132 30W
56	Diyarbakir	37 55N	40 14E
74	Djambala	2 33S	14 45E
64	Djangeru	2 20S	116 29E
72	Djelfa	34 30N	3 20E
74	Djema	6 3N	25 19E
73	Djerba, I. de	33 56N	11 0E
72	Djerid, Chott el, Reg.	35 50N	8 30E
55	Djibouti	11 36N	43 9E
72	Djidjelli	36 52N	5 50E
74	Djolu	0 37N	22 21E
72	Djougou	9 42N	1 40E
73	Djourab, Erg du	16 40N	18 50E
74	Djugu	1 55N	30 30E
46	Djúpivogur	64 40N	14 10W
44	Djursholm	59 24N	18 5E
45	Djursland, Reg.	56 27N	10 40E
49	Dnepr, R.	46 30N	32 18E
49	Dneprodzerzhinsk	48 30N	34 37E
49	Dnepropetrovsk	48 30N	35 0E
49	Dnestr, R.	46 18N	30 17E
49	Dnieper, R.= Dnepr, R.	46 30N	32 18E
49	Dniester, R.= Dnestr, R.	46 18N	30 17E
73	Doba	8 39N	16 51E
24	Döbeln	51 7N	13 7E
65	Dobo	5 46S	134 13E
40	Doboj	44 44N	18 6E
40	Dobra	45 54N	22 36E
41	Dobruja, Reg.	44 30N	28 30E
44	Döda Fallet.	63 4N	16 35E
62	Dodballapur	13 18N	77 32E
101	Dodge City	37 45N	100 1W
74	Dodoma	6 1S	35 45E
93	Dodsland	51 48N	108 49W
16	Doetinchem	51 58N	6 17E
41	Doftana	45 17N	25 45E
92	Dog Creek	51 35N	122 18W
57	Doha	25 15N	51 36E
60	Dohad	22 50N	74 15E
59	Dohazari	22 10N	92 5E
63	Doi Luang, Ra.	18 20N	101 30E
40	Dojransko, J.	41 11N	22 44E
18	Dol	48 34N	1 47W
91	Dolbeau	48 53N	72 14W
21	Dôle	47 6N	5 30E
12	Dolgellau	52 44N	3 53W
38	Dolianova	39 23N	9 11E
74	Dolisie	4 12S	12 41E
41	Dolni Dŭbnik	43 24N	24 26E
37	Dolo, Italy	45 25N	12 5E
55	Dolo, Somali Rep.	4 13N	42 8E
37	Dolomiti, Mts.	46 25N	11 50E
108	Dolores, Arg.	36 19S	57 40W
108	Dolores, Uruguay	33 33S	58 13W
112	Dolphin, C.	51 15S	58 58W
88	Dolphin & Union Str.	69 5N	114 45W
109	Dom Pedrito	31 0S	54 40W
50	Dombarovskiy	50 46N	59 39E
44	Dombås	62 5N	9 8E
19	Dombasle	48 38N	6 21E
21	Dombes, Reg.	46 0N	5 3E
108	Domeyko, Cord.	24 30S	69 0W
18	Domfront	48 37N	0 4W
105	Dominica, I.	15 30N	61 20W
105	Dominica Pass	15 10N	61 20W
105	Dominican Rep. ■	19 0N	70 40W
36	Domodossola	46 7N	8 17E
19	Dompaire	48 13N	6 13E
12	Don, R., Eng.	53 39N	0 59W
14	Don, R., Scot.	57 10N	2 4W
49	Don, R., U.S.S.R.	47 4N	39 18E
31	Don Benito	38 57N	5 52W
15	Donaghadee	54 39N	5 33W
8	Donald	36 22S	143 0E
92	Donalda	52 35N	112 34W
25	Donauwörth	48 43N	10 46E
26	Donawitz	47 22N	15 4E
12	Doncaster	53 32N	1 7W
62	Dondra Hd.	5 55N	80 35E
15	Donegal	54 39N	8 7W
15	Donegal □	54 50N	0 8W
15	Donegal, B.	54 30N	8 30W
49	Donetsk	48 0N	37 48E
63	Dong Hoi	17 18N	106 36E
83	Dongara	29 15S	114 56E
61	Dongargarh	21 11N	80 45E
18	Donges	47 18N	2 4W
73	Dongola	19 9N	30 22E
40	Donji Vakuf	44 8N	17 25E
91	Donnacona	46 40N	71 47W
85	Donnelly's Crossing	35 43S	173 33E
83	Donnybrook	33 35S	115 48E
96	Donora	40 11N	79 52W
80	Donor's Hills	18 42S	140 33E
83	Doodlakine	31 35S	117 28E
14	Doon, R.	55 26N	4 38W
54	Dor	32 37N	34 55E
13	Dorchester	50 43N	2 26W
89	Dorchester, C.	65 29N	77 30W
20	Dordogne □	45 10N	0 45E
20	Dordogne, R.	45 2N	0 35W
16	Dordrecht	51 49N	107 45W
93	Dore Lake	54 56N	107 45W
90	Dorion	45 23N	74 3W
37	Dornberg	45 45N	13 50E
26	Dornbirn	47 25N	9 44E
14	Dornie	57 17N	5 30W
14	Dornoch	57 52N	4 2W
14	Dornoch Firth	57 52N	4 2W
67	Döröö Nuur, L.	47 40N	93 30E
83	Dorre, I.	25 9S	113 7E
81	Dorrigo	30 21S	152 43E
13	Dorset □	50 47N	2 20W
24	Dorsten	51 39N	6 58E
24	Dortmund	51 31N	7 28E
112	Dos Bahias, C.	44 55S	65 32W
31	Dos Hermanas	37 17N	5 55W
57	Doshi	35 37N	68 41E
72	Dosso	13 3N	3 12E
92	Dot	50 12N	121 25W
99	Dothan	31 13N	85 24W
19	Douai	50 22N	3 4E
72	Douala	4 3N	9 42E
18	Douarnenez	48 6N	4 20W
26	Doubrava, R.	49 40N	15 30E
19	Doubs □	47 10N	6 25E
85	Doubtless, B.	34 55S	173 27E
90	Doucet	48 15N	76 35W
12	Douglas, U.K.	54 9N	4 25W
103	Douglas, Ariz	31 21N	109 33W
99	Douglas, Ga.	31 31N	82 51W
100	Douglas, Wyo.	42 45N	105 24W
43	Doukáton, Ákra, Pt.	38 34N	20 30E
19	Doulevant	48 22N	4 53E
19	Doullens	50 9N	2 21E
14	Dounreay	58 40N	3 28W
111	Dourada, Sa.	13 10S	48 45W
30	Douro, R.	41 8N	8 40W
29	Douro Litoral, Reg.	41 5N	8 20W
20	Douze, R.	43 54N	0 30W
12	Dove, R.	54 20N	0 55W
80	Dover, Australia	43 19S	147 1E
13	Dover, U.K.	51 8N	1 19E
98	Dover, Del.	39 10N	75 32W
97	Dover, N.H.	43 12N	70 56W
97	Dover, N.J.	40 53N	74 34W
97	Dover Plains	41 44N	73 35W
13	Dovey, R.	52 32N	4 0W
44	Dovrefjell, Mts.	62 6N	9 25E
98	Dowagiac	41 59N	86 6W
57	Dowlātābad	28 18N	56 40E
15	Down □	54 24N	5 55W
13	Downham Market	52 36N	0 23E
15	Downpatrick	54 20N	5 43W
97	Doylestown	40 19N	75 8W
21	Drac, R.	45 13N	5 41E
41	Drăgăneşti Olt.	44 10N	24 32E
41	Drăgăneşti Vlaşca	44 6N	25 36E
41	Drăgăşani	44 40N	24 16E
40	Dragina	44 30N	19 25E
40	Dragocvet	44 0N	21 15E
21	Draguignan	43 32N	6 28E
5	Drake Pass.	58 0S	70 0W
75	Drakensberg, Mts.	27 0S	30 0E
42	Dráma	41 9N	24 8E
42	Dráma □	41 9N	24 8E
44	Drammen	59 44N	10 15E
26	Drau, R.= Drava R.	45 33N	18 55E
37	Drava, R.	45 33N	18 55E
19	Draveil	48 41N	2 25E
92	Drayton Valley	53 13N	114 59W
16	Drenthe □	52 45N	6 30E
24	Dresden	51 3N	13 44E
24	Dresden □	51 10N	14 0E
18	Dreux	48 44N	1 22E
12	Driffield	54 0N	0 27W
40	Drin, R.	41 60N	19 32E
42	Drin-i-zi	41 37N	20 28E
37	Drniš	43 51N	16 10E
15	Drogheda	53 43N	6 21W
49	Drogobych	49 20N	23 30E
13	Droitwich	52 16N	2 9W
21	Drôme □	44 35N	5 10E
21	Drôme, R.	44 46N	4 46E
84	Dromedary, C.	36 17S	150 10E
80	Dronfield	53 19S	1 27W
20	Dronne, R.	45 2N	0 9W
5	Dronning Maud Ld.	75 0S	10 0E
26	Drosendorf	48 52N	15 37E
84	Drouin	38 8S	145 51E
92	Drumheller	51 28N	112 42W
90	Drummondville	45 53N	72 30W
51	Druzhina	68 11N	14S 19E
28	Drwęca R.	53 0N	18 42E
41	Dryanovo	42 59N	25 28E
93	Dryden	49 47N	92 50W
82	Drysdale, R.	13 59S	126 51E
96	Du Bois	41 7N	78 46W
100	Du Quoin	38 0N	89 10W
80	Duaringa	23 42S	149 42E
56	Dubā	27 10N	35 40E
88	Dubawnt L.	63 0N	102 0W
57	Dubayy	25 18N	55 18E
84	Dubbo	32 15S	148 36E
15	Dublin, Eire	53 20N	6 15W
99	Dublin, U.S.A.	32 32N	82 54W
15	Dublin □	53 20N	6 15W
102	Dubois	44 10N	112 14W
49	Dubovka	49 5N	44 50E
61	Dubrajpur	23 48N	87 23E
72	Dubreka	9 48N	13 31W
40	Dubrovnik	42 38N	18 7E
51	Dubrovskoye	47 28N	42 40E
100	Dubuque	42 30N	90 41W
102	Duchesne	40 10N	110 24W
80	Duchess	21 22S	139 52E
77	Ducie I.	24 47S	124 50W
93	Duck Lake	52 47N	106 13W
93	Duck Mt. Prov. Park	51 36N	100 55W
24	Duderstadt	51 31N	10 16E
51	Dudinka	69 25N	86 15E
13	Dudley	52 30N	2 5W
62	Dudna, R.	19 17N	76 54E
30	Dueñas	41 52N	4 33W
30	Duero, R.	41 37N	4 25W
14	Dufftown	57 26N	3 9W
37	Dugi Otok, I.	44 0N	15 0E
37	Dugo Selo	45 51N	16 18E
24	Duisburg	51 27N	6 42E
57	Dukhan	25 25N	50 50E
72	Duku	10 43N	10 43E
105	Dulce, G.	8 40N	83 20W
41	Dulgopol	43 3N	27 22E
24	Dülmen	51 49N	7 18E
41	Dulovo	43 48N	27 9E
80	Dululu	23 48S	150 15E
100	Duluth	46 48N	92 10W
61	Dum-Dum	22 39N	88 26E
59	Dum Duma	27 40N	95 40E
64	Dumai	1 35N	101 20E
101	Dumas	35 50N	101 58W
14	Dumbarton	55 58N	4 35W
83	Dumbleyung	33 17S	117 42E
41	Dumbrăveni	46 14N	24 34E
14	Dumfries	55 4N	3 37W
14	Dumfries-Galloway □	55 12N	3 30W
84	Dumosa	35 52S	143 6E
73	Dumyât	31 25N	31 48E
15	Dun Laoghaire	53 17N	6 9W
27	Dunaföldvár	46 50N	18 57E
41	Dunarea= Donau, R.	45 20N	29 40E
27	Dunaújváros	47 0N	18 57E
40	Dunav	45 0N	20 21E
40	Dunavtsi	42 57N	22 53E
85	Dunback	42 23S	170 36E
14	Dunbar	56 0N	2 32W
93	Dunblane, Canada	51 11N	106 52W
14	Dunblane, U.K.	56 10N	3 58W
92	Duncan, Canada	48 45N	123 40W
101	Duncan, U.S.A.	34 25N	98 0W
63	Duncan Pass.	11 0N	92 30E
105	Duncan Town	22 20N	75 80W
96	Dundalk, Canada	44 10N	80 24W
15	Dundalk, U.K.	53 55N	6 45W
90	Dundas	43 17N	79 59W
83	Dundas, L.	32 35S	121 50E
82	Dundas, Str.	11 15S	131 35E
75	Dundee, S. Africa	28 11S	30 15E
14	Dundee, U.K.	56 29N	3 0W
15	Dundrum	54 17N	5 50W
15	Dundrum, B.	54 12N	5 40W
60	Dundwara	27 48N	79 9E
85	Dunedin	45 50S	170 33E
14	Dunfermline	56 5N	3 28W
15	Dungannon	54 30N	6 47W
15	Dungannon □	54 30N	6 47W
60	Dungarpur	23 52N	73 45E
15	Dungarvan	52 6N	7 40W
67	Dunbure Shan, Mts.	35 0N	90 0E
13	Dungeness, Pt.	50 54N	0 59E
74	Dungu	3 42N	28 32E
84	Dunkeld, Australia	37 40S	142 22E
14	Dunkeld, U.K.	56 34N	3 36W
19	Dunkerque	51 2N	2 20E
13	Dunkery Beacon	51 15N	3 37W
96	Dunkirk	42 30N	79 18W
72	Dunkwa	6 0N	1 47W
80	Dunmara	16 42S	133 25E
97	Dunmore	41 27N	75 38W
15	Dunmore Hd.	53 37N	8 44W
99	Dunn	35 18N	78 36W
14	Dunnet Hd.	58 38N	3 22W
96	Dunnville	42 57N	79 37W
14	Dunoon	55 57N	4 56W
14	Duns	55 47N	2 20W
102	Dunsmuir	41 0N	122 10W
13	Dunstable	51 53N	0 31W
109	Duque de Caxias	22 45S	43 19W
96	Duquesne	40 22N	79 55W
85	D'Urville, I.	40 50S	173 55E
54	Dūrā	31 30N	35 2E
82	Durack, R.	15 33S	127 52E
21	Durance, R.	43 55N	4 44E
104	Durango, Mexico	24 3N	104 39W
30	Durango, Sp.	43 13N	2 40W
103	Durango, U.S.A.	37 10N	107 50W
104	Durango □	25 0N	105 0W
83	Duranillin	33 30S	116 45E
101	Durant	34 0N	96 25W
30	Duratón, R.	41 37N	4 7W
108	Durazno	33 25S	56 38W
75	Durban	29 49S	31 1E
31	Durcal	37 0N	3 34W
40	Durdevac	46 2N	17 3E
24	Düren	50 48N	6 30E
61	Durg	21 15N	81 22E
90	Durham, Canada	44 10N	80 48W
12	Durham, U.K.	54 47N	1 34W
99	Durham, U.S.A.	36 0N	78 55W
12	Durham □	54 42N	1 45W
40	Durmitor, Mt.	43 18N	19 0E
42	Durrësi	41 19N	19 28E
18	Durtal	47 40N	0 18W
97	Duryea	41 20N	75 45W
50	Dushak	37 20N	60 10E
50	Dushanbe	38 40N	68 50E
85	Dusky, Sd.	45 47S	166 29E
24	Düsseldorf	51 15N	6 46E
88	Dutch Harbor	53 54N	166 35W
56	Duzce	40 50N	31 10E
41	Dve Mogili	43 47N	25 55E
48	Drinskaya Guba	65 0N	39 45E
26	Dvur Králové	50 27N	15 50E
60	Dwarka	22 18N	69 8E
83	Dwellingup	32 38S	115 58E
5	Dyer Plat.	70 0S	65 0W
101	Dyersburg	36 2N	89 20W
13	Dyfed □	52 0N	4 30W
48	Dzerzhinsk	56 15N	43 15E
50	Dzhalal Abad	41 0N	73 0E
51	Dzhalinda	53 50N	124 0E
50	Dzhambul	43 10N	71 0E
49	Dzhankoi	45 40N	34 30E
51	Dzhardzhan	68 43N	124 2E
51	Dzhelinde	70 0N	114 20E
50	Dzhezkazgan	47 10N	67 40E
50	Dzhizak	40 20N	68 0E
51	Dzhugdzur Khrebet, Ra.	57 30N	138 0E
28	Działdowo	53 15N	20 15E
27	Dzierżoniow	50 45N	16 39E
67	Dzungaria, Reg.	44 10N	88 0E
67	Dzungarian Gate= Dzungarskiye Vorota	45 25N	82 25E
67	Dzungarskiye Vorota	45 25N	82 25E
68	Dzuunbulag	46 58N	115 30E
68	Dzuunmod	47 45N	106 58E

E

Page	Name	Lat.	Long.
88	Eagle	64 44N	141 29W
101	Eagle Pass	28 45N	100 35W

Fiñana Fukuyama

33 Fiñana 37 10N 2 50W
14 Findhorn 57 30N 3 45W
98 Findlay 41 0N 83 41W
18 Finistère □ 48 20N 4 20W
30 Finisterre 42 54N 9 16W
30 Finisterre, C. 42 50N 9 19W
80 Finke 25 34S 134 35E
46 Finland ■ 70 0N 27 0E
48 Finland, G. of 60 0N 26 0E
84 Finley 35 38S 145 35E
92 Finnegan 51 7N 112 5W
80 Finnigan, Mt. 15 49S 145 17E
81 Finniss, C. 33 38S 134 51E
46 Finnmark □ 69 30N 25 0E
45 Finspång 58 45N 15 43E
25 Finsteraarhorn, Mt. 46 31N 8 10E
24 Finsterwalde 51 37N 13 42E
36 Fiorenzuola 44 56N 9 54E
37 Firenze 43 47N 11 15E
21 Firminy 45 23N 4 18E
60 Firozabad 27 10N 78 25E
41 Fîrţaneşti 45 48N 27 59E
57 Fīrūzābād 28 52N 52 35E
57 Fīrūzkūh 35 50N 52 40E
83 Fisher 30 30S 131 0E
97 Fishers I. 41 16N 72 2W
13 Fishguard 51 59N 4 59W
97 Fitchburg 42 35N 71 47W
32 Fitero 42 4N 1 52W
112 Fitz Roy 47 10S 67 0W
99 Fitzgerald 31 45N 83 10W
80 Fitzroy, R., Queens. 23 32S 150 52E
82 Fitzroy, R., W. Australia 17 31S 138 35E
82 Fitzroy Crossing 18 9S 125 38E
36 Fivizzana 44 14N 10 8E
74 Fizi 4 17S 28 55E
45 Fjellerup 56 29N 10 34E
44 Fla 60 25N 9 26E
103 Flagstaff 35 10N 111 40W
47 Flåm 60 52N 7 14E
12 Flamborough Hd. 54 8N 0 4W
102 Flaming Gorge L. 41 15N 109 30W
16 Flandre Occidentale □ 51 0N 3 0E
16 Flandre Orientale □ 51 0N 4 0E
16 Flandres, Plaines des 51 10N 3 15E
14 Flannan Is. 58 9N 7 52W
102 Flathead L. 47 50N 114 0W
80 Flattery, C., Australia 14 58S 145 21E
102 Flattery, C., U.S.A. 48 21N 124 31W
12 Fleetwood 53 55N 3 1W
47 Flekkefjord 58 18N 6 39E
44 Flen 59 4N 16 35E
24 Flensburg 54 46N 9 28E
18 Flers 48 47N 0 33W
13 Fletton 52 34N 0 13W
93 Flin Flon 54 46N 101 53W
83 Flinders, B. 34 19S 114 9E
80 Flinders, I. 40 0S 148 0E
81 Flinders, Ras. 31 30S 138 30E
12 Flint, U.K. 53 15N 3 7W
98 Flint, U.S.A. 43 0N 83 40W
77 Flint I. 11 26S 151 48W
32 Flix 41 14N 0 32E
19 Flixecourt 50 0N 2 5E
12 Flodden 55 37N 2 8W
100 Flora 38 40N 88 30W
37 Florence, Italy = Firenze 43 47N 11 15E
99 Florence, Ala. 34 50N 87 50W
103 Florence, Ariz. 33 0N 111 25W
102 Florence, Oreg. 44 0N 124 3W
99 Florence, S.C. 34 5N 79 50W
110 Florencia 1 36N 75 36W
104 Flores 16 50N 89 40W
65 Flores, I. 8 35S 121 0E
65 Flores Sea 6 30S 124 0E
111 Floriano 6 50S 43 0W
109 Florianópolis 27 30S 48 30W
108 Florida 34 7S 56 10W
99 Florida □ 28 30N 82 0W
87 Florida Str. 25 0N 80 0W
27 Floridsdorf 48 15N 16 25E
42 Flórina 40 48N 21 26E
42 Flórina □ 40 45N 21 20E
47 Florø 61 35N 5 1E
32 Flumen, R. 41 50N 0 25W
38 Flumendosa, R. 39 30N 9 25E
16 Flushing = Vlissingen 51 26N 3 34E
5 Flying Fish, C. 72 30S 103 0W
93 Foam Lake 51 40N 103 15W
40 Foča 43 31N 18 47E
41 Focşani 45 41N 27 15E
39 Fóggia 41 28N 15 31E
91 Fogo 49 43N 54 17W
26 Fohnsdorf 47 12N 14 40E
24 Föhr, I. 54 40N 8 30E
20 Foix 42 58N 1 38E
20 Foix, Reg. 43 0N 1 30E
43 Fokís □ 38 30N 22 15E
43 Folégandros, I. 36 37N 24 55E
90 Foleyet 48 15N 82 25W
37 Foligno 42 58N 12 40E
13 Folkestone 51 5N 1 11E
36 Follónica, G. di 42 54N 10 53E
93 Fond du Lac, Canada 59 20N 107 10W
100 Fond-du-Lac, U.S.A. 43 46N 88 26W
38 Fondi 41 21N 13 25E
30 Fonfría 41 37N 6 9W
104 Fonseca, G. de 13 10N 87 40W
19 Fontainebleau 48 24N 2 40E
110 Fonte Boa 2 25S 66 0W
20 Fontenay-le-Comte 46 28N 0 48W
69 Foochow 26 5N 119 18E
19 Forbach 49 10N 6 52E
84 Forbes 33 22S 148 0E
61 Forbesganj 26 17N 87 18E
32 Forcall, R. 40 40N 0 12W
25 Forchheim 49 42N 11 4E
96 Ford City 40 47N 79 11W
4 Forel, Mt. 66 52N 36 55W
92 Forest Lawn 51 4N 114 0W
92 Forestburg 52 35N 112 1W
91 Forestville 48 48N 69 20W
20 Forez, Mts. du 45 40N 3 50E
14 Forfar 56 40N 2 53W
19 Forges-les-Eaux 49 37N 1 30E
37 Forlí 44 14N 12 2E
12 Formby Pt. 53 33N 3 7W
33 Formentera, I. 38 40N 1 30E
32 Formentor, C. 39 58N 3 13E
38 Fórmia 41 15N 13 34E
111 Formiga 20 27S 45 25W
36 Formigine 44 37N 10 51E
108 Formosa, Arg. 26 15S 58 10W
111 Formosa, Brazil 15 32S 47 20W
108 Formosa □ 25 0S 60 0W
69 Formosa = Taiwan ■ 24 0N 121 0E
111 Formosa, Sa. 12 0S 55 0W
69 Formosa Str. 24 40N 124 0E
30 Fornos de Algodres 40 48N 7 32W
36 Fornovo di Taro 44 42N 10 7E
14 Forres 57 37N 3 38W
83 Forrest 38 22S 143 40E
101 Forrest City 35 1N 90 47W
44 Fors 60 14N 16 20E
80 Forsayth 18 33S 143 34E
44 Forsmo 63 16N 17 11E
24 Forst 51 43N 15 37E
102 Forsyth 46 14N 106 37W
90 Fort Albany 52 15N 81 35W
73 Fort-Archambault = Sarh 9 5N 18 23E
92 Fort Assinboine 54 20N 114 45W
14 Fort Augustus 57 9N 4 40W
102 Fort Benton 47 50N 110 40W
102 Fort Bragg 39 28N 123 50W
102 Fort Bridger 41 22N 110 20W
89 Fort Chimo 58 9N 68 12W
93 Fort Chipewyan 58 46N 111 9W
100 Fort Collins 40 30N 105 4W
90 Fort Coulonge 45 50N 76 45W
75 Fort-Dauphin 25 2S 47 0E
100 Fort Dodge 42 29N 94 10W
93 Fort Frances 48 35N 93 25W
88 Fort Franklin 65 30N 123 45W
90 Fort George 53 40N 79 0W
90 Fort George, R. 53 50N 77 0W
88 Fort Good Hope 66 14N 128 40W
92 Fort Graham 56 38N 124 35W
103 Fort Hancock 31 19N 105 56W
90 Fort Hope 51 30N 88 10W
91 Fort Kent 47 12N 68 30W
73 Fort-Lamy = Ndjamena 12 4N 15 8E
100 Fort Laramie 42 15N 104 30W
99 Fort Lauderdale 26 10N 80 5W
92 Fort Liard 60 20N 123 30W
92 Fort Mackay 57 12N 111 41W
91 Fort McKenzie 56 50N 69 0W
92 Fort Macleod 49 45N 113 30W
72 Fort MacMahon 29 51N 1 45E
88 Fort McPherson 67 30N 134 55W
100 Fort Madison 40 39N 91 20W
72 Fort Mirabel 29 31N 2 55E
100 Fort Morgan 40 10N 103 50W
99 Fort Myers 26 30N 82 0W
92 Fort Nelson 58 50N 122 30W
88 Fort Norman 64 57N 125 30W
99 Fort Payne 34 25N 85 44W
102 Fort Peck 47 1N 105 30W
102 Fort Peck Res. 47 40N 107 0W
99 Fort Pierce 27 29N 80 19W
74 Fort Portal 0 40N 30 20E
92 Fort Providence 61 20N 117 30W
93 Fort Qu'Appelle 50 45N 103 50W
92 Fort Resolution 61 10N 114 40W
74 Fort-Rousset 0 29S 15 55E
90 Fort Rupert 51 30N 78 40W
92 Fort St. James 54 30N 124 10W
92 Fort St. John 56 15N 120 50W
60 Fort Sandeman 31 20N 69 25E
92 Fort Saskatchewan 53 40N 113 15W
101 Fort Scott 38 0N 94 40W
88 Fort Selkirk 62 43N 137 22W
90 Fort Severn 56 0N 87 40W
92 Fort Simpson 61 45N 121 30W
50 Fort Slevchenko 44 30N 50 10E
101 Fort Smith 35 25N 94 25W
101 Fort Stockton 30 48N 103 2W
101 Fort Sumner 34 24N 104 8W
99 Fort Valley 32 33N 83 52W
92 Fort Vermilion 58 30N 115 57W
75 Fort Victoria 20 8S 30 55E
98 Fort Wayne 41 5N 85 10W
90 Fort William, Canada = Thunder Bay 48 20N 89 10W
14 Fort William, U.K. 56 48N 5 8W
101 Fort Worth 32 45N 97 25W
88 Fort Yukon 66 35N 145 12W
111 Fortaleza 3 35S 38 35W
105 Fort-de-France 14 36N 61 5W
82 Fortescue, R. 21 20S 116 5E
14 Forth, Firth of 56 5N 2 55W
14 Fortrose 57 35N 4 10W
102 Fortuna 48 38N 124 8W
88 Forty Mile 64 20N 140 30W
21 Fos 43 20N 4 57E
37 Fossacesia 42 15N 14 30E
36 Fossano 44 39N 7 40E
5 Fossil Bluff 71 15S 69 0W
37 Fossombrone 43 41N 12 49E
98 Fostoria 41 8N 83 25W
18 Fougères 48 21N 1 14W
14 Foula, I. 60 10N 2 5W
13 Foulness, I. 51 26N 0 55E
72 Foumban 5 45N 10 50E
20 Fourchambault 47 0N 3 3E
82 Fourcroy, C. 11 45S 130 2E
19 Fourmies 50 1N 4 2E
43 Foúrnoi, I. 37 36N 26 32E
72 Fouta Djalon, Mts. 11 20N 12 10W
85 Foveaux, Str. 46 42S 168 10E
13 Fowey 50 20N 4 39W
83 Fowlers, B. 31 59S 132 34E
69 Fowning 33 30N 119 40E
93 Fox Valley 50 30N 109 25W
89 Foxe Basin 68 30N 77 0W
89 Foxe Chan. 66 0N 80 0W
89 Foxe Pen. 65 0N 76 0W
85 Foxton 40 29S 175 18E
15 Foyle, L. 55 6N 7 18W
15 Foynes 52 37N 9 6W
30 Foz 43 33N 7 20W
109 Foz do Iguaçu 25 30S 54 30W
97 Frackville 40 46N 76 15W
32 Fraga 41 32N 0 21E
97 Framingham 42 17N 71 25W
111 Franca 20 25S 47 30W
37 Francavilla al Mare 42 25N 14 16E
39 Francavilla Fontana 40 32N 17 35E
17 France ■ 47 0N 3 0E
74 Franceville 1 38S 13 35E
19 Franche Comté, Reg. 46 30N 5 50E
91 Francis Harbour 52 34N 55 44W
75 Francistown 21 11S 27 32E
39 Francofonte 37 13N 14 50E
91 François 47 34N 56 44W
24 Frankenberg 51 3N 8 47E
25 Frankenwald, Mts. 50 18N 11 36E
98 Frankfort, Ind. 40 20N 86 33W
98 Frankfort, Ky. 38 12N 85 44W
24 Frankfurt □ 52 30N 14 0E
25 Frankfurt am Main 50 7N 8 40E
24 Frankfurt an der Oder 52 50N 14 31E
25 Fränkishe Alb. 49 20N 11 30E
100 Franklin, Nebr. 40 9N 98 55W
97 Franklin, N.H. 43 28N 71 39W
97 Franklin, N.J. 41 9N 74 38W
96 Franklin, Pa. 41 22N 79 45W
99 Franklin, Tenn. 35 54N 86 53W
98 Franklin, W. Va. 38 38N 79 21W
88 Franklin, Reg. 71 0N 99 0W
102 Franklin D. Roosevelt L. 48 30N 118 16W
88 Franklin Mts. 66 0N 125 0W
88 Franklin Str. 72 0N 96 0W
84 Frankston 38 8S 145 8E
50 Frantsa Iosifa, Zemlya, Is. 76 0N 62 0E
90 Franz 48 25N 85 30W
38 Frascati 41 48N 12 41E
96 Fraser 42 32N 82 57W
81 Fraser, I. 25 15S 153 10E
92 Fraser, R. 49 9N 123 12W
92 Fraser Lake 54 0N 124 50W
14 Fraserburgh 47 41N 2 0W
63 Fraser's Hill 3 43N 101 43E
41 Frăteşti 43 59N 25 59E
25 Frauenfeld 47 34N 8 54E
108 Fray Bentos 33 10S 58 15W
82 Frazier Downs 18 48S 121 42E
45 Fredericia 55 34N 9 45E
98 Frederick, Md. 39 25N 77 23W
101 Frederick, Okla. 34 22N 99 0W
98 Fredericksburg 38 16N 77 29W
91 Fredericton 45 57N 66 40W
45 Frederiksborg □ 55 50N 12 10E
4 Frederikshåb 62 0N 49 30W
45 Frederikshavn 57 28N 10 31E
45 Frederikssund 55 50N 12 3E
45 Frederiksvaerk 55 58N 12 2E
96 Fredonia 42 26N 79 20W
44 Fredrikstad 59 13N 10 57E
97 Freehold 40 15N 74 18W
97 Freeland 41 3N 75 48W
105 Freeport, Bahamas 26 30N 78 35W
100 Freeport, Ill. 42 18N 89 40W
97 Freeport, N.Y. 40 39N 73 35W
101 Freeport, Tex. 28 55N 95 22W
72 Freetown 8 30N 13 10W
31 Fregenal de la Sierra 38 10N 6 39W
24 Freiberg 50 55N 13 20E
25 Freiburg 48 0N 7 50E
112 Freire 39 0S 72 50W
25 Freising 48 24N 11 27E
26 Freistadt 48 30N 14 30E
24 Freital 51 0N 13 40E
21 Fréjus 43 25N 6 44E
83 Fremantle 32 1S 115 47E
100 Fremont, Nebr. 41 30N 96 30W
98 Fremont, Ohio 41 20N 83 5W
84 French, I. 38 20S 145 22E
111 French Guiana ■ 4 0N 53 0W
55 French Terr. of the Afars & Issas ■ 11 30N 42 15E
111 Fresco, R. 6 39S 51 59W
104 Fresnillo 23 10N 103 0W
103 Fresno 36 47N 119 50W
30 Fresno Alhandigo 40 42N 5 37W
25 Freudenstadt 48 27N 8 25E
80 Frewena 19 50S 135 50E
108 Frías 28 40S 65 5W
25 Fribourg 46 49N 7 9E
25 Fribourg □ 45 40N 7 0E
25 Friedberg 50 19N 8 45E
25 Friedrichshafen 47 39N 9 29E
26 Friesach 46 57N 14 24E
16 Friesland □ 53 5N 5 50E
75 Frio, C. 18 0S 12 0E
24 Fritzlar 51 8N 9 19E
37 Friuli Venezia Giulia □ 46 0N 13 0E
89 Frobisher B. 63 0N 67 0W
13 Frome 51 16N 2 17W
98 Front Royal 38 55N 78 10W
31 Fronteira 39 3N 7 39W
104 Frontera 18 30N 92 40W
20 Frontignan 43 27N 3 45E
38 Frosinone 41 38N 13 20E
44 Frösö 63 11N 14 35E
98 Frostburg 39 43N 78 57W
44 Frövi 59 28N 15 24E
41 Frumoasa 46 28N 25 48E
50 Frunze 42 54N 74 36E
111 Frutal 20 0S 49 0W
27 Frýdek Místek 49 40N 18 20E
43 Fthiótis □ 38 50N 22 25E
68 Fuchin 47 10N 132 0E
69 Fuchow 27 50N 116 14E
66 Fuchu 34 34N 133 14E
69 Fuchun Kiang, R. 30 10N 120 9E
31 Fuengirola 36 32N 4 41W
31 Fuente de Cantos 38 15N 6 18W
31 Fuente el Fresno 39 14N 3 46W
31 Fuente Ovejuna 38 15N 5 25W
31 Fuentes de Andalucia 37 28N 5 20W
32 Fuentes de Ebro 31 31N 0 38W
31 Fuentes de León 38 5N 6 32W
30 Fuentes de Oñoro 40 33N 6 52W
108 Fuerte Olimpo 21 0S 58 0W
72 Fuerteventura, I. 28 30N 14 0W
57 Fujaira 25 7N 56 18E
66 Fuji 35 9N 138 39E
66 Fuji-san, Mt. 35 22N 138 44E
66 Fuji-no-miya 35 20N 138 40E
66 Fujisawa 35 22N 139 29E
69 Fukien □ 26 0N 117 30E
66 Fukuchiyama 35 25N 135 9E
66 Fukui 36 0N 136 10E
66 Fukui □ 36 0N 136 12E
66 Fukuoka 33 30N 130 30E
66 Fukuoka □ 33 30N 131 0E
66 Fukushima 37 30N 140 15E
66 Fukushima □ 37 30N 140 15E
66 Fukuyama 34 35N 133 20E

Fulda Giong, Teluk B.

24 Fulda 50 32N 9 41 E
24 Fulda, R. 51 25N 9 39 E
103 Fullerton 33 52N 117 58W
100 Fulton, Mo. 38 50N 91 55W
97 Fulton, N.Y. 43 20N 76 22W
19 Fumay 50 0N 4 40 E
20 Fumel 44 30N 0 58 E
66 Funabashi 35 45N 140 0 E
76 Funafuti, I. 8 30S 179 0 E
72 Funchal 32 45N 16 55W
110 Fundación 10 31N 74 11W
30 Fundão 40 8N 7 30W
91 Fundy, B. of 45 0N 66 0W
72 Funtua 11 31N 7 17 E
56 Furat, Nahr al, R. 33 30N 43 0 E
109 Furnas, Reprêsa de, L. 20 45S 46 0W
12 Furness 54 14N 3 8W
26 Fürstenfeld 47 3N 16 3 E
25 Furstenfeldbruck 48 10N 11 15 E
24 Furstenwalde 52 20N 14 3 E
25 Fürth 49 29N 11 0 E
89 Fury & Hecla Str. 69 40N 81 0W
110 Fusagasugá 4 21N 74 22W
68 Fushan 37 30N 121 5 E
68 Fushun 42 0N 123 59 E
68 Fusin 42 12N 121 33 E
25 Füssen 47 12N 121 33 E
69 Futing 27 15N 120 10 E
69 Futsing 25 46N 119 29 E
76 Futuna, I. 14 25S 178 20 E
69 Fuyang 30 5N 119 56 E
68 Fuyu 45 10N 124 50 E
12 Fylde, R. 53 47N 2 56W
45 Fyn, I. 55 20N 10 30 E
14 Fyne, L. 56 0N 5 20W
45 Fyns □ 55 15N 10 30 E

G

72 Gabès 33 53N 10 2 E
73 Gabès, G. de 34 0N 10 30 E
74 Gabon ■ 0 10S 10 0 E
75 Gaborone 24 37S 25 57 E
97 Gabriels 44 26N 74 12W
41 Gabrovo 42 52N 25 27 E
57 Gach-Sārán 30 15N 50 45 E
40 Gacko 43 10N 18 33 E
62 Gadag 15 30N 75 45 E
60 Gadarwara 22 50N 78 50 E
33 Gádor, Sa. de 36 57N 2 45W
99 Gadsden, Ala. 34 1N 86 0W
103 Gadsden, Ariz. 32 35N 114 47W
62 Gadwal 16 10N 77 50 E
41 Găesti 44 48N 25 14 E
38 Gaeta 41 12N 13 35 E
38 Gaeta, G. di 41 0N 13 25 E
99 Gaffney 35 10N 81 31W
72 Gafsa 34 24N 8 51 E
91 Gagetown 45 46N 66 29W
72 Gagnoa 6 4N 5 55W
91 Gagnon 51 50N 68 5W
20 Gah 43 12N 0 27W
61 Gahmar 25 27N 83 55 E
61 Gaibandha 25 20N 89 36 E
26 Gail, R. 46 36N 13 53 E
20 Gaillac 43 54N 1 54 E
18 Gaillon 49 10N 1 20 E
96 Gaines 41 45N 77 35W
99 Gainesville, Fla. 29 38N 82 20W
99 Gainesville, Ga. 34 17N 83 47W
101 Gainesville, Tex. 33 40N 97 10W
12 Gainsborough 53 23N 0 46W
81 Gairdner, L. 32 0S 136 0 E
14 Gairloch, L. 57 43N 5 45W
75 Galangue 13 48S 16 3 E
77 Galápagos, Is. 0 0N 89 0W
14 Galashiels 55 37N 2 50W
41 Galaţi 45 27N 28 2 E
39 Galatina 40 10N 18 10 E
39 Galátone 40 8N 18 3 E
99 Galax 36 42N 80 57W
43 Galaxídhion 38 22N 22 23 E
83 Galena 27 50S 114 41 E
33 Galera 37 45N 2 33W
100 Galesburg 40 57N 90 23W
48 Galich 58 23N 42 18 E
30 Galicia, Reg. 42 43N 8 0W
54 Galilee= Hagalil, Reg. 32 53N 35 18 E
54 Galilee, Sea of= Kinneret, Yam 32 49N 35 36 E
36 Gallarte 45 40N 8 48 E
99 Gallatin 36 24N 86 27W
62 Galle 6 5N 80 10 E
32 Gállego, R. 41 39N 0 51W
112 Gallegos, R. 51 35S 69 0W
110 Gallinas, Pta. 12 28N 71 40W
39 Gallipoli 40 8N 18 0 E
98 Gallipolis 38 50N 82 10W
46 Gällivare 67 7N 20 32 E
32 Gallocanta, L. de 40 58N 1 30W
14 Galloway, Reg. 55 0N 4 25W
14 Galloway, Mull of 54 38N 4 50W
103 Gallup 35 30N 108 54W
96 Galt= Cambridge 43 21N 80 19W
26 Galtür 46 58N 10 11 E
30 Galve de Sorbe 41 13N 3 10W
101 Galveston 29 15N 94 48W
101 Galveston B. 29 30N 94 50W
108 Gálvez 32 0S 61 20W
15 Galway 53 16N 9 4W
15 Galway, B. 53 10N 9 20W
15 Galway □ 53 16N 9 3W
66 Gamagori 34 50N 137 14 E
72 Gambaga 10 30N 0 28W
72 Gambia ■ 13 20N 15 45W
72 Gambia, R. 13 28N 16 34W
82 Gambier, C. 11 56S 130 57 E
104 Gamboa 9 8N 79 42W
103 Gamerco 35 33N 108 56W
20 Gan 0 10S 71 10 E
54 Gan Shamu'el 32 28N 34 56 E
54 Gan Yavne 31 48N 34 42 E
90 Gananoque 44 20N 76 10W
61 Gandak, R. 25 32N 85 5 E
91 Gander 49 1N 54 33W
32 Gandesa 41 3N 0 26 E
72 Gandi 12 55N 5 49 E
33 Gandía 38 58N 0 9W
61 Ganga, Mouths of the 21 30N 90 0 E
61 Ganga, R. 23 22N 90 32 E
60 Ganganagar 29 56N 73 56 E
60 Gangapur 26 32N 76 37 E
62 Gangavati 15 30N 76 36 E
59 Gangaw 22 5N 94 15 E
61 Ganges, R.= Ganga, R. 23 22N 90 32 E
61 Gangtok 27 20N 88 40 E
60 Ganj 27 45N 78 47 E
20 Gannat 46 7N 3 11 E
27 Ganserdorf 48 20N 16 43 E
72 Gao 18 0N 1 0 E
72 Gaoual 11 45N 13 25W
21 Gap 44 33N 6 5 E
111 Garanhuns 8 50S 36 30W
102 Garberville 40 11N 123 50W
109 Garça 22 14S 49 37W
21 Gard □ 44 2N 4 10 E
36 Garda, L. di 45 40N 10 40 E
24 Gardelegen 52 32N 11 21 E
101 Garden City 38 0N 100 45W
57 Gardez 33 31N 68 59 E
102 Gardiner 45 3N 110 53W
97 Gardner 42 35N 72 0W
55 Gardo 9 18N 49 20 E
102 Garfield 47 3N 117 8W
43 Gargaliánoi 37 4N 21 38 E
39 Gargano, Testa del, Pt. 41 49N 16 12 E
38 Garigliano, R. 41 13N 13 45 E
102 Garland 41 47N 112 10W
50 Garm 39 0N 70 20 E
25 Garmisch-Partenkirchen 47 30N 11 5 E
57 Garmsār 35 20N 52 25 E
61 Garo Hills 25 30N 90 30 E
55 Garoe 8 35N 48 40 E
20 Garonne, R. 45 2N 0 36W
20 Garrigues, Reg. 43 40N 3 30 E
102 Garrison 46 37N 112 56W
100 Garrison Res. 47 30N 102 0W
88 Garry, L. 65 40N 100 0W
90 Garson 50 5N 96 50W
20 Gartempe, R. 46 48N 0 50 E
67 Gartok 31 59N 80 30 E
24 Gartz 54 17N 13 21 E
65 Garut 7 14S 107 53 E
31 Garvão 37 42N 8 21W
85 Garvie, Mts. 45 27S 169 59 E
98 Gary 41 35N 87 20W
110 Garzón 2 10N 75 40W
17 Gascogne, G. de 44 0N 2 0W
20 Gascogne, Reg. 43 45N 0 20 E
83 Gascoyne, R. 24 52S 113 37 E
83 Gascoyne Junction 25 3S 115 12 E
72 Gashaka 7 20N 11 29 E
91 Gaspé 48 52N 64 30W
91 Gaspé, C. 48 48N 64 7W
91 Gaspé Pass. 49 10N 64 0W
91 Gaspé Pen. 48 45N 65 40W
91 Gaspesian Prov. Park 49 0N 66 45W
99 Gastonia 35 17N 81 10W
43 Gastoúni 37 51N 21 15 E
42 Gastoúri 39 34N 19 54 E
112 Gastre 42 10S 69 15W
33 Gata, C. de 36 41N 2 13W
30 Gata, Sa. de 40 20N 6 20W
40 Gătaia 45 26N 21 30 E
14 Gatehouse of Fleet 54 53N 4 10W
12 Gateshead 54 57N 1 37W
19 Gatinais, Reg. 48 5N 2 40 E
20 Gâtine, Hauteurs de 46 40N 0 50W
97 Gatineau 45 28N 75 40W
90 Gatineau Nat. Park 45 30N 75 52W
75 Gatooma 18 21S 29 55 E
104 Gatun 9 16N 79 55W
104 Gatun L. 9 7N 79 56W
31 Gaucín 36 31N 5 19W
61 Gauhati 26 5N 91 55 E
5 Gaussberg, Mt. 66 45S 89 0 E
32 Gavá 41 18N 2 0 E
20 Gavarnie 42 44N 0 3W
57 Gavater 25 10N 61 23 E
43 Gávdhos, I. 34 50N 24 6 E
31 Gavião 39 28N 7 50W
44 Gavle 60 41N 17 13 E
44 Gävleborgs □ 61 20N 16 15 E
36 Gavorrano 42 55N 10 55 E
18 Gavray 49 55N 1 20W
60 Gawilgarh Hills 21 15N 76 45 E
81 Gawler 34 30S 138 42 E
61 Gaya 24 47N 85 4 E
81 Gayndah 25 35S 151 39 E
54 Gaza 31 30N 34 28 E
54 Gaza Strip 31 29N 34 25 E
56 Gaziantep 37 6N 37 23 E
28 Gdańsk 54 22N 18 40 E
28 Gdansk □ 54 10N 18 30 E
28 Gdynia 54 35N 18 33 E
73 Gebeit Mine 21 3N 36 29 E
73 Gedaref 14 2N 35 28 E
54 Gedera 31 49N 34 46 E
20 Gèdre 42 47N 0 2 E
45 Gedser 54 35N 11 55 E
84 Geelong 38 2S 144 20 E
83 Geelvink, Chan. 28 30S 114 10 E
16 Geeraadsbergen 50 45N 3 53 E
24 Geesthacht 53 25N 10 20 E
73 Geili 16 1N 32 37 E
44 Geilo 60 32N 8 14 E
25 Geislingen 47 55N 8 37 E
74 Geita 2 48S 32 12 E
39 Gela 37 3N 14 15 E
39 Gela, G. di 37 0N 14 8 E
16 Gelderland □ 52 5N 6 10 E
16 Geldrop 51 25N 5 32 E
16 Geleen 50 57N 5 49 E
56 Gelibolu 40 28N 26 43 E
25 Gelnhausen 50 12N 9 12 E
24 Gelsenkirchen 51 30N 7 5 E
24 Gelting 54 43N 9 53 E
63 Gemas 2 37N 102 36 E
16 Gembloux 50 34N 4 43 E
74 Gemena 3 20N 19 40 E
37 Gemona del Fruiuli 46 16N 13 7 E
25 Gemünden 50 3N 9 43 E
20 Gençay 46 23N 0 23 E
108 General Acha 37 20S 64 38W
108 General Alvear 36 0S 60 0W
108 General Artigas 26 52S 56 16W
108 General Juan Madariaga 37 0S 57 0W
108 General Martin Miguel de Güemes 24 50S 65 0W
108 General Pico 35 45S 63 50W
108 General Pinedo 27 15S 61 30W
112 General Roca 30 0S 67 40W
41 General Toshevo 43 42N 28 6 E
108 General Viamonte 35 1S 61 3W
108 General Villegas 35 0S 63 0W
96 Genesee, R. 43 16N 77 36W
25 Geneva= Genève, Switz. 46 12N 6 9 E
96 Geneva, U.S.A. 42 53N 77 0W
25 Geneva, L.= Léman, L. 46 26N 6 30 E
25 Genève 46 12N 6 9 E
31 Genil, R. 37 42N 5 19W
21 Génissiat, Barrage de 46 1N 5 48 E
16 Genk 50 58N 5 32 E
38 Gennargentu, Mt. del 39 59N 9 19 E
36 Genova 44 24N 8 56 E
36 Génova, G. di 44 0N 9 0 E
16 Gent 51 2N 3 37 E
24 Genthin 52 24N 12 10 E
83 Geographe, B. 33 30S 115 15 E
83 Geographe, Chan. 24 30S 113 0 E
75 George 33 58S 22 29 E
97 George, L. 43 30N 73 30W
89 George R.=Port Nouveau-Quebec 58 30N 65 50W
80 George Town Australia 41 5S 148 55 E
63 George Town, W. Malaysia 5 25N 100 19 E
80 Georgetown, Australia 18 17S 143 33 E
90 Georgetown, Ont. 43 40N 80 0W
91 Georgetown, P.E.I. 46 13N 62 24W
72 Georgetown, Gambia 13 30N 14 47W
110 Georgetown, Guyana 6 50N 58 12W
99 Georgetown, U.S.A. 33 22N 79 15W
99 Georgia □ 32 0N 82 0W
92 Georgia Str. 49 20N 124 0W
90 Georgian B. 45 15N 81 0W
49 Georgian S.S.R. □ 41 0N 45 0 E
49 Georgiu-Dezh 51 3N 39 20 E
49 Georgiyevsk 44 12N 43 28 E
24 Gera 50 53N 12 5 E
24 Gera □ 50 45N 11 30 E
83 Geraldton, Australia 28 48S 114 32 E
90 Geraldton, Canada 49 44N 86 59W
19 Gérardmer 48 3N 6 50 E
88 Gerdine, Mt. 61 32N 152 50W
56 Gerede 40 45N 32 10 E
33 Gérgal 37 7N 2 31W
25 Gerlafingen 47 10N 7 34 E
55 Gerlogubi 6 53N 45 3 E
92 Germansen Landing 55 43N 124 40W
75 Germiston 26 15S 28 5 E
66 Gero 35 48N 137 14 E
27 Gerlachovka, Mt. 49 11N 20 7 E
32 Gerona 41 58N 2 46 E
32 Gerona □ 42 11N 2 30 E
20 Gers □ 43 35N 0 38 E
20 Gers, R. 44 9N 0 39 E
24 Geseke 51 38N 8 29 E
30 Getafe 40 18N 3 44W
20 Gevaudan, Reg. 44 40N 3 40 E
40 Gevgelija 41 9N 22 30 E
21 Gex 46 21N 6 3 E
102 Geyser 47 17N 110 30W
46 Geysir 64 19N 20 18W
54 Gezer 31 52N 34 55 E
61 Ghaghara, R. 25 45N 84 40 E
72 Ghana ■ 6 0N 1 0W
72 Ghardaîa 32 31N 3 37 E
56 Ghat 24 59N 10 19 E
61 Ghatal 22 40N 87 46 E
62 Ghatprabha, R. 16 21N 75 51 E
73 Ghazal, Bahr el, R. 9 31N 30 25 E
72 Ghazaouet 35 8N 1 50W
60 Ghaziabad 28 42N 77 35 E
61 Ghazipur 25 38N 83 35 E
57 Ghazni 33 30N 68 17 E
57 Ghazni □ 33 0N 68 0 E
36 Ghedi 45 24N 10 16 E
41 Gheorghe Gheorghiu-Dej 46 17N 26 47 E
21 Ghisonaccia 42 1N 9 26 E
57 Ghor □ 34 0N 64 20 E
90 Ghost River 51 25N 83 20W
72 Ghudāmes 30 11N 9 29 E
57 Ghuriān 34 17N 61 25 E
15 Giant's Causeway 55 15N 6 30W
36 Giaveno 45 3N 7 20 E
105 Gibara 21 0N 76 20W
38 Gibellina 37 48N 13 0 E
75 Gibeon 25 7S 17 45 E
31 Gibraléon 37 23N 6 58W
31 Gibraltar ■ 36 7N 5 22W
31 Gibraltar, Str. of 35 55N 5 40W
82 Gibson, Des. 24 0S 126 0 E
19 Gien 47 40N 2 36 E
24 Giessen 50 34N 8 40 E
24 Gifhorn 52 29N 10 32 E
66 Gifu 35 30N 136 45 E
66 Gifu □ 36 0N 137 0 E
104 Giganta, Sa. de la 25 30N 111 30W
14 Gigha, I. 55 42N 5 45W
36 Giglio, I. 42 20N 10 52 E
20 Gignac 43 39N 3 32 E
30 Gijón 43 32N 5 42W
103 Gila, R. 32 43N 114 33W
103 Gila Bend 32 57N 112 43W
56 Gilan □ 37 0N 49 0 E
76 Gilbert Is. 1 0N 176 0 E
93 Gilbert Plains 51 9N 100 28W
80 Gilbert River 18 9S 142 50 E
83 Gilgai 31 15S 119 56 E
84 Gilgandra 31 42S 148 39 E
58 Gilgit 35 50N 74 15 E
93 Gillam 56 20N 94 40W
80 Gilliat 20 40S 141 28 E
13 Gillingham 51 23N 0 34 E
90 Gilmour 44 48N 77 37W
103 Gilroy 37 10N 121 37W
80 Gindie 23 45S 148 10 E
83 Gingin 31 22S 115 37 E
54 Ginnosar 32 51N 35 32 E
39 Ginosa 40 35N 16 45 E
39 Gióia, G. di 38 30N 15 50 E
39 Gióia del Colle 40 49N 16 55 E
39 Gióia Táuro 38 26N 15 53 E
43 Gióna, Mt. 38 38N 22 14 E
65 Giong, Teluk, B. 4 50N 118 20 E

Great Whale, R. Hallands □

90 Great Whale, R. ... 55 20N 77 45 E
90 Great Whale River=Poste de la Baleine ... 55 20N 77 40 E
12 Great Whernside, Mt. ... 54 9N 1 59W
12 Great Yarmouth .. 52 40N 1 45 E
105 Greater Antilles ... 20 0N 74 0W
12 Greater Manchester □ ... 53 35N 2 15W
64 Greater Sunda Is. . 4 30S 113 0 E
30 Gredos, Sa. de ... 40 20N 5 0W
43 Greece ■ ... 40 0N 23 0 E
100 Greeley ... 40 30N 104 40W
98 Green Bay ... 44 30N 88 0W
98 Green B. ... 45 0N 87 30W
85 Green Island ... 45 54S 170 27 E
97 Green Mts. ... 44 0N 72 45W
103 Green River, Utah 39 0N 110 10W
102 Green River, Wyo. 41 32N 109 28W
98 Greencastle ... 39 40N 86 48W
99 Greeneville ... 31 50N 86 38W
98 Greenfield, Ind. ... 39 47N 85 51W
97 Greenfield, Mass. . 42 38N 72 38W
97 Greenfield Park ... 45 26N 73 28W
4 Greenland ■ ... 66 0N 45 0W
4 Greenland Sea ... 73 0N 10 0W
14 Greenock ... 55 57N 4 45W
15 Greenore ... 54 2N 6 8W
83 Greenough, R. ... 28 51S 114 38 E
97 Greenport ... 41 5N 72 23W
99 Greensboro ... 36 7N 79 46W
98 Greensburg, Ind. .. 39 20N 85 30W
96 Greensburg, Pa. ... 40 18N 79 31W
72 Greenville, Liberia 5 7N 9 6W
96 Greenville, Ala. ... 31 50N 86 37 E
98 Greenville, Mich. .. 43 12N 85 14W
101 Greenville, Miss. .. 33 25N 91 0W
99 Greenville, N.C. ... 35 37N 77 26W
96 Greenville, Pa. ... 41 23N 80 22W
99 Greenville, S.C. ... 34 54N 82 24W
101 Greenville, Tex. ... 33 5N 96 5W
13 Greenwich, U.K. .. 51 28N 0 0
97 Greenwich, N.Y. .. 43 2N 73 36W
96 Greenwich, Ohio .. 41 1N 82 32W
101 Greenwood, Miss. . 33 30N 90 4W
99 Greenwood, S.C. .. 34 13N 82 13W
80 Gregory Downs ... 18 35S 138 45 E
82 Gregory L. ... 20 10S 127 30 E
24 Greiffenberg ... 53 6N 13 57 E
24 Greifswald ... 54 6N 13 23 E
24 Greifswalder Bodden ... 54 12N 13 35 E
26 Grein ... 48 14N 14 51 E
24 Greiz ... 50 39N 12 12 E
48 Gremikha ... 67 50N 39 40 E
45 Grenå ... 56 26N 10 53 E
101 Grenada ... 33 45N 89 50W
105 Grenada, I. ... 12 10N 61 40W
84 Grenfell ... 33 52S 148 8 E
21 Grenoble ... 45 12N 5 42 E
65 Gresik ... 9 13S 112 38 E
101 Gretna ... 30 0N 90 2W
14 Gretna Green ... 55 0N 3 3W
24 Greven ... 52 7N 7 36 E
42 Grevená □ ... 40 2N 21 25 E
24 Grevenbroich ... 51 6N 6 32 E
16 Grevenmacher ... 49 41N 6 26 E
45 Grevie ... 56 22N 12 46 E
85 Grey, R. ... 42 27S 171 12 E
91 Grey Res. ... 48 20N 56 30W
102 Greybull ... 44 30N 108 3W
85 Greymouth ... 42 29S 171 13 E
85 Greytown, N.Z. ... 41 5S 175 29 E
75 Greytown, S. Africa ... 29 1S 30 36 E
102 Gridley ... 39 27N 121 47W
99 Griffin ... 33 15N 84 16W
84 Griffith ... 34 14S 145 46 E
93 Griffith Mine ... 50 47N 93 25W
96 Grimsby, Canada .. 43 12N 79 33W
12 Grimsby, U.K. ... 53 35N 0 5W
46 Grimsey, I. ... 66 33N 18 0W
92 Grimshaw ... 56 10N 117 40W
47 Grimstad ... 58 22N 8 35 E
25 Grindelwald ... 46 38N 8 2 E
45 Grindsted ... 55 46N 8 55 E
100 Grinnell ... 41 45N 92 50W
30 Griñon ... 40 13N 3 51W
37 Grintavec, Mt. ... 46 21N 14 32 E
19 Gris Nez, C. ... 50 50N 1 35 E
20 Grisolles ... 43 49N 1 19 E
37 Grmeč Planina ... 44 43N 16 16 E
48 Grodno ... 53 42N 23 52 E
28 Grodzisk Mãzowiecki ... 52 7N 20 37 E
28 Grodzisk Wlkp. ... 52 15N 16 22 E
18 Groix, I. de ... 47 38N 3 28W
24 Gronau ... 52 13N 7 2 E
46 Grong ... 64 25N 12 8 E
16 Groningen ... 53 15N 6 35 E
16 Groningen □ ... 53 16N 6 40 E
75 Groot-Brakrivier .. 34 2S 22 18 E
75 Groot Karoo, Reg. 32 35S 23 0 E
75 Groot Namakwaland= Namaland, Reg. . 26 0S 18 0 E
80 Groote Eylandt, I. . 14 0S 136 50 E
75 Grootfontein ... 19 31S 18 6 E
33 Grosa, Pta. ... 39 6N 1 36 E
26 Gross Glockner, Mt. ... 47 5N 12 40 E
24 Gross Ottersleben . 52 5N 11 33 E
24 Grossenbrode ... 54 21N 11 4 E
24 Grossenhain ... 51 17N 13 32 E
37 Grosseto ... 42 45N 11 7 E
26 Grossgerungs ... 48 34N 14 57 E
97 Groton ... 41 22N 75 5W
39 Grottáglie ... 40 32N 17 25 E
96 Grove City ... 41 10N 80 5W
97 Groveton ... 44 34N 71 30W
37 Grožnjan ... 45 22N 13 43 E
49 Groznyy ... 43 20N 45 45 E
40 Grubišno Polje ... 45 44N 17 12 E
41 Grudovo ... 42 21N 27 10 E
28 Grudziądz ... 53 30N 18 47 E
39 Grumo Appula ... 41 2N 16 43 E
44 Grums ... 59 22N 13 5 E
25 Gruyères ... 46 35N 7 4 E
48 Gryazi ... 52 30N 39 58 E
5 Grytviken ... 53 50S 37 10W
25 Gstaad ... 46 28N 7 18 E
105 Guacanayabo, G. de ... 20 40N 77 20W
104 Guadalajara, Mexico ... 20 40N 103 20W
30 Guadalajara, Sp. .. 40 37N 3 12W
32 Guadalajara □ ... 40 47N 3 0W
31 Guadalcanal ... 38 5N 5 52W
76 Guadalcanal, I. ... 9 32S 160 12 E
31 Guadalén, R. ... 38 5N 3 32W
31 Guadalete, R. ... 36 35N 6 13W
31 Guadalimar, R. ... 37 58W 3 45W
31 Guadalmez, R. ... 38 46N 5 4W
32 Guadalope, R. ... 41 15N 0 3W
29 Guadalquivir, R. .. 36 47N 6 22W
31 Guadalupe, Sp. ... 39 27N 5 17W
103 Guadalupe, U.S.A. 34 59N 120 33W
31 Guadalupe, Sa. de . 39 26N 5 25W
101 Guadalupe Pk. ... 31 50N 105 30W
30 Guadarrama, Sa. de ... 41 0N 4 0W
105 Guadeloupe, I. ... 16 20N 61 40W
105 Guadeloupe Pass. . 16 50N 68 15W
31 Guadiana, R. ... 37 14N 7 22W
33 Guadiana Menor, R. ... 37 56N 3 15W
31 Guadiaro, R. ... 36 17N 5 17W
32 Guadiela, R. ... 40 22N 2 49W
33 Guadix ... 37 18N 3 11W
112 Guafo, B. del ... 43 35S 74 0W
109 Guaíra ... 24 5S 54 10W
112 Guaitecas, Is. ... 44 0S 74 30W
110 Guajira, Pen. de la ... 12 0N 72 0W
37 Gualdo Tadino ... 43 14N 12 46 E
108 Gualeguay ... 33 10S 59 20W
108 Gualeguaychú ... 33 3S 58 31W
76 Guam, I. ... 13 27N 144 45 E
105 Guanabacoa ... 23 8N 82 18W
109 Guanabara □ ... 23 0S 43 25W
105 Guanacaste ... 10 40N 85 30W
105 Guanajay ... 22 56N 82 42W
104 Guanajuato ... 21 0N 101 20W
104 Guanajuato □ ... 20 40N 101 20W
110 Guanare ... 8 42N 69 12W
105 Guantánamo ... 20 10N 75 20W
109 Guaporé ... 12 0S 64 0W
110 Guaporé, R. ... 29 10S 51 54W
110 Guaqui ... 16 41S 68 54W
32 Guara, Sa. de ... 42 19N 0 15W
109 Guarapari ... 20 40S 40 30W
109 Guarapuava ... 25 20S 51 30W
109 Guaratinguetá ... 22 49S 45 9W
109 Guaratuba ... 25 53S 48 38W
30 Guarda ... 40 32N 7 20W
30 Guarda □ ... 40 40N 7 20W
33 Guardamar del Segura ... 38 5N 0 39W
37 Guardiagrele ... 42 11N 14 11 E
30 Guardo ... 42 47N 4 50W
31 Guareña ... 38 51N 6 6W
30 Guareña, R. ... 41 29N 5 23W
109 Guaria □ ... 26 0S 56 30W
109 Guarujá ... 24 2S 46 25W
109 Guarus ... 21 30S 41 20W
110 Guasaualito ... 7 15N 70 44W
110 Guasipati ... 7 28N 61 54W
36 Guastalla ... 44 55N 10 40 E
104 Guatemala ... 14 38N 90 31W
104 Guatemala ■ ... 15 40N 90 30W
110 Guaviare, R. ... 4 3N 67 44W
109 Guaxupé ... 21 10S 47 5W
105 Guayama ... 17 59N 66 7W
110 Guayaquil ... 2 15S 79 52W
110 Guayaquil, G. de .. 3 10S 81 0W
37 Gúbbio ... 43 20N 12 34 E
28 Gubin ... 51 58N 14 45 E
63 Guchil ... 5 35N 102 10 E
68 Guchin-Us ... 45 28N 102 10 E
62 Gudalur ... 11 30N 76 29 E
44 Gudbrandsdalen ... 62 0N 9 14 E
62 Gudivada ... 16 30N 81 15 E
62 Gudiyatam ... 12 57N 78 55 E
62 Gudur ... 14 12N 79 55 E
19 Guebwiller ... 47 55N 7 12 E
30 Guecho ... 43 21N 2 59W
72 Guéckédou ... 8 40N 10 5W
72 Guelma ... 36 25N 7 29 E
96 Guelph ... 43 35N 80 20W
18 Guéméné-sur-Scorff ... 48 4N 3 13W
18 Guer ... 47 54N 2 8W
18 Guérande ... 47 20N 2 26W
20 Guéret ... 46 11N 1 51 E
19 Guérigny ... 47 6N 3 10 E
30 Guernica ... 43 19N 2 40W
13 Guernsey, I. ... 49 30N 2 35W
104 Guerrero □ ... 17 30N 100 0W
21 Gueugnon ... 45 36N 4 3 E
37 Guglionesi ... 51 55N 14 54 E
109 Guia Lopes da Laguna ... 21 26S 56 7W
106 Guiana Highlands, Mts. ... 5 0N 60 0W
75 Guibes ... 26 41S 16 49 E
30 Guijo de Coria ... 40 6N 6 28W
13 Guildford ... 51 14N 0 34W
21 Guillaumes ... 44 5N 6 52 E
18 Guilvinec ... 47 48N 4 17W
111 Guimarães ... 2 9S 44 35W
30 Guimarãis ... 41 28N 8 24W
65 Guimaras, I. ... 10 35N 122 37 E
70 Guinea, Reg. ... 9 0N 3 0 E
72 Guinea ■ ... 10 20N 10 0W
70 Guinea, G. of ... 3 0N 2 30 E
72 Guinea-Bissau ■ .. 12 0N 15 0W
105 Güines ... 22 50N 82 0W
18 Guingamp ... 48 34N 3 10W
18 Guipavas ... 48 26N 4 29W
32 Guipuzcoa □ ... 43 12N 2 15W
110 Guiria ... 10 32N 62 1iw
19 Guiscard ... 49 40N 3 0 E
19 Guise ... 49 52N 3 35 E
30 Guitiriz ... 43 11N 7 50W
65 Guiuan ... 11 2N 125 44 E
20 Gujan-Mestres ... 44 38N 1 4W
60 Gujarat □ ... 23 20N 71 0 E
60 Gujranwala ... 32 10N 74 12 E
60 Gujrat ... 32 40N 74 2 E
62 Gulbarga ... 17 20N 76 50 E
62 Guledgud ... 16 3N 75 48 E
101 Gulfport ... 30 28N 89 3W
93 Gull Lake ... 50 10N 108 55W
50 Gulshad ... 46 45N 74 25 E
44 Gulsvik ... 60 24N 9 38 E
74 Gulu ... 2 48N 32 17 E
84 Gum Lake ... 32 42S 143 9 E
67 Guma ... 37 37N 78 18 E
60 Gumal, R. ... 31 56N 70 22 E
30 Gumiel de Hizán .. 41 46N 3 41W
80 Gumla ... 23 2N 84 32 E
66 Gumma □ ... 36 30N 138 20 E
24 Gummersbach ... 51 2N 7 32 E
72 Gummi ... 12 4N 5 9 E
60 Guna ... 24 40N 77 19 E
84 Gundagai ... 35 3S 148 6 E
81 Gunnedah ... 30 59S 150 15 E
84 Gunning ... 34 47S 149 14 E
103 Gunnison, Colo. ... 38 32N 106 56W
102 Gunnison, Utah ... 39 11N 111 48W
62 Guntakal ... 15 11N 77 27 E
99 Guntersville ... 34 18N 86 16W
62 Guntur ... 16 23N 80 30 E
64 Gunungsitoli ... 1 15N 97 30 E
93 Gunworth ... 51 20N 108 10W
25 Gunzenhausen ... 49 6N 10 45 E
56 Gūrchān ... 34 55N 49 25 E
60 Gurdaspur ... 32 5N 75 25 E
60 Gurgaon ... 28 33N 77 10 E
81 Gurley ... 29 45S 149 48 E
63 Gurun ... 5 49N 100 27 E
111 Gurupá ... 1 20S 51 45W
50 Guryer ... 47 5N 52 0 E
72 Gusau ... 12 18N 6 31 E
38 Gúspini ... 39 32N 8 38 E
27 Güssing ... 47 3N 16 20 E
24 Güstrow ... 53 47N 12 12 E
27 Guta=Kalárovo ... 47 54N 18 0 E
24 Gütersloh ... 51 54N 8 25 E
83 Gutha ... 28 58S 115 55 E
101 Guthrie ... 35 55N 97 30W
110 Guyana ■ ... 5 0N 59 0W
20 Guyenne, Reg. ... 44 30N 0 40 E
81 Guyra ... 30 15S 151 40 E
59 Gwa ... 17 30N 94 40 E
58 Gwādar ... 25 10N 62 18 E
83 Gwalia ... 28 55S 121 20 E
60 Gwalior ... 26 12N 78 10 E
75 Gwanda ... 20 55S 29 0 E
28 Gwda, R. ... 53 4N 16 44 E
15 Gweedore ... 55 4N 8 15W
75 Gwelo ... 19 27S 29 49 E
13 Gwent □ ... 51 45N 3 0W
12 Gwynedd □ ... 53 0N 4 0W
50 Gydanskiy Pol. ... 70 0N 78 0 E
81 Gympie ... 26 11S 152 38 E
27 Gyoma ... 46 56N 20 58 E
27 Gyöngyös ... 47 48N 20 15 E
27 Györ ... 47 41N 17 40 E
27 Györ Sopron □ ... 47 40N 17 20 E
93 Gypsumville ... 51 45N 98 40W
27 Gyula ... 46 38N 21 17 E

H

63 Ha Dong ... 20 58N 105 46 E
63 Ha Giang ... 22 46N 104 56 E
63 Ha Tinh ... 18 20N 105 54 E
25 Haag ... 48 11N 12 12 E
16 Haarlem ... 52 23N 4 39 E
85 Haast, R. ... 43 50S 169 2 E
58 Hab Nadi Chauki . 25 0N 66 50 E
61 Habiganj ... 24 24N 91 30 E
66 Hachinohe ... 40 30N 141 29 E
66 Hachiōji ... 33 3N 139 55 E
92 Hackett ... 52 9N 112 28 E
97 Hackettstown ... 40 51N 74 50W
60 Hadali ... 32 16N 72 11 E
54 Hadar Ramatayim . 52 8N 34 45 E
57 Hadd, Ras al ... 22 35N 59 50 E
14 Haddington ... 55 57N 2 48W
72 Hadejia ... 12 30N 9 59 E
54 Hadera ... 32 27N 34 55 E
45 Haderslev ... 55 17N 9 30 E
55 Hadhramawt, Reg. 15 30N 49 30 E
12 Hadrian's Wall ... 55 0N 2 30 E
68 Haeju ... 38 12N 125 41 E
56 Hafar al Bātin ... 28 25N 46 50 E
60 Hafizabad ... 32 5N 73 40 E
59 Haflong ... 25 10N 93 5 E
46 Hafnarfjördur ... 64 3N 21 55W
54 Hagalil, Reg. ... 32 53N 35 18 E
62 Hagari, R. ... 15 44N 76 56 E
24 Hagen ... 51 21N 7 29 E
98 Hagerstown ... 39 39N 77 46W
20 Hagetmau ... 43 39N 0 37W
44 Hagfors ... 60 3N 13 45 E
46 Hagi, Iceland ... 65 28N 23 25W
66 Hagi, Japan ... 34 30N 131 30 E
18 Hague, C. de la ... 49 43N 1 57W
19 Haguenau ... 48 49N 7 47 E
54 Haifa ... 32 46N 35 0 E
83 Haig ... 30 55S 126 10 E
69 Haikow ... 20 0N 110 20 E
68 Hailar ... 49 12N 119 37 E
68 Hailar, R. ... 49 35N 117 55 E
102 Hailey ... 43 30N 114 15W
90 Haileybury ... 47 30N 79 38W
68 Hailun ... 47 24N 127 0 E
68 Hailung ... 42 46N 125 57 E
69 Haimen ... 31 48N 121 8 E
69 Hainan, I. ... 19 0N 110 0 E
16 Hainaut □ ... 50 30N 4 0 E
27 Hainburg ... 48 9N 16 56 E
92 Haines Junction ... 60 45N 137 30W
26 Hainfeld ... 48 3N 15 48 E
69 Haining ... 30 16N 120 47 E
63 Haiphong ... 20 55N 105 42 E
69 Haitan Tao, I. ... 25 30N 119 45 E
105 Haiti ■ ... 19 0N 72 30W
69 Haiyen ... 30 28N 120 57 E
27 Hajdu-Bihar □ ... 47 30N 21 30 E
27 Hajdúböszörmény . 47 40N 21 30 E
27 Hajdúdurog ... 47 48N 21 30 E
27 Hajdúhadház ... 47 40N 21 40 E
27 Hajdúnánás ... 47 50N 21 26 E
27 Hajdúszoboszló ... 47 27N 21 22 E
61 Hajipur ... 25 45N 85 20 E
28 Hajnówka ... 52 45N 23 36 E
57 Hajr, Reg. ... 24 0N 56 34 E
45 Håkantorp ... 58 18N 12 55 E
66 Hakodate ... 41 45N 140 44 E
66 Haku-San, Mt. ... 36 9N 136 46 E
66 Hakui ... 36 53N 136 47 E
56 Ḩalab ... 36 10N 37 15 E
73 Halaib ... 22 5N 36 30 E
24 Halberstadt ... 51 53N 11 2 E
85 Halcombe ... 40 8S 175 30 E
44 Halden ... 59 7N 11 30 E
24 Haldensleben ... 52 17N 11 30 E
61 Haldwani ... 29 25N 79 30 E
94 Haleakala, Mt. ... 20 42N 156 15W
54 Halhul ... 31 35N 35 7 E
55 Hali ... 18 40N 41 15 E
90 Haliburton ... 45 3N 78 30W
91 Halifax, Canada ... 44 38N 63 35W
12 Halifax, U.K. ... 53 43N 1 51W
26 Hall ... 47 17N 11 30 E
89 Hall Lake ... 68 30N 81 0W
45 Hallands □ ... 57 0N 12 37 E

Hallandsås Mt. Hindukush, Mts.

45 Hallandsås Mt. 56 23N 13 0E
16 Halle, Belgium 50 44N 4 13W
24 Halle, E. Germany 51 29N 12 0E
24 Halle □ 51 28N 11 58E
44 Hällefors 59 46N 14 30E
26 Hallein 47 40N 13 5E
81 Hallett 33 25S 138 55E
5 Halley Bay 76 30S 27 0W
44 Hallingdalselv, R. 60 24N 9 35E
46 Hällnäs 64 18N 19 40E
82 Halls Creek 18 20S 128 0E
44 Hallsberg 59 5N 15 7E
44 Hallstahammar 59 38N 16 15E
26 Hallstatt 47 33N 13 38E
97 Hallstead 41 56N 75 45W
65 Halmahera, I. 0 40N 128 0E
45 Halmstad 56 37N 12 56E
73 Halq el Oued 36 53N 10 10E
24 Haltern 51 44N 7 10E
56 Hamā 35 5N 36 40E
66 Hamada 34 50N 132 10E
56 Hamadān 34 52N 48 32E
56 Hamadān □ 35 0N 48 40E
66 Hamamatsu 34 45N 137 45E
44 Hamar 60 48N 11 7E
24 Hamburg, Germany 53 32N 9 59E
96 Hamburg, U.S.A. 40 37N 95 38W
97 Hamden 41 21N 72 56W
47 Häme □ 61 30N 24 30E
47 Hämeenlinna 61 3N 24 26E
83 Hamelin Pool 26 22S 114 20E
24 Hameln 52 7N 9 24E
82 Hamersley Ra. 22 0S 117 45E
68 Hamhung 40 0N 127 30E
67 Hami 42 54N 93 28E
84 Hamilton, Australia 37 37S 142 0E
105 Hamilton, Bermuda 32 15N 64 45W
96 Hamilton, Canada 43 20N 79 50W
85 Hamilton, N.Z. 37 47S 175 19E
14 Hamilton, U.K. 55 47N 4 2W
102 Hamilton, Mont. 46 20N 114 6W
98 Hamilton, Ohio 39 20N 84 35W
80 Hamilton Hotel 22 45S 140 40E
97 Hamilton Mt. 43 25N 74 22W
93 Hamiota 50 11N 100 38W
99 Hamlet 34 56N 79 40W
24 Hamm 51 40N 7 58E
44 Hammarö, I. 59 20N 13 30E
46 Hammerfest 70 33N 23 50E
98 Hammond, Ind. 41 40N 87 30W
101 Hammond, La. 30 30N 90 28W
85 Hampden 45 18S 170 50E
13 Hampshire □ 51 3N 1 20W
98 Hampton 37 4N 76 8W
56 Hamra 24 2N 38 55E
44 Hamrånge 60 59N 17 5E
69 Han Kiang, R. 30 32N 114 22E
69 Hanchung 33 10N 107 2E
100 Hancock 47 10N 88 35W
55 Handa, Japan 34 53N 137 0E
66 Handa, Somalia 10 37N 51 2E
74 Handeni 5 25S 38 2E
27 Handlová 48 45N 18 35E
54 Hanegev, Reg. 30 50N 35 0E
92 Haney 49 12N 122 40W
103 Hanford 36 25N 119 45W
69 Hangchow 30 12N 120 1E
69 Hangchow Wan, G. 30 30N 121 30E
47 Hangö 59 59N 22 57E
68 Hanh 51 32N 100 35E
54 Hanita 33 5N 35 10E
69 Hankow 30 32N 114 20E
68 Hanku 39 16N 117 50E
85 Hanmer 42 32S 172 50E
92 Hanna 51 40N 112 0W
100 Hannibal 39 42N 91 22W
24 Hannover 52 23N 9 43E
45 Hanö, B. 55 45N 14 60E
45 Hanö, I. 56 0N 14 50E
63 Hanoi 21 5N 150 40E
90 Hanover, Canada 44 9N 81 2W
97 Hanover, N.H. 43 43N 72 17W
98 Hanover, Pa. 39 46N 76 59W
112 Hanover, I. 50 58S 74 40W
60 Hansi 29 10N 75 57E
68 Hantan 36 42N 114 30E
69 Hanyang 30 30N 114 19E
46 Haparanda 65 52N 24 8E
91 Happy Valley 55 53N 60 10W
60 Hapur 28 45N 77 45E
68 Har-Ayrag 45 50N 109 30E
67 Har Us Nuur, L. 48 0N 92 0E
54 Har Yehuda, Reg. 31 40N 35 0E
56 Harad 24 15N 49 0E
55 Haradera 4 33N 47 38E
68 Harbin 45 46N 126 51E
91 Harbour Breton 47 29N 55 50W
91 Harbour Deep 50 25N 56 30W
91 Harbour Grace 47 40N 53 22W
24 Harburg 53 27N 9 58E
60 Harda 22 27N 77 5E
47 Hardanger Fd. 60 15N 6 0E
75 Hardap Dam 24 28S 17 48E
16 Harderwijk 52 21N 5 36E
75 Harding 30 22S 29 55E
60 Hardwar 29 58N 78 16E
112 Hardy, Pen. 55 30S 68 20W
55 Harer 9 20N 42 8E
18 Harfleur 49 30N 0 10E
55 Hargeisa 9 30N 44 2E
62 Harihar 14 32N 75 44E
62 Haripad 9 14N 76 28E
12 Harlech 52 52N 4 7W
102 Harlem 48 29N 108 39W
16 Harlingen, Neth. 53 11N 5 25E
101 Harlingen, U.S.A. 26 30N 97 50W
13 Harlow 51 47N 0 9E
102 Harlowton 46 30N 109 54W
102 Harney L. 43 0N 119 0W
102 Harney Basin 43 30N 119 0W
100 Harney Pk. 43 52N 103 33W
44 Härnösand 62 38N 18 5E
30 Haro 42 35N 2 55W
62 Harpanahalli 14 47N 75 59E
99 Harriman 36 0N 84 35W
91 Harrington Harbour 50 31N 59 30W
14 Harris, I. 57 50N 6 55W
98 Harrisburg, Ill. 37 42N 88 30W
97 Harrison, N.Y. 40 58N 73 43W
101 Harrison, Ohio 36 10N 93 4W
96 Harrisburg, Pa. 40 18N 76 52W
88 Harrison B. 70 25N 151 0W
98 Harrisonburg 38 28N 78 52W
100 Harrisonville 38 45N 93 45W
90 Harriston 43 57N 80 53W
12 Harrogate 53 59N 1 32W
13 Harrow 51 35N 0 15W
97 Hartford 41 47N 72 41W
91 Hartland 46 20N 67 32W
13 Hartland Pt. 51 2N 4 32W
12 Hartlepool 54 42N 1 11W
75 Hartley 18 10S 30 7E
92 Hartley Bay 46 4N 80 45W
93 Hartney 49 30N 100 35W
99 Hartsville 34 23N 80 2W
60 Harunabad 29 35N 73 2E
83 Harvey, Australia 33 4S 115 48E
98 Harvey, U.S.A. 41 40N 87 40W
13 Harwich 51 56N 1 18E
60 Haryana 29 0N 76 10E
24 Harz, Mts. 51 40N 10 40E
13 Haslemere 51 5N 0 41W
20 Hasparren 43 24N 1 18W
62 Hassan 13 0N 76 5E
16 Hasselt 50 56N 5 21E
72 Hassi Messaoud 31 15N 6 35E
72 Hassi R'Mel 32 35N 3 24E
45 Hässleholm 56 9N 13 46E
85 Hastings, N.Z. 39 39S 176 52E
13 Hastings, U.K. 50 51N 0 36E
98 Hastings, Mich. 42 40N 85 20E
100 Hastings, Neb. 40 34N 98 22W
103 Hatch 32 45N 107 8W
40 Hateg 45 36N 22 55E
67 Hatgal 50 40N 100 0E
60 Hathras 27 36N 78 6E
61 Hatia I. 22 50N 91 20E
99 Hatteras, C. 35 10N 75 30W
101 Hattiesburg 31 20N 89 20W
27 Hatvan 47 40N 19 45E
47 Haugesund 59 23N 5 13E
41 Haunţii Sebeşului, Mt. 45 30N 23 30E
55 Haura 13 50N 47 35E
85 Hauraki, G. 36 35S 175 5E
26 Hausruck, Mts. 48 6N 13 30E
19 Haut-Rhin □ 48 0N 7 15E
21 Haute-Corse □ 42 30N 9 20E
20 Haute-Garonne □ 43 28N 1 30E
20 Haute-Loire □ 45 5N 3 50E
19 Haute-Marne □ 48 10N 5 20E
91 Hauterive 49 10N 68 25W
19 Hautmont 50 15N 3 55E
19 Haute-Saône □ 47 45N 6 10E
21 Haute-Savoie □ 46 0N 6 20E
20 Haute-Vienne □ 45 50N 1 10E
21 Hautes-Alpes □ 44 40N 6 30E
20 Hautes-Pyrénées □ 43 0N 0 10E
13 Havant 50 51N 0 59W
90 Havelock 44 26N 77 53W
85 Havelock North 39 42S 176 53E
13 Haverfordwest 51 48N 4 59W
97 Haverhill 42 50N 71 2W
62 Haveri 14 53N 75 24E
13 Havering 51 33N 0 20E
97 Haverstraw 41 12N 73 58W
26 Havlíčkuv Brod 49 36N 15 33E
102 Havre 48 40N 109 34W
91 Havre St. Pierre 50 18N 63 33W
56 Havza 41 0N 35 35E
94 Hawaii □ 20 0N 155 0W
94 Hawaii, I. 20 0N 155 0W
85 Hawea, L. 44 28S 169 19E
85 Hawera 39 35S 174 19E
14 Hawick 55 25N 2 48W
90 Hawk Junction 48 5N 84 35W
85 Hawke, B. 39 25S 177 20E
81 Hawker 31 59S 138 22E
85 Hawke's Bay □ 39 45S 176 35E
91 Hawke's Harbour 53 2N 55 50W
91 Hawkesbury, Nova Scotia 45 40N 61 10W
90 Hawkesbury, Ont. 45 35N 74 40W
102 Hawthorne 38 37N 118 47W
84 Hay, Australia 34 30S 144 51E
13 Hay, U.K. 52 4N 3 9W
92 Hay River 60 50N 115 50W
19 Hayange 49 20N 6 2E
103 Hayden 40 30N 107 22W
80 Haydon 18 0S 141 30E
88 Hayes, Mt. 63 37N 146 43W
93 Hayes, R. 57 3N 92 9W
13 Hayling I. 50 40N 1 0W
100 Hays 38 55N 99 25W
13 Haywards Heath 51 0N 0 5W
57 Hazārān, Kūh-e, Mt. 29 35N 57 20E
98 Hazard 37 18N 83 10W
61 Hazaribagh 23 58N 85 26E
19 Hazebrouck 50 42N 2 31E
92 Hazelton 55 20N 127 42W
97 Hazleton 40 58N 76 0W
54 Hazor 33 2N 35 2E
57 Hazrat Imam 37 15N 68 50E
102 Healdsburg 38 33N 122 51W
12 Heanor 53 1N 1 20W
3 Heard I. 53 0S 74 0E
90 Hearst 49 40N 83 41W
91 Heart's Content 47 54N 53 27W
91 Heath Steele 48 30N 66 20W
81 Hebel 28 59S 147 48E
91 Hebertville 47 0N 71 30W
14 Hebrides, Inner, Is. 57 20N 6 40W
14 Hebrides, Outer, Is. 57 50N 7 25W
89 Hebron, Canada 58 10N 62 50W
54 Hebron, Jordan 31 32N 35 6E
92 Hecate Str. 53 10N 130 30W
44 Hedemora 60 18N 15 58E
44 Hedmark □ 61 45N 11 0E
16 Heemstede 52 19N 4 37E
16 Heerde 52 24N 6 2E
16 Heerenveen 52 57N 5 55E
16 Heerlen 50 55N 6 0E
24 Heide 54 10N 9 7E
25 Heidelberg 49 23N 8 41E
25 Heidenheim 48 40N 10 10E
75 Heilbron 27 16S 27 59E
25 Heilbronn 49 8N 9 13E
24 Heiligenstadt 51 22N 10 9E
68 Heilungkiang □ 47 30N 129 0E
47 Heinola 61 13N 26 10E
93 Heinsburg 53 50N 110 30W
59 Heinze Is. 14 25N 97 45E
46 Hekla, Mt. 63 56N 19 35W
101 Helena, Ark. 34 30N 90 35W
102 Helena, Mont. 46 40N 112 0W
14 Helensburgh 56 0N 4 44W
85 Helensville 36 41S 174 29E
54 Helez 31 36N 34 39E
45 Helgasjön, L. 57 0N 14 54E
24 Heligoland, I. 54 10N 7 51E
75 Hell-Ville 13 25S 48 16E
16 Hellendoorn 52 24N 6 27E
33 Hellín 38 31N 1 40W
57 Helmand, Hamun 31 0N 61 0E
57 Helmand □ 31 0N 64 0E
57 Helmand, R. 31 12N 61 34E
16 Helmond 51 29N 5 41E
14 Helmsdale 58 7N 3 40W
24 Helmstedt 52 16N 11 0E
45 Helsingborg 56 3N 12 42E
47 Helsingfors= Helsinki 60 15N 25 3E
45 Helsingør 56 2N 12 35E
47 Helsinki 60 15N 25 3E
13 Helston 50 7N 5 17W
12 Helvellyn, Mt. 54 31N 3 1W
73 Helwân 29 50N 31 20E
13 Hemel Hempstead 51 45N 0 28W
32 Henares, R. 40 24N 3 30W
20 Hendaye 43 23N 1 47W
98 Henderson, Ky. 37 50N 87 38W
99 Henderson, N.C. 36 18N 78 23W
101 Henderson, Tex. 32 5N 94 49W
99 Hendersonville 35 21N 82 28W
81 Hendon 28 5S 151 50E
16 Hengelo 52 15N 6 48E
69 Hengyang 26 57N 112 28E
19 Hénin Beaumont 50 25N 2 58E
18 Hennebont 47 49N 3 19W
24 Henningsdorf 52 38N 13 13E
90 Henrietta Maria, C. 55 10N 82 30W
74 Henrique de Carvalho 9 39S 20 24E
101 Henryetta 35 2N 96 0W
84 Henty 35 30N 147 0E
59 Henzada 17 38N 95 35E
102 Heppner 45 27N 119 34W
57 Herat 34 20N 62 7E
57 Herat □ 34 20N 62 7E
20 Hérault □ 43 34N 3 15E
20 Hérault, R. 43 17N 3 26E
93 Herbert 50 30N 107 10W
80 Herbert Downs 23 0S 139 11E
40 Hercegnavi 42 30N 18 33E
13 Hereford, U.K. 52 4N 2 42W
101 Hereford, U.S.A. 34 50N 102 28W
13 Hereford and Worcester □ 52 14N 1 42W
16 Herentals 51 12N 4 51E
24 Herford 52 7N 8 40E
19 Héricourt 47 32N 6 55E
25 Herisau 47 22N 9 17E
97 Herkimer 43 0N 74 59W
18 Herm, I. 49 30N 2 28W
26 Hermagor-Pressegger See, L. 46 38N 13 23E
84 Hermidale 31 30S 146 42E
102 Hermiston 45 50N 119 16W
85 Hermitage 43 44S 170 5E
112 Hermite, I. 55 50S 68 0W
56 Hermon, Mt.= Sheikh, Jabal ash 33 20N 26 0E
104 Hermosillo 29 10N 111 0W
27 Hernad R. 47 56N 21 8E
109 Hernandarias 25 20S 54 50W
108 Hernando 32 28S 64 50W
24 Herne 51 33N 7 12E
13 Herne Bay 51 22N 1 8E
45 Herning 56 8N 9 0E
90 Heron Bay 48 40N 85 25W
56 Herowabad 37 37N 48 32E
30 Herrera de Pisuerga 42 35N 4 20W
31 Herrera del Duque 39 10N 5 3W
101 Herrin 37 50N 89 0W
45 Herrljunga 58 5N 13 5E
16 Herstal 50 40N 5 38E
13 Hertford 51 47N 0 4W
13 Hertford □ 51 51N 0 5W
30 Hervás 40 16N 5 52W
77 Hervey Is. 19 30S 159 0W
24 Herzberg 51 38N 10 20E
54 Herzliyya 32 10N 34 50E
26 Herzogenburg 48 17N 15 41E
24 Hessen □ 50 57N 9 20E
24 Hettstedt 51 39N 11 30E
18 Heve, C. de la 49 30N 0 5E
27 Heves □ 47 50N 20 0E
89 Hewett, C. 70 30N 68 0W
12 Hexham 54 58N 2 7W
12 Heysham 54 5N 2 53W
84 Heywood 38 8S 141 37E
100 Hibbing 47 30N 93 0W
99 Hickory 35 46N 81 17W
97 Hicksville 40 46N 73 30W
66 Hida Sammyaku, Mts. 36 0N 137 10E
104 Hidalgo □ 20 30N 99 10W
104 Hidalgo del Parral 26 10N 104 50W
26 Hieflau 47 36N 14 46E
72 Hierro, I. 27 57N 17 56W
69 Hifung 22 59N 115 17E
66 Higashiósaka 34 39N 135 35E
83 Higginsville 31 42S 121 38E
99 High Point 35 57N 79 58W
92 High Prairie 55 30N 116 30W
92 High River 50 30N 113 50W
13 High Wycombe 51 37N 0 45W
70 High Veld 26 30S 30 0E
14 Highland □ 57 30N 4 50W
98 Highland Park, Ill. 42 10N 87 50W
98 Highland Park, Mich. 42 25N 83 6W
32 Hijar 41 10N 0 27W
56 Hijāz, Reg. 26 0N 37 30E
66 Hikari 33 58N 131 56E
66 Hikone 35 15N 136 10E
85 Hikurangi 37 54S 178 5E
24 Hildersheim 52 9N 9 55E
16 Hillegom 52 18N 4 35E
45 Hillerød 55 56N 12 19E
13 Hillingdon 51 33N 0 29W
100 Hillsboro, Kan. 38 28N 97 10W
102 Hillsboro, Oreg. 45 31N 123 0W
101 Hillsboro, Tex. 32 0N 97 10W
90 Hillsport 49 27N 85 34W
84 Hillston 33 30S 145 31E
94 Hilo 19 44N 155 5W
16 Hilversum 52 14N 5 10E
60 Himachal Pradesh □ 31 30N 77 0E
52 Himalaya, Mts. 29 0N 84 0E
66 Himeji 34 50N 134 40E
66 Himi 36 50N 137 0E
45 Himmerland, Reg. 56 50N 9 38E
56 Hims=Homs 34 40N 36 45E
80 Hinchinbrook, I. 18 20S 146 15E
13 Hinckley 52 33N 1 21W
60 Hindaun 26 44N 77 5E
84 Hindmarsh, L. 35 50S 141 55E
57 Hindukush, Mts. 36 0N 71 0E

I

Iesi Jaguarão

37 Iesi 43 32N 13 12 E
72 Ife 7 30N 4 31 E
111 Igarapava 20 3S 47 47W
111 Igarapé Açu 1 4S 47 33W
51 Igarka 67 30N 87 20 E
62 Igatpuri 19 40N 73 35 E
38 Iglésias 39 19N 8 27 E
89 Igloolik Island 69 20N 81 30W
93 Ignace 49 30N 91 40W
42 Igoumenítsa 39 32N 20 18 E
109 Iguaçu, R. 25 30S 53 10W
104 Iguala 18 20N 99 40W
32 Igualada 41 37N 1 37 E
109 Iguape 24 43S 47 33W
111 Iguatu 6 20S 39 18W
109 Iguazú Falls 25 2S 54 26W
68 Ihsien 41 45N 121 3 E
66 Iida 35 35N 138 0 E
46 Iisalmi 63 32N 27 10 E
66 Iizuka 33 38N 130 42 E
72 Ijebu Ode 6 47N 3 52 E
16 Ijmuiden 52 28N 4 35 E
16 Ijsel, R. 52 30N 6 0 E
16 Ijsselmeer, L. 52 45N 5 20 E
43 Ikaría, I. 37 35N 26 10 E
45 Ikast 56 8N 9 10 E
66 Ikeda 34 1N 133 48 E
41 Ikhtiman 42 27N 23 48 E
66 Iki, I. 33 45N 129 42 E
65 Ilagan 17 9N 121 53 E
68 Ilan 46 14N 129 33 E
51 Ilanskiy 56 14N 96 3 E
28 Iława 53 37N 19 33 E
80 Ilbilbie 21 45S 149 20 E
19 Île de France, Reg. 49 0N 2 20 E
74 Ilebo 4 17S 20 47 E
80 Ilfracombe, Australia 23 30S 144 30 E
13 Ilfracombe, U.K. 51 13N 4 8W
109 Ilha Grande, B. de 23 9S 44 30W
111 Ilhéus 15 0S 39 10W
30 Ilhavo 40 33N 8 43W
40 Ilia 45 57N 22 40 E
43 Ilia □ 37 45N 21 35 E
88 Iliamna L. 59 30N 155 0W
88 Iliamna, Mt. 60 5N 153 9W
50 Ilich 41 0N 68 10 E
43 Iliki, L. 38 24N 23 15 E
42 Iliodhrómia, I. 39 12N 23 50 E
37 Ilirska Bistrica 45 34N 14 14 E
50 Iliysk=Kapchagai 44 10N 77 20 E
62 Ilkal 15 57N 76 8 E
12 Ilkeston 52 59N 1 19W
68 Ilkhuri Shan, Mts. 51 30N 124 0 E
108 Illapel 32 0S 71 10W
18 Ille-et-Vilaine □ 48 10 1 30W
25 Iller, R. 48 23N 9 58 E
30 Illescás 40 8N 3 51W
110 Illimani, Mt. 16 30S 67 50W
100 Illinois, R. 38 58N 90 27W
100 Illinois □ 40 15N 89 30W
72 Illizi 26 31N 8 32 E
31 Illora 37 17N 3 53W
48 Ilmen, Oz. 5 15N 31 10 E
24 Ilmenau 50 41N 10 55 E
110 Ilo 17 40S 71 20W
65 Iloilo 10 45N 122 33 E
72 Ilorin 8 30N 4 35 E
65 Ilwaki 7 55S 126 30 E
28 Iłżanka, R. 51 11N 21 14 E
66 Imabari 34 4N 133 0 E
51 Iman 45 50N 133 40 E
48 Imandra, Oz. 67 45N 33 0 E
66 Imari 33 15N 129 52 E
42 Imathía □ 40 30N 22 15 E
12 Immingham 53 37N 0 12W
37 Imola 44 20N 11 42 E
111 Imperatriz 5 30S 47 20W
36 Impéria 43 52N 8 0 E
93 Imperial, Canada 51 21N 105 28W
103 Imperial, U.S.A. 32 52N 115 34W
103 Imperial Dam 32 50N 114 30W
74 Impfondo 1 40N 18 0 E
59 Imphal 24 15N 94 0 E
26 Imst 47 15N 10 44 E
54 Imwas 31 51N 34 59 E
72 In Salah 27 10N 2 32 E
85 Inangahua Junction 41 52S 171 59 E
46 Inari 68 54N 27 5 E
46 Inari, L. 69 0N 28 0 E
32 Inca 39 43N 2 54 E
68 Inchŏn 37 32N 126 45 E
44 Indalsälven, R. 62 31N 17 27 E
59 Indaw 24 15N 96 5 E
101 Independence, Kans. 37 10N 95 50W
100 Independence, Mo. 39 3N 94 25W
102 Independence, Oreg. 44 53N 123 6W
41 Independenţa 45 25N 27 42 E
58 India ■ 23 0N 77 30 E
92 Indian Cabin 59 50N 117 12W
93 Indian Head 50 30N 103 35W
1 Indian Ocean 5 0S 75 0 E
96 Indiana 40 38N 79 9W
98 Indiana □ 40 0N 86 0W
98 Indianapolis 39 42N 86 10W
100 Indianola 41 20N 93 38W
48 Indiga 67 50N 48 50 E
40 Indija 45 6N 20 7 E
64 Indonesia ■ 5 0S 115 0 E
65 Indramaju 6 21S 108 20 E
62 Indravati, R. 18 43N 80 17 E
18 Indre, R. 47 16N 0 19 E
19 Indre □ 46 45N 1 30 E
18 Indre-et-Loire □ 47 12N 0 40 E
60 Indus, Mouths of the 24 20N 67 50 E
60 Indus, R. 24 20N 67 47 E
56 Inebolu 41 55N 33 40 E
56 Inegöl 40 5N 29 31 E
33 Infantes 38 43N 3 1W
30 Infiesto 43 21N 5 21W
108 Ingenio Santa Ana 27 25S 65 40W
90 Ingersoll 43 4N 80 55W
80 Ingham 18 43S 146 10 E
12 Ingleborough, Mt. 54 11N 2 23W
81 Inglewood, N.S.W. 28 25S 151 8 E
84 Inglewood, Vic. 36 29S 143 53 E
85 Inglewood, N.Z. 39 9S 174 14 E
103 Inglewood 33 58N 118 27W
25 Intolstadt 48 45N 11 26W
49 Ingulec 47 42N 33 4 E
75 Inhambane 23 54S 35 30 E
75 Inharrime 24 30S 35 0 E
69 Ining, Kwangsi-Chuang 25 8N 109 57 E
67 Ining Sinkiang-Uigur 43 57N 81 20 E
15 Inishmore, I. 53 8N 9 45W
15 Inishowen, Pen. 55 14N 7 15W
25 Inn, R. 48 35N 13 28 E
26 Inn, R. 48 35N 13 28 E
68 Inner Mongolian Autonomous Rep. □ 44 50N 117 40 E
24 Innerste, R. 52 15N 9 50 E
80 Innisfail, Australia 17 33S 146 5 E
92 Innisfail, Canada 52 0N 114 0W
26 Innsbruck 47 16N 11 23 E
28 Inowrocław 52 50N 18 20 E
83 Inscription, C. 25 29S 112 59 E
59 Insein 16 46N 96 18 E
41 Însurăţei 44 50N 27 40 E
48 Inta 66 2N 60 8 E
108 Intendente Alvear 35 12S 63 32W
25 Interlaken 46 41N 7 50 E
100 International Falls 48 30N 93 25W
112 Inútil, B. 53 30S 70 15W
88 Inuvik 68 25N 133 30W
14 Inverary 56 13N 5 5W
14 Inverbervie 56 50N 2 17W
85 Invercargill 46 24S 168 24 E
81 Inverell 29 48S 151 36 E
14 Invergordon 57 41N 4 10W
92 Invermere 50 51N 116 9W
91 Inverness, Canada 46 15N 61 19W
14 Inverness, U.K. 57 29N 4 12W
14 Inverurie 57 15N 2 21W
82 Inverway 17 50S 129 38 E
81 Investigator, Str. 35 30S 137 0 E
103 Inyokern 35 37N 117 54W
48 Inza 53 55N 46 25 E
42 Ioánnina 39 42N 20 55 E
42 Ioánnina □ 39 50N 20 57 E
101 Iola 38 0N 95 20W
41 Ion Corvin 44 7N 27 50 E
14 Iona, I. 56 20N 6 25W
98 Ionia 42 59N 85 7W
43 Ionian Is.= Iónioi Nísoi 38 40N 20 8 E
43 Ionian Sea 37 30N 17 30 E
43 Iónioi Nísoi 38 40N 20 8 E
43 Íos, I. 36 41N 25 20 E
100 Iowa □ 42 18N 93 30W
100 Iowa City 41 40N 91 35W
100 Iowa Falls 42 30N 93 15W
111 Ipameri 17 44S 48 9W
27 Ipel, R. 47 49N 18 52 E
110 Ipiales 1 0N 77 45W
67 Ipin 28 58N 104 45 E
42 Ipiros □ 39 30N 20 30 E
63 Ipoh 4 36N 101 4 E
81 Ipswich, Australia 27 38S 152 37 E
13 Ipswich, U.K. 52 4N 1 9 E
111 Ipu 4 23S 40 44W
108 Iquique 20 19S 70 5W
110 Iquitos 3 45S 73 10W
111 Iracoubo 5 30N 53 10W
43 Iráklion 35 20N 25 12 E
43 Iráklion □ 35 10N 25 10 E
57 Iran ■ 33 0N 53 0 E
57 Iranshahr 27 75N 60 40 E
104 Irapuato 20 40N 101 40W
56 Iraq ■ 33 0N 44 0 E
109 Irati 25 25S 50 38W
54 Irbid 32 35N 35 48 E
32 Iregua, R. 42 27N 2 24W
15 Ireland 53 0N 8 0W
105 Ireland I. 32 19N 64 50W
51 Iret 60 10N 154 5 E
68 Iri 35 59N 127 0 E
65 Irian Jaya □ 5 0S 140 0 E
73 Iriba 15 7N 22 15 E
74 Iringa 7 48S 33 43 E
111 Iriri, R. 3 52S 52 37W
15 Irish Republic ■ 53 0N 8 0 E
11 Irish Sea 54 0N 145 12 E
51 Irkineyeva 58 30N 96 49 E
51 Irkutsk 52 10N 104 20 E
18 Iroise, B. 48 15N 4 45W
100 Iron Mountain 45 49N 88 4W
13 Ironbridge 52 38N 2 29W
98 Ironton 38 35N 82 40W
100 Ironwood 46 30N 90 10W
90 Iroquois Falls 48 40N 80 40W
59 Irrawaddy, R. 15 50N 95 6 E
68 Irshih 47 8N 119 57 E
39 Irsina 40 45N 16 15 E
50 Irtysh, R. 61 4N 68 52 E
74 Irumu 1 32N 29 53 E
32 Irún 43 20N 1 52W
32 Irurzun 42 55N 1 50W
14 Irvine 55 37N 4 40W
15 Irvinestown 54 28N 7 38W
83 Irwin, Pt. 35 4S 116 56 E
84 Irymple 34 14S 142 8 E
60 Isa Khel 32 42N 71 16 E
46 Ísafjördur 66 5N 23 9W
66 Isahaya 32 50N 130 3 E
41 Işalnita 44 24N 23 44 E
74 Isangi 0 52N 24 10 E
25 Isar, R. 48 49N 12 58 E
37 Isarco, R. 46 27N 11 18 E
43 Isari 37 22N 22 0 E
19 Isbergues 50 36N 2 24 E
38 Íschia, I. 40 45N 13 51 E
55 Iscia Baidoa 3 40N 43 0 E
66 Ise 34 29N 136 42 E
66 Ise-Wan, G. 34 45N 136 45 E
45 Isefjord 55 53N 11 50 E
36 Iseo, L. d' 45 43N 10 4 E
21 Isère, R. 44 59N 4 51 E
21 Isère □ 45 10N 5 50 E
24 Iserlohn 51 22N 7 40 E
39 Isérnia 41 35N 14 12 E
69 Ishan 24 30N 108 41 E
66 Ishikari-Wan 43 20N 141 20 E
66 Ishikawa □ 36 30N 136 30 E
50 Ishim, R. 57 45N 71 10 E
66 Ishinomaki 38 32N 141 20 E
58 Ishkuman 36 40N 73 50 E
100 Ishpeming 46 30N 87 40W
74 Isiro 2 53N 27 58 E
80 Isisford 24 15S 144 21 E
56 Iskenderun 36 32N 36 10 E
41 Iskŭr, R. 43 44N 24 27 E
41 Iskŭr, Yazovir 42 30N 23 29 E
14 Isla, R. 56 30N 3 25W
31 Isla Cristina 37 13N 7 17W
58 Islamabad 33 40N 73 0 E
62 Islampur 17 2N 72 9 E
83 Island, Pt. 30 20S 115 2 E
93 Island L. 53 40N 94 30W
90 Island Falls 49 35N 81 20W
91 Islands, B. of 49 11N 58 15W
112 Islas Malvinas= Falkland Is. 51 30S 59 0W
14 Islay, I. 55 46N 6 10W
20 Isle, R. 44 55N 0 15W
12 Isle of Man □ 54 15N 4 30W
13 Isle of Wight □ 36 54N 76 43W
73 Ismâ'ilîya 30 37N 32 18 E
73 Isna 25 17N 32 30 E
38 Isola del Liri 41 39N 13 32 E
56 Isparta 37 47N 30 30 E
41 Isperikh 43 43N 26 50 E
39 Ispica 36 47N 14 53 E
54 Israel ■ 32 0N 34 50 E
83 Isseka 28 22S 114 35 E
20 Issoire 45 32N 3 15 E
20 Issoudun 46 57N 2 0 E
19 Is-sur-Tille 47 30N 5 10 E
50 Issyk Kul, L. 42 30N 77 30 E
56 Istanbul 41 0N 29 0 E
43 Istíaía 38 57N 23 10 E
37 Istra, Pen. 45 10N 14 0 E
108 Itá 25 29S 57 21W
111 Itabira 19 29S 43 23W
111 Itabuna 1448 E 39 16W
111 Itacaré 14 18S 39 0W
111 Itaeté 13 0S 41 5W
111 Itaituba 4 10S 55 50W
109 Itajaí 27 0S 48 45W
109 Itajubá 22 24S 45 30W
37 Italy ■ 42 0N 13 0 E
111 Itapecuru-Mirim 3 20S 44 15W
111 Itaperaba 12 32S 40 18W
109 Itaperuna 21 10S 42 0W
109 Itapetininga 23 36S 48 7W
109 Itapeva 23 59S 48 59W
109 Itaporanga 23 42S 49 29W
109 Itapuá □ 26 40S 55 40W
109 Itaquari 20 12S 40 25W
110 Itaquatiana 2 58S 58 30W
108 Itaqúi 29 0S 56 30W
109 Itararé 24 6S 49 23W
60 Itarsi 22 36N 77 51 E
97 Ithaca 42 25N 76 30W
43 Itháki, I. 38 25N 20 40 E
66 Ito 34 58N 139 5 E
18 Iton, R. 49 9N 1 12 E
109 Itu 23 10S 47 15W
111 Ituiutaba 19 0S 49 25W
68 Ituliho 50 40N 121 30 E
111 Itumbiara 18 20S 49 10W
93 Ituna 51 10N 103 30W
24 Itzehoe 53 56N 9 31 E
46 Ivalo 68 38N 27 35 E
40 Ivangrad 42 51N 19 50 E
84 Ivanhoe 32 56S 144 20 E
49 Ivano-Frankovsk 49 0N 24 40 E
48 Ivanovo 49 0N 24 40 E
41 Ivaylovgrad 41 32N 26 8 E
72 Ivory Coast ■ 7 30N 5 0 E
45 Ivösjön, L. 56 8N 14 25 E
36 Ivrea 45 30N 7 52 E
89 Ivugivik 62 18N 77 50W
66 Iwaki 37 3N 140 55 E
66 Iwakuni 34 15N 132 8 E
66 Iwata 34 49N 137 59 E
66 Iwate □ 39 30N 141 30 E
72 Iwo 7 39N 4 9 E
104 Ixtepec 16 40N 95 10W
104 Ixtlán 21 5N 104 28W
104 Izamal 20 56N 89 1W
28 Izbica Kujawski 52 25N 18 30 E
16 Izegem 50 55N 3 12 E
48 Izhevsk 56 50N 53 0 E
56 Izmir 38 25N 27 8 E
56 Izmit 40 45N 29 50 E
31 Iznalloz 37 24N 3 30W
54 Izra 32 51N 36 15 E
41 Iztochni Rodopi 41 40N 25 30 E
66 Izumi-sano 34 40N 135 43 E
66 Izumo 35 20N 132 55 E

J

54 Jaba 32 20N 35 13 E
54 Jabalíya 31 32N 34 27 E
31 Jabalón, R. 38 53N 3 35W
61 Jabalpur 23 9N 79 58 E
56 Jablah 35 20N 36 0 E
26 Jablonec 50 43N 15 10 E
28 Jabłonowo 53 23N 19 10 E
109 Jaboticabal 21 15S 48 17W
32 Jaca 42 35N 0 33W
109 Jacareí 23 20S 46 0W
109 Jacarèzinho 23 5S 50 0W
81 Jackson, Australia 26 40S 149 30 E
98 Jackson, Ky. 37 35N 83 22W
98 Jackson, Mich. 42 18N 84 25W
101 Jackson, Minn. 43 35N 95 30W
99 Jackson, Tenn. 35 40N 88 50W
92 Jackson Bay 50 32N 125 57W
85 Jacksons 42 46N 171 32 E
99 Jacksonville, Fla. 30 15N 81 38W
100 Jacksonville, Ill. 39 42N 90 15W
99 Jacksonville, N.C. 34 50N 77 29W
101 Jacksonville, Tex. 31 58N 95 12W
99 Jacksonville Beach 30 19N 81 26W
105 Jacmel 18 20N 72 40W
60 Jacobabad 28 20N 68 29 E
111 Jacobina 11 11S 40 30W
54 Jacob's Well 32 13N 35 13 E
91 Jacques Cartier, Mt. 48 57N 66 0W
91 Jacques Cartier Pass. 49 50N 62 30W
25 Jade-Busen 53 30N 8 15 E
30 Jadraque 40 55N 2 55W
31 Jaén 37 44N 3 43W
33 Jaén □ 37 50N 3 30W
54 Jaffa=Tel Aviv-Yafo 32 4N 34 48 E
62 Jaffna 9 45N 80 2 E
62 Jaffna Lagoon 9 35N 80 15 E
60 Jagadhri 30 10N 77 20 E
62 Jagdalpur 19 3N 82 6 E
75 Jagersfontein 29 44S 25 27 E
73 Jaghbub 29 42N 24 38 E
60 Jagraon 30 50N 75 25 E
62 Jagtial 18 50N 79 0 E
109 Jaguarão 32 30S 53 30W

K

Kalmar □ Kepno

45 Kalmar □ .... 57 25N 16 15 E
49 Kalmyk A.S.S.R. □ 46 5N 46 1 E
50 Kalmykovo .... 49 0N 51 35 E
61 Kalna .... 23 13N 88 25 E
27 Kalocsa .... 46 32N 19 0 E
41 Kalofer .... 42 37N 24 59 E
60 Kalol .... 23 15N 72 33 E
75 Kalomo .... 17 0S 26 30 E
43 Kalonerón .... 37 20N 21 38 E
61 Kalpi .... 26 8N 79 47 E
88 Kaltag 64 20N 158 44W
48 Kaluga .... 54 35N 36 10 E
62 Kalutara .... 6 35N 80 0 E
62 Kalyan .... 20 30N 74 3 E
62 Kalyani .... 17 53N 76 59 E
48 Kama, R. .... 55 45N 52 0 E
66 Kamaishi .... 39 20N 142 0 E
60 Kamalia .... 30 44N 72 42 E
55 Kamaran, I. ...... 15 28N 42 35 E
83 Kambalda .... 31 10S 121 37 E
62 Kambam .... 9 45N 77 16 E
48 Kambarka .... 56 17N 54 12 E
51 Kamchatka Pol. ... 57 0N 160 0 E
50 Kamen .... 53 50N 81 30 E
49 Kamenets
Podolskiy .... 48 40N 26 30 E
40 Kamenica .... 44 25N 19 40 E
37 Kamenjak, Rt. .... 44 46N 13 55 E
48 Kamenka .... 65 58N 44 0 E
41 Kameno .... 42 35N 27 18 E
49 Kamensk
Shakhtinskiy .... 48 23N 40 20 E
50 Kamensk
Uralskiy .... 56 28N 61 54 E
51 Kamenskoye ...... 62 45N 165 30 E
41 Kamenyak .... 43 24N 26 57 E
24 Kamenz .... 51 17N 14 7 E
66 Kameoka .... 35 0N 135 35 E
26 Kamienna Góra ... 50 48N 16 2 E
74 Kamina .... 8 45S 25 0 E
92 Kamloops 50 40N 120 20W
26 Kamp, R. .... 48 35N 15 26 E
74 Kampala .... 0 20N 32 30 E
63 Kampar .... 4 18N 101 9 E
16 Kampen .... 52 33N 5 53 E
63 Kampong Chhnang 12 15N 104 20 E
63 Kampot .... 10 36N 104 10 E
60 Kamptee .... 21 9N 79 19 E
93 Kamsack 51 35N 101 50W
48 Kamskoye Vdkhr. . 58 0N 56 0 E
49 Kamyshin .... 50 10N 45 30 E
69 Kan Kiang, R. ..... 29 45N 116 10 E
103 Kanab 27 3N 112 29W
62 Kanakapura ...... 12 33N 77 28 E
42 Kanália .... 39 30N 22 53 E
74 Kananga .... 5 55S 22 18 E
48 Kanash .... 55 48N 47 32 E
42 Kanastraíon,
Akra .... 39 54N 23 40 E
66 Kanazawa .... 36 30N 136 38 E
63 Kanchanaburi ..... 14 8N 99 31 E
61 Kanchenjunga,
Mt. .... 27 50N 88 10 E
62 Kanchipuram ..... 12 52N 79 45 E
69 Kanchow .... 25 51N 114 59 E
68 Kanchwan .... 36 29N 109 24 E
50 Kandagach .... 49 20N 57 15 E
57 Kandahar .... 31 32N 65 30 E
57 Kandahar □ ...... 31 0N 65 0 E
48 Kandalaksha ...... 67 9N 32 30 E
48 Kandalakshskiy
Zaliv .... 66 0N 35 0 E
64 Kandangan .... 2 50S 115 20 E
85 Kandavu, I. .... 19 0S 178 15 E
60 Kandhla .... 29 18N 77 19 E
61 Kandi .... 23 58N 88 5 E
62 Kandukur .... 15 12N 79 57 E
62 Kandy .... 7 18N 80 43 E
96 Kane 41 39N 78 53W
86 Kane Basin 79 0N 70 0W
37 Kanfanar .... 45 7N 13 50 E
81 Kangaroo, I. ...... 35 45S 137 0 E
56 Kangāvar .... 34 40N 48 0 E
68 Kangnŭng .... 37 45N 128 54 E
69 Kangshan .... 22 43N 120 14 E
67 Kangsu □ .... 38 0N 101 40 E
59 Kangto, Mt. ...... 27 50N 92 35 E
62 Kanhangad .... 12 21N 74 58 E
61 Kanhar, R. .... 24 28N 83 9 E
62 Kanheri .... 19 13N 72 50 E
48 Kanin, Pol. .... 68 0N 45 0 E
84 Kaniva .... 36 22S 141 18 E
40 Kanjiža .... 46 3N 20 4 E
98 Kankakee 41 6N 87 50W
98 Kankakee, R. 41 23N 88 16W
72 Kankan 10 30N 9 15W
99 Kannapolis 35 32N 80 37W
61 Kannauj .... 27 3N 79 26 E
72 Kano .... 12 2N 8 30 E
66 Kanoya .... 31 23N 130 51 E
59 Kanpetlet .... 21 10N 93 59 E
61 Kanpur .... 26 35N 80 20 E
58 Kanrach .... 25 35N 65 20 E
100 Kansas, R. 39 7N 94 36W
100 Kansas □ 38 40N 98 0W
100 Kansas City,
Kans. 39 0N 94 40W
100 Kansas City, Mo. .. 39 3N 94 30W
51 Kansk .... 56 20N 96 37 E
66 Kantō □ .... 36 0N 120 0 E
67 Kantse .... 31 30N 100 29 E
15 Kanturk 52 10N 8 55W
66 Kanuma .... 36 44N 139 42 E
75 Kanye .... 25 0S 25 28 E
69 Kanyu .... 34 53N 119 9 E
69 Kaohsiung .... 22 35N 120 16 E
72 Kaolack 14 5N 16 8W
68 Kaomi .... 36 25N 119 45 E
68 Kaoping .... 35 48N 112 55 E
69 Kaoyu Hu, L. ..... 32 50N 119 25 E
60 Kapadvanj .... 23 5N 73 0 E
43 Kapéllo, Ákra .... 36 9N 23 3 E
26 Kapfenberg .... 47 26N 15 18 E
75 Kapiri Mposha .... 13 59S 28 43 E
57 Kapisa □ .... 34 45N 69 30 E
26 Kaplice .... 48 42N 14 30 E
27 Kaposvár .... 46 25N 17 47 E
64 Kapuas, R. .... 0 25S 109 24 E
81 Kapunda .... 34 20S 138 56 E
60 Kapurthala .... 31 23N 75 25 E
90 Kapuskasing 49 25N 82 30W
81 Kaputar, Mt. ...... 30 15S 130 10 E
50 Kara .... 69 10N 65 25 E
50 Kara Bogaz Gol,
Zaliv .... 41 0N 53 30 E
50 Kara Kalpak
A.S.S.R. □ ..... 43 0N 59 0 E
50 Kara Sea .... 75 0N 70 0 E
56 Karabük .... 41 12N 32 37 E
50 Karabutak .... 49 59N 60 14 E
60 Karachi .... 24 53N 67 0 E
58 Karachi □ .... 25 30N 67 0 E
62 Karad .... 17 54N 74 10 E
56 Karadeniz
Boğazi .... 41 10N 29 5 E
56 Karadeniz
Dağlari, Mts. ... 41 30N 35 0 E
50 Karaganda .... 49 50N 73 0 E
50 Karagayly .... 49 26N 76 0 E
62 Karaikkudi .... 10 0N 78 45 E
57 Karaj .... 35 4N 51 0 E
50 Karakas .... 48 20N 83 30 E
68 Karakorum, Mts. .. 35 20N 76 0 E
58 Karakoram P. ...... 35 33N 77 46 E
56 Karaköse .... 39 44N 43 3 E
51 Karalon .... 57 5N 115 50 E
64 Karambu .... 3 53S 116 6 E
60 Karanja .... 20 29N 77 31 E
75 Karasburg .... 28 0S 18 44 E
50 Karasino .... 66 50N 86 50 E
46 Karasjok .... 69 27N 25 30 E
50 Karasuk .... 53 44N 78 2 E
50 Karatau .... 43 10N 70 28 E
50 Karatau Ra. .... 44 0N 69 0 E
66 Karatsu .... 33 30N 130 0 E
26 Karawanken,
Mts. .... 46 30N 14 40 E
50 Karazhal .... 48 2N 70 49 E
56 Karbalā .... 32 47N 44 3 E
27 Karcag .... 47 19N 21 1 E
42 Kardhítsa .... 39 23N 21 54 E
42 Kardhítsa □ ...... 39 15N 21 50 E
75 Kareeberge .... 30 50S 22 0 E
48 Karelian
A.S.S.R. □ ..... 65 30N 32 30 E
50 Kargasok .... 59 3N 80 53 E
50 Kargat .... 55 10N 80 15 E
58 Kargil .... 34 32N 76 12 E
48 Kargopol .... 61 30N 38 58 E
75 Kariba L. .... 16 40S 28 25 E
62 Karikal .... 10 59N 79 50 E
73 Karima .... 18 30N 21 40 E
64 Karimata,
Selat, Str. ...... 2 0S 108 20 E
62 Karimnagar .... 18 26N 79 10 E
66 Kariya .... 34 58N 137 1 E
50 Karkaralinsk ...... 49 30N 75 10 E
49 Karkinitskiy
Zaliv .... 45 36N 32 35 E
54 Karkur .... 32 29N 34 57 E
24 Karl-Marx-Stadt .. 50 50N 12 55 E
24 Karl-Marx-
Stadt □ .... 50 45N 13 0 E
37 Karlovac .... 45 31N 15 36 E
26 Karlovy Vary ..... 50 13N 12 51 E
45 Karlshamn .... 56 10N 14 51 E
44 Karlskoga .... 59 22N 14 33 E
45 Karlskrona .... 56 10N 15 35 E
25 Karlsruhe .... 49 3N 8 23 E
44 Karlstad .... 59 23N 13 30 E
88 Karluk 57 30N 155 0W
60 Karnal .... 29 42N 77 2 E
59 Karnaphuli Res. ... 22 40N 92 20 E
62 Karnataka □ ...... 13 15N 77 0 E
26 Karnische Alpen,
Mts. .... 46 36N 13 0 E
26 Kärnten □ .... 46 52N 13 30 E
74 Karonga .... 9 57S 33 55 E
81 Karoonda .... 35 1S 139 59 E
43 Kárpathos, I. ..... 35 37N 27 10 E
48 Karpogory .... 63 59N 44 27 E
56 Kars .... 40 40N 43 5 E
50 Karsakpay .... 47 55N 66 40 E
50 Karshi .... 38 53N 65 48 E
42 Karstal Óros ...... 41 15N 25 13 E
50 Kartaly .... 53 3N 60 40 E
74 Karungu .... 0 50S 34 10 E
62 Karur .... 10 59N 78 2 E
27 Karviná .... 49 53N 18 25 E
60 Karwan, R. .... 27 17N 78 5 E
61 Karwi .... 25 12N 80 57 E
63 Kas Kong .... 11 27N 102 12 E
74 Kasai, R. .... 3 2S 16 57 E
74 Kasama .... 10 16S 31 9 E
74 Kasangulu .... 4 15S 15 15 E
62 Kasaragod .... 12 30N 74 58 E
60 Kasganj .... 27 48N 78 42 E
57 Kāshān .... 34 5N 51 30 E
67 Kashgar .... 39 46N 75 52 E
69 Kashing .... 30 45N 120 41 E
60 Kashipur .... 29 15N 79 0 E
53 Kashmir □ .... 34 0N 78 0 E
48 Kasimov .... 54 55N 41 20 E
92 Kaslo 49 55N 117 0W
74 Kasongo .... 4 30S 26 33 E
43 Kásos, I. .... 35 20N 26 55 E
73 Kassala .... 15 23N 36 26 E
73 Kassalâ □ .... 15 20N 36 26 E
42 Kassándra, Pen. ... 40 0N 23 30 E
24 Kassel .... 51 19N 9 32 E
65 Kassue .... 6 58S 139 21 E
56 Kastamonu .... 41 25N 33 43 E
43 Kastélli .... 35 29N 23 38 E
42 Kastoría .... 40 30N 21 19 E
42 Kastoría □ .... 40 30N 21 15 E
42 Kástron .... 39 53N 25 8 E
60 Kasur .... 31 5N 74 25 E
51 Kata .... 58 46N 102 40 E
74 Katako Kombe .... 3 25S 24 20 E
83 Katanning .... 33 40S 117 33 E
42 Kateríni .... 40 18N 22 37 E
59 Katha .... 24 10N 96 30 E
82 Katherine .... 14 27S 132 20 E
60 Kathiawar, Reg. ... 22 0N 71 0 E
64 Katiet .... 2 21S 99 14 E
61 Katihar .... 25 34N 87 36 E
75 Katima Mulilo .... 17 28S 24 13 E
88 Katmai Mt. 58 20N 154 59W
61 Katmandu .... 27 45N 85 12 E
43 Kato Akhaia ...... 38 8N 21 33 E
42 Kato Stavros ...... 40 39N 23 43 E
60 Katol .... 21 17N 78 38 E
75 Katombora .... 18 0S 25 30 E
74 Katompi .... 6 2S 26 23 E
84 Katoomba .... 33 41S 150 19 E
27 Katowice .... 50 17N 19 5 E
27 Katowice □ .... 50 30N 19 0 E
14 Katrine, L. .... 56 15N 4 30 E
44 Katrineholm ...... 59 9N 16 12 E
72 Katsina .... 7 10N 9 20 E
57 Kattawaz
Urgan □ .... 32 10N 62 20 E
45 Kattegat, Str. ..... 57 0N 11 20 E
61 Katwa .... 23 30N 89 25 E
16 Katwijk-aan-Zee .. 52 12N 4 22 E
94 Kauai, I. 19 30N 155 30W
25 Kaufbeuren .... 47 42N 10 37 E
46 Kaukonen .... 67 42N 24 58 E
48 Kaunas .... 54 54N 23 54 E
72 Kaura Namoda .... 12 37N 6 33 E
46 Kautokeino .... 69 0N 23 4 E
51 Kavacha .... 60 16N 169 51 E
40 Kavadarci .... 41 26N 22 3 E
62 Kavali .... 14 55N 80 1 E
42 Kaválla .... 40 57N 24 28 E
42 Kavála □ .... 41 5N 24 30 E
42 Kavállas, Kól. ..... 40 50N 24 25 E
41 Kavarna .... 43 26N 28 22 E
111 Kaw 4 30N 52 15W
66 Kawagoe .... 35 55N 139 29 E
66 Kawaguchi .... 35 52N 138 45 E
94 Kawaihae 20 5N 155 50W
74 Kawambwa .... 9 48S 29 3 E
66 Kawanoe .... 34 1N 133 34 E
61 Kawardha .... 22 0N 81 17 E
66 Kawasaki .... 35 35N 138 42 E
90 Kawene 48 45N 91 15W
85 Kawerau .... 38 7S 176 42 E
85 Kawhia
Harbour .... 38 4S 174 49 E
59 Kawnro .... 22 48N 99 8 E
63 Kawthaung .... 10 5N 98 36 E
59 Kawthoolei □ ..... 18 0N 97 30 E
59 Kayah □ .... 19 15N 97 15 E
62 Kayangulam ...... 9 10N 76 33 E
103 Kayenta .... 36 46N 110 15 E
72 Kayes 14 25N 11 30W
81 Kayrunnera .... 30 40S 142 30 E
56 Kayseri .... 38 45N 35 30 E
64 Kayuagung .... 3 28S 104 46 E
51 Kazachye .... 70 52N 135 58 E
50 Kazakh S.S.R. □ .. 50 0N 58 0 E
48 Kazan .... 55 48N 49 3 E
41 Kazanlŭk .... 42 38N 25 35 E
49 Kazbek, Mt. ...... 42 30N 44 30 E
57 Kāzerūn .... 29 38N 51 40 E
27 Kazincbarcika ..... 48 17N 20 36 E
50 Kazym, R. .... 63 54N 65 50 E
28 Kcynia .... 53 0N 17 30 E
43 Kéa, I. .... 37 30N 24 22 E
100 Kearney 40 45N 99 3W
46 Kebnekaise, Mt. ... 67 48N 18 30 E
55 Kebri Dehar 6 45N 44 17W
65 Kebumen .... 7 42S 109 40 E
27 Kecel .... 46 31N 19 16 E
27 Kecskemet .... 46 57N 19 35 E
63 Kedah □ .... 5 50N 100 40 E
91 Kedgwick 47 40N 67 20W
65 Kediri .... 7 51S 112 1 E
27 Kedzierzyn .... 50 20N 18 12 E
3 Keeling Is.=
Cocos Is. .... 12 12S 96 54 E
69 Keelung=Chilung . 25 3N 121 45 E
97 Keene 42 57N 72 17W
75 Keetmanshoop .... 26 35S 18 8 E
93 Keewatin 47 23N 93 0W
88 Keewatin, Reg. ... 63 20N 94 40W
43 Kefallinía, I. ...... 38 28N 20 30 E
65 Kefamenanu ...... 9 28S 124 38 E
54 Kefar Gil'adi ..... 33 14N 35 35 E
54 Kefar Sava .... 32 11N 34 54 E
54 Kefar Szold ...... 33 11N 35 34 E
54 Kefar Tavor ...... 32 42N 35 24 E
54 Kefar Vitkin ...... 32 22N 34 53 E
54 Kefar Yona .... 32 20N 34 54 E
54 Kefar Zetim ...... 32 49N 35 27 E
72 Keffi .... 8 55N 7 43 E
46 Keflavik 64 2N 22 35W
25 Kehl .... 48 34N 7 50 E
12 Keighley 53 52N 1 54W
81 Keith, Australia ... 36 0S 140 20 E
14 Keith, U.K. 57 33N 2 58W
88 Keith Arm, B. 65 30N 122 0W
60 Kekri .... 26 0N 75 10 E
51 Kël .... 69 30N 124 10 E
63 Kelang .... 3 2N 101 26 E
63 Kelantan, R. ...... 6 11N 102 16 E
63 Kelantan □ .... 5 10N 102 0 E
73 Kelibia .... 36 50N 11 3 E
83 Kellerberrin ...... 31 36S 117 38 E
102 Kellogg 47 30N 116 5W
15 Kells=Ceanannas
Mor 53 42N 6 53W
92 Kelowna 49 50N 119 25W
92 Kelsey Bay 50 25N 126 0W
85 Kelso, N.Z. .... 45 54S 169 15 E
14 Kelso, U.K. 55 36N 2 27W
102 Kelso, U.S.A. 46 10N 122 57W
63 Keluang .... 2 3N 103 18 E
93 Kelvington 52 20N 103 30W
48 Kem .... 65 0N 34 38 E
48 Kem, R. .... 64 57N 34 41 E
50 Kemerovo .... 55 20N 85 50 E
46 Kemi .... 65 47N 24 32 E
46 Kemijärvi .... 66 43N 27 22 E
46 Kemijoki, R. ...... 65 47N 24 30 E
102 Kemmerer 41 52N 110 30W
81 Kempsey .... 31 1S 152 50 E
25 Kempten .... 47 42N 10 18 E
90 Kemptville 45 0N 75 38W
61 Ken, R.,
India 25 46N 80 31W
14 Ken, R., U.K. 54 50N 4 4W
65 Kendal, Indonesia . 6 56S 110 14 E
12 Kendal, U.K. 54 19N 2 44W
65 Kendari .... 3 50S 122 30 E
83 Kendenup .... 34 30S 117 38 E
88 Kendi 60 30N 151 0W
61 Kendrapara .... 20 35N 86 30 E
72 Kenema 7 50N 11 14W
59 Keng Tawng ...... 20 45N 98 18 E
59 Keng Tung .... 21 0N 99 30 E
68 Kenho .... 50 43N 121 30 E
72 Kenitra 34 15N 6 40W
15 Kenmare 51 52N 9 35W
99 Kennedy, C.=
Canaveral, C. ... 28 28N 80 31W
13 Kennet, R. 51 28N 0 57W
101 Kennett 36 7N 90 0W
102 Kennewick 46 11N 119 2W
88 Keno Hill 63 57N 135 25W
93 Kenora 49 50N 94 35W
98 Kenosha 42 33N 87 48W
91 Kensington 46 25N 63 34W
96 Kent 41 8N 81 20W
13 Kent □ .... 51 12N 0 40 E
88 Kent Pen. 68 30N 107 0W
50 Kentau .... 43 32N 68 36 E
98 Kenton 40 40N 83 35W
98 Kentucky, R. 38 41N 85 11W
98 Kentucky □ 37 20N 85 0W
91 Kentville 45 6N 64 29W
74 Kenya ■ .... 2 20N 38 0 E
74 Kenya, Mt. .... 0 10S 37 18 E
100 Keokuk 40 25N 91 30W
28 Kepno .... 51 18N 17 58 E

Kerala □ Knoxville, Tenn.

62 Kerala □ 11 0N 76 15 E
84 Kerang 35 40 S 143 55 E
57 Keray 26 15N 57 30 E
49 Kerch 45 20N 36 20 E
54 Kerem Maharal 32 39N 34 59 E
76 Kerguelan, I. 48 15 S 69 10 E
74 Kericho 0 22 S 35 15 E
64 Kerinci, Mt. 2 5 S 101 0 E
73 Kerkenna, Is. 34 48N 11 1 E
50 Kerki 37 10N 65 0 E
42 Kerkintis, L. 41 12N 23 10 E
42 Kérkira 39 38N 19 50 E
42 Kérkira, I. 39 35N 19 45 E
16 Kerkrade 50 53N 6 4 E
76 Kermadec Is. 31 8 S 175 16W
57 Kermān 30 15N 57 1 E
57 Kermān □ 30 0N 57 0 E
56 Kermānshāh 34 23N 47 0 E
56 Kermānshāh □ 34 0N 46 30 E
101 Kermit 31 56N 103 3W
93 Kerrobert 52 0N 109 11W
101 Kerrville 30 1N 99 8W
15 Kerry □ 52 7N 9 35W
15 Kerry Hd. 52 26N 9 56W
68 Kerulen, R. 48 48N 117 0 E
72 Kerzaz 29 29N 1 25W
46 Keski-Suomen □ 63 0N 25 0 E
12 Keswick 54 35N 3 9W
27 Keszthely 46 50N 17 15W
72 Keta 5 49N 1 0 E
64 Ketapang 1 55 S 110 0 E
92 Ketchikan 55 25N 131 40W
28 Kętrzyn 54 7N 21 22 E
13 Kettering 52 24N 0 44W
102 Kettle Falls 48 41N 118 2W
100 Kewanee 41 18N 90 0W
100 Keweenaw B. 47 0N 88 0W
100 Keweenaw Pt. 47 26N 87 40W
97 Keyport 40 26N 74 12W
98 Keyser 39 26N 79 0W
51 Kezhma 59 15N 100 57 E
50 Khabarovo 69 30N 60 30 E
51 Khaborovsk 48 20N 135 0 E
60 Khachraud 23 25N 75 20 E
61 Khagaria 25 18N 86 32 E
61 Khairabad 27 33N 80 47 E
60 Khairpur □ 23 30N 69 8 E
57 Khalij-e Fars 28 20N 51 45 E
42 Khálki 39 26N 22 30 E
42 Khalkidhikí □ 40 25N 23 20 E
43 Khalkís 38 27N 23 42 E
48 Khalmer Yu 67 58N 65 1 E
48 Khalturin 58 40N 48 50 E
61 Khamaria 23 10N 80 52 E
60 Khambhalia 22 14N 69 41 E
60 Khamgaon 20 42N 76 37 E
55 Khamir 16 10N 43 45 E
62 Khammam 17 11N 80 6 E
67 Khan Tengri, Mt. 42 25N 80 10 E
54 Khān Yūnis 31 21N 34 18 E
57 Khanabad 36 45N 69 5 E
56 Khānaqin 34 23N 45 25 E
60 Khandwa 21 49N 76 22 E
51 Khandyga 62 30N 134 50 E
60 Khanewal 30 20N 71 55 E
43 Khaniá 35 30N 24 4 E
43 Khaniá □ 35 0N 24 0 E
43 Khaníon, Kól. 35 33N 23 55 E
51 Khanka, Oz. 45 0N 132 30 E
60 Khanna 30 42N 76 16 E
60 Khanpur 28 42N 70 35 E
50 Khanty-Mansiysk 61 0N 69 0 E
51 Khapcheranga 49 40N 112 0 E
61 Kharagpur 22 20N 87 25 E
62 Kharda 18 40N 75 40 E
56 Kharfa 22 0N 46 35 E
60 Khargon 21 45N 75 40 E
49 Kharkov 49 58N 36 20 E
41 Kharmanli 41 55N 25 55 E
48 Kharovsk 59 56N 40 13 E
56 Kharsaniya 27 10N 49 10 E
73 Khartoum=El Khartûm 15 31N 32 35 E
57 Khasab 26 14N 56 15 E
57 Khāsh 28 15N 61 5 E
73 Khashm el Girba 14 59N 35 58 E
61 Khasi Hills 25 30N 91 30 E
41 Khaskovo 41 56N 25 30 E
51 Khatanga 72 0N 102 20 E
73 Khatanga, R. 73 30N 109 0 E
60 Khatauli 29 14N 77 43 E
56 Khavari □ 37 20N 46 0 E
62 Khed 18 51N 73 56 E
60 Khekra 28 52N 77 20 E
72 Khemis Miliana 36 11N 2 14 E
72 Khenchela 35 28N 7 11 E
72 Khenifra 32 58N 5 46W
49 Kherson 46 35N 32 35 E
43 Khersónisos Akrotíri 35 30N 24 10 E
67 Khetinsiring 32 54N 92 50 E
43 Khiliomódhion 37 48N 22 51 E
51 Khilok 51 30N 110 45 E
43 Khíos 38 27N 26 9 E
43 Khíos, I. 38 20N 26 0 E
50 Khiva 41 30N 60 18 E
41 Khlebarovo 43 38N 26 17 E
49 Khmelnitisky 49 23N 27 0 E
63 Khmer Rep.■=Cambodia ■ 12 15N 105 0 E
60 Khojak P. 30 55N 66 30 E
48 Kholm 57 10N 31 15 E
51 Kholmsk 35 5N 139 48 E
63 Khon Kaen 16 30N 102 47 E
63 Khong, R. 14 7N 105 51 E
51 Khonu 66 30N 143 25 E
48 Khoper, R. 52 0N 43 20 E
43 Khóra Sfakion 35 15N 24 9 E
57 Khorasan □ 34 0N 58 0 E
63 Khorat, Cao Nguyen 15 30N 102 50 E
63 Khorat=Nakhon Ratchasima 14 59N 102 12 E
50 Khorog 37 30N 71 36 E
56 Khorramābād 33 30N 48 25 E
56 Khorromshahr 30 29N 48 15 E
72 Khouribga 32 58N 6 50W
57 Khugiani 31 28N 66 14 E
61 Khulna 22 45N 89 34 E
61 Khulna □ 22 45N 89 35 E
60 Khurai 24 3N 78 23 E
60 Khurja 28 15N 77 58 E
60 Khushab 32 20N 72 20 E
56 Khuzestan □ 31 0N 50 0 E
57 Khvor 33 45N 55 0 E
57 Khvormūj 28 40N 51 30 E
56 Khvoy 38 35N 45 0 E
57 Khyber P. 34 10N 71 8 E
69 Kialing Kiang, R. 30 2N 106 18 E
84 Kiama 34 40 S 150 50 E
84 Kiamal 34 58 S 142 18 E
68 Kiamusze 46 45N 130 30 E
69 Kian 27 1N 114 58 E
69 Kiangling 30 28N 113 16 E
69 Kiangsi □ 27 45N 115 0 E
69 Kiangsu □ 33 0N 119 50 E
69 Kiangyin 31 51N 120 0 E
68 Kiaohsien 36 20N 120 0 E
43 Kiáton 38 1N 22 44 E
74 Kibombo 3 57 S 25 53 E
74 Kibwezi 2 27 S 37 57 E
40 Kičevo 41 34N 20 59 E
51 Kichiga 59 50N 163 5 E
92 Kicking Horse P. 51 27N 116 25W
13 Kidderminster 52 24N 2 13W
24 Kiel 54 16N 10 8 E
24 Kiel Canal=Nord Ostsee Kanal 54 15N 9 40 E
27 Kielce 50 58N 20 42 E
27 Kielce □ 50 40N 20 40 E
69 Kienko 31 50N 105 30 E
69 Kienow 27 0N 118 16 E
67 Kienshui 23 57N 102 45 E
69 Kiensi 26 58N 106 0 E
69 Kienteh 29 30N 119 28 E
69 Kienyang 27 30N 118 0 E
49 Kiev=Kiyev 50 30N 30 28 E
72 Kiffa 16 50N 11 15W
43 Kifisiá 38 4N 23 49 E
43 Kifissós, R. 38 6N 23 45 E
74 Kigali 1 5 S 30 4 E
74 Kigoma-Ujiji 5 30 S 30 0 E
66 Kii-Suido, Chan. 33 0N 134 50 E
69 Kikiang 28 58N 106 44 E
40 Kikinda 45 50N 20 30 E
43 Kikládhes, Is. 37 20N 24 30 E
44 Kil 59 30N 13 20 E
62 Kilakarai 9 12N 78 47 E
81 Kilcoy 26 59 S 152 30 E
15 Kildare 53 10N 6 50W
15 Kildare □ 53 10N 6 50W
74 Kilembe 0 15N 30 3 E
101 Kilgore 32 22N 94 40W
74 Kilimanjaro 3 7 S 37 20 E
74 Kilindini 4 4 S 39 40 E
56 Kilis 36 50N 37 10 E
15 Kilkee 52 41N 9 40W
15 Kilkenny 52 40N 7 17W
15 Kilkenny □ 52 35N 7 15W
42 Kilkís 40 58N 22 57 E
15 Killala 54 13N 9 12W
15 Killaloe 52 48N 8 28W
93 Killarney, Canada 49 10N 99 40W
15 Killarney, Eire 52 2N 9 30W
15 Killary Harbour 53 38N 9 52W
14 Killiecrankie, P. of 56 44N 3 46W
14 Killin 56 27N 4 20W
43 Killíni, Mt. 37 54N 22 25 E
15 Killybegs 54 38N 8 26W
84 Kilmany 38 8 S 146 55 E
14 Kilmarnock 55 36N 4 30W
84 Kilmore 37 25 S 144 53 E
74 Kilosa 6 48 S 37 0 E
15 Kilrush 52 39N 9 30W
74 Kilwa Kivinje 8 45 S 39 25 E
81 Kimba 33 8 S 136 23 E
100 Kimball 41 17N 103 20W
93 Kimberley, Canada 49 40N 116 10W
75 Kimberley, S. Africa 28 43 S 24 46 E
82 Kimberley Downs 17 24 S 124 22 E
102 Kimberly 42 33N 114 25W
68 Kimchaek 40 41N 129 12 E
68 Kimchon 36 11N 128 4 E
48 Kimry 56 55N 37 15 E
64 Kinabalu, Mt. 6 0N 116 0 E
93 Kincaid 49 40N 107 0W
90 Kincardine 44 10N 81 40W
93 Kindersley 51 30N 109 10W
72 Kindia 10 0N 12 52W
74 Kindu 2 55 S 25 50 E
48 Kineshma 57 30N 42 5 E
80 King, I. 39 50 S 144 0 E
80 King, Mt. 25 10 S 147 31 E
82 King Edward, R. 14 14 S 126 35 E
112 King George B. 51 30 S 60 30W
89 King George Is. 53 40N 80 30W
82 King Leopold, Ras. 17 20 S 124 20 E
82 King Sd. 16 50 S 123 20 E
88 King William I. 69 0N 98 0W
75 King William's Town 32 51 S 27 22 E
81 Kingaroy 26 32 S 151 51 E
67 Kingku 23 49N 100 30 E
103 Kingman 35 12N 114 2W
81 Kingoonya 30 54N 135 18 E
68 Kingpeng 43 30N 117 25 E
103 Kings Canyon Nat. Park 37 0N 118 45W
12 Kings Lynn 52 45N 0 25 E
97 Kings Park 40 53N 73 16 E
13 Kingsbridge 50 14N 3 46W
15 Kingscourt 53 55N 6 48W
90 Kingston, Canada 44 20N 76 30W
105 Kingston, Jamaica 18 0N 76 50W
85 Kingston, N.Z. 45 20 S 168 43 E
97 Kingston, N.Y. 41 55N 74 0W
97 Kingston, Pa. 41 19N 75 58W
97 Kingston, R.I. 41 29N 71 30W
81 Kingston South East 36 52 S 139 51 E
105 Kingstown 13 10N 61 10W
90 Kingsville, Canada 42 3N 82 45W
101 Kingsville, U.S.A. 27 30N 97 53W
68 Kingtai 37 4N 103 59 E
69 Kingtehchen 29 8N 117 21 E
69 Kingtzekwan 33 25N 111 10 E
14 Kingussie 47 5N 4 2W
68 Kinhsien 36 6N 107 49 E
69 Kinhwa 29 5N 119 32 E
93 Kinistino 52 59N 105 0W
74 Kinkala 4 18 S 14 49 E
66 Kinki □ 33 30N 136 0 E
85 Kinleith 38 20 S 175 56 E
85 Kinloch 44 51 S 168 20 E
69 Kinmen, I. 24 25N 118 24 E
45 Kinna 57 32N 12 42 E
54 Kinneret 32 44N 35 34 E
54 Kinneret, Yam, L. 32 49N 35 36 E
14 Kinross 56 13N 3 25W
15 Kinsale 51 42N 8 31W
15 Kinsale, Old Hd. 51 37N 8 32W
67 Kinsha, R. 32 30N 98 0 E
74 Kinshasa 4 20 S 15 15 E
69 Kinsiang 35 4N 116 25 E
99 Kinston 35 18N 77 35W
14 Kintyre, Pen. 55 30N 5 35W
69 Kioshan 32 50N 114 0 E
43 Kiparissía 37 15N 21 40 E
43 Kiparissiakós Kól. 37 25N 21 25 E
90 Kipawa Reserve Prov. Park 47 0N 78 30W
60 Kiratpur 29 32N 78 12 E
25 Kirchheim 48 38N 9 20 E
51 Kirensk 57 50N 107 55 E
50 Kirgiz S.S.R. □ 42 0N 75 0 E
56 Kirikkale 39 51N 33 32 E
48 Kirillov 59 51N 38 14 E
68 Kirin 43 58N 126 31 E
68 Kirin □ 43 45N 125 20 E
14 Kirkcaldy 56 7N 3 10W
14 Kirkcudbright 54 50N 4 3W
62 Kirkee 18 34N 73 56 E
46 Kirkenes 69 40N 30 5 E
14 Kirkintilloch 55 57N 4 10W
90 Kirkland Lake 48 15N 80 0W
100 Kirksville 40 8N 92 35W
56 Kirkūk 35 30N 44 21 E
14 Kirkwall 58 59N 2 59W
62 Kirlampudi 17 12N 82 12 E
48 Kirov 58 35N 49 40 E
49 Kirovabad 40 45N 46 10 E
49 Kirovakan 41 0N 44 0 E
49 Kirovograd 48 35N 32 20 E
48 Kirovsk 67 48N 33 50 E
51 Kirovskiy 45 51N 48 11 E
14 Kirriemuir 56 41N 3 0W
48 Kirsanov 52 35N 42 40 E
60 Kirthar Ra. 27 0N 67 0 E
46 Kiruna 67 50N 20 20 E
83 Kirup 33 40 S 115 50 E
66 Kiryū 36 25N 139 20 E
45 Kisa 57 58N 15 37 E
43 Kisámou, Kól. 35 30N 23 38 E
74 Kisangani 0 35N 25 15 E
64 Kisaran 2 47N 99 29 E
66 Kisaratzu 35 25N 139 59 E
50 Kiselevsk 54 5N 86 6 E
74 Kisengwa 6 0 S 25 50 E
61 Kishanganj 26 3N 88 14 E
60 Kishangarh 27 50N 70 30 E
49 Kishinev 47 0N 28 50 E
66 Kishiwada 34 28N 135 22 E
54 Kishon 32 33N 35 12 E
61 Kishorganj 24 26N 90 40 E
58 Kishtwar 33 20N 75 48 E
68 Kisi 45 21N 131 0 E
74 Kisii 0 40 S 34 45 E
88 Kiska I. 52 0N 177 30 E
27 Kiskörös 46 37N 19 20 E
27 Kiskundorozsma 46 16N 20 5 E
27 Kiskunfélegyháza 46 42N 19 53 E
27 Kiskunhalas 46 28N 19 37 E
27 Kiskunmajsa 46 30N 19 48 E
49 Kislovodsk 43 50N 42 45 E
66 Kiso-Gawa, R. 35 2N 136 45 E
27 Kispest 47 27N 19 9 E
72 Kissidougou 9 5N 10 0W
62 Kistna, R.=Krishna, R. 15 43N 80 55 E
27 Kisújszállzás 47 12N 20 50 E
74 Kisumu 0 3 S 34 45 E
27 Kisvárda 48 14N 22 4 E
67 Kitai 44 0N 89 27 E
66 Kitaibaraki 36 50N 140 45 E
66 Kitakyūshū 33 50N 130 50 E
74 Kitale 1 0N 35 12 E
83 Kitchener, Australia 30 55 S 124 8 E
96 Kitchener, Canada 43 30N 80 30W
74 Kitega 3 30 S 29 58 E
43 Kíthira 36 9N 23 0 E
43 Kíthnos, I. 37 26N 24 27 E
92 Kitimat 53 55N 129 0W
42 Kitros 40 22N 22 34 E
66 Kitsuki 33 35N 131 37 E
96 Kittanning 40 49N 79 30W
97 Kittatinny Mts. 41 0N 75 0W
97 Kittery 43 7N 70 42W
75 Kitwe 12 54 S 28 7 E
69 Kityang 23 30N 116 29 E
26 Kitzbühel 47 27N 12 24 E
69 Kiukiang 29 37N 116 2 E
69 Kiuling Shan, Mts. 28 40N 115 0 E
69 Kiungchow 19 57N 110 17 E
69 Kiungchow-Haihsia, Str. 20 40N 110 0 E
74 Kivu, L. 1 48 S 29 0 E
69 Kiyang 26 36N 111 42 E
49 Kiyev 50 30N 30 28 E
49 Kiyevskoye, Vdkhr. 51 0N 30 0 E
48 Kizel 59 3N 57 40 E
49 Kizlyar 43 51N 46 40 E
50 Kizyl-Arvat 38 58N 56 15 E
50 Kizyl Kiva 40 20N 72 35 E
40 Kladanj 44 14N 18 42 E
26 Kladno 50 10N 14 7 E
26 Klagenfurt 46 38N 14 20 E
48 Klaipeda 55 43N 21 10 E
102 Klamath Falls 42 20N 121 50W
37 Klanjec 46 3N 15 45 E
65 Klaten 7 43 S 110 36 E
26 Klatovy 49 23N 13 18 E
92 Klawak 55 35N 133 0W
92 Kleena Kleene 52 0N 124 50W
37 Klekovača, Mt. 44 25N 16 32 E
75 Klerksdorp 26 51 S 26 38 E
24 Kleve 51 46N 6 10 E
45 Klippan 56 8N 13 10 E
75 Klipplaat 33 0 S 24 22 E
41 Klisura 42 40N 24 28 E
27 Kłobuck 50 55N 19 5 E
27 Kłodzko 50 28N 16 38 E
88 Klondike 64 0N 139 40W
27 Klosterneuburg 48 18N 16 19 E
88 Kluane, L. 61 25N 138 50W
12 Knaresborough 54 1N 1 29W
41 Knezha 43 30N 23 56 E
13 Knighton 52 21N 3 2W
37 Knin 44 1N 16 17 E
26 Knittelfeld 47 13N 14 51 E
40 Knjaževac 43 35N 22 18 E
16 Knokke 51 20N 3 17 E
100 Knoxville, Iowa 41 20N 93 5W
99 Knoxville, Tenn. 35 58N 83 57W

Liard, R. Loughrea

88 Liard, R. 61 52N 121 18W
101 Liberal 37 4N 101 0W
108 Libertador General San Martin 25 30S 64 45W
26 Liberec 50 47N 15 7E
72 Liberia ■ 6 30N 9 30W
97 Liberty 41 48N 74 45W
73 Lîbîya, Sahrâ', Des. 27 35N 25 0E
20 Libourne 44 55N 0 14W
42 Librazhdi 41 12N 20 22E
74 Libreville 0 25N 9 26E
73 Libya ■ 28 30N 17 30E
38 Licata 37 6N 13 55E
12 Lichfield 52 40N 1 50W
75 Lichinga 13 13S 35 11E
75 Lichtenburg 26 8S 26 8E
25 Lichtenfels 50 7N 11 4E
39 Licosa, Pta. 40 15N 14 53E
44 Lidingo 59 22N 18 8E
45 Lidkoping 58 31N 13 14E
38 Lido di Ostia 45 25N 12 23E
28 Lidzbark Warminski 54 7N 20 34E
82 Liebenwalde 52 51N 13 23E
26 Liechtenstein ■ 47 8N 9 35E
16 Liège 50 38N 5 35E
16 Liège □ 50 32N 5 35E
26 Lienz 46 50N 12 46E
48 Liepaja 56 30N 21 0E
16 Lier 51 7N 4 34E
41 Lieşti 45 38N 27 34E
19 Liévin 45 40N 75 40W
26 Liezen 47 34N 14 15E
15 Liffey, R. 53 21N 6 16W
15 Lifford 54 50N 7 30W
37 Lignano 45 42N 13 8E
19 Ligny-en-Barrois 48 36N 5 20E
36 Ligùria □ 44 30N 9 0E
79 Lihou Reef and Cays 17 25S 151 40E
94 Lihue 21 59N 152 24W
74 Likasi 10 55S 26 48E
67 Likiang 26 50N 100 15E
74 Likati 3 20N 24 0E
21 L'Île Rousse 42 38N 8 53E
69 Liling 27 47N 113 30E
19 Lille 50 38N 3 3E
18 Lillebonne 49 30N 0 32E
44 Lillehammer 61 8N 10 30E
45 Lillerød 55 52N 12 22E
19 Lillers 50 35N 2 28E
47 Lillesand 58 15N 8 23E
44 Lillestrøm 59 58N 11 5E
92 Lillooet 50 42N 121 56W
75 Lilongwe 14 0S 33 48E
40 Lim, R. 43 0N 19 40E
110 Lima, Peru 12 0S 77 0W
102 Lima, Mont. 44 41N 112 38W
98 Lima, Ohio 40 42N 84 5W
30 Lima, R. 41 50N 8 18W
15 Limavady □ 55 0N 6 55W
15 Limavady 55 3N 6 58W
112 Limay, R. 39 0S 68 0W
60 Limbdi 22 34N 71 51E
25 Limburg 50 22N 8 4E
16 Limburg □ 51 20N 5 55E
109 Limeira 22 35S 47 28W
15 Limerick 52 40N 8 38W
15 Limerick □ 52 30N 8 50W
45 Limfjorden 56 55N 9 0E
45 Limmared 57 34N 13 20E
43 Limni 38 43N 23 18E
42 Límnos, I. 39 50N 25 5E
111 Limoeiro do Norte 5 5S 38 0W
111 Limoera 7 52S 35 27W
20 Limoges 45 50N 1 15E
105 Limón 10 0N 83 2W
20 Limousin, Plateaux 46 0N 1 0E
20 Limousin, Reg. 46 0N 1 0E
20 Limoux 43 4N 2 12E
75 Limpopo, R. 25 15S 33 30E
74 Limuru 1 2S 36 35E
108 Linares, Chile 35 50S 71 40W
104 Linares, Mexico 24 50N 99 40W
31 Linares, Sp. 38 10N 3 40W
108 Linares □ 36 0S 71 0W
38 Línas, Mt. 39 25N 8 38E
68 Lincheng 37 26N 114 34E
12 Lincoln □ 53 14N 0 32W
108 Lincoln, Arg. 34 55N 61 30W
85 Lincoln, N.Z. 43 38S 172 30E
12 Lincoln, U.K. 53 14N 0 32W
100 Lincoln, Ill. 40 10N 89 20W
100 Lincoln, Neb. 40 50N 96 42W
4 Lincoln Sea 84 0N 55 0W
12 Lincoln Wolds 53 20N 0 5W
25 Lindau 47 33N 9 41E
45 Linderod 55 56N 13 47E
45 Linderödsåsen, Reg. 55 53N 13 53E
44 Lindesberg 59 36N 15 15E
74 Lindi 9 58S 39 38E
30 Lindoso 41 52N 8 11W
90 Lindsay, Canada 44 22N 78 43W
103 Lindsay, U.S.A. 36 14N 119 6W
68 Linfen 36 5N 111 32E
65 Lingayen 16 1N 120 14E
65 Lingayen G. 16 10N 120 15E
24 Lingen 52 32N 7 21E
64 Lingga, Kep. 0 10E 104 30E
69 Lingling 26 13N 111 37E
69 Linglo 24 20N 105 25E
69 Lingshui 18 27N 110 0E
72 Linguéré 15 25N 15 5W
63 Linh Cam 18 31N 105 31E
69 Linhai 28 51N 121 7E
68 Linho 40 50N 107 30E
69 Lini 35 5N 118 20E
69 Linkao 19 56N 109 42E
68 Linkiang 46 2N 133 56E
45 Linköping 58 28N 15 36E
68 Linkow 45 16N 130 18E
14 Linlithgow 55 58N 3 38W
14 Linnhe, L. 56 36N 5 25W
69 Linping 24 25N 114 32E
109 Lins 21 40S 49 44W
68 Linsi 43 30N 118 5E
67 Linsia 35 50N 103 0E
67 Lintan 34 59N 103 49E
98 Linton 39 0N 87 10W
68 Lintsing 36 50N 115 45W
81 Linville 26 50S 152 11E
26 Linz, Austria 48 18N 14 18E
24 Linz, Germany 50 33N 7 18E
39 Lípari, I. 38 40N 15 0E
48 Lipetsk 52 45N 39 35E
69 Liping 26 16N 109 8E
28 Lipno 52 49N 19 15E
24 Lippe, R. 51 39N 6 38E
24 Lippstadt 51 40N 8 19E
27 Liptovsky Svaty Mikuláš 49 6N 19 35E
84 Liptrap, C. 38 50S 145 55E
74 Lira 2 17N 32 57E
32 Liria 39 37N 0 35W
74 Lisala 2 12N 21 38E
31 Lisboa 38 42N 9 10W
31 Lisboa □ 39 0N 9 12W
15 Lisburn 54 30N 6 9W
15 Lisburn □ 54 30N 6 5W
88 Lisburne, C. 68 50N 166 0W
69 Lishui 28 20N 119 48W
18 Lisieux 49 10N 0 12E
20 L'Isle 43 52N 1 49E
20 L'Isle-Jourdain 43 37N 1 5E
19 l'Isle-sur-le-Doubs 47 28N 6 33E
81 Lismore, Australia 28 44S 153 21E
15 Lismore, Eire 52 8N 7 58W
90 Listowel, Canada 44 4N 80 58W
15 Listowel, Eire 52 27N 9 30W
100 Litchfield 39 10N 89 40W
84 Lithgow 33 25S 150 8E
43 Líthinon, Ákra 34 55N 24 44E
48 Lithuanian S.S.R. □ 55 30N 24 0E
37 Litija 46 3N 14 50E
97 Lititz 40 9N 76 18W
42 Litókhoron 40 8N 22 34E
26 Litoměřice 50 33N 14 10E
26 Litschav 48 58N 15 4E
105 Little Abaco I. 26 50N 77 30W
63 Little Andaman, I. 10 40N 92 15E
85 Little Barrier, I. 36 12S 175 8E
90 Little Current 45 55N 82 0W
103 Little Colorado, R. 36 11N 111 48W
100 Little Falls, Minn. 45 58N 94 19W
97 Little Falls, N.Y. 43 3N 74 50W
105 Little Inagua I. 21 40N 73 50W
90 Little Longlac 49 42N 86 58W
13 Little Ouse, R. 52 30N 0 22E
60 Little Rann 23 25N 71 25E
85 Little River 43 45S 172 49E
101 Little Rock 34 41N 92 10W
101 Littlefield 33 57N 102 17W
13 Littlehampton 50 48N 0 32W
69 Liuan 31 45N 116 30E
69 Liucheng 24 39N 109 14E
69 Liuchow 24 10N 109 10E
75 Liuwa Plain 14 20S 22 30E
101 Livermore, Mt. 30 45N 104 8W
84 Liverpool, Australia 33 55S 150 52E
91 Liverpool, Canada 44 5N 64 41W
12 Liverpool, U.K. 53 25N 3 0W
104 Livingston, Guatemala 15 50N 88 50W
102 Livingston, U.S.A. 45 40N 110 40W
74 Livingstonia 10 38S 34 5E
75 Livingstone 17 46S 25 52E
40 Livno 43 50N 17 0E
48 Livny 52 30N 37 30E
36 Livorno 43 32N 10 18E
21 Livron-sur Drôme 44 46N 4 51E
13 Lizard Pt. 49 57N 5 11W
40 Ljig 44 13N 20 18E
37 Ljubljana 46 4N 14 33E
44 Ljungan, R. 62 19N 17 23E
45 Ljungby 56 49N 13 55E
44 Ljusdal 61 46N 16 3E
44 Ljusnan, R. 61 12N 17 8E
37 Ljutomer 46 31N 16 11E
13 Llandeilo 50 54N 4 0W
13 Llandovery 51 59N 3 49W
13 Llandrindod Wells 52 15N 3 23W
12 Llandudno 53 19N 3 51W
13 Llanelli 51 41N 4 11W
30 Llanes 43 25N 4 50W
12 Llangollen 52 58N 3 10W
13 Llanidloes 52 28N 3 31W
86 Llano Estacado, Reg. 34 0N 103 0W
106 Llanos, Reg. 3 25N 71 35W
112 Llanquihue, L. 41 10S 72 50W
31 Llerena 38 17N 6 0W
32 Llobregat, R. 41 17N 2 8E
32 Lloret de Mar 41 41N 2 53E
93 Lloydminster 53 20N 110 0W
33 Lluchmayor 39 29N 2 53E
108 Llullaillaco, Mt. 24 30S 68 30W
36 Loano 44 8N 8 14E
75 Lobatse 25 12S 25 40E
24 Löbau 51 5N 14 42E
108 Lobería 38 10S 58 40W
75 Lobito 12 18S 13 35E
31 Lobón, Canal de 38 50N 6 55W
108 Lobos 35 2S 59 0W
63 Loc Ninh 11 50N 106 34E
25 Locarno 46 10N 8 47E
14 Lochaber, Reg. 56 55N 5 0W
14 Lochalsh, Kyle of 57 17N 5 43W
14 Lochboisdale 57 10N 7 20W
14 Lochgilphead 56 2N 5 37W
14 Lochmaddy 57 36N 7 10W
14 Lochnagar, Mt. 56 57N 3 14W
14 Lochy, L. 56 58N 4 55W
81 Lock 33 34S 135 46E
96 Lock Haven 41 7N 77 31W
91 Lockeport 43 47N 65 4W
14 Lockerbie 55 7N 3 21W
101 Lockhart 29 55N 97 40W
96 Lockport 43 12N 78 42W
39 Locri 38 14N 16 14E
54 Lod 31 57N 34 54E
20 Lodève 43 44N 3 19E
36 Lodi, It. 45 19N 9 30E
102 Lodi, U.S.A. 38 12N 121 16W
74 Lodja 3 30S 23 23E
32 Lodosa 42 25N 2 4W
28 Łódź 51 45N 19 27E
28 Łódź □ 51 45N 19 27E
63 Loei 17 29N 101 35E
26 Lofer 47 35N 12 41E
46 Lofoten, Is. 68 10N 13 0E
98 Logan, Ohio 39 35N 82 22W
102 Logan, Utah 41 45N 111 50W
98 Logan, W. Va. 37 51N 81 59W
88 Logan, Mt. 60 40N 140 0W
98 Logansport 31 58N 93 58W
57 Logar □ 33 50N 69 0E
32 Logrono 42 28N 2 32W
32 Logroño □ 42 28N 2 27W
31 Logrozán 39 20N 5 32W
61 Lohardaga 23 27N 84 45E
55 Loheia 15 45N 42 40E
69 Loho 33 33N 114 5E
25 Lohr 50 0N 9 35E
47 Loimaa 60 50N 23 5E
18 Loir, R. 47 33N 0 32W
18 Loir-et-Cher □ 47 40N 1 20E
21 Loire □ 45 40N 4 5E
18 Loire, R. 47 16N 2 11W
18 Loire-Atlantique □ 47 25N 1 40W
19 Loiret □ 47 58N 2 10E
110 Loja, Ecuador 3 59S 79 16W
31 Loja, Sp. 37 10N 4 10W
16 Lokeren 51 6N 3 59E
74 Lokitaung 4 12N 35 48E
46 Lokka, L. 68 0N 27 50E
45 Løkken 57 22N 9 41E
44 Lokkenverk 63 8N 9 45E
72 Lokoja 7 47N 6 45E
74 Lokolama 2 35S 19 50E
69 Lokwei 19 12N 110 30E
45 Lolland, L. 54 45N 11 30E
24 Lollar 50 39N 8 43E
41 Lom 43 48N 23 20E
74 Lomami, R. 0 46N 24 16E
108 Lomas de Zamora 34 45S 58 25W
36 Lombardia □ 45 35N 9 45E
65 Lomblen, I. 8 30S 116 20E
64 Lombok, I. 8 35S 116 20E
72 Lomé 6 9N 1 20E
74 Lomela 2 5S 23 52E
74 Lomela, R. 0 14S 20 42E
45 Lomma 55 43N 13 6E
92 Lomond 50 24N 112 36W
14 Lomond, L. 56 8N 4 38W
103 Lompoc 34 41N 120 32W
28 Łomza 53 10N 22 2E
28 Łomza □ 53 20N 22 0E
62 Lonavla 18 46N 73 29E
112 Loncoche 39 20S 72 50W
96 London, Canada 43 0N 81 15W
13 London, U.K. 51 30N 0 5W
13 London □ 51 30N 0 5W
15 Londonderry 55 0N 7 20W
15 Londonderry □ 55 0N 7 20W
82 Londonderry, C. 13 45S 126 55E
112 Londonderry, I. 55 0S 71 0W
109 Londrina 23 0S 51 10W
103 Lone Pine 36 35N 118 2W
103 Long Beach, Calif. 33 46N 118 12W
97 Long Beach, N.Y. 40 35N 73 40W
97 Long Branch 40 19N 74 0W
12 Long Eaton 52 54N 1 16W
105 Long I., Bahamas 23 20N 75 10W
90 Long I., Canada 44 23N 66 19W
97 Long I., U.S.A. 40 50N 73 20W
97 Long Island Sd. 41 10N 73 0W
91 Long Range Mts. 48 0N 58 30W
63 Long Xuyen 10 19N 105 28E
43 Longá 36 53N 21 55E
19 Longeau 47 47N 5 20E
15 Longford 53 43N 7 50W
15 Longford □ 53 42N 7 45W
64 Longiram 0 5S 115 45E
100 Longmont 40 10N 105 4W
80 Longreach 23 28S 144 14E
97 Longueuil 45 32N 73 28W
19 Longuyon 49 27N 5 35E
101 Longview, Tex. 32 30N 94 45W
102 Longview, Wash. 46 9N 122 58W
19 Longwy 49 30N 5 45W
37 Lonigo 45 23N 11 22E
24 Löningen 54 43N 7 44E
37 Lonja, R. 45 27N 16 41E
21 Lons-le-Saunier 46 40N 5 31E
46 Lønsdal 66 46N 15 26E
13 Looe 50 21N 4 26W
93 Loomis 49 15N 108 45W
93 Loon Lake 44 50N 77 15W
83 Loongana 30 52S 127 5E
15 Loop Hd. 52 34N 9 55W
67 Lop Nor, L. 40 30N 90 30E
74 Lopez, C. 0 47S 8 40E
31 Lora del Río 37 39N 5 33W
96 Lorain 41 20N 82 5W
33 Lorca 37 41N 1 42W
76 Lord Howe I. 31 33S 159 6E
103 Lordsburg 32 15N 108 45W
56 Lorestan □ 33 0N 48 30E
111 Loreto 7 5S 45 30W
18 Lorient 47 45N 3 23N
14 Lorn, Firth of 56 20N 5 40W
14 Lorne, Reg. 56 26N 5 10W
25 Lörrach 47 36N 7 38E
19 Lorraine, Reg. 49 0N 6 0E
90 Lorrainville 47 21N 79 23W
103 Los Alamos 35 57N 106 17W
108 Los Andes 32 50S 70 40W
108 Los Angeles, Chile 37 28S 72 23W
103 Los Angeles, U.S.A. 34 0N 118 10W
103 Los Angeles Aqueduct 35 0N 118 20W
103 Los Banos 37 8N 120 56W
31 Los Barrios 36 11N 5 30W
110 Los Hermanos, Is. 11 45N 64 25W
112 Los Lagos 39 51S 72 50W
104 Los Mochis 25 45N 109 5W
32 Los Monegros 41 29N 0 3W
31 Los Palacios Villafranca 37 10N 5 55W
110 Los Roques, Is. 11 50N 66 45W
31 Los Santos de Maimona 38 37N 6 22W
110 Los Testigos, Is. 11 23N 63 6W
51 Loshkalakh 62 45N 147 20E
37 Losinj 44 35N 14 28E
14 Lossiemouth 57 43N 3 17W
20 Lot □ 44 39N 1 40E
20 Lot, R. 44 18N 0 20E
20 Lot-et-Garonne □ 44 22N 0 30E
108 Lota 37 5S 73 10W
14 Lothian □ 55 55N 3 35W
20 Lothiers 46 42N 1 33E
74 Loto 28 50S 22 28E
25 Lotschbergtunnel 46 26N 7 43E
18 Loudéac 48 11N 2 47W
20 Loudun 35 41N 84 22W
12 Loughborough 52 46N 1 11W
15 Loughrea 53 11N 8 33W

Louis Trichardt Maiduguri

75 Louis Trichardt ... 23 0s 25 55 E
91 Louisbourg 45 55N 60 0W
90 Louiseville 46 20N 73 0W
76 Louisiade Arch. ... 11 10s 153 0 E
101 Louisiana □ 30 50N 92 0W
98 Louisville, Ky. 38 15N 85 45W
101 Louisville, Miss. ... 33 7N 89 3W
20 Loulay 46 3N 0 30W
31 Loulé 37 9N 8 0W
26 Louny .... 50 20N 13 48 E
100 Loup City .... 41 19N 98 57 E
20 Lourdes 43 6N 0 3W
75 Lourenço
Marques=
Maputo .... 25 58s 32 32 E
31 Lourinha 39 14N 9 17W
30 Lousã 40 7N 8 14W
81 Louth, Australia .. 30 30s 145 8 E
15 Louth, Eire 53 47N 6 33W
12 Louth, U.K. 53 23N 0 0
15 Louth □ 53 55N 6 30W
43 Loutra-Aidhipsoú . 38 54N 23 2 E
18 Louviers .... 49 12N 1 10 E
93 Love 53 29N 104 9W
41 Lovech .... 43 8N 24 43 E
100 Loveland 40 27N 105 4W
102 Lovelock 40 17N 118 25W
30 Lovios .... 41 55 E 8 4W
47 Lovisa .... 60 28N 26 12 E
26 Lovosice .... 50 30N 14 2 E
37 Lovran .... 45 18N 14 15 E
40 Lovrin .... 45 58N 20 48 E
97 Lowell 42 38N 71 19W
85 Lower Hutt .... 41 10s 174 55 E
13 Lowestoft .... 52 29N 1 44 E
28 Łowicz .... 52 6N 19 55 E
97 Lowville 43 48N 75 30W
81 Loxton .... 34 28s 140 31 E
76 Loyalty Is .... 21 0s 167 30 E
69 Loyang .... 34 41N 112 28 E
69 Loyung .... 24 25N 109 25 E
20 Lozère □ .... 44 35N 3 30 E
40 Loznica .... 44 32N 19 14 E
68 Lu-ta .... 39 0N 121 31 E
74 Lualaba, R. .... 0 26N 25 20 E
74 Luanda .... 8 58s 13 9 E
63 Luang Prabang .... 19 45N 102 10 E
75 Luangwa, R. ...... 15 40N 30 25 E
75 Luanshya .... 13 3s 28 28 E
30 Luarca 43 32N 6 32W
28 Lubań .... 51 5N 15 15 E
65 Lubang Is. .... 13 50N 120 12 E
28 Lubartów .... 51 28N 22 42 E
54 Lubban .... 32 9N 35 14 E
24 Lübben .... 51 56N 13 54 E
101 Lubbock 33 40N 102 0W
24 Lübeck .... 53 52N 10 41 E
74 Lubefu .... 4 47s 24 27 E
28 Lubin .... 51 24N 16 11 E
28 Lublin .... 51 12N 22 38 E
28 Lublin □ .... 51 5N 22 30 E
27 Lubliniec .... 50 43N 18 45 E
56 Lubnān, Mts. ..... 34 0N 36 0 E
28 Lubon .... 52 21N 16 51 E
28 Lubsko .... 51 45N 14 57 E
64 Lubuklinggau ..... 3 15s 102 55 E
64 Lubuksikaping .... 0 10N 100 15 E
75 Lubumbashi ...... 11 32s 27 28 E
74 Lubutu .... 0 45s 26 30 E
88 Lucania, Mt. 60 48N 141 25W
36 Lucca .... 43 50N 10 30 E
14 Luce B. 54 45N 4 48W
65 Lucena, Philippines 13 56N 121 37 E
31 Lucena, Sp. 37 27N 4 31W
32 Lucena del Cid ... 40 9N 0 17W
27 Lučenec .... 48 18N 19 42 E
39 Lucera .... 41 30N 15 20 E
33 Luchena, R. 37 44N 1 50W
24 Lüchow .... 52 58N 11 8 E
69 Luchow .... 29 2N 105 10 E
24 Luckenwalde ..... 52 5N 13 11 E
61 Lucknow .... 26 50N 81 0 E
20 Luçon 46 28N 1 10W
37 Ludbreg .... 46 15N 16 38 E
24 Lüdenscheid ...... 51 13N 7 37 E
75 Lüderitz .... 26 41s 15 8 E
60 Ludhiana .... 30 57N 75 56 E
98 Ludington 43 58N 86 27W
13 Ludlow 52 23N 2 42W
41 Ludus .... 46 29N 24 5 E
44 Ludvika .... 60 8N 15 14 E
25 Ludwigsburg ...... 48 53N 9 11 E
25 Ludwigshafen ..... 49 27N 8 27 E
24 Ludwigslust ...... 53 19N 11 28 E
101 Lufkin 31 25N 94 40W
48 Luga .... 58 40N 29 55 E
25 Lugano .... 46 0N 8 57 E
25 Lugano, L. di ..... 46 0N 9 0 E
49 Lugansk=
Voroshilovgrad .. 48 35N 39 29 E
55 Lugh Ganana ..... 3 48N 42 40 E
30 Lugo, Sp. 43 2N 7 35W
37 Lugo, It. .... 44 25N 11 53 E
30 Lugo □ 43 0N 7 30W
40 Lugoj .... 45 42N 21 57 E
30 Lugones 43 26N 5 50W
50 Lugovoy .... 43 0N 72 20 E
36 Luino .... 46 0N 8 24 E
111 Luis Correia 3 0s 41 35W
108 Luján 34 45s 59 5W
69 Lukang .... 24 0N 120 19 E
61 Lukhisarai .... 27 11N 86 5 E
41 Lukovit .... 43 13N 24 11 E
28 Łuków .... 51 56N 22 23 E
75 Lukulu .... 14 35s 23 25 E
46 Luleå .... 65 35N 22 10 E
74 Lulonga, R. ...... 0 43N 18 23 E
74 Lulua, R. .... 5 2s 21 7 E
74 Luluabourg=
Kananga .... 5 55s 22 18 E
99 Lumberton 34 37N 78 59W
85 Lumsden .... 45 44s 168 27 E
68 Lun .... 47 55N 105 1 E
60 Lunavada .... 23 8N 73 37 E
45 Lund .... 55 41N 13 12 E
75 Lundazi .... 12 20s 33 7 E
13 Lundy, I. 51 10N 4 41W
12 Lune, R. 54 2N 2 50W
24 Lüneburg .... 53 15N 10 23 E
24 Lüneburger
Heide, Reg. .... 53 0N 10 0 E
21 Lunel .... 43 39N 7 31 E
24 Lunen .... 51 36N 7 31 E
91 Lunenburg 44 22N 64 18W
19 Lunéville .... 48 36N 6 30 E
68 Lunghwa .... 41 15N 117 51 E
68 Lungkiang .... 47 22N 123 4 E
68 Lungkow .... 37 40N 120 25 E
59 Lungleh .... 22 55N 92 45 E
68 Lungsi .... 35 0N 104 35 E
60 Luni, R. .... 24 40N 71 15 E
74 Luofu .... 0 1s 29 15 E
41 Lupeni .... 45 21N 23 13 E
108 Luque 37 35N 4 16W
19 Lure .... 47 40N 6 30 E
15 Lurgan 54 28N 6 20W
75 Lusaka .... 15 28s 28 16 E
42 Lushnja .... 40 55N 19 41 E
74 Lushoto .... 4 47s 38 20 E
68 Lushun .... 38 48N 121 16 E
75 Luso .... 11 47s 19 52 E
20 Lussac-les-
Châteaux .... 46 24N 0 43 E
13 Luton 51 53N 0 24W
64 Lutong .... 4 30N 114 0 E
48 Lutsk .... 50 50N 25 15 E
5 Lützow Holnbukta,
B. .... 69 0s 38 0 E
16 Luxembourg ...... 49 37N 6 9 E
16 Luxembourg ■ .... 50 0N 6 0 E
16 Luxembourg □ .... 49 58N 5 30 E
19 Luxeuil-les-Bains .. 47 49N 6 24 E
73 Luxor=El Uqsur .. 25 41N 32 38 E
20 Luy, R. 43 39N 1 8W
48 Luza .... 60 39N 47 10 E
25 Luzern .... 47 3N 8 18 E
25 Luzern □ .... 47 2N 7 55 E
111 Luziania 16 20s 48 0W
65 Luzon, I. .... 16 0N 121 0 E
20 Luzy .... 46 47N 3 58 E
49 Lvov .... 49 40N 24 0 E
68 Lwanhsien .... 39 45N 118 45 E
28 Lwówek Śl .... 51 7N 15 38 E
51 Lyakhovskiye Os. . 73 40N 141 0 E
60 Lyallpur .... 31 30N 73 5 E
41 Lyaskovets .... 43 6N 25 44 E
14 Lybster 58 18N 3 16W
45 Lyckeby .... 56 12N 15 37 E
46 Lycksele .... 64 38N 18 40 E
54 Lydda=Lod ...... 31 57N 34 54 E
75 Lydenburg .... 25 10s 30 29 E
85 Lyell .... 41 48s 172 4 E
85 Lyell, Ra. .... 41 38s 172 20 E
13 Lyme Regis 50 44N 2 57W
13 Lymington 50 46N 1 32W
98 Lynchburg 37 23N 79 10W
84 Lyndhurst, N.S.W. . 33 41N 149 2 E
80 Lyndhurst, Queens. 18 56s 144 30 E
97 Lyndonville 44 32N 72 1W
97 Lynn 42 28N 70 57W
93 Lynn Lake 56 51N 101 3W
13 Lynton 51 14N 3 50W
21 Lyon .... 45 46N 4 50 E
21 Lyonnais, Reg. .... 45 45N 4 15 E
83 Lyons, R. 25 2N 115 9W
97 Lyons Falls 43 37N 75 22W
26 Lysá .... 50 11N 14 51 E
45 Lysekil .... 58 17N 11 26 E
48 Lysra .... 57 7N 57 47 E
12 Lytham
St. Annes 53 45N 2 58W
85 Lyttelton .... 43 35s 172 44 E
41 Lyubimets .... 41 50N 26 5 E

M

54 Ma'ad .... 32 37N 35 36 E
69 Maanshan .... 31 40N 118 30 E
16 Maas, R. .... 51 49N 5 1 E
16 Maastricht .... 50 50N 5 40 E
12 Mablethorpe ...... 53 21N 0 14 E
109 Macaé 20 20s 41 55W
101 McAllen 26 12N 98 15W
101 McAlester 34 57N 95 40W
111 Macapá 0 5N 51 10W
80 McArthur, R. ..... 15 54s 136 40 E
111 Macau 5 0s 36 40W
69 Macau ■ .... 22 16N 113 35 E
92 McBride 53 20N 120 10W
102 McCammon 42 41N 112 11W
12 Macclesfield 53 16N 2 9W
93 McClintock 57 45N 94 15W
88 M'Clintock Chan. . 71 0N 103 0W
101 McComb 31 20N 90 30W
100 McCook 40 15N 100 35W
3 McDonald I. .... 54 0s 73 0 E
82 Macdonnell, Ras. .. 23 40s 133 0 E
81 McDouall Peak ... 29 51s 134 55 E
88 Macdougall, L. 66 20N 98 30W
14 Macduff 57 40N 2 30W
90 Mace 48 55N 80 0W
30 Maceda 42 16N 7 39W
30 Macedo de
Cavaleiros 41 31N 6 57W
111 Maceió 9 40s 35 41W
72 Macenta 8 35N 9 20W
37 Macerata .... 43 19N 13 28 E
102 McGill 35 27N 114 50W
15 Macgillycuddy's
Reeks, Mts. 52 2N 9 45W
108 Machagai 26 56s 60 2W
74 Machakos .... 1 30s 37 15 E
110 Machala 3 10s 79 50W
51 Machel'na .... 61 20N 172 20 E
30 Machichaco, C. ... 43 28N 2 47W
110 Machiques 10 4N 72 34W
13 Machynlleth 52 36N 3 51W
72 Macias Nguema
Biyoga, I. ...... 3 30N 8 40 E
81 Macintyre, R. ..... 28 38s 150 47 E
30 Macizo Galaico ... 42 30N 7 30W
80 Mackay, Australia .. 21 36s 148 39 E
102 Mackay, U.S.A. ... 43 58N 113 37W
82 Mackay, L. .... 22 40s 128 35 E
96 McKees Rocks 40 27N 80 3W
96 McKeesport 40 21N 79 50W
92 Mackenzie 55 20N 123 5W
88 Mackenzie, Reg. .. 61 30N 144 30W
88 Mackenzie, R. 69 15N 134 8W
110 Mackenzie City ... 6 0N 58 10W
88 Mackenzie Mts. ... 64 0N 130 0W
80 McKinlay .... 21 16s 141 17 E
88 McKinley, Mt. 63 10N 151 0W
4 McKinley Sea 84 0N 10 0W
101 McKinney 33 10N 96 40W
93 Macklin 52 20N 109 56W
81 Macksville .... 30 40s 152 56 E
81 Maclean .... 29 26s 153 16 E
75 Maclear .... 31 2s 28 23 E
81 Macleay, R. ...... 30 52s 153 1 E
92 McLennan 55 42N 116 50W
83 McLeod, L. .... 24 9s 113 47 E
92 McLure 50 55N 120 20W
86 M'Clure Str. 74 40N 117 30W
102 McMinnville,
Oreg. 45 16N 123 11W
99 McMinnville,
Tenn. 35 43N 85 45W
93 McMurray 56 45N 111 27W
103 McNary 34 4N 109 53W
100 Macomb 40 25N 90 40W
38 Macomer .... 40 16N 8 48 E
21 Mâcon .... 46 19N 4 50 E
99 Macon 32 50N 83 37W
100 McPherson 38 25N 97 40W
76 Macquarie Is. 54 36s 158 55s
84 Macquarie, R. .... 30 7s 147 24 E
5 Mac Robertson
Coast .... 68 30s 63 0 E
15 Macroom 51 54N 8 57W
56 Madā'in Sālih ..... 26 51N 37 58 E
75 Madagascar ■ .... 20 0s 47 0 E
73 Madama .... 22 0N 14 0 E
62 Madanapalle ..... 13 33N 78 34 E
76 Madane .... 5 0s 145 46 E
61 Madaripur .... 23 2N 90 15 E
59 Madauk .... 17 56N 96 52 E
96 Madawaska 45 30N 77 55W
59 Madaya .... 22 20N 96 10 E
38 Maddalena, I. ..... 41 15N 9 23 E
39 Maddaloni .... 41 4N 14 23 E
104 Madden L. 9 20N 79 37W
72 Madeira, I. 32 50N 17 0W
110 Madeira, R. 3 22s 58 45W
103 Madera 37 0N 120 1W
61 Madhupur .... 24 18N 86 37 E
60 Madhya Pradesh □ 21 50N 81 0 E
55 Madinat al
Shaab .... 12 50N 45 0 E
74 Madingou .... 4 10s 13 33 E
98 Madison, Ind. 38 42N 85 20W
100 Madison, S.D. 44 0N 97 8W
100 Madison, Wis. 43 5N 89 25W
98 Madisonville 37 42N 86 30W
65 Madiun .... 7 38s 111 32 E
62 Madras, India ..... 13 8N 80 19 E
102 Madras, U.S.A. ... 44 40N 121 10W
104 Madre, Laguna 25 0N 97 30W
110 Madre de Dios, R. 10 59s 66 8W
112 Madre de Dios,
I. 50 20s 75 10W
104 Madre del
Sur, Sa. 17 30N 100 0W
104 Madre Occidental,
Sa. 27 0N 107 0W
104 Madre Oriental,
Sa. 25 0N 100 0W
30 Madrid 40 25N 3 45W
30 Madrid □ 40 30N 3 45W
31 Madridejos 39 28N 3 33W
31 Madrona, Sa. 38 27N 4 16W
31 Madroñera 39 26N 5 42W
65 Madura, I. .... 7 0N 113 20 E
65 Madura, Selat ..... 7 30s 113 20 E
83 Madura Motel .... 31 55s 127 0 E
62 Madurai .... 9 55N 78 10 E
62 Madurantakam .... 12 30N 79 50 E
66 Maebashi .... 36 23N 139 4 E
41 Măeruş .... 45 53N 25 31 E
13 Maesteg 51 36N 3 40W
105 Maestra, Sa. 20 15N 77 0W
32 Maestrazgo, Mts.
de 40 30N 0 25W
75 Maevatanana ..... 16 56s 46 49 E
93 Mafeking, Canada . 52 40N 101 10W
75 Mafeking, S.Africa 25 50s 25 38 E
74 Mafia I. .... 7 45s 39 50 E
109 Mafra 36 10N 50 0W
51 Magadan .... 59 30N 151 0 E
74 Magadi .... 1 54s 36 19 E
112 Magallanes,
Estrecho de, Str. 52 30s 75 0W
110 Magangue 9 14N 74 45W
91 Magdalen Is. 47 30N 61 40W
104 Magdalena,
Mexico 30 50N 112 0W
103 Magdalena, U.S.A. 34 10N 107 20W
112 Magdalena, I.,
Chile 44 42s 73 10W
104 Magdalena, I.,
Mexico 24 40N 112 15W
24 Magdeburg ...... 52 8N 11 36 E
24 Magdeburg □ ..... 52 20N 11 40 E
54 Magdi'el .... 32 10N 34 54 E
15 Magee, I. 54 48N 5 44W
65 Magelang .... 7 29s 110 13 E
36 Maggiorasca, Mt. .. 44 33N 9 29 E
36 Maggiore, L. ..... 46 0N 8 35 E
54 Maghar .... 32 54N 35 24 E
15 Magherafelt 54 45N 6 36W
15 Magherafelt □ 54 45N 6 36W
37 Magione .... 43 10N 12 12 E
39 Máglie .... 40 8N 18 17 E
43 Magnisía □ ...... 39 24N 22 46 E
50 Magnitogorsk ..... 53 20N 59 0 E
101 Magnolia 33 18N 93 12W
91 Magog 45 18N 72 9W
92 Magrath 49 25N 112 50W
33 Magro, R. 39 11N 0 25W
111 Maguarinho, C. ... 0 15s 48 30W
59 Magwe .... 20 10N 95 0 E
56 Mahābād .... 36 50N 45 45 E
61 Mahabharat Lekh,
Mts. .... 28 30N 82 0 E
62 Mahad .... 18 6N 73 29 E
55 Mahaddei Uen .... 3 0N 45 32 E
60 Mahadeo Hills .... 22 20N 78 30 E
75 Mahalapye .... 23 1s 26 51 E
57 Mahallāt .... 33 55N 50 30 E
61 Mahanadi, R. ..... 20 0N 86 25 E
61 Mahananda, R. ... 24 29N 88 18 E
97 Mahanoy City 40 48N 76 10W
60 Maharashtra □ .... 19 30N 75 30 E
62 Mahboobabad .... 17 42N 80 2 E
62 Mahbubnagar ..... 16 45N 77 59 E
73 Mahdia .... 35 28N 11 0 E
62 Mahé .... 11 42N 75 34 E
85 Maheno .... 45 10s 170 50 E
85 Mahia Pen. .... 39 9s 177 55 E
61 Mahoba .... 25 15N 79 55 E
32 Mahón .... 39 50N 4 18 E
91 Mahone Bay 44 27N 64 23W
60 Mahuva .... 25 7N 71 46 E
74 Mai-Ndombe, L. .. 2 0s 18 0 E
13 Maidenhead 51 31N 0 42W
93 Maidstone,
Canada 53 5N 109 20W
13 Maidstone, U.K. .. 51 16N 0 31 E
73 Maiduguri .... 12 0N 13 20 E

Maijdi Martapura, Kalimantan

61 Maijdi 22 48N 91 10 E
61 Maikala Ra. 22 0N 81 0 E
19 Mailly-le-Camp 48 41N 4 12 E
15 Main, R. 54 43N 6 18W
25 Main, R. 50 0N 8 18 E
99 Maine □ 45 20N 69 0W
18 Maine, Reg. 48 0N 0 0 E
18 Maine-et-Loire □ 47 31N 0 30W
59 Maingkwan 26 15N 96 45 E
14 Mainland, I., Orkney 59 0N 3 10W
14 Mainland, I., Shetland 60 15N 1 22W
60 Mainpuri 27 18N 79 4 E
25 Mainz 50 0N 8 17 E
108 Maipú 37 0S 58 0W
110 Maiquetía 10 36N 66 57W
59 Mairabari 26 30N 92 30 E
105 Maisí, C. 20 10N 74 10W
19 Maisse 48 24N 2 21 E
84 Maitland 32 44S 151 36 E
66 Maizuru 35 25N 135 22 E
65 Majalengka 6 55S 108 14 E
54 Majd el Kurum 32 56N 35 15 E
65 Majene 3 27S 118 57 E
40 Majevica, Mts. 44 45N 18 50 E
75 Majunga 17 0S 47 0 E
61 Makalu, Mt. 27 54N 87 6 E
51 Makarovo 57 40N 107 45 E
40 Makarska 43 18N 17 2 E
65 Makasar, Selat, Str. 1 0S 118 20 E
50 Makat 47 39N 53 19 E
42 Makedhonia □ 40 39N 53 19 E
72 Makeni 8 55N 12 5W
49 Makeyevka 48 0N 38 0 E
75 Makgadikgadi Salt Pans 20 40S 25 45 E
49 Makhachkala 43 0N 47 15 E
74 Makindu 2 17S 37 49 E
50 Makinsk 52 37N 70 26 E
56 Makkah 21 30N 39 54 E
91 Makkovik 55 0N 59 10W
51 Maklakovo 58 16N 92 29 E
27 Makó 46 14N 20 33 E
74 Makokou 0 40N 12 50 E
58 Makran Coast Ra. 25 40N 4 0 E
56 Māku 39 15N 44 31 E
66 Makurazaki 31 15N 130 20 E
72 Makurdi 7 45N 8 32 E
49 Mal Usen, R. 48 50N 49 39 E
37 Mala Kapela, Mts. 44 45N 15 30 E
62 Malabar Coast, Reg. 11 0N 75 0 E
63 Malacca, Str. of 3 0N 101 0 E
27 Malacky 48 27N 17 0 E
102 Malad City 41 10N 112 20W
31 Málaga 36 43N 4 23W
31 Málaga □ 36 38N 4 58W
75 Malagasy Rep.= Madagascar ■ 19 0S 46 0 E
31 Malagón 39 11N 3 52W
31 Malagón, R. 37 35N 7 29W
73 Malakâl 9 33N 31 50 E
58 Malakand 34 40N 71 55 E
51 Malamyzh 50 0N 136 50 E
65 Malang 7 59S 112 35 E
74 Malanje 9 30S 16 17 E
44 Mälaren, L. 59 30N 17 10 E
90 Malartic 48 9N 78 9W
56 Malatya 38 25N 38 20 E
75 Malawi ■ 13 0S 34 0 E
75 Malawi, L. 12 30S 34 30 E
63 Malay Pen. 5 0N 102 0 E
63 Malaya □ 4 0N 102 0 E
56 Malayer 28 22N 56 38 E
64 Malaysia ■ 5 0N 110 0 E
80 Malbon 21 5S 140 17 E
31 Malbooma 30 41S 134 11 E
28 Malbork 54 3N 19 10 E
24 Malchow 53 29N 12 25 E
83 Malcolm 28 51S 121 25 E
97 Malden 42 26N 71 5W
77 Malden I. 4 3S 154 59W
53 Maldive Is. 2 0N 73 0W
109 Maldonado 35 0S 55 0W
27 Malé Karpaty, Mts. 48 30N 17 20 E
60 Malegaon 20 30N 74 30 E
60 Malerkotla 30 32N 75 58 E
19 Malesherbes 48 15N 2 24 E
32 Malgrat 41 39N 2 46 E
73 Malha 15 8N 26 12 E
72 Mali ■ 15 0N 10 0W
40 Mali, Kanal 45 36N 19 24 E
15 Malin Hd. 55 18N 7 16W
74 Malindi 3 12S 40 5 E
65 Malingping 6 45S 106 2 E
84 Mallacoota, Inlet 34 40S 149 40 E
14 Mallaig 57 0N 5 50W
61 Mallawan 27 4N 80 12 E
73 Mallawi 27 44N 30 44 E
43 Mállia 35 17N 25 27 E
32 Mallorca, I. 39 30N 3 0 E
15 Mallow 52 8N 8 39W
46 Malmberget 67 11N 20 40 E
45 Malmö 55 36N 12 59 E
45 Malmöhus □ 55 45N 13 30 E
41 Malnaş 46 2N 25 49 E
65 Malolos 14 50N 21 2 E
97 Malone 44 50N 74 19W
31 Malpartida 39 26N 6 30W
30 Malpica 43 19N 8 50W
102 Malta 48 20N 107 55W
73 Malta ■ 35 50N 14 30 E
12 Malton 54 9N 0 48W
65 Maluku, Is. 3 0S 128 0 E
44 Malung 60 42N 13 44 E
62 Malvalli 12 28N 77 8 E
62 Malvan 16 2N 73 30 E
13 Malvern, U.K. 52 7N 2 19W
101 Malvern, U.S.A. 34 22N 92 50W
13 Malvern Hills 52 0N 2 19W
111 Mamanguape 6 50S 35 4W
65 Mamasa 2 55S 119 20 E
18 Mamers 48 21N 0 22 E
39 Mámmola 38 23N 16 13 E
103 Mammoth 32 46N 110 43W
69 Mamoi 26 0N 119 25 E
110 Mamoré, R. 10 23S 65 53W
72 Mamou 10 15N 12 0W
64 Mampawah 0 30N 109 5 E
28 Mamry, L. 54 8N 21 42 E
72 Man 7 30N 7 40W
12 Man, I. of 54 15N 4 30W
59 Man Na 23 27N 97 19 E
111 Mana 5 45N 53 55W
62 Manaar, G. of 8 30N 79 0 E
110 Manacapuru 3 10S 60 50W
32 Manacor 39 32N 3 12 E
65 Manado 1 40N 124 45 E
105 Managua 12 0N 86 20W
105 Managua, L. de 12 20N 86 30W
75 Mananjary 21 13S 48 20 E
85 Manapouri, L. 45 32S 167 32 E
61 Manaslu, Mt. 28 33N 84 33 E
67 Manass 44 20N 86 21 E
59 Manaung Kyun, I. 18 45N 93 40 E
110 Manaus 3 0S 60 0W
31 Mancha Real 37 48N 3 39W
18 Manche □ 49 10N 1 20W
12 Manchester, U.K. 53 30N 2 15W
97 Manchester, Conn. 41 47N 72 30W
97 Manchester, N.H. 42 58N 71 29W
68 Manchouli 49 46N 117 24 E
109 Mandaguari 23 32S 51 42W
47 Mandal 58 2N 7 25 E
65 Mandala, Puncak, Mt. 4 30S 141 0 E
59 Mandalay 22 0N 96 10 E
68 Mandalgovi 45 40N 106 22 E
56 Mandali 33 52N 45 28 E
100 Mandan 46 50N 101 0W
65 Mandar, Teluk, G. 3 35S 119 4 E
75 Mandimba 14 22S 35 33 E
61 Mandla 22 39N 80 30 E
45 Mandø, I. 55 18N 8 33 E
75 Mandritsara 15 50S 48 49 E
60 Mandsaur 24 3N 75 8 E
83 Mandurah 32 32S 115 43 E
39 Mandúria 40 25N 17 38 E
60 Mandvi 22 51N 69 22 E
62 Mandya 12 30N 77 0 E
73 Manfalût 27 20N 30 52 E
39 Manfredónia 41 40N 15 55 E
39 Manfredónia, G. di 41 30N 16 10 E
62 Mangalagiri 16 26N 80 36 E
41 Mangalia 43 50N 28 35 E
62 Mangalore 12 55N 74 47 E
30 Manganeses 41 45N 5 43W
85 Mangaweka 39 48S 175 47 E
64 Manggar 2 50S 108 10 E
58 Mangla Dam 33 32N 73 50 E
65 Mangole, I. 1 50S 125 55 E
85 Mangonui 35 1S 173 32 E
30 Mangualde 40 38N 7 48W
109 Mangueira, L. 33 0S 52 50W
67 Mangyai 38 6N 91 37 E
50 Mangyshlak Pol. 43 40N 52 30 E
100 Manhattan 39 10N 96 40W
111 Manhuaçu 20 15S 42 2W
37 Maniago 46 11N 12 40 E
110 Manicoré 6 0S 61 10W
91 Manicouagan, L. 51 25N 68 15W
77 Manihiki, I. 11 0S 161 0W
65 Manila 14 40N 121 3 E
65 Manila B. 14 0N 120 0 E
84 Manildra 33 11S 148 41 E
81 Manilla 30 45S 150 43 E
59 Manipur □ 24 30N 94 0 E
56 Manisa 38 38N 27 30 E
98 Manistee 44 15N 86 20W
98 Manistique 45 59N 86 18W
93 Manitoba □ 55 30N 97 0W
93 Manitoba, L. 50 40N 98 30W
100 Manitou Springs 38 52N 104 55W
90 Manitoulin I. 45 40N 82 30W
98 Manitowoc 44 8N 87 40W
110 Manizales 5 5N 75 32W
62 Manjeri 11 7N 76 11 E
56 Manjil 36 46N 49 30 E
83 Manjimup 34 15S 116 6 E
62 Manjra, R. 18 49N 77 52 E
100 Mankato, Kans. 39 49N 98 11W
100 Mankato, Minn. 44 8N 93 59W
72 Mankono 8 10N 6 10W
32 Manlleu 42 2N 2 17 E
84 Manly 33 48S 151 14 E
81 Mannahill 32 26S 139 59 E
62 Mannargudi 10 45N 79 32 E
25 Mannheim 49 28N 8 29 E
92 Manning 56 53N 117 39W
38 Mannu, C. 40 2N 8 24 E
38 Mannu, R. 40 50N 8 23 E
81 Mannum 34 57S 139 12 E
65 Manokwari 0 54N 134 0 E
74 Manono 7 18S 27 25 E
21 Manosque 43 49N 5 47 E
32 Manresa 41 48N 1 50 E
60 Mansa, India 30 0N 75 27 E
74 Mansa, Zambia 11 13S 28 55 E
89 Mansel I. 62 0N 80 0W
84 Mansfield, Australia 37 0S 146 0 E
12 Mansfield, U.K. 53 8N 1 12W
96 Mansfield, U.S.A. 40 45N 82 30W
97 Mansfield, Mt. 44 33N 72 49W
30 Mansilla de las Mules 42 30N 5 25W
20 Mansle 45 52N 0 9 E
110 Manta 1 0S 80 40W
103 Manteca 37 50N 121 12W
19 Mantes-la-Jolie 49 0N 1 41 E
102 Manti 39 23N 111 32W
109 Mantiqueira, Sa. da 22 0S 44 0W
36 Mántova 45 10N 10 47 E
65 Manukan 8 14N 123 3 E
85 Manukau 37 2S 174 54 E
62 Manwath 19 19N 76 32 E
49 Manych-Gudilo, Oz. 46 24N 42 38 E
74 Manyoni 5 45S 34 55 E
60 Manzai 32 20N 70 15 E
30 Manzaneda, Cabeza de 42 12N 7 15W
105 Manzanillo, Cuba 20 20N 77 10W
104 Manzanillo, Mexico 19 0N 104 20W
105 Manzanillo, Pta. 9 30N 79 40W
73 Mao 14 4N 15 19 E
93 Maple Creek 49 55N 109 27W
100 Maplewood 38 33N 90 18W
62 Mapuca 15 36N 73 46 E
57 Maputo 25 58S 32 32 E
56 Maqnā 28 25N 34 50 E
112 Maquinchao 41 15S 68 50W
109 Mar Sa. do 25 30S 49 0W
108 Mar Chiquita, L. 30 40S 62 50W
108 Mar del Plata 38 0S 57 30W
111 Marabá 5 20S 49 5W
110 Maracaibo 10 40N 71 37W
110 Maracaibo, L. de 9 40N 71 30W
109 Maracaju 21 38S 55 9W
110 Maracay 10 15N 67 36W
73 Maradah 29 4N 19 4 E
72 Maradi 13 35N 8 10 E
56 Maragheh 37 30N 46 12 E
111 Marajó, I. de 1 0S 49 30W
56 Marand 38 30N 45 45 E
75 Marandellas 18 5S 31 42 E
111 Maranguape 3 55S 38 50W
111 Maranhão=São Luís 2 39S 44 15W
111 Maranhão □ 5 0S 46 0W
37 Marano, L. di 45 42N 13 13 E
110 Marañón, R. 4 50S 75 35W
56 Maraş 37 37N 36 53 E
41 Mărăşeşti 45 52N 27 5 E
31 Marateca 38 34N 8 40W
43 Marathókambos 37 43N 26 42 E
80 Marathon 20 51S 143 32 E
55 Marbat 17 0N 54 45 E
31 Marbella 36 30N 4 57W
82 Marble Bar 21 9S 119 44 E
97 Marblehead 42 29N 70 51W
24 Marburg 50 49N 8 44 E
27 Marcal, R. 47 41N 17 32 E
36 Marcaria 45 7N 10 34 E
13 March 57 33N 0 5 E
37 Marche □ 43 22N 13 10 E
20 Marche, Reg. 46 5N 2 10 E
16 Marche-en-Famenne 50 14N 5 19 E
31 Marchena 37 18N 5 23W
39 Marcianise 41 3N 14 16 E
19 Marck 50 57N 1 57 E
108 Marcos Juárez 32 42S 62 5W
76 Marcus I. 24 0N 153 45 E
97 Marcy, Mt. 44 7N 73 55W
58 Mardan 34 12N 72 2 E
56 Mardin 37 20N 40 36 E
14 Maree, L. 57 40N 5 30W
80 Mareeba 16 59S 145 28 E
37 Maremma, Reg. 42 45N 11 15 E
62 Margao 14 12N 73 58 E
92 Margaret Bay 51 20N 127 20W
82 Margaret River 18 0S 126 30 E
20 Margaride, Mts. de la 44 43N 3 38 E
110 Margarita, Is. de 11 0N 64 0W
13 Margate 51 23N 1 24 E
39 Margharita d'Savoia 41 25N 16 5 E
48 Mari A.S.S.R. □ 56 30N 48 0 E
85 Maria van Diemen, C. 34 29S 172 40 E
45 Mariager, Fd. 56 42N 10 19 E
76 Mariana Is. 17 0N 145 0 E
105 Marianao 23 8N 82 24W
99 Marianna 30 45N 85 15W
75 Mariano Machado 13 2S 14 40 E
26 Mariánské Lázně 49 57N 12 41 E
26 Mariazell 47 47N 15 19 E
55 Marib 15 25N 45 20 E
45 Maribo 54 48N 11 30 E
37 Maribor 46 36N 15 40 E
89 Maricourt 61 36N 71 57W
105 Marie-Galante, I. 15 56N 61 16W
47 Mariehamn 60 5N 19 57 E
75 Mariental 24 36S 18 0 E
96 Marienville 41 27N 79 8W
45 Mariestad 58 43N 13 50 E
99 Marietta, Ga. 34 0N 84 30W
98 Marietta, Ohio 39 27N 81 27W
105 Marigot 15 32N 61 18W
50 Marniisk 56 10N 87 20 E
109 Marília 22 0S 50 0W
65 Marinduque, I. 13 25N 122 0 E
98 Marinette 45 4N 87 40W
109 Maringá 23 35S 51 50W
101 Marion, Ill. 37 45N 88 55W
98 Marion, Ind. 40 35N 85 40W
100 Marion, Iowa 42 2N 91 36W
98 Marion, Ohio 40 38N 83 8W
99 Marion, S.C. 34 11N 79 22W
99 Marion, Va. 36 51N 81 29W
21 Maritimes, Alpes, Mts. 44 10N 7 10 E
41 Maritsa 42 1N 25 50 E
57 Marjan 32 5N 68 20 E
62 Markapur 15 44N 79 19 E
45 Markaryd 56 28N 13 35 E
12 Market Drayton 52 55N 2 30W
13 Market Harborough 52 29N 0 55W
12 Market Rasen 53 24N 0 20W
5 Markham, Mt. 83 0S 164 0 E
28 Marki 52 20N 21 2 E
43 Markoupoulon 37 53N 23 57 E
40 Markovac 44 14N 21 7 E
48 Marks 51 45N 46 50 E
25 Marktredwitz 50 1N 12 2 E
97 Marlboro 42 19N 71 33W
80 Marlborough 22 46S 149 52 E
85 Marlborough □ 41 45S 173 33 E
13 Marlborough Downs 51 25N 1 55W
19 Marle 49 43N 3 47 E
101 Marlin 31 25N 96 50W
62 Marmagao 15 25N 73 56 E
20 Marmande 44 30N 0 10 E
56 Marmara Denizi, Sea 40 45N 28 15 E
37 Marmolada, Mt. 46 25N 11 55 E
90 Marmora 44 28N 77 41W
19 Marne □ 49 0N 4 10 E
19 Marne, R. 48 49N 2 24 E
75 Maroantsetra 15 26S 49 44 E
81 Maroochydore 26 35S 153 10W
27 Maros, R. 46 15N 20 13 E
75 Marovoay 16 6S 46 39 E
77 Marquesas Is. 9 0S 139 30W
98 Marquette 46 30N 87 21W
73 Marra, J. 7 20N 27 35 E
72 Marrakech 31 40N 8 0W
80 Marrawah 40 56S 144 41 E
81 Marree 29 39S 138 1 E
31 Marroqui, Pta. 36 0N 5 37W
73 Marsa Brega 30 30N 19 20 E
73 Marsa Susa 32 52N 21 59 E
74 Marsabit 2 18N 38 0 E
38 Marsala 37 48N 12 25 E
37 Marsciano 42 54N 12 20 E
84 Marsden 33 47N 147 32 E
21 Marseille 43 18N 5 23 E
100 Marshall, Minn. 44 25N 95 45W
100 Marshall, Mo. 39 8N 93 15W
101 Marshall, Tex. 32 29N 94 20W
76 Marshall Is. 9 0N 171 0 E
100 Marshalltown 42 0N 93 0W
100 Marshfield 44 42N 90 10W
44 Märsta 59 37N 17 52 E
59 Martaban 16 30N 97 35 E
59 Martaban, G. of 15 40N 96 30 E
64 Martapura, Kalimantan 3 22S 114 56 E

Martapura, Sumatera — Metropolis

64 Martapura, Sumatera 4 19S 104 22E
73 Marte 12 23N 13 46E
33 Martes, Sa. 39 20N 1 0W
81 Marthaguy Creek 30 16S 147 35E
97 Marha's Vineyard 41 25N 70 35W
25 Martigny 46 6N 7 3E
21 Martigues 43 24N 5 4E
27 Martin 49 6N 18 48E
32 Martín, R. 41 18N 0 19W
7 Martin Vaz, I. 20 30S 28 15W
39 Martina Franca 40 42N 17 20E
105 Martinique, I. 14 40N 61 0W
105 Martinique Pass. 15 15N 61 0W
109 Martinópolis 22 11S 51 12W
96 Martins Ferry 40 5N 80 46W
26 Martinsberg 48 22N 15 9E
98 Martinsburg 39 30N 77 57W
98 Martinsville, Ind. 39 29N 86 23W
99 Martinsville, Va. 36 41N 79 52W
85 Marton 40 4S 175 23E
31 Martos 37 44N 3 58W
66 Marugame 34 15N 133 55E
84 Marulan 34 43S 150 3E
20 Marvejols 44 33N 3 19E
60 Marwar 25 43N 73 45E
50 Mary 37 40N 61 50E
80 Mary Kathleen 20 35S 139 48E
89 Mary River 70 30N 78 0W
81 Maryborough, Queens. 25 31S 152 37E
84 Maryborough, Vic. 37 0S 143 44E
98 Maryland □ 39 10N 76 40W
12 Maryport 54 43N 3 30W
91 Marystown 47 10N 55 10W
103 Marysvale 38 25N 112 17W
102 Marysville 39 14N 121 40W
99 Maryville 35 50N 84 0W
73 Marzūq 25 53N 14 10E
72 Mascara 35 26N 0 6E
57 Mashhad 36 20N 59 35E
32 Masnou 41 28N 2 20E
92 Masset 54 0N 132 0W
57 Masqat 23 37N 58 36E
56 Mastura 23 7N 38 52E
62 Masulipatnam 16 12N 81 12E
74 Masaka 0 21S 31 45E
65 Masamba 2 30S 120 15E
68 Masan 35 11N 128 32E
33 Masanasa 39 25N 0 25W
57 Masandam, Ras. 26 30N 56 30E
74 Masasi 10 45S 38 52E
105 Masaya 12 0N 86 7W
65 Masbate 12 20N 123 30E
65 Masbate, I. 12 20N 123 30E
75 Maseru 29 18S 27 30E
90 Mashkode 47 2N 84 7W
74 Masindi 1 40N 41 43E
56 Masjed Soleyman 31 55N 49 25E
15 Mask, L. 53 36N 9 24W
100 Mason City 48 0N 119 0W
36 Massa 44 2N 10 7E
36 Massa Maríttima 43 3N 10 52E
97 Massachusetts □ 42 25N 72 0W
97 Massachusetts B. 42 30N 70 0W
39 Massafra 40 35N 17 8E
36 Massarossa 43 53N 10 17E
73 Massawa=Mitsiwa 15 35N 39 25E
97 Massena 44 52N 74 55W
20 Massiac 45 15N 3 11E
20 Massif Central Reg. 45 30N 2 21E
96 Massillon 40 47N 81 30W
85 Masterton 40 56S 175 39E
43 Mástikho, Ákra 38 10N 26 2E
66 Masuda 34 40N 131 51E
65 Mataboor 1 41S 138 3E
31 Matachel, R. 38 50N 6 17W
90 Matachewan 47 50N 80 55W
68 Matad 47 12N 115 29E
74 Matadi 5 52S 13 31E
105 Matagalpa 13 10N 85 40W
90 Matagami 49 45N 77 34W
62 Matale 7 30N 80 44E
104 Matamoros 18 2N 98 17W
91 Matane 48 50N 67 33W
88 Matanuska 61 38N 149 0W
105 Matanzas 23 0N 81 40W
62 Matara 5 58N 80 30E
64 Mataram 8 41S 116 10E
82 Mataranka 14 55S 133 4E
32 Mataró 41 32N 2 29E
32 Matarraña, R. 41 14N 0 22E
85 Mataura 46 11S 168 51E
104 Matehuala 23 40N 100 50W
37 Matélica 43 15N 13 0E
39 Matera 40 40N 16 37E
27 Mátészalka 47 58N 22 20E
60 Mathura 27 30N 77 48E
28 Matkinia Grn 52 42N 22 2E
12 Matlock 53 8N 1 32W
72 Matmata 33 30N 9 59E
111 Mato Grosso □ 14 0S 54 0W
70 Matopo 20 36S 28 20E
30 Matosinhos 41 11N 8 42W
57 Matrah 23 37N 58 30E
73 Matrûh 31 19N 27 9E
69 Matsu, I. 26 9N 119 56E
66 Matsue 35 25N 133 10E
66 Matsumoto 36 15N 138 0E
66 Matsusaka 34 34N 136 32E
66 Matsuyama 33 45N 132 45E
62 Mattancheri 9 50N 76 15E
90 Mattawa 46 20N 78 45W
25 Matterhorn, Mt. 45 58N 7 39E
105 Matthew Town 20 57N 73 40W
100 Mattoon 39 30N 88 20W
64 Matua 2 58S 110 52E
110 Maturín 9 45N 63 11W
60 Mau Ranipur 25 16N 79 8E
19 Maubeuge 50 17N 3 57E
20 Maubourguet 43 29N 0 1E
110 Maués 3 20S 57 45W
94 Maui, I. 20 45N 156 20E
59 Maulamyaing 16 30N 97 40E
108 Maule □ 36 5S 72 30W
65 Maumere 8 38S 122 13E
75 Maun 20 0S 23 26E
94 Mauna Loa, Mt. 19 50N 155 28E
61 Maunath Bhanjan 25 56N 83 33E
59 Maungmagan Is. 41 0S 97 48E
21 Maures, Mts. 43 15N 6 15E
21 Maurienne 45 15N 6 20E
72 Mauritania ■ 20 50N 10 0W
71 Mauritius 20 0S 57 0E
21 Maurienne, Reg. 45 15N 6 20E
20 Maurs 44 43N 2 12E
26 Mauterndorf 47 9N 13 40E
62 Mavelikara 9 14N 76 32E
54 Mavqi'im 31 38N 34 32E
59 Mawkmai 20 14N 97 50E
59 Mawlaik 23 40N 94 26E
80 Maxwelton 39 51S 174 49E
105 May Pen 17 58N 77 15W
32 Maya 43 12N 1 29W
104 Maya Mts. 16 30N 89 0W
105 Mayaguana I. 21 30N 72 44W
105 Mayagüez 18 12N 67 9W
83 Mayanup 33 58S 116 25E
80 Maydena 42 45S 146 39E
25 Mayen 50 18N 7 10E
18 Mayenne 48 20N 0 38W
18 Mayenne □ 48 10N 0 40W
18 Mayenne, R. 47 30N 0 33W
92 Mayerthorpe 53 57N 115 15W
99 Mayfield 36 45N 88 40W
49 Maykop 44 35N 40 25E
97 Maynard 42 30N 71 33W
90 Maynooth, Canada 45 14N 77 56W
15 Maynooth, Eire 53 22N 6 38W
88 Mayo 63 38N 135 57W
15 Mayo □ 43 47N 9 7W
30 Mayorga 42 10N 5 16W
98 Maysville 38 43N 84 16W
74 Mayumba 3 25S 10 39E
62 Mayuram 11 3N 79 42E
51 Mayya 61 44N 130 18E
75 Mazabuka 15 52S 27 44E
111 Mazagão 0 20S 51 50W
92 Mazama 49 43N 120 8W
20 Mazamet 43 30N 2 20E
57 Mazan Deran □ 36 30N 53 30E
38 Mazara del Vallo 37 40N 12 34E
57 Mazar-i-Sharif 36 41N 67 0E
112 Mazarredo 47 10S 66 50W
33 Mazarrón 37 38N 1 19W
33 Mazarrón, G. de 37 27N 1 19W
104 Mazatenango 14 35N 91 30W
104 Mazatlán 23 10N 106 30W
39 Mazzarino 37 19N 14 12E
75 Mbabane 26 18S 31 6E
74 M'Baiki 3 53N 18 1E
74 Mbala 8 46S 31 17E
74 Mbale 1 8N 34 12E
74 Mbandaka 0 1S 18 18E
74 Mbarara 0 35S 30 25E
74 Mbeya 8 54S 33 29E
74 Mbuji-Mayi 6 9S 23 40E
74 Mbulu 3 45S 35 30E
75 Mchinji 13 47S 32 58E
103 Mead, L. 36 10N 114 10W
83 Meadow 26 35S 114 30E
93 Meadow Lake 54 10N 108 10W
93 Meadow Lake Prov. Park 52 25N 109 0W
96 Meadville 41 39N 80 9W
90 Meaford 44 40N 80 36W
15 Meath □ 53 32N 6 40W
20 Meaulne 46 36N 2 28E
19 Meaux 48 58N 2 50E
56 Mecca=Makkah 21 30N 39 54E
96 Mechanicsburg 40 12N 77 0W
97 Mechanicville 42 54N 73 41W
16 Mechelen 51 2N 4 29E
24 Mecklenburger, B. 54 20N 11 40E
82 Meda P.O. 17 20S 123 59E
62 Medak 18 1N 78 15E
64 Medan 3 40N 98 38E
112 Medanosa, Pta. 48 0S 66 0W
72 Médéa 36 12N 2 50E
110 Medellín 6 15N 75 35W
72 Médenine 33 21N 10 30E
72 Mederdra 17 0N 15 38W
102 Medford 42 20N 122 52W
41 Medgidia 44 15N 28 19E
41 Mediaş 46 9N 24 22E
37 Medicina 44 29N 11 38E
102 Medicine Bow 41 56N 106 11W
102 Medinine Bow Ra. 41 10N 106 25W
93 Medicine Hat 50 0N 110 45W
96 Medina 43 15N 78 27W
30 Medina de Rioseco 41 53N 5 3W
30 Medina del Campo 41 18N 4 55W
31 Medina-Sidonia 36 28N 5 57W
32 Medinaceli 41 12N 2 30W
34 Mediterranean Sea 35 0N 15 0E
20 Médoc, Reg. 45 10N 0 56W
49 Medveditsa, R. 49 0N 43 58E
51 Medvezhi Oshova 71 0N 161 0E
48 Medvezhyegorsk 63 0N 34 25E
13 Medway, R. 51 27N 0 44E
83 Meeberrie 26 57S 116 0E
83 Meekatharra 26 32S 118 29E
24 Meerane 50 51N 12 30E
60 Meerut 29 1N 77 50E
74 Mega 3 57N 38 30E
43 Megalópolis 37 25N 22 7E
91 Mégantic 45 36N 70 56W
43 Mégara 37 58N 23 22E
21 Mégève 45 51N 6 37E
61 Meghalaya □ 25 50N 91 0E
61 Meghna, R. 22 50N 90 50E
54 Megiddo 32 36N 15 11E
40 Mehadia 44 56N 22 23E
60 Mehsana 23 39N 72 26E
20 Mehun-sur-Yèvre 47 10N 2 13E
68 Meihokow 42 37N 125 46E
69 Meihsien 24 20N 116 0E
59 Meiktila 21 0N 96 0E
24 Meiningen 50 32N 10 25E
30 Meira, Sa. de 43 15N 7 15W
25 Meiringen 46 43N 8 12E
24 Meissen 51 10N 13 29E
24 Meissner, Mt. 51 12N 9 50E
20 Méjean, Causse 44 15N 3 30E
73 Mekele 13 33N 39 30E
72 Meknès 33 57N 5 33W
63 Mekong, R. 10 33N 105 24E
63 Melaka 2 15N 102 15E
63 Melaka □ 2 17N 102 18E
64 Melalap 5 10N 116 5E
43 Mélambes 35 8N 24 40E
76 Melanesia, Arch. 4 0S 155 0E
62 Melapalaiyam 8 39N 77 44E
84 Melbourne 37 40S 145 0E
104 Melchor Múzquiz 27 50N 101 40W
37 Méldola 44 7N 12 3E
24 Meldorf 54 5N 9 5E
36 Melegnano 45 21N 9 20E
48 Melekess= Dimitrovgrad 54 25N 49 33E
39 Melfi 41 0N 15 40E
93 Melfort 52 50N 105 40W
30 Melgar de Fernamental 42 27N 4 17W
43 Meligalá 37 15N 21 59E
72 Melilla 35 21N 2 57W
54 Melilot 31 22N 34 37E
108 Melipilla 33 42S 71 15W
93 Melita 49 15N 101 5W
49 Melitopol 46 50N 35 22E
26 Melk 48 13N 15 20E
20 Melle 46 14N 0 10W
45 Mellerud 58 41N 12 28E
26 Mělník 50 22N 14 23E
109 Melo 32 20S 54 10W
14 Melrose 55 35N 2 44W
12 Melton Mowbray 52 46N 0 52W
19 Melun 48 32N 2 39E
62 Melur 10 2N 78 23E
93 Melville 32 2S 115 48E
82 Melville, I., Australia 11 30S 131 0E
86 Melville, I., Canada 75 30N 111 0W
91 Melville, L. 53 45N 59 40W
89 Melville Pen. 68 0N 84 0W
48 Memel=Klaipeda 55 43N 21 10E
25 Memmingen 47 59N 10 12E
101 Memphis 35 7N 90 0W
97 Memphremagog L. 45 8N 72 17W
12 Menai Str. 53 7N 4 20W
100 Menasha 44 13N 88 27W
64 Menate 0 12S 112 47E
69 Mencheng 33 27N 116 45E
20 Mende 44 31N 3 30E
13 Mendip Hills 51 17N 2 40W
102 Mendocino 39 26N 123 50W
103 Mendota 36 46N 120 24W
108 Mendoza 32 50S 68 52W
108 Mendoza □ 33 0S 69 0W
110 Mene de Mauroa 10 45N 70 50W
110 Mene Grande 9 49N 70 56W
56 Menemen 38 36N 27 4E
16 Menen 50 47N 3 7E
38 Menfi 37 36N 12 57E
64 Menggala 4 20S 105 15E
31 Mengíbar 37 58N 3 48W
67 Mengtz 23 20N 103 20E
84 Menindee 32 20N 142 25E
100 Menominee 45 9N 87 39W
100 Menomonie 44 50N 91 54W
32 Menorca, I. 40 0N 4 0E
64 Mentawai, Kep. 2 0S 99 0E
21 Menton 43 50N 7 29E
73 Menzel Temime 36 46N 11 0E
48 Menzelinsk 55 43N 53 8E
83 Menzies 29 40S 120 58E
54 Me'ona 33 1N 35 15E
16 Meppel 52 42N 6 12E
24 Mepper 52 41N 7 20E
32 Mequinenza 41 22N 0 17E
43 Merabéllou, Kól. 35 10N 25 50E
65 Merak 5 55S 106 1E
37 Merano 46 40N 11 10E
65 Merauke 8 29S 120 24E
55 Merca 1 48N 44 50E
32 Mercadal 39 59N 4 5E
37 Mercato Saraceno 43 57N 12 11E
103 Merced 37 25N 120 30W
108 Mercedes, Buenos Aires 34 40S 59 30W
108 Mercedes, Corrientes 29 10S 58 5W
108 Mercedes, San Luis 33 40S 65 30W
108 Mercedes, Uruguay 33 12S 58 0W
85 Mercer 37 16S 175 5E
89 Mercy, C. 65 0N 62 30W
13 Mere 51 5N 2 16W
112 Meredith, C. 52 15S 60 40W
41 Merei 45 7N 26 43E
19 Méréville 48 20N 2 5E
63 Mergui 12 30N 98 35E
63 Mergui Arch.= Myeik Kyunzu 11 30N 97 30E
104 Mérida, Mexico 20 50N 89 40W
31 Mérida, Sp. 38 55N 6 25W
110 Mérida, Ven. 8 36N 71 8W
97 Meriden 41 33N 72 47W
102 Meridian, Id. 43 41N 116 20W
101 Meridian, Miss. 32 20N 88 42W
111 Meriruma 1 15N 54 50W
16 Merksem 51 16N 4 25E
19 Merlebach 49 5N 6 52E
73 Merowe 18 29N 31 46E
83 Merredin 31 28S 118 18E
100 Merrill 45 11N 89 41W
97 Merrimack, R. 42 49N 70 49W
92 Merritt 50 10N 120 45W
83 Merroe 27 53S 117 50E
74 Mersa Fatma 14 57N 40 17E
13 Mersea I. 51 48N 0 55E
24 Merseburg 51 20N 12 0E
12 Mersey, R. 53 25N 3 0W
12 Merseyside □ 53 25W 2 55W
56 Mersin 36 51N 34 36E
63 Mersing 2 25N 103 50E
13 Merthyr Tydfil 51 45N 3 23W
31 Mértola 37 40N 7 40E
101 Mertzon 31 17N 100 48W
19 Méru 49 13N 2 8E
74 Meru 0 3N 37 40E
19 Méry 48 30N 3 52E
25 Merzig 49 26N 6 37E
103 Mesa 33 20N 111 56W
39 Mesagne 40 33N 17 49E
43 Mesaras, Kól. 35 6N 24 47E
57 Meshed=Mashhad 36 20N 59 35E
103 Mesilla 32 20N 107 0W
18 Meslay-du-Maine 47 58N 0 33W
43 Mesolóngion 38 27N 21 28E
56 Mesopotamia, Reg.=Al Jazirah, Reg. 33 30N 44 0E
39 Messina, It. 38 10N 15 32E
75 Messina, S.Africa 22 20S 30 12E
39 Messina, Str. di 38 5N 15 35E
43 Messíni 37 4N 22 1E
43 Messinía □ 37 10N 22 0E
43 Messiniakós Kól. 36 45N 22 5E
37 Mestre 45 30N 12 13E
110 Meta, R. 6 12N 67 28W
90 Metagama 47 0N 81 55W
108 Metán 25 30S 65 0W
85 Methven 43 38S 171 40E
41 Metkovets 43 37N 23 10E
40 Metković 43 6N 17 39E
92 Metlakatia 55 8N 131 35W
37 Metlika 45 40N 15 20E
101 Metropolis 37 10N 88 47W

Métsovon Monchique

42 Métsovon 39 48N 21 12E
62 Mettuppalaiyam 11 18N 76 59E
62 Mettur 11 48N 77 47E
54 Metulla 33 17N 35 34E
19 Metz 49 8N 6 10E
64 Meulaboh 4 11N 96 3E
19 Meulan 49 0N 1 52E
64 Meureudu 5 19N 96 10E
19 Meurthe, R. 48 47N 6 9E
19 Meuse □ 49 8N 5 25E
16 Meuse, R. 51 49N 5 1E
25 Meuselwitz 51 3N 12 18E
19 Meurthe-et-Moselle □ 48 52N 6 0E
101 Mexia 31 38N 96 32W
111 Mexiana, I. 0 0 49 30W
104 Mexicali 32 40N 115 30W
104 Mexico, Mexico 19 20N 99 10W
100 Mexico, U.S.A. 39 10N 91 55W
104 Mexico ■ 20 0N 100 0W
104 México □ 19 20N 99 10W
24 Meyenburg 53 19N 12 15E
20 Meymac 45 32N 2 10E
48 Mezen, R. 66 11N 43 59E
41 Mezdra 43 12N 23 35E
20 Mèze 43 27N 3 36E
48 Mezen 65 50N 44 20E
18 Mézidon 49 5N 0 1W
20 Mézin 44 4N 0 16E
27 Mezóberény 46 49N 21 3E
27 Mezökövesd 47 49N 20 35E
27 Mezötur 47 0N 20 41E
60 Mhow 22 33N 75 50E
104 Miahuatlán 16 21N 96 36W
31 Miajadas 39 9N 5 54W
99 Miami 25 52N 80 15W
99 Miami Beach 25 49N 80 6W
56 Miandowāb 37 0N 46 5E
56 Miāneh 37 30N 47 40E
60 Mianwali 32 38N 71 28E
69 Miaoli 24 34N 120 48E
50 Miass 54 59N 60 6E
41 Micăsasa 46 7N 24 7E
27 Michalovce 48 44N 21 54E
88 Michelson, Mt. 69 19N 144 17W
98 Michigan □ 44 40N 85 40W
98 Michigan, L. 44 0N 87 0W
98 Michigan City 41 42N 86 56W
91 Michikamau L. 54 0N 6 0W
90 Michipicoten I. 47 55N 85 45W
90 Michipicoten River 47 50N 84 58W
104 Michoacán □ 19 0N 102 0W
41 Michurin 42 9N 27 51E
48 Michurinsk 52 58N 40 27E
76 Micronesia, Arch. 17 0N 160 0E
13 Mid Glamorgan □ 51 40N 3 25W
16 Middelburg, Neth. 51 30N 3 36E
75 Middelburg, S. Africa 31 30S 25 0E
45 Middelfart 55 30N 9 43E
63 Middle Andaman, I. 12 30N 92 30E
91 Middle Brook 48 40N 54 20W
97 Middleboro 41 56N 70 52W
99 Middlesboro 36 40N 83 40W
12 Middlesbrough 54 35N 1 14W
97 Middlesex 40 36N 74 30W
97 Middletown, Conn. 41 37N 72 40W
97 Middletown, N.Y. 41 28N 74 28W
98 Middletown, Ohio 39 29N 84 25W
97 Middletown, Pa. 40 12N 76 44W
91 Middleton 44 50N 65 5W
80 Middleton P.O. 22 22S 141 32E
20 Midi, Canal du 43 45N 1 21E
83 Midland, Australia 31 54S 115 59E
90 Midland, Canada 44 45N 79 50W
98 Midland, Mich. 43 37N 84 17W
96 Midland, Pa. 40 39N 80 27W
101 Midland, Tex. 32 0N 102 3W
61 Midnapore 22 25N 87 21E
76 Midway Is. 28 13N 177 22W
102 Midwest 43 27N 106 11W
40 Midžor, Mt. 43 24N 22 40E
66 Mie □ 34 20N 136 20E
28 Międzychod 52 35N 15 53E
28 Międzyrzec Podlaski 51 58N 22 45E
28 Międzyrzecz 52 26N 15 35E
27 Mielec 50 18N 21 25E
69 Mienyang 31 18N 104 26E
41 Miercurea Ciuc 46 21N 25 48E
30 Mieres 43 18N 5 48W
54 Migdal 32 51N 35 30E
54 Migdal Ha'Emeq 32 41N 35 14E
19 Migennes 47 58N 3 31E
37 Migliarino 44 54N 11 56E
66 Mihara 34 25N 133 5E
32 Mijares, R. 39 55N 0 1W
31 Mijas 36 36N 4 40W
41 Mikhaylovgrad 43 27N 23 16E
43 Mikínai 37 43N 22 46E
74 Mikindani 10 15S 40 2E
46 Mikkeli □ 61 56N 28 0E
43 Míkonos, I. 37 30N 25 25E
27 Mikołow 50 10N 18 50E
42 Mikrí Prespa, L. 40 46N 21 4E
Límní 40 46N 21 4E
48 Mikun 62 20N 50 0E
110 Milagro 2 0S 79 30W
81 Milang 35 20S 138 55E
36 Milano 45 28N 9 10E
39 Milazzo 38 13N 15 13E
13 Mildenhall 52 20N 0 30E
84 Mildura 34 13S 142 9E
42 Miléai 39 20N 23 9E
81 Miles 26 37S 150 10E
100 Miles City 46 30N 105 50W
93 Milestone 50 0N 104 30W
87 Milford, Conn. 41 13N 73 4W
98 Milford, Del. 38 52N 75 26W
97 Milford, Mass. 42 8N 71 30W
103 Milford, Utah 38 20N 113 0W
13 Milford Haven 51 43N 5 2W
28 Milicz 51 31N 17 19E
83 Miling 30 30S 116 17E
39 Militello in Val di Catania 37 16N 14 46E
20 Millau 44 8N 3 4E
97 Millerton 41 57N 73 32W
91 Millertown Junction 48 49N 56 28W
20 Millevaches, Plat. de 45 45N 2 0E
81 Millicent 37 34S 140 21E
99 Millinocket 45 45N 68 45W
12 Millom 54 13N 3 16W
98 Millville 39 22N 74 0W
89 Milne Inlet 72 30N 80 0W
92 Milo 24 28N 103 23E
43 Mílos, I. 36 44N 24 25E
85 Milton, N.Z. 46 7S 169 59E
96 Milton, U.S.A. 41 0N 76 53W
96 Milton West 43 33N 79 53W
13 Milton Keynes 52 3N 0 42W
15 Miltown Malbay 52 51N 9 25W
96 Milverton 43 35N 80 43W
98 Milwaukee 43 9N 87 58W
102 Milwaukie 45 33N 122 39W
20 Mimizan 44 12N 1 13W
26 Mimoň 50 38N 14 45E
56 Minā al Ahmadī 29 5N 48 10E
56 Mina Saud 28 45N 48 20E
57 Mīnāb 27 10N 57 1E
66 Minamata 32 10N 130 30E
109 Minas 34 20S 55 15W
31 Minas de Rio Tinto 37 42N 6 22W
111 Minas Gerais □ 18 50S 46 0W
104 Minatitlán 17 58N 94 35W
59 Minbu 20 10N 95 0E
14 Minch, Little, Chan. 57 40N 6 50W
14 Minch, North, Chan. 58 0N 6 0W
65 Mindanao, I. 8 0N 125 0E
65 Mindanao Sea 9 0 124 0E
65 Mindanao Trench 8 0N 128 0E
24 Minden 52 18N 8 54E
101 Minden 32 40N 93 20W
65 Mindoro, I. 13 0N 121 0E
65 Mindoro Str. 12 30N 120 30E
13 Minehead 51 12N 3 29W
101 Mineral Wells 32 50N 98 5W
97 Minersville 40 40N 76 17W
39 Minervino Murge 41 6N 16 4E
91 Mingan 50 20N 64 0W
49 Mingechaurskoye, Vdkhr. 40 56N 47 20E
80 Mingela 19 52S 146 38E
83 Mingenew 29 12S 115 21E
33 Minglanilla 39 34N 1 38W
30 Mingorria 40 42N 4 40N
29 Minho Reg. 41 40N 8 30W
69 Minhow=Foochow 26 5N 119 18E
40 Minićevo 43 42N 22 18E
83 Minilya 23 55S 114 0E
69 Min Kiang, R. 26 0N 119 30E
69 Minkiang 32 30N 114 10E
72 Minna 9 37N 6 30E
100 Minneapolis 44 58N 93 20W
93 Minnedosa 50 20N 99 50W
100 Minnesota □ 46 40N 94 0W
81 Minnipa 32 51S 135 9E
66 Mino 35 32N 136 55E
30 Miño, R. 41 52N 8 51W
100 Minot 48 10N 101 15W
48 Minsk 53 52N 27 30E
28 Mińsk Mazowiecki 52 10N 21 33E
91 Minto 34 1S 150 51E
89 Minto, L. 48 0N 84 45W
102 Minturn 39 45N 106 25W
38 Minturno 41 15N 13 43E
51 Minusinsk 53 50N 91 20E
59 Minutang 28 15N 96 30E
67 Minya Konka, Mt. 29 34N 101 53E
91 Miquelon, I. 47 8N 56 24W
37 Mira 45 26N 12 9E
31 Mira, R. 37 43N 8 47W
39 Mirabella Eclano 41 3N 14 59E
62 Miraj 16 50N 74 45E
108 Miramar 38 15S 57 50W
21 Miramas 43 33N 4 59E
20 Miramont 44 37N 0 21E
111 Miranda 20 10S 50 15W
30 Miranda de Ebro 42 41N 2 57W
30 Miranda do Corvo 40 6N 8 20W
30 Miranda do Douro 41 30N 6 16W
30 Mirandela 41 32N 98 59W
36 Mirandola 44 53N 11 2E
109 Mirandópolis 21 9S 51 6W
37 Mirano 45 29N 12 6E
109 Mirassol 20 46S 49 28W
19 Mirecourt 48 20N 6 10E
64 Miri 4 18N 114 0E
80 Miriam Vale 24 20S 151 39E
109 Mirim, L. 32 45S 52 50W
61 Mirzapur 25 10N 82 45E
68 Mishan 45 31N 132 2E
98 Mishawaka 41 40N 86 8W
66 Mishima 35 10N 138 52E
54 Mishmar Alyalon 31 52N 34 57E
54 Mishmar Ha 'Emeq 32 37N 35 7E
54 Mishmar Ha Negev 31 22N 34 48E
54 Mishmar Ha Yarden 33 0N 35 56E
38 Misilmeri 38 2N 13 25E
109 Misiones, Arg. □ 27 0S 54 0W
108 Misiones, Paraguay □ 27 0S 57 0W
57 Miskīn 23 44N 56 52E
105 Miskitos, Cayos 14 26N 82 50W
27 Miskolc 48 7N 20 50E
65 Misool, I. 2 0S 130 0E
73 Misrātah 32 18N 15 3E
101 Mission 26 15N 98 30W
92 Mission City 49 10N 122 15W
101 Mississippi □ 33 0N 90 0W
101 Mississippi, R. 29 0N 89 15W
101 Mississippi, Delta of the 29 10N 89 15W
102 Missoula 47 0N 114 0W
100 Missouri □ 38 25N 92 30W
100 Missouri, Plat. du Coteau du 46 0N 99 30W
100 Missouri, R. 38 50N 90 8W
90 Mistassini, L. 51 0N 73 40W
39 Misterbianco 37 32N 15 0E
39 Mistretta 37 56N 14 20E
81 Mitchell, Australia 26 29S 147 58E
100 Mitchell, U.S.A. 43 40N 98 0W
99 Mitchell, Mt. 35 40N 82 20W
15 Mitchelstown 52 16N 8 18W
60 Mitha Tiwana 32 13N 72 6E
42 Míthimna 39 20N 26 12E
43 Mitilíni 39 6N 26 35E
104 Mitla 16 55N 96 17W
66 Mito 36 20N 140 30E
73 Mitsiwa 15 35N 39 25E
84 Mittagong 34 28S 150 29E
24 Mittelland-kanal 52 23N 7 45E
25 Mittwelda 50 59N 13 0E
84 Mittyack 35 8S 142 36E
74 Mitumba, Chaîne des 10 0S 26 20E
66 Miyagi □ 38 15N 140 45E
66 Miyako 39 40N 141 75E
66 Miyakonojo 31 32N 131 5E
66 Miyazaki 31 56N 131 30E
66 Miyazaki 32 0N 131 30E
54 Miyet, Bahr el 31 30N 35 30E
66 Miyoshi 34 48N 132 32E
68 Miyun 40 22N 116 49E
15 Mizen Hd., Cork 51 27N 9 50W
15 Mizen Hd., Wicklow 52 52N 6 4W
41 Mizil 44 59N 26 29E
59 Mizoram □ 23 0N 92 40E
54 Mizpe Ramon 20 36N 34 48E
45 Mjölby 58 20N 15 10E
75 Mkushi 14 20S 29 20E
26 Mladá Boleslav 50 27N 14 53E
40 Mladenovac 44 28N 20 44E
28 Mława 53 9N 20 25E
70 Mlanje, Mt. 16 2S 35 33E
40 Mljet, I. 42 43N 17 30E
40 Mljetski, Kanal 42 48N 17 35E
46 Mo 66 15N 14 8E
65 Moa, I. 8 0S 128 0E
103 Moab 38 40N 109 35W
84 Moama 36 3S 144 45E
74 Moba 7 3S 29 47E
74 Mobaye 4 25N 21 5E
100 Moberly 39 25N 92 25W
90 Mobert 48 41N 85 40W
99 Mobile 30 41N 88 3W
45 Møborg 56 24N 8 21E
74 Mobutu Sese Seko, L. 1 30N 31 0E
75 Moçambique 15 3S 40 42E
75 Moçâmedes 16 35S 12 30E
75 Mochudi 24 27S 26 7E
45 Möckeln, L. 56 40N 14 15E
110 Mocoa 1 15N 76 45W
109 Mococa 21 28S 47 0W
104 Moctezuma, R. 21 59N 98 34W
75 Mocuba 16 54S 37 25E
36 Módcna 44 39N 10 55E
103 Modesto 37 43N 121 0W
39 Módica 36 52N 14 45E
37 Modigliana 44 9N 11 48E
27 Mödling 48 5N 16 17E
84 Moe 38 12S 146 19E
18 Moélan-sur-Mer 47 49N 3 38W
44 Moelv 60 56N 10 43E
111 Moengo 5 45N 54 20W
74 Moero, L. 9 0S 28 45E
14 Moffat 55 20N 3 27W
60 Moga 30 48N 75 8E
55 Mogadiscio 2 2N 45 25E
55 Mogadishu= Mogadiscio 2 2N 45 25E
72 Mogador= Essaouira 31 32N 9 42W
59 Mogaung 25 20N 97 0E
33 Mogente 38 52N 0 45W
109 Mogi das Cruzes 23 45S 46 20W
109 Mogi Mirim 22 20S 47 0W
48 Mogilev 53 55N 30 18E
49 Mogilvev Podolskiy 48 20N 27 40E
37 Mogliano Venteto 45 33N 12 15E
51 Mogocha 53 40N 119 50E
103 Mogollon Mesa 43 40N 110 0W
83 Mogumber 31 2S 116 3E
27 Mohács 45 58N 18 41E
97 Mohawk, R. 42.47N 73 42W
24 Möhne, R. 51 27N 7 57E
68 Moho 53 15N 122 27E
19 Mohon 49 45N 4 44E
62 Moinabad 17 44N 77 16E
50 Mointy 47 40N 73 45E
20 Moissac 44 7N 1 5E
31 Moita 38 38N 8 58W
33 Mojácar 37 6N 1 55W
103 Mojave 35 8N 118 8W
103 Mojave Des. 35 0N 117 30W
65 Mojokerto 7 29S 112 25E
61 Mokameh 25 24N 85 55E
85 Mokau, R. 38 42S 174 37E
43 Mokhós 35 16N 25 27E
69 Mokpo 34 50N 126 30E
40 Mokra Gora 42 50N 20 30E
16 Mol 51 11N 5 5E
39 Mola di Bari 41 3N 17 5E
12 Mold 53 10N 3 10W
49 Moldanan S.S.R. □ 47 0N 28 0E
40 Moldova Nouă 44 45N 21 41E
41 Moldoveanu, Mt. 45 36N 24 45E
75 Molepolole 24 28S 25 28E
39 Molfetta 41 12N 16 35E
32 Molina de Aragón 40 46N 1 52W
100 Moline 41 30N 90 30W
37 Molinella 44 38N 11 40E
39 Molise □ 41 45N 14 30E
30 Molledo 43 8N 4 6W
110 Mollendo 17 0S 72 0W
32 Mollerusa 41 37N 0 54E
31 Mollina 37 8N 4 38W
24 Mölln 53 37N 10 41E
45 Mölndal 57 40N 12 3E
94 Molokai, I. 21 8N 156 0W
84 Molong 33 5S 148 54E
75 Molopo, R. 28 30S 20 13E
43 Mólos 38 47N 22 37E
65 Molucca Sea 4 0S 124 0E
65 Moluccas, Is.= Maluku, Is. 1 0S 127 0E
74 Mombasa 4 2S 39 43E
30 Mombuey 42 3N 6 20W
41 Momchilgrad 41 33N 25 23E
62 Mominabad 18 43N 76 23W
110 Mompos 9 14N 74 26W
45 Møn, I. 54 57N 12 15E
105 Mona, Pta. 9 37N 82 36W
105 Mona, I. 18 5N 67 54W
14 Monach Is. 57 32N 7 40W
21 Monaco ■ 43 46N 7 23E
14 Monadhliath Mts. 57 10N 4 4W
97 Monadnock Mt. 42 52N 72 7W
15 Monaghan 54 15N 6 58W
15 Monaghan □ 54 10N 7 0W
101 Monahans 31 35N 102 50W
73 Monastir 35 50N 10 49E
32 Moncada 39 30N 0 24W
30 Monção 42 4N 8 27W
32 Moncayo, Sa. del 41 48N 1 50W
48 Monchegorsk 67 54N 32 58E
24 Mönchengladbach 51 12N 6 23E
31 Monchique 37 19N 8 38W

Moza Nasser, L.=Naser, Buheiret en

54 Moza 31 48N 35 8 E
75 Mozambique ■ 19 0S 35 0 E
70 Mozambique Chan. 20 0S 39 0 E
48 Mozyr 52 0N 29 15 E
74 Mpanda 6 23S 31 40 E
75 Mpika 11 51S 31 25 E
28 Mrągowo 53 57N 21 18 E
73 Msaken 35 49N 10 33 E
75 Msoro 13 35S 31 50 E
74 Mtwara 10 20S 40 20 E
111 Muaná 1 25S 49 15W
63 Muang Chiang Rai 19 52N 99 50 E
63 Muang Lamphun 18 40N 98 53 E
63 Muang Phichit 16 29N 100 21 E
63 Muar=Bandar Maharani 2 3N 102 34 E
64 Muarabungo 1 40S 101 10 E
64 Muarakaman 0 2S 116 45 E
64 Muaratembesi 1 42S 103 2 E
64 Muaratewe 0 50S 115 0 E
56 Mubairik 23 22N 39 8 E
74 Mubende 0 33N 31 22 E
73 Mubi 10 18N 13 16 E
25 Mücheln 51 18N 11 49 E
14 Muck, I. 56 50N 6 15W
111 Mucuri 18 0S 40 0W
75 Mufulira 12 32S 28 15W
30 Mugardos 43 27N 8 15W
31 Muge 39 3N 8 40W
30 Mugia 43 3N 9 17W
73 Muhammad Qol 20 53N 37 9 E
25 Mühldorf 48 14N 12 23 E
24 Mühlhausen 51 12N 10 29 E
15 Muine Bheag 52 42N 6 59W
30 Muiños 41 58N 7 59W
55 Mukalla 14 33N 49 2 E
68 Mukden=Shenyang 41 48N 123 27 E
55 Mukeiras 13 59N 45 52 E
83 Mukinbudin 30 55S 118 5 E
64 Mukomuko 2 20S 101 10 E
60 Muktsar 30 30N 74 30 E
33 Mula 38 3N 1 33W
105 Mulatas, Arch. de las 6 51N 78 31W
108 Mulchén 37 45S 72 20W
24 Mulde, R., 51 10N 12 48 E
91 Mulgrave 45 38N 61 31W
31 Mulhacén, Mt. 37 4N 3 20W
24 Mülheim 51 26N 6 53W
19 Mulhouse 47 40N 7 20 E
14 Mull of Galloway, Pt. 54 40N 4 55W
14 Mull of Kintyre, Pt. 55 20N 5 45W
14 Mull, I. 56 27N 6 0W
84 Mullengudgery 31 43S 147 29 E
15 Mullet, Pen. 54 10N 10 2W
83 Mullewa 28 29S 115 30 E
15 Mullingar 53 31N 7 20W
81 Mullumbimby 28 30S 153 30 E
60 Multan □ 30 29N 72 29 E
60 Multan 30 15N 71 30 E
84 Mulwala 35 59S 146 0 E
63 Mun, R. 15 19N 105 31 E
65 Muna, I. 5 0S 122 30 E
25 Munchberg 50 11N 11 48 E
24 Muncheberg 52 30N 14 9 E
25 München 48 8N 11 33 E
98 Muncie 40 10N 85 20W
62 Mundakayam 9 30N 76 32 E
24 Münden 51 25N 9 42 E
82 Mundiwindi 23 47S 120 9 E
33 Mundo, R. 38 30N 2 15W
111 Mundo Novo 11 50S 40 29W
60 Mundra 22 54N 69 26 E
83 Mundrabilla 31 52S 127 51 E
33 Munera 39 2N 2 29W
81 Mungallala 26 25S 147 34 E
80 Mungana 17 8S 144 27 E
81 Mungindi 28 58S 149 1 E
75 Munhango 12 9S 18 36 E
25 Munich= München 48 8N 11 33 E
45 Munkedal 58 28N 11 40 E
44 Munkfars 59 50N 13 30 E
112 Muñoz Gamero, Pen. 52 30S 73 5 E
19 Munster 48 2N 7 8 E
15 Munster □ 52 20N 8 40W
24 Münster, Niedersachsen 52 59N 10 5 E
24 Münster, Nordrhein-Westfalen 51 58N 7 37 E
83 Muntadgin 31 48S 118 30 E
64 Muntok 2 5S 105 10 E
46 Muonio, R. 67 48N 23 25 E
26 Mur, R. 46 18N 16 53 E
37 Mura, R. 46 18N 16 53 E
112 Murallón, Mt. 49 55S 73 30W
74 Murangá 0 45S 37 9 E
48 Murashi 59 30N 49 0 E
20 Murat 45 7N 2 53 E
26 Murau 47 6N 14 10 E
38 Muravera 39 25N 9 35 E
30 Murça 41 24N 7 28W
84 Murchison, Australia 36 39S 145 14 E
85 Murchison, N.Z. 41 49S 172 21 E
83 Murchison, R. 26 1S 117 6 E
33 Murcia 38 2N 1 10W
33 Murcia □ 37 50N 1 30W
33 Murcia, Reg. 38 35N 1 50W
41 Mureş 46 45N 24 40 E
41 Mureşul, R. 46 15N 20 13 E
20 Muret 43 30N 1 20 E
99 Murfreesboro 35 50N 86 21W
50 Murgab 38 10N 73 59 E
81 Murgon 26 15S 151 54 E
109 Muriaé 21 8S 42 23W
24 Müritzsee 53 25N 12 40 E
48 Murmansk 68 57N 33 10 E
32 Muro 39 45N 3 3 E
48 Murom 55 35N 42 3 E
66 Muroran 42 25N 141 0 E
30 Muros 42 45N 9 5W
39 Muro Lucano 40 45N 15 30 E
101 Murphysboro 37 50N 89 20W
99 Murray, Ky. 36 40N 88 20W
102 Murray, Utah 40 41N 111 58W
81 Murray, R. 35 22S 139 22 E
81 Murray Bridge 35 6S 139 14 E
84 Murrayville 35 16S 141 11 E
58 Murree 33 56N 73 28 E
83 Murrin Murrin 28 50S 121 45 E
84 Murrumbidgee, R. 34 43S 143 12 E
84 Murrurundi 31 42S 150 51 E
61 Murshidabad 24 11N 88 19 E
60 Murtazapur 20 40N 77 25 E
84 Murtoa 36 35S 142 28 E
30 Murtosa 40 44N 8 40W
85 Murupara 38 30S 178 40 E
61 Murwara 23 46N 80 28 E
81 Murwillumbah 28 18S 153 27 E
26 Mürzzuschlag 47 36N 15 41 E
41 Musala, Mt. 41 13N 23 27 E
57 Muscat=Masqat 23 37N 58 36 E
100 Muscatine 41 25N 91 5W
74 Mushie 2 56S 17 4 E
98 Muskegon 43 15N 86 17W
98 Muskegon Heights 43 12N 86 17W
101 Muskogee 35 50N 95 25W
73 Musmar 18 6N 35 40 E
74 Musoma 1 30S 33 48 E
14 Musselburgh 55 57N 3 3W
20 Mussidan 45 2N 0 22 E
38 Mussomeli 37 35N 13 43 E
112 Musters, L. 45 20S 69 25W
84 Muswellbrook 32 16S 150 56 E
73 Mût 25 28N 28 58 E
68 Mutankiang 44 35N 129 30 E
80 Muttaburra 22 38S 144 29 E
91 Mutton Bay 50 50N 59 2W
62 Muvatupusha 9 53N 76 35 E
51 Muya 56 27N 115 39 E
58 Muzaffarabad 34 25N 73 30 E
60 Muzaffargarh 30 5N 71 14 E
60 Muzaffarnagar 29 26N 77 40 E
61 Muzaffarpur 26 7N 85 32 E
50 Muzhi 65 25N 64 40 E
18 Muzillac 47 35N 2 30W
67 Muztagh, Mt. 36 30N 87 22 E
74 Mvadhi Ousye 1 13N 13 12 E
74 Mwanza, Tanzania 2 30S 32 58 E
74 Mwanza, Zaire 7 55S 26 43 E
74 Mweka 4 50S 21 40 E
74 Mweru, L. 9 0S 28 45 E
63 My Tho 10 29N 106 23 E
59 Myanaung 18 25N 95 10 E
59 Myaungmya 16 30N 95 0 E
59 Myingyan 21 30N 95 30 E
59 Myitkyina 25 30N 97 26 E
27 Myiava 48 41N 17 37 E
61 Mymensingh= Nasirabad 24 42N 90 30 E
102 Myrtle Creek 43 0N 123 19W
102 Myrtle Point 43 0N 124 4W
28 Myślibórz 52 55N 14 50 E
27 Mystowice 50 15N 19 12 E
62 Mysore 12 17N 76 41 E
27 Myszkow 50 45N 19 22 E
46 Mývatn, L. 65 36N 17 0W
26 Mže, R. 49 46N 13 24 E

N

54 Na'an 31 53N 34 52 E
47 Naantali 60 27N 21 57 E
15 Naas 53 12N 6 40W
61 Nabadwip 23 34N 88 20 E
73 Nabenl 36 30N 10 51 E
60 Nabha 30 26N 76 14 E
54 Nabi Rubin 31 56N 34 44 E
54 Nābulus 32 14N 35 15 E
74 Nachingwea 10 49S 38 49 E
27 Náchod 50 25N 16 8 E
44 Nacka 59 17N 18 12 E
81 Nackara 32 48S 139 12 E
101 Nacogdoches 31 33N 95 30W
104 Nacozari 30 30N 109 50W
60 Nadiad 22 41N 72 56 E
57 Nadūshan 32 2N 53 35 E
48 Nadvoitsy 63 52N 34 15 E
50 Nadym 63 35N 72 42 E
45 Næstved 55 13N 11 44 E
72 Nafada 11 8N 11 20 E
65 Naga 13 38N 123 15 E
59 Nagaland □ 26 0N 95 0 E
66 Nagano 36 40N 138 10 E
66 Nagano □ 36 15N 138 0 E
66 Nagaoka 32 27N 138 51 E
62 Nagappattinam 10 46N 79 51 E
66 Nagasaki 32 47N 129 50 E
66 Nagasaki □ 32 50N 129 40 E
66 Nagato 36 15N 138 16 E
60 Nagaur 27 15N 73 45 E
62 Nagercoil 8 12N 77 33 E
60 Nagina 29 30N 78 30 E
51 Nagornyy 55 58N 124 57 E
66 Nagoya 35 10N 136 50 E
60 Nagpur 21 8N 79 10 E
27 Nagykanizsa 46 28N 17 0 E
27 Nagykörös 47 2N 19 48 E
69 Naha 26 12N 127 40 E
88 Nahannai Butte 61 5N 123 30W
54 Nahariyya 33 1N 35 5 E
56 Nahavand 34 10N 48 30 E
54 Nahf 32 56N 35 18 E
112 Nahuel Huapi, L. 41 0S 71 32W
93 Naicam 52 30N 104 30W
25 Naila 50 19N 11 43 E
91 Nain 56 34N 61 40W
18 Naintré 46 46N 0 29 E
14 Nairn 57 35N 3 54W
74 Nairobi 1 17S 36 48 E
74 Naivasha 0 40S 36 30 E
57 Najafābād 32 40N 51 15 E
56 Najd, Reg. 26 30N 42 0 E
30 Najerilla, R. 42 15N 2 45W
60 Najibabad 29 40N 78 20 E
66 Nakamura 33 0N 133 0 E
56 Nakhi Mubarak 24 10N 38 10 E
49 Nakhichevan 39 14N 45 30 E
51 Nakhodka 43 10N 132 45 E
63 Nakhon Phanom 17 23N 104 43 E
63 Nakhon Ratchasima 14 59N 102 12 E
63 Nakhon Sawan 15 35N 100 12 E
63 Nakhon Si Thammarat 8 29N 100 0 E
90 Nakina 50 10N 86 40W
60 Nakodar 31 8N 75 31 E
45 Nakskov 54 50N 11 8 E
74 Nakuru 0 15S 35 5 E
92 Nakusp 50 20N 117 45W
58 Nal, R. 26 2N 65 19 E
68 Nalayh 47 43N 107 22 E
49 Nalchik 43 30N 43 33 E
62 Nalgonda 17 6N 79 15 E
62 Nallamalai Hills 15 30N 78 50 E
30 Nalon, R. 43 32N 6 4W
73 Nālūt 31 54N 11 0 E
63 Nam Dinh 20 25N 106 5 E
63 Nam-Phan, Reg. 10 30N 106 0 E
63 Nam Tha 20 58N 101 30 E
63 Nam Tok 14 21N 99 0 E
67 Nam Tso, L. 30 40N 90 30 E
62 Namakkal 11 13N 78 13 E
75 Namaland, Reg. 29 43S 19 5 E
50 Namangan 41 30N 71 30 E
75 Namapa 13 43S 39 50 E
65 Namber 1 2S 134 57 E
81 Nambour 26 38S 152 49 E
81 Nambucca Heads 30 40S 152 48 E
67 Namcha Barwa, Mt. 29 30N 95 10 E
75 Namib Des.= Namibwoestyn 22 30S 15 0W
75 Namibia ■ 22 0S 18 9 E
75 Namibwoestyn 22 30S 15 0W
65 Namlea 3 10S 127 5 E
102 Nampa 43 40N 116 40W
75 Nampula 15 6S 39 7 E
65 Namrole 3 46S 126 46 E
46 Namsen, R. 64 27N 11 28 E
46 Namsos 64 29N 11 30 E
59 Namtu 23 5N 97 28 E
16 Namur 50 27N 4 52 E
16 Namur □ 50 17N 5 0 E
75 Namutoni 18 49S 16 55 E
75 Namwala 15 44S 26 30 E
28 Namysłów 51 6N 17 42 E
69 Namyung 25 15N 114 5 E
67 Nan Shan, Mts. 38 0N 98 0 E
92 Nanaimo 49 10N 124 0W
81 Nanango 26 40S 152 0 E
66 Nanao 37 0N 137 0 E
69 Nanchang 28 34N 115 48 E
69 Nancheng 27 30N 116 28 E
69 Nancheng= Hanchung 33 10N 107 2 E
69 Nanchung 30 47N 105 59 E
19 Nancy 48 42N 6 12 E
61 Nanda Devi, Mt. 30 30N 80 30 E
62 Nander 19 10N 77 20 E
85 Nandi 17 25S 176 50 E
62 Nandikotkur 15 52N 78 18 E
60 Nandura 20 52N 76 25 E
60 Nandurbar 21 20N 74 15 E
62 Nandyal 15 30N 78 30 E
58 Nanga Parbat, Mt. 35 10N 74 35 E
57 Nangarhar □ 34 15N 70 30 E
19 Nangis 48 33N 3 0 E
62 Nanjangud 12 6N 76 43 E
60 Nankana Sahib 31 27N 73 38 E
69 Nankang 25 42N 114 35 E
69 Nanking 32 10N 118 50 E
66 Nankoku 33 39N 133 44 E
83 Nannine 26 51S 118 18 E
69 Nanning 22 51N 108 18 E
83 Nannup 33 59S 115 45 E
61 Nanpara 27 52N 81 33 E
69 Nanping 26 45N 118 5 E
66 Nansei-Shotō, Is. 29 0N 129 0 E
83 Nanson 28 34S 114 46 E
20 Nant 44 1N 3 18 E
69 Nantan 25 0N 107 35 E
18 Nantes 47 12N 1 33W
19 Nanteuil-le-Haudouin 49 9N 2 48 E
20 Nantiat 46 1N 1 11 E
97 Nanticoke 41 12N 76 1W
92 Nanton 50 20N 113 50W
69 Nantou 23 57N 120 35 E
21 Nantua 46 10N 5 35 E
86 Nantucket I. 41 16N 70 3W
69 Nantung 32 0N 120 50 E
111 Nanuque 17 50S 40 21W
69 Nanyang 33 2N 112 35 E
68 Nanyuan 39 48N 116 23 E
74 Nanyuki 0 2N 37 4 E
33 Nao, C. de la 38 44N 0 14 E
66 Naoetsu 37 12N 138 10 E
61 Naogaon 24 52N 88 52 E
42 Náousa 40 42N 22 9 E
102 Napa 38 18N 122 17W
90 Napanee 44 15N 77 0W
85 Napier 39 30S 176 56 E
82 Napier Broome, B. 14 0S 127 0 E
82 Napier Downs 16 20S 124 30 E
110 Napo, R. 3 20S 72 40W
100 Napoleon 46 32N 99 49W
39 Nápoli 40 50N 14 5 E
66 Nara 34 40N 135 49 E
66 Nara □ 34 30N 136 0 E
60 Nara, R. 24 7N 69 7 E
84 Naracoorte 36 50S 140 44 E
62 Narasapur 16 26N 81 50 E
62 Narasaraopet 16 14N 80 4 E
63 Narathiwat 6 40N 101 55 E
61 Narayanganj 23 31N 90 33 E
62 Narayanpet 16 45N 77 30 E
20 Narbonne 43 11N 3 0 E
30 Narcea, R. 43 28N 6 6W
39 Nardo 40 10N 18 0 E
83 Narembeen 32 4S 118 24 E
83 Naretha 31 0S 124 50 E
28 Narew 52 55N 23 30 E
28 Narew, R. 52 26N 20 42 E
60 Narmada, R. 21 35N 72 35 E
60 Narnaul 28 5N 76 11 E
37 Narni 42 30N 12 30 E
38 Naro 37 18N 13 48 E
60 Narowal 32 6N 74 52 E
81 Narrabri 30 19S 149 46 E
81 Narran, R. 29 45S 147 20 E
84 Narrandera 34 42S 146 31 E
83 Narrogin 32 58S 117 14 E
84 Narromine 32 12S 148 12 E
66 Naruto 35 36N 140 25 E
46 Narvik 68 28N 17 26 E
60 Narwana 29 39N 76 6 E
31 Naryilco 28 37S 141 53 E
50 Narym 59 0N 81 58 E
50 Narymskoye 49 10N 84 15 E
50 Naryn 41 30N 76 10 E
72 Nasarawa 8 32N 7 41 E
73 Naser, Buheiret en 23 0N 32 30 E
102 Nashua, Mont. 48 10N 106 25W
97 Nashua, N.H. 42 50N 71 25W
99 Nashville 36 12N 86 46W
40 Nasice 45 32N 18 4W
60 Nasik 20 2N 73 50 E
60 Nasirabad, Bangladesh 26 15N 74 45 E
60 Nasirabad, India 26 15N 74 45 E
61 Nasirabad, Pak. 28 25N 68 25 E
105 Nassau 25 0N 77 30W
112 Nassau, B. 55 20S 68 0W
73 Nasser, L.=Naser, Buheiret en 23 0N 32 30 E

Nipigon, L. — Oakville, Man.

90 Nipigon, L. 49 40N 88 30W
111 Niquelandia 14 27S 48 27W
62 Nira, R. 17 58N 7 8E
66 Nirasaki 35 42N 138 27E
62 Nirmal 19 3N 78 20E
40 Niš 43 19N 21 58E
31 Nisa 39 30N 2 41W
55 Nisab 14 25N 46 29E
40 Nišava, R. 43 22N 21 46E
39 Niscemi 37 8N 14 21E
66 Nishinomiya 34 45N 135 20E
43 Nísiros, I. 36 35N 27 12E
45 Nissan, R. 43 22N 21 46E
45 Nissum, Fd. 56 20N 8 11E
109 Niterói 22 52S 43 0W
14 Nith, R. 55 0N 3 35W
27 Nitra 48 19N 18 4E
27 Nitra, R. 47 46N 18 10E
16 Nivelles 50 35N 4 20E
19 Nivernais, Reg. 47 0N 3 40E
62 Nizamabad 18 45N 78 7E
59 Nizamghat 28 20N 95 45E
51 Nizhne Kolymsk 68 40N 160 55E
50 Nizhne-Vartovskoye 60 56N 76 38E
51 Nizhneangarsk 56 0N 109 30E
51 Nizhneudinsk 55 0N 99 20E
50 Nizhniy Tagil 57 45N 60 0E
56 Nizip 37 1N 37 46E
27 Nizké Tatry, Mts. 48 55N 20 0E
54 Nizzanim 31 42N 34 37E
74 Njombe 9 0S 34 35E
72 Nkambe 6 35N 10 40E
72 Nkawkaw 6 36N 0 49W
74 Nkhata Bay 11 33S 34 16E
75 Nkhota Kota 12 55S 34 15E
72 Nkongsamba 4 55N 9 55E
88 Noatak 67 34N 162 59W
66 Nobeoka 32 36N 131 41E
30 Noblejas 39 58N 3 26W
39 Nocera Inferiore 40 45N 14 37E
39 Noci 40 47N 17 7E
66 Noda 47 30N 142 5E
104 Nogales, Mexico 31 36N 94 29W
103 Nogales, U.S.A. 31 33N 110 59W
66 Nōgata 33 48N 130 54E
18 Nogent-le-Rotrou 48 20N 0 50E
19 Nogent-sur-Seine 48 30N 3 30E
83 Noggerup 33 32S 116 5E
51 Noginsk 55 50N 38 25E
108 Nogoya 32 24S 59 50W
27 Nograd □ 48 0N 19 30E
30 Nogueira de Ramuin 42 21N 7 43W
32 Noguera Pallaresa, R. 42 15N 0 54E
32 Noguera Ribagorzana, R. 41 40N 0 43E
60 Nohar 29 11N 74 49E
63 Noi, R. 17 5N 105 2E
18 Noire, Mts., Finistere 48 11N 3 40W
20 Noire, Mts., Tarn 43 26N 2 12W
20 Noirétable 45 48N 3 46E
20 Noirmoutier 47 0N 2 15W
20 Noirmoutier, Î. de 46 58N 2 10W
58 Nok Kundi 28 50N 62 45E
51 Nokhhuysk 60 0N 117 45E
39 Nola 40 54N 14 29E
21 Nolay 46 58N 4 35E
36 Noli, C. di 44 12N 8 26E
88 Nome 64 30N 165 30W
18 Nonancourt 48 47N 1 11E
18 Nonant-le-Pin 48 42N 0 12E
80 Nonda 20 40S 142 28E
63 Nong Khae 14 29N 100 53E
63 Nong Khai 17 50N 102 46E
20 Nontron 45 31N 0 40E
82 Noonamah 12 38S 131 4E
81 Noondoo 28 35S 148 30E
16 Noord Beveland, I. 51 45N 3 50E
16 Noord Brabant □ 51 40N 5 0E
16 Noord Holland □ 52 30N 4 45E
16 Noordoost-Polder 52 45N 5 45E
16 Noordwijk 52 14N 4 26E
92 Nootka I. 49 40N 126 50W
44 Nora 59 32N 15 2E
90 Noranda 48 20N 79 0E
44 Norberg 60 4N 15 56E
37 Nórcia 42 50N 13 5E
19 Nord □ 50 15N 3 30E
24 Nord-Friesische, Is. 54 50N 8 20E
24 Nord-Ostsee Kanal 54 5N 9 15E
24 Nord-Süd Kanal 53 0N 10 32E
4 Nordaustlandet 79 55N 23 0E
45 Nordborg 55 5N 9 50E
24 Norddeich 53 37N 7 10E
92 Nordegg 52 29N 116 5W
24 Norden 53 35N 7 12E
24 Nordenham 53 29N 8 28E
24 Norderney 53 42N 7 9E
24 Norderney, I. 53 42N 7 15E
24 Nordhausen 51 29N 10 47E
24 Nordhorn 52 27N 7 4E
46 Nordkapp, Norway 71 11N 25 48E
4 Nordkapp, Svalbard 80 31N 20 0E
46 Nordland □ 65 40N 13 0E
25 Nördlingen 48 50N 10 30E
24 Nordrhein Westfalen □ 51 45N 7 30E
24 Nordstrand, I. 54 27N 8 50E
51 Nordvik 73 40N 110 57E
45 Nordyllands □ 57 0N 10 0E
15 Nore, R. 52 25N 6 58W
100 Norfolk, Nebr. 42 3N 97 25W
98 Norfolk, Va. 36 52N 76 15W
12 Norfolk □ 52 39N 1 0E
76 Norfolk I. 28 58S 168 3E
51 Norilsk 69 20N 88 0E
100 Normal 40 30N 89 0W
101 Norman 35 12N 97 30W
88 Norman Wells 65 40N 126 45W
18 Normandie, Reg. 48 45N 0 10E
18 Normandie, Collines de 48 55N 0 45W
90 Normandin 48 49N 72 31W
80 Normanton 17 40S 141 10E
83 Nornalup 35 0S 116 49E
112 Norquinco 41 51S 70 55W
45 Norrahammar 57 43N 14 7E
46 Norrbotten □ 66 45N 23 0E
45 Nørresundby 57 5N 9 52E
97 Norristown 40 9N 75 15W
45 Norrköping 58 37N 16 11E
44 Norrtälje 59 46N 18 42E
83 Norseman 32 8S 121 43E
45 Norsholm 58 31N 15 59E
51 Norsk 52 30N 130 0E
111 Norte, C. do 1 40N 49 55W
85 North, C. 34 23S 173 4E
85 North I. 38 0S 176 0E
97 North Adams 42 42N 73 6W
1 North America 45 0N 100 0W
63 North Andaman, I. 13 15N 92 40E
6 North Atlantic Ocean 30 0N 50 0W
93 North Battleford 52 50N 108 10W
90 North Bay 46 20N 79 30W
90 North Belcher Is. 56 30N 79 0W
92 North Bend, Canada 49 50N 121 35W
102 North Bend, Oreg. 43 28N 124 7W
96 North Bend, Pa. 41 20N 77 42W
14 North Berwick 56 4N 2 44W
99 North Carolina □ 35 30N 80 0W
14 North Channel 55 0N 5 30W
98 North Chicago 42 19N 87 50W
100 North Dakota □ 47 30N 100 0W
83 North Dandalup 32 31S 115 58E
15 North Down □ 54 40N 5 45W
13 North Downs 51 17N 0 30W
9 North European Plain 55 0N 25 0E
13 North Foreland, Pt. 51 22N 1 28E
92 North Kamloops 50 40N 120 25W
68 North Korea ■ 40 0N 127 0E
59 North Lakhimpur 27 15N 94 10E
14 North Minch 58 5N 5 55W
100 North Platte 41 10N 100 50W
4 North Pole 90 0N 0 0E
14 North Ronaldsay, I. 59 20N 2 30W
93 North Saskatchewan, R. 53 15N 105 6W
8 North Sea 56 0N 4 0E
91 North Sydney 46 12N 60 21W
97 North Syracuse 43 8N 76 8W
96 North Tonawanda 43 5N 78 50W
101 North Truchas Pk. 36 0N 105 30W
12 North Tyne, R. 54 59N 2 8W
14 North Uist, I. 57 40N 7 15W
92 North Vancouver 49 25N 123 20W
105 North Village 32 15N 64 45W
12 North Walsham 52 49N 1 22E
82 North West, C. 21 45S 114 9E
14 North West Highlands, Mts. 57 35N 5 2W
88 North West Territories □ 65 0N 100 0W
12 North York Moors 54 25N 0 50W
12 North Yorkshire □ 54 10N 1 25W
12 Northallerton 54 20N 1 26W
83 Northam 31 35S 116 42E
83 Northampton, Australia 28 21S 114 33E
13 Northampton, U.K. 52 14N 0 54W
97 Northampton, Mass. 42 22N 72 39W
97 Northampton, Pa. 40 38N 75 24W
13 Northampton □ 52 16N 0 55W
80 Northampton Downs 24 35S 145 48E
83 Northcliffe 34 36S 116 7E
24 Northeim 51 42N 10 0E
15 Northern Ireland ■ 54 45N 7 0W
78 Northern Territory □ 16 0S 133 0E
100 Northfield 44 37N 93 10W
97 Northport 45 8N 85 39W
12 Northumberland □ 55 12N 2 0W
80 Northumberland, Is. 21 45S 150 20E
91 Northumberland Str. 46 20N 64 0W
12 Northwich 53 16N 2 30W
88 Norton Sd. 64 0N 165 0W
24 Nortorf 54 14N 10 47E
97 Norwalk, Conn. 41 7N 73 27W
96 Norwalk, Ohio 41 15N 82 37W
46 Norway ■ 67 0N 11 0E
93 Norway House 53 55N 98 50W
5 Norwegian Dependency 75 0S 15 0E
4 Norwegian Sea 66 0N 1 0E
12 Norwich, U.K. 52 38N 1 17E
97 Norwich, Conn. 41 33N 72 5W
97 Norwich, N.Y. 42 32N 75 30W
97 Norwood 42 10N 71 10W
50 Nosok 70 10N 82 20E
57 Nosratabad 29 55N 60 0E
14 Noss Hd. 58 29N 3 4W
75 Nossob, R. 26 55S 20 37E
28 Noteć R. 52 44N 15 26E
43 Notios Evvoïkos, Kól. 38 20N 24 0E
92 Notikewin 57 15N 117 5W
39 Noto 36 52N 15 4E
44 Notodden, Reg. 59 35N 9 17E
91 Notre Dame B. 49 45N 55 30W
89 Notre Dame de Koartac=Koartac 60 55N 69 40W
89 Notre Dame d'Ivugivik= Ivugivik 62 20N 78 0W
96 Nottawasaga B. 44 40N 80 30W
12 Nottingham 52 57N 1 10W
12 Nottinghamshire □ 53 10N 1 0W
72 Nouadhibou 21 0N 17 0W
72 Nouakchott 18 20N 15 50W
76 Noumea 22 17S 166 30E
75 Nouport 31 10S 24 57E
90 Nouveau Comptoir 53 2N 78 55W
19 Nouzonville 49 48N 4 44E
27 Nová Bana 48 28N 18 39E
26 Nová Bystrice 49 2N 15 8E
111 Nova Cruz 6 28S 35 25W
109 Nova Esperança 23 8S 52 13W
109 Nova Friburgo 22 10S 42 30W
111 Nova Granada 20 29S 49 19W
40 Nova Gradiška 45 17N 17 28E
109 Nova Iguaçu 22 45S 43 28W
75 Nova Lisboa= Huambo 12 42S 15 54E
26 Nova Paka 50 29N 15 30E
91 Nova Scotia □ 45 10N 63 0W
75 Nova Sofola 20 7S 34 48E
111 Nova Venecia 18 45S 40 24E
41 Nova Zagora 42 32N 25 59E
41 Novaci 45 10N 23 42E
36 Novara 45 27N 8 36E
48 Novaya Ladoga 60 7N 32 16E
50 Novaya Lyalya 58 50N 60 35E
51 Novaya Sibir, Os. 75 10N 150 0E
50 Novaya Zemlya, I. 75 0N 56 0E
27 Nové Mesto 49 33N 16 7E
27 Nové Zámky 47 59N 18 11E
33 Novelda 38 24N 0 45W
36 Novellara 44 50N 10 43E
48 Novgorod 58 30N 31 25E
40 Novi Bečej 45 36N 20 10E
40 Novi Kneževac 46 4N 20 8E
41 Novi Krichim 42 22N 24 31E
36 Novi Lígure 44 45N 8 47E
41 Novi Pazar, Bulgaria 43 25N 27 15E
40 Novi Pazar, Yug. 43 12N 20 28E
40 Novi-Sad 45 18N 19 52E
37 Novi Vinodolski 45 10N 14 48E
109 Nôvo Hamburgo 29 37S 51 7W
109 Novo Horizonte 21 28S 49 13W
74 Novo Redondo 11 10S 13 48E
49 Novocherkassk 47 27N 40 5E
50 Novokazalinsk 45 40N 61 40E
48 Novokiybyshevsk 53 7N 49 58E
50 Novo-kuznetsk 54 0N 87 10E
48 Novomoskovsk 54 5N 38 15E
49 Novorossiyk 44 43N 37 52E
49 Novoshakhtinsk 47 39N 39 58E
50 Novosibirsk 55 0N 83 5E
51 Novosibirskiye Os. 75 0N 140 0E
48 Novotroitsk 51 10N 58 15E
49 Novouzensk 50 32N 48 17E
40 Novska 45 19N 17 0E
26 Novy Bydžov 50 14N 15 29E
28 Nõvy Dwór 52 26N 20 44E
27 Nový Jičín 49 15N 18 0E
57 Now Shahr 36 40N 51 40E
84 Nowa Nowa 37 44S 148 3E
28 Nowa Sól 51 48N 15 44E
28 Nowe Warpno 53 42N 14 18E
59 Nowgong 26 20N 92 50E
28 Nowogrod 53 14N 21 53E
84 Nowra 34 53S 150 35E
27 Nowy Sącz 49 40N 20 41E
30 Noya 42 48N 8 53W
18 Noyant 47 30N 0 6E
19 Noyers 47 40N 4 0E
19 Noyon 49 34N 3 0E
18 Nozay 47 34N 1 38W
75 Nsanje 16 55S 35 12E
72 Nsawam 5 50N 0 24W
75 Nuanetsi 21 22S 30 45E
70 Nubian Des. 21 30N 33 30E
73 Nûbîya, Es Sahrâ en 21 30N 33 30E
108 Ñuble □ 37 0S 72 0W
108 Nueva Palmira 33 52S 58 20W
104 Nueva Rosita 28 0N 101 20W
108 Nueve de Julio 35 30S 60 50W
105 Nuevitas 21 30N 77 20W
112 Nuevo, G. 43 0S 64 30W
104 Nuevo Laredo 27 30N 99 40W
104 Nuevo León □ 25 0N 100 0W
85 Nuhaka 39 3S 177 45E
19 Nuits 47 10N 4 56E
21 Nuits St. Georges 47 10N 4 56E
73 Nukheila 19 1N 26 21E
50 Nukus 42 20N 59 40E
88 Nulato 64 43N 158 6W
32 Nules 39 51N 0 9W
82 Nullagine 21 53S 120 6E
83 Nullarbor 31 26S 130 55E
83 Nullarbor Plain 31 20S 128 0E
66 Numata 36 38N 139 3E
66 Numazu 35 7N 138 51E
44 Numedal 60 6N 9 6E
84 Numurkah 36 0S 145 26E
13 Nuneaton 52 32N 1 29W
88 Nunivak I. 60 0N 166 0W
68 Nunkiang 49 11N 125 12E
16 Nunspeet 52 21N 5 45E
38 Núoro 40 20N 9 20E
25 Nürnberg 49 26N 11 5E
64 Nusa Tenggara Barat 8 50S 117 30E
65 Nusa Tenggara Timur □ 9 30S 122 0E
58 Nushki 29 35N 65 59E
89 Nutak 57 30N 61 59W
62 Nuwara Eliya 6 58N 80 55E
75 Nuweveldberge 32 10S 21 45E
62 Nuzvid 16 47N 80 51E
83 Nyabing 33 30S 118 7E
97 Nyack 41 5N 73 57W
74 Nyahanga 2 20S 33 37E
73 Nyâlâ 12 2N 24 58E
75 Nyasa, L. 12 0S 34 30E
45 Nyborg 55 18N 10 47E
45 Nybro 56 44N 15 55E
50 Nyda 66 40N 73 10E
67 Nyenchen, Ra. 30 30N 95 0E
74 Nyeri 0 23S 36 56E
27 Nyirbátor 47 49N 22 9E
27 Nyíregyháza 48 0N 21 47E
46 Nykarleby 63 32N 22 31E
45 Nykøbing 54 56N 11 52E
45 Nykøbing Mors 56 49N 8 51E
45 Nyköping 58 45N 17 0E
75 Nylstroom 24 42S 28 22E
26 Nymburk 50 10N 15 1E
44 Nynäshamn 58 54N 17 57E
84 Nyngan 31 30S 147 8E
25 Nyon 46 23N 6 14E
21 Nyons 44 22N 5 10E
84 Nyora 38 20S 145 41E
27 Nysa 50 40N 17 22E
28 Nysa, R. 52 4N 14 46E
51 Nyurba 63 17N 118 20E
74 Nzega 4 10S 33 12E
72 Nzérékoré 7 49N 8 48W

O

100 Oahe Dam 44 28N 100 25W
100 Oahe Res. 45 30N 100 15W
94 Oahu, I. 21 30N 158 0W
102 Oak Creek 40 15N 106 59W
98 Oak Park 41 55N 87 45W
99 Oak Ridge 36 1N 84 5W
101 Oakdale 30 50N 92 28W
12 Oakengates 52 42N 2 29W
102 Oakesdale 47 11N 117 9W
81 Oakey 27 25S 151 43E
12 Oakham 52 40N 0 43W
103 Oakland 37 50N 122 18W
84 Oakleigh 37 54S 145 6E
96 Oakmont 40 31N 79 50W
82 Oakover, R. 20 43S 120 33E
102 Oakridge 43 47N 122 31W
93 Oakville, Man. 49 56N 97 58W

Osby Paranavaí

45 Osby 56 23N 13 59E
101 Osceola 35 40N 90 0W
25 Oschatz 51 17N 13 8E
24 Oschersleben 52 2N 11 13E
38 Oschiri 40 43N 9 7E
40 Osečina 44 23N 19 34E
96 Oshawa 43 50N 78 45W
100 Oshkosh 44 3N 88 35W
72 Oshogbo 7 48N 4 37E
41 Osica de Jos 44 14N 24 20E
28 Osieczna 51 55N 16 40E
40 Osijek 45 34N 18 41E
37 Osimo 43 40N 13 30E
49 Osipenko= Berdyansk 46 45N 36 49E
100 Oskaloosa 41 18N 92 40W
45 Oskarshamn 57 15N 16 27E
44 Oslo 59 55N 10 45E
44 Oslofjorden 58 30N 10 0E
62 Osmanabad 18 5N 76 10E
56 Osmaniye 37 5N 36 10E
24 Osnabrück 52 16N 8 2E
109 Osorio 29 53S 50 17W
112 Osorno 40 25S 73 0W
16 Oss 51 46N 5 32E
80 Ossa, Mt. 41 80S 146 0E
33 Ossa de Montiel 38 58N 2 45W
97 Ossining 41 9N 73 50W
24 Oste, R. 53 33N 9 10E
16 Ostend=Oostende 51 15N 2 50E
24 Osterburg 52 47N 11 44E
44 Østerdalen 62 0N 10 40E
45 Östergötlands □ 58 24N 15 34E
24 Osterholz-Scharmbeck 53 14N 8 48E
44 Östersund 63 10N 14 38E
44 Østfold □ 59 25N 11 25E
24 Ostfriesische Is. 53 45N 7 15E
25 Ostfriesland, Reg. 53 20N 7 40E
44 Östhammar 60 16N 18 22E
27 Ostrava 49 51N 18 18E
28 Ostrgog 52 37N 16 33E
28 Ostróda 53 42N 19 58E
28 Ostrołeka 53 4N 21 38E
28 Ostrołeka □ 53 0N 21 30E
41 Ostrov 43 40N 24 9E
28 Ostrów Mazowiecka 52 50N 21 51E
28 Ostrów Wielkopolski 51 39N 17 49E
27 Ostrowiec-Swietokrzyski 50 57N 21 23E
40 Ostrozac 43 43N 17 49E
28 Ostrzeszów 51 25N 17 52E
39 Ostuni 40 44N 17 34E
42 Osumi, R. 40 48N 19 52E
66 Ōsumi-Kaikyō, Str. 30 55N 131 0E
66 Ōsumi-Shotō, Is. 30 30N 130 45E
31 Osuna 37 14N 5 8W
97 Oswego 43 29N 76 30W
97 Oswego, R. 43 28N 76 31W
12 Oswestry 52 52N 3 3W
27 Oświęcim 50 2N 19 11E
85 Otago □ 44 45S 169 10E
66 Ōtake 34 27N 132 25E
85 Otaki 40 45S 175 10E
66 Otaru 43 13N 141 0E
26 Otava 61 39N 27 4E
110 Otavalo 0 20N 78 20W
42 Otelec 45 36N 20 50E
30 Otero de Rey 43 6N 7 36W
102 Othello 46 53N 119 8W
85 Otira Gorge 42 53S 171 33E
75 Otjiwarongo 20 30S 16 33E
85 Otorohanga 38 11S 175 12E
39 Otranto 40 9N 18 28E
39 Otranto, C. d' 40 7N 18 30E
66 Ōtsu 42 35N 143 40E
44 Otta 61 46N 9 32E
62 Ottapalam 10 46N 76 23E
90 Ottawa, Canada 45 27N 75 42W
100 Ottawa, Ill. 41 20N 88 55W
100 Ottawa, Kans 38 40N 95 10W
89 Ottawa Is. 59 50N 80 0W
90 Ottawa, R. 45 20N 73 58W
24 Otterndorf 53 47N 8 52E
93 Otter Rapids 55 42N 104 46W
26 Ottersheim 48 21N 14 12E
45 Otterup 55 30N 10 22E
100 Ottumwa 41 0N 92 25W
72 Oturkpo 7 10N 8 15E
112 Otway, B. 53 30S 74 0W
84 Otway, C. 38 52S 143 31E
112 Otway, Seno de 53 5S 71 30W
28 Otwock 52 5N 21 20E
26 Ötz 47 13N 10 53E
26 Ötztaler Alpen, Mts. 46 58N 11 0E
72 Ouagadougou 12 25N 1 30W
72 Ouallene 24 41N 1 11E
72 Ouargla 31 59N 5 25E
72 Ouarzazate 30 55N 6 55W
74 Oubangi, R. 0 30S 17 42E
19 Ouche, R. 47 6N 5 16E
16 Oudenaarde 50 50N 3 37E
18 Oudon 47 22N 1 19W
75 Oudtshoorn 33 35S 22 14E
18 Ouessant, I. d' 48 28N 5 6W
74 Ouesso 1 37N 16 5E
72 Ouezzane 34 51N 5 42W
72 Ouidah 6 25N 2 0E
72 Oujda 34 41N 1 45W
72 Ouled Djellal 34 28N 5 2E
46 Oulu 65 1N 25 29E
46 Oulu □ 64 36N 27 20E
46 Oulujärvi, L. 64 25N 27 0E
16 Our, R. 49 53N 6 18E
111 Ouricuri 7 53S 40 5W
109 Ourinhos 23 0S 49 54W
109 Ouro Fino 22 16S 46 25W
109 Ouro Prêto 20 20S 43 30W
80 Ouse 42 25S 146 42E
13 Ouse, R., E. Sussex 50 47N 0 3E
12 Ouse, R., N. Yorks 53 42N 0 41W
18 Oust, R. 47 39N 2 6W
75 Outjo 20 5S 16 7E
93 Outlook 51 30N 107 0W
19 Outreau 50 40N 1 36E
84 Ouyen 35 1S 142 22E
36 Ovada 44 39N 8 40E
85 Ovalau, I. 17 40S 178 48E
108 Ovalle 30 33S 71 18W
75 Ovamboland, Reg. 17 20S 16 30E
30 Ovar 40 51N 8 40E
16 Over Flakkee, I. 51 45N 4 5E
16 Overijssel □ 52 25N 6 35E
16 Overpelt 51 12N 5 20E
30 Oviedo 43 25N 5 50W
30 Oviedo □ 43 20N 6 0W
44 Oviksfjällen, Mts. 63 0N 13 49E
85 Owaka 46 27S 169 40E
66 Owase 34 7N 136 5E
100 Owatonna 44 3N 93 17W
97 Owego 42 6N 76 17W
90 Owen Sound 44 35N 80 55W
74 Owendo 0 17N 9 30E
98 Owensboro 37 40N 87 5W
72 Owo 7 18N 5 30E
98 Owosso 43 0N 84 10W
45 Oxelösund 58 43N 17 15E
13 Oxford, U.K. 51 45N 1 15W
97 Oxford, Mass. 42 7N 71 52W
99 Oxford, N.C. 36 19N 78 36W
13 Oxford □ 51 45N 1 15W
93 Oxford House 54 46N 95 16W
103 Oxnard 34 10N 119 14W
66 Oyama 36 18N 139 48E
74 Oyem 1 37N 11 35E
51 Oymyakon 63 25N 143 10E
72 Oyo 7 46N 3 56E
21 Oyonnax 46 16N 5 40E
97 Oyster Bay 40 52N 73 32W
65 Ozamiz 8 15N 123 50E
99 Ozark 31 29N 85 39W
86 Ozark Plat. 37 20N 91 40W
100 Ozarks, L. of the 38 10N 93 0W
38 Ozieri 40 35N 9 0E
28 Ozorków 51 57N 19 16E
41 Ozun 45 47N 25 50E

P

63 Pa Sak, R. 14 11 100 40E
67 Paan 30 0N 99 3E
59 Pa-an 16 45N 97 40E
75 Paarl 13 45S 18 46E
28 Pabianice 51 40N 19 20E
61 Pabna 24 1N 89 18E
110 Pacaraima, Sa. 5 0N 63 0W
110 Pacasmayo 7 20S 79 35W
38 Paceco 37 59N 12 32E
60 Pachhar 24 40N 77 42E
39 Pachino 36 43N 15 4E
60 Pachora 20 38N 75 29E
104 Pachuca 20 10N 98 40W
103 Pacific Groves 37 36N 121 58W
77 Pacific Ocean 10 0N 140 0W
18 Pacy 49 2N 1 22E
65 Padalarang 7 50S 107 30E
64 Padang 1 0S 100 20E
93 Paddockwood 53 30N 105 30W
24 Paderborn 51 42N 8 44E
88 Padlei 62 10N 97 5W
89 Padloping Island 67 0N 63 0W
62 Padmanabhapuram 8 16N 77 17E
37 Pádova 45 24N 11 52E
60 Padra 22 15N 73 7E
61 Padrauna 26 54N 83 59E
13 Padstow 50 33N 4 57W
98 Paducah, Ky. 37 0N 88 40W
101 Paducah, Tes. 34 3N 100 16W
85 Paeroa 37 23S 175 41E
37 Pag, I. 44 50N 15 0E
65 Pagadian 7 55N 123 30E
71 Pagalu, I. 1 35S 3 35E
43 Pagastikós Kól. 39 15N 23 12E
103 Page 47 11N 97 37W
57 Paghman 34 36N 68 57E
37 Paglieta 42 10N 14 30E
85 Pago Pago 14 16S 170 43W
103 Pagosa Springs 37 16N 107 1W
90 Pagwa River 50 2N 85 14W
94 Pahala 20 25N 156 0W
63 Pahang, R. 3 32N 102 28E
63 Pahang □ 3 30N 103 9E
85 Pahiatua 40 27S 175 50E
68 Paicheng 45 40N 122 52E
13 Paignton 50 26N 3 33W
18 Paimboeuf 47 17N 2 0W
18 Paimpol 48 48N 3 4W
96 Painesville 41 42N 81 18W
90 Paint Hills= Nouveau Comptoir 53 2N 78 55W
103 Painted Des. 36 40N 112 0W
14 Paisley 55 51N 4 27W
110 Paita 5 5S 81 0W
68 Paiyin 36 45N 104 4E
30 Pajares 43 0N 5 48W
63 Pak Lay 18 15N 101 27E
63 Pak Sane 18 22N 103 39E
62 Pakala 13 29N 79 8E
64 Pakanbaru 0 30N 101 15E
69 Pakhoi 21 30N 109 10E
58 Pakistan ■ 30 0N 70 0E
59 Pakokku 21 30N 95 0E
69 Pakongchow 23 50N 113 0E
60 Pakpattan 30 25N 73 16E
60 Pakrac 45 27N 17 12E
27 Paks 46 38N 18 55E
63 Pakse 15 5N 105 52E
57 Paktya □ 33 0N 69 15E
32 Palafrugell 41 55N 3 10E
39 Palagonía 37 20N 14 43E
43 Palaiokastron 35 12N 26 18E
62 Palakol 16 31N 81 46E
32 Palamós 41 50N 3 10E
51 Palana 59 10N 160 10E
64 Palangkaraya 2 16S 113 56E
60 Palanpur 24 10N 72 25E
75 Palapye 22 30S 27 7E
62 Palar, R. 12 28N 80 9E
99 Palatka 29 40N 81 40W
65 Palau Is. 7 30N 134 30E
63 Palauk 13 10N 98 40E
63 Palaw 13 0N 98 50E
64 Palawan, I. 10 0N 119 0E
64 Palawan Is. 10 0N 115 0E
62 Palayancottai 8 45N 77 45E
40 Pale 43 50N 18 38E
65 Paleleh 1 10N 121 50E
64 Palembang 3 0S 104 50E
30 Palencia 42 1N 4 34W
30 Palencia □ 42 31N 4 33W
38 Palermo 38 8N 13 20E
101 Palestine 31 42N 95 35W
59 Paletwa 21 30N 92 50E
62 Palghat 10 46N 76 42E
60 Pali 25 50N 73 20E
72 Palimé 6 57N 0 37E
100 Palisade 40 35N 101 10W
60 Palitana 21 32N 71 49E
62 Palk B. 9 30N 79 30E
62 Palkonda 18 36N 83 48E
62 Palkonda Ra. 13 50N 79 20N
80 Palm, Is. 18 40S 146 35E
103 Palm Springs 33 51N 116 35W
32 Palma 39 33N 2 39E
33 Palma, B. de 39 30N 2 39E
8 Palma, I. 28 45N 17 50W
31 Palma del Rio 37 43N 5 17W
38 Palma di Montechiaro 37 12N 13 46E
105 Palma Soriano 20 15N 76 0W
111 Palmares 8 41S 35 36W
109 Palmas 26 29S 52 0W
72 Palmas, C. 4 27N 7 46W
109 Palmeira 25 25S 50 0W
111 Palmeira dos Indios 9 25S 36 30W
31 Palmela 38 32N 8 57W
88 Palmer 61 35N 149 10W
5 Palmer Ld. 73 0S 60 0W
85 Palmerston 45 29S 170 43E
85 Palmerston North 40 21S 175 39E
97 Palmerton 40 47N 75 36W
39 Palmi 38 21N 15 51E
108 Palmira, Arg. 32 59S 68 25W
110 Palmira, Col. 3 32N 76 16W
97 Palmyra 34 5N 77 18W
77 Palmyra Is. 5 52N 162 5W
62 Palni 10 30N 77 30E
62 Palni Hills 10 14N 77 33E
103 Palo Alto 37 25N 122 8W
39 Palo del Colle 41 4N 16 43E
65 Palopo 3 0S 120 16E
33 Palos, C. de 37 38N 0 40W
56 Palu 38 45N 40 0E
60 Palwal 28 8N 77 19E
65 Pamekason 7 10S 113 29E
68 Pamiencheng 43 16N 124 4E
20 Pamiers 43 7N 1 39E
99 Pamlico Sd. 35 20N 76 0W
101 Pampa 35 35N 100 58W
65 Pampanua 4 22S 120 14E
106 Pampas, Reg. 34 0S 64 0W
110 Pamplona 7 23N 72 39W
32 Pana 39 25N 89 0W
41 Panagyurishte 42 49N 24 15E
62 Panaji 15 25N 73 50E
104 Panama 9 0N 79 25W
105 Panamá ■ 8 48N 79 55W
104 Panamá, B. de 8 50N 79 20W
105 Panamá, G. de 8 4N 79 20W
104 Panama Canal 9 10N 79 56W
99 Panama City 30 10N 105 41W
65 Panarukan 7 40S 113 52E
65 Panay, I. 11 10N 122 30E
65 Panay G. 11 0N 122 30E
40 Pančevo 44 52N 20 41E
30 Pancorbo, P. 42 32N 3 5W
62 Pandharpur 17 41N 75 20E
60 Pandhurna 21 36N 78 35E
109 Pando 34 30S 56 0W
50 Panfilov 44 30N 80 0E
59 Pang-Long 23 11N 98 45E
42 Pangaíon Óros 40 50N 24 0E
74 Pangani 5 25S 38 58E
64 Pangkalanberandan 4 1N 98 20E
64 Pangkalansusu 4 2N 98 42E
89 Pangnirtung 66 8N 65 44W
103 Panguitch 37 52N 112 30W
59 Pangyang 22 10N 98 45E
60 Panipat 29 25N 77 2E
84 Panitya 35 15S 141 0E
57 Panjao 34 21N 67 0E
58 Panjgur 27 0N 64 5E
62 Panjim=Panaji 15 25N 73 50E
64 Pankalpinang 2 0S 106 0E
61 Panna 24 40N 80 15E
62 Pannuru 16 5N 80 34E
109 Panorama 21 21S 51 51W
62 Panruti 11 46N 79 35E
68 Panshih 42 55N 126 3E
38 Pantellaria, I. 36 52N 12 0E
104 Pánuco 22 0N 98 25W
62 Panvel 18 59N 73 10E
72 Panyam 9 27N 9 8E
68 Paochang 41 46N 115 30E
69 Paoki 34 25N 107 15E
39 Páola 39 21N 16 2E
67 Paoshan 25 7N 99 9E
68 Paoting 38 50N 115 30E
68 Paotow 40 35N 110 3E
69 Paoying 33 10N 119 20E
27 Papá 47 22N 17 30E
105 Papagayo, G. del 10 4N 85 50W
62 Papagni, R. 14 10N 78 30E
85 Papakura 37 45S 174 59E
104 Papantla 20 45N 97 41W
64 Papar 5 45N 116 0E
43 Papas, Ákra 38 13N 21 6E
24 Papenburg 53 7N 7 25E
76 Papua New Guinea ■ 8 0S 145 0E
37 Papuča 44 22N 15 30E
40 Papuk, Mts. 45 30N 17 30E
111 Pará=Belém 1 20S 48 30W
111 Pará □ 3 20S 52 0W
111 Paracatú 17 10S 46 50W
81 Parachilna 31 10S 138 21E
40 Paraćin 43 54N 21 27E
31 Paradas 37 18N 5 29W
61 Paradip 20 15N 86 35E
102 Paradise 47 27N 114 54W
101 Paragould 36 5N 90 30W
109 Paraguaçu Paulista 22 22S 50 35W
110 Paraguaipoa 11 21N 71 57W
110 Paraguaná, Penide 12 0N 70 0W
108 Paraguari 25 36S 57 0W
108 Paraguarí □ 26 0S 57 10W
107 Paraguay ■ 23 0S 57 0W
108 Paraguay, R. 27 18S 58 38W
111 Paraiba □ 7 0S 36 0W
109 Paraíba do Sul, R. 21 37S 41 3W
47 Parainen 60 18N 22 18E
72 Parakou 9 25N 2 40E
43 Parálion-Astrous 37 25N 22 45E
62 Paramagudi 9 31N 78 39E
111 Paramaribo 5 50N 55 10W
108 Paraná, Arg. 32 0S 60 30W
111 Paraná, Brazil 12 30S 47 40W
108 Paraná, R. 33 43S 59 15W
109 Paraná □ 24 30S 51 0W
109 Paranaguá 25 30S 48 30W
109 Paranapanema, R. 22 40S 53 9W
109 Paranavaí 23 4S 52 28W

Port Chalmers Pulaski, N.Y.

85 Port Chalmers 45 49S 170 30E
97 Port Chester 41 0N 73 41W
90 Port Colborne 42 50N 79 10W
92 Port Coquitlam 49 20N 122 45W
96 Port Credit 43 34N 79 35W
78 Port Darwin 12 18S 130 55E
105 Port de Paix 19 50N 72 50W
63 Port Dickson 2 30N 101 49E
80 Port Douglas 16 30S 145 30E
92 Port Edward 54 14N 130 18W
90 Port Elgin 44 25N 81 25W
75 Port Elizabeth 33 58S 25 40E
14 Port Ellen 55 39N 6 12W
12 Port Erin 54 5N 4 45W
72 Port Étienne= Nouadhibou 21 0N 17 0W
84 Port Fairy 38 22S 142 12E
74 Port-Gentil 0 47S 8 40E
14 Port Glasgow 55 57N 4 40W
72 Port Harcourt 4 43N 7 5E
92 Port Hardy 50 41N 127 30W
89 Port Harrison= Inoucdouac 58 25N 78 15W
82 Port Hedland 20 25S 118 35E
97 Port Henry 44 0N 73 30W
91 Port Hood 46 0N 61 32W
90 Port Hope 44 0N 78 20W
96 Port Huron 43 0N 82 28W
97 Port Jervis 41 22N 74 42W
84 Port Kembla 34 29S 150 56E
63 Port Klang 3 0N 101 21E
20 Port La Nouvelle 43 1N 3 3E
15 Port Laoise 53 2N 7 20W
101 Port Lavaca 28 38N 96 38W
81 Port Lincoln 34 42S 135 52E
72 Port-Lyautey= Kenitra 34 15N 6 40W
81 Port Macquarie 31 25S 152 54E
91 Port Maitland 44 0N 66 2W
92 Port Mellon 49 32N 123 31W
91 Port Menier 49 51N 64 15W
76 Port Moresby 9 24S 147 8E
93 Port Nelson 57 5N 92 56W
75 Port Nolloth 29 17S 16 52E
89 Port Nouveau-Quebec 58 30N 65 50W
105 Port of Spain 10 40N 61 20W
102 Port Orchard 47 31N 122 47W
90 Port Perry 44 6N 78 56W
81 Port Pirie 33 10S 137 58E
88 Port Radium 66 10N 117 40W
73 Port Said= Bûr Saîd 31 16N 32 18E
75 Port St. Johns= Umzimvubu 31 38S 29 33E
21 Port-St.-Louis 43 23N 4 50E
91 Port St. Servain 51 21N 58 0W
75 Port Shepstone 30 44S 30 28E
92 Port Simpson 54 30N 130 20W
90 Port Stanley 42 40N 81 10W
73 Port Sudan= Bûr Sûdân 19 32N 37 9E
13 Port Talbot 51 35N 3 48W
102 Port Townsend 48 0N 122 50W
20 Port-Vendres 42 32N 3 8E
48 Port Vladimir 69 25N 33 6E
81 Port Wakefield 34 12S 138 10E
63 Port Weld 4 50N 100 38E
15 Portadown 54 27N 6 26W
100 Portage 43 31N 89 25W
93 Portage la Prairie 49 58N 98 18W
31 Portalegre 39 19N 7 25W
31 Portalégre □ 39 15N 7 40W
101 Portales 34 12N 103 25W
15 Portarlington 53 10N 7 10W
105 Port-au-Prince 18 40N 72 20W
21 Port-de-Bouc 43 24N 4 59E
18 Port-en-Bessin 49 20N 0 45W
103 Porterville 36 5N 119 0W
20 Portet 43 31N 1 25E
13 Porthcawl 51 28N 3 42W
31 Portimão 37 8N 8 32W
84 Portland, Australia 33 13S 149 59E
97 Portland, Conn. 41 34N 72 39W
99 Portland, Me. 43 40N 70 15W
102 Portland, Oreg. 45 35N 122 30W
13 Portland Bill 50 31N 2 27W
13 Portland I. 50 32N 2 25W
89 Portland Promontory 59 0N 78 0W
12 Portmadoc 52 51N 4 8W
91 Portneuf 46 43N 71 55W
21 Porto, Fr. 42 16N 8 38E
30 Porto, Port. 41 8N 8 40W
30 Porto □ 41 8N 8 20W
21 Porto, G. de 42 17N 8 34E
109 Pôrto Alegre 30 5S 51 3W
75 Porto Amélia= Pemba 12 58S 40 30E
111 Pôrto de Móz 1 41S 52 22W
38 Porto Empédocle 37 18N 13 30E
111 Porto Franco 9 45S 47 0W
111 Porto Grande 0 42N 51 24W
108 Pôrto Murtinho 21 45S 57 55W
111 Porto Nacional 10 40S 48 30W
72 Porto-Novo 6 23N 2 42E
37 Porto Recanati 43 26N 13 40E
37 Porto San Giórgio 43 11N 13 49E
111 Porto Seguro 16 20S 39 0W
37 Porto Tolle 44 57N 12 20E
38 Porto Torres 40 50N 8 23E
109 Porto União 26 10S 51 0W
21 Porto-Vecchio 41 35N 9 16E
110 Porto Velho 8 46S 63 54W
36 Portoferráio 42 50N 10 20E
37 Portogruaro 45 57N 12 50E
102 Portola 39 49N 120 28W
37 Portomaggiore 44 41N 11 47E
36 Portovénere 44 2N 9 50E
110 Portoviejo 1 0S 80 20W
14 Portpatrick 54 50N 5 7W
14 Portree 57 25N 6 11W
15 Portrush 55 13N 6 40W
13 Portsmouth, U.K. 50 48N 1 6W
97 Portsmouth, N.H. 43 5N 70 45W
98 Portsmouth, Ohio 38 45N 83 0W
97 Portsmouth, R.I. 41 35N 71 44W
98 Portsmouth, Va. 36 50N 76 50W
14 Portsoy 57 41N 2 41W
46 Porttipahta, I. 68 5N 26 40E
30 Portugalete 43 19N 3 4W
29 Portugal ■ 40 0N 7 0W
72 Portuguese Guinea ■= Guinea Bissau ■ 12 0N 15 0W
15 Portumna 53 5N 8 12W
112 Porvenir 53 10S 70 30W
47 Provoo 60 27N 25 50E
109 Posadas, Arg. 27 30S 56 0W
31 Posadas, Sp. 37 47N 5 11W
69 Poseh 23 50N 106 0E
65 Poso 1 20S 120 55E
111 Posse 14 4S 46 18W
24 Pössneck 50 42N 11 34E
90 Poste de la Baleine 55 20N 77 40W
72 Poste Maurice Cortier 22 14N 1 2E
37 Postojna 45 46N 14 12E
75 Potchefstroom 26 41S 27 7E
39 Potenza 40 40N 15 50E
37 Potenza, R. 43 25N 13 40E
37 Potenza Picena 43 22N 13 37E
30 Potes 43 15N 4 42W
75 Potgietersrus 24 10S 29 3E
49 Poti 42 10N 41 38E
72 Potiskum 11 39N 11 2E
98 Potomac, R. 38 0N 76 20W
110 Potosí 19 38S 65 50W
108 Potosí □ 20 30S 67 0W
65 Potatan 10 56N 122 38E
68 Potow 38 8N 116 31E
24 Potsdam, E. Germany 52 23N 13 4E
97 Potsdam, U.S.A. 44 40N 74 59W
24 Potsdam □ 52 40N 13 30E
97 Pottersville 42 38N 84 45W
97 Pottsdown 40 17N 75 40W
97 Pottsville 40 39N 76 12W
92 Pouce Coupe 55 40N 120 10W
97 Poughkeepsie 41 40N 73 57W
19 Pouilly 47 18N 2 57E
109 Pouso Alegre 11 55S 57 0W
85 Poverty B. 38 43S 178 0E
30 Póvoa de Varzim 41 25N 8 46W
48 Povenets 62 48N 35 0E
90 Powassan 46 5N 79 25W
100 Powder, R. 46 44N 105 26W
102 Powder River 43 5N 107 0W
102 Powell 44 45N 108 45W
103 Powell, L. 37 25N 110 45W
92 Powell River 49 48N 125 20W
13 Powys □ 52 20N 3 30W
69 Poyang 28 59N 116 40E
69 Poyang Hu, L. 29 10N 116 10E
51 Poyarkovo 49 38N 128 45E
30 Poza de la Sal 42 35N 3 31W
40 Požarevac 44 35N 21 18E
40 Požega 45 21N 17 41E
28 Poznań 52 25N 17 0E
28 Poznań □ 52 30N 18 0E
33 Pozo Alcón 37 42N 2 56W
110 Pozo Almonte 20 10S 69 50W
31 Pozoblanco 38 23N 4 51W
39 Pozzallo 36 44N 15 40E
39 Pozzuoli 40 49N 14 7E
40 Praca 43 47N 18 43E
63 Prachin Buri 14 0N 101 25E
20 Prades 42 38N 2 23E
111 Prado 17 20S 39 20W
37 Pragerska 46 27N 15 42E
26 Prague=Praha 50 5N 14 22E
26 Praha 50 5N 14 22E
20 Prahecq 46 19N 0 26W
41 Prahova, R. 44 43N 26 27E
40 Prahovo 44 18N 22 39E
41 Praid 46 32N 25 10E
111 Prainha 1 45S 53 30W
80 Prairie 20 50S 144 35E
102 Prairie City 45 27N 118 44W
100 Prairie du Chien 43 1N 91 9W
100 Prairies, Coteau des 44 0N 97 0W
64 Praja 8 39S 116 37E
111 Prata 19 25S 49 0W
37 Prato 43 53N 11 5E
37 Prátola Peligna 42 7N 13 51E
101 Pratt 37 40N 98 45W
30 Pravia 43 30N 6 12W
108 Precordillera 30 0S 69 1W
37 Predáppio 44 7N 11 58E
40 Predejane 42 51N 22 9E
93 Preeceville 52 0N 102 50W
92 Premier 56 4N 130 1W
40 Prenj, Mt. 43 33N 17 53E
24 Prenzlau 53 19N 13 51E
40 Prepansko, J. 40 45N 21 0E
63 Preparis North Chan. 15 12N 93 40E
63 Preparis South Chan. 14 36N 93 40E
27 Prerov 49 28N 17 27E
90 Prescott, Canada 44 45N 75 30W
103 Prescott, U.S.A. 34 35N 112 30W
40 Preševo 42 19N 21 39E
108 Presidencia Roque Saenz Peña 26 50S 60 30W
108 Presidente de la Plaza 27 0S 60 0W
109 Presidente Epitácio 21 46S 52 6W
108 Presidente Hayes □ 24 0S 59 0W
109 Presidente Prudente 15 45S 54 0W
41 Preslav 43 10N 26 52E
27 Prešov 49 0N 21 15E
99 Presque Isle 46 40N 68 0W
72 Prestea 5 22N 2 7W
13 Presteign 52 17N 3 0W
96 Preston, Canada 43 25N 80 20W
12 Preston, U.K. 53 46N 2 42W
14 Prestonpans 55 58N 3 0W
14 Prestwick 55 30N 4 38W
75 Pretoria 25 44S 28 12E
43 Préveza 38 57N 20 47E
88 Pribilov Is. 56 0N 170 0W
26 Příbram 49 41N 14 2E
102 Price 39 40N 110 48W
32 Priego 40 38N 2 21W
31 Priego de Córdoba 37 27N 4 12W
75 Prieska 29 40S 22 42E
27 Prievidza 48 46N 18 36E
40 Prijedor 44 58N 16 41E
49 Prikaspiyskaya Nizmennost 47 30N 50 0E
49 Prikumsk 44 30N 44 10E
40 Prilep 41 21N 21 37E
49 Priluki 50 30N 32 15E
93 Prince Albert 53 15N 105 50W
93 Prince Albert Nat. Park 54 0N 106 25W
88 Prince Albert Pen. 72 0N 116 0W
88 Prince Albert Sd. 70 25N 115 0W
89 Prince Charles I. 68 0N 76 0W
3 Prince Edward Is. 45 15S 39 0E
91 Prince Edward I. □ 44 2N 77 20W
92 Prince George 53 50N 122 50W
86 Prince of Wales, C. 53 50N 131 30W
80 Prince of Wales, I., Australia 10 35S 142 0E
88 Prince of Wales I., Canada 73 0N 99 0W
92 Prince of Wales I., U.S.A. 53 30N 131 30W
92 Prince Rupert 54 20N 130 20W
80 Princess Charlotte, B. 14 15S 144 0E
5 Princesse Astrid Kyst 71 0S 10 0E
5 Princesse Ragnhild Kyst 71 0S 30 0E
92 Princeton, Canada 49 27N 120 30W
98 Princeton, Ind. 38 20N 87 35W
98 Princeton, Ky. 37 6N 87 55W
97 Princeton, N.J. 40 18N 74 40W
98 Princeton, W.Va. 37 21N 81 8W
71 Principé, I. 1 37N 7 25E
30 Prior, C. 43 34N 8 17W
48 Priozersk 61 2N 30 4E
48 Pripyat, R. 51 20N 30 20E
40 Priština 42 40N 21 13E
99 Pritchard 30 47N 88 5W
24 Pritzwalk 53 10N 12 11E
38 Priverno 41 29N 13 10E
40 Prizren 42 13N 20 45E
38 Prizzi 37 44N 13 24E
65 Probolinggo 7 46S 113 13E
62 Proddatur 14 45N 78 30E
104 Progreso 21 20N 89 40W
42 Prokletije, Mt. 42 30N 19 45E
50 Prokopyevsk 54 0N 87 3E
40 Prokuplje 43 16N 21 36E
59 Prome 18 45N 95 30E
111 Propriá 10 13S 36 51W
21 Propriano 41 41N 8 52E
80 Proserpine 20 21S 148 36E
102 Prosser 46 11N 119 52W
27 Prostějov 49 30N 17 9E
41 Provadiya 43 12N 27 30E
21 Provence, Reg. 43 40N 5 45E
97 Providence 41 41N 71 15W
90 Providence Bay 45 41N 82 15W
105 Providencia, I. de 13 25N 81 26W
51 Provideniya 64 23N 173 18W
92 Provincial Cannery 51 33N 127 36W
19 Provins 48 33N 3 15E
102 Provo 40 16N 111 37W
93 Provost 52 25N 110 20W
40 Prozor 43 50N 17 34E
109 Prudentópolis 25 12S 50 57W
80 Prudhoe, I. 21 23S 149 45E
88 Prudhoe Bay 70 10N 148 0W
93 Prudhomme 52 22N 105 47W
27 Prudnik 50 20N 17 38E
28 Pruszez Gdańska 54 17N 19 40E
28 Pruszków 52 9N 20 49E
49 Prut, R. 45 28N 28 12E
5 Prydz B. 69 0S 74 0E
28 Przasnysz 53 2N 20 45E
27 Przemysl 49 50N 22 45E
27 Przemysl □ 50 0N 22 0E
50 Przhevalsk 42 30N 78 20E
43 Psará, I. 38 37N 25 38E
48 Pskov 57 50N 28 25E
27 Pszczyna 49 59N 18 58E
42 Ptolemaís 40 30N 21 43E
110 Pucallpa 8 25S 74 30W
69 Puchi 29 42N 113 54E
41 Pucioasia 45 4N 25 26E
62 Pudukkottai 10 28N 78 47E
104 Puebla 19 0N 98 10W
104 Puebla □ 18 30N 98 0W
31 Puebla de Guzman 37 33N 7 15W
30 Puebla de Sanabria 42 4N 6 38W
100 Pueblo 38 20N 104 40W
108 Puente Alto 33 32S 70 35W
31 Puente Genil 37 22N 4 47W
32 Puente la Reina 42 40N 1 49W
30 Puenteareas 42 10N 8 28W
30 Puentedeume 43 24N 8 10W
67 Puerh 23 11N 100 56E
105 Puerto Armuelles 8 20N 83 10W
110 Puerto Asís 0 30N 76 30W
110 Puerto Ayacucho 5 40N 67 35W
104 Puerto Barrios 15 40N 88 40W
110 Puerto Berrío 6 30N 74 30W
110 Puerto Bolívar 3 10S 79 55W
110 Puerto Cabello 10 28N 68 1W
105 Puerto Cabezas 14 0N 83 30W
110 Puerto Carreño 6 12N 67 22W
105 Puerto Cortes 15 51N 88 0W
104 Puerto Cortés 8 20N 82 20W
112 Puerto Coyle 50 54S 69 15W
110 Puerto Cumarebo 11 29N 69 21W
31 Puerto de Santa María 36 35N 6 15W
72 Puerto del Rosario 28 30N 13 52W
112 Puerto Deseado 47 45S 66 0W
110 Puerto Páez 6 13N 67 28W
110 Puerto Leguizamo 0 12S 74 46W
112 Puerto Lobos 42 0S 65 3W
33 Puerto Lumbreras 37 34N 1 48W
112 Puerto Madryn 42 48S 65 4W
33 Puerto Mazarrón 37 34N 1 15W
112 Puerto Montt 41 28S 72 57W
112 Puerto Natales 51 45S 72 25W
105 Puerto Padre 21 13N 76 35W
108 Puerto Pinasco 22 30S 57 50W
112 Puerto Pirámides 42 35S 64 20W
110 Puerto Piritu 10 5N 65 0W
105 Puerto Plata 19 40N 70 45W
65 Puerto Princesa 9 55N 118 50E
112 Puerto Quellón 43 7S 73 37W
31 Puerto Real 36 33N 6 12W
105 Puerto Rico, I. 18 15N 66 45W
112 Puerto Saavedra 38 47S 73 24W
110 Puerto Suárez 18 58S 57 52W
112 Puerto Varas 41 19S 72 59W
31 Puertollano 38 43N 4 7W
112 Pueyrredón, L. 47 20S 72 0W
48 Pugachev 52 0N 48 55E
102 Puget Sd. 47 15N 123 30W
39 Puglia □ 41 0N 16 30E
40 Pui 45 30N 23 4E
32 Puig Mayor, Mt. 39 49N 2 47E
32 Puigcerda 42 24N 1 50E
19 Puisaye, Collines de la 47 35N 3 30E
85 Pukaki, L. 44 5S 170 1E
93 Pukatawagan 55 45N 101 20W
85 Pukekohe 37 12S 174 55E
37 Pula 39 0N 9 0E
108 Pulacayo 20 25S 66 41W
68 Pulantien 39 25N 122 0E
97 Pulaski, N.Y. 43 32N 76 9W

Pulaski, Tenn. Reading, U.K.

99 Pulaski, Tenn. 35 10N 87 0W
98 Pulaski, Va. 37 4N 80 49W
28 Puławy 51 23N 21 59E
62 Pulicat L. 13 40N 80 15E
62 Puliyangudi 9 11N 77 24E
102 Pullman 46 49N 117 10W
64 Puloraja 4 55N 95 24E
28 Pułtusk 52 43N 21 6E
67 Puluntohai 47 2N 87 29E
61 Punakha 27 42N 89 52E
62 Punalur 9 0N 76 56E
58 Punch 33 48N 74 4E
58 Pune 18 29N 73 57E
60 Punjab □ 31 0N 76 0E
110 Puno 15 55S 70 3W
108 Punta Alta 38 53S 62 4W
112 Punta Arenas 53 0S 71 0W
112 Punta Delgada 42 43S 63 38W
104 Punta Gorda 16 10N 88 45W
81 Puntabie 32 12S 134 5E
105 Puntarenas 10 0N 84 50W
110 Punto Fijo 11 42N 70 13W
110 Purace, Mt. 2 21N 76 23W
13 Purbeck, I. of 50 40N 2 5W
33 Purchena Tetica 37 21N 2 21W
61 Puri 19 50N 85 58E
62 Purli 18 50N 76 35E
60 Purna, R. 21 5N 76 0E
61 Purnea 25 45N 87 31E
63 Pursat 12 34N 103 50E
61 Purulia 23 17N 86 33E
110 Purus, R. 3 42S 61 28W
41 Pŭrvomay 42 8N 25 17E
65 Purwakarta 6 35S 107 29E
65 Purwodadi, Jawa 7 7S 110 55E
65 Purwodadi, Jawa 7 51S 110 0E
65 Purwokerto 7 25S 109 14E
65 Purworedjo 7 43S 110 2E
68 Pusan 35 5N 129 0E
51 Pushchino 54 20N 158 10E
49 Pushkino 51 16N 47 9E
27 Püspökladány 47 19N 21 6E
59 Putao 27 28N 97 30E
85 Putaruru 38 3S 175 47E
68 Putehachi 48 4N 122 45E
69 Putien 22 28N 119 0E
39 Putignano 40 50N 17 5E
41 Putna, R. 45 35N 27 30E
97 Putnam 41 55N 71 55W
24 Puttgarden 54 28N 11 15E
62 Puttur 12 46N 75 12E
110 Putumayo, R. 3 7S 67 58E
20 Puy de Dôme, Mt. 45 46N 2 57E
20 Puy de Sancy, Mt. 45 32N 2 41E
20 Puy l'Evêque 44 31N 1 9E
102 Puyallup 47 10N 122 22W
20 Puy-de-Dôme □ 45 47N 3 0E
20 Puyoô 43 33N 0 56W
49 Pyatigorsk 44 2N 43 0E
59 Pyinmana 19 45N 96 20E
68 Pyŏngyang 39 0N 125 30E
17 Pyrenees, Mts. 42 45N 0 20E
20 Pyrénées-Atlantiques □ 43 15N 0 45W
20 Pyrénées-Orientales □ 42 35N 2 25E
28 Pyrzyce 53 10N 14 55E
59 Pyu 18 30N 96 35E

Q

54 Qabatiya 32 25N 35 16E
57 Qadam 32 55N 66 45E
56 Qadhima 22 20N 39 13E
60 Qadian 31 51N 74 19E
56 Qal'at al Mu'azzam 27 43N 37 27E
56 Qal'at Sālih 31 31N 47 16E
56 Qal'at Sura 26 10N 38 40E
57 Qala-i-Kirta 32 15N 63 0E
57 Qala Nau 35 0N 63 5E
54 Qalqīlya 32 12N 34 58E
73 Qâra 29 38N 26 30E
57 Qasr-e Qand 26 15N 60 45E
73 Qasr Farâfra 27 0N 28 1E
55 Qasr Hamam 21 5N 46 5E
57 Qatar ■ 25 30N 51 15E
73 Qattara, Munkhafed el 29 30N 27 30E
56 Qazvin 36 15N 50 0E
73 Qena 26 10N 32 43E
54 Qesari 32 30N 34 53E
57 Qeshm 26 55N 56 10E
57 Qeshm, I. 26 50N 56 0E
57 Qeys, Jazireh-ye 26 32N 53 56E
54 Qezi'ot 30 52N 34 28E
58 Qila Safed 29 0N 61 30E
54 Qiryat Bialik 32 50N 35 5E
54 Qiryat 'Eqron 31 52N 34 49E
54 Qiryat Gat 31 36N 35 47E
54 Qiryat Hayyim 32 49N 35 4E
54 Qiryat Mal'akhi 31 44N 34 45E
54 Qiryat Shemona 33 13N 35 35E
54 Qiryat Tiv'om 32 43N 35 8E
54 Qiryat Yam 32 51N 35 4E
55 Qīzān 16 57N 42 3E
57 Qom 34 40N 51 4E
97 Quabbin Res. 42 22N 72 18W
24 Quackenbrück 52 40N 7 59E
83 Quairading 32 0S 117 21E
97 Quakerstown 40 27N 75 20W
83 Qualeup 33 48S 116 48E
63 Quang Ngai 15 13N 108 58E
63 Quang Tri 16 45N 107 13E
63 Quang Yen 21 3N 106 52E
13 Quantock Hills 51 8N 3 10W
108 Quaraí 30 15S 56 20W
38 Quartu Sant'Elena 39 15N 9 10E
57 Qūchān 37 10N 58 27E
75 Que Que 18 58S 29 48E
84 Queanbeyan 35 17S 149 14E
91 Québec 46 52N 71 13W
91 Québec □ 50 0N 70 0W
24 Quedlinburg 51 47N 11 9E
5 Queen Alexandra Ra. 85 0S 170 0E
92 Queen Charlotte 53 28N 132 2W
92 Queen Charlotte Is. 53 10N 132 0W
92 Queen Charlotte Str. 51 0N 128 0W
86 Queen Elizabeth Is. 75 0N 95 0W
5 Queen Mary Coast 70 0S 95 0E
88 Queen Maud G. 68 15N 102 0W
5 Queen Maud Ra. 86 0S 160 0W
79 Queensland □ 15 0S 142 0E
80 Queenstown, Australia 42 4S 145 35E
85 Queenstown, N.Z. 45 1S 168 40E
75 Queenstown, S.Africa 31 52S 26 52E
111 Queimadas 11 0S 39 38W
74 Quela 9 10S 16 56E
75 Quelimane 17 53S 36 58E
69 Quemoy, I. = Kinmen, I. 24 25N 118 25E
108 Quenquèn 38 30S 58 30W
104 Querêtaro 20 40N 100 23W
104 Querêtaro □ 20 30N 100 30W
33 Quesada 37 51N 3 4W
92 Quesnel 53 5N 122 30W
18 Questembert 47 40N 2 28W
90 Quetico 48 45N 90 55W
90 Quetico Prov. Park 48 15N 91 45W
60 Quetta 30 15N 66 55E
60 Quetta □ 30 15N 68 30E
104 Quezaltenango 14 40N 91 30W
65 Quezon City 14 38N 121 0E
63 Qui Nhon 13 40N 109 13E
110 Quibdo 5 42N 76 40W
18 Quiberon 47 29N 3 9W
108 Quiindy 25 58S 57 16W
112 Quilân, C. 43 15S 74 30W
75 Quilengues 14 12S 15 12E
20 Quillan 42 53N 2 10E
108 Quillota 32 54S 71 16W
108 Quilmes 34 50S 58 0W
62 Quilon 8 50N 76 38E
81 Quilpie 26 35S 144 11E
108 Quilpué 33 3S 71 27W
18 Quimper 48 0N 4 9W
18 Quimperlé 47 53N 3 33W
97 Quincy, Mass. 42 14N 71 0W
99 Quincy, Fla. 30 34N 84 34W
100 Quincy, Ill. 39 55N 91 20W
104 Quintana Roo □ 19 0E 88 0W
32 Quintanar de la Orden 39 36N 3 5W
33 Quintanar del Rey 39 21N 1 56W
108 Quintero 32 45S 71 30W
32 Quinto 41 25N 0 32W
30 Quiroga 42 28N 7 18W
21 Quissac 43 55N 4 0E
108 Quitilipi 26 50S 60 13W
110 Quito 0 15S 78 35W
111 Quixadá 4 55S 39 0W
54 Qumran 31 43N 35 27N
82 Quoin, I. 14 54S 129 32E
81 Quorn 32 25S 138 0E
67 Qurug-Tagh, Mts. 41 30N 90 0E
73 Qûs 25 55N 32 50E
73 Quseir 26 7N 34 16E
42 Qytet Stalin 40 47N 19 57E

R

26 Raab 47 42N 17 38E
54 Ra'anana 32 12N 34 52E
46 Raane 64 40N 24 28E
14 Raasay, I. 57 25N 6 4W
37 Rab, I. 44 45N 14 45E
27 Raba, R. 50 9N 20 30E
65 Raba 8 36S 118 55E
30 Rabaçal, R. 41 30N 7 12W
20 Rabastens 43 50N 1 43E
72 Rabat 34 2N 6 48W
76 Rabaul 4 24S 152 18E
56 Rabigh 22 50N 39 5E
27 Rabka 49 37N 19 59E
38 Racalmuto 37 25N 13 41E
40 Răcăşdia 44 59N 21 36E
91 Race, C. 46 40N 53 18W
27 Racibórz 50 7N 18 18E
98 Racine 42 41N 87 51W
26 Radbuza, R. 49 46N 13 24E
24 Radeburg 51 6N 13 45E
98 Radford 37 8N 80 32W
27 Radlin 50 3N 18 29E
28 Radom 51 23N 21 12E
28 Radom □ 51 20N 21 0E
40 Radomir 42 37N 23 4E
28 Radomka R. 51 43N 21 26E
28 Radomsko 51 5N 19 28E
37 Radovljica 46 22N 14 12E
26 Radstadt 47 24N 13 28E
13 Radstock 51 17N 2 25W
40 Raduša 42 7N 21 15E
93 Radville 49 30N 104 15W
92 Rae 62 45N 115 50W
61 Rae Bareli 26 18N 81 20E
89 Rae Isthmus 66 40N 87 30W
85 Raetihi 39 25S 175 17E
108 Rafaela 31 10S 61 30W
38 Raffadali 37 23N 13 29E
56 Rafhā 29 35N 43 35E
57 Rafsanjān 30 30N 56 5E
73 Rågå 8 28N 25 41E
80 Raglan, Australia 23 42S 150 49E
85 Raglan, N.Z. 37 55S 174 55E
39 Ragusa 36 56N 14 42E
73 Rahad el Bardi 11 20N 23 40E
60 Rahimyar Khan 28 30N 70 25E
62 Raichur 16 10N 77 20E
61 Raiganj 25 37N 88 10E
61 Raigarh 21 56N 83 25E
60 Raikot 30 38N 75 36E
80 Railton 41 25S 146 28E
102 Rainier, Mt. 46 50N 121 50W
93 Rainy River 48 50N 94 30W
61 Raipur 21 17N 81 45E
90 Raith 48 50N 90 0W
62 Rajahmundry 17 1N 81 48E
62 Rajapalaiyam 9 25N 77 35E
60 Rajasthan □ 26 45N 73 30E
60 Rajasthan Can. 30 31N 71 0E
61 Rajbari 23 47N 89 41E
60 Rajgarh, Mad. P. 24 2N 76 45E
60 Rajgarh, Rajasthan 28 40N 75 25E
37 Rajhenburg 46 1N 15 29E
60 Rajkot 22 15N 70 56E
61 Rajmahal Hills 24 30N 87 30E
61 Rajnandgaon 21 5N 81 5E
60 Rajpipla 21 50N 73 30E
60 Rajpura 30 32N 76 32E
61 Rajshahi 24 22N 88 39E
61 Rajshahi □ 25 0N 89 0E
85 Rakaia 43 45S 172 1E
85 Rakaia, R. 43 54S 172 12E
27 Rákospalota 47 30N 19 5E
26 Rakovník 50 6N 13 42E
41 Rakovski 42 21N 24 57E
93 Raleigh, Australia 30 27S 153 2E
99 Raleigh, Canada 49 30N 92 5W
40 Ralja 44 33N 20 34E
54 Rám Alláh 31 55N 35 10E
84 Ram Head 37 47S 149 30E
54 Rama 32 56N 35 21E
39 Ramacca 37 24N 14 40E
62 Ramachandrapuram 16 50N 82 4E
62 Ramanathapuram 9 25N 78 55E
54 Ramat Gan 32 4N 34 48E
54 Ramat Ha Sharon 32 7N 34 50E
54 Ramat Ha Shofet 32 36N 35 5E
19 Rambervillers 48 20N 6 38E
19 Rambouillet 48 40N 1 48E
59 Rambre Kyun, I. 19 0N 94 0E
62 Ramdurg 15 58N 75 22E
65 Ramelau, Mt. 8 55S 126 22E
56 Râmhormoz 31 15N 49 35E
54 Ramla 31 55N 34 52E
60 Ramnaga 32 47N 75 18E
103 Ramona 33 1N 116 56W
88 Rampart 65 30N 150 10W
60 Rampur 23 25N 73 53E
60 Rampura 24 30N 75 27E
61 Rampurhat 24 10N 87 50E
90 Ramsey, Canada 47 25N 82 20W
12 Ramsey, U.K. 54 20N 4 21W
13 Ramsgate 51 20N 1 25E
61 Ranaghat 23 15N 88 35E
108 Rancagua 34 10S 70 50W
18 Rance, R. 48 31N 1 59W
109 Rancharia 22 15S 50 55W
102 Ranchester 44 57N 107 12W
61 Ranchi 23 19N 85 27E
112 Ranco, L. 40 15S 72 25W
41 Rancu 44 32N 24 15E
39 Rándazzo 37 53N 14 56E
45 Randers 56 29N 10 1E
45 Randers, Fd. 56 37N 10 20E
97 Randolph 43 55N 72 39W
44 Randsfjorden 60 25N 10 24E
46 Råneå 65 53N 22 18E
85 Rangaunu, B. 34 51S 173 15E
85 Rangitaiki, R. 37 54S 176 53E
85 Rangitata, R. 44 11S 171 30E
65 Rangkasbitung 6 22S 106 16E
59 Rangoon 16 45N 96 20E
61 Rangpur 25 42N 89 22E
62 Ranibennur 14 35N 75 30E
62 Ranipet 12 56N 79 23E
88 Rankin Inlet 62 30N 93 0W
84 Rankins Springs 33 49S 146 14E
14 Rannoch, L. 56 41N 4 20W
63 Ranong 9 56N 98 40E
64 Rantauprapat 2 15N 99 50E
65 Rantemario, Mt. 3 15S 119 57E
54 Rantis 32 4N 35 3E
98 Rantoul 40 18N 88 10W
77 Rapa Iti, Is. 27 35S 144 20W
36 Rapallo 44 21N 9 12E
65 Rapang 3 45S 119 55E
100 Rapid City 44 0N 103 0W
97 Raquette, R. 45 0N 74 42W
77 Rarotonga, I. 21 30S 160 0W
112 Rasa, Pte. 40 55S 63 20N
57 Ras al Khaima 25 50N 56 5E
73 Ra's Al-Unuf 30 25N 18 15E
56 Ra's al Tannūrah 26 40N 50 10E
73 Rashad 11 55N 31 0E
73 Rashîd 31 21N 30 22E
56 Rasht 37 20N 49 40E
62 Rasipuram 11 30N 78 25E
40 Raška 43 19N 20 39E
61 Rasra 25 50N 83 50E
25 Rastatt 48 50N 8 12E
63 Rat Buri 13 30N 99 54E
88 Rat Is. 51 50N 178 15E
60 Ratangarh 28 5N 74 35E
61 Rath 25 36N 79 37E
15 Rath Luirc 52 21N 8 40W
15 Rathdrum, Eire 52 57N 6 13W
102 Rathdrum, U.S.A 47 50N 116 58W
24 Rathenow 52 38N 12 23E
15 Rathkeale 52 32N 8 57W
15 Rathlin, I. 55 18N 6 14W
26 Ratikon, Ra. 47 3N 9 50E
60 Ratlam 23 20N 75 0E
62 Ratnagiri 16 57N 73 18E
62 Ratnapura 6 40N 80 20E
101 Raton 37 0N 104 30W
26 Ratten 47 28N 15 44E
14 Rattray Hd. 57 38N 1 50W
24 Ratzeburg 53 41N 10 46E
63 Raub 3 47N 101 52E
108 Rauch 36 45S 59 5W
85 Raukumara, Ra. 38 5S 177 55E
47 Rauma 61 10N 21 30E
61 Raurkela 22 14N 84 50E
38 Ravanusa 37 16N 13 58E
57 Rāvar 31 20N 56 51E
37 Ravenna, Italy 44 28N 12 15E
96 Ravenna, U.S.A. 41 11N 81 15W
25 Ravensburg 47 48N 9 38E
80 Ravenshoe 17 37S 145 29E
83 Ravensthorpe 33 35S 120 2E
60 Raver 21 15N 76 5E
44 Ravfoss 60 44N 10 37E
28 Rawa Mazowiecka 51 46N 20 12E
58 Rawalpindi 33 38N 73 8E
58 Rawalpindi □ 33 38N 73 8E
63 Rawang 3 19N 101 35E
90 Rawdon 46 3N 73 40W
85 Rawene 35 25S 173 32E
28 Rawicz 51 36N 16 52E
28 Rawka R. 52 9N 20 8E
83 Rawlinna 30 58S 125 28E
102 Rawlins 41 50N 107 20W
112 Rawson 43 15S 65 0W
91 Ray, C. 47 33N 59 15W
62 Rayachoti 14 4N 78 50E
62 Rayadrug 14 40N 76 50E
51 Raychikhinsk 49 46N 129 25E
92 Raymond, Canada 49 30N 112 35W
102 Raymond, U.S.A. 46 45N 123 48W
101 Raymondville 26 30N 97 50W
93 Raymore 50 25N 104 31W
101 Rayne 30 16N 92 16W
18 Raz, Pte. du 48 2N 4 47W
40 Ražana 44 6N 19 55E
40 Ražanj 43 40N 21 31E
41 Razdelna 43 13N 27 41E
41 Razelm, L. 44 50N 29 0E
41 Razgrad 43 33N 26 34E
41 Razlog 41 53N 23 28E
20 Ré, I. de 46 12N 1 30W
13 Reading, U.K. 51 27N 0 57W

Reading, U.S.A. Ronsard, C.

97 Reading, U.S.A. 40 20N 75 53W
108 Realicó 35 0S 64 15W
20 Réalmont 43 48N 2 10E
65 Rebi 5 30S 134 7E
37 Recanati 43 24N 13 32E
40 Recas 45 46N 21 30E
60 Rechna Doab, Reg. 31 35N 73 30E
111 Recife 8 0S 35 0W
24 Recklinghausen 51 36N 7 10E
108 Reconquista 29 10S 59 45W
101 Red, R. 48 10N 97 0W
97 Red Bank 40 21N 74 4W
102 Red Bluff 40 11N 122 11W
92 Red Deer 52 20N 113 50W
93 Red Lake 51 1N 94 1W
100 Red Oak 41 0N 95 10W
100 Red Wing 44 32N 92 35W
28 Reda 54 40N 18 19E
13 Redbridge 51 35N 0 7E
12 Redcar 54 37N 1 4W
93 Redcliff 50 10N 110 50W
81 Redcliffe 27 12S 153 0E
84 Redcliffs 34 16S 142 10E
102 Redding 40 30N 122 25W
13 Redditch 52 18N 1 57W
103 Redlands 34 0N 117 0W
83 Redmond, Australia 34 55S 117 40E
102 Redmond, U.S.A. 44 19N 121 11W
18 Redon 47 40N 2 6W
105 Redonda, I. 16 58N 62 19W
30 Redondela 42 15N 8 38W
31 Redondo 38 39N 7 37W
103 Redondo Beach 33 52N 118 26W
13 Redruth 50 14N 5 14W
92 Redstone 52 8N 123 42W
93 Redvers 49 35N 101 40W
92 Redwater 53 55N 113 0W
103 Redwood City 37 30N 122 15W
15 Ree, L. 53 35N 8 0W
103 Reedley 34 40N 119 27W
102 Reedsport 43 45N 124 4W
85 Reefton 42 6S 171 51E
28 Rega, R. 53 52N 15 16E
39 Regalbuto 37 40N 14 38E
54 Regavim 32 32N 35 2E
25 Regen 48 58N 13 9E
25 Regen, R. 49 1N 12 6E
25 Regensburg 49 1N 12 7E
36 Reggio nell'Emilia 44 42N 10 38E
39 Réggio di Calábria 38 7N 15 38E
93 Regina 50 30N 104 35W
57 Registan, Reg. 30 15N 65 0E
109 Registro 24 30S 47 50W
31 Reguengos de Monsaraz 38 25N 7 32W
75 Rehoboth 17 55S 15 5E
54 Rehovot 31 54N 34 48E
24 Reichenbach 50 36N 12 19E
83 Reid 35 17S 149 8E
80 Reid River 19 40S 146 48E
99 Reidsville 36 21N 79 40W
13 Reigate 51 14N 0 11W
32 Reillo 39 54N 1 53W
19 Reims 49 15N 4 0E
54 Reina 32 43N 35 18E
112 Reina Adelaida, Arch. 52 20S 74 0W
93 Reindeer L. 57 20N 102 20W
85 Reinga, C. 34 25S 172 43E
30 Reinosa 43 2N 4 15W
30 Reinosa, P. 42 56N 4 10W
51 Rekinniki 60 38N 163 50E
111 Remanso 9 41S 42 4W
65 Rembang 6 42S 111 21E
57 Remeshk 26 55N 58 50E
19 Remiremont 48 0N 6 36E
24 Remscheid 51 11N 7 12E
97 Remsen 43 19N 75 11W
24 Rendsburg 54 18N 9 41E
51 Rene 66 2N 179 25W
90 Renfrew, Canada 45 30N 76 40W
14 Renfrew, U.K. 55 52N 4 24W
64 Rengat 0 30S 102 45E
108 Rengo 34 25S 70 52W
62 Renigunta 13 38N 79 30E
73 Renk 11 47N 32 49E
16 Renkum 51 58N 5 43E
81 Renmark 34 11S 140 43E
18 Rennes 48 7N 1 41W
18 Rennes, Bassin de 48 0N 2 0W
102 Reno 39 30N 119 0W
32 Rentería 43 19N 1 54W
102 Renton 47 30N 122 9W
61 Reotipur 25 33N 83 45E
62 Repalle 16 2N 80 45E
100 Republican, R. 39 3N 96 48W
89 Repulse Bay 66 30N 86 30W
32 Requena 39 30N 1 4W
40 Resen 41 5N 21 0E
93 Reserve 33 50N 108 54W
108 Resistencia 27 30S 59 0W
40 Reşiţa 45 18N 21 53E
89 Resolution I., Canada 61 30N 65 0W
85 Resolution, I., N.Z. 45 40S 166 40E
104 Retalhulen 14 33N 91 46W
19 Rethel 49 30N 4 20E
43 Réthímnon 35 15N 24 40E
43 Réthímnon □ 35 23N 24 28E
18 Rétiers 47 55N 1 25W
71 Réunion, Í. 22 0S 56 0E
32 Reus 41 10N 1 5E
25 Reutlingen 48 28N 9 13E
26 Reutte 47 29N 10 42E
20 Revel 43 28N 2 0E
61 Revelganj 25 50N 84 40E
92 Revelstoke 51 0N 118 0W
19 Revigny 48 50N 5 0E
77 Revilla Gigedo Is. 18 40N 112 0W
19 Revin 49 55N 4 39E
61 Rewa 24 33N 81 25E
60 Rewari 28 15N 76 40E
102 Rexburg 43 45N 111 50W
72 Rey Malabo 3 45N 8 50E
46 Reykanes, Pen. 63 48N 22 40W
46 Reykjavik 64 10N 21 57E
104 Reynosa 26 5N 98 18W
56 Reza'iyeh 37 40N 45 0E
13 Rhayader 52 19N 3 30W
16 Rheden 52 0N 6 3E
24 Rheine 52 17N 7 25E
25 Rheinland-Pfalz □ 50 50N 7 0E
24 Rheydt 51 10N 6 24E
19 Rhinau 48 19N 7 43E
100 Rhinelander 45 38N 89 29W
72 Rhir, C. 30 38N 9 54W
36 Rho 45 31N 9 2E
97 Rhode Island □ 41 38N 71 37W
75 Rhodesia ■ 20 0S 28 30E
41 Rhodope, Mts. = Rhodopi Planina 41 40N 24 20E
41 Rhodopi Planina 41 40N 24 20E
13 Rhondda 51 39N 3 30W
21 Rhône □ 45 54N 4 35E
21 Rhône, R. 43 28N 4 42E
14 Rhum, I. 57 0N 6 20W
12 Rhyl 53 19N 3 29W
111 Riachão 7 20S 46 37W
30 Riansares, R. 39 32N 3 18W
64 Riau □ 1 0N 102 35E
64 Riau, Kep. 0 30N 104 20E
30 Riaza, R. 41 16N 3 29W
30 Ribadavia 42 17N 8 8W
30 Ribadeo 43 35N 7 5W
30 Ribadesella 43 30N 5 7W
32 Ribas 42 19N 2 15E
111 Ribas do Rio Pardo 20 27S 53 46W
29 Ribatejo, Reg. 39 15N 8 30W
12 Ribble, R. 54 13N 2 20W
45 Ribe □ 55 34N 8 30E
45 Ribe 55 19N 8 44E
19 Ribeauville 48 10N 7 20E
19 Ribécourt 49 30N 2 55E
30 Ribeira 42 36N 8 58W
109 Ribeirão Prêto 21 10S 47 50W
38 Ribera 37 30N 13 13E
24 Ribnitz-Damgarten 54 14N 12 24E
26 Říčany 50 0N 14 40E
85 Riccarton 43 32S 172 37E
37 Riccione 44 0N 12 39E
100 Rice Lake 44 10N 78 10W
75 Richards B. 28 48S 32 6E
97 Richford 45 0N 72 40W
91 Richibucto 46 42N 64 54W
102 Richland 44 49N 117 9W
80 Richmond, Australia 20 43S 143 8E
85 Richmond, N.Z. 41 4S 173 12E
75 Richmond, S. Africa 29 54S 30 8E
13 Richmond, Surrey 51 28N 0 18W
12 Richmond, Yorks. 54 24N 1 43W
102 Richmond, Calif. 38 0N 122 30W
98 Richmond, Ind. 39 50N 84 50W
98 Richmond, Ky. 37 40N 84 20W
102 Richmobd, Utah 41 55N 111 48W
98 Richmond, Va. 37 33N 77 27W
90 Richmond Gulf, L. 56 20N 75 50W
96 Richmond Hill 43 52N 79 27W
98 Richwood 38 17N 80 32W
32 Ricla 41 31N 1 24W
93 Ridgedale 53 0N 104 10W
90 Ridgetown 42 26N 81 52W
97 Ridgewood 40 59N 74 7W
96 Ridgway 41 25N 78 43W
93 Riding Mountain Nat. Park 50 55N 100 25W
26 Ried 48 14N 13 30E
37 Rienza, R. 46 49N 11 47E
24 Riesa 51 19N 13 19E
39 Riesi 37 16N 14 4E
37 Rieti 42 23N 12 50E
102 Rifle 39 40N 107 50W
48 Riga 56 53N 24 8E
91 Rigolet 54 10N 58 23W
37 Rijeka 45 20N 14 21E
40 Rijeka Crnojevica 42 24N 19 1E
16 Rijssen 52 19N 6 30E
16 Rijswijk 52 4N 4 22E
102 Riley 39 18N 96 50W
19 Rilly 49 11N 4 3E
27 Rimavaská Sobota 48 22N 20 2E
44 Rimbo 59 44N 18 21E
37 Rimini 44 3N 12 33E
41 Rîmnicu Sărat 45 26N 27 3E
41 Rîmnicu Vîlcea 45 9N 24 21E
91 Rimouski 48 27N 68 30W
15 Rineanna 52 42N 85 7W
45 Ringe 55 13N 10 28E
44 Ringerike 60 7N 10 16E
45 Ringkøbing 56 5N 8 15E
45 Ringköbing □ 56 15N 8 30E
45 Ringsjön, L. 55 55N 13 30E
45 Ringsted 55 25N 11 46E
24 Rinteln 52 11N 9 3E
33 Rio, Pta. del 36 49N 2 24W
111 Rio Amazonas, Estuario do 1 0N 49 0W
110 Rio Branco, Brazil 9 58S 67 49W
109 Rio Branco, Uruguay 32 34S 53 25W
109 Rio Brilhante 21 48S 54 33W
105 Rio Claro 10 20N 61 25W
109 Rio Claro 22 19S 47 35W
108 Rio Cuarto 33 10S 64 25W
109 Rio de Janeiro 23 0S 43 12W
109 Rio de Janeiro □ 22 50S 43 0W
109 Rio do Sul 27 95S 49 37W
112 Rio Gallegos 51 35S 69 15W
109 Rio Grande, Arg. 53 50S 67 45W
112 Rio Grande, Brazil 32 0S 52 20W
94 Rio Grande, R. 37 47N 106 15W
111 Rio Grande do Norte □ 5 45S 36 0W
109 Rio Grande do Sul □ 30 0S 54 0W
111 Rio Largo 9 28S 35 50W
110 Rio Mulatos 19 40S 66 50W
74 Rio Muni □ 1 30N 10 0E
109 Rio Negro 26 0S 50 0W
109 Rio Pardo 15 55S 42 30W
108 Río Segundo 31 40S 63 58W
108 Río Tercero 32 10S 64 5W
30 Rio Tinto 41 11N 8 34W
111 Rio Verde, Brazil 17 43S 50 56W
104 Río Verde, Mexico 21 56N 99 59W
102 Rio Vista 38 11N 121 44W
110 Riobamba 1 50S 78 45W
20 Riom 45 54N 3 7E
110 Ríohacha 11 33N 72 55W
39 Rionero in Vulture 40 55N 15 40E
110 Ríosucio 5 30N 75 40W
110 Rioscio 7 27N 77 7W
96 Ripley 44 4N 81 32W
32 Ripoll 42 15N 2 13E
12 Ripon, U.K. 54 8N 1 31W
100 Ripon, U.S.A. 43 51N 88 50W
39 Riposto 37 44N 15 12E
40 Risan 42 32N 18 42E
20 Riscle 43 39N 0 5W
54 Rishon Le Zion 31 58N 34 48E
54 Rishpon 32 12N 34 49E
18 Risle, R. 49 26N 0 23E
41 Rîsnov 45 35N 25 27E
45 Risør 58 43N 9 13E
63 Ritchies Arch. 12 10N 93 5E
96 Rittman 40 57N 81 48W
102 Ritzville 47 10N 118 21W
36 Riva 45 53N 10 50E
18 Riva Bella-Ouistreham 49 17N 0 18W
108 Rivadavia 29 50S 70 35W
105 Rivas 11 30N 85 50W
21 Rive-de-Gier 45 32N 4 37E
109 Rivera 31 0S 55 50W
97 Riverhead 40 53N 72 40W
93 Riverhurst 50 55N 106 50W
75 Riversale 34 7S 21 15E
103 Riverside, Calif. 34 0N 117 15W
102 Riverside, Wyo. 41 12N 106 57W
81 Riverton, Australia 34 10S 138 46E
93 Riverton, Canada 51 5N 97 0W
85 Riverton, N.Z. 46 21S 168 0E
102 Riverton, U.S.A. 43 1N 108 27W
20 Rivesaltes 42 47N 2 50E
36 Riviera 44 0N 8 30E
91 Rivière Bleue 47 26N 69 2W
91 Rivière du Loup 47 50N 69 30W
91 Rivière Pentecôte 49 57N 67 1W
36 Rivoli 45 3N 7 31E
56 Riyadh = Ar Riyád 24 41N 46 42E
56 Rize 41 0N 40 30E
44 Rjukan 59 54N 8 33E
30 Roa 41 41N 3 56W
21 Roanne 46 3N 4 4E
99 Roanoke, Ala. 33 9N 85 23W
98 Roanoke, Va. 37 19N 79 55W
99 Roanoke Rapids 36 36N 77 42W
105 Roatán, I. de 16 23N 86 26W
75 Robertson 33 46S 19 50E
90 Roberval 48 32N 72 15W
77 Robinson Crusoe, I. 33 50S 78 30W
93 Roblin 51 21N 101 25W
92 Robson, Mt. 53 10N 119 10W
101 Robstown 27 47N 97 40W
31 Roca, C. da 38 40N 9 31W
111 Rocas, Is. 4 0S 34 1W
37 Roccastrada 43 0N 11 10E
109 Rocha 34 30S 54 25W
12 Rochdale 53 36N 2 10W
20 Rochefort 45 56N 0 57W
100 Rochelle 41 55N 89 5W
92 Rocher River 61 12N 114 0W
84 Rochester, Australia 36 22S 144 41E
13 Rochester, U.K. 51 22N 0 30E
100 Rochester, Minn. 44 1N 92 28W
97 Rochester, N.H. 43 19N 70 57W
96 Rochester, N.Y. 43 10N 77 40W
96 Rochester, Pa. 40 41N 80 17W
99 Rock Hill 34 55N 81 2W
100 Rock Island 41 30N 90 35W
105 Rock Sound 24 54N 76 12W
102 Rock Springs 46 55N 106 11W
8 Rockall, I. 57 37N 13 42W
5 Rockefeller Plat. 84 0S 130 0W
100 Rockford, Ill. 42 20N 89 0W
100 Rockford, Mich. 43 7N 85 33W
80 Rockhampton 23 22S 150 32E
83 Rockingham 32 15S 115 38E
97 Rockville, Conn. 41 51N 72 27W
99 Rockland, Ma. 44 6N 69 8W
98 Rockville, Md. 39 7N 77 10W
83 Rocky Gully 34 30S 117 0E
99 Rocky Mount 35 55N 77 48W
92 Rocky Mountain House 52 22N 114 55W
86 Rocky Mts. 48 0N 113 0W
96 Rocky River 41 30N 81 40W
92 Rockyford 51 13N 113 8W
44 Rødberg 60 17N 8 56E
45 Rødby 54 41N 11 23E
45 Rødbyhavn 54 39N 11 22E
91 Roddickton 50 51N 56 8W
20 Rodez 44 21N 2 33E
42 Rodhópi □ 41 10N 25 30E
43 Ródhos 36 15N 28 10E
43 Ródhos, I. 36 15N 28 10E
85 Rodney, C. 36 17S 174 50E
3 Rodriguez, I. 20 0S 65 0E
82 Roebourne 20 44S 117 9E
82 Roebuck, B. 18 5S 122 20E
82 Roebuck Plains P.O. 17 56S 122 28E
16 Roermond 51 12N 6 0E
89 Roes Welcome Sd. 65 0N 87 0W
16 Roeselare 50 57N 3 7E
47 Rogaland □ 59 12N 6 20E
37 Rogaska Slatina 46 15N 15 42E
101 Rogers 36 20N 94 0W
90 Roggan River 54 24N 78 5W
21 Rogliano 42 57N 9 30E
60 Rohtak 28 55N 76 43E
19 Roisel 49 58N 3 6E
108 Rojas 34 10S 60 45W
26 Rokycany 49 43N 13 35E
109 Rolândia 23 5S 52 0W
101 Rolla 38 0N 91 42W
80 Rollingstone 19 2S 146 24E
80 Rolleston 43 35S 172 24E
105 Rolleville 23 41N 76 0W
37 Roma, Italy 41 54N 12 30E
81 Roma, Australia 26 32S 148 49E
51 Roman 43 8N 23 54E
21 Romans 45 3N 5 3E
88 Romanzof, C. 61 49N 165 56W
37 Rome, Italy = Roma 41 54N 12 30E
99 Rome, Ga. 34 20N 85 0W
97 Rome, N.Y. 43 14N 75 29W
45 Romeleåsen, Reg. 55 34N 13 33E
19 Romilly 48 31N 3 44E
13 Romney Marsh 51 0N 1 0E
45 Rømø, I. 55 10N 8 30E
19 Romorantin-Lanthenay 47 21N 1 45E
44 Romsdal 62 25N 7 50E
14 Ronaldsay, North I. 59 23N 2 26W
14 Ronaldsay, South I. 58 47N 2 56W
111 Roncador, Sa. do 12 30S 52 30W
31 Ronda 36 46N 5 12W
31 Ronda, Sa. de 36 44N 5 3W
44 Rondane, Reg. 61 57N 9 50E
96 Rondeau Prov. Park 42 16N 81 51W
110 Rondônia □ 11 0S 63 0W
111 Rondonópolis 16 28S 54 38W
45 Rønne 55 6N 14 44E
5 Ronne Ld. 83 0S 70 0W
45 Ronneby 56 12N 15 17E
83 Ronsard, C. 24 46S 113 10E

Ronse St. George's Chan.

16 Ronse 50 45N 3 35E
75 Roodepoort-Maraisburg 26 11S 27 54E
60 Roorkee 29 52N 77 59E
16 Roosendaal 51 32N 4 29E
103 Roosevelt Res. 33 46N 111 0W
80 Roper, R. 14 43S 135 27E
20 Roquefort 44 2N 0 20W
32 Roquetas 40 50N 0 30E
110 Roraima □ 2 0N 61 30W
110 Roraima, Mt. 5 10N 60 40W
44 Røros 62 35N 11 23E
31 Rosal de la Frontera 37 59N 7 13W
108 Rosario, Arg. 33 0S 60 50W
111 Rosário, Brazil 3 0S 44 15W
104 Rosario, Mexico 23 0S 105 52W
108 Rosario, Urug. 34 20S 57 20W
108 Rosario de la Frontera 25 50S 65 0W
108 Rosario del Tala 32 20S 59 10W
109 Rosário do Sul 30 15S 54 55W
32 Rosas 42 19N 3 10E
18 Roscoff 48 44N 4 0W
15 Roscommon 53 38N 8 11W
15 Roscommon □ 53 40N 8 15W
15 Roscrea 52 57N 7 47W
91 Rose Blanche 47 38N 58 45W
92 Rose Harbour 52 15N 131 10W
93 Rose Valley 52 19N 103 49W
105 Roseau 48 56N 96 0W
101 Rosenberg 29 30N 95 48W
102 Rosebud 31 5N 97 0W
102 Roseburg 43 10N 123 10W
84 Rosedale 38 11S 146 48E
19 Rosendaël 51 3N 2 24E
25 Rosenheim 47 51N 12 9E
37 Roseto degli Abruzzi 42 40N 14 2E
93 Rosetown 57 33N 108 0E
73 Rosetta = Rashid 31 21N 30 22E
102 Roseville 38 46N 121 41W
81 Rosewood 35 38S 147 52E
54 Rosh Ha'Ayin 32 5N 34 47E
54 Rosh Pinna 32 58N 35 32E
45 Roshage, C. 57 7N 8 35E
19 Rosières 48 36N 6 20E
36 Rosignano 43 23N 10 28E
110 Rosignol 6 15N 57 30W
45 Roskilde 55 38N 12 3E
45 Roskilde □ 55 35N 12 5E
45 Roskilde, Fd. 55 50N 12 2E
48 Roslavl 53 57N 32 55E
85 Ross, N.Z. 42 53S 170 49E
13 Ross, U.K. 51 55N 2 34W
15 Ross □ 70 0S 170 5W
5 Ross Ice Shelf 80 0S 180 0W
5 Ross Sea 74 0S 178 0E
39 Rossano Cálabro 39 36N 16 39E
92 Rossland 49 6N 117 50W
15 Rosslare 52 17N 6 23W
25 Rosslau 57 52N 12 15E
72 Rosso 16 30N 15 49W
49 Rossosh 50 15N 39 20E
93 Rosthern 52 40N 106 20W
24 Rostock 54 4N 12 9E
24 Rostock □ 54 10N 12 30E
49 Rostov 47 15N 39 45E
101 Roswell 33 26N 104 32W
14 Rosyth 56 2N 3 26W
31 Rota 36 37N 6 20W
24 Rotenburg 53 6N 9 24E
25 Rothenburg ob der Tauber 49 21N 10 11E
13 Rother, R. 50 59N 0 40W
12 Rotherham 53 26N 1 21W
14 Rothes 57 31N 3 12W
14 Rothesay 55 50N 5 3W
65 Roti, I. 10 50S 123 0E
84 Roto 33 0S 145 30E
85 Rotorua 38 9S 176 16E
85 Rotorua, L. 38 5S 176 18E
26 Rottenmann 47 31N 14 22E
16 Rotterdam 51 55N 4 30E
83 Rottnest, I. 32 0S 115 27E
25 Rottweil 48 9N 8 38E
76 Rotuma, I. 12 25S 177 5E
19 Roubaix 50 40N 3 10E
26 Roudnice 50 25N 14 15E
18 Rouen 49 27N 1 4E
20 Rouergue, Reg. 44 20N 2 20E
81 Round, Mt. 30 26S 152 16E
102 Roundup 46 25N 108 35W
14 Rousay, I. 59 10N 3 2W
97 Rouses Point 44 58N 73 22W
20 Roussillon, Reg. 45 24N 4 49E
90 Rouyn 48 20N 79 0W
46 Rovaniemi 66 29N 25 41E
36 Rovereto 45 53N 11 3E
37 Rovigo 45 4N 11 48E
41 Rovinari 44 55N 23 11E
37 Rovinj 45 18N 13 40E
49 Rovno 50 40N 26 10E
65 Roxas 11 36N 122 49E
85 Roxburgh 45 33S 169 19E
45 Roxen, L. 58 30N 15 41E
82 Roy Hill 22 37S 119 58E
32 Roya, Peña 40 25N 0 40W
98 Royal Oak 42 30N 83 5W
100 Royale, I. 48 0N 89 0W
20 Royan 45 37N 1 2W
19 Roye 47 40N 6 31E
27 Rožnava 48 37N 20 35E
48 Rtishchevo 52 35N 43 50E
30 Rúa 42 24N 7 6W
85 Ruapehu, Mt. 39 18S 175 35E
110 Rubio 7 43N 72 22W
50 Rubtsovsk 51 30N 80 50E
88 Ruby 38 27S 145 55E
27 Ruda Slaska 50 16N 18 50E
81 Rudall 33 43S 136 17E
24 Rüdersdorf 52 28N 13 48E
45 Rudkøbing 54 56N 10 41E
48 Rudnichny 59 38N 52 26E
51 Rudnogorsk 57 15N 103 42E
50 Rudnyy 52 57N 63 7E
74 Rudolf, L. = Turkana, L. 4 10N 36 10E
24 Rudolstädt 50 44N 11 20E
19 Rue 50 15N 1 40E
73 Rufa'a 14 44N 33 32E
20 Ruffec 46 2N 0 42E
74 Rufiji, R. 8 0S 39 20E
108 Rufino 34 20S 62 50W
72 Rufisque 14 43N 17 17W
13 Rugby, U.K. 52 23N 1 16W
100 Rugby, U.S.A. 48 21N 100 0W
24 Rügen, I. 54 22N 13 25E
54 Ruhāma 31 31N 34 43E
24 Ruhla 50 53N 10 21E
24 Ruhr, R. 51 27N 6 44E
74 Ruki, R. 0 5N 18 17E
74 Rukwa, L. 7 50S 32 10E
82 Rum Jungle 13 0S 130 59E
40 Ruma 45 8N 19 50E
41 Rumania ■ 46 0N 25 0E
80 Rumbalara 25 20S 134 29E
97 Rumford 44 30N 70 30W
21 Rumilly 45 53N 5 56E
66 Rumoi 43 56N 141 39W
97 Rumson 40 22N 74 0W
85 Runanga 42 25S 171 15E
12 Runcorn 53 20N 2 44W
74 Rungwa 6 55S 33 32E
60 Rupar 31 2N 76 38E
64 Rupat, I. 1 45N 101 40E
90 Rupert House = Fort Rupert 51 30N 78 40W
75 Rusape 18 35S 32 8E
41 Ruse 43 48N 25 59E
13 Rushden 52 17N 0 37W
98 Rushville 39 38N 85 22W
84 Rushworth 36 32S 145 1E
111 Russas 4 56S 37 58W
93 Russell, Canada 50 50N 101 20W
100 Russell, Kans. 38 56N 98 55W
97 Russell, N.Y. 44 26N 75 11W
99 Russellville, Ala. 34 30N 87 44W
101 Russellville, Ark. 35 15N 93 0W
50 Russkaya Polyana 53 47N 73 53E
75 Rustenburg 25 41S 27 14E
101 Ruston 32 30N 92 40W
31 Rute 37 19N 4 29W
65 Ruteng 8 26S 120 30E
102 Ruth 39 15N 115 1W
84 Rutherglen, Australia 36 5S 146 29E
14 Rutherglen, U.K. 55 50N 4 11W
39 Rutigliano 41 1N 17 0E
97 Rutland 43 38N 73 0W
74 Rutshuru 1 13S 29 25E
39 Ruvo di Púglia 41 7N 16 27E
74 Ruvuma, R. 10 29S 40 28E
74 Ruwenzori, Mts. 0 30N 29 55E
27 Ruzomberok 49 3N 19 17E
74 Rwanda ■ 2 0S 30 0E
14 Ryan, L. 55 0N 5 2W
48 Ryazan 54 38N 39 44E
48 Ryazhsk 53 40N 40 7E
50 Rybache 46 40N 81 20E
48 Rybachiy Pol. 69 43N 32 0E
48 Rybinsk 58 3N 38 52E
48 Rybinskoye, Vdkhr. 58 30N 38 25E
27 Rybnik 50 6N 18 32E
13 Ryde 50 44N 1 9W
27 Rydułtowy 50 4N 18 23E
13 Rye 50 57N 0 46E
12 Rye, R. 54 12N 0 53W
28 Rypin 53 3N 19 32E
69 Ryūkyū, Is. 26 0N 128 0E
27 Rzeszów 50 5N 21 58E
27 Rzeszów □ 50 0N 22 0E
28 Rzepin 52 20N 14 49E
48 Rzhev 56 15N 34 18E

S

54 Sa'ad 31 28N 34 33E
57 Sa'ādatābād 30 10N 53 5E
24 Saale, R. 51 57N 11 55E
24 Saaler Bodden 54 20N 12 25E
24 Saalfeld 50 39N 11 21E
26 Saalfelden 47 26N 12 51E
25 Saanen 46 29N 7 15E
25 Saarbrücken 49 15N 6 58E
25 Saarburg 49 36N 6 32E
48 Saaremaa, I. 58 30N 22 30E
25 Saarland □ 49 20N 0 75E
25 Saarlouis 49 19N 6 45E
105 Saba, I. 17 30N 63 10W
40 Šabac 44 48N 19 42E
32 Sabadell 41 28N 2 7E
64 Sabah □ 6 0N 117 0E
56 Sabalan, Kuhha-ye 38 15N 47 49E
110 Sabanalargo 10 38N 74 55W
64 Sabang 5 50N 95 15E
111 Sabará 19 55S 43 55W
60 Sabarmati, R. 22 25N 73 20E
54 Sabastiya 32 17N 35 12E
38 Sabáudia 41 17N 13 2E
73 Sabhah 27 9N 14 29E
60 Sabi, R. 36 48N 140 4E
33 Sabinal, Pta. del 36 43N 2 44W
104 Sabinas 27 50N 101 10W
104 Sabinas Hidalgo 26 40N 100 10W
101 Sabine, R. 30 0N 93 45W
18 Sablé 47 50N 0 21W
87 Sable, C., Canada 43 29N 65 38W
91 Sable, C., U.S.A. 25 5N 81 0W
91 Sable I. 44 0N 60 0W
20 Sables-d'Olonne, Les 46 30N 1 45W
30 Sabôr, R. 41 10N 7 7W
30 Sabugal 40 20N 7 5W
57 Sabzevār 36 15N 57 40E
57 Sabzvāran 28 45N 57 50E
32 Sacedón 40 29N 2 41W
97 Sackets Harbor 43 57N 76 7W
25 Säckingen 47 34N 7 56E
99 Saco 43 29N 70 28W
102 Sacramento 38 39N 121 30E
102 Sacramento, R. 38 3N 121 56W
103 Sacramento Mts. 32 30N 105 30W
31 Sacratif, C. 36 42N 3 28W
30 Sada 43 22N 8 15W
32 Sádaba 2 19N 1 12W
62 Sadasivpet 17 38N 77 50E
73 Sadd el Aali 24 5N 32 54E
66 Sado, I. 38 15N 138 30E
31 Sado, R. 38 29N 8 55W
60 Sadri 24 28N 74 30E
45 Sæby 57 20N 10 32E
32 Saelices 39 55N 2 49W
56 Safaniya 28 5N 48 42E
57 Safed Koh 34 15N 64 0E
44 Säffle 59 8N 12 55E
103 Safford 32 54N 109 52W
13 Saffron Walden 52 5N 0 15E
72 Safi 32 20N 9 17W
65 Saga, Indonesia 2 40S 132 55E
66 Saga, Japan 33 15N 130 18E
66 Saga □ 33 15N 130 20E
59 Sagaing 22 0N 96 0E
60 Sagar 23 50N 78 50E
62 Sagara 14 14N 75 6E
67 Sagil 50 15N 91 15E
98 Saginaw 43 26N 83 55W
98 Saginaw B. 43 50N 83 40W
89 Saglouc 62 30N 74 15W
21 Sagone 42 7N 8 42E
21 Sagone, G. de 42 4N 8 40E
31 Sagres 37 0N 8 58W
105 Sagua la Grande 22 50N 80 10W
103 Saguache 38 10N 106 4W
91 Saguenay, R. 48 10N 69 45W
32 Sagunto 39 42N 0 18W
30 Sahagun 42 18N 5 2W
72 Sahara 23 0N 5 0W
60 Saharanpur 29 58N 77 33E
60 Sahaswan 28 5N 78 45E
61 Sahibganj 25 12N 87 55E
60 Sahiwal 30 45N 73 8E
27 Sahy 48 4N 18 55E
27 Saîda 34 50N 0 11E
57 Sa'idābād 29 30N 55 45E
62 Saidapet 13 0N 80 15E
58 Saidu 34 50N 72 15E
57 Saighan 35 10N 67 55E
20 Saignes 45 20N 2 31E
63 Saigon = Phan Bho Ho Chi Minh 10 58N 106 40E
55 Saihut 15 12N 51 10E
66 Saijō 34 0N 133 5E
66 Saiki 32 35N 131 50E
14 St. Abbs Hd. 55 55N 2 10W
26 St. Aegyd 47 52N 15 33E
20 St. Affrique 43 57N 2 53E
18 St. Aignan 47 16N 1 22E
13 St. Albans, U.K. 51 46N 0 21W
97 St. Albans, U.S.A. 44 49N 73 5W
13 St. Albans Hd. 50 34N 2 3W
19 St. Amand 50 25N 3 6E
20 St. Amand-Mont-Rond 46 43N 2 30E
19 St. Amarin 47 54N 7 0E
21 St. Amour 46 26N 5 21E
26 St. Andra 46 46N 14 50E
20 St. André-de-Cubzac 44 59N 0 26W
21 St. André-les-Alpes 43 58N 6 30E
14 St. Andrews 56 20N 2 48W
84 St. Arnaud 36 32S 143 16E
12 St. Asaph 53 15N 3 27W
20 St. Astier 45 8N 0 31E
18 St. Aubin de Cormier 48 15N 1 26W
91 St. Augustin 51 19N 58 48W
99 St. Augustine 29 52N 81 20W
13 St. Austell 50 20N 4 48W
19 St. Avold 49 7N 6 40E
105 St. Barthelémy, I. 17 50N 62 50W
12 St. Bees Hd. 54 30N 3 38E
20 St. Benoit-du-Sault 46 26N 1 24E
93 St. Boniface 49 50N 97 10W
21 St. Bonnet 44 40N 6 5E
18 St. Brice en Coglès 48 25N 1 22W
13 St. Bride's B. 51 48N 5 15W
18 St. Brieuc 48 30N 2 46W
18 St. Cast 48 37N 2 18W
96 St. Catherines 43 10N 79 15W
13 St. Catherine's Pt. 50 34N 1 18W
20 St. Céré 44 51N 1 54E
21 St. Chamond 45 28N 4 31E
100 St. Charles 38 46N 90 30W
20 St. Chély-d'Apcher 44 48N 3 17E
20 St. Chinian 43 25N 2 56E
105 St. Christopher, I. 17 20N 62 40W
20 St. Ciers sur Gironde 45 17N 0 37W
97 St. Clair 40 42N 76 12W
90 St. Clair, L. 42 30N 82 45W
20 St. Claud 45 54N 0 28E
93 St. Claude, Canada 49 40N 98 22W
21 St. Claude, Fr. 46 22N 5 52E
100 St. Cloud 45 30N 94 11W
91 St. Cœur de Marie 48 39N 71 43W
83 St. Cricq, C. 25 17S 113 6E
20 St. Cyprien 42 37N 3 0E
21 St. Cyr 43 11N 5 43E
13 St. Davids 51 54N 5 16W
13 St. David's Hd. 51 54N 5 16W
105 St. David's I. 32 22N 64 39W
19 St. Denis 48 56N 2 22E
18 St. Denis d'Orques 48 2N 0 17W
19 St. Dié 48 17N 6 56E
19 St. Dizier 48 40N 5 0E
21 St.-Egrève 45 14N 5 41E
88 St. Elias, Mt. 60 20N 141 59W
20 St. Eloy 46 10N 2 51E
20 St. Émilion 44 53N 0 9W
21 St. Étienne 45 27N 4 22E
21 St. Étienne de Tinée 44 16N 6 56E
90 St. Félicien 48 40N 72 25W
91 St. Fintan's 48 10N 58 50W
21 St. Florent 42 41N 9 18E
20 St. Florent-sur-Cher 46 59N 2 15E
19 St. Florentin 48 0N 3 45E
20 St. Flour 45 2N 3 6E
21 St. Fons 45 42N 4 52E
20 St. Foy-la Grande 44 50N 0 13E
75 St. Francis, C. 34 14S 24 49E
97 St. Francis, L. 45 10N 74 20W
90 St. Gabriel de Brandon 46 17N 73 24W
25 St. Gallen 47 25N 9 23E
25 St. Gallen □ 47 10N 9 8E
20 St. Gaudens 43 6N 0 44E
20 St. Gaultier 46 39N 1 26E
81 St. George, Australia 28 1S 148 41E
105 St. George, Bermuda 32 24N 64 42W
91 St. George, Canada 45 11N 66 57W
103 St. George, U.S.A. 37 10N 113 35W
99 St. George, C. 29 36N 85 2W
84 St. George Hd. 35 11S 150 45E
93 St. George West 50 33N 96 7W
16 St. Georges, Belgium 50 37N 4 20E
90 St. Georges, Canada 46 42N 72 35W
111 St. George's, Fr. Guiana 4 0N 52 0W
105 St. Georges, Grenada 12 5N 61 43W
91 St. George's B. 48 20N 59 0W
11 St. George's Chan. 52 0N 6 0W

São João do Araguaia Seyðisfjörður

111 São João do Araguaia 5 23S 48 46W
111 São João do Piaui 8 10S 42 15W
109 São Leopoldo 29 50S 51 10W
109 São Lourenço 16 30S 55 5W
111 São Luís 2 39S 44 15W
109 São Luís Gonzaga 28 25S 55 0W
111 São Marcos, B. de 2 0S 44 0W
111 São Mateus 18 44S 39 50W
8 São Miguel, I. 37 33N 25 27W
109 São Paulo 23 40S 56 50W
109 São Paulo □ 22 0S 49 0W
30 São Pedro do Sul 40 46N 8 4W
111 São Roque, C. de 5 30S 35 10W
74 São Salvador do Congo 6 18S 14 16E
109 São Sebastião, I. de 23 50S 45 18W
109 São Sebastião do Paraíso 20 54S 46 59W
71 São Tomé, I. 0 10N 7 0E
109 São Vicente 23 57S 46 23W
31 São Vicente, C. de 37 0N 9 0W
21 Saône, R. 45 44N 4 50E
21 Saône-et-Loire □ 46 25N 4 50E
72 Sapele 5 50N 5 40E
110 Saposoa 6 55S 76 30W
66 Sapporo 43 0N 141 15E
39 Sapri 40 5N 15 37E
61 Sapt Kosi, R. 26 30N 86 55E
101 Sapulpa 36 0N 96 40W
56 Saqqez 36 15N 46 20E
32 Saragossa 41 39N 0 53W
40 Sarajevo 43 52N 18 26E
97 Saranac Lake 44 20N 74 10W
42 Saranda 39 59N 19 55E
109 Sarandí del Yi 33 21S 55 58W
108 Sarandí Grande 33 20S 55 50W
65 Sarangani B. 6 0N 125 13E
48 Saransk 54 10N 45 10E
48 Sarapul 56 28N 53 48E
99 Sarasota 27 10N 82 30W
97 Saratoga Springs 43 5N 73 47W
48 Saratov 51 30N 46 2E
64 Sarawak □ 2 0S 113 0E
57 Sarbāz 26 38N 61 19E
57 Sarbisheh 32 30N 59 40E
27 Sårbogård 46 55N 18 40E
61 Sarda, R. 27 22N 81 23E
60 Sardarshahr 28 30N 74 29E
38 Sardegna, I. 39 57N 9 0E
60 Sardhana 29 9N 77 39E
38 Sardinia, I.= Sardegna, I. 39 57N 9 0E
6 Sargasso Sea 27 0N 67 0W
60 Sargodha 32 10N 72 40E
73 Sarh 9 5N 18 23E
57 Sarī 36 30N 53 11E
56 Sarikamiş 40 22N 42 35E
64 Sarikei 2 8N 111 30E
80 Sarina 21 22S 149 13E
32 Sariñena 41 47N 0 10W
68 Sariwon 38 31N 125 44E
13 Sark, I. 49 25N 2 20W
27 Sarkad 46 47N 21 17E
20 Sarlat-la-Canéda 44 54N 1 13E
112 Sarmiento 45 35S 69 5W
37 Sarnano 43 2N 13 17E
96 Sarnia 43 0N 82 30W
39 Sarno 40 48N 14 35E
48 Sarny 51 17N 26 40E
43 Saronikós Kól. 37 45N 23 45E
36 Saronno 45 38N 9 2E
27 Sárospatak 58 18N 21 33E
44 Sarpsborg 59 16N 11 12E
30 Sarracín 42 15N 3 45W
19 Sarralbe 48 55N 7 1E
19 Sarrebourg 48 43N 7 3E
19 Sarreguemines 49 1N 7 4E
30 Sarriá 42 41N 7 49W
32 Sarrión 40 9N 0 49W
21 Sartène 41 38N 9 0E
18 Sarthe □ 47 58N 0 10E
18 Sarthe, R. 47 30N 0 32W
50 Sartynya 63 30N 62 50E
57 Sarur 23 17N 58 4E
50 Sary Tash 39 45N 73 40E
50 Saryshagan 46 12N 73 48E
18 Sarzeau 47 31N 2 48W
36 Sarzana 44 7N 9 57E
55 Sasabeneh 7 59N 44 43E
61 Sasaram 24 57N 84 5E
40 Sasca Montană 44 41N 21 45E
66 Sasebo 33 15N 129 50E
93 Saskatchewan □ 53 40N 103 30W
93 Saskatchewan, R. 53 12N 99 16W
93 Saskatoon 52 10N 106 45W
51 Saskylakh 71 55N 114 1E
48 Sasovo 54 25N 41 55E
72 Sassandra 5 0N 6 8W
72 Sassandra, R. 4 58N 6 5W
38 Sássari 40 44N 8 33E
24 Sassnitz 54 29N 13 39E
36 Sassuolo 44 31N 10 47E
62 Satara 17 44N 73 58E
48 Satka 55 3N 59 1E
61 Satkhira 22 43N 89 8E
60 Satmala Hills 20 15N 74 40E
61 Satna 24 35N 80 50E
27 Sátoraljaújhely 48 25N 21 41E
60 Satpura Ra. 21 40N 75 0E
63 Sattahip 12 41N 100 54E
62 Sattenapalle 16 25N 80 6E
27 Satu Mare 47 48N 22 53E
27 Satu-Mare □ 47 45N 23 0E
47 Sauda 59 38N 6 21E
46 Sauđarkrókur 65 45N 19 40W
55 Saudi Arabia ■ 26 0N 44 0E
24 Sauerland, Mts. 51 0N 8 0E
20 Saujon 45 41N 0 55W
19 Sauldre, R. 47 16N 1 30E
19 Saulieu 47 17N 4 14E
90 Sault Ste. Marie, Canada 46 30N 84 20W
98 Saulte Ste. Marie, U.S.A. 46 27N 84 22W
18 Saumur 47 15N 0 5W
46 Saurbaer 64 24N 21 35W
40 Sava, R. 44 50N 20 26E
85 Savaii, I. 13 35S 172 25W
72 Savalou 7 57N 2 4E
100 Savanna 42 5N 90 10W
99 Savannah 32 4N 81 4W
99 Savannah, R. 32 2N 80 53W
63 Savannakhet 16 30N 104 49E
90 Savant Lake 50 20N 90 40W
62 Savantvadi 15 55N 73 54E
62 Savanur 14 59N 75 28E
60 Savda 21 9N 75 56E
72 Savé 8 2N 2 17E
20 Save, R. 43 47N 1 17E
56 Sāveh 35 2N 50 20E
72 Savelugu 9 38N 0 54W
18 Savenay 47 20N 1 55W
19 Saverne 48 39N 7 20E
36 Savigliano 44 39N 7 40E
30 Saviñao 42 35N 7 38W
21 Savoie □ 45 26N 6 35E
21 Savoie, Reg. 45 30N 5 20E
36 Savona 44 19N 8 29E
45 Sävsjö 57 20N 14 40E
45 Sävsjöström 57 1N 15 25E
65 Sawai 3 0S 129 5E
63 Sawankhalok 17 19N 99 54E
103 Sawatch Mts. 38 30N 106 30W
73 Sawknah 29 4N 15 47E
75 Sawmills 19 30S 28 2E
65 Sawu Sea 9 30S 121 50E
91 Sayabec 38 35N 67 41W
56 Sayda 33 35N 35 25E
68 Saynshand 44 55N 110 11E
97 Sayre 42 0N 76 30W
97 Sayville 40 45N 73 7W
26 Sazava 49 50N 15 0E
58 Sazin 35 35N 73 30E
12 Sca Fell, Mt 54 27N 3 14W
18 Scaër 48 2N 3 42E
36 Scandiano 44 36N 10 40E
14 Scapa Flow 58 52N 3 0W
12 Scarborough 54 17N 0 24W
25 Schaal See 53 40N 10 57E
25 Schaffhausen 47 42N 8 36E
26 Schärding 48 27N 13 27E
26 Scharnitz 47 23N 11 15E
91 Schefferville 54 50N 66 40W
26 Scheibbs 48 1N 15 9E
16 Schelde, R. 51 22N 4 15E
97 Schenectady 42 50N 73 58W
16 Scheveningen 52 6N 4 18E
16 Schiedam 51 55N 4 25E
25 Schifferstadt 49 22N 8 23E
19 Schiltigheim 48 35N 7 45E
37 Schio 45 42N 11 21E
26 Schladming 47 23N 13 41E
24 Schleswig 54 32N 9 34E
24 Schleswig-Holstein □ 54 10N 9 40E
24 Schmalkalden 50 43N 10 28E
24 Schmölln 50 54N 12 22E
24 Schneeberg 47 53N 15 55E
24 Schönebeck 52 2N 11 42E
65 Schouten, Kep. 1 0S 136 0E
25 Schramberg 48 12N 8 24E
90 Schreiber 48 45N 87 20W
26 Schruns 47 5N 9 56E
90 Schumacher 48 30N 81 16W
102 Schurz 38 59N 118 57W
97 Schuykill Haven 40 37N 76 11W
25 Schwabach 49 19N 11 3E
25 Schwäbisch Gmund 48 49N 9 48E
25 Schwabisch Hall 49 7N 9 45E
25 Schwäbische Alb, Mts. 48 30N 9 30E
68 Schwangcheng 45 27N 126 27E
68 Schwangyashan 46 35N 131 15E
26 Schwarzach R. 50 30N 11 30E
24 Schwarzenberg 50 31N 12 49E
25 Schwarzwald 48 0N 8 0E
26 Schwaz 47 20N 11 44E
25 Schweinfurt 50 3N 10 12E
25 Schwenningen 48 3N 8 32E
24 Schwerin 53 37N 11 22E
24 Schwerin □ 53 35N 11 20E
24 Schweriner See, L. 53 45N 11 26E
25 Schwetzingen 49 22N 8 35E
25 Schwyz 47 2N 8 39E
25 Schwyz □ 47 2N 8 39E
38 Sciacca 37 30N 13 3E
39 Scicli 36 48N 14 41E
55 Scillave 6 22N 44 32E
13 Scilly Is. 49 55N 6 15W
28 Scinawa 51 25N 16 26E
100 Scobey 48 47N 105 30W
84 Scone, Australia 32 0S 150 52E
14 Scone, U.K. 56 25N 3 26W
4 Scoresbysund 70 20N 23 0W
5 Scotia Sea 56 5S 56 0W
14 Scotland ■ 57 0N 4 0W
5 Scott, C. 71 30S 168 0E
100 Scott City 38 30N 100 52W
100 Scottsbluff 41 55N 103 35W
80 Scottsdale 41 9S 147 31E
97 Scranton 41 22N 75 41W
12 Scunthorpe 53 35N 0 38W
84 Sea Lake 35 28S 142 55E
90 Seaforth 43 35N 81 25W
93 Seal, R. 59 4N 94 48W
103 Searchlight 35 31N 111 57W
101 Searcy 35 15N 91 45W
102 Seattle 47 41N 122 15W
104 Sebastián Vizcaíno, B. 28 0N 114 0W
102 Sebastopol 38 16N 122 56W
41 Sebeş 45 58N 23 34E
99 Sebring 27 36N 81 47W
40 Sečanj 45 25N 20 47E
19 Seclin 50 33N 3 2E
85 Secretary, I. 45 15S 166 56E
62 Secunderabad 17 28N 78 30E
100 Sedalia 38 40N 93 18W
19 Sedan 49 43N 4 57E
85 Seddon 41 40S 174 7E
85 Seddonville 41 33E 172 1E
54 Sede Ya'aqov 32 43N 35 7E
92 Sedgewick 52 48N 111 41W
54 Sedom 31 5N 35 20E
102 Sedro Woolley 48 30N 122 15W
26 Seefeld 51 53N 13 17E
75 Seeheim 26 32S 17 52E
18 Sées 48 38N 0 10E
24 Seesen 51 35N 10 10E
63 Segamat 2 30N 102 50E
32 Segorbe 39 50N 0 30W
72 Ségou 13 30N 6 10W
30 Segovia 40 57N 4 10W
30 Segovia □ 40 55N 4 10W
18 Segré 47 40N 0 52W
72 Séguéla 7 57N 6 40W
101 Seguin 29 34N 97 58W
33 Segura, R. 38 6N 0 54W
33 Segura, Sa. de 38 5N 2 45W
57 Sehkonj, Kuh-e 30 0N 57 30E
60 Sehore 23 10N 77 5E
41 Şeica Mare 46 1N 24 7E
21 Seille, R. 49 7N 6 11E
46 Seinäjoki 62 47N 22 50E
18 Seine, B. de la 49 30N 0 30W
18 Seine, R. 49 26N 0 26E
19 Seine-et-Marne □ 48 45N 3 0E
18 Seine-Maritime □ 49 40N 1 0E
72 Sekondi-Takoradi 5 2N 1 48W
63 Selangor □ 3 20N 101 30E
64 Selatan □, Kalimantan 3 0S 115 0E
65 Selatan □, Sulawesi 3 0S 120 0E
64 Selatan □, Sumatera 3 0S 105 0E
25 Selb 50 9N 12 9E
12 Selby 53 47N 1 5W
88 Seldovia 59 27N 151 43W
75 Selebi-Pikwe 22 0S 27 45E
68 Selenge 49 25N 103 59E
19 Sélestat 48 10N 7 26E
72 Sélibaby 15 20N 12 15W
93 Selkirk, Canada 50 10N 97 20W
14 Selkirk, U.K. 55 33N 2 50W
92 Selkirk Mts. 51 0N 117 10W
99 Selma, Ala. 32 30N 87 0W
103 Selma, Calif. 36 39N 119 30W
19 Seltz 48 48N 8 4W
75 Selukwe 19 40S 30 0E
65 Semarang 7 0S 110 26E
65 Semeru, Mt. 8 4S 113 3E
102 Seminoe Res. 42 0N 107 0W
101 Seminole, Okla. 35 15N 96 45W
101 Seminole, Tex. 32 41N 102 38W
50 Semiozernoye 52 35N 64 0E
50 Semipalatinsk 50 30N 80 10E
26 Semmering P. 47 41N 15 45E
57 Semnān 35 55N 53 25E
57 Semnān □ 36 0N 54 0E
65 Semporna 4 30N 118 33E
110 Sena Madureira 9 5S 68 45W
111 Senador Pompeu 5 40S 39 20W
63 Senai 1 38S 103 38E
75 Senanga 16 2S 23 14E
66 Sendai, Kagoshima 31 50N 130 20E
66 Sendai, Miyagi 38 15N 141 0E
102 Seneca 44 10N 119 2W
96 Seneca L. 42 40N 76 58W
72 Senegal ■ 14 30N 14 30W
72 Senegal, R. 16 30N 15 30W
70 Senegambia, Reg. 14 0N 14 0W
25 Senftenberg 51 30N 13 51E
111 Senhor-do Bonfim 10 30S 40 10W
37 Senigállia 43 42N 13 12E
37 Senj 45 0N 14 58E
73 Sennâr 13 30N 33 35E
90 Senneterre 48 25N 77 15W
19 Sens 48 11N 3 15E
40 Senta 45 55N 20 3E
65 Sentolo 7 55S 110 13E
32 Seo de Urgel 42 22N 1 23E
60 Seohara 29 15N 78 33E
61 Seonath, R. 21 44N 82 27E
61 Seoni 22 5N 79 30E
68 Seoul=Soul 37 20N 126 15E
91 Separation Pt. 53 40N 57 16W
63 Sepone 16 45N 106 13E
91 Sept Iles 50 13N 66 22W
41 Septemvri 42 13N 24 6E
102 Sequim 48 3N 123 9W
103 Sequoia Nat. Park 36 20N 118 30W
16 Seraing 50 35N 5 32E
65 Seram, I. 3 10S 129 0E
65 Seram Sea 3 0S 130 0E
61 Serampore 22 44N 88 30E
65 Serang 6 8S 106 10E
48 Serdobsk 52 28N 44 10E
36 Seregno 45 40N 9 12E
63 Seremban 2 43N 101 53E
75 Serenje 13 11S 30 52E
111 Sergipe □ 10 30S 37 30W
64 Seria 4 37N 114 30E
64 Serian 1 10N 110 40E
19 Sérifontaine 49 20N 1 45E
43 Sérifos, I. 37 9N 24 30E
37 Sérmide 45 0N 11 17E
50 Serov 59 40N 60 20E
75 Serowe 22 25S 26 43E
75 Serpa Pinto 14 48S 17 52E
83 Serpentine 32 22S 115 59E
38 Serpeddi, Pta. 39 19N 9 28E
33 Serpis, R. 38 45N 0 21W
48 Serpukhov 54 55N 37 28E
42 Sérrai 41 5N 23 32E
42 Sérrai □ 41 5N 23 37E
38 Serramanna 39 26N 8 56E
111 Serrinha 11 39E 39 0W
111 Sertania 8 5S 37 20W
75 Serule 21 57S 27 11E
42 Sérvia 40 9N 21 58E
31 Sesimbra 38 28N 9 20W
30 Sestao 43 18N 3 0W
36 Sesto S. Giovanni 45 32N 9 14E
36 Sestri Levante 44 17N 9 22E
20 Sète 43 25N 3 42E
111 Sete Lagôas 19 27S 44 16W
72 Sétif 36 9N 5 26E
66 Seto 35 14N 137 6E
66 Setonaikai 34 10N 133 10E
72 Settat 33 0N 7 40W
74 Setté Cama 2 32S 9 57E
36 Séttimo Tor 45 9N 7 46E
12 Settle 54 5N 2 18W
31 Setúbal 38 30N 8 58W
31 Setúbal □ 38 25N 8 35W
31 Setúbal, B. de 38 40N 8 56W
64 Seulimeum 5 27N 95 15E
49 Sevastopol 44 35N 33 30E
20 Sévérac-le-Château 44 20N 3 5E
90 Severn, R., Canada 56 2N 87 36W
13 Severn, R., U.K. 51 25N 3 0W
51 Severnaya Zemlya, I. 79 0N 100 0E
48 Severnyye Uvaly, Reg. 58 0N 48 0E
26 Severoceský □ 50 35N 14 15E
48 Severodvinsk 64 27N 39 58E
27 Severomoravsky □ 49 38N 17 40E
31 Sevilla 37 23N 6 0W
31 Sevilla □ 37 0N 6 0W
41 Sevlievo 43 1N 25 6E
18 Sèvre Nantaise, R. 47 12N 1 30W
20 Sèvre Niortaise, R. 46 20N 1 12W
88 Seward 60 0N 149 40W
88 Seward Pen. 65 0N 164 0W
108 Sewell 34 10S 70 45W
53 Seychelles, Is. 5 0S 56 0E
46 Seyđisfjörđur 65 16N 14 0W

Síwa Sretensk

73 Síwa 29 11N 25 31E
60 Siwalik Ra. 28 0N 83 0E
61 Siwan 26 13N 84 27E
13 Sizewell 52 13N 1 38E
45 Sjaelland, I. 55 30N 11 30E
40 Skadarsko, J. 42 10N 19 15E
Jezero, L. 42 10N 19 15E
45 Skaerbaek 55 31N 9 38E
45 Skagen 57 43N 10 35E
47 Skagerrak, Str. 57 30N 9 0E
92 Skagway 59 30N 135 20W
45 Skanderborg 56 2N 9 55E
45 Skanör 55 24N 12 50E
45 Skara 58 25N 13 30E
45 Skaraborg □ 58 20N 13 30E
58 Skardu 35 20N 73 35E
44 Skarnes 50 15N 11 41E
28 Skarzysko
Kamienna 51 7N 20 52E
92 Skenna Mts. 56 40N 128 0W
12 Skegnwss 53 9N 0 20E
110 Skeldon 6 0N 57 20W
46 Skellefteå 64 45N 20 59E
46 Skelleftehamn 64 41N 21 14E
42 Skíathos, I. 39 12N 23 30E
15 Skibbereen 51 33N 9 16W
12 Skiddaw, Mt. 54 39N 3 9W
44 Skien 59 12N 9 35E
28 Skierniewice 51 58N 20 19E
28 Skierniewice □ 51 50N 20 10E
72 Skikda 36 50N 6 58E
12 Skipton 53 57N 2 1W
43 Skíros, I. 38 55N 24 34E
45 Skive 56 33N 9 2E
45 Skjern 55 57N 8 30E
44 Skoghall 59 20N 13 30E
44 Skönsberg 62 25N 17 21E
43 Skópelos, I. 39 9N 23 47E
40 Skopje 42 1N 21 32E
28 Skórcz 43 47N 18 30E
45 Skövde 58 24N 13 50E
51 Skovorodino 53 59N 123 55E
99 Skowhegan 44 49N 69 40W
47 Skudeneshavn 59 10N 5 10E
15 Skull 51 32N 9 40W
45 Skurup 55 28N 13 30E
44 Skutskär 60 37N 17 25E
28 Skwierzyna 52 46N 15 30E
14 Skye, I. 57 15N 6 10W
45 Slagelse 55 23N 11 19E
15 Slaney, R. 52 52N 6 45W
40 Slano 42 48N 17 53E
26 Slaný 50 13N 14 6E
41 Slatina 44 28N 24 22E
101 Slaton 33 27N 101 38W
70 Slave Coast 6 0N 2 30E
92 Slave Lake 55 25N 114 50W
50 Slavgorod 53 10N 78 50E
40 Slavonska Požega 45 20N 17 41E
40 Slavonski Brod 45 11N 18 0E
49 Slavyansk 45 15N 38 11E
12 Sleaford 53 0N 0 22W
14 Sleat, Sd. of 57 5N 5 47W
97 Slide Mt. 42 0N 74 23W
16 Sliedrecht 51 50N 4 45E
15 Sligo 54 17N 8 28W
15 Sligo □ 54 10N 8 40W
63 Slim River 3 48N 101 25E
41 Sliven 42 42N 26 19N
40 Slivnitsa 42 50N 23 0E
37 Sljeme, Mt. 45 57N 15 58E
97 Sloansville 42 45N 74 22W
48 Slobodskoy 58 40N 50 6E
41 Slobozia 44 34N 27 23E
13 Slough 51 30N 0 35W
37 Slovenija □ 45 58N 14 30E
37 Slovenska Bistrica 46 24N 15 35E
27 Slovenská
Socialistická
Rep. □ 48 40N 19 0E
27 Slovenské
Rudohorie, Mts. 50 25N 13 0E
27 Slovensko, Reg. 48 50N 20 0E
28 Słubice 52 50N 14 35E
28 Słubia, R. 54 35N 16 50E
28 Słupsk 54 28N 17 1E
28 Słupsk □ 54 20N 17 20E
41 Slunchev Bryag 42 40N 27 41E
51 Slyudyanka 51 40N 103 30E
93 Smeaton 53 30N 105 49W
40 Smederevo 44 40N 20 57E
44 Smedjebacken 60 8N 15 25E
92 Smith 55 10N 114 0W
88 Smith Arm, B. 66 30N 123 0W
92 Smithers 54 45N 127 10W
99 Smithfield 35 31N 78 16W
90 Smiths Falls 44 55N 76 0W
80 Smithton 40 53S 145 6E
31 Smoky Bay 32 22S 133 56E
90 Smoky Falls 50 10N 82 10W
100 Smoky Hill, R. 39 3N 96 48W
48 Smolensk 54 45N 32 0E
42 Smolikas, Mt. 40 9N 20 58E
41 Smolyan 41 36N 24 38E
90 Smooth Rock Falls 49 17N 81 37W
12 Snaefell, Mt. 54 18N 4 26W
46 Snaefellsjökull.Mt. 64 50N 23 49W
102 Snake, R. 46 12N 119 2W
102 Snake River Plain 43 13N 113 0W
16 Sneek 53 2N 5 40E
28 Sniardwy,
Sezero, L. 53 46N 21 44E
93 Snow Lake 54 53N 101 2W
12 Snowdon, Mt. 53 4N 4 8W
103 Snowflake 34 30N 110 4W
102 Snowshoe Pk. 48 13N 115 41W
31 Snowtown 33 47S 138 13E
84 Snowy, Mts. 36 15S 148 20E
101 Snyder 32 45N 100 57W
102 Soap Lake 47 29N 119 31W
111 Sobral 3 50S 40 30W
30 Sobreira Formosa 39 46N 7 51W
28 Sochaczew 52 15N 20 13E
67 Soche 38 24N 77 20E
49 Sochi 43 35N 39 40E
77 Society Is. 17 0S 151 0W
110 Socorro, Col. 6 29N 73 16W
103 Socorro, U.S.A. 34 3N 106 58W
55 Socotra, I. 12 30N 54 0E
33 Socúellamas 39 16N 2 47W
92 Soda Creek 52 25N 122 10W
102 Soda Springs 42 4N 111 40W
44 Söderhamn 61 18N 17 10E
45 Söderköping 58 31N 16 35E
44 Södermanlands □ 59 10N 16 30E
44 Södertälje 59 12N 17 50E
74 Sodo 7 0N 37 57E
16 Soest, Neth. 52 9N 5 19E
24 Soest, W. Germany 51 34N 8 7E
42 Sofádhes 39 28N 22 4E
75 Sofala = Beira 19 50S 34 52E
41 Sofiya 42 45N 23 20E
110 Sogamoso 5 43N 72 56W
47 Sogn og Fjordane □ 61 40N 6 0E
73 Sohâg 26 27N 31 43E
16 Soignes 50 35N 4 5E
19 Soissons 49 25N 3 19E
60 Sojat 25 55N 73 38E
56 Soke 37 48N 27 28E
72 Sokodé 9 0N 1 11E
48 Sokol 59 30N 40 5E
28 Sokólka 53 25N 23 30E
26 Sokolov 50 12N 22 7E
72 Sokoto 13 2N 5 16E
65 Solano 16 25N 121 15E
30 Solares 43 23N 3 43W
28 Solec Kujawski 53 6N 18 14E
110 Soledad, Col. 10 55N 74 46W
103 Soledad, U.S.A. 36 27N 121 16W
110 Soledad, Ven. 8 10N 63 34W
21 Solenzara 41 53N 9 23E
19 Solesmes 50 10N 3 30E
48 Soligalich 59 5N 42 10E
48 Solikamsk 59 38N 56 50E
24 Solingen 51 10N 7 4E
44 Sollefteå 63 10N 17 20E
44 Sollentuna 59 26N 17 56E
32 Sóller 39 43N 2 45E
44 Solna 59 22N 18 1E
19 Sologne, Reg. 47 40N 2 0E
64 Solok 0 55S 100 40E
104 Sololá 14 49N 91 10E
76 Solomon Is. 8 0S 159 0E
25 Solothurn 47 13N 7 32E
25 Solothrun □ 47 18N 7 40E
37 Solta, I. 43 24N 16 15E
57 Soltanābād 36 29N 58 5E
56 Soltāniyeh 36 20N 48 55E
24 Soltau 52 59N 9 50E
97 Solvay 43 5N 76 17W
45 Sölvesborg 56 5N 14 35E
48 Solvychegodsk 61 21N 46 52E
75 Solwezi 12 20S 26 26E
14 Solway Firth 54 45N 3 38W
55 Somali Rep. ■ 7 0N 47 0E
40 Sombor 45 46N 19 17E
105 Somerset, Bermuda 32 20N 64 55W
97 Somerset, Mass. 41 45N 71 10W
98 Somerset, Ky. 37 5N 84 40W
13 Somerset □ 51 9N 3 0W
75 Somerset East 32 42S 25 35E
105 Somerset I.,
Bermuda 32 20N 64 55W
88 Somerset I., Canada 73 30N 93 0W
97 Somersworth 43 15N 70 51W
97 Somerville 40 34N 74 36W
39 Somma Vesuvianna 40 52N 14 23E
19 Somme □ 40 0N 2 15E
18 Somme, B. de la 5 22N 1 30E
19 Somme, R. 50 11N 1 39E
45 Sommen, L. 58 0N 15 15E
19 Sommesous 48 44N 4 12E
27 Somogy □ 46 19N 17 30E
30 Somosierra, P. de 41 9N 3 35W
20 Somport, Col du 42 48N 0 31W
61 Son, R. 25 40N 84 51E
36 Soncino 45 24N 9 52E
45 Sønderborg 54 55N 9 49E
25 Sondershausen 51 22N 10 50E
45 Sonderyllands □ 55 10N 9 10E
36 Sóndrio 46 10N 9 53E
60 Sonepat 29 0N 77 5E
63 Song Cau 13 20N 109 18E
74 Songea 10 40S 35 40E
47 Songefjorden 61 10N 5 30E
63 Songkhla 7 13N 100 37E
58 Sonmiani 25 25N 66 40E
25 Sonneberg 50 22N 11 11E
101 Sonora 30 33N 100 37W
104 Sonora □ 37 59N 120 27W
104 Sonsonate 13 45N 89 45W
25 Sonthofen 47 31N 10 16E
69 Soochow 31 18N 120 41E
28 Sopot 54 27N 18 31E
40 Sopotnica 41 23N 21 13E
27 Sopron 47 41N 16 37E
91 Sop's Arm 49 46N 56 56W
44 Sør Trøndelag □ 63 0N 11 0E
38 Sora 41 45N 13 36E
110 Sorata 15 50S 68 50W
33 Sorbas 37 6N 2 7W
90 Sorel 46 0N 73 10W
36 Soresina 45 17N 9 51E
21 Sorgues 44 1N 4 53E
32 Soria 41 43N 2 32W
32 Soria □ 41 46N 2 28W
57 Sorkh, Kuh-e 35 40N 58 30E
45 Sorø 55 26N 11 32E
109 Sorocaba 23 31S 47 35W
27 Soroksar 47 24N 19 9E
60 Soron 27 55N 78 45E
65 Sorong 0 55S 131 15E
74 Soroti 1 43N 33 35E
46 Sørøya, I. 70 35N 22 45E
31 Sorraia, R. 38 56N 8 53W
39 Sorrento 40 38N 14 23E
46 Sorsele 65 31N 17 30E
48 Sortavala 61 42N 30 41E
48 Sosnogorsk 63 37N 53 51E
51 Sosnovka 54 9N 109 35E
27 Sosnowiec 50 20N 19 10E
18 Sotteville 49 24N 1 5E
74 Souanke 2 10N 14 10E
43 Soúdas, Kól. 35 28N 24 10E
97 Souderton 40 19N 75 19W
42 Souflíon 41 12N 26 18E
20 Souillac 44 53N 1 29E
68 Soul 37 33N 126 58E
20 Soulac 45 30N 1 4W
75 Sources, Mt. aux 28 45S 28 50E
111 Soure, Brazil 0 35S 48 30W
30 Soure, Port. 40 4N 8 38W
93 Souris 49 40N 100 20W
93 Souris, R. 49 39N 99 34W
111 Sousa 7 0S 38 10W
111 Sousel 2 38S 52 29W
73 Sousse 35 50N 10 33E
75 South Africa ■ 30 0S 25 0E
1 South America 10 0S 60 0W
63 South Andaman, I. 11 50N 92 45E
7 South Atlantic
Ocean 20 0S 20 0W
78 South Australia □ 32 0S 139 0E
98 South Bend, Ind.
U.S.A. 41 38N 86 20W
102 South Bend,
Wash. 46 44N 123 52W
99 South Boston 36 42N 78 58W
99 South Carolina □ 33 45N 81 0W
98 South Charleston 38 20N 81 40W
100 South Dakota □ 45 0N 100 0W
5 South Georgia, I. 54 30S 37 0W
13 South Glamorgan □ 51 28N 3 26W
81 South Grafton 42 11S 71 42W
98 South Haven 42 22N 86 20W
74 South Horr 2 12N 36 56E
85 South Invercargill 46 26N 168 23E
85 South Island 43 50S 171 0E
68 South Korea ■ 36 0N 128 0E
5 South Magnetic
Pole 66 30S 139 30E
98 South Milwaukee 42 50N 87 52W
5 South Orkney Is. 63 0S 45 0W
100 South Platte, R. 41 7N 100 42W
5 South Pole 90 0S 0 0E
90 South Porcupine 48 30N 81 12W
90 South River 45 52N 79 21W
93 South
Saskatchewan, R. 53 15N 105 5W
5 South Shetland Is. 62 0S 59 0W
12 South Shields 54 59N 1 26W
100 South Sioux City 42 30N 96 30W
12 South Tyne, R. 54 59N 2 8W
75 South West Africa
= Nambia ■ 22 0S 18 9E
96 South Williamsport 41 14N 77 1W
55 South Yemen ■ 15 0N 48 0E
12 South Yorkshire □ 52 45N 1 25W
90 Southampton,
Canada 44 30N 81 25W
13 Southampton,
U.K. 50 54N 1 23W
97 Southampton,
U.S.A. 40 54N 72 22W
89 Southampton I. 64 30N 84 0W
97 Southbridge 42 4N 72 2W
13 Southend 51 32N 0 43E
85 Southern Alps, Mts. 43 41S 170 11E
83 Southern Cross 31 12S 119 15E
7 Southern Mid-
Atlantic Ridge 30 0S 15 0W
5 Southern Ocean 62 0S 160 0W
14 Southern
Uplands, Mts. 55 30N 4 0W
97 Southington 41 37N 72 53W
81 Southport,
Australia 28 0S 153 25E
12 Southport, U.K. 53 38N 3 1W
13 Southwold 52 19N 1 41E
75 Soutpansberge 22 55S 29 30E
20 Souvigny 46 33N 3 10E
48 Sovetsk 57 38N 48 53E
51 Sovetskaya Gavan 48 50N 140 0E
29 Spain ■ 40 0N 5 0W
12 Spalding 52 47N 0 9W
91 Spaniard's Bay 47 38N 53 20W
102 Spanish Fork 40 10N 111 37W
105 Spanish Pt. 32 12N 64 45W
105 Spanish Town 18 0N 77 20W
102 Sparks 39 30N 119 45W
100 Sparta 43 55N 91 10W
99 Spartanburg 35 0N 82 0W
43 Spárti 37 5N 22 25E
39 Spartivento,
C., Italy 37 56N 16 4E
38 Spartivento,
C., Sardinia 38 52N 8 50E
51 Spassk-Dal'niy 44 40N 132 40E
43 Spátha, Ákra 35 42N 23 43E
100 Spearfish 44 32N 103 52W
84 Speed 35 21S 142 27E
105 Speightstown 13 18N 59 30W
88 Spenard 61 0N 149 50W
88 Spence Bay 69 32N 93 31W
100 Spencer 43 5N 95 3W
81 Spencer, G. 34 30S 137 0E
85 Spenser, Mts. 42 15S 172 45E
15 Sperrin Mts. 54 50N 7 0W
25 Spessart, Mts 50 0N 9 20E
43 Spétsai 37 16N 23 9E
14 Spey, R. 57 40N 3 6W
25 Speyer 49 19N 8 26E
39 Spinazzola 40 58N 16 5E
92 Spirit River 55 45N 119 0W
27 Spišska Nová Ves 48 58N 20 34E
26 Spittal 46 48N 13 31E
37 Split 43 31N 16 26E
37 Splitski Kan. 43 31N 16 20E
25 Splugenpass 46 30N 9 20E
102 Spokane 47 45N 117 25W
37 Spoleto 42 44N 12 44E
97 Spotswood 40 23N 74 23W
24 Spree, R. 52 32N 13 13E
24 Spremberg 51 33N 14 21E
97 Spring Valley 41 7N 74 4W
75 Springbok 29 42S 17 54E
85 Springburn 43 40S 171 32E
91 Springdale, Canada 49 30N 56 6W
101 Springdale, U.S.A. 36 10N 94 5W
103 Springerville 34 10N 109 16W
85 Springfield, N.Z. 43 19S 171 56E
100 Springfield, Ill. 39 58N 89 40W
97 Springfield, Mass. 42 8N 72 37W
101 Springfield, Mo. 37 15N 93 20W
98 Springfield, Ohio 39 50N 83 48W
102 Springfield, Ore. 44 2N 123 0W
99 Springfield, Tenn. 36 35N 86 55W
97 Springfield, Vt. 43 20N 72 30W
75 Springfontein 30 15S 25 40E
91 Springhill 45 40N 64 4W
75 Springs 26 13S 28 25E
80 Springsure 24 8S 148 6E
80 Springvale,
Queens. 23 33S 140 42E
82 Springvale,
W.Australia 17 48S 127 41E
102 Springville 40 14N 111 35W
12 Spurn Hd. 53 34N 0 8W
40 Spuž 42 32N 19 10E
92 Squamish 49 45N 123 10W
39 Squillace, G. di 38 43N 16 35E
39 Squinzano 40 27N 18 1E
65 Sragen 7 28S 110 59E
40 Srbobran 45 32N 19 48E
63 Sre Umbell 11 8N 103 46E
51 Sredinnyy Khrebet 57 0N 160 0E
41 Sredna Gora 42 40N 25 0E
51 Sredne
Tamborskoye 50 55N 137 45E
51 Srednekolymsk 67 20N 154 40E
51 Srednevilyuysk 63 50N 123 5E
41 Sredni Rodopi 41 40N 24 45E
28 Śrem 52 6N 17 2E
40 Sremska 44 58N 19 37E
63 Srépok, R. 13 33N 106 16E
51 Sretensk 52 10N 117 40E

Swords Te Puke

15 Swords 53 27N 6 15W
84 Sydney, Australia 33 53S 151 10E
91 Sydney, Canada 46 7N 60 7W
91 Sydney Mines 46 18N 60 15W
4 Sydprøven 60 30N 45 35W
25 Syke 52 55N 8 50E
48 Syktyvkar 61 45N 50 40E
99 Sylacauga 33 10N 86 15W
59 Sylhet 24 43N 91 55E
24 Sylt, I. 54 50N 8 20E
92 Sylvan Lake 52 20N 114 10W
50 Sym 60 20N 87 50E
50 Syr Darya, R. 46 3N 61 0E
97 Syracuse 38 0N 101 40W
56 Syria ■ 35 0N 38 0E
51 Syul'dzhyukyor 63 25N 113 40E
48 Syzran 53 12N 48 30E
27 Szabolcs-Szatmar □ 48 2N 21 45E
27 Szarvas 46 50N 20 38E
28 Szczecin 53 27N 14 27E
28 Szczecin □ 53 27N 14 32E
28 Szczecinek 53 43N 16 41E
28 Szczythna 53 33N 21 0E
69 Szechwan □ 30 15N 103 15E
27 Szeged 46 16N 20 10E
27 Szeghalom 47 1N 21 10E
27 Székesfehérvár 47 15N 18 25E
27 Szekszárd 46 22N 18 42E
67 Szemao 22 50N 101 0E
69 Szengen 24 50N 108 0E
27 Szentendre 47 39N 19 4E
27 Szentes 46 39N 20 21E
68 Szeping 43 10N 124 18E
27 Szolnok 47 10N 20 15E
27 Szolnok □ 47 15N 20 30E
27 Szombathely 47 14N 16 38E
28 Szprotawa 51 33N 15 35E

T

68 Ta Hingan Ling, Mts. 48 0N 120 0E
67 Ta Liang Shan, Mts. 28 0N 103 0E
108 Tabacal 23 15S 64 15W
14 Tabasco □ 17 45N 93 30W
92 Taber 49 48N 111 5W
33 Tabernas 37 4N 2 26W
33 Tabernes de Valldigna 39 5N 0 13W
65 Tablas, I. 12 20N 122 10E
75 Table Mt. 34 0S 18 22E
82 Tableland 17 16S 126 51E
80 Tabletop, Mt. 23 30S 147 0E
26 Tábor 49 25N 14 39E
74 Tabora 5 2S 32 57E
72 Tabou 4 30N 7 20W
56 Tabriz 38 7N 56 20E
56 Tabuk 28 30N 36 25E
44 Täby 59 29N 18 4E
110 Tachira 8 7N 72 21W
65 Tacloban 11 1N 125 0E
110 Tacna 18 0S 70 20W
102 Tacoma 47 15N 122 30W
109 Tacuarembó 31 45S 56 0W
72 Tademait, Plateau du 28 30N 2 30E
55 Tadjoura 11 50N 44 55E
85 Tadmor, N.Z. 41 27S 172 45E
56 Tadmor, Syria 34 30N 37 55E
91 Tadoussac 48 11N 69 42W
62 Tadpatri 14 55N 78 1E
50 Tadzhik S.S.R. □ 35 30N 70 0E
68 Taegu 35 50N 128 25E
68 Taejon 35 30N 127 22E
32 Tafalla 42 30N 1 41W
75 Tafelbaai 33 35S 18 25E
13 Taff, R. 51 27N 3 9W
108 Tafi Viejo 26 43S 67 17W
57 Taftan, Kūh-e, Mt. 28 36N 61 6E
49 Taganrog 47 12N 38 50E
65 Tagbilaran 9 42N 124 3E
36 Tággia 43 52N 7 50E
37 Tagliacozzo 42 4N 13 13E
111 Taguatinga 12 26S 45 40W
85 Tahakopa 46 30S 169 23E
67 Tahcheng 46 50N 83 1E
77 Tahiti, I. 17 45S 149 30W
102 Tahoe, L. 39 6N 120 0W
72 Tahoua 14 57N 5 16E
69 Tahsien 31 12N 108 13E
73 Tahta 26 44N 31 32E
69 Tai Hu 31 10N 120 0E
69 Taichow 32 30N 119 50E
69 Taichung 24 10N 120 35E
68 Taihan Shan, Mts. 36 0N 114 0E
85 Taihape 39 41S 175 48E
69 Taiho 26 50N 114 54E
68 Taiku 37 46N 112 28E
68 Tailai 46 28N 123 18E
81 Tailem Bend 35 12S 139 29E
25 Tailfingen 48 15N 9 1E
56 Taima 27 35N 38 45E
14 Tain 57 49N 4 4W
69 Tainan 23 0N 120 15E
43 Taínaron, Ákra 36 22N 22 27E
69 Taipei 25 2N 121 30E
63 Taiping 4 50N 100 43E
112 Taitao, Pen. de 46 30S 75 0W
69 Taitung 22 43N 121 4E
69 Taiwan ■ 23 30N 121 0E
43 Táiyeto Óros, Mts. 37 0N 22 23E
54 Taiyiba, Israel 32 36N 35 27E
54 Taiyiba, Jordan 31 55N 35 17E
68 Taiyuan 38 0N 112 30E
55 Ta'izz 13 38N 44 4E
30 Tajuña, R. 40 7N 3 35W
73 Tājūra 32 51N 13 27E
63 Tak 17 0N 99 10E
66 Takachiho 32 42N 131 18E
66 Takada 37 7N 138 15E
85 Takaka 40 51S 172 50E
66 Takamatsu 34 20N 134 5E
66 Takaoka 36 40N 137 0E
85 Takapuna 36 47S 174 47E
66 Takasaki 36 20N 139 0E
66 Takatsuki 34 40N 135 37E
74 Takaungu 3 38S 39 52E
66 Takayama 36 10N 137 5E
66 Takefu 35 50N 136 10E
63 Takeo 11 3N 104 50E
57 Takhar □ 36 30N 69 30E
67 Takla Makan, Reg. 39 40N 85 0E
109 Tala 34 21S 55 46W
108 Talagante 33 40S 70 50W
110 Talara 4 30S 81 10W
65 Talaud, Kep. 4 30N 127 10E
30 Talavera de la Reina 39 55N 4 46W
108 Talca 35 20S 71 46W
108 Talca □ 35 20S 71 46W
108 Talcahuano 36 40S 73 10W
50 Taldy Kurgan 45 10N 78 45E
54 Talfit 32 5N 35 17E
69 Tali, Shensi 34 48N 109 48E
67 Tali, Yunnan 25 50N 100 0E
65 Taliabu, I. 1 45S 125 0E
68 Talien 38 53N 121 37E
62 Talikoti 16 29N 76 17E
64 Taliwang 8 50S 116 55E
88 Talkeetna 62 20N 149 50W
99 Talladega 33 28N 86 2W
99 Tallahassee 30 25N 84 15W
84 Tallangatta 36 10S 147 14E
48 Tallinn 59 29N 24 58E
101 Tallulah 32 25N 91 12W
54 Talluza 32 17N 35 18E
41 Talmaciu 45 38N 24 19E
108 Taltal 25 23S 70 40W
81 Talwood 28 27S 149 20E
72 Tamale 9 22N 0 50W
66 Tamano 34 35N 133 59E
72 Tamanrasset 22 56N 5 30E
97 Tamaqua 40 46N 75 58W
13 Tamar, R. 50 22N 4 10W
66 Tamashima 34 27N 133 18E
72 Tamatave 18 10S 49 25E
104 Tamaulipas □ 24 0N 99 0W
72 Tambacounda 13 55N 13 45W
83 Tambellup 34 4S 117 37E
80 Tambo 24 54S 146 14E
64 Tambora, I. 8 14S 117 55E
48 Tambov 52 45N 41 20E
30 Tambre, R. 42 49N 8 53W
72 Tamchaket 17 25N 10 40W
30 Tamega, R. 41 5N 8 21W
104 Tamiahua, Laguna de 21 30N 97 30W
62 Tamil Nadu □ 11 0N 77 0E
68 Taming 36 20N 115 10E
61 Tamluk 22 18N 87 58E
54 Tammun 32 18N 35 23E
99 Tampa 27 57N 82 30W
47 Tampere 61 30N 23 50E
104 Tampico 22 20N 97 50W
63 Tampin 2 28N 102 13E
55 Tamra 32 51N 35 12E
68 Tamsagbulag 47 15N 117 5E
26 Tamsweg 47 7N 13 49E
31 Tamuja, R. 39 33N 6 8W
81 Tamworth, Australia 31 0S 150 58E
13 Tamworth, U.K. 52 38N 1 2W
46 Tana 70 23N 28 13E
73 Tana, L. 12 0N 37 20E
74 Tana, R. 2 32S 40 31E
66 Tanabe 33 44N 135 22E
88 Tanacross 63 40N 143 30W
64 Tanahgrogot 1 55S 116 15E
65 Tanahmeroh 6 0S 140 7E
82 Tanami, Des. 23 15S 132 20E
88 Tanana 65 10N 152 15W
88 Tanana, R. 64 25N 145 30W
75 Tananarive = Antananarivo 18 55S 47 31E
18 Tancarville 46 50N 0 55W
60 Tanda, Ut.P. 28 57N 78 56E
61 Tanda, Ut.P. 26 33N 82 35E
41 Tandarei 44 39N 27 40E
108 Tandil 37 15S 59 6W
60 Tandlianwala 31 3N 73 9E
60 Tando Adam 25 45N 48 40E
60 Tando Mohommad Khan 25 8N 68 32E
62 Tandur 19 11N 79 30E
85 Taneatua 38 4S 177 1E
66 Tane-ga-Shima, I. 30 30N 131 0E
59 Tanen Tong Dan, Mts. 19 40N 99 0E
72 Tanezrouft 23 9N 0 11E
74 Tanga 5 5S 39 2E
61 Tangail 24 15N 90 0E
74 Tanganyika, L. 6 40S 30 0E
72 Tanger 35 50N 5 49W
65 Tangerang 6 12S 106 39E
24 Tangermünde 52 32N 11 57E
67 Tanghla Shan, Mts. 33 10N 90 0E
69 Tangshan, Anhwei 34 23N 116 34E
68 Tangshan, Hopei 39 40N 118 10E
69 Tangtu 31 37N 118 39E
69 Tangyang 30 50N 111 45E
65 Tanimbar, Kep. 7 30S 131 30E
63 Tanjong Malim 3 44N 101 27E
62 Tanjore = Thanjavur 10 48N 79 12E
64 Tanjung 2 10S 115 25E
64 Tanjungbalai 2 55N 99 44E
64 Tanjungkarang 5 25S 105 16E
64 Tanjungpandan 2 45S 107 39E
64 Tanjungredeb 2 12N 117 35E
64 Tanjungselor 2 55N 117 25E
90 Tannin 49 40N 91 0E
45 Tannis, B. 57 40N 10 10E
73 Tanta 30 45N 30 57E
62 Tanuku 16 45N 81 44E
81 Tanunda 34 30S 139 0E
62 Tanur 11 1N 75 46E
20 Tanus 44 8N 2 19E
74 Tanzania ■ 6 40S 34 0E
68 Taonan 45 30N 122 20E
69 Taoyuan 25 0N 121 4E
69 Tapa Shan, Mts. 31 45N 109 30E
104 Tapachula 14 54N 92 17W
64 Tapaktuan 3 30N 97 10E
85 Tapanui 45 56N 169 18E
30 Tapia 43 34N 6 56W
27 Tápiószele 47 45N 19 55E
60 Tapti, R. 21 5N 72 40E
85 Tapuaenuka, Mt. 41 55S 173 50E
109 Taquara 29 36S 50 46W
109 Taquaritinga 21 24S 48 30W
50 Tara 56 55N 74 30E
50 Tara, R. 56 42N 74 36E
51 Tarabagatay, Khrebet, Mts. 47 30N 84 0E
56 Tarābulus, Lebanon 34 31N 33 52E
73 Tarābulus, Libya 32 49N 13 7E
84 Tarago 35 6S 149 39E
64 Tarakan 3 20N 117 35E
85 Taranaki □ 39 5S 174 51E
30 Tarancón 40 1N 3 1W
60 Taranga Hill 24 0N 72 40E
39 Táranto 40 30N 17 11E
39 Táranto, G. di 40 0N 17 15E
110 Tarapaca 2 56S 69 46W
108 Tarapaca □ 20 45S 69 30W
110 Tarapoto 6 30S 76 20W
21 Tarare 45 55N 4 26E
20 Tarascon 42 50N 1 37E
85 Tarawera 39 2S 176 36E
85 Tarawera, L. 38 13S 176 27E
32 Tarazona 41 55N 1 43W
33 Tarazona de la Mancha 39 16N 1 55W
14 Tarbat Ness 57 52N 3 48W
58 Tarbela Dam 34 0N 72 52E
14 Tarbert 57 54N 6 49W
20 Tarbes 43 15N 0 3E
37 Tarcento 46 12N 13 12E
20 Tardets 43 7N 0 53W
84 Taree 31 50S 152 30E
21 Tarentaise, Reg. 45 30N 6 35E
31 Tarifa 36 1N 5 36W
108 Tarija 21 30S 64 40W
108 Tarija □ 21 30S 63 30W
67 Tarim, R. 41 5N 86 40E
49 Tarkhankut, Mys. 45 25N 32 30E
50 Tarko Sale 64 55N 77 50E
72 Tarkwa 5 20N 2 0W
65 Tarlac 15 30N 120 25E
80 Tarlton Downs 22 40S 136 45E
20 Tarn, R. 44 5N 1 6E
20 Tarn □ 43 50N 2 8E
27 Tarna, R. 47 31N 19 59E
45 Tarnby 55 37N 12 36E
20 Tarn-et-Garonne □ 44 8N 1 20E
27 Tarnobrzeg 50 35N 21 41E
28 Tarnobrzeg □ 50 40N 22 0E
27 Tarnów 50 3N 21 0E
27 Tarnow □ 50 0N 21 0E
27 Tarnowskie Góry 50 27N 18 54E
57 Tārom 28 11N 55 42E
37 Tarquínia 42 15N 11 45E
32 Tarragona 41 5N 1 17E
32 Tarragona □ 41 0N 1 0E
32 Tarrasa 41 26N 2 1E
32 Tárrega 41 39N 1 9E
97 Tarrytown 41 5N 73 52W
73 Tarso Emissi 21 27N 18 36E
56 Tarsus 36 58N 34 55E
108 Tartagal 22 30S 63 50W
20 Tartas 43 50N 0 48W
48 Tartu 58 25N 26 58E
56 Tartūs 34 55N 35 55E
64 Tarutung 2 0N 99 0E
37 Tarvisio 46 31N 13 35E
73 Tasāwah 26 0N 13 37E
90 Tashereau 48 40N 78 40W
62 Tasgaon 17 2N 74 39E
50 Tashauz 42 0N 59 20E
67 Tashigong 33 0N 79 30E
50 Tashkent 41 20N 69 10E
67 Tashkurgan 37 51N 74 57E
57 Tashkurghan 36 45N 67 40E
50 Tashtagol 52 47N 87 53E
65 Tasikmalaya 7 18S 108 12E
45 Tåsinge, I. 55 0N 10 36E
51 Taskan 63 5N 150 5E
85 Tasman, B. 40 59S 173 25E
85 Tasman Glacier 43 45S 170 20E
76 Tasman Sea 42 30S 168 0E
80 Tasmania, I. 49 0S 146 30E
27 Tata 47 37N 18 19E
27 Tatabánya 47 32N 18 25E
48 Tatar A.S.S.R. □ 55 30N 51 30E
50 Tatarsk 55 50N 75 20E
66 Tateyama 35 0N 139 50E
69 Tatien 25 45N 118 0E
27 Tatry, Mts. 49 20N 20 0E
67 Tatsaitan 37 55N 95 0E
109 Tatui 23 25S 48 0W
68 Tatung 40 10N 113 10E
68 Tatungkow 39 55N 124 10E
109 Taubaté 23 5S 45 30W
85 Taumarunui 38 53S 175 15E
110 Taumaturgo 9 0S 73 50W
59 Taungdwingyi 20 1N 95 40E
59 Taunggyi 20 50N 97 0E
59 Taungup Taunggya 18 20N 93 40E
13 Taunton, U.K. 51 1N 3 7W
97 Taunton, U.S.A. 41 54N 71 6W
25 Taunus, Mts. 50 15N 8 20E
85 Taupo 38 41S 176 7E
85 Taupo, L. 38 46S 175 55E
85 Tauranga 37 35S 176 11E
39 Taurianova 38 22N 16 1E
56 Taurus Mts. = Toros Daglari 37 0N 35 0E
32 Tauste 41 58N 1 18W
69 Tava Wan, G. 22 40N 114 40E
88 Tavani 62 10N 93 30W
50 Tavda 58 7N 65 8W
50 Tavda, R. 57 47N 67 16E
19 Taverny 49 2N 2 13E
74 Taveta 3 31N 37 37E
85 Taveuni, I. 16 51S 179 58W
21 Tavignano, R. 42 14N 9 20E
31 Tavira 37 8N 7 40W
13 Tavistock 50 33N 4 9W
30 Távora, R. 41 0N 7 30W
59 Tavoy 14 7N 98 18E
13 Taw, R. 51 4N 4 11W
60 Tawa, R. 22 48N 77 48E
65 Tawitawi, I. 5 2N 120 0E
14 Tay, Firth of 56 25N 3 8W
14 Tay, L. 56 30N 4 10W
14 Tay, R. 56 37N 3 58W
63 Tay Ninh 11 20N 106 5E
110 Tayabamba 8 15S 77 10E
101 Taylor 30 30N 97 30W
103 Taylor, Mt. 35 16N 107 50W
100 Taylorville 39 32N 29 20W
51 Taymyr Pol. 75 0N 100 0E
14 Tayport 56 27N 2 52W
51 Tayshet 55 58N 97 25E
14 Tayside □ 56 30N 3 35W
65 Taytay 10 45N 119 30E
69 Tayu 25 38N 114 9E
67 Tayulehsze 29 15N 98 1E
72 Taza 34 10N 4 0W
50 Tazovskiy 67 28N 78 42E
49 Tbilisi 41 50N 44 50E
73 Tchad ■ 12 30N 17 15E
73 Tchad, L. 13 30N 14 30E
74 Tchibanga 2 45S 11 12E
28 Tczew 54 8N 18 50E
85 Te Anau, L. 45 15S 167 45E
85 Te Aroha 37 32S 175 44E
85 Te Awamutu 38 1S 175 20E
85 Te Horo 40 48S 175 6E
85 Te Kuiti 38 20S 175 11E
85 Te Puke 37 46S 176 22E

Teano Tocopilla

39 Teano 41 15N 14 1E
31 Teba 36 59N 4 55W
72 Tébessa 35 28N 8 9E
64 Tebingtinggi 3 38S 102 1E
20 Tech, R. 42 36N 3 3E
104 Tecuala 22 24N 105 30W
41 Tecuci 45 51N 27 27E
50 Tedzhen 37 23N 60 31E
12 Tees, R. 54 34N 1 16W
12 Teesside 54 37N 1 13W
110 Tefé 3 25S 64 50W
65 Tegal 6 52S 109 8E
16 Tegelen 51 20N 6 9E
61 Teghra 25 30N 85 34E
105 Tegucigalpa 14 10N 87 0W
68 Tehchow 37 28N 116 18E
57 Tehrān 35 44N 51 30E
57 Tehrān □ 35 30N 51 0E
67 Tehtsin 28 45N 98 58E
104 Tehuacán 18 20N 97 30W
104 Tehuantepec 16 10N 95 19W
104 Tehuntepec, Istmo de 17 0N 94 30W
13 Teifi, R. 52 7N 4 42W
13 Teign, R. 50 33N 3 29W
13 Teignmouth 50 33N 3 30W
41 Teiuş 46 12N 23 40E
75 Teixeira da Silva 12 12S 15 52E
74 Teixeira de Sousa 10 42S 22 12E
31 Tejo, R. 38 40N 9 24W
85 Tekapo, L. 43 48S 170 32E
104 Tekax 20 20N 89 30W
50 Tekeli 44 50N 79 0E
56 Tekirdag 40 58N 27 30E
62 Tekkali 18 43N 84 24E
54 Tel Aviv-Yafo 32 4N 34 48E
54 Tel Mond 32 15N 34 56E
104 Tela 15 40N 87 28W
64 Telanaipura = Jambi 1 38S 103 30E
49 Telavi 42 0N 45 30E
92 Telegraph Creek 58 0N 131 10W
44 Telemark □ 59 30N 8 30E
30 Teleno 42 23N 6 22W
12 Telford 52 42N 2 29W
26 Telfs 47 19N 11 4E
68 Telisze 39 50N 112 0E
92 Telkwa 54 41N 126 56W
98 Tell City 38 0N 86 44W
62 Tellicherry 11 45N 75 30E
63 Telok Anson 4 0N 101 10E
112 Telsen 42 30S 66 50W
24 Teltow 52 24N 13 15E
64 Telukbetung 5 29S 105 17E
64 Telukbutun 4 5N 108 7E
64 Telukdalem 0 45N 97 50E
72 Tema 5 41N 0 0E
65 Temanggung 7 18S 110 10E
63 Tembeling, R. 4 4N 102 20E
31 Tembleque 39 41N 3 30W
13 Teme, R. 52 9N 2 18W
63 Temerloh 3 27N 102 25E
50 Temir 49 8N 57 6E
50 Temirtou 53 10N 87 20E
90 Temiskaming 46 44N 79 5W
84 Temora 34 30S 147 30E
103 Tempe 33 26N 111 59W
64 Tempino 1 55S 103 23E
38 Témpio Pausania 40 53N 9 6E
101 Temple 31 5N 97 28W
15 Templemore 52 48N 7 50W
24 Templin 53 8N 13 31E
112 Temuco 38 50S 72 50W
85 Temuka 44 14S 171 17E
62 Tenali 16 15N 80 35E
104 Tenancingo 18 98N 99 33W
104 Tenango 19 0N 99 40W
63 Tenasserim 12 6N 99 3E
21 Tenay 45 55N 5 30E
13 Tenby 51 40N 4 42W
21 Tenda 44 5N 7 34E
72 Tenerife, I. 28 20N 16 40W
65 Tengah□, Java 7 0S 110 0E
64 Tengah□, Kalimantan 2 20S 113 0E
67 Tengchung 24 58N 98 30E
69 Tenghsien 35 10N 117 10E
50 Tengiz, Oz. 50 30N 69 0E
62 Tenkasi 8 55N 77 20E
80 Tennant Creek 19 30S 134 0E
99 Tennessee, R. 37 0N 88 20W
99 Tennessee □ 36 0N 86 30W
66 Tenryū-Gawa, R. 34 39N 137 47E
81 Tenterfield 29 0S 152 0E
111 Teófilo Otoni 17 15S 41 30W
104 Teotihuacan 19 44N 98 50W
104 Tepic 21 30N 104 54W
26 Teplice 50 39N 13 48E
32 Ter, R. 42 1N 3 12E
30 Tera, R. 38 56N 8 3W
37 Téramo 42 40N 13 40E
84 Terang 38 3S 142 59E
8 Terceira, I. 38 43N 24 13W
62 Terdal 16 33N 75 9E
40 Teregova 45 10N 22 16E
49 Terek, R. 43 44N 46 33E
63 Terengganu □ 4 53N 103 0E
111 Teresina 5 2S 42 45W
28 Terespol 52 5N 23 36E
19 Tergnier 49 40N 3 17E
63 Teriang 3 15N 102 26E
39 Terlizzi 41 8N 16 32E
50 Termez 37 0N 67 15E
38 Términi Imerese 37 59N 13 51E
104 Términos, L. de 18 35N 91 30W
65 Ternate 0 45N 127 25E
16 Terneuzen 51 20N 3 50E
37 Terni 42 34N 12 38E
26 Ternitz 47 43N 16 2E
81 Terowie 38 10S 138 50E
92 Terrace 54 30N 128 35W
38 Terracina 41 17N 13 12E
37 Terranuova 43 38N 11 35E
20 Terrasson 45 7N 1 19E
5 Terre Adélie 67 0S 140 0E
98 Terre Haute 46 30N 75 13W
101 Terrell 32 44N 96 19W
97 Terryville 41 41N 73 1W
16 Terschelling, I. 53 25N 5 20E
32 Teruel 40 22N 1 8W
32 Teruel □ 40 48N 1 0E
41 Tervel 43 45N 27 28E
46 Tervola 66 6N 24 59E
40 Tešica 43 27N 21 45E
72 Tessalit 20 12N 1 0E
13 Test, R. 51 7N 1 30W
20 Tet, R. 42 44N 3 2E
75 Tete 16 13S 33 33E
41 Teteven 42 58N 24 17E
72 Tetouan 35 30N 5 25W
40 Tetovo 42 1N 21 2E
51 Tetyukhe = Dalnergorsk 44 40N 135 50E
93 Teulon 50 30N 97 20W
14 Teviot, R. 55 36N 2 26W
81 Tewantin 26 27S 153 3E
13 Tewkesbury 51 59N 2 8W
101 Texarkana, Ark. 33 25N 94 0W
101 Texarkana, Tex. 33 25N 94 0W
81 Texas 28 49S 151 15E
101 Texas □ 31 30N 98 30W
101 Texas City 27 20N 95 20W
16 Texel, I. 53 5N 4 50E
104 Teziutlán 19 50N 97 30W
59 Tezpur 26 40N 92 45E
75 Thabana Ntlenyana 29 30S 29 9E
75 Thabazimbi 24 40S 26 4E
63 Thailand ■ 16 0N 101 0E
63 Thakhek 17 25 104 45E
58 Thal 33 28N 70 33E
60 Thal Desert 31 0N 71 30E
81 Thallon 28 30S 148 57E
25 Thalwil 47 17N 8 35E
13 Thame, R. 51 52N 0 47W
85 Thames 37 7S 175 34E
90 Thames, R., Canada 42 19N 82 28W
13 Thames, R., U.K. 51 28N 0 43E
62 Thana 19 12N 72 59E
60 Thanesar 30 1N 76 52E
13 Thanet, I. 51 21N 1 20E
63 Thang Binh 15 50N 108 20E
82 Thangoo P.O. 18 10S 122 22E
80 Thangool 24 29S 150 35E
63 Thanh Hoa 19 35N 105 40E
62 Thanjavur 10 48N 79 12E
19 Thann 47 48N 7 5E
19 Thaon 48 15N 6 25E
81 Thargomindah 27 58S 143 46E
59 Tharrawaddy 17 30N 96 0E
42 Thásos, I. 40 40N 24 40E
103 Thatcher 32 54N 109 46W
59 Thaton 17 0N 97 39E
20 Thau, Étang de 43 23N 3 36E
59 Thaungdut 24 30N 94 30E
59 Thayetmyo 19 19N 95 11E
59 Thazi 21 0N 96 5E
105 The Bight 24 19N 75 24W
102 The Dalles 45 40N 121 11W
105 The Flatts 32 19N 64 45W
68 The Great Wall of China 37 30N 109 0E
105 The Grenadines 12 40N 61 15W
16 The Hague = s'Gravenhage 52 7N 7 14E
83 The Johnston Lakes 32 25S 120 30E
93 The Pas 53 45N 101 15W
81 Theebine 26 0S 152 30E
20 Thenon 45 9N 1 4E
80 Theodore 24 55S 150 3E
42 Thermaikós Kól. 40 15N 22 45E
102 Thermopolis 43 14N 108 10E
43 Thermopylae 38 48N 22 45E
42 Thesprotia □ 39 27N 20 22E
42 Thessalía □ 39 30N 22 0E
90 Thessalon 46 20N 83 30W
42 Thessaloníki 40 38N 23 0E
42 Thessaloníki □ 40 45N 23 0E
13 Thetford 52 25N 0 44E
91 Thetford Mines 46 8N 71 18W
81 Thevenard 32 9S 133 38E
101 Thibodaux 29 48N 90 49W
93 Thicket Portage 55 25N 97 45W
100 Thief River Falls 48 15N 96 10W
37 Thiene 45 42N 11 29E
19 Thierache, Reg. 49 51N 3 45E
20 Thiers 45 52N 3 33E
72 Thiès 14 50N 16 51W
74 Thika 1 1S 37 5E
19 Thionville 49 20N 6 10E
43 Thíra, I. 36 23N 25 27E
12 Thirsk 54 15N 1 20W
45 Thisted 56 57N 8 42E
43 Thíval 38 19N 23 19E
20 Thiviers 45 25N 0 54E
99 Thomasville, Ala. 31 55N 87 42W
99 Thomasville, Fla. 30 50N 84 0W
99 Thomasville, N.C. 35 5N 80 4W
93 Thompson 55 50N 97 34W
97 Thompsonville 42 0N 72 37W
63 Thonburi 13 50N 100 36W
21 Thonon 46 22N 6 29E
12 Thornaby on Tees 54 36N 1 19W
96 Thorold 43 8N 79 13W
20 Thouars 46 59N 0 13W
42 Thráki □ 41 9N 25 30E
42 Thrakikón Pélagos 40 30N 25 0E
102 Three Forks 45 5N 111 40W
92 Three Hills 51 43N 113 15W
97 Three Rivers 28 30N 98 10W
4 Thule 76 0N 68 0W
25 Thun 46 45N 7 38E
90 Thunder Bay 48 25N 89 10E
92 Thunder River 52 13N 119 20W
25 Thunersee 46 42N 7 42E
63 Thung Song 8 10N 99 40E
25 Thurgau □ 47 34N 9 10E
24 Thüringer Wald 50 35N 11 0E
15 Thurles 52 40N 7 53W
26 Thurn P. 47 19N 12 24E
90 Thurso, Canada 45 36N 75 15W
14 Thurso, U.K. 58 34N 3 31W
5 Thurston I. 72 0S 100 0W
45 Thy, Reg. 57 0N 8 30E
72 Tiaret 35 28N 1 21E
72 Tiassalé 5 58N 4 57W
109 Tibaji 24 19S 50 19W
37 Tiber, R. 41 44N 12 14E
54 Tiberias 32 47N 35 32E
73 Tibesti 21 0N 17 30E
67 Tibet □ 32 30N 86 0E
52 Tibet, Plateau of 35 0N 90 0E
81 Tibooburra 29 26S 142 1E
45 Tibro 58 28N 14 10E
104 Tiburón, I. 29 0N 112 30W
36 Ticino, R. 45 9N 9 14E
25 Ticino □ 46 20N 8 45E
97 Ticonderoga 43 40N 73 28E
104 Ticul 20 20N 89 50W
45 Tidaholm 58 12N 13 55E
72 Tidjikdja 18 4N 11 35W
68 Tiehling 42 25N 123 51E
16 Tiel 51 54N 5 5E
16 Tielt 51 0N 3 20E
52 Tien Shan, Mts. 42 0N 80 0E
16 Tienen 50 48N 4 57E
69 Tienshui 34 30N 105 34E
68 Tientsin 39 10N 117 0E
69 Tientung 23 47N 107 2E
31 Tierra de Barros 38 40N 6 30W
30 Tierra de Campos 42 5N 4 45W
112 Tierra del Fuego, I. 54 0S 69 0W
30 Tiétar, R. 39 55N 5 50W
109 Tietê, R. 20 40S 51 35W
98 Tiffin 41 8N 83 10W
54 Tifrah 31 19N 34 42E
99 Tifton 31 28N 83 32W
65 Tifu 3 39S 126 18E
41 Tigăneşti 44 44N 26 8E
93 Tignish 46 58N 63 57W
56 Tigris, R. = Dijlah, Nahr 31 0N 47 25E
51 Tigu 29 48N 91 38E
59 Tigyaing 23 45N 96 10E
104 Tijuana 32 30N 117 10W
104 Tikal 17 2N 89 35W
49 Tikhoretsk 45 56N 40 5E
51 Tiksi 71 50N 129 0E
16 Tilburg 51 31N 5 6E
90 Tilbury, Canada 42 17N 84 23E
13 Tilbury, U.K. 51 27N 0 24E
61 Tilhat 28 0N 79 45E
51 Tilichiki 61 0N 166 5E
90 Tillsonburg 42 53N 80 55W
43 Tílos, I. 36 27N 27 27E
81 Tilpa 30 58S 144 30E
48 Timanskiy Kryazh 65 58N 50 5E
85 Timaru 44 23S 171 14E
43 Timbákion 35 4N 24 45E
72 Timbuktu = Tombouctou 16 50N 3 0W
42 Timfi Oros, Mt. 39 59N 20 45E
43 Timfristós, Mt. 38 57N 21 50E
40 Timiş, R. 44 51N 20 39E
40 Timişoara 4543 1 21 15E
90 Timmins 48 28N 81 25W
40 Timok, R. 44 13N 22 40E
111 Timon 5 8S 42 52W
65 Timor, I. 9 0S 125 0E
82 Timor, Sea 10 0S 127 0E
72 Timris, C. 19 15N 16 30W
65 Timur□, Java 7 20S 112 0E
64 Timur□, Kalimantan 1 15N 117 0E
62 Tindivanam 12 15N 79 35E
72 Tindouf 27 50N 8 4W
45 Tinglev 54 57N 9 13E
83 Tinkurrin 33 0S 117 38E
43 Tínos, I. 37 33N 25 8E
33 Tiñoso, C. 37 32N 1 6W
69 Tinpak 21 40N 111 15E
81 Tintinara 35 48S 140 2E
31 Tinto, R. 37 12N 6 55W
63 Tioman, Pulau 2 50N 104 10E
59 Tipongpani 27 20N 95 55E
15 Tipperary 52 28N 8 10W
15 Tipperary □ 52 37N 7 55W
13 Tipton 52 32N 2 4W
62 Tiptur 13 15N 76 26E
54 Tīra 32 14N 34 56E
57 Tirān 32 45N 51 0E
42 Tirana 41 18N 19 49E
42 Tirana-Durresi □ 41 35N 20 0E
36 Tirano 46 13N 10 11E
49 Tiraspol 46 55N 29 35E
54 Tirat Karmel 32 46N 34 58E
54 Tirat Tsevi 32 26N 35 51E
54 Tirat Yehuda 32 1N 34 56E
56 Tire 38 5N 27 50E
56 Tirebolu 40 58N 38 45E
14 Tiree, I. 56 31N 6 49W
41 Tîrgovişte 44 55N 25 27E
41 Tîrgu-Cârbuneşti 44 58N 23 31E
41 Tîrgu-Jiu 45 5N 23 19E
41 Tîrgu-Mureş 46 31N 24 38E
41 Tîrgu Ocna 46 15N 26 37E
41 Tîrgu Sacuesc 46 0N 26 8E
58 Tirich Mir, Mt. 36 15N 71 35E
41 Tîrnaveni 46 19N 24 13E
42 Tírnavos 39 45N 22 18E
26 Tirol □ 47 3N 10 43E
38 Tirso, L. del 40 8N 8 56E
38 Tirso, R. 39 52N 8 33E
62 Tiruchchirappalli 10 45N 78 45E
62 Tiruchendur 8 29N 78 7E
62 Tirunelveli 8 45N 77 45E
62 Tirupati 13 45N 79 30E
62 Tiruppur 11 6N 77 21E
62 Tiruppattur 12 30N 78 30E
62 Tiruturaipundi 10 32N 79 41E
62 Tiruvalla 9 23N 76 33E
62 Tiruvallur 13 9N 79 57E
62 Tiruvannamalai 12 10N 79 12E
62 Tiruvarur 10 46N 79 38E
62 Tiruvatipuram 12 39N 79 33E
62 Tiruvottiyur 13 10N 80 22E
40 Tisa, R. 45 15N 20 17E
93 Tisdale 52 50N 104 0W
27 Tisza, R. 45 15N 20 17E
27 Tiszaföldvár 46 59N 20 15E
27 Tiszafüred 47 38N 20 50E
51 Tit-Ary 71 58N 127 1E
110 Titicaca, L. 15 30S 69 30W
40 Titigrad 42 30N 19 19E
40 Titov Veles 41 46N 21 47E
40 Titovo Uzice 43 55N 19 50E
74 Titule 3 15N 25 31E
96 Titusville 41 35N 79 39W
40 Tivat 42 28N 18 43E
13 Tiverton 50 54N 3 30W
37 Tívoli 41 58N 12 45E
57 Tiwī 22 45N 59 12E
72 Tizi-Ouzou 36 48N 4 2E
104 Tizimín 21 0N 88 1W
45 Tjörn, I. 58 0N 11 35E
104 Tlaxcala □ 19 30N 98 20W
104 Tlaxiaco 17 10N 97 40W
72 Tlemcen 34 52N 1 15W
28 Tłuszcz 52 25N 21 25E
60 Toba Tek Singh 31 30N 69 0E
105 Tobago, I. 11 10N 60 30W
33 Tobarra 38 35N 1 41W
65 Tobelo 1 25N 127 56E
80 Tobermorey, Australia 22 12S 138 0E
90 Tobermory, Canada 45 12N 81 40W
14 Tobermory, U.K. 56 37N 6 4W
50 Tobolsk 58 0N 68 10E
73 Tobruk = Tubruq 32 7N 23 55E
111 Tocantinopolis 6 20S 47 25W
111 Tocantins, R. 1 45S 49 10W
99 Toccoa 34 35N 83 19W
66 Tochigi 36 25N 139 45E
66 Tochigi □ 36 45N 139 45E
31 Tocina 37 37N 5 44W
44 Töckfors 59 30N 11 50E
108 Tocopilla 22 5S 70 10W

Tobarão Utiel

109 Tubarão 28 30s 49 0w
54 Tubas 32 20n 35 22e
56 Tubayq, Jabal at 29 40n 37 30e
25 Tübingen 48 31n 9 4e
73 Tubruq 32 7n 23 55e
77 Tubuai Is. 23 20s 151 0w
110 Tucacas 10 48n 68 19w
28 Tuchola 53 33n 17 52e
83 Tuckanarra 27 8s 118 1e
105 Tucker's Town 32 19n 64 43w
103 Tucson 32 14n 110 59w
108 Tucumán □ 26 48s 66 2w
101 Tucumcari 35 12n 103 45w
110 Tucupita 9 4n 62 0w
111 Tucuruí 3 45s 49 48w
32 Tudela 42 4n 1 39w
30 Tudela de Duero 41 37n 4 39w
65 Tuguegarao 17 35n 121 42e
51 Tugur 53 50n 136 45e
69 Tuhshan 25 40n 107 30e
88 Tuktoyaktuk 69 15n 133 0w
48 Tula 54 13n 37 32e
67 Tulan 37 24n 98 1e
103 Tulare 36 15n 119 26w
103 Tularosa 33 4n 106 1w
75 Tulbagh 33 16s 19 6e
110 Tulcán 0 48n 77 43w
41 Tulcea 45 13n 28 46e
75 Tuléar 23 21s 43 40e
75 Tuli 1 24s 122 26e
54 Tūlkarm 32 19n 35 10e
99 Tullahoma 35 23n 86 12w
15 Tullamore 53 17n 7 30w
20 Tulle 45 16n 1 47e
26 Tulln 48 20n 16 4e
15 Tullow 52 48n 6 45w
80 Tully 17 30s 141 0e
73 Tulymaythah 32 40n 20 55e
41 Tulovo 42 33n 25 32e
101 Tulsa 36 10n 96 0w
110 Tulua 4 6n 76 11w
51 Tulun 54 40n 100 10e
65 Tulungagung 8 5s 111 54e
105 Tuma, R. 13 6n 84 35w
110 Tumaco 1 50n 78 45w
110 Tumatumari 5 20n 58 55w
44 Tumba 59 12n 17 48e
74 Tumba, L. 0 50s 18 0e
110 Tumbes 3 30s 80 20w
81 Tumby Bay 34 21s 136 8e
68 Tumen 42 46n 129 59e
110 Tumeremo 7 18n 61 30w
62 Tumkur 13 18n 77 12w
14 Tummel, L. 56 43n 3 55w
58 Tump 26 7n 62 16e
63 Tumpat 6 11n 102 10e
111 Tumucumaque South 2 0n 55 0w
84 Tumut 35 16s 148 13e
13 Tunbridge Wells 51 7n 0 16e
74 Tunduru 11 0s 37 25e
62 Tungabhadra Dam 15 21n 76 23e
69 Tungcheng 31 0n 117 3e
68 Tungchow 39 58n 116 50e
69 Tungchuan 35 4n 109 2e
69 Tungfanghsien 18 50n 108 33e
68 Tunghwa 41 46n 126 0e
68 Tungkiang 47 40n 132 30e
69 Tungkwanshan 31 0n 117 45e
68 Tungliao 43 42n 122 11e
69 Tunglu 29 50n 119 35e
68 Tungping 35 50n 116 20e
69 Tungshan 29 36n 144 28e
69 Tungshan, I. 23 40n 117 31e
92 Tungsten 61 52n 128 1w
69 Tungtai 32 55n 120 15e
69 Tungting Hu, L. 28 30n 112 30e
69 Tungtze 27 59n 106 56e
68 Tunhwa 43 27n 128 16e
67 Tunhwang 40 5n 94 46e
62 Tuni 17 22n 82 43e
72 Tunis 36 50n 10 11e
72 Tunisia ■ 33 30n 9 0e
110 Tunja 5 40n 73 25e
108 Tunuyán 33 55s 69 0w
51 Tuoy-khaya 62 30n 111 0w
109 Tupã 21 57s 50 28w
99 Tupelo 34 15n 88 42w
51 Tupik 54 26n 119 57e
108 Tupiza 21 30s 65 40w
97 Tupper Lake 44 18n 74 30w
108 Tupungato, Mt. 33 15s 69 50w
110 Túquerres 1 5n 77 37w
54 Tur 31 47n 35 14e
61 Tura 25 30n 90 16e
56 Turayf 31 45n 38 30e
110 Turbaco 10 20n 75 25w
40 Turbe 44 15n 17 35e
110 Turbo 8 6n 76 43e
41 Turda 46 35n 23 48e
28 Turek 52 3n 18 30e
67 Turfan 43 6n 89 24e
67 Turfan Depression 43 0n 88 0e
41 Tŭrgovishte 43 17n 26 38e
56 Turgutlu 38 30n 27 48e
56 Turhal 40 24n 36 19e
32 Turia, R. 39 27n 0 19w
111 Turiaçu 1 40s 45 28w
36 Turin=Torino 45 3n 7 40e
74 Turkana, L. 4 10n 36 10e
50 Turkestan 43 10n 68 10e
27 Túrkeve 47 6n 20 44e
56 Turkey ■ 39 0n 36 0e
82 Turkey Creek P.O. 17 2s 128 12e
50 Turkmen S.S.R. 39 0n 59 0e
105 Turks Is. 21 20n 71 20w
47 Turku 60 27n 22 14e
103 Turlock 37 30n 122 55w
104 Turneffe Is. 17 20n 87 50w
16 Turnhout 51 19n 4 57w
26 Türnitz 47 55n 15 29e
26 Turnov 50 34n 15 10e
41 Tûrnovo 43 5n 25 41e
41 Turnu Măgurele 43 46n 24 56e
40 Turnu-Severin 44 39n 22 41e
14 Turriff 57 32n 2 58w
93 Turtle 48 52n 92 40w
93 Turtleford 53 30n 108 50w
56 Turūbah 28 20n 43 15e
47 Turun ja Pori □ 61 0n 22 30e
27 Turzovka 49 25n 18 41e
99 Tuscaloosa 33 13n 87 31w
96 Tuscarora Mt. 40 10n 77 45w
99 Tuskegee 32 26n 85 42w
96 Tussey Mt. 40 25n 78 7w
62 Tuticorin 8 50n 78 12e
111 Tutoja 2 45s 42 20w
41 Tutrakan 44 2n 26 40e
25 Tuttlingen 47 59n 8 50e
65 Tutuala 8 25s 127 15e
77 Tutuila, I. 14 19s 170 50w
51 Turukhansk 65 55n 88 5e
51 Tava, A.S.S.R. 52 0n 95 0e
76 Tuvalu ■ 8 0s 176 0e
56 Tuwaiq, Jabal 23 0n 46 0e
104 Tuxpan 20 50n 97 30w
104 Tuxtla Gutiérrez 16 50n 93 10w
30 Tuy 42 3n 8 39w
63 Tuy Hoa 13 5n 109 17e
63 Tuyen Hoa 17 55n 106 3e
69 Tuyun 26 5n 107 20e
56 Tuz Gölü 38 45n 33 30e
56 Tuz Khurmātu 34 50n 44 45e
40 Tuzla 44 34n 18 41e
45 Tvedestrand 58 38n 8 58e
41 Tvŭrditsa 42 42n 25 53e
12 Tweed, R. 55 46n 2 0w
92 Tweedsmuir Prov. Park 52 55n 126 5w
102 Twin Falls 42 30n 114 30w
98 Two Rivers 44 10n 87 31w
27 Tychy 50 9n 18 59e
101 Tyler 32 20n 95 15w
26 Týn nad Vltavou 49 13n 14 26e
51 Tyndinskiy 55 10n 124 43e
12 Tyne, R. 55 1n 1 26w
12 Tyne & Wear □ 54 55n 1 35w
12 Tynemouth 55 1n 1 27w
44 Tynset 62 27n 10 47e
56 Tyre =Sur 33 19n 35 16e
96 Tyrone 40 39n 78 10w
84 Tyrendarra 38 12s 141 50e
44 Tyrifjorden 60 2n 10 3e
38 Tyrrhenian Sea 40 0n 12 30e
50 Tyumen 57 0n 65 18e
13 Tywi, R. 51 46n 4 22w
75 Tzaneen 23 47s 30 9e
69 Tzeki 27 40n 117 5e
69 Tzekung 29 25n 104 30e
69 Tzekwei 31 0n 110 46e
68 Tzepo 36 28n 117 58e
68 Tzeyang 32 47n 108 58e
42 Tzoumérka, Mt. 39 30n 21 26e

U

55 Uarsciek 2 28n 45 55e
110 Uaupés 0 8s 67 5w
109 Ubá 21 0s 43 0w
111 Ubaitaba 14 18s 39 20w
21 Ubaye, R. 44 28n 6 18e
66 Ube 34 6n 131 20e
31 Ubeda 38 3n 3 23w
111 Uberaba 19 50s 48 0w
111 Uberlândia 19 0s 48 20w
63 Ubon Ratchathani 15 15n 104 50e
31 Ubrique 36 41n 5 27w
74 Ubundu 0 22s 25 30e
110 Ucayali, R. 4 30s 73 30w
93 Uchi Lake 51 10n 92 40w
66 Uchiura-Wan, G. 42 25n 140 40e
92 Ucluelet 48 57n 125 32w
60 Udaipur 24 36n 73 44e
62 Udamalpet 10 35n 77 15e
37 Udbina 44 31n 15 47e
45 Uddevalla 58 21n 11 55e
46 Uddjaur, L. 65 55n 17 50e
62 Udgir 18 25n 77 5e
60 Udhampur 33 0n 75 5e
72 Udi 6 23n 7 21e
37 Údine 46 5n 13 10e
62 Udipi 13 25n 74 42e
48 Udmurt A.S.S.R. □ 57 30n 52 30e
63 Udon Thani 17 29n 102 46e
41 Udvoy, Mts. 42 50n 26 50e
24 Ueckermünde 53 45n 14 1e
66 Ueda 36 30n 138 10e
51 Uelen 66 10n 170 0w
24 Uelzen 53 0n 10 33e
74 Uere, R. 3 42n 25 24e
48 Ufa 54 45n 55 55e
74 Uganda ■ 2 0n 32 0e
88 Ugashik Lakes 57 0n 157 0w
21 Ugine 45 45n 6 25e
51 Uglegorsk 49 10n 142 5e
41 Ugûrchin 43 6n 24 26e
27 Uherské Hradiště 49 4n 17 30e
27 Uhersky Brod 49 1n 17 40e
26 Uhlava, R. 49 45n 13 20e
96 Uhrichsville 40 23n 81 22w
75 Uitenhage 33 40s 25 28e
27 Újfehértó 47 49n 21 41e
60 Ujhani 28 0n 79 6e
60 Ujjain 23 9n 75 43e
27 Ujpest 47 33n 19 6e
65 Ujung Pandang 5 10s 119 0e
51 Uka 57 50n 162 0e
74 Ukerewe I. 2 0s 33 0e
59 Ukhrul 25 10n 94 25e
48 Ukhta 63 55n 54 0e
102 Ukiah 39 10n 123 9w
49 Ukrainian S.S.R. □ 48 0n 35 0e
68 Ulaanbaatar 48 0n 107 0e
68 Ulan Bator =Ulaanbaatar 48 0n 107 0e
51 Ulan Ude 52 0n 107 30e
68 Ulanhot 46 5n 122 1e
40 Ulcinj 41 58n 19 10e
62 Ulhasnagar 19 15n 73 10e
40 Uljma 45 2n 21 10e
30 Ulla, R. 42 39n 8 44w
84 Ulladulla 35 21s 150 29e
14 Ullapool 57 54n 5 10w
32 Ulldecona 40 36n 0 20e
12 Ullswater, L. 54 35n 2 52w
25 Ulm 48 23n 10 0e
41 Ulmeni 45 4n 46 40e
45 Ulricehamn 57 46n 13 26e
44 Ulsberg 62 45n 10 3e
15 Ulster □ 54 45n 6 30w
12 Ulverston 54 13n 3 7w
80 Ulverstone 41 11s 146 11e
48 Ulyanovsk 54 25n 48 25e
49 Uman 48 40n 30 12e
4 Umanak 70 40n 52 0w
62 Umarkhed 19 37n 77 38e
37 Umbertide 43 18n 12 20e
37 Umbria □ 42 53n 12 30e
46 Umeå 63 45n 20 20e
57 Umm al Qaiwain 25 30n 55 35e
54 Umm el Fahm 32 31n 35 9e
73 Umm Keddada 13 36n 26 42e
56 Umm Lajj 25 0n 37 23e
57 Umm Said 25 0n 51 40e
88 Umnak I. 53 0n 168 0w
75 Umniati, R. 17 30s 29 23e
60 Umrer 20 51n 79 18e
60 Umreth 22 41n 73 4e
75 Umtali 18 58s 32 38e
75 Umtata 31 36s 28 49e
75 Umvuma 19 16s 30 30e
75 Umzimvubu 31 38s 29 33e
60 Una 20 46n 71 8e
37 Unac, R. 44 30n 16 9e
97 Unadilla 42 20n 75 17w
88 Unalakleet 63 53n 160 50w
88 Unalaska I. 54 0n 164 30w
103 Uncompahgre Pk. 38 5n 107 32w
84 Underbool 35 10s 141 51e
84 Ungarie 33 38s 146 56e
89 Ungava B. 59 30n 67 0w
89 Ungava Pen. 60 0n 75 0w
111 União 4 50s 37 50w
109 União da Vitória 26 5s 51 0w
88 Unimak I. 54 30n 164 30w
99 Union 34 49n 81 39w
97 Union City, N.J. 40 47n 74 5w
101 Union City, Tenn. 36 35n 89 0w
102 Union Gap 46 38n 120 29w
53 Union of Soviet Socialist Republics ■ 60 0n 60 0e
98 Uniontown 39 54n 79 45w
57 United Arab Emirates ■ 24 0n 54 30e
11 United Kingdom ■ 55 0n 3 0w
94 United States of America ■ 37 0n 96 0w
93 Unity 52 30n 109 5w
60 Unjha 23 46n 72 24e
61 Unnao 26 35n 80 30e
14 Unst, I. 60 50n 0 55w
25 Unterwalden □ 46 50n 8 15e
56 Ünye 41 5n 37 15e
66 Uozu 36 48n 137 24e
110 Upata 8 1n 62 24w
4 Upernavik 72 45n 56 0w
75 Upington 28 25s 21 15e
60 Upleta 21 46n 70 16e
85 Upolu, I. 13 58s 172 0w
85 Upper Hutt 41 8s 175 5e
91 Upper Musquodoboit 45 10n 62 58w
72 Upper Volta ■ 12 0n 0 30w
44 Uppsala 59 53n 17 42e
44 Uppsala □ 60 0n 17 30e
56 Ur 30 55n 46 25e
110 Uracará 2 20s 57 50w
84 Ural, Mt. 33 21s 146 12e
48 Ural Mts. = Uralskie Gory 60 0n 59 0e
50 Ural, R. 47 0n 51 48e
81 Uralla 30 37s 151 29e
50 Uralsk 51 20n 51 20e
48 Uralskie Gory 60 0n 59 0e
80 Urandangi 21 32s 138 14e
93 Uranium City 59 28n 108 40w
62 Uravakonda 14 57n 77 12e
66 Urawa 35 50n 139 40e
50 Uray 60 5n 65 15e
100 Urbana, Ill. 40 7n 88 12w
98 Urbana, Ohio 40 9n 83 44w
37 Urbino 43 43n 12 38e
30 Urbión, Picos de 42 1n 2 52w
20 Urdos 42 51n 0 35w
12 Ure, R. 54 1n 1 12w
50 Urengoy 66 0n 78 0e
56 Urfa 37 12n 38 50e
26 Urfahr 48 19n 14 17e
50 Urgench 41 40n 60 30e
25 Uri □ 46 43n 8 35e
110 Uribia 11 43n 72 16w
54 Urim 31 18n 34 32e
41 Urlati 44 59n 26 15e
56 Urmia, L. = Daryâcheh-ye Reza'iyeh 37 30n 45 30e
40 Uroševac 42 23n 21 10e
28 Ursus 52 12n 20 53
111 Uruaca 14 35s 49 16w
104 Uruapán 19 30n 102 0w
111 Uruçui 7 20s 44 28w
108 Uruguay ■ 32 30s 55 30w
108 Uruguay, R. 34 12s 58 18w
108 Uruguaiana 29 50s 57 0w
67 Urungu, R. 46 30n 88 50e
57 Uruzgan □ 33 30n 66 0e
41 Urziceni 44 46n 26 42e
48 Usa, R. 65 57n 56 55e
56 Uşak 38 43n 29 28e
24 Usedom, I. 53 50n 13 55e
56 Usfan 21 58n 39 27e
50 Ush-Tobe 45 16n 78 0e
112 Ushuaia 54 50s 68 23w
51 Ushuman 52 47n 126 32e
13 Usk, R. 51 36n 2 58w
56 Üsküdar 41 0n 29 5e
48 Usman 52 5n 39 48e
51 Usolye Sibirskoye 52 40n 103 40e
50 Uspenskiy 48 50n 72 55e
20 Ussel 45 32n 2 18e
51 Ussuriysk 43 40n 131 50e
51 Ust-Ilga 55 5n 104 55e
51 Ust-Ilimsk 58 3n 102 39e
50 Ust Ishim 57 45n 71 10e
51 Ust-Kamchatsk 56 10n 162 0e
50 Ust Kamenogorsk 50 0n 82 20e
51 Ust-Kut 56 50n 105 10e
51 Ust Kuyga 70 1n 135 36e
51 Ust Maya 60 30n 134 20e
51 Ust Olenck 73 0n 120 10e
50 Ust Post 70 0n 84 10e
48 Ust Tsilma 65 25n 52 0e
51 Ust-Tungir 55 25n 120 15e
48 Ust Usa 66 0n 56 30e
44 Ustaoset 60 30n 8 2e
51 Ustchaun 68 47n 170 30e
27 Ustí na Orlici 49 58n 16 38e
26 Ustí nad Labem 50 41n 14 3e
38 Ustica, I. 38 42n 13 10e
51 Ustye 55 30n 97 30e
104 Usulután 13 25n 88 28w
102 Utah □ 39 30n 111 30w
65 Utara □, Sulawesi 1 0n 120 3e
64 Utara □, Sumatera 2 0n 99 0e
24 Ütersen 53 40n 9 40e
63 Uthai Thani 15 22n 100 3e
56 Uthmaniya 25 5n 49 6e
97 Utica 43 5n 75 18w
32 Utiel 39 37n 1 11w

Utrecht, Neth. Vila Nova de Gaia

16 Utrecht, Neth. 52 3N 5 8E
75 Utrecht, S. Africa 27 38S 30 20E
16 Utrecht, Netherlands □ 52 6N 5 7E
31 Utrera 37 12N 5 48W
66 Utsunomiya 36 30N 139 50E
61 Uttar Pradesh □ 27 0N 80 0E
63 Uttaradit 17 36N 100 5E
12 Uttoxeter 52 53N 1 50W
47 Uudenmaa □ 60 25N 23 0E
68 Uuldza 49 8N 112 10E
47 Uusikaupunki 60 47N 21 28E
101 Uvalde 29 15N 99 48W
50 Uvat 59 5N 68 50E
74 Uvinza 5 5S 30 24E
74 Uvira 3 22S 29 3E
67 Uvs Nuur, L. 50 20N 92 30E
66 Uwajima 33 10N 132 35E
104 Uxmal 20 22N 89 46W
108 Uyuni 20 35S 66 55W
108 Uyuni, Salar de 20 10S 68 0W
50 Uzbek S.S.R. 40 5N 65 0E
20 Uzerche 45 25N 1 35E
21 Uzès 44 1N 4 26E

V

75 Vaal, R. 29 4S 23 38E
46 Vaasa 63 10N 21 35E
46 Vaasa □ 63 6N 23 0E
27 Vác 47 49N 19 10E
109 Vacaria 28 31S 50 52W
21 Vaccares, Étang de 43 32N 4 34E
60 Vadnagar 23 47N 72 40E
46 Vadsø 70 3N 29 50E
26 Vaduz 47 8N 9 31E
45 Vaggeryd 57 30N 14 10E
30 Vagos 40 33N 8 42W
27 Váh, R. 47 55N 18 0E
5 Vahsel B. 75 0S 35 0W
50 Vaigach 70 10N 59 0E
62 Vaigai, R. 9 20N 79 0E
18 Vaiges 48 2N 0 30W
60 Vaijapur 19 58N 74 45E
62 Vaikam 9 45N 76 25E
41 Vakarel 42 35N 23 40E
90 Val d'Or 48 7N 77 47W
93 Val Marie 49 15N 107 45W
30 Valadares 41 5N 8 38W
41 Valahia □ 44 35N 25 0E
25 Valais □ 46 12N 7 45E
27 Valasské Meziříčí 49 29N 17 59E
44 Valbo 60 40N 17 4E
112 Valchete 40 40S 66 20W
19 Val-d'Oise □ 49 5N 2 0E
37 Valdagno 45 38N 11 18E
48 Valdayskaya Vozvyshennost 57 0N 33 40E
31 Valdeazogues, R. 38 45N 4 55W
45 Valdemarsvik 58 14N 16 40E
31 Valdepeņas, Ciudad Real 38 43N 3 25W
31 Valdepeņas, Jaen 31 33N 3 47W
30 Valderaduey, R. 41 31N 5 42W
32 Valderrobres 40 53N 0 9E
112 Valdés, Pen. 42 30S 63 45W
88 Valdez 61 14N 146 10W
112 Valdivia 39 50S 73 14W
37 Valdobbiádene 45 53N 12 0E
99 Valdosta 30 50N 83 48W
44 Valdres 61 0N 91 3E
111 Valença, Brazil 13 20S 39 5W
30 Valença, Port. 42 1N 8 34W
111 Valença da Piaui 6 20S 41 45W
21 Valence 44 57N 4 54E
20 Valence-d'Agen 44 8N 0 54E
33 Valencia, Sp. 39 27N 0 23W
110 Valencia, Ven. 10 11N 68 0W
33 Valencia, G. de 39 30N 0 20E
33 Valencia, Reg. 39 25N 0 45W
33 Valencia □ 39 20N 0 40W
31 Valencia de Alcantara 39 25N 7 14W
30 Valencia de Don Juan 42 17N 5 31W
31 Valencia del Ventoso 38 15N 6 29W
19 Valenciennes 50 20N 3 34E
41 Vălenii-de-Munte 45 12N 26 3E
15 Valentia, I. 51 54N 10 22W
100 Valentine 42 50N 100 35W
36 Valenza 45 2N 8 39E
110 Valera 9 19N 70 37W
39 Valguarnera Caropepe 37 30N 14 22E
21 Valinco, G. de 41 40N 8 52E
40 Valjevo 44 18N 19 53E
16 Valkenswaard 51 21N 5 29E
32 Vall de Uxó 40 49N 0 15W
104 Valladolid, Mexico 20 30N 88 20W
30 Valladolid, Sp. 41 38N 4 43W
30 Valladolid □ 41 38N 4 43W
36 Valle d'Aosta □ 45 45N 7 22E
110 Valle de la Pascua 9 13N 66 0W
104 Valle de Santiago 20 25N 101 15W
30 Vallecas 40 23N 3 41W
102 Vallejo 38 12N 122 15W
108 Vallenar 28 30S 70 50W
100 Valley City 46 57N 98 0W
90 Valleyfield 45 15N 74 8W
92 Valleyview 55 5N 117 25W
32 Valls 41 18N 1 15E
30 Valmaseda 43 11N 3 12W
19 Valmy 49 5N 4 45E
18 Valognes 49 30N 1 28W
108 Valparaíso 33 2S 71 40W
108 Valparaíso □ 33 2S 71 40W
75 Valsbaai 34 15S 18 40E
36 Valtellino 46 9N 10 2E
31 Valverde del Camino 37 35N 6 47W
30 Valverde del Fresno 40 15N 6 51W
43 Vamos 35 24N 24 13E
62 Vamsadhara, R. 18 21N 84 8E
101 Van Buren, Ark. 35 28N 94 18W
91 Van Buren, Me. 47 10N 68 1W
82 Van Diemen, C. 16 30S 139 46E
82 Van Diemen, G. 12 0S 132 0E
56 Van Gölü 38 30N 43 0E
98 Van Wert 40 52N 84 31W
92 Vancouver, Canada 49 20N 123 10W
102 Vancouver, U.S.A. 45 44N 122 41W
92 Vancouver I. 49 50N 126 30W
100 Vandalia 38 57N 89 4W
45 Vandborg 56 32N 8 10E
92 Vanderhoof 54 0N 124 0W
80 Vandyke 24 8S 142 45E
45 Vänern, L. 58 47N 13 50E
45 Vänersborg 58 26N 12 27E
63 Vang Vieng 18 58N 102 32E
74 Vanga 4 35S 39 12E
62 Vaniyambadi 12 46N 78 44E
51 Vankarem 67 51N 175 50W
90 Vankleek Hill 45 32N 74 40W
46 Vännäs 63 58N 19 48E
18 Vannes 47 40N 2 47W
44 Vansbro 60 32N 14 15E
85 Vanua Levu, I. 15 45S 179 10E
21 Var, R. 43 39N 7 12E
21 Var □ 43 27N 6 18E
62 Varada, R. 14 56N 75 41E
18 Varades 47 25N 1 1W
61 Varanasi 25 22N 83 8E
37 Varaždin 46 20N 16 20E
36 Varazze 44 21N 8 36E
45 Varberg 57 17N 12 20E
40 Vardar, R. 40 35N 22 50E
45 Varde 55 38N 8 29E
24 Varel 53 23N 8 9E
20 Varennes-sur-Allier 49 12N 5 0E
40 Vareš 44 12N 18 23E
36 Varese 45 49N 8 50E
109 Varginha 21 33S 45 25W
44 Värmdö, I. 59 18N 18 45E
44 Värmlands □ 59 45N 13 0E
41 Varna 43 13N 27 56E
45 Värnamo 57 10N 14 3E
26 Varnsdorf 49 56N 14 38E
40 Varvarin 43 43N 21 20E
19 Varzy 47 22N 3 20E
27 Vas □ 47 10N 16 55E
31 Vascâo, R. 37 31N 7 31W
32 Vascongadas, Reg. 42 50N 2 45W
43 Vasilikón 38 25N 23 40E
44 Västerås 59 37N 16 38E
46 Västerbotten □ 64 58N 18 0E
44 Västerdalälven, R. 60 33N 15 8E
46 Västernorrlands □ 63 30N 17 40E
45 Västervik 57 43N 16 43E
44 Västmanlands □ 89 5N 16 20E
37 Vasto 42 8N 14 40E
20 Vatan 47 4N 1 50E
37 Vatican City 41 54N 12 27E
39 Vaticano, C. 38 38N 15 50E
46 Vatnajökull 64 30N 16 30W
45 Vättern, L. 58 25N 14 30E
21 Vaucluse □ 44 3N 5 10E
19 Vaucouleurs 48 37N 5 40E
25 Vaud □ 46 35N 6 30E
103 Vaughan 34 37N 105 12W
21 Vauvert 43 42N 4 17E
92 Vauxhall 50 5N 112 9W
45 Växjö 56 52N 14 50E
50 Vaygach, Os. 70 0N 60 0E
24 Vechta 52 47N 8 18E
16 Vechte, R. 52 35N 6 5E
27 Vecsés 47 26N 19 19E
62 Vedaraniam 10 25N 79 50E
16 Veendam 53 5N 6 25E
16 Veenendaal 52 2N 5 34E
46 Vefsna, R. 65 50N 13 12E
30 Vegadeo 45 27N 7 4W
46 Vegafjord 65 37N 12 0E
92 Vegreville 53 30N 112 5W
31 Vejer de la Frontera 36 15N 5 59W
45 Vejle □ 55 2N 11 22E
37 Vela Luka 42 59N 16 44E
20 Velay, Mts. du 45 0N 3 40E
37 Velebit Planina, Mts. 44 50N 15 20E
37 Velebitski Kanal 44 45N 14 55E
42 Velestínon 39 23N 22 45E
110 Vélez 6 2N 73 43W
33 Velez Blanco 37 41N 2 5W
31 Vélez Málaga 36 48N 4 5W
33 Vélez Rubio 37 41N 2 5W
37 Velika Kapela, Mts. 45 10N 15 5E
40 Velika Morava, R. 44 43N 21 3E
40 Velika Plana 44 20N 21 1E
40 Veliki Backu, Kanal 45 45N 19 15E
48 Velikiy Ustyug 60 47N 46 20E
48 Velikiye Luki 56 25N 30 32E
62 Velikonda Ra. 14 45N 79 10E
41 Velingrad 42 4N 23 58E
37 Velino, Mt. 42 10N 13 20E
26 Velke Meziřiči 49 21N 16 1E
38 Velletri 41 43N 12 43E
45 Vellinge 55 29N 13 0E
62 Vellore 12 57N 79 10E
16 Velsen 52 27N 4 40E
48 Velsk 61 10N 42 5E
24 Velten 52 40N 13 11E
62 Vembanad L. 9 36N 76 15E
21 Venaco 42 14N 9 10E
108 Venado Tuerto 33 50S 62 0W
21 Vence 43 43N 7 6E
31 Vendas Novas 38 39N 8 27W
20 Vendée □ 46 40N 1 20W
19 Vendeuvre 48 14N 4 27E
18 Vendôme 47 47N 1 3E
32 Vendrell 41 10N 1 30E
45 Vendsyssel, Reg. 57 22N 10 15E
37 Véneta, L. 45 19N 12 13E
37 Veneto □ 45 30N 12 0E
37 Venézia 45 27N 12 20E
110 Venezuela ■ 8 0N 65 0W
110 Venezuela, G. de 11 30N 71 0W
62 Vengurla 15 53N 73 45E
37 Venice = Venézia 45 27N 12 20E
21 Vénissieux 45 43N 4 53E
62 Venkatagiri 14 0N 79 35E
62 Venkatapuram 18 20N 80 30E
16 Venlo 51 22N 6 11E
16 Venraij 51 31N 6 0E
30 Venta de S. Rafael 40 42N 4 12W
36 Ventimiglia 43 50N 7 39E
13 Ventnor 50 35N 1 12W
21 Ventoux, Mt. 44 10N 5 17E
48 Ventspils 57 25N 21 32E
103 Ventura 34 16N 119 25W
108 Vera, Arg. 29 30S 60 20W
33 Vera, Sp. 37 15N 1 15W
104 Veracruz 19 10N 96 10W
104 Veracruz □ 19 0N 96 15W
60 Veraval 20 53N 70 27E
36 Vercelli 45 19N 8 25E
112 Verde, R. 41 56S 65 5W
24 Verden 52 56N 9 15E
21 Verdon, R. 43 43N 5 46E
19 Verdun 49 12N 5 24E
21 Verdun-sur-le-Doubs 46 54N 5 0E
75 Vereeniging 26 38S 27 57E
32 Vergara 43 9N 2 28W
42 Vergoritis, L. 40 45N 21 45E
30 Verín 41 57N 7 27W
49 Verkhniy Baskunchak 48 5N 46 50E
51 Verkhoyansk 67 50N 133 50E
51 Verkhoyanskiy Khrebet 66 0N 129 0E
19 Vermenton 47 40N 3 42E
93 Vermilion 53 20N 110 50W
93 Vermilion, R. 53 44N 110 18W
93 Vermilion Bay 49 50N 93 20W
100 Vermillion 42 50N 96 56W
97 Vermont □ 43 40N 72 50W
102 Vernal 40 28N 109 35W
90 Verner 46 25N 80 8W
18 Verneuil 48 45N 0 56E
92 Vernon, Canada 50 20N 119 15W
18 Vernon, Fr. 49 5N 1 30E
101 Vernon, U.S.A. 34 0N 99 15W
42 Véroia 40 34N 22 18E
38 Véroli 41 43N 13 24E
36 Verona 45 27N 11 0E
19 Versailles 48 48N 2 8E
72 Verte, C. 14 45N 17 30W
18 Vertou 47 10N 1 28W
19 Vertus 48 54N 4 0E
16 Verviers 50 37N 5 52E
19 Vervins 49 50N 3 53E
21 Vescovato 42 30N 9 26E
26 Veselí n Luž 49 12N 14 43E
49 Veselovskoye, Vdkhr. 47 0N 41 0E
19 Vesle, R. 49 23N 3 38E
19 Vesoul 60 40N 6 11E
47 Vest-Agde □ 58 30N 7 0E
44 Vestfold □ 59 15N 10 0E
45 Vestjællands □ 55 30N 11 20E
46 Vestmannaejar, Is. 63 27N 20 15W
4 Vestspitsbergen, I. 78 40N 17 0E
39 Vesuvio, Mt. 40 50N 14 22E
27 Veszprém 47 8N 17 57E
27 Veszprém □ 47 5N 17 55E
27 Vésztö 46 55N 21 16E
62 Vetapalem 15 47N 80 18E
45 Vetlanda 57 24N 15 3E
41 Vetovo 43 42N 26 16E
37 Vettore, Mt. 44 38N 7 5E
25 Vevey 46 28N 6 51E
20 Vézère, R. 44 53N 0 53E
110 Viacha 16 30S 68 5W
36 Viadana 44 55N 10 30E
111 Viana 3 0S 44 40W
30 Viana del Bollo 42 10N 7 10W
31 Viana do Alentejo 38 20N 8 0W
30 Viana do Castelo 41 42N 8 50W
30 Vianna do Castelo □ 41 50N 8 30W
111 Vianopolis 16 40S 48 35W
31 Viar, R. 37 36N 5 50W
36 Viaréggio 43 52N 10 13E
39 Vibo Valéntia 38 40N 16 5E
45 Viborg 56 27N 9 23E
45 Viborg □ 56 30N 9 20E
20 Vic-Fézensac 43 47N 0 19E
37 Vicenza 45 32N 11 31E
32 Vich 41 58N 2 19E
20 Vichy 46 9N 3 26E
101 Vicksburg 32 22N 90 56W
39 Vico del Gargano 41 54N 15 57E
111 Vicosa 9 28S 36 25W
20 Vic-sur-Cère 44 59N 2 38E
96 Victor 42 58N 77 24W
81 Victor Harbour 35 30S 138 37E
108 Victoria, Arg. 32 40S 60 10W
79 Victoria, Australia 21 16S 149 3E
72 Victoria, Cameroon 4 1N 9 10E
92 Victoria, Canada 48 30N 123 25W
112 Victoria, Chile 38 22S 72 29W
69 Victoria, Hong Kong 22 25N 114 15E
64 Victoria, Malaysia 5 20N 115 20E
101 Victoria, U.S.A. 28 50N 97 0W
74 Victoria, L. 1 0S 33 0E
82 Victoria, R. 15 12S 129 43E
93 Victoria Beach 50 45N 96 32W
105 Victoria de las Tunas 20 58N 76 59W
75 Victoria Falls 17 58S 25 45E
88 Victoria I. 71 0N 11 0W
15 Victoria Ld. 75 0S 160 0E
59 Victoria Taungdeik, Mt. 21 15N 93 55E
75 Victoria West 31 25S 23 4E
91 Victoriaville 46 4N 71 56W
103 Victorville 34 32N 117 18W
99 Vidalia 32 13N 82 25W
21 Vidauban 43 25N 6 27E
40 Vidin 43 59N 22 52E
30 Vidio, C. 43 35N 6 14W
112 Viedma 40 50S 63 0W
112 Viedma, L. 49 30S 72 30W
30 Vieira 41 38N 8 8W
32 Viella 42 43N 0 44E
24 Vienenburg 51 57N 10 35E
27 Vienna = Wien 48 12N 16 22E
21 Vienne 45 31N 4 53E
18 Vienne, R. 47 13N 0 5E
20 Vienne □ 45 53N 0 42E
63 Vientiane 18 7N 102 35E
24 Viersen 51 15N 6 23E
25 Vierwald-stättersee, L. 47 0N 8 30E
19 Vierzon 47 13N 2 5E
39 Vieste 41 53N 16 10E
63 Vietnam ■ 16 0N 108 0E
21 Vif 45 5N 5 41E
65 Vigan 17 35N 120 28E
36 Vigévano 45 18N 8 50E
111 Vigia 0 50S 48 5W
20 Vignemale, Pic de 42 47N 0 10W
36 Vignola 44 29N 11 0E
30 Vigo 42 12N 8 41W
30 Vigo, Ria de 42 15N 8 45W
62 Vijayadurg 16 30N 73 25E
62 Vijayawada 16 31N 80 39E
62 Vikramasingapuram 8 40N 76 47E
50 Vikulovo 56 50N 70 40E
75 Vila Cabral = Lichinga 13 13S 35 11E
31 Vila de Rei 39 41N 8 9W
30 Vila do Conde 41 21N 8 45W
31 Vila Franca de Xira 38 57N 8 59W
75 Vila Machado 19 15S 34 14E
30 Vila Nova de Foscôa 41 5N 7 9W
30 Vila Nova de Gaia 41 4N 8 40W

Vila Nova de Ourém Wallaceburg

31 Vila Nova de Ourém 39 40N 8 35W
30 Vila Pouca de Aguiar 41 30N 7 38W
30 Vila Real 41 17N 7 48W
31 Vila Real de Sto. António 37 10N 7 28W
109 Vila Velha 20 20S 40 17W
31 Vila Viçosa 38 45N 7 27W
30 Vilaboa 42 21N 8 39W
18 Vilaine, R. 47 30N 2 27W
30 Vilar Formosa 40 38N 6 45W
30 Vilareal □ 41 36N 7 35W
51 Viliga 60 2N 156 56 E
108 Villa Ana 28 28S 59 40W
108 Villa Ángela 27 34S 60 45W
108 Villa Cañás 34 0S 61 35W
72 Villa Cisneros = Dakhla 23 50N 15 53W
108 Villa Colón 31 38S 68 20W
108 Villa Constitución 33 15S 60 20W
108 Villa Dolores 31 58S 65 15W
108 Villa Guillermina 28 15S 59 29W
108 Villa Hayes 25 0S 57 20W
105 Villa Julia Molina 19 5N 69 45W
108 Villa María 32 20S 63 10W
108 Villa Ocampo 28 30S 59 20W
36 Villa Minozzo 44 21N 10 30 E
108 Villa San José 32 12 E 58 15W
30 Villablino 42 57N 6 19W
31 Villacañas 39 38N 3 20W
32 Villacarlos 39 53N 4 17 E
30 Villacarriedo 43 14N 3 48W
33 Villacarrillo 38 7N 3 3W
30 Villacastín 40 46N 4 25W
26 Villach 46 37N 13 51 E
30 Villada 42 15N 4 59W
32 Villafeliche 41 10N 1 30W
32 Villafranca 42 17N 1 46W
31 Villafranca de los Barros 38 35N 6 18W
31 Villafranca de los Caballeros 39 26N 3 21W
30 Villafranca del Bierzo 42 38N 6 50W
32 Villafranca del Panadés 41 21N 1 40 E
36 Villafranca di Verona 45 20N 10 51 E
30 Villagarcia de Arosa 42 34N 8 46W
108 Villaguay 32 0S 58 45W
104 Villahermosa, Mexico 17 45N 92 50W
33 Villahermosa, Sp. 38 46N 2 52W
33 Villajoyosa 38 30N 0 12W
30 Villalba 40 36N 3 59W
30 Villalba de Guardo 42 42N 4 49W
30 Villalón de Campos 42 5N 5 4W
30 Villalpando 41 51N 5 25W
30 Villaluenga 40 2N 3 54W
30 Villamañán 42 19N 5 35W
31 Villamartín 36 52N 5 38W
32 Villamayor 41 42N 0 43W
103 Villanueva 35 16N 105 31W
33 Villanueva de Castellón 39 5N 0 31W
31 Villanueva de Córdoba 38 20N 4 38W
31 Villanueva de la Serena 38 59N 5 50W
33 Villanueva del Arzobispo 38 10N 3 0W
31 Villanueva del Fresno 38 23N 7 10W
32 Villanueva y Geltrú 41 13N 1 40 E
30 Villarcayo 42 56N 3 34W
39 Villaroso 37 36N 14 9 E
112 Villarrica 39 15S 72 30W
33 Villarrobledo 39 18N 2 36W
32 Villarroya de la Sierra 41 27N 1 46W
31 Villarrubia de los Ojos 39 14N 3 36W
31 Villarta de San Juan 39 15N 3 25W
30 Villatobas 39 54N 3 20W
110 Villavicencio 4 9N 73 37W
108 Villazón 22 0S 65 35W
90 Ville Marie 47 20N 79 30W
101 Ville Platte 30 45N 92 17W
18 Villedieu 48 50N 1 12W
20 Villefort 44 28N 3 56 E
19 Villefranche 47 19N 146 0 E
20 Villefranche-de-Lauragais 43 25N 1 44 E
20 Villefranche-de-Rouergue 44 21N 2 2 E
21 Villefranche-sur-Saône 45 59N 4 43 E
32 Villel 40 14N 1 12W
19 Villemaur 48 14N 3 40 E
33 Villena 38 39N 0 52W
19 Villeneuve 48 42N 2 25 E
19 Villeneuve-l'Archevèque 48 14N 3 32 E
21 Villeneuve-lès-Avignon 43 57N 4 49 E
20 Villeneuve-sur-Lot 44 24N 0 42 E
18 Villers-Bocage 49 3N 0 40W
19 Villers-Cotterets 49 15N 3 4 E
18 Villers-sur-Mer 49 21N 0 2W
19 Villerupt 49 28N 5 55 E
21 Villeurbanne 45 46N 4 55 E
25 Villingen 48 3N 8 29 E
62 Villupuram 11 59N 79 31 E
92 Vilna 54 7N 111 55W
48 Vilnius 54 38N 25 25 E
26 Vils 47 33N 10 37 E
16 Vilvoorde 50 56N 4 26 E
51 Vilyuysk 63 40N 121 20 E
36 Vimercate 45 38N 9 25 E
45 Vimmerby 57 40N 15 55 E
108 Viña del Mar 33 0S 71 30W
32 Vinaroz 40 30N 0 27 E
98 Vincennes 38 42N 87 29W
60 Vindhya Ra. 22 50N 77 0 E
63 Vinh 18 45N 105 38 E
37 Vinica 45 28N 15 16 E
101 Vinita 36 40N 95 12W
40 Vinkovci 45 19N 18 48 E
49 Vinnitsa 49 15N 28 30 E
44 Vinstra 61 37N 9 44 E
41 Vinţu de Jos 46 0N 23 30 E
84 Violet Town 36 19S 145 37 E
37 Vipava 45 51N 13 38 E
37 Vipiteno 46 55N 11 25 E
65 Viqueque 8 42S 126 30 E
93 Virden 49 50N 101 0W
112 Vírgenes, C. 52 19S 68 21W
105 Virgin Gorda, I. 18 45N 64 26W
105 Virgin Is., Br. 18 40N 64 30W
105 Virgin Is., U.S. 18 20N 64 50W
100 Virginia 47 30N 92 32W
98 Virginia □ 37 45N 78 0W
98 Virginia Beach 36 54N 75 58W
102 Virginia City 45 25N 111 58W
40 Virje 46 4N 16 59 E
40 Virovitica 45 51N 17 21 E
40 Virpazar 42 15N 19 5 E
16 Virton 49 35N 5 32 E
62 Virudunagar 9 30N 78 0 E
37 Vis, I. 43 0N 16 10 E
103 Visalia 36 25N 119 18W
65 Visayan Sea 11 30N 123 30 E
45 Visby 57 37N 18 18 E
86 Viscount Melville Sd. 78 0N 108 0W
16 Visé 50 44N 5 41 E
40 Višegrad 43 47N 19 17 E
111 Viseu, Brazil 1 10S 46 20W
30 Viseu, Port. 40 40N 7 55W
30 Viseu □ 40 40N 7 55W
62 Vishakhapatnam 17 45N 83 20 E
61 Vishnupur 23 8N 87 20 E
45 Vislanda 56 46N 14 30 E
60 Visnagar 23 45N 72 32 E
37 Višnja Gora 45 58N 14 45 E
48 Vitebsk 55 10N 30 15 E
37 Viterbo 42 25N 12 8 E
85 Viti Levu, I. 17 30S 177 30 E
51 Vitim 59 45N 112 25 E
51 Vitim, R. 59 26N 112 34 E
109 Vitoria, Brazil 20 20S 40 22W
32 Vitória, Sp. 42 50N 2 41W
111 Vitória da Conquista 14 51S 40 51W
111 Vitoria de Santo Antão 8 10S 37 20W
18 Vitré 48 8N 1 12W
19 Vitry-le-François 48 43N 4 33 E
42 Vitsi, Mt 40 40N 21 25 E
19 Vitteaux 47 24N 4 30 E
39 Vittória 36 58N 14 30 E
37 Vittório Véneto 45 59N 12 18 E
32 Viver 39 55N 0 36W
30 Vivero 43 39N 7 38W
20 Vivonne 46 36N 0 15 E
44 Vivsta 62 30N 17 18 E
30 Vizcaya □ 43 15N 2 45W
62 Vizianagaram 18 6N 83 10 E
21 Vizille 45 5N 5 46 E
41 Viziru 45 0N 27 43 E
27 Vizovice 49 12N 17 56 E
39 Vizzini 37 9N 14 43 E
16 Vlaardingen 51 55N 4 21 E
40 Vladicin Han 42 42N 22 1 E
48 Vladimir 56 0N 40 30 E
40 Vladimirovac 45 1N 20 53 E
51 Vladivostok 43 10N 131 53 E
40 Vlasenica 44 11N 18 59 E
26 Vlasim 49 40N 14 53 E
16 Vlissingen 51 26N 3 34 E
42 Vlóra 40 32N 19 28 E
42 Vlora □ 40 12N 20 0 E
26 Vltava, R. 49 35N 14 10 E
36 Vobarno 45 38N 10 30 E
26 Vöcklabruck 48 1N 13 39 E
37 Vodnjan 44 59N 13 52 E
24 Vogelsberg, Mts. 50 30N 9 15 E
36 Voghera 44 59N 9 1 E
75 Vohémar 13 25S 50 0 E
74 Voi 3 25S 38 32 E
43 Voíotía □ 38 20N 23 0 E
21 Voiron 45 22N 5 35 E
26 Voitsberg 47 3N 15 9 E
42 Voïviïs, L. 39 30N 22 45 E
45 Vojens 55 16N 9 18 E
76 Volcano Is. 25 0N 141 0 E
49 Volga, R. 45 55N 47 52 E
49 Volga Heights, Mts. 51 0N 46 0 E
49 Volgograd 48 40N 44 25 E
49 Volgogradskoye, Vdkhr. 50 0N 45 20 E
26 Völkermarkt 46 34N 14 39 E
25 Völkingen 49 15N 6 50 E
16 Vollenhove 52 40N 5 58 E
51 Volochanka 71 0N 94 28 E
48 Vologda 59 25N 40 0 E
42 Vólos 39 24N 22 59 E
48 Volsk 52 5N 47 28 E
72 Volta, L. 7 30N 0 15 E
72 Volta Noire, R. 8 41N 1 33W
109 Volta Redonda 22 31S 44 5W
36 Volterra 43 24N 10 50 E
36 Voltri 44 25N 8 43 E
38 Volturno, R. 41 1N 13 55 E
42 Vólvi, L. 40 40N 23 34 E
49 Volzhskiy 48 56N 44 46 E
16 Voorburg 52 5N 4 24 E
26 Voralberg □ 47 20N 10 0 E
42 Vóras Oros, Mt. 40 57N 21 45 E
45 Vordingborg 55 0N 11 54 E
43 Voríai Sporádhes, Is. 39 15N 23 30 E
42 Vóras Evvoïkos Kól. 38 45N 23 15 E
48 Vorkuta 67 48N 64 20 E
48 Voronezh 51 40N 39 10 E
49 Voroshilovgrad 48 38N 39 15 E
19 Vosges, Mts. 48 20N 7 10 E
19 Vosges □ 48 12N 6 20 E
47 Voss 60 38N 6 26 E
51 Vostochnyy Sayan 54 0N 96 0 E
77 Vostok, I. 10 5S 152 23W
48 Votkinsk 57 0N 53 55 E
48 Votkinskoye, Vdkhr. 57 30N 55 0 E
30 Vouga, R. 40 41N 8 40W
30 Vouzela 40 43N 8 7W
19 Vouziers 49 22N 4 40 E
48 Vozhe, Oz. 60 45N 39 0 E
51 Voznesenka 46 51N 35 26 E
49 Voznesensk 47 35N 31 15 E
48 Voznesenye 61 0N 35 45 E
41 Vrancei, Mt. 46 0N 26 30 E
51 Vrangelya, Os. 71 0N 180 0 E
40 Vranica, Mt. 43 59N 18 0 E
40 Vranje 42 34N 21 54 E
27 Vranov 48 53N 21 40 E
37 Vransko 46 17N 14 58 E
41 Vratsa 43 13N 23 30 E
40 Vrbas 45 0N 17 27 E
40 Vrbas, R. 45 6N 17 31 E
37 Vrbnik 45 4N 14 32 E
37 Vrbovsko 45 24N 15 5 E
26 Vrchlabí 49 38N 15 37 E
75 Vredenburg 32 51S 18 0 E
62 Vriddhachalam 11 30N 79 10 E
60 Vrindaban 27 37N 77 40 E
43 Vrondádhes 38 25N 26 7 E
40 Vrpolje 43 42N 16 1 E
40 Vršac 45 8N 21 18 E
40 Vrsacki, Kanal 45 15N 21 0 E
75 Vryburg 26 55S 24 45 E
75 Vryheid 27 54S 30 47 E
27 Vsetín 49 20N 18 0 E
16 Vught 51 38N 5 20 E
40 Vukovar 45 21N 18 59 E
92 Vulcan, Canada 50 25N 113 15W
41 Vulcan, Rumania 45 23N 23 17 E
37 Vulci 42 23N 11 37 E
62 Vuyyuru 16 28N 80 50 E
60 Vyara 21 8N 73 28 E
48 Vyatskiye 56 5N 51 0 E
48 Vyazma 55 10N 34 15 E
48 Vyborg 60 42N 28 45 E
27 Vyehodné Beskydy, Mts. 49 30N 22 0 E
26 Vychodoceský □ 50 20N 15 45 E
27 Východoslovenský □ 48 50N 21 0 E
48 Vyg, Oz. 63 30N 34 0 E
12 Vyrnwy, L. 52 48N 3 30W
27 Vyškov 49 17N 17 0 E
26 Vyšší Brod 48 36N 14 20 E
48 Vytegra 61 15N 36 40 E

W

72 Wa 10 7N 2 25W
16 Waal, R. 51 55N 4 30 E
91 Wabana 47 40N 53 0W
98 Wabash 40 48N 85 46W
98 Wabash, R. 37 46N 88 2W
93 Wabowden 54 55N 98 35W
28 Wabrzeźno 53 16N 18 57 E
91 Wabush City 52 40N 67 0W
101 Waco 31 33N 97 5W
73 Wad Banda 13 10N 27 50 E
73 Wad Hamid 16 20N 32 45 E
73 Wâd Medanî 14 28N 33 30 E
66 Wadayama 35 19N 134 52 E
16 Waddeniladen, Is. 53 30N 5 30 E
16 Waddenzee 53 15N 5 15 E
83 Wadderin Hill 32 0S 118 25 E
97 Waddington 44 51N 75 12W
92 Waddington, Mt. 51 10N 125 20W
31 Waddy, Pt. 24 58S 153 21 E
93 Wadena, Canada 52 0N 103 50W
100 Wadena, U.S.A. 46 25N 95 2W
25 Wadenswil 47 14N 8 30 E
73 Wadi Halfa 21 53N 31 19 E
27 Wadowice 49 52N 19 30 E
96 Wadsworth 39 44N 119 22W
16 Wageningen 51 58N 5 40 E
89 Wager Bay 66 0N 91 0W
84 Wagga Wagga 35 7S 147 24 E
83 Wagin 33 17S 117 25 E
28 Wagrowiec 52 48N 17 19 E
65 Wahai 2 48S 129 35 E
100 Wahpeton 46 20N 96 35W
62 Wai 17 56N 73 57 E
85 Waiau 42 39S 173 5 E
85 Waiau, R. 42 46S 173 23 E
26 Waidhofen, Austria 48 49N 15 17 E
26 Waidhofen, Austria 47 57N 14 46 E
65 Waigeo, I. 0 20S 130 40 E
85 Waihi 37 23S 175 52 E
85 Waihou, R. 37 10S 175 32 E
85 Waikaremoana, L. 38 49S 177 9 E
85 Waikari 42 58S 172 41 E
85 Waikato, R. 37 23S 174 43 E
85 Waikerie 34 9S 140 0 E
85 Waikokopu 39 3S 177 52 E
85 Waikouaiti 45 36S 170 41 E
85 Waimakariri, R. 43 24S 172 42 E
85 Waimarino 40 40S 175 20 E
85 Waimate 44 53S 171 3 E
65 Waingapu 9 35S 120 11 E
93 Wainwright 52 50N 110 50W
85 Waiouru 39 29S 175 40 E
85 Waipara 43 3N 172 46 E
85 Waipawa 39 56S 176 38 E
85 Waipiro 38 2S 176 22 E
85 Waipu 35 59S 174 29 E
85 Waipukurau 40 1S 176 33 E
85 Wairakei 38 37S 176 6 E
85 Wairau, R. 41 32S 174 7 E
85 Wairoa 39 3S 177 25 E
85 Waitaki, R. 44 56S 171 7 E
85 Waitara 38 59S 174 15 E
85 Waiuku 37 15S 174 45 E
69 Waiyeung 23 12N 114 32 E
66 Wajima 37 30N 137 0 E
74 Wajir 1 42N 40 20 E
66 Wakasa 35 20N 134 24 E
66 Wakasa-Wan 34 45N 135 30 E
85 Wakatipu, L. 45 6S 168 30 E
93 Wakaw 52 39N 105 44W
66 Wakayama 34 15N 135 15 E
66 Wakayama □ 34 50N 135 30 E
76 Wake, I. 19 18N 166 36 E
12 Wakefield, U.K. 53 41N 1 31W
85 Wakefield, N.Z. 41 24S 173 5 E
97 Wakefield 42 30N 71 3W
89 Wakeham Bay = Maricourt 61 36N 71 57W
66 Wakkanai 45 28N 141 35 E
65 Wakre 0 30S 131 5 E
41 Walachia = Valahia □ 44 40N 25 0 E
27 Walbrzych 50 45N 16 18 E
28 Walbrzych □ 50 50N 16 30 E
13 Walbury Hill 51 22N 1 28W
81 Walcha 30 55S 151 31 E
16 Walcheren, I. 51 30N 3 35 E
28 Wałcz 53 17N 16 28 E
24 Waldbröl 50 52N 7 36 E
102 Walden 40 47N 106 20W
93 Waldron 50 53N 102 35W
83 Walebing 30 40S 116 15 E
11 Wales ■ 52 30N 3 30W
81 Walgett 30 0S 148 5 E
83 Walkaway 28 59S 114 48W
90 Walkerton 44 10N 81 10W
102 Walla Walla 46 3N 118 25W
102 Wallace 47 30N 116 0W
90 Wallaceburg 42 40N 82 30W

Wallal Willimantic

81 Wallal 26 32S 146 7E
82 Wallal Downs 19 47S 120 40E
81 Wallaroo 33 56S 137 39E
12 Wallasey 3 26S 3 2W
84 Wallerawang 33 25S 150 4E
80 Wallahallow 17 50S 135 50E
97 Wallingford 43 27N 72 58W
76 Wallis Arch. 13 20S 176 20E
102 Wallowa 45 40N 117 35W
12 Wallsend 54 59N 1 30W
81 Wallumbilla 26 33S 149 9E
12 Walney, I 54 5N 3 15W
84 Walpeup 35 10S 142 2E
13 Walsall 52 36N 1 59W
101 Walsenburg 37 42N 104 45W
24 Walsrode 52 51N 9 37E
62 Waltair 17 44N 83 23E
24 Waltershausen 50 53N 10 33E
90 Waltham, Canada 45 57N 76 57W
97 Waltham, U.S.A. 42 22N 71 12W
75 Walvisbaai 23 0S 14 28E
75 Walvis Bay = Walvisbaai 23 0S 14 28E
74 Wamba 2 10N 27 57E
31 Wanaaring 29 38S 144 0E
85 Wanaka, L. 44 33S 169 7E
65 Wanapiri 4 30S 135 50E
97 Wanaque 41 3N 74 17W
81 Wanbi 34 46S 140 17E
62 Wandiwash 12 30N 79 30E
81 Wandoan 26 5S 149 55E
85 Wanganui 39 35S 175 3E
84 Wangaratta 36 21S 146 19E
81 Wangary 34 33S 135 29E
68 Wangtu 38 42N 115 4E
69 Wanhsien 30 45N 108 20E
75 Wankie 18 18S 26 30E
93 Wanless 54 11N 101 21W
69 Wanning 18 45N 110 28E
69 Wantsai 28 1N 114 5E
69 Wanyang Shan, Mts. 26 30N 113 30E
69 Wanyuan 32 3N 108 16E
102 Wapato 46 30N 120 25W
55 Warandab 7 20N 44 2E
62 Warangal 17 58N 79 45E
85 Ward 41 49S 174 11E
57 Wardak □ 34 15N 68 0E
60 Wardha 20 45N 78 39E
97 Ware 42 16N 72 15W
24 Waren 53 30N 12 41E
24 Warendorf 51 57N 8 0E
81 Warialda 29 29S 150 33E
65 Warkopi 1 12S 134 9E
85 Warkworth 36 24S 174 41E
13 Warley 52 30N 2 0W
93 Warman 52 25N 106 30W
75 Warmbad, S.W. Africa 28 25S 18 42E
75 Warmbad, S.W. Africa 19 14S 13 51E
84 Warncoort 38 30S 143 45E
102 Warner Ra. 41 30S 120 20W
99 Warner Robins 32 41N 83 36W
24 Warnermünde 54 9N 12 5E
83 Waroona 32 50S 115 55E
60 Warora 20 14N 79 1E
84 Warracknabeal 36 9S 142 26E
84 Warragul 38 10S 145 58E
81 Warrego, R. 30 24S 145 21E
84 Warren, Australia 31 42S 147 51E
96 Warren, Ohio 41 18N 80 52W
96 Warren, Pa. 41 52N 79 10W
101 Warren 33 35N 92 3W
15 Warrenpoint 54 7N 6 15W
100 Warrensburg 38 45N 93 45W
75 Warrenton, S. Africa 28 9S 24 47E
102 Warrenton, U.S.A. 46 11N 123 59W
72 Warri 5 30N 5 41E
12 Warrington, U.K. 53 25N 2 38W
99 Warrington, U.S.A. 30 22N 87 16W
84 Warrnambool 38 25S 142 30E
58 Warsak Dam 34 10N 71 25E
98 Warsaw 41 14N 85 50W
28 Warszawa 52 13N 21 0E
28 Warszawa □ 52 35N 21 0E
28 Warta, R. 52 35N 14 39E
13 Warwick □ 52 20N 1 30W
81 Warwick, Australia 28 10S 152 1E
13 Warwick, U.K. 52 17N 1 36W
97 Warwick, U.S.A. 41 43N 71 25W
92 Wasa 49 45N 115 50W
86 Wasatch Mts. 40 30N 111 15W
103 Wasco, Calif. 35 37N 119 16W
102 Wasco, Oreg. 45 45N 120 46W
100 Waseca 44 3N 93 31W
12 Wash, The 52 58N 0 20W
96 Washago 44 46N 79 21W
102 Washington □ 47 45N 120 30W
98 Washington, D.C. 38 52N 77 0W
98 Washington, Ind. 38 40N 87 8W
100 Washington, Iowa 41 20N 91 45W
100 Washington, Mo. 38 33N 91 1W
97 Washington, N.J. 40 45N 74 59W
99 Washington, N.C. 35 35N 77 1W
98 Washington, Ohio 39 34N 83 26W
96 Washington, Pa. 40 10N 80 20W
77 Washington I. 4 43N 160 24W
97 Washington, Mt. 44 15N 71 18W
16 Wassenaar 52 8N 4 24E
24 Wasserkuppe, Mt. 50 30N 9 56E
90 Waswanipi 49 30N 77 0W
65 Watangpone 4 29S 120 25E
97 Waterbury 41 32N 73 0W
15 Waterford 52 16N 7 8W
15 Waterford □ 51 10N 7 40W
16 Waterloo, Belgium 50 43N 4 25E
100 Waterloo, Iowa 42 27N 92 20W
96 Waterloo, N.Y. 42 54N 76 53W
97 Watertown, N.Y. 43 58N 75 57W
100 Watertown, S.D. 44 57N 97 5W
100 Watertown, Wis. 43 15N 88 45W
99 Waterville 44 35N 69 40W
97 Watervliet 42 46N 73 43W
65 Wates 7 53S 110 6E
13 Watford 51 38N 0 23W
83 Watheroo 30 15S 116 0W
105 Watling, I. 24 0N 74 30W
93 Watrous 51 40N 105 25W
74 Watsa 3 4N 29 30E
83 Watson 30 19S 131 41E
92 Watson Lake 60 12N 129 0W
103 Watsonville 37 58N 121 49W
25 Wattwil 47 18N 9 6E
84 Waubra 37 21S 143 39E
84 Wauchope 31 28S 152 45E
93 Waugh 49 40N 95 20W
98 Waukegan 42 22N 87 54W
100 Waukesha 43 0N 88 15W
100 Waupun 43 38N 88 44W
100 Wausau 44 57N 89 40W
98 Wauwatosa 43 6N 87 59W
82 Wave Hill 17 32N 131 0E
13 Waveney, R. 52 28N 1 45E
85 Waverley 39 46S 174 37E
100 Waverly 42 40N 92 30W
16 Wavre 50 43N 4 38E
73 Wâw 7 45N 28 1E
101 Waxahachie 32 22N 96 53W
80 Wayatinah 42 19S 146 27E
99 Waycross 31 12N 82 25W
98 Waynesboro, Pa. 39 46N 77 32W
98 Waynesboro, Va. 38 4N 78 57W
99 Waynesville 35 31N 83 0W
57 Wazirabad, Afghanistan 36 44N 66 47E
60 Wazirabad, Pak. 32 30N 74 8E
13 Weald, The 51 7N 0 9E
12 Wear, R. 54 55N 1 22W
101 Weatherford 32 45N 97 48W
97 Webster 42 4N 71 54W
100 Webster City 42 30N 93 50W
100 Webster Green 38 38N 90 20W
65 Weda 0 30N 127 50E
112 Weddell I. 51 50S 61 0W
5 Weddell Sea 72 30S 40 0W
84 Wedderburn 36 20S 143 33E
91 Wedgeport 43 44N 65 59W
81 Wee Waa 30 11S 149 26E
102 Weed 41 29N 122 22W
16 Weert 51 15N 5 43E
28 Wegliniec 51 18N 15 10E
69 Wei Ho, R. 35 45N 114 30E
24 Weida 50 47N 12 3E
68 Weifang 36 47N 119 10E
68 Weihai 37 30N 122 10E
25 Weilheim 47 50N 11 9E
24 Weimar 51 0N 11 20E
69 Weinan 34 30N 109 35E
25 Weingarten 47 49N 9 39E
25 Weinheim 47 50N 11 9E
80 Weipa 12 24S 141 50E
93 Weir River 57 0N 94 10W
96 Weirton 40 22N 80 35W
102 Weiser 44 10N 117 0W
25 Weissenburg 49 2N 10 58E
24 Weissenfels 51 11N 11 58E
24 Weisswasser 51 30N 14 36E
26 Wêitra 48 41N 14 54E
26 Weiz 47 13N 15 39E
28 Wejherow 54 35N 18 12E
93 Wekusko 54 45N 99 45W
31 Welbourn Hill 27 21S 134 6E
98 Welch 37 29N 81 36W
25 Welden 48 27N 10 40E
75 Welkom 28 0S 26 50E
96 Welland 43 0N 79 10W
12 Welland, R. 52 53N 0 2E
80 Wellesley, Is. 17 20S 139 30E
13 Wellingborough 52 18N 0 41W
84 Wellington, Australia 32 30S 149 0E
90 Wellington, Canada 43 57N 77 20W
85 Wellington, N.Z. 41 19S 174 46E
12 Wellington, U.K. 52 42N 2 31W
101 Wellington, U.S.A. 37 15N 97 25W
85 Wellington □ 40 8S 175 36E
112 Wellington, I. 49 30S 75 0W
12 Wells, Norfolk 52 57N 0 51E
13 Wells, Somerset 51 12N 2 39W
102 Wells, U.S.A. 41 8N 115 0W
83 Wells, L. 26 44S 123 15W
97 Wells River 44 9N 72 4W
96 Wellsburg 40 15N 80 36W
28 Wełna, R. 42 9N 77 53W
26 Wels 48 9N 14 1E
84 Welshpool, Australia 38 42S 146 26E
13 Welshpool, U.K. 52 40N 3 9W
12 Wem 52 52N 2 45W
102 Wenatchee 47 30N 120 17W
69 Wenchang 19 38N 110 42E
72 Wenchi 7 46N 2 8W
69 Wenchow 28 0N 120 35E
102 Wendell 42 50N 114 51W
69 Wensiang 34 35N 110 40E
12 Wensleydale 54 20N 2 0W
67 Wensu 41 15N 80 14E
68 Wenteng 25 15S 23 16E
84 Wentworth 34 2S 141 54E
75 Wepener 29 42S 27 3E
75 Werda 25 15S 23 16E
24 Werdau 50 45N 12 20E
24 Werder 52 23N 12 56E
24 Werdohl 51 15N 7 47E
25 Werne 51 38N 7 38E
24 Wernigerode 51 49N 0 45E
84 Werribee 37 54S 144 40E
84 Werris Creek 31 8S 150 38E
25 Wertheim 49 44N 9 32E
24 Wesel 51 39N 6 34E
24 Weser, R. 53 32N 8 34E
91 Wesleyville 49 8N 53 36W
80 Wessel, Is. 11 10S 136 45E
98 West Bend 43 25N 88 10W
61 West Bengal □ 25 0N 90 0E
13 West Bromwich 52 32N 2 1W
100 West Des Moines 41 30N 93 45W
112 West Falkland, I. 51 30S 60 0W
100 West Frankfort 37 56N 89 0W
24 West Germany ■ 51 0N 9 0E
13 West Glamorgan □ 51 40N 3 55W
97 West Hartford 41 45N 72 45W
97 West Haven 41 18N 72 57W
101 West Helena 34 30N 90 40W
101 West Memphis 35 5N 90 3W
13 West Midlands □ 52 30N 2 0W
101 West Monroe 32 32N 92 7W
99 West Palm Beach 26 44N 80 3W
97 West Pittston 41 19N 75 49W
105 West Pt. 18 14N 78 30W
101 West Point, Miss. 33 36N 88 38W
98 West Point, Va. 37 35N 76 47W
13 West Sussex □ 50 55N 0 30W
98 West Virginia □ 39 0N 18 0W
84 West Wyalong 33 56S 147 10E
12 West Yorkshire □ 53 45N 1 40W
99 Westbrook 43 41N 70 21W
80 Westbury 41 30S 146 51E
24 Westerland 54 51N 8 20E
78 Western Australia □ 25 0S 118 0E
62 Western Ghats, Mts. 15 30N 74 30E
14 Western Isles □ 57 30N 7 10W
63 Western Malaysia □ 4 0N 10 2E
85 Western Samoa ■ 14 0S 172 0W
16 Westerschelde, R. 51 25N 4 0E
24 Westerstede 51 15N 7 55E
24 Westerwald, Mts. 50 39N 8 0E
97 Westfield 42 9N 72 49W
85 Westland □ 43 33S 169 59E
92 Westlock 54 20N 113 55W
15 Westmeath □ 53 30N 7 30W
98 Westminster 39 34S 77 1W
103 Westmorland 33 2N 115 42W
64 Weston, Malaysia 5 10N 115 35E
98 Weston, U.S.A. 39 3N 80 29W
13 Weston-super-Mare 51 20N 2 59W
15 Westport, Eire 53 44N 9 31W
85 Westport, N.Z. 41 46S 171 37E
14 Westray, I. 59 18N 3 0W
92 Westview 49 50N 124 31W
102 Westwood 40 26N 121 0W
65 Wetar, I. 7 30S 126 30E
92 Wetaskiwin 52 55N 113 24W
97 Wethersfield 41 43N 72 40W
16 Wetteren 51 0N 3 53E
24 Wetzlar 50 33N 8 30E
101 Wewaka 35 10N 96 35W
15 Wexford 52 20N 6 28W
15 Wexford □ 52 20N 6 40W
93 Weyburn 49 40N 103 50W
26 Weyer 47 51N 14 40E
13 Weymouth, U.K. 50 36N 2 28W
97 Weymouth, U.S.A. 42 13N 70 53W
85 Whakatane 37 57S 177 1E
89 Whale, R. 57 40N 67 0W
93 Whale Cove 62 10N 93 0W
14 Whalsay, I. 60 22N 1 0W
85 Whangamomona 39 8S 174 44E
85 Whangarei 35 43S 174 21E
85 Whangaroa, Harbour 35 4S 173 46E
12 Wharfe, R. 53 51N 1 7W
100 Wheatland 42 4N 105 58W
103 Wheeler Pk. 38 57N 114 15W
96 Wheeling 40 2N 80 41W
12 Whernside, Mt. 54 14N 2 24W
96 Whitby, Canada 43 50N 78 50W
12 Whitby, U.K. 54 29N 0 37W
98 White, R., Ind. 38 25N 87 44W
101 White, R., Ark. 33 53N 91 3W
81 White Cliffs 30 50S 143 10E
13 White Horse, Vale of 51 37N 1 30W
97 White Mts. 44 15N 71 15W
73 White Nile, R. = Nîl el Abyad 9 30N 31 40E
97 White Plains 41 2N 73 44E
90 White River 48 35N 85 20W
97 White River Junc. 43 28N 72 20W
48 White Sea = Beloye More 66 30N 38 0E
102 White Sulphur Springs 46 35N 111 0W
85 Whitecliffs 43 26S 171 55E
97 Whitefield 44 23N 71 37W
102 Whitefish 48 25N 114 22W
97 Whitehall, N.Y. 43 32N 73 28W
102 Whitehall, Wis. 44 20N 91 19W
12 Whitehaven 54 33N 3 35W
92 Whitehorse 60 45N 135 10W
93 Whiteshell Prov. Park 50 0N 95 25W
80 Whitewood 21 28S 143 30E
93 Whitewood 50 20N 102 20W
14 Whithorn 54 55N 4 25W
85 Whitianga 36 47S 175 41E
97 Whitman 42 4N 70 55W
103 Whitney, Mt. 36 35N 118 14W
97 Whitney Point 42 19N 75 59W
13 Whitstable 51 21N 1 2E
80 Whitsunday, I. 20 15S 149 4E
88 Whittier 60 46N 148 48W
91 Whittle, C. 50 11N 60 8W
81 Whyalla 33 2S 137 30E
90 Wiarton 44 50N 81 10W
101 Wichita 37 40N 97 29W
101 Wichita Falls 33 57N 98 30W
14 Wick 58 26N 3 5W
103 Wickenburg 33 58N 112 45W
83 Wickepin 32 50S 117 30E
96 Wickliffe 41 46N 81 29W
15 Wicklow 53 0N 6 2W
15 Wicklow □ 52 59N 6 25W
15 Wicklow Mts. 53 0N 6 30W
83 Widgiemooltha 31 30S 121 34E
12 Widnes 53 22N 2 44W
28 Wiecbork 53 22N 17 30E
25 Wiedenbrück 51 50N 8 18E
28 Wielbark 53 24N 20 55E
28 Wieluń 51 15N 18 40E
27 Wien 48 12N 16 22E
27 Wiener Neustadt 47 49N 16 16E
28 Wieprz, R. 51 34N 21 49E
16 Wierden 52 22N 6 35E
25 Wiesbaden 50 7N 8 17E
12 Wigan 53 33N 2 38W
14 Wigtown 54 52N 4 27W
14 Wigtown B. 54 46N 4 15W
84 Wilcannia 31 30S 143 26E
24 Wildeshausen 52 54N 8 25E
26 Wildon 46 52N 15 31E
98 Wildwood 39 5N 74 46W
26 Wilhelmsburg, Austria 48 6N 15 36E
24 Wilhelmsburg, W. Germany 53 28N 10 1E
24 Wilhelshaven 53 30N 8 9E
97 Wilkes-Barre 41 15N 75 52W
15 Wilkes Ld. 69 0S 120 0E
5 Wilkes Sub-Glacial Basin 68 0S 140 0E
93 Wilkie 52 27N 108 42W
96 Wilkinsburg 40 26N 79 50W
96 Willard 41 3N 82 44W
103 Willcox 32 13N 109 53W
105 Willemstad 12 5N 69 0W
82 Willeroo 15 14S 131 37E
81 William Creek 28 58S 136 22E
83 Williams, Australia 33 0S 117 0E
103 Williams, U.S.A. 35 16N 112 11W
92 Williams Lake 52 20N 122 10W
98 Williamsburg 37 17N 76 44W
98 Williamson 37 46N 82 17W
96 Williamsport 41 18N 77 1W
84 Williamstown, Australia 37 46S 144 58E
97 Williamstown, U.S.A. 42 41N 73 12W
97 Willimantic 41 45N 72 12W